The Pilot's Handbook of Aeronautical Knowledge

Fourth Edition

Paul E. Illman

McGraw-Hill

New York San Francisco Washington, D.C. Auckland Bogotá
Caracas Lisbon London Madrid Mexico City Milan
Montreal New Delhi San Juan Singapore
Sydney Tokyo Toronto

Library of Congress Cataloging-in-Publication Data

Illman, Paul E.
    The pilot's handbook of aeronautical knowledge / Paul E. Illman.—4th ed.
        p.   cm.
    Includes index.
    ISBN 0-07-134519-1 (hc.)—ISBN 0-07-134518-3 (pbk.)
    1. Airplanes—Piloting.   2. Aeronautics.   I. Title.
TL710.I45   1999
629.132'52—dc21   99-054046
                                                                          CIP

McGraw-Hill

A Division of The McGraw·Hill Companies

    3 4 5 6 7 8 9 0   DOC/DOC   0 4 3 2 1

ISBN 0-07-134519-1

The sponsoring editor for this book was Shelley Carr, the editing supervisor was Sally Glover, and the production supervisor was Pamela Pelton. It was set in Garamond per the Gen1-AV1 design by Paul Scozzari of McGraw-Hill's Hightstown, N.J., Professional Book Group composition unit.

Printed and bound by R. R. Donnelley & Sons Company.

McGraw-Hill books are available at special quantity discounts to use as premiums and sales promotions, or for use in corporate training programs. For more information, please write to the Director of Special Sales, McGraw-Hill, Two Penn Plaza, New York, NY 10121-2298. Or contact your local bookstore.

This book is printed on recycled, acid-free paper containing a minimum of 50% recycled, de-inked fiber.

Contents

Introduction

This fourth edition of the *Pilot's Handbook of Aeronautical Knowledge* is based on the FAA publication of the same name (Advisory Circular 61-23B), originally issued in 1980. In 1990, at the request of Tab Books, Inc., I revised, reorganized, and added to that handbook, which had never been edited or updated. I did not, however, rewrite it in any major way. The second edition thus appeared in 1990, under its original title.

Since 1990, many aviation-related changes have occurred, which, when combined, warranted more revising and updating, thus resulting in a third and now fourth edition. Hopefully, the update properly reflects the various changes and presents to the reader facts, procedures, and regulations that are current at the turn of the century.

As was true with the previous edition, the basic content of some of the original chapters remains unchanged. After all, the fundamentals of how an airplane flies don't change, nor do the principles of reciprocating engines, flight instruments, aircraft performance, weather, and the like. However, each chapter has been rewritten, with the intent of making it more readable while, at the same time, eliminating what I considered superfluous or unrelated information.

Since this book is primarily designed for the training of pilots, I suppose you might feel that certain sections are unnecessarily technical, with the reaction something akin to, "Why do I need all this stuff about lift, drag, carburetors, instrument systems, warm fronts, cold fronts, and the rest? If I can get an airplane off the ground and bring it back, that's all that counts, isn't it?"

Well, maybe, but that is a house built on sand! Knowing how and why an airplane flies, knowing its operational limits and the dangers of exceeding them, understanding the theories of flight, the basics of weather, how to calculate aircraft performance under varying surface and atmospheric conditions—these and more constitute the foundation on which safe flying skills are constructed.

You really don't have to know much about an automobile to drive it, but an automobile is hardly an airplane. Because of the forces that act upon it and the environment in which it functions, the latter is a far more complex means of getting from here to there. Were the basic principles not so essential for proficient and safe flight, they would not be part of all ground school courses and written pilot exams.

No one book on the subject, however, and certainly not this one, can contain the whole depth and breadth of information required of the complete pilot. Sections of this book will presumably need further explanation by a qualified instructor. And certainly no one book can keep up with the changes that are taking place in aviation. Consequently, knowledge growth, skill growth, and currency maintenance have to be the responsibility of each student pilot and each licensed pilot.

Subscribe to aviation publications, study the *Aeronautical Information Manual*, read the FAA circulars, buy or rent videos, read books, attend the periodic FAA-sponsored safety seminars, join aviation-oriented organizations. Whatever you do, though, don't stop learning. Pilot training has a beginning, but it has no end.

Paul E. (Pete) Illman

1

Earning your wings: rewards and responsibilities

A logical assumption: You bought or borrowed this book because you're considering learning to fly or are perhaps in the early stages of doing so. If either is the case, I'd like to offer a few introductory thoughts about what being a pilot could or should mean to you. In addition, I've included some suggestions on choosing a flight training school, what you should expect of an instructor, and your own feelings and behaviors during the training period. I hope you won't look on this as a preaching chapter but rather one that touches on some matters not always discussed either before or during the flight-training program. So, to get underway, let's begin with...

A few among many

Becoming a pilot means that you are joining a group of about 620,000 certificated pilots in the United States, the majority of whom hold private or commercial certificates and make up what is referred to as "general aviation," (versus airline and military). Relatively speaking, 620,000 is not a very large group—about the equivalent of a midsized American city—which is not a particularly meaningful comparison, but it does point out that those who have earned their pilot ratings are only a very small segment of the nation's 260 million citizens.

Which leads to the next point: It's probably fair to say that from way back in ancient times man has searched for ways to break the "surly bonds" and soar unfettered above all that lies below. Discounting, of course, the millions of airline passengers who are doing that very thing every year, those of us who have earned our pilots' wings are infinitely small drops in the ocean of past and present humanity. At the same time, we are the fortunate few given the opportunity to enjoy the freedom of flight as well as the ability to learn what needs to be learned and do what needs to be done to earn those wings. That doesn't mean that we're all Phi Beta Kappas or Mensa members. Pilots aren't superhumans, physically or mentally. They're mostly just average people with the determination and the ability to achieve something that is of meaning and consequence to them.

Okay, but so what? You ask. The "so what" is this: Once you pass the FAA's written exam, the oral exams, the examiner's flight test, and have your signed private pilot's certificate in hand, you will have accomplished something countless others never even tried or didn't have what it takes to succeed. If you can look on the accomplishment in that light, you ought to be proud of whom you are and what you have done. Your achievement should be a self-esteem builder—if it ever needed building.

Self-esteem and the younger student pilot

Relating this to the matter at hand, perhaps for the emotionally mature adult who learns to fly, increased self-esteem may not be that important (although I've never yet met a pilot, whatever the age, who wasn't proud to have it known that, yes, he was a pilot). In this day when we hear so much about teenagers' behaviors, their lack of discipline, peer pressure, their need for attention, their lack of self-esteem, and all the rest, learning to fly could be one of the solutions to a disturbing problem. To be more explicit, let me put it this way:

A youngster doesn't have to be of any minimum age to take flying lessons—7, 10, 14; it doesn't matter. As long as he or she can physically reach the controls (control column, rudder pedals, throttle, instrument panel, and the like), he or she can do the necessary homework and take flight lessons. This same student, though, cannot solo an airplane until the age of 16 and cannot get a private pilot's certificate until he or she is 17. Whatever the case, the matter of self-esteem and self-discipline now enters the picture.

In the middle-school and high-school environment where peer pressure, attention, self-confidence, self-esteem, pride, acceptance, and all the rest are so important, that young student pilot is doing something that most likely no one else in his or her peer group is doing: He or she is learning to fly. If at least 16, this student has soloed; taken off and landed dozens of times; put the airplane though stalls, steep turns, and a variety of other in-flight maneuvers; and has made several cross-country flights. If the student is 17 or more, he or she is a certificated private pilot; has passed the various FAA exams; can now carry passengers; and already has logged 50, 60, 80, 100 hours of flight time.

These youngsters don't need to do oddball things to get attention or build their self-esteem. They don't need to pop pills, gulp down booze, and rely on dress style or body adornments. They're getting their kicks and jollies from flying airplanes. And, as long as they don't flaunt their accomplishments, they should have a level of self-esteem that eliminates the need for questionable or harmful behaviors.

Flying and discipline

Something else to consider about flying is self-discipline. Simply put, flying demands it. While this subject alone could take up a couple of chapters, suffice it to say that a pilot who fails to go by the book, who disregards rules, procedures, or instructions is unlikely to be flying very long. If his or her own foolish lack of discipline doesn't do him in, the FAA surely will. The earlier this absolute requirement for self-discipline is learned, the more deeply it will become ingrained as an unconscious behavior pattern. And, once that point is reached, the behavior will tend to carry over to ground activities like study habits, substance usage, or getting behind the wheel of an automobile.

The careful, rule-obedient pilot is usually, but not inevitably, a careful, accident-free driver If you think about it, airplane accidents resulting from dumb flying, such as buzzing Aunt Abigail's house, doing acrobatics at 500 feet, or trying to fly formation with another unqualified formation pilot, are very rare occurrences. Pilots do have accidents, but most are caused by other factors such as weather, fuel exhaustion, a communications failure, or a mechanical failure rather than the lack of discipline.

Self-esteem, discipline, and drugs

Another aspect of this self-esteem/discipline discussion is the issue of alcohol and drugs in the aviation environment. If your self-esteem is healthy, and if you truly understand the dangers of alcohol and drugs, peer pressure urging you to "just try once" any of such substances should have zero influence on you.

One additional deterrent to substance use, or abuse, ought to be the FAA's position on it in pilot certification. This is touched on in the later chapter on medical facts for pilots, but when you go for your FAA physical exam, you will be asked to fill out a medical history form. On the form is a question relative to substance abuse, and specifically a question that asks if you have ever been convicted of driving under the influence. There is also a place for you to sign your approval authorizing the FAA to verify your driving record through your state's National Driver Registry. If you don't sign the authorization, you won't get your certificate, be you a student pilot or an airline captain. So whatever your previous driving record relative to substance abuse, tell the truth. You might as well, because the FAA is going to check that record anyway.

Selecting the flight school and the instructor

Unless you've already selected the flight school or FBO (Fixed Base Operator) for your training, I'd suggest that you shop around a little. That assumes, of course, that you're in an area where you have the option of several schools or airports from which to choose. Whatever the case, you might evaluate a few things like the following before you commit yourself:

- What does the office look like? Neat, clean, businesslike, or sloppy, disorganized, ill kempt?
- What was your initial impression of how you were greeted? How thoroughly were your questions answered? Did you get the feeling that people wanted to help you?
- Did you meet your potential instructor? If so, how would you evaluate the person's attitude and observable behaviors?
- What could you learn about him or her? How long had he/she been instructing? How many hours had he/she logged? What ratings did he/she have? What is his charge per hour? What is the per-hour rate for the airplane? Can you buy block time, as 10 hours of time for the cost of 9 hours? Does the FBO accept credit cards? If so, which? Does the instructor charge for instructing time he/she spends with you on the ground? If, so, how much per hour? As a first impression, do you think you would be comfortable, compatible with this individual?
- What type of aircraft does the FBO have? Were you able to inspect the planes close-up? How would you describe their

exterior and interior condition? Clean, painted, seat upholstery and carpet in good shape, exterior free of oil streaks, dents? (Note: a dirty, in-need-of-paint aircraft with worn seat covers, etc., doesn't mean the aircraft is poorly maintained mechanically, but its condition should raise some questions about the rest of the operation.)

Just a few points to consider when selecting a flying school and an instructor: Keep this in mind, though. You and the instructor have to be compatible—you have to be able to trust him or her; you have to feel free to ask questions; and you have the right to expect clear and full answers. If any element of that relationship is lacking at any point in the training process, ask for another instructor or take your business elsewhere. You have to be satisfied; you have to feel comfortable in every relationship with the instructor; you should look forward eagerly to the next lesson; you should be having fun during every lesson; you should feel satisfied with the progress you're making; and you should know that your instructor knows how to teach and knows what he or she is teaching. You're paying good money for the privilege of learning and you have the right to get the best in return. Are you? Or, if you're just starting out, do you think you will?

Some questions about you

And now, what about you? Some random questions you should perhaps ask of yourself:

- Can you be counted on to keep scheduled flight or ground school appointments?
- If you can't meet a certain schedule, do you always advise the FBO or your instructor as far in advance as possible?
- Are you always on time or early for your scheduled appointments?
- Have you done whatever homework the instructor has assigned? (Reading, problem solving, preflight planning, cross-country flight plotting, etc.)
- If it isn't offered, do you ask for a clear briefing on what you will be doing during the upcoming lesson?
- Do you ask questions about doubtful areas left over from the previous lesson or from the homework?
- Do you always bring your logbook with you for each lesson?

- Do you always make a thorough preflight inspection of the airplane you are about to fly—even though somebody just flew it?
- Do you always use checklists for preflight aircraft inspections, engine start-up, pretakeoff checks, and prelanding checks?
- Are you rested, fed, and ready to go for each lesson?
- Do you ask questions during flight about maneuvers or what you are doing right or incorrectly?
- If your instructor makes you nervous or uncomfortable in the air, do you feel free to discuss that with him or her back on the ground?
- Do you pay your bills on time?
- Are you clean and properly dressed for each lesson? (Remember that cockpits in small planes are rather tight—and hot during summer days.)
- Do you ask your instructor for ongoing feedback on how you are doing? On your progress?
- Do you reflect genuine interest before, during, and after each lesson?
- If you were your instructor, how would you rate you? Would you enjoy having you as a student?

One other suggestion for you, if you are a student pilot, whatever your age: Once you begin the training, don't let too much time lapse between lessons. The closer together you can schedule your flying sessions, the better. Otherwise, after a long period off—say three weeks, four weeks, or more—you'll find that you'll have considerable relearning to do, and that it will take some time to regain the feel of things.

The unexpected is inevitable. Schedules will have to be revised; appointments postponed or canceled; weather will throw the best of plans out of kilter. Recognizing the inevitability of the inevitables, you should try to get as much flying time as you can in the most condensed period of time. If you have never flown before, you should be able to solo after 10 to 14 hours of instruction and complete the training for your private pilot certificate in 40 to 50 hours or so. If, however, you drag out the time between lessons and fly, say, only 2 or 3 hours a month, it will take a lot more time to solo or get the certificate. Plus that added time, don't forget the added cost. Flight training can get rather expensive if you allow it to drag on and on.

In the interests of time management and money conservation, you might want to consider setting some specific achievement objectives, such as, "To solo by X date"; "To be scheduled for the FAA written exam by Y date"; "To be approved by my instructor for the FAA flight test by Z date."

Make these challenging but attainable targets, write them down, and then go back to the solo objective and develop a schedule or timetable to reach the objective. If you need to, discuss the objectives with your instructor, your family, or whomever to be sure that each objective is practical from their point of view. Once you've met the solo challenge, develop a set of plans that will lead to the attainment of the second objective...and so on until you have that long-hoped-for certificate safely in hand.

But enough of the preaching and suggesting. Let's now get to the nittty-gritty of it, starting with the Principles of Flight in Chapter 2.

2

Principles of flight

With the preliminary comments and observations out of the way, it's time to get to heart of the matter by discussing how a heavier-than-air machine, of whatever size or description, is able to defy the law of gravity and apparently soar effortlessly through the atmosphere. Oh, sure, we know it's because the vehicle has a wing and the equivalent of tail feathers at its back end. Also, we know that it has an engine of some sort that provides the force necessary to propel the vehicle into flight. And we know that the vehicle will remain airborne until some other force is exerted and causes the vehicle to succumb to the gravity that it had earlier overcome.

In between departure from the earth and return to it, certain laws of nature or physics—both favorable and unfavorable—have come into play. Consequently, to understand and be able to predict aircraft performance under various operating conditions, every pilot needs as much knowledge as possible of those laws and principles that so directly affect the aircraft from takeoff to landing.

In moving into the subject, however, I'd ask you to keep in mind that the principles discussed in the chapter are primarily directed to those just beginning their flight-training program. Accordingly, what follows does not pretend to be a complete examination of all of the complexities of aerodynamics. I do hope, however, that the discussion will encourage you to delve more deeply into the subject as you gain flight experience and move into larger and more complex aircraft.

Forces acting on the airplane in flight

Among the aerodynamic forces acting on an airplane during flight, four are considered basic because they affect the aircraft in all of its maneuvers. These forces are lift—the upward-acting force; weight

9

(or gravity)—the downward-acting force; thrust—the forward-acting force; and drag—the retarding or rearward-acting force (Fig. 2-1). Lift and thrust are the positive (1) forces, and weight and drag the negative (2) forces.

While in steady flight, the altitude, direction, and speed of the airplane will remain constant *until* one or more of the basic forces changes in magnitude. In unaccelerated (steady) flight, the opposing forces are in equilibrium. In other words, lift equals weight, thrust equals drag, and the sum of the opposing forces is zero.

When pressure is applied to the airplane controls, one or more of the basic forces changes in magnitude and becomes greater than the opposing force. This causes the airplane to accelerate or move in the direction of the applied force. For example, if power is applied (increasing thrust) and altitude is maintained, the airplane will accelerate. As speed increases, drag increases, until a point is reached where drag again equals thrust. At that point, the airplane will continue in steady flight but at a higher speed.

Another example: If power is applied while in level flight, and a climb attitude is established, the force of lift would increase during the time back elevator pressure is applied. After a steady rate of climb is established, though, the force of lift would be approximately equal to the force of weight. The airplane climbs not because lift is greater than in level flight, but because thrust is greater than drag. At

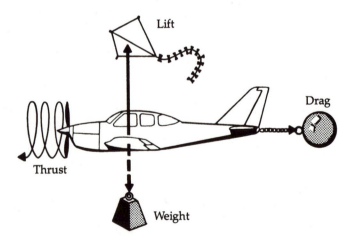

Fig. 2-1. *The four forces acting on an airplane in flight.*

the same time, it climbs because a component of thrust is developed that acts upward, perpendicular to the flight path.

Airplane designers always try to increase aircraft performance by increasing the efficiency of the desirable forces of lift and thrust while reducing, as much as possible, the undesirable forces of weight and drag. Nonetheless, compromises must be made to meet the function and desired performance of the airplane.

Before discussing the four forces further, it might be helpful to define some of the terms used extensively in this section:

acceleration—This force is involved in overcoming inertia, and it is defined as a change of velocity per unit of time. It means changing speed and/or direction, including starting from rest (positive acceleration) and stopping (deceleration or negative acceleration).

airfoil—An airfoil is any surface, such as an airplane wing, that is designed to obtain reaction such as lift from the air through which it moves. Typical airfoil sections are shown in Fig. 2-2.

angle of attack—The acute angle between the chord line of the wing and the direction of the relative wind (Fig. 2-3).

angle of incidence—The acute angle formed by the chord line of the wing and the longitudinal axis of the airplane (Fig. 2-4). It is determined during the design of the airplane and is the angle at which

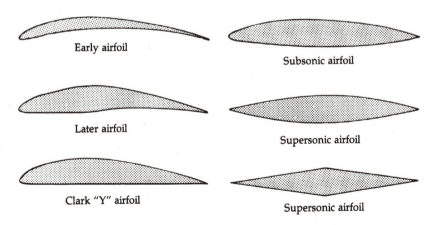

Fig. 2-2. *Typical airfoil sections.*

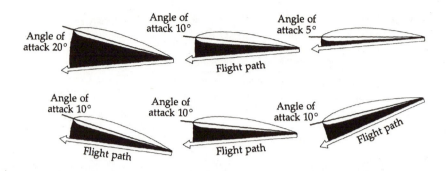

Fig. 2-3. *(Above) The angle of attack is the angle between the wing chord and the flight path. (Below) The angle of attack is always based on the flight path, not the ground.*

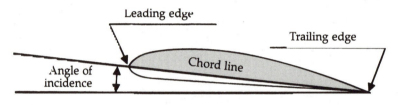

Line parallel to longitudinal axis

Fig. 2-4. *A cross-sectional view of an airfoil illustrating the chord line.*

the wing is attached to the fuselage. Therefore, it's a fixed angle and can't be changed by the pilot. Don't confuse this angle with the angle of attack.

chord—An imaginary straight line drawn from the leading edge to the trailing edge of a cross section of an airfoil (Fig. 2-4).

camber—Camber is the curvature of the airfoil from the leading edge to the trailing edge. "Upper camber" refers to the curvature of the upper surface, "lower camber" to the curvature of the lower surface, and "mean camber" to the mean line that is equidistant at all points between the upper and lower surfaces (Fig. 2-5).

component—A component is one of the various forces or parts of a combination of forces. See Fig. 2-6, which illustrates the component of lift vertically and the component of drag horizontally.

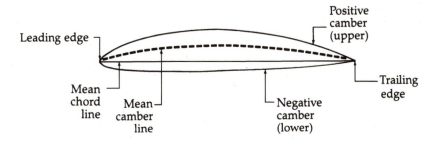

Fig. 2-5. *The structure of an airfoil section, in terms of the three types of camber (upper, lower, and "mean").*

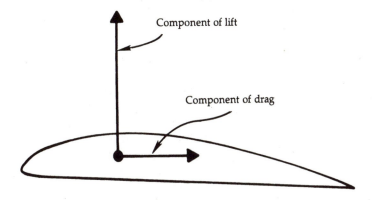

Fig. 2-6. *Two of the component forces that act upon an aircraft in flight.*

relative wind—The direction of the airflow produced by an object moving through the air (Fig. 2-7). The relative wind for an airplane in flight flows in a direction parallel with and opposite to the direction of flight. Accordingly, the actual flight path of the airplane determines the direction of the relative wind.

speed—Rather obviously, speed is the distance traveled in a certain period of time.

vector—A vector is the graphic representation of a force drawn in a straight line that indicates direction by an arrow and magnitude by its length. When an object is being acted on by two or more forces, the combined effect of these forces is represented by a *resultant* vector. After the vectors have been resolved, the resultant can be

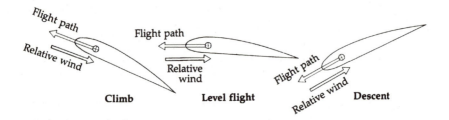

Fig. 2-7. *An illustration of the relationship between an aircraft's flight path and relative wind.*

measured to determine the direction and magnitude of the combined forces (Fig. 2-8).

velocity—The speed or rate of movement in a certain direction.

wing area—The wing area is the plan surface of the wing and control surfaces. It may also include the wing area covered by the fuselage (main body of the airplane) and engine nacelles.

wing planform—The shape or form of a wing as viewed from above. It may be long and tapered, short and rectangular, or various other shapes (Fig. 2-9).

wingspan—Wingspan is simply the length of the wing from wing tip to wing tip.

Lift

Lift is the upward force created by an airfoil when it is moved through the air. Although lift may be exerted to some extent by many external parts, an airplane has three principal airfoils—the wing, the propeller, and the horizontal tail surfaces.

In explaining how a wing produces lift, Bernoulli's principle and one of Newton's laws come into play:

Bernoulli's principle states, in part, that "the internal pressure of a fluid (liquid or gas) decreases at points where the speed of the fluid increases." In other words, high speed flow is associated with low pressure, and low speed flow with high pressure.

This principle is made apparent by changes in pressure of fluid flowing within a pipe where the inside diameter of the pipe decreases,

similar to a venturi tube (Fig. 2-10). In the wide section of the gradually narrowing pipe, the fluid flows at a lower speed, producing a
higher pressure. As the pipe narrows it still contains the same
amount of fluid, but because the passageway is constricted, the fluid
flows at a higher speed producing a lower pressure.

The same principle applies to an airplane wing, since it is designed
and constructed with a curve or camber (Fig. 2-10). When air flows

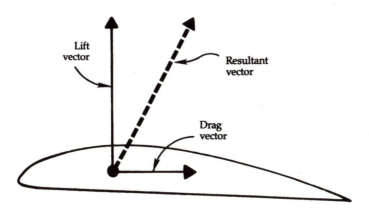

Fig. 2-8. *How two or more forces acting on an object produce the
resultant vector.*

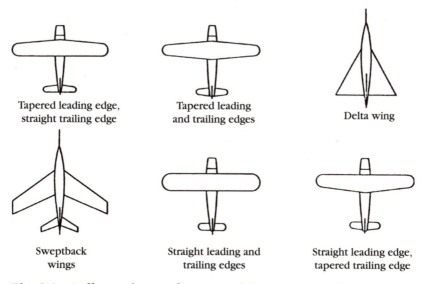

Fig. 2-9. *Different shapes of wings and their wing planforms.*

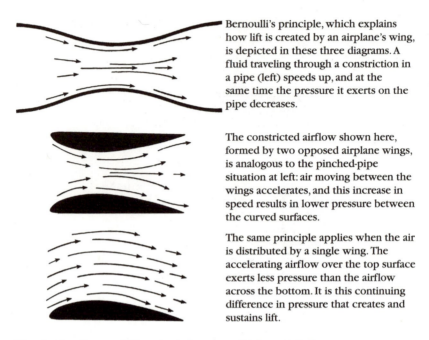

Bernoulli's principle, which explains how lift is created by an airplane's wing, is depicted in these three diagrams. A fluid traveling through a constriction in a pipe (left) speeds up, and at the same time the pressure it exerts on the pipe decreases.

The constricted airflow shown here, formed by two opposed airplane wings, is analogous to the pinched-pipe situation at left: air moving between the wings accelerates, and this increase in speed results in lower pressure between the curved surfaces.

The same principle applies when the air is distributed by a single wing. The accelerating airflow over the top surface exerts less pressure than the airflow across the bottom. It is this continuing difference in pressure that creates and sustains lift.

Fig. 2-10. *Bernoulli's principle as applied to airfoils.*

along the upper wing surface, it travels a greater distance in the same period of time as the airflow along the lower wing surface. Therefore, as established by Bernoulli's principle, the pressure above the wing is less than it is below the wing, generating a lift force over the upper curved surface of the wing in the direction of the low pressure.

Because for every action there is an equal and opposite reaction (Newton's third law of motion), an additional upward force is generated as the lower surface of the wing deflects the air downward (Fig. 2-11). Thus both the development of low pressure above the wing and reaction to the force and direction of air as it is deflected from the wing's lower surface contribute to the total lift generated.

The amount of lift generated by the wing depends upon several factors:

1. Speed of the wing through the air
2. Angle of attack
3. Planform of the wing

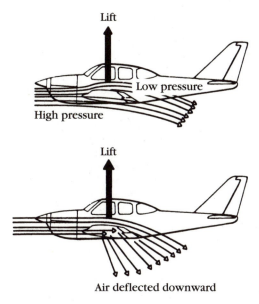

Fig. 2-11. *How the lower surface of the wing deflects air downward to contribute to the total lift generated.*

4. Wing area

5. The density of the air

Lift acts upward and perpendicular to the relative wind and to the wingspan (Fig. 2-12). Although lift is generated over the entire wing, an imaginary point is established that represents the resultant of all lift forces. This single point is the center of lift, sometimes referred to as the center of pressure (CP). The location of the center of pressure relative to the center of gravity (weight) is very important from the standpoint of airplane stability. Stability is covered in more detail later in this chapter.

Gravity (weight)

Gravity is the downward force that tends to draw all bodies vertically toward the center of the earth. The airplane's center of gravity (CG) is the point on the airplane at which all weight is considered to be concentrated. It is the point of balance. As an example, if an airplane were suspended from a rope attached at its center of gravity, the airplane would hang (or should) in perfect balance (Fig. 2-13).

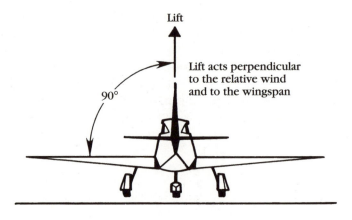

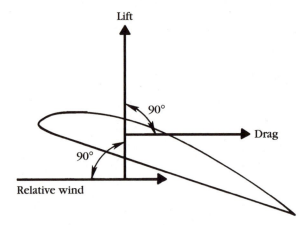

Fig. 2-12. *The relationship between relative wind, lift, and drag.*

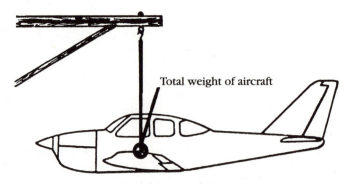

Fig. 2-13. *An airplane suspended from its center of gravity should hang in perfect balance.*

The center of gravity is located along the longitudinal centerline of the airplane (the imaginary line from the nose to the tail) and somewhere near the center of lift of the wing. The location of the center of gravity depends on the location and weight of the load placed in the airplane. This is determined and controlled through weight and balance calculations made by the pilot prior to flight. The exact location of the center of gravity is important during flight because of its effect on airplane stability and performance.

Thrust

The propeller, itself an airfoil, produces the thrust, or forward force, that drives the airplane through the air. It receives its power directly from the engine and is designed to displace a large mass of air to the rear. It is the rearward displacement that develops the forward thrust that carries the airplane through the air. This thrust, though, must be strong enough to counteract the forces of drag and to give the airplane the desired forward motion. The direction of this thrust force is referred to as the *thrust line.*

Drag

Drag is the rearward acting force that resists the forward movement of the airplane through the air. Drag acts parallel to and in the same direction as the relative wind (Fig. 2-14).

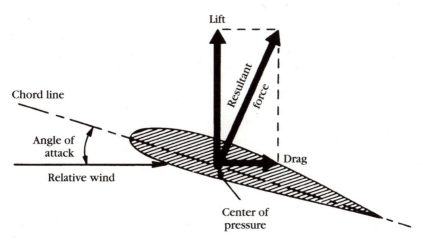

Fig. 2-14. *Drag acts parallel to and in the same direction as the relative wind.*

Every part of the airplane that is exposed to the air while the airplane is in motion produces some resistance and contributes to the total drag. Total drag can be classified into two main types: *induced drag* and *parasite drag.*

Induced drag is the undesirable but unavoidable by-product of lift, and it increases in direct proportion to increases in angle of attack. The greater the angle of attack, up to the critical angle, the greater the amount of lift developed, and the greater the induced drag. The airflow around the wing is deflected downward, producing a rearward component to the lift vector that is induced drag. The amount of air deflected downward increases greatly at higher angles of attack; consequently, the higher the angle of attack or the slower the airplane is flown, the greater the induced drag.

Parasite drag is the resistance of the air produced by any part of the airplane that does not produce lift. Several factors affect parasite drag. When each factor is considered independently, it must be assumed that other factors remain constant:

1. The more streamlined an object, the less the parasite drag.
2. The more dense the air moving past the airplane, the greater the parasite drag.
3. The larger the size of the object in the airstream, the greater the parasite drag.
4. As speed increases, the amount of parasite drag increases; if the speed is doubled, four times as much drag is produced.

Parasite drag can be further classified into *form drag, skin friction,* and *interference drag.* Form drag is caused by the frontal area of the airplane components being exposed to the airstream. A similar reaction is illustrated by Fig. 2-15, where the side of a flat plate is exposed to the airstream. The drag is caused by the form of the plate and is the reason streamlining is necessary to increase airplane efficiency and speed. Fig. 2-15 also illustrates that when the face of the plate is parallel with the airstream, the largest part of the drag is skin friction.

Skin friction drag is caused by air passing over the airplane's surfaces, and it increases considerably if the airplane surfaces are rough and dirty.

Interference drag is caused by interference of the airflow between adjacent parts of the airplane such as the intersection of wings and tail sections with the fuselage. Fairings are used to streamline these intersections and decrease interference drag.

In the final analysis, it's the airplane's total drag that determines the amount of thrust required at a given airspeed. Figure 2-16 illustrates the variation in parasite, induced, and total drag with speed for a typical airplane in steady level flight. Thrust must equal drag in steady flight; therefore the curve for the total drag also represents

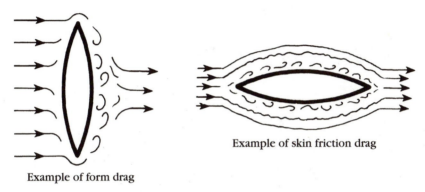

Example of skin friction drag

Example of form drag

Fig. 2-15. *Two types of drag—form and skin friction—that affect aircraft speed and efficiency.*

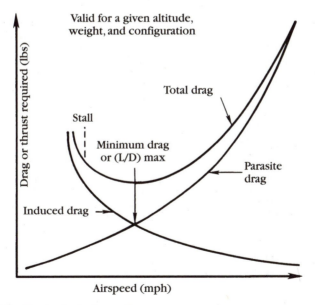

Fig. 2-16. *Typical airplane drag curves.*

the thrust required. Also note in Fig. 2-16 that the airspeed at which minimum drag occurs is the same airspeed at which the maximum lift/drag ratio (L/D) takes place. At this point, the least power is required for both maximum lift and minimum total drag. This becomes important in determining maximum endurance and range for the airplane.

The force of drag can be controlled to a certain extent by the pilot. Loading the airplane properly, retracting the landing gear (if so equipped) and flaps when not used, and keeping the surface of the airplane clean, all help to reduce the total drag.

Relationship of forces on flight

As one might expect, the relationships of some of these forces inevitably have material effects on the aircraft in flight. The following, then, illustrates the key relationships, after which are additional factors that can have particular effects on both lift and drag.

Relationship between angle of attack and lift

As mentioned previously, the angle of attack is the acute angle between the relative wind and the chord line of the wing. At small angles of attack, most of the wing lift is a result of the difference in pressure between the upper and lower surfaces of the wing (Bernoulli's principle). Additional lift is generated by the equal and opposite reaction of the airstream being deflected downward from the wing (Newton's law).

As the angle of attack is increased, the airstream is forced to travel faster because of the greater distance over the upper surface of the wing, thus creating a greater pressure differential between the upper and lower surfaces. At the same time, the airstream is deflected downward at a greater angle, causing an increased opposite reaction. Both the increased pressure differential and increased opposite reaction increase lift as well as drag. Thus as angle of attack is increased, lift is increased up to the *critical angle of attack* (Fig. 2-17).

When the angle of attack is increased to approximately 18° to 20° (critical angle of attack) on most airfoils, the airstream can no longer follow the upper curvature of the wing because of the excessive change in direction and begins separating from the rear of the upper wing surface. As the angle of attack is further increased, the

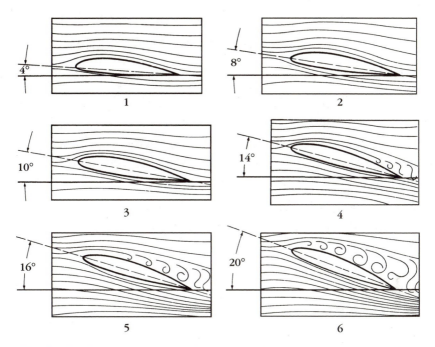

Fig. 2-17. *The patterns of airflow around a wing at various angles of attack.*

airstream is forced to flow straight back, away from the top surface of the wing and from the area of highest camber. This causes a swirling or burbling of the air as it attempts to follow the upper surface of the wing. When the critical angle of attack is reached, the turbulent airflow, which appeared near the trailing edge of the wing at lower angles of attack, quickly spreads forward over the entire upper wing surface as Fig. 2-17, frame 6, illustrates. This results in a sudden increase in pressure on the upper wing surface and a considerable loss of lift. Due to the loss of lift and increase in form drag, the remaining lift is insufficient to support the airplane, and the wing stalls. To recover from a stall, the angle of attack must be decreased so that the airstream can once again flow smoothly over the wing surface.

Remember that the angle of attack is the angle between the chord line and the relative wind, not the chord line and the horizon. Therefore, an airplane can be stalled in any attitude of flight with respect to the horizon, if the angle of attack is increased up to and beyond the critical angle of attack.

Relationship of thrust and drag in straight-and-level flight

During straight-and-level flight, thrust and drag are equal in magnitude if a constant airspeed is being maintained. When the thrust of the propeller is increased, thrust momentarily exceeds drag and the airspeed increases, provided straight-and-level flight is maintained. As said earlier, as airspeed increases, drag increases very rapidly. Eventually, if all available power is used, thrust will reach its maximum, the airspeed will increase until drag equals thrust, and the airspeed will become constant. This will be the top speed for that airplane in that configuration and attitude.

When thrust becomes less than drag, the airplane decelerates to a slower airspeed, provided straight-and-level flight is maintained, until thrust and drag again become equal. Of course, if the airspeed becomes too slow, or more precisely, if the angle of attack is too great, in an effort to maintain the current altitude, the airplane will stall.

Relationship of lift weight in straight-and-level flight

The upward force on the wing, which is a component of lift, always acts perpendicular to the direction of the relative wind. In straight-and-level flight (constant altitude), lift counterbalances the airplane weight. When lift and weight are equal, the airplane neither gains nor loses altitude. If lift becomes less than weight, the airplane enters a descent; if lift becomes greater than weight, the airplane enters a climb. Once a steady rate of climb or descent is established, the relationship of the four forces won't be quite the same as in straight-and-level flight, but for all practical purposes, lift still equals weight for small angles of climb or descent.

In summary, when the aircraft is flying at a constant airspeed and a constant altitude, thrust equals drag and lift equals weight. The aircraft is neither losing nor gaining airspeed and is neither losing nor gaining altitude.

Factors affecting lift and drag

Some of the factors that influence lift and drag include wing area, shape of the airfoil, angle of attack, speed of the air passing over the wing (airspeed), and density of the air moving over the wing. A change in any of these factors affects the relationship between lift and drag because when lift is increased, drag is increased, and when lift is decreased, drag is decreased.

Effect of wing area on lift and drag

The lift and drag acting on a wing are proportional to the wing area. This means that if the wing area is doubled, other variables remaining the same, the lift and drag created by the wing are also doubled.

Effect of airfoil shape on lift and drag

Generally, the more curvature there is to the upper surface of an airfoil, the more lift is produced (up to a point). High-lift wings have a large convex curvature on the upper surface and a concave lower surface. Most airplanes have wing flaps that, when lowered, cause an ordinary wing to approximate the high-lift condition by increasing the curvature of the upper surface and creating a concave lower surface, thus increasing the wing's lift (Fig. 2-18).

A lowered aileron also produces that same effect by extending the curvature of a portion of the wing and thereby increasing the angle of attack, which in turn increases lift and also drag. A raised aileron reduces lift on the wing by decreasing the curvature of a portion of the wing and decreasing the angle of attack. The elevators alter the curvature and angle of attack of the horizontal tail surfaces by changing the amount and direction of lift, while the rudder does the same thing for the vertical tail surfaces.

It's often thought by the uninitiated that the only danger of in-flight icing is the weight of the ice that forms on the wings. It's true that ice can increase the weight, but more important is the fact that an ice formation can alter the shape of the airfoil and, with sufficient accumulation, seriously affect all aspects of airplane performance and control. As the ice forms on the airfoil, especially the leading edge, the flow of air over the wing is disrupted. This disruption of the smooth airflow causes the wing to lose part or all of its lifting efficiency—while drag, at the same time, is increased substantially.

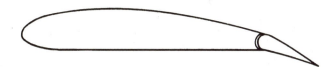

Fig. 2-18. *The use of flaps increases lift and drag.*

Even a slight coating of frost on the wings could prevent an airplane from becoming airborne for the same reason: The smooth flow of air over the wing surface is disrupted and the lift capability of the wing is destroyed. Even more hazardous is becoming airborne with frost on the wing because, again, performance and control could be adversely affected. This is why it is *extremely* important that all frost, snow, and ice be removed from the airplane before takeoff.

Effect of wing design on aircraft stalls

The type of wing design for a particular airplane depends almost entirely on the purpose for which that airplane is to be used. If speed is the prime consideration, a tapered wing is more desirable than a rectangular wing, but a tapered wing with no twist has undesirable stall characteristics. Assuming equal wing area, the tapered wing produces less drag than the rectangular wing because it has less area at its tip. The elliptical wing is more efficient (greater lift for the amount of drag), but doesn't have as good stall characteristics as the rectangular wing.

To achieve those good stall characteristics, the root of the wing should stall first, with the stall pattern progressing outward to the tip. This type of pattern decreases undesirable rolling tendencies and increases lateral control when approaching the stall itself. It's not desirable for a wing tip to stall first, particularly if the tip of one wing stalls before the tip of the other wing, which usually happens.

A desirable stall pattern can be accomplished by:

1. Designing the wing with a twist so that the tip has a lower angle of incidence and therefore a lower angle of attack when the root of the wing approaches the critical angle of attack (Fig. 2-19).
2. Designing slots near the leading edge of the wing tip to allow air to flow smoothly over that part of the wing at higher angles of attack, thereby stalling the root of the wing first (Fig. 2-20).
3. Attaching stall or spoiler strips on the leading edge near the wing root. This strip breaks up the airflow at higher angles of attack and produces the desired effect of the root area of the wing stalling first (Fig. 2-21).

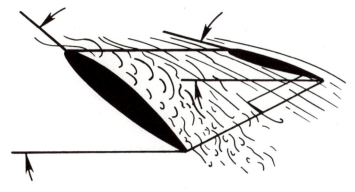

Fig. 2-19. *A view of wing tip twist. Ailerons are still effective even though the wing root is in a stalled condition.*

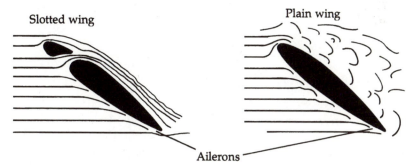

Fig. 2-20. *Slotted wing tip, its effect on airflow and wing stalling, versus the plain wing at equal angles of attack.*

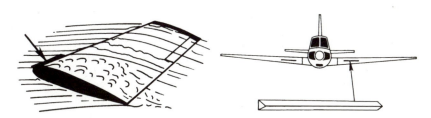

Fig. 2-21. *The stall strip—another means to ensure that the root section stalls first.*

Effect of airspeed on lift and drag

An increase in the velocity of the air passing over the wing (airspeed) increases lift and drag. Lift is increased because:

1. The increased impact of the relative wind on the wing's lower surface creates a greater amount of air being deflected downward.

2. The increased speed of the relative wind over the upper surface creates a lower pressure on top of the wing (Bernoulli's principle).

3. A greater pressure differential between the upper and lower wing surface is created. Drag is also increased, since any change that increases lift also increases drag.

Tests show that lift and drag vary as the square of the velocity. The velocity of the air passing over the wing in flight is determined by the airspeed of the airplane. If an airplane doubles its speed, it quadruples the lift and drag (assuming that the angle of attack remains the same).

Effect of air density on lift and drag

Lift and drag vary directly with the density of the air: As air density increases, lift and drag increase; as air density decreases, lift and drag decrease. Air density is affected by pressure, temperature, and humidity. At an altitude of 18,000 feet, the density of the air is half the density at sea level. Consequently, if an airplane is to maintain the same lift at high altitudes, the amount of air flowing over the wing must be the same as at lower altitudes. To achieve this, the speed of the air over the wings (airspeed) must be increased. This is why an airplane requires a longer takeoff distance to become airborne at higher altitudes than with similar conditions at lower altitudes (Fig. 2-22).

Because air expands when heated, warm air is less dense than cool air. When other conditions remain the same, an airplane requires a longer takeoff run on a hot day than on a cool day (Fig. 2-22).

Similarly, because water vapor weighs less than an equal amount of dry air, moist air (high relative humidity) is less dense than dry air (low relative humidity). Therefore, when other conditions remain the same, the airplane requires a longer takeoff run on a humid day

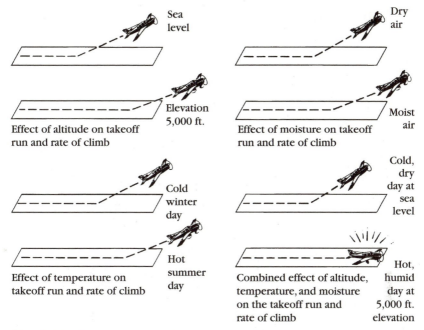

Fig. 2-22. *The various combinations of altitude, temperature, and humidity and their effects on takeoff runs and rates of climb.*

than on a dry day (Fig. 2-22). This is especially true on a hot, humid day because the air can hold much more water vapor than on a cool day. The more moisture in the air, the less dense the air.

Less dense air also causes other performance losses besides the loss of lift. Engine horsepower falls off and propeller efficiency decreases because of power loss, and propeller blades, being airfoils themselves, are less effective when air is less dense. Because the propeller is not pulling with its normal force and efficiency, it takes longer to build up the necessary forward speed to produce the required lift for takeoff. The result? The airplane needs a longer takeoff run. The rate of climb is also less for the same reasons.

Considering these factors, it's obvious that a pilot should beware of the three Hs: High, Hot, and Humid—high altitudes, hot temperatures, and high moisture content (high relative humidity). A combination of these three conditions could be disastrous, especially if combined with a short runway, a heavily loaded airplane, or other takeoff-limiting conditions.

Turning tendency (torque effect)

By definition, torque is a force, or combination of forces, that produces, or tends to produce, a twisting or rotating motion of an airplane.

An airplane propeller spinning clockwise, as seen from the cockpit, produces forces that tend to twist or rotate the airplane in the opposite direction, thus turning the airplane to the left. Fortunately, airplanes are designed so that the torque effect is not noticeable to the pilot when the airplane is in straight-and-level flight with a cruise power setting.

The effect of torque increases in direct proportion to engine power, airspeed, and airplane attitude. If the power setting is high, the airspeed slow, and the angle of attack high, the torque is greater. During takeoffs and climbs, when torque is most pronounced, the pilot must apply sufficient right rudder pressure to counteract the left-turning tendency and maintain a straight takeoff path.

Several forces are involved in the insistent tendency of an airplane of standard configuration to turn to the left. All of these forces are created by the rotating propeller. How they are actually created varies greatly from one explanation to the next, hence an individual explanation of each is perhaps the best approach to understanding the reason for this left-turning tendency.

The four forces are: *reactive force, spiraling slipstream, gyroscopic precession*, and *"P" factor*.

Reactive force. This is based on Newton's law of action and reaction. Applying the law to an airplane with a propeller rotating in a clockwise direction, as seen from the cockpit, a force is produced that tends to roll the entire airplane about its longitudinal axis in a counterclockwise direction. To better understand this concept, consider the air through which the propeller rotates as a restraining force. This restraining force acts opposite to the direction the propeller rotates, creating a tendency for the airplane to roll to the left (Fig. 2-23).

Spiraling slipstream. This theory is based on the reaction of the air to a rotating propeller blade. As the airplane propeller rotates through the air in a clockwise direction (viewed from the rear), the propeller blade forces the air rearward in a spiraling clockwise direction of flow around the fuselage. A portion of this spiraling slipstream strikes the left side of the vertical stabilizer, forcing the

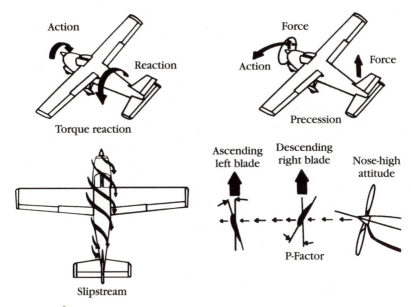

Torque reaction

Precession

Slipstream

P-Factor

Fig. 2-23. *Factors that cause an airplane's left-turning tendency.*

airplane's tail to the right and the nose to the left, causing the airplane to rotate around the vertical axis (Fig. 2-23). The portion of the spiraling slipstream traveling under the fuselage is not obstructed, thus creating a different resistance between the obstructed and the unobstructed flow which causes the left-turning tendency.

Gyroscopic precession. This theory is based on one of the gyroscopic properties that applies to any object spinning in space, even a rotating airplane propeller. As the nose of the airplane is raised, lowered, moved left or right, a deflective force is applied to the spinning propeller, resulting in a reactive force known as *precession*. Precession is the resultant action or deflection of a spinning wheel (propeller in this case) when a force is applied to its rim. This resultant force occurs 90° ahead in the direction of rotation and in the direction of the applied force (Fig. 2-23).

"P" factor, or asymmetric propeller loading. The effects of "P" factor, or asymmetric propeller loading, usually occur when the airplane is flown at a high angle of attack.

The downward-moving blade, which is on the right side of the propeller arc, as seen from the rear, has a higher angle of attack, greater action and reaction, and therefore higher thrust than the upward-moving blade on the left (Fig. 2-23). This results in a tendency for the airplane to yaw around the vertical axis to the left. Again this tendency is most pronounced when the engine is operating at a high power setting and the airplane is flown at a high angle of attack.

Corrections for turning tendency or torque during flight

Because the airplane is flown in cruising flight most of the time, manufacturers design airplanes with certain built-in corrections that counteract, primarily only during straight-and-level cruising flight, the left-turning tendency, or torque effect. The corrections eliminate the necessity of applying constant right rudder pressure. Because the effect of torque varies so much during climbs and changes in angle of attack, it's impractical for designers to try to correct for torque other than during normal cruise conditions. For operations other than straight-and-level, the pilot has alternate means, such as rudder and trim controls, to offset the turning effect.

A couple of examples of built-in corrections: Many manufacturers *cant* the engine so that the thrust line of the propeller points slightly to the right. This counteracts much of the left-turning tendency of the airplane during various conditions of flight. Other manufacturers increase the angle of incidence of the left wing slightly, which increases the angle of attack and therefore increases the lift on this wing. The increased lift counteracts left-turning tendency in cruising flight. The increase in lift, however, increases drag on the left wing, so, to compensate for this, the vertical stabilizer is offset slightly to the left.

Torque corrections in flight conditions, other than cruising flight, must be accomplished by the pilot. This is normally done by applying enough rudder to overcome the left-turning tendency, as in a straight climb where right rudder pressure is necessary.

When thinking of "torque," such things as reactive force, spiraling slipstream, gyroscopic precession, and asymmetric propeller loading ("P" factor) must be considered, as well as any other power-induced forces that tend to turn the airplane.

Airplane stability

Stability is the inherent ability of a body, after its equilibrium is disturbed, to develop forces or moments that tend to return the body to its original position. In other words, a stable airplane tends to return to the original condition of flight if disturbed by a force such as turbulent air. This means that a stable airplane is easy to fly, but it does not mean that a pilot can always depend solely on that built-in stability to return the airplane to its original straight-and-level flight. Even in the most stable craft, some conditions require the use of controls to get the plane back to the desired attitude. You will find, though, that a well-designed plane requires a lot less effort to control it because of its inherent stability.

Stability is classified as *positive, neutral,* or *negative.*

Positive stability can be illustrated by a ball inside of a bowl (Fig. 2-24). If the ball is displaced from its normal resting place at the bottom of the bowl, it eventually returns to that position.

Neutral stability, again using the ball in Fig. 2-24 as an example, is when the ball is on a flat plane. If the ball is displaced, it comes to rest at some new, neutral position and shows no tendency to return to its original position.

Negative stability is, in fact, instability, and can be illustrated by a ball on the top of an inverted bowl (Fig. 2-24). Even the slightest displacement of the ball activates greater forces that cause the ball to continue to move in the direction of the applied force. From this, it's obvious that airplanes should display positive stability, or perhaps neutral stability, but never negative stability.

Stability can be further classified as *static* or *dynamic.* Static stability means that if the airplane's equilibrium is disturbed, forces are activated that initially tend to return the airplane to its original position, as in Example A in Fig. 2-25. In this instance, a positive dynamic stability is a property that dampens the oscillations set up by a statically stable airplane, thus enabling the oscillations to become smaller and smaller in magnitude until the airplane eventually settles down to its original condition of flight.

On the other hand, even with a positive static stability, if a negative dynamic force exists, oscillation would be undamped and increasingly greater displacements would result, as illustrated in Example B, Fig. 2-25 Here, the dynamic might be so great that, if left uncontrolled by the pilot, it could force the airplane well beyond its original straight and level position.

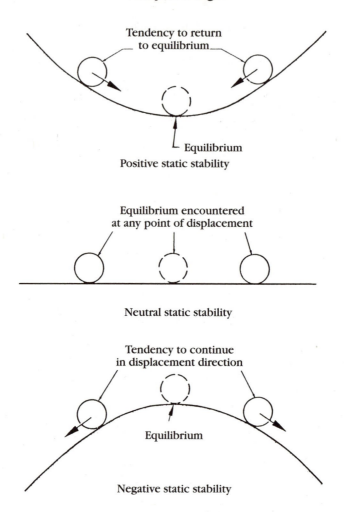

Fig. 2-24. *Illustrations of Positive, Neutral, and Static stability.*

In the third instance (Example C, Fig. 2-25), where the aircraft has a positive static and a neutral dynamic stability, a state of divergent oscillation exists. Here, the various displacements would be approximately the same, being neither damped nor undamped by the neutral dynamics of the aircraft.

With these displacement and oscillation possibilities, it's obvious that a well-designed airplane would possess a stability that is both positive static and positive dynamic in nature—not the positive/negative or positive/neutral conditions depicted in Fig. 2-25's Examples B and C.

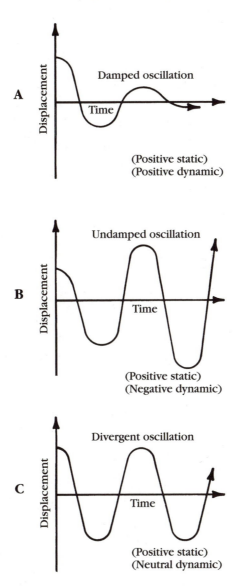

Fig. 2-25. *Relationship of oscillation and static and dynamic stability.*

Before any further discussion of stability, I should first review the axes of rotation because it is around them that stability has its effect. Said simply, an airplane has three axes where movement takes place:

1. The *lateral axis* is an imaginary line from wing tip to wing tip.

2. The *longitudinal axis* is also an imaginary line from the tip of the nose to the tail.

3. The *vertical axis* is another imaginary line extending vertically through the intersection of the lateral and longitudinal lines.

The airplane can rotate around all three axes simultaneously or it can rotate around just one axis (Fig. 2-26). Think of these axes as imaginary axles around which the airplane turns, much as a wheel would turn around axles positioned in these same three planes. The three axes intersect at the center of gravity and each one is perpendicular to the other two.

Rotation about the lateral axis is called *pitch*, and is controlled by the elevators. This rotation is referred to as *longitudinal control* or *longitudinal stability.*

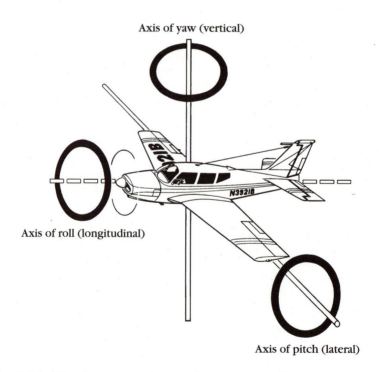

Fig. 2-26. *The three axes of aircraft rotation—roll, yaw, and pitch.*

Rotation about the longitudinal axis is called *roll*, is controlled by the ailerons, and is referred to as *lateral control* or *lateral stability*.

Rotation about the vertical axis is called *yaw*, is controlled by the rudder, and is referred to as *directional control* or *directional stability*.

Stability of the airplane, then, is the combination of forces that act around these three axes to keep the pitch attitude of the airplane in a normal level flight attitude with respect to the horizon, the wings level, and the nose of the airplane directionally straight along the desired path of flight.

Longitudinal stability about the lateral axis

Longitudinal stability is important to the pilot because it determines to a great extent the pitch characteristics of the airplane, particularly as they relate to the stall characteristics. It would be unsafe and uncomfortable for the pilot if an airplane continually displayed a tendency either to stall or dive when his or her attention was diverted for some reason. If properly designed, the airplane does not display these unstable tendencies, assuming it is loaded according to the manufacturer's recommendations. Suffice it to say that the location of the center of gravity, with respect to the center of lift, determines to a great extent the longitudinal stability of the airplane.

Figure 2-27 illustrates neutral longitudinal stability. Note that the center of lift is directly over the center of gravity or weight. An airplane with this caliber of stability produces no inherent pitch moments around the center of gravity.

Figure 2-28 illustrates the center of lift in front of the center of gravity. This plane would display negative stability and an undesirable pitchup moment during flight. If disturbed, the up and down pitching moment would tend to increase in magnitude. This condition can especially occur if the airplane is loaded so that the center of gravity is rearward of the airplane's aft loading limits.

Figure 2-29 shows an airplane with the center of lift behind the center of gravity. Again, this produces negative stability. Some force must balance the down force of the weight. This is accomplished by designing the airplane in such a manner that the air flowing downward

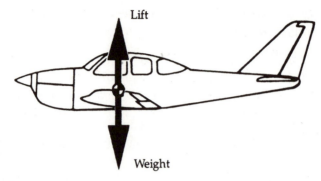

Fig. 2-27. *An airplane with neutral stability and no inherent pitch potential.*

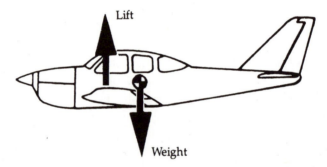

Fig. 2-28. *Another plane with negative stability and upward pitch tendencies.*

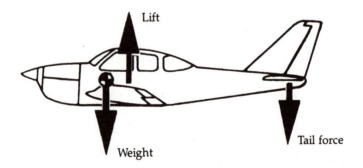

Fig. 2-29. *A third plane with potential negative stability until redesigned to counteract pitch-down tendency.*

behind the trailing edge of the wing strikes the upper surface of the horizontal stabilizer (except on T-tails). This creates a downward tail force that counteracts the tendency to pitch down and provides positive stability.

To further explain: If the nose is pitched down and the control released, the airspeed will increase. In turn, this will increase the downwash on the tail's horizontal stabilizer, forcing the nose up (except on T-tails). Conversely, if the nose is pitched up and the control released, the airspeed will diminish, thus decreasing the downwash on the horizontal stabilizer. This permits the nose to pitch downward. There is one speed only for each degree of angle of attack and eventually, after several pitch oscillations, the airplane tends to stabilize at the airspeed (angle of attack) for which it is trimmed.

The above concept is of prime importance to the pilot because a common misconception about longitudinal stability is that an airplane is stable in respect to the horizon. Instead, keep in mind that longitudinal stability is with respect only to airspeed (angle of attack).

This explanation of longitudinal stability needs some qualification because during certain flight maneuvers the airplane is not entirely "speed seeking," but "angle of attack seeking." This can be demonstrated by placing the airplane in a power-off glide and trimming it for a specific speed. Then if the throttle is opened suddenly, the airplane will nose up and finally assume an attitude that results in a speed considerably less than that of the power-off glide. It does this because of additional forces developed by the propeller blast over the horizontal stabilizer (except T-tails) and the fact that the airplane is stable only with relation to the airflow, or the relative wind. In other words, the stable airplane is not concerned with its own attitude relative to the earth or horizon but with the relative wind with which it always tends to maintain an alignment.

Longitudinal control (pitch) about the lateral axis

In the previous discussion, the single-speed, or angle of attack, concept has been used to explain how longitudinal stability is attained. It's important, though, to realize that the airplane is stable at various speeds or angles of attack—not just one. The controls that allow the pilot to depart from the one speed or angle of attack concept are the elevators (Fig. 2-30) and the elevator trim tab (Fig. 2-31).

The function of the elevator control is to provide a means by which the wing's angle of attack can be changed.

On most airplanes the elevators are movable control surfaces hinged to the horizontal stabilizer and attached to the control column in the cockpit by mechanical linkage. This allows the pilot to change the angle of attack of the entire horizontal stabilizer. The horizontal stabilizer normally has a negative angle of attack to provide a downward force rather than a lifting force. If the pilot applies back elevator pressure, the elevator is raised, increasing the horizontal stabilizer's negative angle of attack and consequently increasing the downward

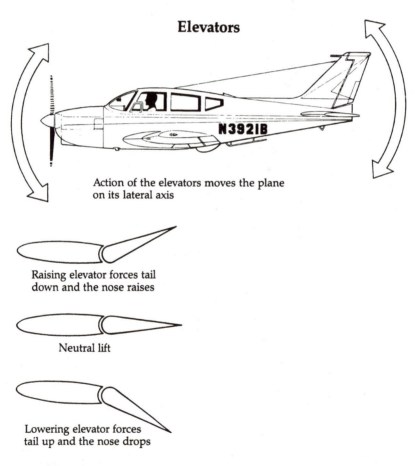

Elevators

Action of the elevators moves the plane on its lateral axis

Raising elevator forces tail down and the nose raises

Neutral lift

Lowering elevator forces tail up and the nose drops

Fig. 2-30. *The effect of elevators on the angle of attack.*

tail force. This forces the tail down, increasing the angle of attack of the wings. Conversely, if forward pressure is applied to the elevator control, the elevators are lowered, decreasing the horizontal stabilizer's negative angle of attack and consequently decreasing the downward force on the tail. This decreases the angle of attack of the wings (Fig. 2-30).

The elevator trim tab is a small auxiliary control surface hinged at the trailing edge of the elevators. The tab acts on the elevators, which in turn act upon the entire airplane. The tab is a part of the elevator but may be moved upward or downward independently of the elevator itself. It is adjusted from the cockpit by a trim crank or button or trim wheel, which is separate from the elevator/aileron control column itself. When activated, it allows the pilot to adjust the angle of attack for a constant setting and, in effect, "trims" the airplane, thus eliminating the need to exert

Trim tab

Elevators in the neutral position

Up position of the elevators is required to hold the nose in the level flight attitude

Trim tab must be adjusted downward to hold elevators in this position to relieve the pressure on the control wheel

Fig. 2-31. *Trim tabs ease pressure on the elevator controls.*

continuous pressure on the control column to maintain a constant angle of attack. An upward deflection of the trim tab forces the elevator downward with the same result as moving the elevator downward with the elevator control, and conversely a downward deflection of the trim tab forces the elevator upward. The direction the trim tab is deflected always causes the entire elevator to be deflected in the opposite direction (Fig. 2-31).

Lateral stability about the longitudinal axis

Lateral stability is the stability displayed around the longitudinal axis of the airplane. An airplane that tends to return to a wings-level attitude after being displaced from a level attitude by a force such as turbulent air is considered to be laterally stable.

Three factors affect lateral stability: (1) *dihedral*, (2) *sweepback*, and (3) *keel effect.*

Dihedral is the angle at which the wings are slanted upward from the root to the tip (Fig. 2-32). The stabilizing effect of dihedral occurs when the airplane sideslips slightly as one wing is forced down in turbulent air. This sideslip results in a difference in the angle of attack between the higher and lower wing, with the greatest angle of attack on the lower wing. The increased angle produces increased lift on the lower wing, with a tendency to return the airplane to

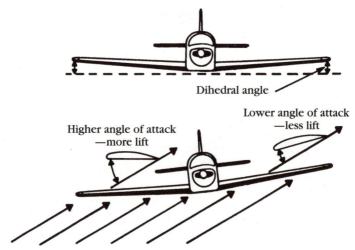

Fig. 2-32. *The effect of dihedral.*

wings-level flight. Note the direction of the relative wind during a slip by the arrows in Fig. 2-32.

Sweepback is the angle at which the wings are slanted rearward from the root to the tip (Fig. 2-33). The effect of sweepback in producing lateral stability is similar to that of dihedral, but not as pronounced. If one wing lowers in a slip, the angle of attack on the low wing increases, producing greater lift. This results in a tendency for the lower wing to rise and return the airplane to level flight. Sweepback augments dihedral to achieve lateral stability. Another reason for sweepback is to place the center of lift farther rearward, which affects longitudinal stability more than it does lateral stability.

Keel effect depends upon the action of the relative wind on the side area of the airplane fuselage. With the wing in a slight slip, the relative wind acting on the fuselage and tail is so distributed that it produces a force acting above the aircraft center of gravity (CG) that tends to roll the aircraft to a wings-level position. Figure 2-34 illustrates this tendency and also illustrates the relationship of the relative wind to directional stability, or *yaw*, as is discussed momentarily.

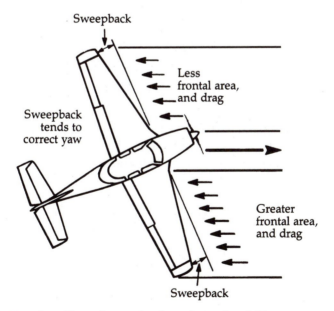

Fig. 2-33. *The effect of sweepback on lateral stability.*

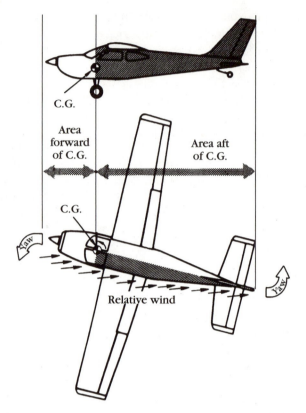

Fig. 2-34. *How the relative wind can produce the keel effect.*

Lateral control (roll) about the longitudinal axis

Lateral control is obtained through the use of *ailerons* and the *aileron trim tabs*. The ailerons are movable surfaces hinged to the outer trailing edge of the wings and attached to the cockpit control column by mechanical linkage. Moving the control wheel or stick to the right to bank to the right raises the aileron on the right wing and lowers the aileron on the left wing. Moving the wheel or stick to the left to bank to the left reverses this and raises the aileron on the left wing and lowers the aileron on the right wing. When an aileron is lowered, the angle of attack on that wing increases, which increases the lift. This permits rolling the airplane laterally around the longitudinal axis (Fig. 2-35).

Most airplanes are equipped with aileron trim tabs, which are small movable parts of each aileron hinged to the aileron's trailing edges.

The tabs, which can be moved independently of the ailerons, have the purpose of "trimming up" the airplane so that it maintains its lateral stability with little or no control column pressure. Call it "fine-tuning." Moving the tabs produces an effect on the aileron that in turn affects the entire airplane. If the trim tab is deflected upward, the aileron is slightly deflected downward, increasing the angle of attack on that wing, resulting in greater lift on that wing. The reverse is true if the trim tab is deflected downward.

Lateral stability or instability in turns

Because of lateral stability, most airplanes tend to recover from shallow banks automatically. However, as the bank is increased, the wing on the outside of the turn travels faster than the wing on the inside of the turn. The increased speed increases the lift on the outside wing, causing a destabilizing rolling moment or an overbanking tendency. The angle of bank will become steeper and steeper unless the pilot applies a slight amount of control pressure to counteract this tendency. The overbanking tendency becomes increasingly significant when the angle of bank reaches more than 30 degrees.

During a medium banked turn (a bank angle between the shallow bank and steep bank), an airplane tends to hold its bank constant and requires less control input on the part of the pilot. This is

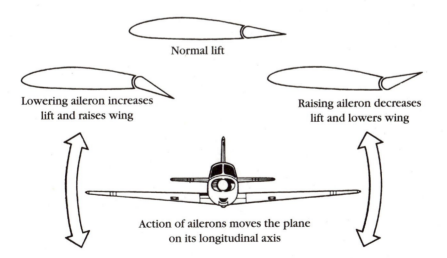

Fig. 2-35. *How ailerons and trim tabs control the aircraft's roll about its longitudinal axis.*

because the stabilizing moments of lateral stability and the destabilizing moments of overbanking very nearly cancel each other out. You can easily discover these various areas of bank through experimentation.

Directional stability about the vertical axis (yaw)

Directional stability is displayed around the vertical axis and depends to a great extent on the quality of lateral stability. If the longitudinal axis of an airplane tends to follow and parallel the flight path of the airplane through the air, whether in straight flight or curved flight, that airplane is considered to be directionally stable.

Directional stability is achieved by placing a vertical stabilizer, or fin, to the rear of the center of gravity on the upper portion of the tail section. The surface of this fin acts similar to a weathervane and causes the airplane to weathercock into the relative wind. If the airplane is yawed out of its flight path during straight flight or turns, either by pilot action or turbulence, the relative wind would exert a force on one side of the vertical stabilizer and tend to return the airplane to its original direction of flight.

Wing sweepback aids in directional stability. If the airplane is rotated about the vertical axis, the airplane will be forced sideways into the relative wind. Because of sweepback, this causes the leading wing to present more frontal area to the relative wind than the trailing wing. The increased frontal area then creates more drag, which tends to force the airplane to return to its original direction of flight (Fig. 2-33). Figure 2-34 also enters the picture again, illustrating the effect of the relative wind hitting the side of the aircraft, as in a slip. As the wind strikes the fuselage, it tends to force the aircraft to return to its normal direction of flight and to parallel the relative wind. In that sense, lateral and directional stability are related, with the keel effect playing a part in both "stabilities."

Disregarding the effects of the relative wind, the combined effects of the vertical stabilizer (fin) and sweepback on directional stability can be compared with feathers of an arrow: It's rather difficult to picture an arrow traveling sideways through the air at any appreciable rate of speed.

Directional control about the vertical axis (yaw)

Directional control of the airplane is obtained through the use of the rudder. The rudder is a movable surface hinged to the trailing edge of the vertical stabilizer (fin) and attached by mechanical linkage to the rudder pedals in the cockpit. By pressing the right rudder pedal, the rudder is deflected to the right, which causes the relative wind to deflect the tail to the left and the nose to the right. If left rudder pressure is applied, the reverse action occurs and the nose is deflected to the left (Fig. 2-36). Keep in mind that the purpose of the rudder during flight is primarily to control yaw and not to turn the airplane. That is the function of the ailerons, in conjunction with the rudder to ensure a coordinated turn.

Some airplanes are equipped with a rudder trim tab, which reacts in a similar manner on the rudder as does the aileron trim tab on the aileron and the elevator trim tab on the elevator.

The amount of directional control the pilot has over the airplane depends on the speed of the airflow striking the rudder. Similar to a

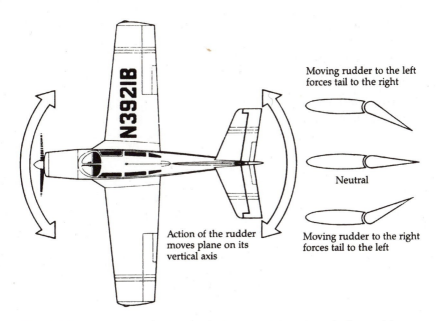

Fig. 2-36. *Maintaining directional control (yaw) with the rudder.*

motor boat, the forward speed must be great enough to permit a positive rudder response to the pilot's (boat or airplane) command.

Load and load factors

An airplane is designed and flight-certificated for a certain maximum weight, usually referred to as the "maximum certificated gross weight." It's critical that *all* airplanes be loaded within their specified weight limits, with the reason probably self-evident: Certain flight conditions or maneuvers could impose extra loads on the airplane structure. Should that occur, and the aircraft is over its maximum gross weight, the extra load could easily exert a level of stress that exceeded the airplane's design capabilities. The end result? Inflight structural failure.

Overstressing the airplane can also occur if the pilot engages in maneuvers creating high loads, regardless of how the airplane is loaded. These maneuvers not only increase the load that the airplane structure must support but also increase the airplane's stalling speed.

During normal flight, the wings of an airplane will support the maximum allowable gross weight of the airplane without any problem. As the airplane is moving at a steady rate of speed and in a straight line, the load imposed on the wings remains constant.

A change in speed during straight flight won't produce any appreciable change in load, but when a change is made in the airplane's flight path, an additional load is imposed upon the airplane structure. This is particularly true if a change in direction is made at high speeds with rapid forceful control movements.

According to certain laws of physics, a mass (airplane in this case) continues to move in a straight line unless some force intervenes, causing the mass (airplane) to assume a curved path. During the time the airplane is in a curved flight path, it still attempts, because of inertia, to force itself to follow straight flight. This tendency to follow straight flight, rather than curved flight, generates a force known as *centrifugal force* that acts toward the outside of the curve.

Any time the airplane is flying in a curved flight path with a positive load, the load the wings must support will be equal to the weight of the airplane plus the load imposed by centrifugal force. A positive load occurs when back pressure is applied to the elevator, causing centrifugal force to act in the same direction as the force of weight. A negative load occurs when forward pressure is applied to the elevator control, causing centrifugal force to act in a direction opposite to that of the force of weight.

Curved flight producing a positive load is a result of increasing the angle of attack and consequently the lift. Increased lift always increases the positive load imposed on the wings. The load, however, is increased only at the time the angle of attack is being increased. Once the angle of attack is established, the load remains constant. The loads imposed on the wings in flight, in these instances, are stated as load factor. (Note: The meaning of *load factor* here is not the same as in the airline industry, where the term refers to the percentage of seats occupied on a flight versus the number of seats available.)

Instead, load factor is the ratio of the total load supported by the airplane's wing to the actual weight of the airplane and its contents; i.e., the actual load supported by the wings divided by the total weight of the airplane. For example, if an airplane has a gross weight of 2000 pounds and, during flight, is subjected to aerodynamic forces that increase the total load the wing must support to 4000 pounds, the load factor would be 2.0 (4000 divided by 2000). In this example the airplane wing is producing "lift" that is equal to twice the gross weight of the airplane.

Another way of expressing load factor is the ratio of a given load to the pull of gravity; i.e., to refer to a load factor of three, as "three Gs," where "G" refers to the pull of gravity. In this case the weight of the airplane is equal to "one G," and if a load of three times the actual weight of the airplane were imposed upon the wing due to curved flight, the load factor would be equal to "three Gs."

Load factors and airplane design

To be certificated by the Federal Aviation Administration, the structural strength (load factor) of airplanes must conform to prescribed standards set forth by Federal Aviation Regulations.

All airplanes are designed to meet certain strength requirements, depending on their intended use. Classification of airplanes as to strength and operational use is known as the *category system.*

The category of each airplane can be readily identified by a placard or document (airworthiness certificate) in the cockpit that states the operational category or categories in which that airplane is certificated.

The category, maneuvers that are permitted, and the maximum safe load factors (limit load factors) specified for these airplanes are identified as:

Category	Permissible maneuvers	Limit load factor*
Normal	1—Any maneuver incident to normal flying.	3.8
	2—Stalls (except whip stalls).	
	3—Lazy eights, chandelles, and steep turns in which the angle of bank does not exceed 60°.	
Utility	1—All operations in the normal category.	4.4
	2—Spins (if approved for that airplane).	
	3—Lazy eights, chandelles, and steep turns in which the angle of the bank is more than 60°.	
Acrobatic	No restrictions except those shown to be necessary as a result of required flight tests.	6.0

*To the limit loads given, a safety factor of 50 percent is added.

Small airplanes might be certificated in more than one category, if the requirements for each category are met. Also note that there is an increase in load factor limits with an increasing severity of maneuvers permitted.

This system provides a means for pilots to determine what operations can be performed in a given airplane without exceeding the load limit. At the same time, all pilots are cautioned to operate any airplane they fly within the load limit for which the airplane is designed. Exceeding those limits is inviting disaster.

Effect of turns on load factor

A turn is made by banking the airplane so that lift from the wings pulls the airplane from its straight flight path. In a constant altitude coordinated turn, the load factor (resultant load) is the result of two forces: pull of gravity and centrifugal force (Fig. 2-37).

Without getting into the mathematics of the turn (which is beyond the scope of this handbook), in any airplane at any *airspeed*, if a constant altitude is maintained during the turn, the load factor for a given *degree* of bank is the same—that load factor being the

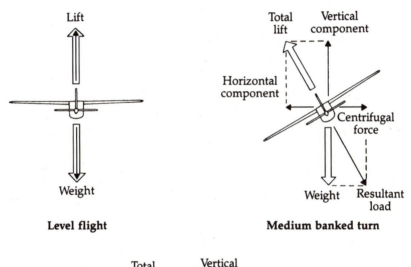

Level flight   **Medium banked turn**

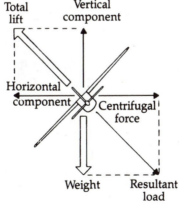

Steep banked turn

Fig. 2-37. *Forces acting on an airplane in a bank.*

resultant of gravity and centrifugal force. Another principle is that for any given *angle* of bank, the rate of turn varies with the airspeed. In other words, if the angle of bank is held constant and the airspeed is increased, the rate of turn will decrease; if the airspeed is decreased, the rate of turn will increase. Because of this, there is no change in centrifugal force for any given bank. Therefore, the load factor remains the same.

Figures 2-38 and 2-39 reveal an important fact about load factor in turns. The load factor increases at a rapid rate after the angle of bank reaches 60°. The wing must produce lift equal to this load factor if altitude is to be maintained. Also, note how rapidly the load factor increases as the angle of bank approaches 90°. At that angle, maintaining a constant-altitude turn is not mathematically possible. An airplane can be banked to 90°, but a continued coordinated turn is impossible at this point without losing altitude. Note, too, that at a bank of slightly more than 80°, the load factor exceeds 6, which is the limit load factor of an acrobatic airplane.

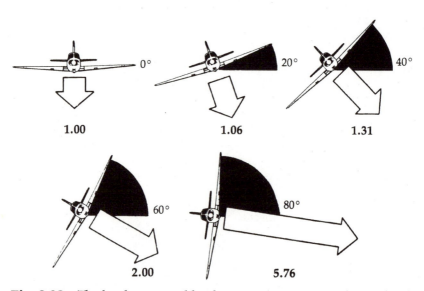

Fig. 2-38. *The load supported by the wings increases as the angle of bank increases. The increase is shown by the relative lengths of the white arrows. Figures below the arrows indicate the increase in load factor. For example, the load factor during a 60-degree bank is 2.00, and the load supported by the wings is twice the weight of the airplane in level flight.*

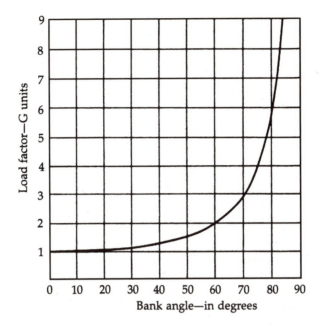

Fig. 2-39. *An illustration of how the angle of bank affects the load factor and G-forces.*

The approximate maximum bank for conventional light airplanes is 60°, which produces a load factor of 2. This bank reaches the limit of a normal category airplane. An additional 10° of bank will increase the load factor by approximately 1 G (Fig. 2-39), bringing it dangerously close to the point at which structural damage or complete failure might occur.

Effect of load factor on stalling speed

Any airplane, within the limits of its structure and the strength of the pilot, can be stalled at any airspeed. At a given airspeed, the load factor increases as the angle of attack increases, and the wing stalls because the angle of attack has been increased to a certain angle. Therefore, there is a direct relationship between the load factor imposed on the wing and its stalling characteristics.

When a sufficiently high angle of attack is reached, the smooth flow of air over an airfoil breaks up and tears away, producing the abrupt change of characteristics and loss of lift that is defined as a stall. A rule for determining the speed at which a wing will stall is that the stalling speed increases in proportion to the square root of the load factor.

To explain further: The load factor produced in a 75° banked turn is 4 (Fig. 2-39). Applying the rule, the square root of 4 is 2. This means that by inducing a load factor of 4, an airplane with a normal unaccelerated stalling speed of 50 knots can be stalled at twice that speed, or 100 knots. If the airplane were capable of withstanding a load factor of 9, the same airplane could be stalled at a speed of 150 knots.

Because the load factor squares as the stalling speed doubles, tremendous loads might be imposed on structures by stalling an airplane at relatively high airspeeds. An airplane that has a normal unaccelerated stalling speed of 50 knots will be subjected to a load factor of 4 Gs when forced into an accelerated stall at 100 knots. As this example shows, it's easy to impose a load beyond the design strength of the conventional airplane.

Reference to the chart in Fig. 2-40 will show that banking an airplane just over 75° in a steep turn increases the stalling speed by

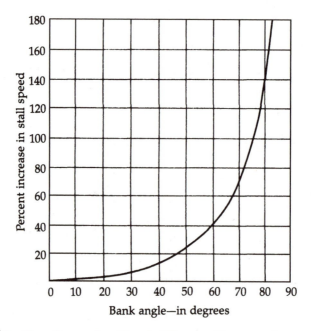

Fig. 2-40. *How the angle of bank affects stalling speed.*

100 percent. If the normal stalling speed is 45 knots, the pilot must keep the airspeed above 90 knots in a 75° bank to prevent sudden entry into a violent power stall. This same effect will take place in a quick pullup from a dive or a maneuver producing load factors above 1 G. Deadly accidents have resulted from sudden, unexpected loss of control, particularly in a steep turn near the ground.

The maximum speed at which an airplane can be safely stalled is the *design maneuvering speed.* That speed is a valuable reference point for the pilot. When operating below it, a damaging positive flight load shouldn't be produced because the airplane would undoubtedly stall before the load became excessive. Any combination of flight control usage, including full deflection of the controls, or gust loads created by turbulence, should not create an excessive air load if the airplane is operated below maneuvering speed. (Be aware, though, pilots, that certain wind shears or gusts can cause excessive loads, even at below-maneuvering speeds.)

The design maneuvering speed for a particular aircraft can be found in the Pilot's Operating Handbook or on a placard in the cockpit. It can also be determined by multiplying the normal unaccelerated stall speed by the square root of the limit load factor. A rule of thumb to determine the maneuvering speed is approximately 1.7 times the normal stalling speed. Thus, an airplane that normally stalls at 60 mph should never be stalled when the airspeed is above 102 mph (60 mph × 1.7 = 102 mph).

The two main points of concern here for the new or experienced pilot:

1. The dangers of inadvertently stalling the airplane by increasing the load factor, as in a steep turn or spiral.
2. Intentionally stalling an airplane above its design maneuvering speed imposes a tremendous and dangerous load factor on the structure.

Effect of speed on load factor

The amount of excess load that can be imposed on the wing depends on how fast the airplane is flying. At slow speeds, the maximum available lifting force of the wing is only slightly greater than the amount necessary to support the weight of the airplane. Consequently, as previously stated, the load factor should not become excessive even if the controls are moved abruptly or the airplane encounters severe gusts. The reason for this is that the airplane will stall before the load can become excessive.

At high speeds, however, the lifting capacity of the wing is so great that a sudden movement of the elevator controls or a strong gust could increase the load factor beyond safe limits. Because of this relationship between speed and safety, certain "maximum" speeds have been established. Each airplane is restricted in the speed at which it can safely execute maneuvers, withstand abrupt application of the controls, or fly in rough air. This speed, once again, is the design maneuvering speed.

Summarizing, at speeds below design maneuvering speed, the airplane should stall before the load factor can become excessive. At speeds above maneuvering speed, the limit load factor for which an airplane is stressed can be exceeded by abrupt or excessive application of the controls or by strong turbulence.

Effect of flight maneuvers on load factor

Load factors apply to all flight maneuvers. In straight-and-level, unaccelerated flight, a load factor of 1 G is always present, but certain maneuvers are known to involve relatively high load factors.

Turns. As already discussed, increased load factors are a characteristic of all banked turns. Load factors become significant both to flight performance and to the load on wing structure as the bank increases beyond approximately 45°.

Stalls. The normal stall entered from straight-and-level flight, or an unaccelerated straight climb, should not produce added load factors beyond the 1 G of straight-and-level flight. As the stall occurs, however, this load factor might be reduced toward zero, the factor at which nothing seems to have weight, and the pilot has the feeling of floating free in space. If recovery is made by abruptly moving the elevator control forward, a negative load is created, which raises the pilot from the seat. This is a *negative wing load* and usually is so slight that there is little effect on the airplane structure. You should be cautioned, however, to avoid sudden and forceful control movements because of the possibility of exceeding the structural load limits.

During the pullup following stall recovery, significant load factors are often encountered. These may be increased by excessively steep diving, high airspeed, and abrupt pullups to level flight. One usually leads to the other, thus increasing the resultant load factor. The abrupt pullup at a high diving speed can easily produce critical loads on structures and create recurrent or secondary stalls by building up the load factor to the point that the speed of the airplane reaches the stalling airspeed during the pullup.

Advanced maneuvers. I'm not covering spins, chandelles, lazy eights, and snap maneuvers in this handbook, but before attempting any of these maneuvers, you should be familiar with the airplane you are flying and know whether or not these maneuvers can be safely performed.

Effect of turbulence on load factor

Turbulence in the form of vertical air currents can, under certain conditions, cause severe load stress on an airplane wing.

When an airplane is flying at a high speed with a low angle of attack and suddenly encounters a vertical current of upward moving air, the relative wind changes to an upward direction as it meets the airfoil. This increases the angle of attack of the wing. If the air current is well defined and travels at a significant rate of speed upward (15 to 30 feet per second), a sharp vertical gust is produced, which would have the same effect on the wing as applying sudden sharp back pressure on the elevator control.

All certificated airplanes are designed to withstand loads imposed by turbulence of considerable intensity. Nevertheless, gust load factors increase with increasing airspeed, so it's always wise in rough air to reduce the speed to the design maneuvering speed, as found in the Pilot's Operating Handbook (POH), or the placard in the cockpit. This is the speed least likely to result in structural damage to the airplane and yet provide a sufficient margin of safety above stalling speed in turbulent air.

Placarded "never exceed" speeds are determined for smooth air only. High dive speeds or abrupt maneuvering in gusty air at airspeeds above the maneuvering speed could well place damaging stress on the whole structure of an airplane.

Stress on the structure means stress on any vital part of the airplane. The most common failures due to load factors involve rib structure within the leading and trailing edges of wings. The cumulative effect of these loads over a long period of time may tend to loosen and weaken vital parts so that actual failure could occur later when the airplane is being operated in a normal manner.

Determining load factors in flight

Load factors are best judged by feel through experience. They can be measured by an instrument called an accelerometer, but since this is not a commonly used instrument in general aviation-type airplanes, developing the ability to judge load factors from the feel of their effect on the body is important. One indication the pilot has of increased load factor is the feeling of increased body weight. In a 60° bank, the body weight doubles. Along with feel and experience, though, a knowledge of the principles outlined previously is essential to estimate load factors, to know their limits, and to stay safely within them. Serious repercussions are possible otherwise.

In view of the foregoing, a few suggestions are offered to avoid overstressing the structure of the airplane:

1. Operate the airplane in conformance with the Pilot's Operating Handbook.
2. Avoid abrupt control usage at high speeds.
3. Reduce speed if turbulence of any severe intensity is encountered in flight or abrupt maneuvers are to be performed.
4. Reduce weight of airplane before flight if intensive turbulence or abrupt maneuvering is anticipated.
5. Avoid turns using an angle of bank in excess of 60°.

Forces on the airplane at airspeeds slower than cruise

At a constant cruise airspeed and straight-and-level flight, the forces of thrust and drag act opposite to each other and parallel to the flight path. These opposing forces are equal in magnitude. Also, the force of lift is equal in magnitude to the force of weight.

While maintaining straight-and-level flight at constant airspeeds slower than normal cruise, the opposing forces must still be equal in magnitude, but some of these forces are separated into components. In this flight condition the actual thrust no longer acts parallel and opposite to the flight path and drag. Actual thrust is inclined upward, as illustrated in Fig. 2-41. Note that now thrust has two components; one acting perpendicular to the flight path in the direction of lift, while the other acts along the flight path itself. Because the actual thrust is inclined, its magnitude must be greater than drag if its component of thrust along the flight path is to equal drag. Also note that a component of thrust acts 90° to the flight

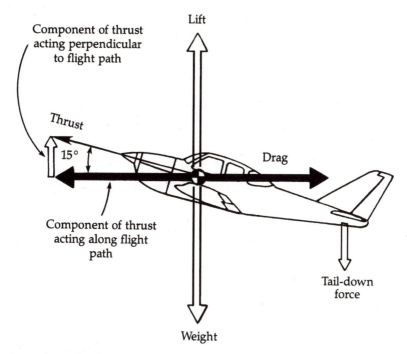

Lift

Component of thrust
acting perpendicular
to flight path

Thrust

15°

Drag

Component of thrust
acting along flight
path

Tail-down
force

Weight

Fig. 2-41. *The forces on the airplane in straight-and-level flight at airspeeds slower than cruise.*

path, and is thus in the same direction as wing lift. Figure 2-41 also illustrates that the forces acting upward (wing lift and the component of thrust) equal the forces acting downward (weight and tail-down force).

Wing loading (wing lift) is actually less at slow speeds than at cruise speeds because the vertical component of thrust helps support the airplane.

In summary, then, in straight-and-level flight at slow speeds, the actual thrust is greater than drag and wing lift is less than at cruise speed.

Forces in a climb

The forces acting on an airplane during a climb are illustrated in Fig. 2-42. When the airplane is in equilibrium, the weight can be resolved into two components—one opposing the lift, and the other acting in the same direction as the drag along the line of the relative wind. The requirements for equilibrium: The thrust must equal the sum of the drag and the opposing component of the weight, and the lift must equal its opposing component of the weight. The steeper the angle of climb, the shorter becomes the length of the component of lift, and simultaneously the component of drag becomes longer. Therefore, the lift requirement decreases steadily as the angle of climb steepens until, in a true vertical climb, if this were possible, the wings would supply no lift and the thrust would be the only force opposing both the drag and the weight, which would be acting downward in opposition.

At a constant power setting, a given rate of climb can be obtained either by climbing steeply at a low airspeed or by climbing on a shallow path at high airspeed. At one extreme, if the airspeed is too low, the induced drag rises to a figure at which all thrust available is required to overcome the drag and none is available for climbing. At the other extreme, if the speed is the maximum obtainable in level flight, all the power is again being used to overcome the drag and there is no rate of climb. Between these two extremes lies a speed, or a small band of speeds, that achieve the best rate of climb. The best rate of climb is achieved not at the steepest angle, but at some combination of moderate angle and optimum airspeed at which the

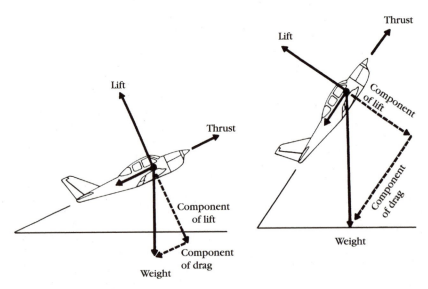

Fig. 2-42. *Forces acting on an airplane in a climb.*

greatest amount of excess power is available to climb the airplane after the drag has been balanced.

Figure 2-43 shows that the speed for minimum drag, or the lowest point on the power-required curve, although low, is not the lowest possible that can be flown without stalling. The increase in power required at the lowest speeds (to the left of the minimum power-required point) is caused by the rapidly rising effects of induced drag at the lower speeds.

The propeller-driven airplane, under the same set of circumstances and for a given rated horsepower, suffers a gradual loss of propeller efficiency and, therefore, a gradual loss of thrust at both ends of its speed range.

The vertical distance between the power-available and power-required curves (Fig. 2-43) represents the power available for climbing at the particular speed. The best climbing airspeed is that at which excess power is at a maximum so that after expending some power in overcoming drag, the maximum amount of power remains available for climbing the airplane. At the intersection of the curves all the available power is being used to overcome drag, leaving none available for climbing. Of course, at the lower range, excess power

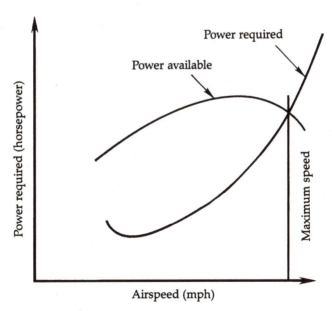

Fig. 2-43. *Power available versus power required.*

for climb soon becomes available if the angle of attack is reduced to allow an increase in speed.

The thrust horsepower of piston engines decreases with altitude. Even if it is possible to prolong sea-level power to some greater altitude by supercharging, or some other method of power boosting, the power inevitably declines when the boosting method employed reaches an altitude at which it can no longer maintain a set power. At higher altitudes the power-available curves are lowered. Since power required increases with true airspeed (velocity), the thrust horsepower required to fly at any desired indicated airspeed increases with altitude.

In essence, then, don't think that an airplane climbs because of "excess lift." It does not; it climbs because of power available over power required.

Forces in a glide

The forces acting on an airplane in a glide are illustrated in Fig. 2-44. For a steady glide with the engine providing no thrust, the lift, drag, and weight forces must be in equilibrium. The illustration shows that weight is balanced by the resultant of lift and drag. The lift vector, acting as it does at right angles to the path of flight, is now tilted forward, while the drag vector is tilted upward and continues to act opposite to the path of flight. From the illustration it can be seen that the geometry of the vectors is such that the angle between the lift vector and the resultant is the same as that between the glide path and the horizontal. This angle (X) between the glide path and the horizontal is called the *glide angle.* Further examination of this diagram shows that as drag is reduced and speed increased, the smaller is the glide angle; therefore,

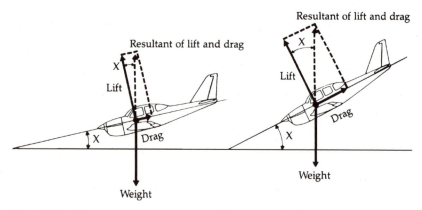

Fig. 2-44. *Forces acting on an airplane in a glide.*

the steepness of the glide path depends on the ratio of lift to drag. When gliding at the angle of attack for best lift-drag ratio, least drag is experienced, and the flattest glide results. The *lift-drag ratio* (L/D) is a measure of the gliding efficiency or aerodynamic cleanness of the airplane. If the L/D is 11/1, it means that lift is 11 times greater than drag.

If the gliding airplane is flying at an airspeed just above the stall, it is operating at maximum angle of attack and therefore, maximum lift. This, however, does not produce the best glide angle for maximum glide distance because the induced drag at this point is high. By reducing the angle of attack, the airspeed increases and, although lift is less at the lower angle of attack, the airplane travels farther per increment of altitude lost because of greatly reduced drag. The increased range can be accomplished, up to a point, by decreasing the angle of attack and induced drag. At some point, the best glide angle will be achieved. If airspeed continues to increase, the parasite drag begins to rise sharply and the airplane again starts losing more altitude per increment of distance traveled. The extreme of this is when the nose is pointed straight down.

The best glide distance is obtained when L/D is at maximum. This optimum condition is determined for each type of airplane, and the speed at which it occurs is used as the recommended best-range glide speed for the airplane. It varies somewhat for different airplane weights, so the airspeed for a representative operational condition is generally selected.

If several instances of the optimum glide path were plotted by an observer on the ground under varying conditions of wind, they would be found to be inconsistent. However, the actual gliding angle of the airplane with respect to the moving air mass remains unchanged. Starting from a given altitude, a glide into the wind at optimum glide airspeed covers less distance over the ground than a glide downwind. Because in both cases the rate of descent is the same, the measured angle, as seen by a ground observer, is governed only by the groundspeed, being steeper at the lower groundspeed when gliding into the wind. The effect of wind, therefore, is to decrease range when gliding with a headwind component, and to increase it when gliding downwind. The endurance of the glide is unaffected by wind.

Variations in gross weight do not affect the gliding angle, provided the optimum indicated airspeed for each gross weight is used. The fully loaded airplane will sink faster but at a greater forward speed, and, although it would reach the ground much quicker, it would have traveled exactly the same distance as the lighter airplane, and its glide angle would have been the same.

A study of Fig. 2-44 shows that an increase in the weight factor is equivalent to adding thrust to the weight component along the glide path. This means more speed and, therefore, more lift and drag, which lengthen the resultant vector until the geometric balance of the diagram is restored. This is done without affecting the gliding angle. The higher speed corresponding to the increased weight is provided automatically by the larger component of weight acting along the glide path, and this component grows or diminishes in proportion to the weight. Because the gliding angle is unaffected, range also is unchanged.

Although range is not affected by changes in weight, endurance decreases with the addition of weight and increases with reduction of weight. If two airplanes having the same lift-drag ratio but different weights start a glide from the same altitude, the heavier airplane, gliding at a higher airspeed, will cover the distance between the starting point and touchdown in a shorter time, but both planes will cover the same distance. Therefore, the endurance of the heavier airplane is less.

Turns during flight

Many pilots never completely understand what makes an airplane turn. Such an understanding is more than of just passing importance because accidents often occur as a direct result of losing control of the airplane while in turning flight.

In review, the airplane is capable of movement around the three axes. It can be pitched around the lateral axis, rolled around the longitudinal axis, and yawed around the vertical axis. Yawing around the vertical axis causes the most misunderstanding about how and why an airplane turns. First, though, remember that the rudder *does not* turn the airplane in flight.

Although pilots know that an airplane is banked to make a turn, few know the reason why. The answer is quite simple. The airplane must be banked because the same force (lift) that sustains the airplane in flight is used to make the airplane turn. The airplane is banked and back elevator pressure is applied. This changes the direction of lift and increases the angle of attack on the wings, which increases the lift. The increased lift pulls the airplane around the turn. The amount of back elevator pressure applied, and therefore the amount of lift, varies directly with the angle of bank used. As the angle of bank is steepened, the amount of back elevator pressure must be increased to hold altitude.

In level flight, the force of lift acts opposite to and exactly equal in magnitude to the force of gravity. As gravity tends to pull all bodies to the center of the earth, that force always acts in a vertical plane with respect to the earth. On the other hand, total lift always acts perpendicular to the relative wind, which for the purpose of this discussion, is considered to be the same as acting perpendicular to the lateral axis of the wind.

With the wings level, lift acts directly opposite to gravity. However, as the airplane is banked, gravity still acts in a vertical plane, but lift now acts in an inclined plane.

As illustrated in Fig. 2-45, the force of lift can be resolved into two components: vertical and horizontal. During the turn entry, the vertical component of lift still opposes gravity, and the horizontal

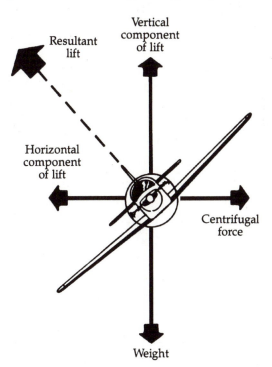

Fig. 2-45. *Forces acting on an airplane in a turn.*

component must overcome centrifugal force; consequently, the total lift must be sufficient to counteract both of these forces. The airplane is then pulled around the turn, not sideways, because the tail section acts as a weathervane that continually keeps the airplane streamlined with the curved flight path.

Also note in Fig. 2-45 that as the turn develops, centrifugal force acts opposite to the horizontal component of lift, and the vertical component of lift acts opposite to gravity. The total resultant lift acts opposite to the total resultant load. So long as these opposing forces are equal to each other in magnitude, the airplane maintains a constant rate of turn. If the pilot moves the controls in a way that changes the magnitude of any of the forces, the airplane accelerates or decelerates in the direction of the applied force. This results in changing the rate at which the airplane turns.

Now for a quick chance to spot check your understanding of some of the principles of flight—the answers to all chapter quickie quizzes are in the appendix.

Quickie quiz questions
Chapter 2

1. What is the relationship of lift, drag, thrust, and weight when an airplane is in straight-and-level flight and flying at a constant air speed?
   A. Lift equals drag and thrust equals weight.
   B. Lift equals weight and thrust equals drag.
   C. Lift and weight equal drag and thrust.
   D. Lift, drag, and weight equal thrust.

2. What are the three axes of rotation that affect an aircraft's stability?

3. What makes an airplane turn or bank?

4. Describe the effects that high density altitude has on an aircraft's takeoff and landing performance.

5. The purpose of a rudder on an airplane is to
   A. control yaw.
   B. control the overbanking tendency.
   C. maintain a crab angle to control drift.
   D. maintain the turn after the airplane is banked.

6. How would you define "angle of attack"?

7. What are the three factors that affect an aircraft's lateral stability?

8. "Load factor" is defined as

   A. The ratio of the total weight of a loaded aircraft to the aircraft's maximum approved operating weight.

   B. The ratio of the number of seats occupied on the aircraft to the number of seats available.

   C. The ratio of the total load supported by the aircraft's wing to the actual weight of the aircraft and its contents.

   D. The ratio of the empty weight of the aircraft to its approved gross weight load.

9. List at least four conditions that can affect an aircraft's load factor.

10. List at least four factors that affect the amount of lift generated by the wing.

Answers in Appendix, page 571.

3

Airplanes and engines

One of the most important activites in promoting aviation safety is the *airworthiness* of airplanes. Each airplane certificated by the Federal Aviation Administration has been manufactured under rigid specifications of design, materials, workmanship, construction, and performance. This certification process provides the best possible assurance that the airplane will not fail from a structural standpoint if it is properly maintained and flown within its clearly specified limitations.

The goal of designers and manufacturers is to obtain maximum aircraft efficiency, combined with adequate strength. Those two qualities, however, must be balanced, because excessive strength means more weight, and more weight lowers efficiency by reducing speed and the amount of useful load the aircraft can carry. The fact that the efficiency/strength goal has been reached is borne out by the almost infinitesimal number of accidents due solely to aircraft structural failure. When well maintained, flown within its published limitations, and operated in reasonable weather (meaning avoiding thunderstorms, known areas of excessive turbulence, icing, and the like), even 50- or 60-year-old planes continue to provide dependable, problem-free service.

This chapter, with the purpose of familiarizing those new to aviation, discusses airplane structure, including flight control systems, wing flaps, landing gear, engine operation, engine accessories, and associated engine instruments. Also included is material related to aircraft documents, aircraft maintenance, and inspection procedures.

The concept here is that if you're going to rely on a machine to take you off the ground and return you safely, it only makes sense to know as much about that machine as possible. Oh, you could probably get by if you only knew how to start and stop the engine and maybe switch fuel tanks, but that's precious little information about a piece of equipment that holds your life in its hands at X-number of feet above the earth. Knowledge is the foundation of proficiency—and knowledge is the purpose of this chapter, as well as of the whole book.

Airplane structure

As I said in Chapter 2, the required structural strength of an airplane is based on its intended use. An aircraft built for normal, routine flying doesn't need the strength of one designed for acrobatic flight, crop-dusting, or other special purposes, some of which involve severe inflight stresses.

Numerous wing designs have been developed in an effort to determine the best type for a specific purpose. Basically, all wings are similar to those used by the Wright brothers and other pioneers. Many modifications, however, have been made to increase lifting capacity, reduce friction, increase structural strength, and generally improve flight characteristics. Whatever the new designs may be, they are subjected to thorough analysis and strength tests before being approved for use on certificated airplanes.

Airplane strength is basically measured by the total load that the wings are capable of carrying without permanent damage to the wing structure. The load imposed on the wings depends on the type of flight in which the airplane is engaged. The wing must support not only the weight of the airplane but the additional loads created during certain flight maneuvers, such as turns and pullouts from rapid descents. Turbulent air also adds loads—loads that increase as the severity of the turbulence increases.

To permit utmost efficiency of construction without sacrificing safety, the FAA has established several categories of airplanes with minimum strength requirements for each. Operating limitations of each plane are made known by markings on instruments, placards on instrument panels, airworthiness certificates, the Aircraft Flight Manual, and/or the Pilot's Operating Handbook.

Flight control systems

The flight control systems in most general aviation airplanes consist of the cockpit controls, cables, pulleys, and linkages connected to the movable surfaces outside the airplane.

There are three primary and two secondary flight control systems. The primary systems consist of the elevator, aileron, and rudder, which are essential in controlling the aircraft. The secondary systems are the trim tabs and wing flaps. As you'll recall from the last chapter, the trim tabs enable the pilot to trim out, and thus ease, control pressures. The flaps, on the other hand, are used to change the lifting characteristics of the wing and to decrease the speed at which the wing stalls. Since flaps weren't really covered in Chapter 2, now is a good time to bring them into the picture.

Wing flaps

Wing flaps are movable parts of the wings, normally hinged to the inboard trailing edges, and are extended or retracted by the pilot. Extending the flaps increases the wing camber, the wing area (some types of flaps), and the wing's angle of attack—all of which increases lift as well as induced drag. The increased lift enables the pilot to make steeper approaches to a landing without an increase in airspeed and shorter takeoff runs from short runways or soft fields. The pilot retracts the flaps when they are no longer needed.

The major precaution is to operate the flaps within the airspeed limitations established for the aircraft being flown. If those limitations are exceeded, the increased drag forces could result in structural damage to the plane.

Figure 3-1 shows the three types of flaps in general use: (A) the *plain*, or *simple flap*, is a portion of the trailing edge of the wing on a hinged pivot that allows the flap to be moved downward, thereby changing the chord line, the angle of attack, and the camber of the wing; (B) the *split flap* is a hinged portion of the bottom surface of the wing only, which when extended, increases the angle of attack by changing the chord line; (C) the *Fowler flap*, when extended, not only tilts downward but also slides rearward on tracks. This increases the angle of attack, wing camber, and wing area, thereby providing added lift without significantly increasing drag.

With all three types of flaps, the practical effect is to permit a steeper angle of descent without an increase in airspeed. Extended flaps also allow a slower speed to be used on an approach and landing, thus reducing the distance of the landing roll.

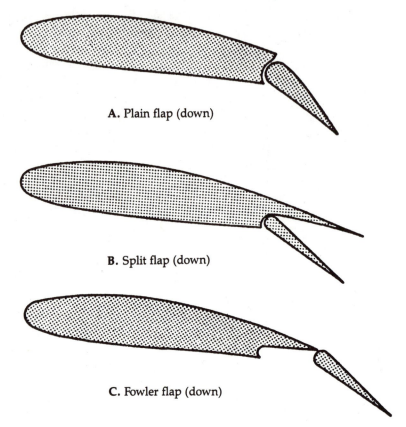

A. Plain flap (down)

B. Split flap (down)

C. Fowler flap (down)

Fig. 3-1. *Three types of wing flaps.*

Landing gear

The landing gear system supports the airplane during the takeoff run, landing, taxiing, and when parked. These ground operations require that the landing gear be capable of steering, braking, and absorbing shock.

A steerable nose gear or tail wheel permits you to control the airplane throughout all operations on the ground. With individual brakes on each main wheel, you can use either brake by itself as an aid to steering or, by applying both brakes simultaneously, decelerate or stop the airplane. Hydraulic shock struts or leaf springs are installed in the various types of landing gear systems to absorb the impact of landings or the shock of taxiing over rough ground.

There are two basic types of landing gears used on light airplanes: the *conventional* gear and the *tricycle* gear.

The conventional gear, which was used on most airplanes manufactured years ago, is still found on certain makes of light airplanes. Typically, referred to as a "tail dragger," the gear system consists of two main wheels and a tailwheel. Shock absorption on the main landing gear is usually provided by inflated tires and shock absorbers and on the tailwheel by the spring assembly to which the tailwheel is bolted. The tailwheel is usually steerable, by pushing on the left or right rudder pedal, through at least 15 degrees on each side of a center point. Beyond that point, the wheel typically becomes full-swiveling.

The tricycle landing gear is used on most airplanes produced today. This gear has advantages over the conventional gear because it offers easier ground handling characteristics and better forward taxiing visibility over the nose. Depending on the aircraft make, the main gear is similar to that of the tail dragger system but is located farther rearward. The nose gear is usually steerable by the rudder pedals through at least 10 degrees on each side of the center. Shock absorption is provided on the nose gear by a shock strut.

Some makes or types of light planes are equipped with retractable landing gears, which, when retracted, help reduce drag and increase airspeed without the need for additional power. This type of gear normally retracts into wing or fuselage openings that are covered by doors after the retraction. The retraction or extension is accomplished either electrically or hydraulically by controls within the cockpit. Green or red panel lights in the cockpit indicate whether the wheels are extended and locked or retracted. Many aircraft are also equipped with an audible warning signal that comes on when power is reduced and the gear has not been extended, as for landing. Additionally, a system is provided for emergency gear extension in the event the hydraulic or electrical gear-extension mechanism fails to function.

Electrical system

Electrical energy is required to operate navigation and communication radios, lights, and other airplane equipment. In the earlier days of aviation, though, most light planes had only a magneto that supplied electrical energy to the engine ignition system, and that was all. Today's airplanes still use independent magnetos but have electrical systems as well. The magneto system, however, is separate from the electrical. In other words, the pilot can turn the electrical system off in flight and the engine will continue to operate efficiently by utilizing the electrical energy generated by the magnetos.

Most light airplanes are equipped with a 12-volt direct-current electrical system. Larger planes have a 24-volt system to provide a reserve capacity for, among other things, more complex avionics and additional energy for starting.

A basic airplane electrical system consists of these components:

1. Alternator or generator
2. Battery
3. Master switch or battery switch
4. Bus bar, fuses, and circuit breakers
5. Voltage regulator
6. Ammeter
7. Starting motor
8. Associated electrical wiring
9. Accessories

Engine-driven generators or alternators supply electric current to the electrical system and also maintain a sufficient electrical charge in the battery that is used primarily for starting.

There are several basic differences between generators and alternators. Most generators do not produce a sufficient amount of electrical current at low engine rpms to operate the entire electrical system. Therefore, during low rpm operations, the electrical needs must be drawn from the battery, which, in a short time, could be depleted.

An alternator, however, produces a sufficient amount of electrical current at slower engine speeds by first producing alternating current, which is converted to direct current. Another advantage is that the electrical output of an alternator is more constant throughout the ranges of engine speeds. Alternators are also lighter in weight, less expensive to maintain, and less prone to become overloaded during conditions of heavy electrical loads. Because of these superior characteristics, most aircraft use alternators rather than generators.

Electrical energy stored in a battery provides a source of power for starting the engine and a limited supply for use in the event the alternator or generator fails. As a general rule, you can count on about two hours of battery life after an alternator failure.

Some airplanes are equipped with receptacles to which external *auxiliary power units* (APUs) can be connected to provide electrical energy for starting. APUs are not only useful but often essential, especially during cold weather. But be careful using an APU when the battery is dead. The danger is that electrical energy will be forced into the dead battery, which could cause the battery to overheat and possibly explode, resulting in damage to the airplane.

A *master switch* is installed to turn the electrical system "on" and "off." Turning the switch "on" provides energy to all the electrical equipment circuits with the exception of the ignition system. For the most part, the following is the equipment most commonly found in light aircraft that use the electrical system for their source of energy:

1. Position lights
2. Landing lights
3. Taxi lights
4. Anticollision lights
5. Interior cabin lights
6. Instrument lights
7. Radio equipment
8. Turn indicator
9. Fuel gauges
10. Stall warning system
11. Pitot heat
12. Cigarette lighter

Some airplanes are equipped with a split-type master switch. One-half controls the master solenoid that disconnects the battery from the electrical system, and the other half controls the alternator circuit. The master switch can be turned on or off, regardless of the position of the alternator switch, but the latter can't be turned on unless the master switch is on. The split switch lets the pilot exclude the alternator from the electrical system in the event of alternator failure. With the alternator switch "off," the entire electrical load is placed on the battery. If the alternator fails in flight (which you can determine simply by checking the ammeter gauge), all nonessential electrical equipment should be turned off to conserve the energy stored in the battery. Again, you've got about a two-hour energy supply before all lights, radios, and everything electrical die.

A bus bar is used as a terminal in the plane's electrical system to connect the main system to the equipment using electricity as a source of

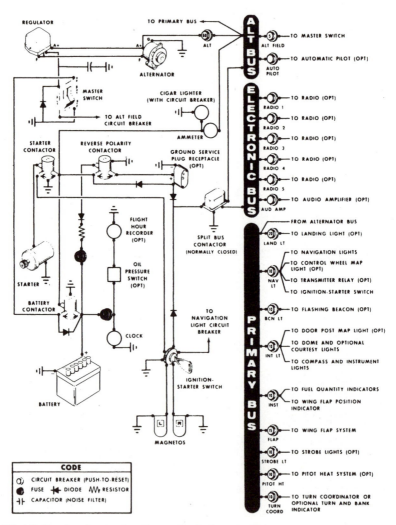

Fig. 3-2. *A schematic of a typical electrical system.*

power. The bus bar simplifies the wiring and provides a common point from which voltage can be distributed throughout the system (Fig. 3-2).

Fuses or circuit breakers are used to protect the circuits and equipment from electrical overload. Spare fuses of the proper amperage limit should be carried in the airplane to replace any that have blown or are defective. Circuit (Fig. 3-3) breakers have the same function as a fuse but can be manually reset, rather than replaced, if an overload condition occurs in the electrical system. Placards at the fuse or circuit breaker location identify the circuit by name and, if fuses are used, show the amperage limit of the fuse.

The *ammeter,* referred to above, is an instrument that monitors the performance of the plane's electrical system. Not all airplanes have one but, instead, are equipped with a light that, when lighted, indicates a discharge in the system as an alternator malfunction.

On most aircraft, though, the ammeter shows one of two conditions: whether the alternator is producing an adequate supply of electrical power to the system, or whether the battery is charging or discharging. For the most part, pilots are primarily concerned about alternator output, so that type of ammeter is commonplace in today's light aircraft.

Fig. 3-3. *An example of a circuit breaker panel, designed to protect circuits and equipment from electrical overloads.*

While the faces of ammeters differ, the one in Fig. 3-4 illustrates the basic elements of the instrument. This has a zero point in the upper center of the dial, a plus value to the right of center, and a negative value to the left. A vertical needle swings to the right or left, depending on the performance of the electrical system. If the needle indicates a plus value, it means that the battery is being charged. After power is drawn from the battery for starting, the needle will indicate a noticeable plus charge value for several minutes and then stabilize to a lower plus charge value.

If the needle indicates a minus value, it means that the alternator output is inadequate and energy is being drawn from the battery to supply the system. This could be caused by either a defective alternator or by an overload in the system, or both. Full scale ammeter discharge or rapid fluctuation of the needle usually means an alternator malfunction. If such occurs, the pilot should cut the alternator out of the system and conserve battery power by turning off all nonessential lights and radios to reduce the load on the electrical system.

A *voltage regulator* controls the rate of charge to the battery by stabilizing the generator or alternator electrical output. The alternator voltage output is usually slightly higher than the battery voltage. For

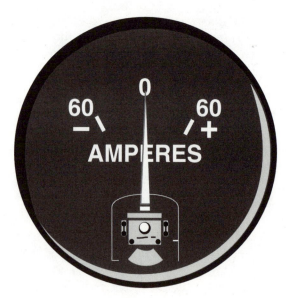

Fig. 3-4. *One variation of the face of an ammeter.*

example, a 12-volt battery system would be fed by an alternator system of approximately 14 volts. The difference in voltage keeps the battery charged.

An inverter is installed on some airplanes to change direct current to alternating current.

Engine operation

Knowledge of a few basic principles of engine operation helps a pilot obtain increased dependability and efficiency from the engine. At the same time, this knowledge can play a major role in avoiding real or potential engine problems.

In this short chapter, it's impractical to discuss in detail the various types of engines and the finer points of operation that can be learned only over time and through experience. Information from the manufacturer's instruction manual, familiarity with the operating limitations of the specific aircraft engine, and guidance from a flight instructor, coupled with the information contained within this section, should provide the information necessary to operate an aircraft engine satisfactorily.

How an engine operates

Most light airplane engines are internal combustion reciprocating engines that operate on the same principle as those in automobiles. They are called "reciprocating" because certain parts move back and forth, in contrast to a circular motion such as a turbine. Some smaller airplanes are equipped with turbine engines, but those are beyond the scope of this handbook.

As shown in Fig. 3-5, the reciprocating engine consists of cylinders, pistons, connecting rods, and a crankshaft. One end of a connecting rod is attached to a piston and the other end to the crankshaft. This converts the straight-line motion of the piston to the rotary motion of the crankshaft, which turns the propeller. At the closed end of the cylinder there are normally two spark plugs that ignite the fuel and two openings over which valves open and close. One valve (the intake valve), when open, admits the mixture of fuel and air, and the other (the exhaust valve), when open, permits the burned gases to escape. For the engine to go through one cycle, the piston must complete four strokes. This requires two revolutions of the crankshaft.

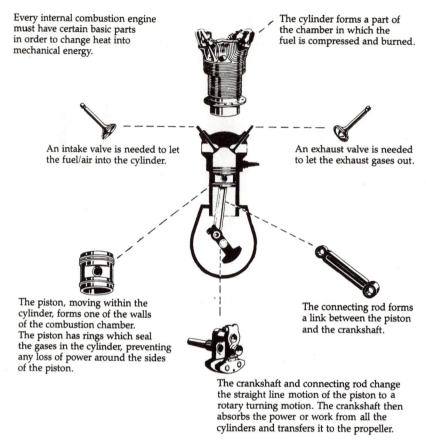

Every internal combustion engine must have certain basic parts in order to change heat into mechanical energy.

The cylinder forms a part of the chamber in which the fuel is compressed and burned.

An intake valve is needed to let the fuel/air into the cylinder.

An exhaust valve is needed to let the exhaust gases out.

The piston, moving within the cylinder, forms one of the walls of the combustion chamber. The piston has rings which seal the gases in the cylinder, preventing any loss of power around the sides of the piston.

The connecting rod forms a link between the piston and the crankshaft.

The crankshaft and connecting rod change the straight line motion of the piston to a rotary turning motion. The crankshaft then absorbs the power or work from all the cylinders and transfers it to the propeller.

Fig. 3-5. *Basic parts of a reciprocating engine.*

The four strokes are the *intake, compression, power,* and *exhaust.* The following describes one cycle of engine operation.

Diagram A of Fig. 3-6: The piston is moving away from the cylinder head. The intake valve is opened and the fuel/air mixture is drawn into the cylinder. This is the *intake stroke.*

Diagram B: The piston is returning to the top of the cylinder. Both valves are closed, and the fuel/air mixture is compressed. This is the *compression stroke.*

Diagram C: When the piston is approximately at the top of the cylinder head, a spark from the plugs ignites the mixture, which burns at a controlled rate. Expansion of the burning gas exerts pressure on the piston, forcing it downward. This is the *power stroke.*

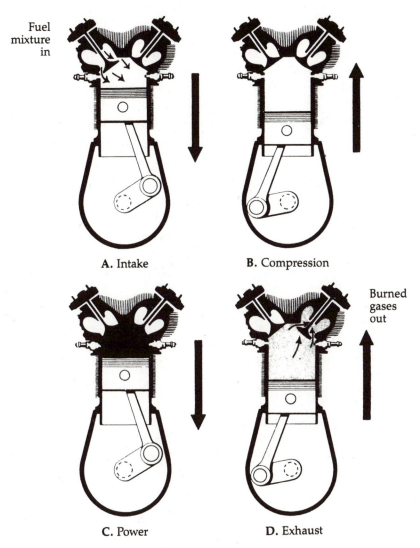

Fuel
mixture
in

A. Intake

B. Compression

Burned
gases
out

C. Power

D. Exhaust

Fig. 3-6. *The four strokes of the piston: (A) Fuel mixture is drawn into cylinder by downward stroke; (B) Mixture is compressed by upward stroke; (C) Spark ignites mixture, forcing piston downward and producing power that turns propeller; (D) Burned gases pushed out of cylinder by upward stroke.*

Diagram D: Just before the piston completes the power stroke, the exhaust valve starts to open, and the burned gases are forced out as the piston returns to the top of the cylinder. This is the *exhaust stroke.* The cycle is then ready to begin again, starting with Diagram A.

From this description, notice that each cylinder of the engine delivers power only once in every four strokes of the piston or every two revolutions of the crankshaft. The momentum of the crankshaft carries the piston through the other three strokes, although the diagram shows the action of only one cylinder. To increase power and gain smoothness of operation, other cylinders are added, and the power strokes are timed to occur at successive intervals during the revolution of the crankshaft.

Aircraft engines are classified by the various ways the cylinders are arranged around the central crankcase. Most general aviation airplane engines are classed as the *horizontally opposed*, meaning that a four-cylinder engine has the cylinder banks arranged in two rows, directly opposite each other and using the same crankshaft.

Larger and more powerful reciprocating engines are classed as *radial engines*. In these, the cylinders are placed in a circular pattern around the crankcase, which is located in the center of the circle.

Other engine classifications are the *in-line*, with the cylinders placed in one straight row, and the *vee* type, with the cylinders located in two rows, forming a "V" similar to the V-8 automobile engine.

Cooling system

The burning fuel within the cylinders produces intense heat, most of which is expelled through the exhaust. Much of the remaining heat, however, must be removed to prevent the engine from overheating. In practically all automobile engines, excess heat is carried away by water circulating around the cylinder walls.

Most light airplane engines, however, are *air cooled*. The cooling process is accomplished by outside air being forced into the engine compartment through openings in front of the engine cowl. This ram air is routed by baffles over fins attached to the engine cylinders and other parts of the engine, where the air absorbs the engine heat. Expulsion of the hot air takes place through one or two openings at the rear bottom of the engine cowling.

Some airplanes are equipped with a device known as *cowl flaps* that are used to control engine temperatures during various flight operations. Cowl flaps are hinged covers that fit over the opening through which the hot air is expelled. By adjusting the cowl flap opening, the pilot can regulate the engine temperature during flight. If the engine temperature is low, the cowl flaps can be closed, thus restricting the flow of expelled hot air and increasing engine temperature. If the temperature is high, the flaps are opened to permit a greater flow of air through the system to decrease the temperature. Usually during low airspeed and high power operations such as takeoffs and climbs, the cowl flaps are opened. At higher speeds and lower power operations, such as cruising flight and descents, they are closed. If the plane is not equipped with cowl flaps, engine temperature is controlled by the only other means possible—changing the airspeed or the power output of the engine.

The *oil temperature gauge* indicates the temperature of the oil that is heated by the engine. It thus gives an indirect and delayed indication of engine temperatures. Regardless, if it's the only means available, the gauge should definitely be used to determine engine temperature.

For a more accurate reading, many planes are equipped with a *cylinder head temperature* gauge. This is an additional instrument that indicates a direct and immediate engine temperature change. It is calibrated in degrees Celsius or Fahrenheit and is usually color coded with a green arc to identify the normal operating range. A red line indicates maximum allowable engine temperature.

To avoid excessive cylinder head temperatures, you can open the cowl flaps (if you have them), increase airspeed, enrich the mixture, or reduce power. Any of these procedures aids in reducing the engine temperature. Establishing a shallow climb also increases the airflow through the cooling system and helps prevent excessively high engine temperatures.

When an airplane engine is operated on the ground, very little air flows past the cylinders (particularly if the engine is closely cowled). Overheating is thus likely to occur, especially on a warm day. For that reason, if it's possible to do so, turn the airplane directly into the wind for the various pretakeoff checks and while waiting takeoff clearance. That wind may not help a lot, but every little added breeze contributes to the cooling process. After takeoff, overheating can also occur during a prolonged climb to your cruising altitude because the engine is usually developing high power at relatively slow airspeed.

Operating the engine at higher than its designed temperature can cause loss of power, excessive oil consumption, and detonation. It can also lead to serious permanent damage, scoring of the cylinder walls, damaging the pistons and rings, and burning and warping the valves. Needless to say, to avoid excessive temperatures, you should closely monitor the cockpit engine temperature instruments.

Ignition system

The *ignition system* provides a spark to ignite the fuel/air mixture in the cylinder. The magneto ignition system is used on most modern aircraft engines because it produces a hotter spark at high engine speeds than the battery system used in automobiles. Also, it doesn't depend on an external source of energy, such as the electrical system. Magnetos are self-contained engine-driven units supplying ignition current. The magneto, however, must be actuated by rotating the engine before current is supplied to the ignition system.

What happens here is that the aircraft battery furnishes electrical power to operate the starter system; the starter system actuates the rotating element of the magneto; and the magneto then furnishes the spark to each cylinder to ignite the fuel/air mixture. After the engine starts, the starter system is disengaged, and the battery no longer has any part in the actual operation of the engine. If the battery (or master) switch is turned OFF, the engine will continue to run. This shouldn't be done, though, because battery power is necessary at low engine rpms to operate other electrical equipment (radio, lights, etc.). Also, when the alternator is operating, the battery is storing up a charge, if it's not already fully charged.

Most aircraft engines are equipped with a *dual ignition* system; that is, two magnetos supply the electrical current to two spark plugs for each combustion chamber. One magneto system supplies the current to one set of plugs; the second magneto system supplies the current to the other set. This is why the ignition switch has four positions: OFF, LEFT, RIGHT, and BOTH. With the switch in the "L" or "R" position, only one magneto is supplying current and only one set of spark plugs is firing. With the switch in the BOTH position, both magnetos are supplying current and both sets of spark plugs are firing. The main advantages of the dual system are:

- Increased safety. In case one magneto system fails, the engine can be operated on the other system until a landing can be made.

Note: To ensure that both ignition systems are operating properly, each system is checked during the engine runup prior to flight. This check should be accomplished in accordance with the manufacturer's recommendations in the Aircraft Flight Manual or Pilot's Operating Handbook.

- Improved burning and combustion of the mixture and, consequently, improved performance.

Be sure to turn the ignition switch to "BOTH" for flight and completely "OFF" when shutting down the engine after flight. Even with the electrical master switch "OFF" and the ignition switch on either "BOTH" or "LEFT" or "RIGHT" magnetos, the engine could fire if the propeller is moved from outside the airplane. Also, if the magneto switch ground wire is disconnected, the magneto is "ON," even though the ignition switch is in the "OFF" position.

Fuel system

The *fuel system* provides a means of storing fuel in the airplane and then transferring it to the airplane engine. Fuel systems are classified according to the method used to furnish fuel to the engine from the fuel tanks. The two classifications are the "gravity feed" and the "fuel pump system."

The gravity feed system utilizes the force of gravity to transfer the fuel from the tanks to the engine. This system can be used on high-wing airplanes, assuming the fuel tanks are installed in the wings, which places the tanks above the carburetor. The fuel is then gravity fed through the system and into the carburetor.

If the design of the airplane is such that gravity cannot be used to transfer fuel, fuel pumps are installed. This is the case on low-wing airplanes, where the fuel tanks in the wings are located below the carburetor.

In this instance, two systems are typically used. The main pump system is engine-driven, while an auxiliary electric-driven pump is available if the main pump fails. The auxiliary pump, commonly known as the "boost pump," is controlled by a switch in the cockpit, and, as well as increasing the reliability of the fuel system, it is also used in engine-starting.

Because of variations in fuel-system operating procedures, you should always consult the Aircraft Flight Manual or Pilot's Operating Handbook for specific procedures pertaining to the type of aircraft you are going to fly.

Fuel tanks, selectors, and strainers. Most airplanes are designed to use space in the wings to mount fuel tanks. All tanks have filler openings that are covered by a cap. The system also includes lines connecting to the engine, a *fuel gauge, strainers*, and *vents* that permit air to replace the fuel consumed during flight. Fuel overflow vents are provided to discharge fuel in the event the fuel expands because of high temperatures. *Drain plugs* or *valves (sumps)* are located at the bottom of the tanks so that water and other sediment can be drained.

Fuel lines pass through a *selector assembly*, located in the cockpit, that provides a means for the pilot to turn the fuel "off," "on," or to select a particular tank, say, "left" or "right," from which to draw fuel. The fuel selector assembly may be a simple on/off valve, or a more complex arrangement that permits the pilot to select individual tanks or use all tanks at the same time.

Most planes are equipped with fuel strainers, called *sumps*, which are located at the low point in the fuel lines between the fuel selector and the carburetor. The sumps filter the fuel and trap water and sediment in a container that can be drained to remove any foreign matter that might exist.

Fuel primer. A manual fuel primer is usually installed to help in starting the engine, particularly in cold weather. Activating the primer draws fuel from the tanks (through the fuel lines) and vaporizes the fuel directly into one or two of the cylinders through small fuel lines. When engines are cold and don't generate sufficient heat to vaporize the fuel, the primer is used not only to start the engine, but to keep it running until adequate engine heat is developed.

Fuel pressure gauge. If a fuel pump is installed in the fuel system, a fuel pressure gauge is also included. This gauge indicates the pressure in the fuel lines. The normal operating pressure can be found in the airplane operating manual or on the gauge itself by color coding.

Induction, carburetion, and injection systems

In reciprocating aircraft engines, the induction system completes the process of taking in outside air, mixing it with fuel, and delivering the mixture to the cylinders. The system includes the *air scoops* and *ducts,* the *carburetor* or *fuel injection system,* the *intake manifold,* and (if installed) the *turbocharger* or *supercharger.*

Two types of induction systems are commonly used in light airplane engines: (1) the *carburetor system,* which mixes the fuel and air in the carburetor before the mixture enters the intake manifold; and (2) the *fuel injection system,* whereby the fuel and air are mixed just prior to entering each cylinder. This system does not utilize a carburetor.

The carburetor system has one of two types of carburetor: (1) the *float type,* which is generally installed in airplanes equipped with small-horsepower engines, and (2) the *pressure type,* used in higher-horsepower engines. Although the pressure type won't be discussed in this book, many aspects of each are similar.

In the operation of the carburetor system, the outside air first flows through an air filter, usually located at an air intake in the front part of the engine cowling. This filtered air then enters the carburetor through a *venturi,* a narrow throat in the carburetor. When the air flows rapidly through the venturi, a low pressure area is created, which forces the fuel to flow through a main fuel jet located at the throat and into the airstream where it is mixed with the flowing air (Fig. 3-7). The fuel/air mixture is then drawn through the intake manifold and into the combustion chambers where it is ignited.

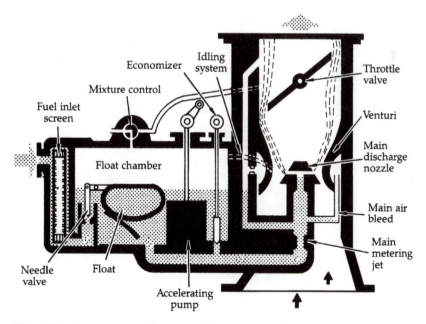

Fig. 3-7. *A cut-away of a typical float-type carburetor.*

The "float-type carburetor" gets its name from a float that rests on fuel within the float chamber. A needle attached to the float opens and closes an opening in the fuel line. This meters the correct amount of fuel into the carburetor, depending on the position of the float, which is controlled by the level of fuel in the float chamber. When the level of the fuel forces the float to rise, the needle closes the fuel opening and shuts off the fuel flow to the carburetor. It opens when the engine requires additional fuel.

Mixture control

A mixture control in the cockpit is provided to change the fuel flow to the engine to compensate for varying air densities as the airplane changes altitude.

Carburetors are normally calibrated at sea level pressure to meter the correct amount of fuel with the mixture control in a "full rich" position. As altitude increases, air density decreases. This means that a given volume of air does not weigh as much at higher altitudes because it does not contain as many air molecules. At the same time, the *weight* of air decreases, even though the volume of air entering the carburetor remains the same. To compensate for this difference, the mixture control is used to adjust the ratio of fuel-to-air mixture entering the combustion chamber. This also regulates fuel consumption.

If the fuel/air mixture is too rich (too much fuel in terms of the weight of air), excessive fuel consumption, rough engine operation, and appreciable loss of power occurs. Because of excessive fuel, a cooling effect takes place that causes below normal temperatures in the combustion chambers. This cooling results in spark plug fouling. Conversely, operation with an excessively lean mixture (too little fuel in terms of the weight of air) results in rough engine operation, detonation, overheating, and a loss of power.

To summarize: As the aircraft climbs and the atmospheric pressure decreases, there is a corresponding decrease in the weight of air passing through the induction system. The volume of air, however, remains constant, and because it is the *volume* of airflow that determines the pressure drop at the throat of the venturi, the carburetor tends to meter the same amount of fuel to this thin air as to the dense air at sea level. Consequently, the mixture becomes richer as the airplane gains altitude. The use of the mixture control prevents this by decreasing the rate of fuel discharge to compensate for the decrease in air density. The mixture must be enriched, however, when descending from altitude.

The manufacturer's recommendation for the particular airplane being flown can help you follow the proper leaning/enriching procedures.

Exhaust gas temperature (EGT) gauge

If the aircraft you fly is equipped with an *exhaust gas temperature gauge*, and if it is properly used, this engine instrument can reduce fuel consumption by 10 percent. The reason is that its accuracy indicates to the pilot the exact amount of fuel that should be metered to the engine.

An EGT measures, in degrees Celsius or Fahrenheit, the temperature of the exhaust gases at the exhaust manifold. This temperature measurement varies with the ratio of fuel to air entering the cylinders and can thus be used as a basis for regulating the fuel/air mixture. This is possible because the EGT is very sensitive to temperature changes.

Although the manufacturer's recommendation for leaning the mixture should be followed, the usual leaning procedure for lower horsepower engines when an EGT is available is this:

Lean the mixture slowly while noting the increase in exhaust gas temperature on the gauge. When the EGT reaches a peak, enrich the mixture until the EGT gauge shows a decrease in temperature. The number of degrees of drop recommended by the engine manufacturer is usually in the 25° to 75° range. Engines equipped with carburetors run rough when leaned to the peak EGT reading but smooth out after the mixture is slightly enriched.

Carburetor icing

Carburetor icing, a potentially serious condition, is caused by the vaporization of fuel, combined with the expansion of air as it flows through the carburetor. This produces a sudden cooling of the mixture, with the temperature of the air passing through the carburetor dropping as much as 15°C (60°F) within a fraction of a second. Water vapor in the air is "squeezed out" by this cooling and, if the temperature in the carburetor reaches 0°C (32°F) or lower, the moisture is deposited as frost or ice inside the carburetor passages. Even a slight accumulation of this deposit reduces power and can lead to a complete engine failure, particularly when the throttle is partly or fully closed (Fig. 3-8).

Conditions conducive to carburetor icing. On dry days, or when the temperature is well below freezing, the moisture in the air is not generally enough to cause trouble. But if the temperature is between –7°C (20°F) and 21°C (70°F), with visible moisture or high humidity, you should be constantly on the alert for carburetor ice. Be particularly watchful when this temperature range exists and you are operating with low or closed throttle settings (as in the traffic pattern or on final approach).

Indications of carburetor icing. For airplanes with fixed-pitch propellers, the first indication of carburetor icing is a loss of rpms. With variable-pitch (constant-speed) propellers, a drop in manifold pressure is an early warning. There is no rpm reduction in constant-speed propeller aircraft because the propeller pitch is automatically adjusted to compensate for any loss of power. It thus maintains a constant rpm. In both instances, though, engine roughness will probably develop rather quickly.

Use of carburetor heat. The carburetor heater is an anti-icing device that preheats the air before it reaches the carburetor. This preheating

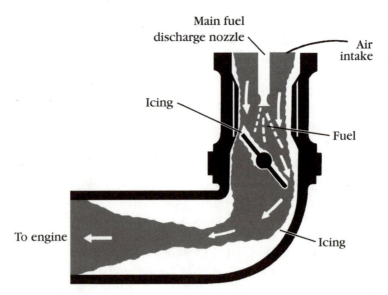

Fig. 3-8. *Formation of ice while in the fuel intake system can reduce or block fuel flow to the engine.*

melts any ice or snow entering the intake and/or ice that forms in the carburetor passages, *provided* the accumulation is not too great. Of equal, or even greater importance, carb heat can be applied to keep the fuel mixture above the freezing temperature so that ice won't form in the first place.

When conditions are conducive to carburetor icing during flight, periodic checks should be made to detect its presence. If icing is suspected because of an rpm drop, a manifold pressure drop, or engine roughness, full carburetor heat should be applied immediately and left in the "on" position until you are certain that all the ice has been removed. Be careful, though: If ice was present, applying partial heat, or not leaving it on long enough, might only aggravate the situation.

When carburetor heat is first applied, there is an rpm drop in airplanes with fixed-pitch propellers and a manifold pressure drop with variable-pitch props. If there is *no* carburetor ice present, no further change in rpm or manifold pressure occurs until the carburetor heat is turned off. At that point, rpms or manifold pressure return to their original reading before heat was applied. If carburetor ice *is* present, the rpms or manifold pressure normally rise after the initial drop (often accompanied by intermittent engine roughness). Then, when the carburetor heat is turned off, the rpms or manifold pressure rise to a setting greater than that before application of the heat. The engine should also run more smoothly once the ice has been removed.

Whenever the throttle is closed during flight, the engine cools rapidly and vaporization of the fuel is less complete than if the engine were warm. Also, in this cooler condition, the engine is more susceptible to carburetor icing. Consequently, if you suspect carburetor-icing conditions and anticipate a closed-throttle operation, the carburetor heat should be turned to "full-on" before closing the throttle and left on during the closed-throttle operation. This is a simple but highly effective ice-preventing measure. Periodically, though, during the closed-throttle operation, the throttle should be opened smoothly for a few seconds to keep the engine warm. Otherwise, the carburetor heater might not produce enough heat to prevent icing.

Use of carburetor heat tends to reduce the output of the engine and increase operating temperatures. The heat, then, should *not* be used when full power is required (as during takeoff) or during normal engine operation, other than to check for the presence or removal of ice. In extreme cases of icing, after the ice has been removed, it may be necessary to apply just enough heat to prevent further ice formation. But, this must be done with caution. Just be sure to check the manufacturer's recommendations for the correct use of carburetor heat in *that* engine. Procedures vary, and what might be right for one engine type could be wrong for another.

One other thing: Always check the carb heat during the preflight engine runup. Here again, follow the engine manufacturer's step-by-step recommendations.

Carburetor air temperature gauge

Certain airplanes are equipped with a carburetor air temperature gauge that is useful in detecting potential icing conditions. Usually, the face of the gauge is calibrated in degrees Celsius (C), with a yellow arc indicating the carburetor air temperature at which icing might occur. This yellow arc ranges between –15°C and +5°C. If the air temperature and moisture content of the air are such that the carburetor icing is improbable, the engine can be operated with the indicator in the yellow range with no adverse effects. However, if the atmospheric conditions are conducive to carburetor icing, the indicator must be kept outside the yellow arc by application of carburetor heat.

Certain carburetor air temperature gauges have a red radial that indicates the maximum permissible carburetor inlet air temperature recommended by the engine manufacturer. They also have a green arc that indicates the normal operating range.

Outside air temperature gauge (OAT)

Almost all airplanes are equipped with an outside air temperature gauge that is calibrated in both degrees Celsius and Fahrenheit. It's used not only for obtaining the outside or ambient air temperature for calculating true airspeed, but is also helpful in detecting potential icing conditions.

Fuel injection system

Fuel injectors have replaced carburetors in certain airplanes. In this system, the fuel is normally injected either directly into the cylinders or just ahead of the intake valve. Fuel injection is generally considered to be less susceptible to icing than the carburetor system, but impact icing of the air intake is a possibility in either system. Impact icing occurs when ice forms on the exterior of the airplane and clogs openings, such as the carburetor's air intake.

Several types of fuel injection systems are in use today. Although there are variations in design, the operational methods of each are generally similar. Most designs include an engine-driven fuel pump, a fuel/air control unit, a fuel distributor, and discharge nozzles for each cylinder.

The advantages of fuel injection are:
- Reduction in evaporative icing
- Better fuel flow
- Faster throttle response
- Precise control of mixture
- Better fuel distribution
- Easier cold weather starts

Disadvantages are usually associated with:
- Difficulty in starting a hot engine
- Vapor locks during ground operations on hot days
- Problems associated with restarting an engine that quits because of fuel starvation

The air intake of the fuel injection system is somewhat similar to that of the carburetor system. The fuel injection system, however, is equipped with an alternate air source located within the engine cowling and comes into play if the external source is obstructed by ice or other matter. This alternate air source is usually operated automatically but has a backup manual system if the automatic feature malfunctions.

Proper fuel is essential

Several grades of aviation fuel are available, and care must be exercised to ensure that the correct aviation grade is being used for the specific type of engine. It can be harmful to the engine and dangerous to flight if the wrong kind of fuel is used. The proper grade is stated in the Aircraft Flight Manual or Pilot's Operating Handbook, often on placards in the cockpit, and usually on the wing next to or encircling the filler caps. Making sure that the right grade is pumped aboard is the pilot's responsibility. Don't leave it up to a perhaps untrained line boy to decide whether your plane takes 100LL or auto fuel. If it requires the former and he fills it with auto gas, you might end up with a problem. It's okay to use a *higher* octane fuel than recommended, when necessary, but *never* use a lower grade. To do so could cause extensive damage to the engine.

In addition to the usual numbering system to identify their octane ratings, dyes have been added to help visually determine the ratings or grades. For example, 80 octane is red in color, 100LL blue, 100 green, 115 (for military use only) is purple, and jet fuel is clear or strawberry.

The classification system identifies the fuels by octane and performance numbers (grades) that designate the antiknock value or knock resistance of the fuel mixture in the engine cylinder. The higher the grade of fuel, the more pressure the fuel can withstand without detonating. For fuels that have two numbers, the first number indicates the lean-mixture rating and the second the rich-mixture rating. Thus, grade 100/130 fuel has a lean mixture rating of 100 and a rich mixture rating of 130.

Airplane engines are designed to use a specific grade of fuel. Lower compression engines take lower numbered octane fuel because these fuels ignite at a lower temperature. Higher octane fuels are used in higher compression engines as they must ignite at higher temperatures, but not prematurely. Repeating an above comment, if the proper grade of fuel is not available, it's possible, although not desirable, to use the next higher grade as a temporary substitute. So, in a pinch, it's okay to step up a grade, but never down!

The right fuel for an engine burns smoothly from the spark plug outward, exerting a smooth pressure downward on the piston. Using low-grade fuel or too lean a mixture can cause detonation. Detonation, or knock, is a sudden explosion or shock to a small area of the piston top, similar to striking it with a fist or banging it with a hammer (Fig. 3-9).

Detonation produces extreme heat that often progresses into preignition, causing severe structural stresses on parts of the engine. Preventing detonation means that the pilot should use the recommended

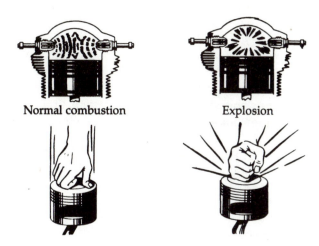

Normal combustion   Explosion

Fig. 3-9. *Illustrations of normal combustion and explosive combustion.*

grade of fuel, maintain a sufficiently rich mixture, and keep the engine temperatures within the established limits.

A knock inhibitor is used to improve the antiknock qualities of a fuel. Such inhibitors must have a minimum of corrosive or other undesirable qualities. Perhaps one of the better inhibitors is, and has been, tetraethyl lead (TEL), which provides a thin layer of protective material to prevent undesirable corrosion.

Fuel contamination

To say that water and dirt in fuel systems are dangerous is, at best, a serious understatement. Of the accidents attributed to powerplant failure from fuel contamination, most have been traced to:

1. Inadequate preflight inspection by the pilot
2. Servicing of aircraft with improperly filtered fuel from small tanks or drums
3. Storing aircraft with partially filled fuel tanks
4. Lack of proper maintenance

To help minimize the fuel-related causes, thorough preflight actions are necessary to ensure that the fuel is as contaminant-free as possible. Those actions, in effect, are as follows:

Drain into a transparent container (a small bottle, vial, or tube) a substantial amount of fuel from the fuel strainer (gascolator) quick drain and from the fuel tank sumps. From each, check for dirt and water. There is often the possibility that when the gascolator is being drained, water existing in the tank(s) might not appear until all the fuel has been drained from the lines leading from the tank(s). Consequently, drain enough fuel to be certain that it is free from contamination. The amount drawn depends on the length of fuel line from the tank to the drain, but if water is found in the first sample, keep on draining until you're drawing only pure fuel.

During the draining process, you should be able to identify suspended water droplets in the fuel by a cloudy appearance of the sample you have collected or by the clear separation of the water from the fuel itself. This separation occurs after the water has settled to the bottom of the tank. Inasmuch as water is the principal contaminant of fuel, and considering the threat that such contamination poses, draining all fuel sumps is an essential and critical step in every preflight inspection.

Along with these measures, the following preventive actions should be considered: For one, be sure the tanks are filled after the last flight of the day. So doing prevents moisture condensation within the tanks because no air space is left. Partially-filled tanks invite such condensation, which only results in an increasing accumulation of water. Even then, though, and even if it's your own airplane that was refueled, don't assume anything; go through the draining process outlined above. You can never be certain that the refill was as free of contaminates as the pumper or supplier might promise.

Another preventive measure is to avoid refueling from cans and drums. This practice introduces a major possibility of fuel contamination—no matter how pure the fuel might have been before it was poured into the container.

Also, avoid the old practice of using a funnel and a chamois skin— if, for some reason, you *have* to refuel from cans or drums. This is risky and should be discouraged, simply because a worn-out chamois, a new chamois that is water-wet or damp, and most imitation chamois skins do *not* filter water.

That said, in remote areas or in emergency situations, you may have no alternative but to refuel from sources with inadequate anticontamination systems. If so, perhaps a chamois skin and funnel are the only possible means of fuel filtering. Just remember the risks, though, and be super careful in the preflight draining process.

Refueling procedures

Static electricity, formed by the friction of air passing over the surfaces of an airplane in flight and by the flow of fuel through the hose and nozzle, creates a fire hazard during refueling. To guard against the possibility of a spark igniting fuel fumes, a ground wire should be attached to the aircraft before the cap is removed from the tank; the refueling nozzle should be grounded to the aircraft before refueling is begun and throughout the refueling process; and the fuel truck, if one is used, should be grounded to the aircraft and the ground. It's amazing, though, to see the number of times these precautions are not followed, especially at the smaller, uncontrolled airports. If there's a way around it, don't let such careless refueling practices happen to any airplane you own or are renting.

If fueling from drums or cans is necessary, proper bonding and grounding connections are extremely important, because there is the ever-present danger of static discharge and fuel vapor explosion. Nylon, dacron, or wool clothing is especially prone to the accumulation and discharge of static electricity from the wearer to the funnel or nozzle. Drums should be placed near grounding posts and the following sequence of connections observed:

1. Drum to ground
2. Ground to aircraft
3. Drum to aircraft
4. Nozzle to aircraft before the aircraft tank cover is opened. When disconnecting, reverse the order—4, 3, 2, 1

Back to the chamois situation again: The passage of fuel through a chamois increases the charge of static electricity and the danger of sparks. Thus, if you have to use a chamois, the aircraft must be properly grounded and the nozzle, chamois filter, and funnel bonded to the aircraft. If a can is used, it should be connected to either the grounding post or the funnel. Under no circumstances should a plastic bucket or similar nonconductive container be used in this operation.

Oil system

Proper lubrication of the engine is essential to the extension of engine life and prevention of excessive maintenance. The oil system provides the means of storing and circulating oil throughout the internal components of a reciprocating engine.

Lubricating oil serves two purposes: (1) Quite obviously, it furnishes a coating over the surfaces of the moving parts, preventing direct metal-to-metal contact and the generation of heat, and (2) it absorbs and dissipates, through the oil cooling system, part of the engine heat produced by the internal combustion process.

Usually, engine oil is stored in a sump at the bottom of the engine crankcase. It is added through an opening to the sump, and a dip stick measures its level. A pump forces the oil from the sump to the various parts of the engine that require lubrication. The oil then drains back to the sump for recirculation.

Each engine is equipped with an oil pressure gauge and an oil temperature gauge that the pilot should monitor regularly to be sure that the oil system is functioning properly. The pressure gauge indicates pounds of pressure per square inch (PSI) and is color-coded with a green arc to indicate the normal operating range. At each end of the arc, some gauges have a red line to indicate high oil pressure and another red line to indicate low oil pressure. The pressure indication varies with the temperature of the oil. If the temperature is cold, the pressure is higher than if the oil is hot.

A loss of oil pressure is usually followed fairly quickly by total engine failure. If pressure is lost while on the ground, shut the engine down immediately; if in the air, land at a suitable emergency landing site as quickly as possible.

The oil temperature gauge is calibrated in either Celsius or Fahrenheit and color coded in green to indicate the normal temperature operating range. This gauge should be monitored regularly in flight, and if it gets up into the red area, you either have a faulty gauge or an oil problem. Don't take a chance that it's the gauge, though. Consider it a serious situation and get on the ground as soon as you can.

Be very sure to check the oil level before each flight. Starting out with an insufficient supply can lead to serious consequences. The engine burns off a certain amount during normal operations, and, if you plan to be out any period of time, taking off with a low oil level is inviting trouble.

With all of the different types of oil on the market for aviation use, follow the engine manufacturer's recommendation as to the type and weight to use. You can find this information in the Aircraft Flight Manual, Pilot's Operating Handbook, or on placards on or near the oil filler cap.

Propeller

A detailed discussion of the propeller is quite complex and beyond the intended scope of this handbook. The following, however, is offered as an introduction to and an overview of a critical component of the piston engine aircraft.

A propeller is a rotating airfoil and is thus subject to induced drag, stalls, and other aerodynamic principles that apply to any airfoil. In providing the necessary thrust to pull, or in some cases push, the airplane through the air, it uses engine power for rotation, which, in turn, generates thrust in much the way a wing produces lift. The propeller has an angle of attack that is the angle between the chord line of the propeller's airfoil and its relative wind (airflow opposite to the motion of the blade). Other factors affecting propellers are illustrated in Fig. 3-10.

A propeller blade is twisted. The blade angle changes from the hub to the tip, with the greatest angle of incidence, or highest pitch, at

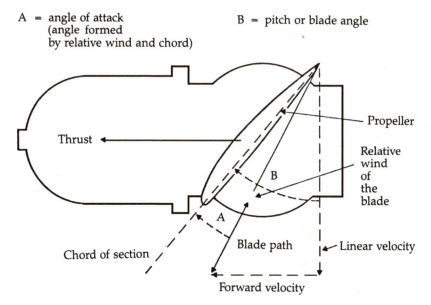

A = angle of attack (angle formed by relative wind and chord)   B = pitch or blade angle

Fig. 3-10. *Factors affecting propellers.*

the hub and the smallest at the tip (Fig. 3-11). The reason for the twist is to produce uniform lift from the hub to the tip. As the blade rotates, there is a difference in the actual speed of the various portions of the blade. The tip of the blade travels faster than that part near the hub because the tip travels a greater distance than the hub in the same length of time (Fig. 3-12). Changing the *angle of incidence (pitch)* from the hub to the tip to correspond with the speed produces uniform lift throughout the length of the blade. If the propeller blade were designed with the same angle of incidence throughout its entire length, it would be extremely inefficient because, as airspeed increased in flight, the portion near the hub would have a negative angle of attack while the blade tip would be stalled.

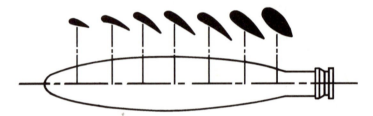

Fig. 3-11. *Changes in propeller blade angle from hub to tip.*

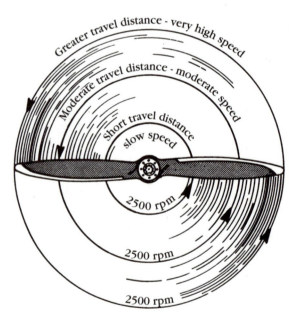

Fig. 3-12. *Relationship of travel distance and speed of various portions of the propeller blade.*

The typical general aviation airplane is equipped with one of two types of propellers. The first are those manufactured as solid units with blades that are fixed at a certain pitch. This type is characteristic of the smaller two- or four-place, single-engine aircraft with up to approximately 180 horsepower—those aircraft that are commonly used as trainers or for recreational, nonbusiness purposes. The second type is the variable pitch propeller, meaning, quite obviously, that the pitch of the blades can be changed, or varied, to produce the desired performance under the various conditions of flight. More on the variable-pitch propeller in a moment, though.

Fixed-pitch propellers

As to the fixed pitch, again there are two types: a *climb propeller* and a *cruise propeller*. Which one is installed depends on its intended use. The climb propeller has a lower pitch, meaning that it has a "flatter" blade angle, thus producing less drag as far as the engine is concerned. With less drag to overcome, the engine has a greater capability to develop higher rpms and more horsepower. Because of the increased takeoff and climb performance, this lower pitched propeller is better suited for short field or high altitude operations. It is not, however, as efficient in cruise flight.

The cruise propeller, on the other hand, has a higher pitch, which produces more drag in terms of engine output. The effect of the higher pitch, then, is better cruise performance with lower rpms and less horsepower capability. Takeoff and climb performance, however, are decreased.

While the propeller is indeed fixed, a qualified shop can change its pitch from climb to cruise or vice versa. The only warning is to be sure that the shop has the expertise to make the adjustment, check the propeller for cracks, balance it, and stand behind its work. It's too critical a piece of equipment to entrust it to anyone but a recognized professional in the field.

The propeller on a low-horsepower engine is typically mounted on a shaft that is usually an extension of the engine crankshaft. In this case, the revolutions per minute of the propeller would be the same as the engine rpm.

On higher-horsepower engines, the propeller is mounted on a shaft geared to the engine crankshaft. Here, the rpm of the propeller is different than that of the engine.

If the propeller is fixed-pitch and the speed of the engine and propeller is the same, a *tachometer* is the only indicator of engine power.

A tachometer is calibrated in hundreds of revolutions per minute and gives a direct indication of the engine and propeller rpm. The instrument is color coded with a green arc denoting the normal operating range and a red line denoting the maximum continuous operating rpm. Some tachometers have additional markings or interrupted arcs. With the possible design variations, be sure to follow the manufacturer's recommendations relative to the meaning of any tachometer markings.

The engine revolutions per minute are regulated by a cockpit throttle that controls the fuel/air flow to the engine. At a given altitude, the higher the tachometer reading, the higher the power output of the engine, which also means higher airspeed but greater fuel consumption—just like an automobile.

There is a condition under which the tachometer does not reflect the correct power output of the engine. This is when the operating altitude increases. For example, 2300 rpm at 5000 feet produce less horsepower than 2300 rpm at sea level. The reason, of course, is that air density decreases as altitude increases. Power output depends on air density, therefore decreasing the density decreases the power output of the engine. As altitude changes, the pilot has to adjust the throttle to maintain the same rpm. Climbing to a higher altitude means the throttle must be opened farther to indicate the same rpm as at a lower altitude.

Variable-pitch propellers

Two other types of propellers fall under the broad heading of *variable pitch*. One is the *adjustable pitch* propeller, the other the *controllable-pitch*. Since both are normally associated with higher performance aircraft, only passing reference to them is made here. As the student of today gains experience and moves up from the fixed-gear, fixed-pitch aircraft to more advanced types, these higher performance propellers will take on considerable significance and warrant a depth of study that is not appropriate for this book.

The main gist of the variable pitch is that the pitch on these propellers can be changed in flight, varying from a simple two-position propeller (the "adjustable-pitch") to the more complex automatic "controllable" propeller. With the adjustable pitch, the number of pitch positions at which the propeller can be set are basically limited to two—high or low. The controllable pitch, however, can be adjusted to any angle between a minimum and a maximum setting.

Described simply, the controllable pitch system involves a throttle in the cockpit that controls the power output of the engine, which is registered on a *manifold pressure* gauge. The manifold pressure gauge is a simple barometer that measures the air pressure in the engine intake manifold in inches of mercury. It is color coded with a green arc indicating the normal operating range.

The other part of the system is a propeller control that regulates the engine rpm and, in turn, the propeller rpm, which is registered on the tachometer. The pilot can then set the throttle control and propeller control at any desired manifold pressure and rpm setting within the engine operating limitation.

Whatever power setting the pilot selects, the propeller governor automatically changes the pitch (blade angle) to counteract any tendency for the engine to vary from that rpm. For example, if the manifold pressure or engine power is increased, the propeller governor automatically increases the pitch of the blade (more propeller drag) to maintain the same rpm.

The advantages of these constant-speed props are that they are more efficient than the fixed-pitch propellers, they stabilize fuel consumption, and they can be adjusted to meet the pilot's preference for a given flight, such as achieving the highest rate of climb, the fastest airspeed, lowest fuel consumption, least engine wear, or whatever combination is important at the time.

One disadvantage over the fixed-pitch prop is, of course, cost, including the basic purchase price, routine maintenance, and overhaul expenses. Ding one of these guys and you'll have a fair outlay of cash to look forward to. For the higher performance aircraft, though, whether it be single- or twin-engine, the variable propeller is essential for operating efficiency and realization of the full potential of the aircraft.

Starting the engine

Before starting the engine, the airplane should be in an area where the propeller will not stir up gravel or dust that could cause damage to the propeller or property. Be sure the brakes are firmly set, and *always* alert anyone who might be in the vicinity of the aircraft that you are about to start the engine. This alert is given by opening a cockpit window, door, or wing window and loudly calling out "CLEAR PROP!" or just plain "CLEAR!" Rules of safety and courtesy must be strictly observed to avoid personal injury or annoyance.

Engines equipped with a starter

Before attempting to start the engine on any airplane, be sure to read or review the manufacturer's recommended starting procedures. These can, and do, vary by type of aircraft and type of engine. And, by all means, follow the engine-starting checklist that should be in every cockpit. *It's inviting trouble to rely solely on memory*, but especially so if you rent airplanes and fly different makes or models, depending on what is available.

After going through the prestart procedures (brakes set, throttle and mixture control set, proper switches on, engine primed, making a 180° visual sweep of the ramp area around your plane, calling "CLEAR PROP," and completing any other checklist items), you should be ready to engage the starter.

If all is well, the engine should catch after only a couple of turns of the propeller. If it doesn't, after 10 seconds or so, turn the starter key off and wait a moment or two. Continuous cranking beyond 30 seconds may damage the starter. If the engine refuses to start under normal circumstances after a reasonable number of attempts, the possibility of problems with ignition or fuel flow should be investigated.

As soon as the engine does start, set the power to the recommended warmup rpm, which is probably somewhere around 1000 rpm. Immediately, check the oil pressure to determine that the oil system is functioning properly. If the gauge does not indicate oil pressure within 30 seconds, stop the engine and find out what the problem is. If oil is not circulating properly, the engine can be seriously damaged in a very short time. Keep in mind, though, that there will be a much slower response in oil pressure indications during cold weather than in the summer. Colder temperatures cause the oil to congeal (thicken) to a greater extent.

Once the engine has started, barring other intermediate checklist actions, you should be ready to taxi to the takeoff runway hold area. As you do so, continue to monitor the operating temperature gauges. If the aircraft has a cylinder-head temperature gauge, that will give you a reliable indication of whether the engine has warmed enough to perform smoothly and dependably. If the airplane isn't equipped with this gauge, then use the oil temperature gauge.

Before takeoff, complete all necessary checks for engine and airplane operation. Once again, use the checklist—DON'T rely on memory.

Engines not equipped with a starter

Although it's a relatively rare requirement these days, the matter of starting, or "hand-propping," an aircraft that is not battery-equipped should be addressed. It warrants attention, too, because it raises the issue of turning the propeller of a battery-equipped engine and safeguards that should be taken.

Because of the dangers involved in hand-starting airplane engines, every precaution should be exercised. In addition to putting the brakes on and placing chocks under the wheels, it's extremely important that a competent pilot be at the controls in the cockpit. Plus that, the person turning the propeller should be thoroughly familiar with the technique. The following are a few suggestions to increase the hand-propping safety factor.

The person who turns the propeller is in charge. He is the one who calls out the commands: "Gas on, switch off, throttle closed, brakes set." The cockpit pilot checks these items and repeats back the commands to ensure that there is no misunderstanding. The person doing the propping then should push slightly on the airplane to be certain that the brakes *are* set and are holding firmly. From this point on, the cockpit pilot must not touch the switch or throttle again until the person swinging the prop calls "Contact." The pilot repeats "Contact," and then turns the switch on—and in that sequence. *Never* turn the switch on and then call "Contact."

For the person swinging the prop, a few simple precautions can help avoid accidents.

- When touching a propeller, always assume that the switch is on, even though the pilot may have confirmed otherwise with "switch off." The switches on many engine installations operate on the principle of short-circuiting the current. If the switch is faulty, as sometimes happens, it can be in the "off" position and still permit the current to flow to the spark plugs.

- Be sure to stand on firm ground. Slippery grass, mud, grease, snow, ice, or loose gravel could cause a slip or a fall into or under the propeller.

- Never allow any portion of the body to get into the propeller arc of rotation. This applies even though the engine is not being cranked; occasionally, a hot engine backfires after shutdown when the propeller has almost stopped rotating.

- Stand close enough to the propeller to be able to step away as it is pulled down. Standing too far away from the propeller requires leaning forward to reach it. This is an off-balance position and it's possible to fall into the blades as the engine starts. Stepping away after cranking is also a safeguard in the event the brakes don't hold when the engine starts.

- When swinging the propeller, always move the blade downward by pushing with the palms of the hands. If the blade is moved upward, or gripped tightly with the fingers and backfiring occurs, it could cause broken fingers or the body to be pulled into the path of the propeller blades.

- When removing the chocks from in front of the wheels, remember that the propeller, when revolving, is almost invisible. It's happened more than once that someone intending to remove the chocks has walked directly into the propeller.

Unsupervised hand-propping should never be attempted by inexperienced persons. But regardless of the experience level, no one should try to hand-prop without strictly following the necessary safety measures. Similarly, uninformed individuals, inexperienced bystanders, or nonpilot passengers should never be allowed to handle the throttle, brakes, or switches during starting procedures. And be sure the airplane is securely chocked or tied down and braked before initiating any hand-propping procedures.

While the above essentially addresses hand-propping a non-starter-equipped plane, similar precautions must be exercised when doing the same with a starter-equipped engine. Frankly, the best advice, as far as the latter situation is concerned, is DON'T. If you can't start this type engine by following the normal procedures, you'd be better off finding a mechanic to troubleshoot the problem. Failing that, at least find someone on the airport property who is experienced at this sort of thing. Hand-propping is not something the beginning or casual pilot should attempt.

Idling the engine during flight

It might be wise to briefly mention the potential problems that could be created by excessive idling of the engine during flight, particularly for long periods of time, as in an extended power-off descent.

Whenever the throttle is closed during flight, the engine cools rapidly and vaporization of fuel is less complete. The airflow through the carburetor system under such conditions may not be of sufficient volume to assure a uniform mixture of fuel and air. Consequently, the engine could cease to operate because the mixture is too lean or too rich. Suddenly opening or closing the throttle could aggravate this condition, and the engine might cough once or twice, sputter, and stop.

Three precautions should be taken to prevent the engine from stopping while idling. First, make sure that the ground-idling speed is properly adjusted. Second, don't open or close the throttle abruptly. Third, keep the engine warm during glides by frequently opening the throttle for a few seconds.

Aircraft documents, maintenance, and inspections

An aircraft owner assumes responsibilities similar to those of an automobile owner. An automobile is usually registered in the state where the owner resides and state license plates must be obtained. The registered owner of an aircraft that he or she is continuing to fly is also responsible for certain items such as:

1. Having a current Airworthiness Certificate and Aircraft Registration Certificate in the aircraft
2. Maintaining the aircraft in an airworthy condition
3. Assuring that maintenance is properly recorded

4. Keeping abreast of current regulations concerning the operation and maintenance of the aircraft

5. Notifying the FAA Aircraft Registry immediately of any change of permanent mailing address, the sale or export of the aircraft, or the loss of U.S. citizenship

Some states require that an automobile be inspected periodically to assure that it is in a safe operating condition. In the same way, but not by state law, an aircraft must be inspected in accordance with an FAA annual inspection program.

Some similarities between automobile and aircraft responsibilities are these:

Automobile/Aircraft Comparison Chart		
Responsibility	**Automobile**	**Aircraft**
Registration	Yes	Yes
Inspection (most states)	Yes	Yes (FAA regulation)
Compulsory insurance (most states)	Yes	No
Reporting of accidents	Yes	Yes
Required maintenance records	No	Yes
Controlled maintenance	No	Yes
Maximum speed restrictions	Yes	Yes

Certificate of aircraft registration

Before an aircraft can be legally flown, it must be registered with the FAA Aircraft Registry. It is also required that the aircraft owner keep that Certificate of Registration (Fig. 3-13) in the airplane at all times.

The Certificate expires when:

1. The aircraft is registered under the laws of a foreign country.

2. The registration of the aircraft is canceled at the written request of the owner.

3. The aircraft is totally destroyed or scrapped.

4. The ownership of the aircraft is transferred.

5. The holder of the certificate loses United States citizenship.

6. Thirty days have elapsed since the death of the holder of the certificate.

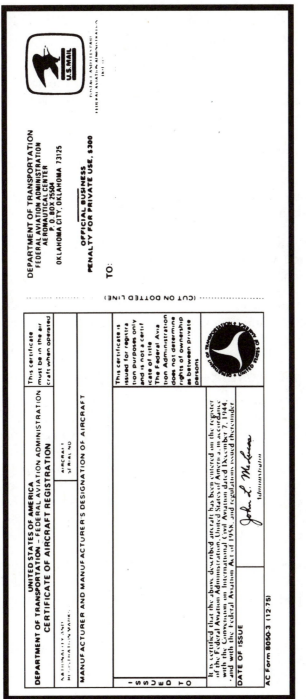

Fig. 3-13. *Certificate of aircraft registration.*

109

When the aircraft is destroyed or scrapped, the owner must notify the FAA by filling in the back of the Certificate of Aircraft Registration and mailing it to the FAA Aircraft Registry.

When a U.S. civil aircraft is transferred to a person who is not a U.S. citizen, the U.S.-registered owner is required to remove the United States registration and nationality marks from the aircraft before the aircraft is delivered.

A Dealers Aircraft Registration Certificate is another form of registration certificate, but it is valid only for required flight tests by the manufacturer or in flights that are necessary for the sale of the aircraft by the manufacturer or a dealer. It must be removed by the dealer when the aircraft is sold.

The FAA does not issue any certificate of ownership or endorse any information with respect to ownership on a Certificate of Aircraft Registration.

Note: For additional information concerning the Aircraft Registration Application or the Aircraft Bill of Sale, contact the nearest Flight Standards District Office.

Airworthiness certificate

An Airworthiness Certificate is issued by the Federal Aviation Administration only after the aircraft has been inspected, is found to meet the requirements of the Federal Aviation Regulations (FARs), and is in a condition for safe operation. Under all circumstances, the aircraft must meet the requirements of the original type certificate, which must be displayed in the aircraft so that it is legible to passengers or crew whenever the aircraft is operated. The Airworthiness Certificate can be transferred with the aircraft except when it is sold to a foreign purchaser.

The *Standard Airworthiness Certificate*, Fig. 3-14, is issued for the aircraft type certificated in the *normal, utility, acrobatic,* or *transport* categories or for *manned free balloons.* An explanation of each item in the certificate follows:

Item 1. Nationality: The "N" indicates the aircraft is of United States registry. Registration Marks: The number is the registration number assigned to the aircraft.

Item 2. Indicates the make and model of the aircraft.

Item 3. Is the serial number assigned to the aircraft, as noted on the aircraft data plate.

Item 4. Indicates that the aircraft must be operated in accordance with the limitations specified for the Normal category.

Item 5. Indicates the aircraft is considered in a condition for safe operation at the time of inspection and issuance of the certificate. Any exemptions from the applicable airworthiness standards are briefly noted here, as is the exemption number. The word "None" is entered if no exemption exists.

Item 6. Indicates the Airworthiness Certificate is in effect indefinitely if the aircraft is maintained in accordance with Parts 21, 43, and 91 of the Federal Aviation Regulations and the aircraft is registered in the United States. Also included are the date the certificate was issued and the signature and office identification of the FAA representative.

A *Special Airworthiness Certificate* is issued for all aircraft certificated in other than the Standard classifications—in other words, for aircraft classified as *Experimental, Restricted, Limited,* or *Provisional.*

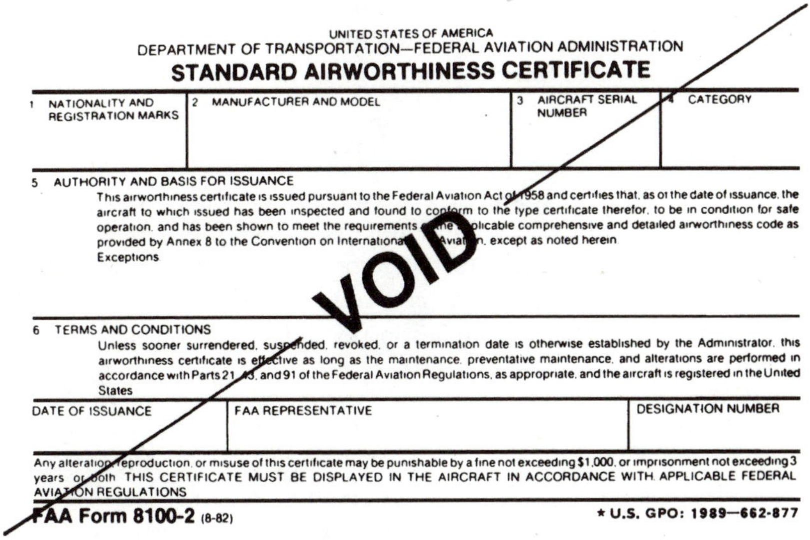

UNITED STATES OF AMERICA
DEPARTMENT OF TRANSPORTATION—FEDERAL AVIATION ADMINISTRATION
STANDARD AIRWORTHINESS CERTIFICATE

1 NATIONALITY AND REGISTRATION MARKS	2 MANUFACTURER AND MODEL	3 AIRCRAFT SERIAL NUMBER	4 CATEGORY

5 AUTHORITY AND BASIS FOR ISSUANCE

This airworthiness certificate is issued pursuant to the Federal Aviation Act of 1958 and certifies that, as of the date of issuance, the aircraft to which issued has been inspected and found to conform to the type certificate therefor, to be in condition for safe operation, and has been shown to meet the requirements of the applicable comprehensive and detailed airworthiness code as provided by Annex 8 to the Convention on International Civil Aviation, except as noted herein

Exceptions

VOID

6 TERMS AND CONDITIONS

Unless sooner surrendered, suspended, revoked, or a termination date is otherwise established by the Administrator, this airworthiness certificate is effective as long as the maintenance, preventative maintenance, and alterations are performed in accordance with Parts 21, 43, and 91 of the Federal Aviation Regulations, as appropriate, and the aircraft is registered in the United States

DATE OF ISSUANCE	FAA REPRESENTATIVE	DESIGNATION NUMBER

Any alteration, reproduction, or misuse of this certificate may be punishable by a fine not exceeding $1,000, or imprisonment not exceeding 3 years or both. THIS CERTIFICATE MUST BE DISPLAYED IN THE AIRCRAFT IN ACCORDANCE WITH APPLICABLE FEDERAL AVIATION REGULATIONS

FAA Form 8100-2 (8-82)   ★ U.S. GPO: 1989—662-877

Fig. 3-14. *Standard airworthiness certificate.*

In purchasing an aircraft classed as other than Standard, it is suggested that the local FAA Flight Standards District Office be contacted for an explanation of the pertinent airworthiness requirements and the limitations of such a certificate.

In summary, the FAA initially determines that an aircraft is in a condition for safe operation and conforms to type design and then issues an Airworthiness Certificate. A Standard Airworthiness Certificate remains in effect so long as the aircraft receives the required maintenance and is properly registered in the United States.

Aircraft maintenance

Maintenance means the inspection, overhaul, and repair of aircraft, including the replacement of parts. Its purpose is to ensure that an aircraft is kept to an acceptable standard of airworthiness throughout its operational life.

Although maintenance requirements vary for different types of aircraft, experience shows that most aircraft need some type of preventive maintenance every 25 hours of flying time or less and minor maintenance at least every 100 hours. These figures are, of course, influenced by the kind of operation, the climatic conditions, storage facilities, age, and construction of the aircraft. Most manufacturers provide service information that should be used to help keep the airplane in the desired state of airworthiness and minimize the need for major repairs and maintenance.

Inspections

Federal Aviation Regulations (FARs) Part 91 places primary responsibility on the owner or operator for maintaining an aircraft in an airworthy condition. Certain inspections must be performed on the aircraft and the owner must maintain the airworthiness of the aircraft during the time between required inspections by having any unsafe defects corrected.

FARs require the inspection of all civil aircraft at specific intervals for the purpose of determining their overall condition, with the intervals depending generally on the type of operation in which the aircraft is engaged. Certain aircraft have to be inspected at least once each 12 calendar months, while inspection of others is required after each

100 hours of operation. In still other instances, an aircraft may be inspected in accordance with a system that requires a major inspection and overhaul of the aircraft based on time in service, number of system operations, or any combination thereof.

To determine the specific inspection requirements and rules for the performance of inspections, FAR Part 43 and Appendices A through F detail the requirements for various types of maintenance and preventive actions. The basic inspections are:

Annual inspection. A reciprocating-powered single-engine aircraft flown for pleasure is required to be inspected at least annually by a *certificated airframe and powerplant mechanic* holding an *inspection authorization*, or by a *certificated repair station* that is appropriately rated, or by the manufacturer of the aircraft. The aircraft cannot be flown unless the annual inspection has been performed within the preceding 12 calendar months. A period of 12 calendar months extends from any day of any month to the last day of the same month the following year. An aircraft with an overdue annual inspection, however, may be operated under a special flight permit for the purpose of flying the aircraft to a location where the inspection can be performed.

100-hour inspection. A reciprocating-powered single-engine aircraft that is used to carry passengers for hire or for flight instruction for hire must be inspected within each 100 hours of time in service by a certificated airframe and powerplant mechanic, a certificated repair station that is appropriately rated, or the aircraft manufacturer. An annual inspection is acceptable as a 100-hour inspection, but the reverse is not true.

Preflight inspection. Although not required by Federal Aviation Regulations, you should always conduct a thorough aircraft inspection before every flight to be sure that the aircraft is mechanically sound and can be operated with safety. The specific steps in this inspection are reviewed in a moment.

Engine overhaul. Depending on the engine type, manufacturers have established certain recommended hours of flight time between major engine overhauls. Although there are several exceptions both ways, a general recommended time is every 2000 hours. This is the "time between overhauls," or TBOs.

There is no regulation that requires an overhaul at or before expiration of the TBO, say 2000 hours, and if the engine is functioning well, with normal oil consumption and healthy compression, many owners keep their planes flying another 200 or 300 hours—or more—before committing to a fairly steep overhaul bill. But, if you're an aircraft owner, around TBO time you'd be wise to start thinking quite seriously about when you'll ground the plane for its overhaul, who will do it, and what it will cost. As to "who," just be sure that you opt for quality work and dependability. Ask questions, shop around, and don't necessarily go with the lowest bidder or price-quoter. Bargains in overhauls are rare, and this is too serious an investment to be cutting corners unnecessarily, financially or otherwise.

Preventive maintenance

Simple or minor preservation operations and replacing small standard parts, not involving complex assembly operations, are considered preventive maintenance. A certificated pilot may perform preventive maintenance on any aircraft he or she owns or operates that is not used in air carrier service. Typical preventive maintenance operations are found in FAR Part 43, Maintenance, Preventive Maintenance, Rebuilding, and Alteration. Part 43 also contains other rules related to aircraft maintenance.

Repairs and alterations

Except as noted under "Preventive Maintenance," all repairs and alterations are classed as either *major* or *minor*. Major repairs or alterations must be approved for return to service by an appropriately rated certificated repair station, an airframe and powerplant mechanic holding an inspection authorization, or a representative of the Administrator. Minor repairs and alterations may be approved for return to service by a certificated airframe and powerplant mechanic or an appropriately certificated repair station.

Airworthiness directives

A primary safety function of the Federal Aviation Administration is to require correction of unsafe conditions found in an aircraft, an aircraft engine, propeller, or appliance when such conditions exist and are likely to exist or develop in other products of the same design. The condition may be the result of a design defect, improper maintenance, or other causes. FAR Part 39, Airworthiness Directives, defines the authority and responsibility of the Administrator for requiring the necessary corrective action. The Airworthiness Directive (AD) is the means used to notify aircraft owners and other interested persons of the unsafe condition and to advise the recipients of what further action they are to take to correct the condition or how to operate under it.

Airworthiness Directives are divided into two categories: (1) those of an emergency nature requiring immediate compliance upon receipt, and (2) those of an urgent nature requiring compliance within a relatively longer period of time.

Airworthiness Directives are Federal Aviation Regulations and must be complied with, unless specific exemption is granted. It's thus the aircraft owner or operator's responsibility to assure compliance, including those ADs that require recurrent or continuing action. For example, an AD might require a repetitive inspection each 50 hours of an operation, which means that every 50 hours the inspection must be made and recorded.

The FARs require that the owner maintain a record showing the current status of applicable airworthiness directives, including the method of compliance, and the signature and certificate number of the repair station or mechanic who performed the work. For ready reference, many aircraft owners have—and should have—a chronological listing of the pertinent ADs in their logbooks.

Preflight inspection

The importance of a thorough preflight inspection of the airplane is one of the pilot's duties that can't be overemphasized. Too many serious accidents have been traced directly to hasty, incomplete, or careless inspections—or to no inspection at all. This has to be a systematic process by which you totally satisfy yourself that the airplane is safe and ready to fly.

To ensure thoroughness, Fig. 3-15, in conjunction with the following Preflight Checklist, is an illustration of an inspection pattern that can be used on almost any single-engine or light twin-engine aircraft, provided it is modified to suit the airplane type and the manufacturer's recommendations.

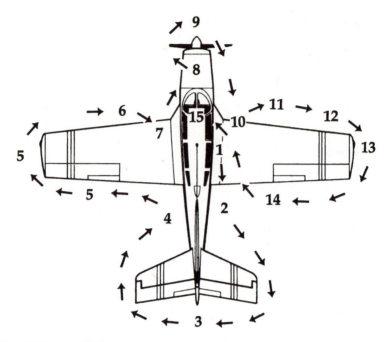

Fig. 3-15. *Preflight inspection chart.*

Which way you go around the airplane doesn't make any real difference. You can move towards the tail first, as the figure shows, or begin with the right wing and move counterclockwise around the plane. What's more important is that you follow the same pattern every time and check all items the same way every time. Doing it this way will develop a habit, a regimen, that ensures completeness.

The numbers on the inspection chart in Fig. 3-15 correspond to the numbers indicated on the itemized list on pages 117, 118, and 119. Quite apparently, no one checklist can fit all airplanes, and certainly the one that follows doesn't. It is, however, reasonably representative of the typical list for a low-wing, fixed gear, single-engine aircraft. Please view it as such, and if it doesn't conform exactly to the plane(s) you are flying, don't fault it for omissions or inaccuracies.

Preflight checklist

Before entering the airplane, stand off and observe the general overall appearance of the airplane for obvious defects and discrepancies. Then proceed as the following suggests.

1. Cockpit/Cabin:
- ☐ Battery and ignition switches—OFF
- ☐ Control locks—REMOVE
- ☐ Flaps—LOWER

2. Fuselage:
- ☐ Baggage compartment—contents secure and door locked
- ☐ Static source—free from obstructions
- ☐ Condition of covering—missing or loose rivets, cracks, tears

3. Empennage:
- ☐ Control surface locks—REMOVE
- ☐ Fixed and movable control surfaces—dents, cracks, excess play, hinge pins and bolts for security and condition
- ☐ Lights—navigation anticollision lights for condition and security

4. Fuselage:
- ☐ Same as item 2, as applicable

5. Wing:
- ☐ Control surface locks—REMOVE
- ☐ Control surfaces, including flaps—dents, cracks, excess play, hinge pins and bolts for security and condition
- ☐ General condition of wings and covering—bulges or wrinkles, loose or missing rivets, cleanliness, freedom from frost, snow, ice, etc.
- ☐ Wing tip and navigation light—security and damage
- ☐ Landing light—condition, cleanliness, and security
- ☐ Stall warning vane—freedom of movement. Prior to inspection turn master switch ON so that stall warning signal can be checked when vane is deflected
- ☐ Pitot cover—"REMOVE"
- ☐ Pitot and static ports—remove obstructions
- ☐ Pitot tube general condition and alignment

6. Fuel tank (left wing):
- ☐ Fuel quantity in tank
- ☐ Fuel tank filler cap and fairing covers—secure
- ☐ Fuel tank vents—obstructions
- ☐ When fuel tank is equipped with a quick or snap-type drain valve, drain a sufficient amount of fuel into a container to check for the presence of water and sediment

7. Landing gear:
  ☐ Wheels and brakes—condition and security, indications of fluid leakage at fittings, fluid lines, and adjacent area. Tires—cuts, bruises, excessive wear, and proper inflation
  ☐ Oleos and shock struts—cleanliness and proper inflation
  ☐ Wheel fairing—general condition and security. On streamline wheel fairings, look inside, if possible, for accumulation of mud, ice, etc.

8. Engine:
  ☐ Engine oil quantity—secure filler cap
  ☐ General condition—check for fuel and oil leaks
  ☐ Cowling, access doors, and cowl flaps—condition and security
  ☐ Drain a sufficient quantity of fuel from the main fuel sump drain to determine that there is no water or sediment remaining in the system.
  ☐ Nose landing gear—wheel and tire—cuts, bruises, excessive wear, and proper inflation
  ☐ Oleo and shock strut—proper inflation and cleanliness
  ☐ Wheel well and fairing—general condition and security

9. Propeller:
  ☐ Propeller and spinner—security, oil leakage, and condition. Be particularly observant for deep nicks and scratches.

  ☐ Assure that ground area under propeller is free of loose stones, cinders, etc.

10. Fuel tank:
  ☐ Same as item 6.

11. Landing gear:
  ☐ Same as item 7

12. Wing tip and navigation lights:
  ☐ Same as item 5

13. Wing:
  ☐ To the extent applicaple, same as item 5

14. Wing:
- [ ] To the extent applicaple, same as item 5

15. Cockpit:
- [ ] Cleanliness and loose articles
- [ ] Windshield and windows—obvious defects and cleanliness
- [ ] Safety belt and shoulder harness—condition and security
- [ ] Parking brake—ON
- [ ] Flaps retracted
- [ ] Check all switches and controls
- [ ] Trim tabs—SET
- [ ] Pilot's seat—LOCKED

Engine start, ground runup, and functional check

Having completed Step 15, above, you're now ready to start the engine, per the following:

- Navigation and communication equipment—OFF
- Fuel tank selector valve—ON
- Brakes—ON
- Start engine in accordance with manufacturer's recommended procedure—including throttle setting, mixture control setting, priming, etc.
- Turn on radios and navigation equipment and check all instruments for proper operation and readings.

If all is well following engine start, taxi to the takeoff runway hold area for the pretakeoff check. (There will be radio communications required before you start taxiing, whether you are at a tower-controlled airport or otherwise. These are discussed later in the book, however.)

At the hold area, turn the aircraft into the wind, if possible, and follow the manufacturer's pretakeoff checklist, including these items:

After checking the left and right magnetos for the proper rpm drop (about 50 to 75 rpms), retard the throttle to idle, momentarily switch the magnetos to OFF to check for proper grounding. If the engine continues to run after the switch is turned to OFF, it indicates a faulty ground circuit between the magneto and switch that should be corrected before further engine operation. Then:

- Check flight controls, including flaps, for free and smooth operation in proper direction.
- Check radio receiver and tune to proper frequency.
- Set altimeter setting and clock—if you have not done so before now.

If all is in order, taxi to the taxiway hold line, look both upwind and downwind for landing or departing traffic, make the necessary departure radio call—and get ready to go. You've done all you could to be sure you're about to fly in a plane that's ready to fly!

After storage. A *thorough* inspection is recommended of aircraft that have been tied down or stored for an extensive period of time. Inactive aircraft are frequently used for nesting by insects and animals. Birds' nests in air intake scoops impair airflow, resulting in excessively rich mixtures and could cause engine stoppage. Nests lodged between engine cylinders and engine baffles cause overheating, preignition, and detonation. Insect nests obstructing fuel tank vents cause lean mixtures and fuel starvation. Excretions from rodents are highly corrosive to aluminum alloy metals and harmful to fabric and wood. Deterioration of fuel, oil, hydraulic, or induction hoses could easily cause leaks and faulty operation.

Among other items, be sure to inspect:

- Oil coolers (intake scoops)
- Carburetors (intake screen and passages)
- Fuel tank vents (free of obstruction)
- Pitot tubes (free of obstruction)
- Fuselage (interior and baggage areas)
- Wings (interior of wings and control surfaces)
- Static vents (free of obstructions)

Now for another test-yourself quiz.

Quickie Quiz Questions
Chapter 3

1. What are the primary and secondary flight control systems?
2. List the elements of a reciprocating engine.
3. What is meant by a "dual ignition" system?
4. What are the purposes of flaps?
5. If the oil temperature gauge indicates an excessively high engine temperature, what are at least four actions the pilot should take to help lower the temperature?
6. What can the pilot do to minimize the possibility of fuel contamination?
7. List the performance differences between a cruise-pitch and a climb-pitch propeller.
8. What are the two most noticeable early symptoms of carburetor icing in an engine with a fixed-pitch propeller?
9. If an ammeter indicates a minus value or displays rapid fluctuations of the needle, what should the pilot do?
10. What operating conditions are most conducive to the formation of carburetor icing?

Answers in Appendix, pages 572-573.

4

Flight instruments

Whether flying on visual or instrument flight rules, the cockpit flight instruments are essential if the airplane is to be operated with precision and produce the expected level of performance. This is particularly true when flying longer distances where, among other things, the ability to stay on altitude and on course are both time- and money-savers. Presumably, the aircraft is equipped with the essential instruments. If so, the next step is to gain the necessary knowledge about the instruments so that they can be referenced and interpreted effectively.

The pitot-static system and associated instruments

Two major elements form the pitot-static system: (1) the *impact pressure chamber* and lines, and (2) the *static pressure chamber* and lines. The two, combined, provide the source of air pressure for the operation of the *altimeter, vertical speed indicator,* and *airspeed indicator.*

In older planes, one common source known as the *pitot-static tube* generated the impact pressure and the static pressure. Now, however, the two sources are separated.

In today's system, the impact air pressure (air striking the airplane because of its forward motion) is taken from a pitot tube, aligned to the relative wind, and mounted either under or on the leading edge of the wing or on the nose. On some airplanes, it's located on the vertical stabilizer. These locations provide minimum disturbance or turbulence caused by the motion of the airplane through the air.

The *static pressure* (pressure of the still air) is usually taken from a static line attached to a vent, or vents, mounted flush with the side of the fuselage. On most airplanes using the flush-type source, each side of the fuselage has one vent. This compensates for any possible variation in static pressure due to erratic changes in airplane attitude.

The openings of both the pitot tube and the static vent should be checked during the preflight inspections to be sure that they are free from obstructions. Clogged or partially clogged openings should be cleaned by a certificated mechanic. Blowing into these openings is not recommended because that could damage any of the three instruments sketched in Fig. 4-1.

Briefly, the pitot-static system operates as follows: As the airplane moves through the air, the impact pressure on the open pitot tube affects the pressure in the pitot chamber. Any change of pressure in the pitot chamber is transmitted through a line connected to the airspeed indicator, which utilizes impact pressure for its operation. The static chamber is vented through small holes to the free undisturbed air, and, as the atmospheric pressure increases or decreases, the pressure in the static chamber changes accordingly. Again, this pressure change is transmitted through lines to the instruments that utilize static pressure as illustrated in Fig. 4-1.

An alternate source for static pressure is provided in some airplanes in the event the static ports become clogged. This source usually is vented to the pressure inside the cockpit. Because of the venturi effect of the flow of air over the cockpit, the alternate static pressure is usually lower than that produced by the normal static source. When the alternate source is used, these differences in instrument indications usually occur: The altimeter reads higher than the actual

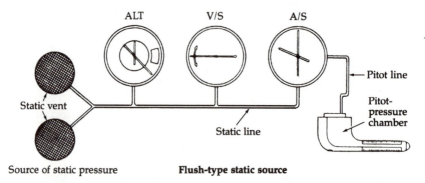

Fig. 4-1. *Pitot-static system and the instruments it affects.*

altitude, the airspeed indicates greater than actual, and the vertical speed shows a climb while the plane is in level flight.

The altimeter

The altimeter (Fig. 4-2) measures the height of the airplane above a given level. Because it's the only instrument that gives altitude information, it's one of the most important instruments in the airplane. To use it effectively, you must thoroughly understand its principle of operation and the effect that atmospheric pressure and temperature have on it.

Principle of operation. The pressure altimeter, using static pressure as its source of operation, is simply an aneroid barometer that measures the pressure of the atmosphere at the level where it is located and presents an altitude indication in feet. Air is more dense at the surface of the earth than aloft, so as altitude increases, atmospheric pressure decreases. This difference in pressure at various levels causes the aneroid "bellows" built within the instrument to expand as the aircraft climbs or contract in descents and thus indicate altitude changes.

The dial of a typical altimeter is graduated with numerals arranged clockwise from 0 to 9 inclusive as shown in Fig. 4-2. Movement of the aneroid element is transmitted through a gear train to the three pointers (or "hands") that sweep the calibrated dial to indicate the altitude. The shortest pointer (barely visible in the center of Fig. 4-2)

Fig. 4-2. *Sensitive altimeter. The instrument is adjusted by the knob (lower left) so the current altimeter setting appears in the window to the right.*

indicates altitude in tens of thousands of feet; the intermediate pointer, in thousands of feet; and the longest pointer in hundreds of feet, subdivided into 20-foot increments.

Whatever altitude is indicated on the instrument is correct, however, only when the sea level barometric pressure is standard (29.92 inches of mercury), the sea level free air temperature is standard (+15°C or 59°F), and the pressure and temperature decrease at a standard rate as the altitude increases.

Because atmospheric pressure continually changes, a means is provided to adjust the altimeter to compensate for nonstandard conditions. The pilot can do this with the small knob in the lower left of the altimeter (between the 6 and the 7 positions in Fig. 4-2). All the pilot has to do is turn the knob until the barometric scale at the airport—say it's 30.32—as per the figure, appears in the small window. As the knob is turned, so is the barometric scale. When the current scale appears, the altimeter pointers are automatically calibrated to indicate the altitude of the aircraft above mean sea level—whether the aircraft is on the ground at an airport or in the air.

So when an air traffic controller, in abbreviated aviation language, advises that ". . . altimeter three zero three two," or whatever, turn the small knob until "30.32" shows in the window. Then check the position of the pointers for your current altitude above *sea level*—not above the ground.

Effects of nonstandard pressure and temperature. If no means were provided for adjusting altimeters to nonstandard pressure, flying could be hazardous. For example, if you were flying from a high pressure to a low pressure area, without adjusting the altimeter, your actual altitude would be *lower* than the indicated altitude. Conversely, when going from a low to a high pressure area, without an altimeter adjustment, you'd be *higher* than the indicated altitude. Both "errors" fortunately can be corrected by setting the altimeter properly.

Variations in air temperature also affect the altimeter. On a warm day, the expanded air is lighter in weight per unit volume than on a cold day; consequently the pressure levels are raised. For example, the pressure level where the altimeter indicates 10,000 feet is HIGHER on a warm day than under standard conditions. On a cold day the reverse is true, and the 10,000-foot level would be LOWER. Adjusting the altimeter for nonstandard pressures, does not, however, compensate for nonstandard temperatures. So if terrain or obstacle clearance is a factor in selecting a VFR flight level, particularly at higher altitudes, remember to anticipate that COLDER-THAN-STANDARD TEMPERATURES place the aircraft LOWER than the altimeter indicates. A higher altitude, then, should be chosen to ensure adequate terrain clearance.

Setting the altimeter. A bit more on this, plus a couple of other points: As explained a moment ago, to adjust the altimeter for variations in atmospheric pressure, set the pressure scale in the small window, which is calibrated in inches of mercury (Hg), to correspond with the announced altimeter setting. Altimeter settings are defined as "station pressure reduced to sea level," expressed in inches of mercury.

The station reporting the altimeter setting takes hourly measurements of its current atmospheric pressure and corrects that value to sea level pressure. Since these altimeter settings reflect height above sea level only in the vicinity of the reporting station, it's necessary to adjust the setting as a flight progresses from one station to the next.

FAA regulations, copied almost verbatim, provide the following concerning altimeter settings: "The cruising altitude of an aircraft below 18,000 feet msl shall be maintained by reference to an altimeter that is set to the current reported altimeter setting of a station located along the route of flight and within 100 nautical miles of the aircraft. If there is no such station, the current reported altimeter setting of an appropriate available station shall be used. In an aircraft having no radio, the altimeter shall be set to the elevation of the departure airport or an appropriate altimeter setting available before departure." (That's clear, isn't it?)

Don't be lulled into believing that the current reported altimeter setting compensates for irregularities in atmospheric pressure at all altitudes. It doesn't, necessarily, because the setting broadcast by ground stations is the *station* pressure corrected to mean sea level. It does not take into account distortion at higher levels, particularly the effect of nonstandard temperatures.

It should be pointed out, however, that if each pilot in a given area used the same altimeter setting, each altimeter would be equally affected by temperature and pressure variation errors, making it possible to maintain the desired altitude separation between aircraft.

When flying over high mountainous terrain, certain atmospheric conditions can cause the altimeter to indicate an altitude of 1000 feet, or more, HIGHER than the actual altitude. For that reason, if you do any mountain climbing, allow a generous margin of extra altitude—not only for possible altimeter error, but also for downdrafts that are particularly prevalent if high winds are encountered.

To illustrate the use of the altimeter-setting system, visualize that you're on a flight from Alpha Airport, which is 485 feet above sea level, to Charlie Municipal, located 1800 feet msl, and your route takes you over the Bravo VOR. Before departing Alpha, the tower or Automatic Terminal Information Service (ATIS) gives you the current altimeter setting of 29.85. When you enter this value in the altimeter-setting window, the altimeter indication (the position of the pointers) should read the same as the actual Alpha Airport elevation of 485 feet msl. This assumes that the altimeter is perfectly calibrated. Most aren't, though, so a small error is possible. If a reading varies more than 75 feet from the actual field elevation, the overall accuracy of the instrument is questionable and it should be checked by an instrument technician for recalibration.

But back to the mythical flight: When over the Bravo VOR, you receive the current area altimeter setting of 29.94, so you reset the altimeter accordingly. Approaching Charlie Municipal, you tune to the Charlie ATIS about 15 miles out and learn, among other things, that the airport altimeter reading there is 29.69, so, once again, you reset the altimeter. Keeping in mind that the field elevation at Charlie is 1800 feet, you should be flying the traffic pattern at an indicated altitude of 800 feet above the airport. And if your altimeter is accurate and 29.69 is the current barometric pressure, the altimeter should read exactly 1800 when you're on the ground and parked at the ramp.

Now let's assume that you did *not* insert the 29.69 reading from the Charlie ATIS and continued to use the Bravo VOR setting of 29.94. If that happened, you'd be approximately 250 feet *below* the proper Charlie traffic pattern altitude while indicating an altitude of 2600 feet, and, on landing, the altimeter would read approximately 250 feet higher, or 2050 feet msl, than the actual field elevation.

The explanation of these figures is this: Your altimeter setting, arriving at Charlie, is 29.94 (the Bravo setting); the correct setting is 29.69. The difference between the two is .25 of one inch of pressure. One inch of pressure is equal to approximately 1000 feet of altitude; consequently, .25 × 1000 feet = 250 feet.

These calculations might be a little confusing, particularly when trying to determine whether to add or subtract the amount of altimeter error. The following, then, might add some clarity and help in solving this type of problem:

The altimeter pointers are moved, as you know, by two means: one, by changes in air pressure, the other, mechanically by the pilot and rotation of the altimeter setting knob.

Remember, when the airplane changes altitude, the changing static pressure within the altimeter case allows the aneroid barometer to expand or contract, which, through linkage, rotates the pointers. A decrease in pressure causes the altimeter to indicate an increase in altitude, while an increase in pressure causes it to indicate a decrease in altitude. Consequently, if the plane is flown from a pressure level of 28.75 inches of Hg to a pressure level of 29.75 inches of Hg, the altimeter would show a decrease of approximately 1000 feet in altitude.

The other method of moving the pointers relies on the mechanical construction of the altimeter. When a pilot rotates the knob on the altimeter, the altimeter setting pressure scale moves simultaneously with the altimeter pointers. This might be confusing because the numerical values of pressure indicated in the window increase while the altimeter indicates an increase in altitude. In effect, then, the two values increase or decrease together—which is contrary to the reaction on the pointers when air pressure changes, but it is based solely on the mechanical makeup of the altimeter.

To explain this a little more, assume that the proper altimeter setting is 29.50 and the actual setting is 30.00, or a .50 difference. This would cause a 500-foot error in altitude. If the altimeter setting is then adjusted from 30.00 to 29.50, the numerical value decreases and the altimeter indicates a decrease of 500 feet in altitude. Before the correction was made, the airplane was flying at an altitude 500 feet higher than it should have been with the correct altimeter setting.

Types of altitude

Knowing the aircraft's altitude is vitally important for several reasons, some of which are obvious. The most apparent is that you have to know that you're flying high enough to clear the highest terrain or obstruction along your intended route. Especially must you know this when visibility is restricted. To keep above mountain peaks, however high they may be, you have to be aware of your altitude and the elevation of the surrounding terrain at all times. To avoid a midair collision, maintaining altitudes in accordance with air traffic rules is essential. In another vein, altitudes are often selected to take advantage of favorable winds and weather conditions. And then, a knowledge of altitudes is necessary to calculate true airspeeds.

As you might expect, "altitude" could be defined as the vertical distance above some point or level that is used as a reference. As you might not expect, though, there are several kinds of altitude, each of which pilots can use for specific reasons. The five that pilots are most usually concerned with are:

1. *Absolute Altitude.* The vertical distance of an aircraft above the terrain

2. *Indicated Altitude.* The altitude read directly from the altimeter after it has been set to the current altimeter setting

3. *Pressure Altitude.* The altitude indicated when the altimeter setting window is adjusted to 29.92. This is the standard datum plane, a theoretical plane where air pressure (corrected to 15°C) is equal to 29.92 inches of mercury. Pressure altitude is used for computer solutions to determine density altitude, true altitude, true airspeed, etc.

4. *True Altitude.* The true vertical distance of the aircraft above sea level—the actual altitude (often expressed in this manner: 10,900 ft. msl.) Airport, terrain, and obstacle elevations found on aeronautical charts are true altitudes.

5. *Density Altitude.* This is pressure altitude corrected for nonstandard temperature variations. When conditions are standard, pressure altitude and density altitude are the same. Consequently, if the temperature is above standard, the density altitude will be higher than pressure altitude. If the temperature is below standard, the density altitude will be lower than pressure altitude. This is an important altitude because it is directly related to the aircraft's takeoff and climb performance.

Fig. 4-3. *The vertical speed indicator—another static pressure instrument.*

Vertical speed indicator

The vertical speed, or vertical velocity, indicator (Fig. 4-3), tells whether the aircraft is climbing, descending, or in level flight. The rate of climb or descent is reported in feet per minute, and, if properly calibrated, the instrument registers zero in level flight.

Principle of operation. Although the vertical speed indicator (VSI) operates solely from static pressure, it is a differential pressure instrument.

The case of the instrument is airtight except for a small connection through a restricted passage to the static line of the pitot-static system. A diaphragm, with connecting linkage and gearing to the indicator pointer, is located inside the sealed case. Both the diaphragm and the case receive air from the static line at existing atmospheric pressure. When the aircraft is on the ground or in level flight, the pressures inside the diaphragm and the instrument case remain the same, and the pointer is at the zero indication. When the aircraft climbs or descends the diaphragm pressure changes immediately, but, due to the metering action of the restricted passage, the case pressure remains higher or lower for a short time, thus causing the diaphragm to contract or expand. This creates a differential pressure that is indicated on the instrument needle as a climb or descent.

The airspeed indicator

The airspeed indicator (Fig. 4-4) is a sensitive, differential pressure gauge that measures and shows promptly the difference between (1) pitot, or impact pressure, and (2) static pressure, the undisturbed atmospheric pressure at flight level. These two pressures are equal when the aircraft is parked on the ground in calm air. When the aircraft moves through the air, the pressure in the pitot line is greater than the pressure in the static lines. That pressure difference is then registered in miles per hour, knots, or both by the airspeed pointer on the face of the instrument.

The three kinds of airspeed the pilot needs to understand are: *indicated*, *calibrated*, and *true* airspeeds.

Indicated airspeed (IAS). This is the direct instrument reading obtained from the airspeed indicator, uncorrected for variations in atmospheric density, installation error, or instrument error.

Calibrated airspeed (CAS). Calibrated airspeed is the indicated airspeed corrected for installation error and instrument error. Although manufacturers try to keep them to a minimum, it's not possible to eliminate

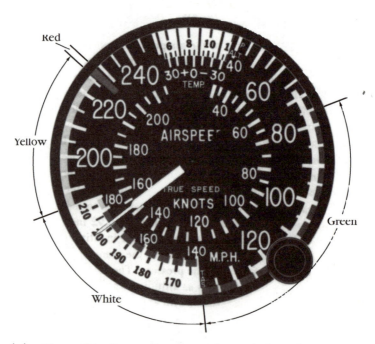

Fig. 4-4. *Airspeed indicator showing color-coded marking system.*

all errors throughout the airspeed operating range. At certain speeds and with certain flap settings, the installation and instrument error might be several miles per hour—errors that are generally greatest at low airspeeds. In the cruising and higher airspeed ranges, indicated and calibrated airspeeds are approximately the same.

It might be important to refer to an airspeed calibration chart to correct for possible airspeed errors, because airspeed limitations, such as those found on the color-coded face of the airspeed indicator, on placards in the cockpit, or in the Owner's Handbook, are usually calibrated airspeeds. Some manufacturers, however, use indicated rather than calibrated airspeed to denote the airspeed limitations mentioned.

The airspeed indicator should be calibrated periodically because leaks could develop or moisture might collect in the tubing. Dirt, dust, ice, or snow collecting at the mouth of the pitot tube could easily obstruct air passage and prevent correct indications. Also, vibrations (and there are lots of them in piston-powered aircraft) can destroy the sensitivity of the diaphragm.

True airspeed. The airspeed indicator is calibrated to indicate true airspeed under standard sea level conditions—that is, 29.92 inches of Hg and 15°C. Because air density decreases with an altitude increase, the airplane has to be flown faster at higher altitudes to create the same pressure difference between pitot impact pressure and static pressure. Consequently, for a given true airspeed, *indicated* airspeed decreases as altitude increases, or, for a given indicated airspeed, true airspeed increases with an increase in altitude.

As a pilot, you can find true airspeed by two methods. The first, which is the more accurate, involves using a computer. In this method, the calibrated airspeed is corrected for temperature and pressure variation by using the airspeed correction scale on the computer.

The second method is by rule of thumb. Here you merely add two percent of the indicated airspeed to the indicated airspeed for each 1000 feet of altitude. As an example, your indicated airspeed is 140 mph at an altitude of 6000 feet. Problem: Find the true airspeed. Solution: 2% × 6 = 12% (.12); 140 × .12 = 16.8; 140 + 16.8 = 156.8 mph (TAS).

The airspeed indicator markings. Airplanes weighing 12,500 pounds or less, manufactured after 1945, and certificated by FAA, are required to have airspeed indicators that conform to a standard color-coded marking system. This marking system, pictured in Fig. 4-4, enables the pilot to determine at a glance certain airspeed limitations that are important for the safe operations of the aircraft. For example, if during the execution of a maneuver, you see that the airspeed needle is in the yellow arc and is rapidly approaching the red line, you need to take immediate action to reduce the airspeed. (Remember, though, that smooth control pressures are essential at high speeds to avoid severe stresses on the aircraft structure.)

Because you'll probably be flying airplanes with these color-coded indicators, the following descriptions of the standard markings may be of help:

- Flap operating range (the white arc)
- Power-off stalling speed with the wing flaps and landing gear in the landing position (the lower limit of the white arc)
- Maximum flaps-extended speed (the upper limit of the white arc). This is the highest airspeed at which you should extend full flaps. If they are lowered at higher airspeeds, severe strain or structural failure could result.
- Normal operating range (the green arc)
- Power-off stalling speed with the wing flaps and landing gear retracted (the lower limit of the green arc)
- Maximum structural cruising speed (the upper limit of the green arc). This is the maximum speed for normal operation.
- Caution range (the yellow arc). The pilot should avoid this area unless in smooth air.
- Never-exceed speed (the red line). This is the maximum speed at which the airplane can be operated in smooth air. This speed should never be intentionally exceeded.

Other airspeed limitations. Other important airspeed limitations are not marked on the face of the airspeed indicator. These speeds are generally found on placards in view of the pilot and in the Airplane Flight Manual or Owner's Handbook.

One example is maneuvering speed, which is usually placarded on this instrument panel and is the maximum "rough air" speed and the maximum speed for abrupt maneuvers. If rough air or heavy turbulence is encountered, the airspeed should be reduced to maneuvering speed or less to minimize the stress on the airplane structure.

Other important airspeeds include:

- Landing gear operating speed: the maximum speed for extending or retracting the landing gear
- Best *angle* of climb speed: important when a short field takeoff to clear an obstacle is required
- Best *rate* of climb speed: the airspeed that gives the pilot the most altitude in a given period of time

Pilots who fly the more complex single- or twin-engine aircraft must know other speeds, such as the aircraft's minimum control speed, minimum flight speed at which the aircraft is satisfactorily controllable if an engine suddenly fails and the remaining engine is at takeoff power. And the list goes on, as the types of performance airspeeds for either or both single- and twin-engine aircraft and their "V" (velocity) coding indicates:

V_a	Design maneuvering speed
V_c	Design cruising speed
V_f	Design flap speed
V_{fe}	Maximum flap extended speed
V_{le}	Maximum landing gear extended speed
V_{lo}	Maximum landing gear operating speed
V_{lof}	Lift-off speed
V_{ne}	Never-exceed speed
V_r	Rotation speed
V_s	The stalling speed or the minimum steady flight speed at which the airplane is controllable
V_{so}	The stalling speed or the minimum steady flight speed in the landing configuration
V_{s1}	The stalling speed or the minimum steady flight speed obtained in a specified configuration
V_x	Speed for best angle of climb
V_y	Speed for best rate of climb

The gyroscopic flight instruments—in general

Several flight instruments utilize the properties of a gyroscope for their operation. The most common are the *turn indicator, turn co-ordinator, heading indicator,* and the *attitude indicator.* To under-stand how these instruments operate requires a bit of knowledge about the instrument power systems, gyroscopic principles, and the operating principles of each instrument.

Sources of power for gyroscopic operation

Gyroscopic instruments are operated either by a vacuum or an elec-trical system. In some airplanes, all the gyros are either vacuum or electrically operated, while in others, vacuum systems provide the power for the heading and attitude indicators and the electrical system drives the gyroscope of the turn needle.

The vacuum or pressure system. The vacuum or pressure system spins the gyro by drawing a stream of air against the instrument's rotor vanes to spin the rotor at high speeds, essentially the same as a water wheel or a turbine operates. Either a venturi tube or a vacuum pump can be used to produce the required vacuum.

The amount of vacuum required for instrument operation is usu-ally between 3.5" to 4.5" Hg. These values are obtained by inserting regulating valves in the individual instrument supply line.

Venturi-tube systems. The venturi tube was used to operate the gyroscopes in many airplanes manufactured years ago. The advantages of a venturi as a suction source are its relatively low cost and simplicity of installation and operation. In this system, the tube is mounted on the exterior of the aircraft fuselage. Then, throughout the aircraft's normal operating airspeed range, the velocity of the air through the venturi creates sufficient suction to spin the gyro.

While the venturi has its advantages, it also has its limitations. To mention just a couple, the venturi is designed to produce the desired vacuum at approximately 100 mph, under standard sea level condi-tions. But, wide variations in airspeed, air density, or restrictions to airflow by ice accretion affect the pressure at the venturi throat and thus the vacuum driving the gyro rotor. Also, because the rotor can't reach normal operating speed until after takeoff, preflight opera-tional checks of venturi-powered gyro instruments are impossible.

For these reasons, the system is adequate only for light aircraft instrument training and very limited flying under instrument weather conditions. Aircraft flown throughout wider ranges of speed, altitude, and weather conditions require a more effective source of power that is independent of airspeed and less susceptible to adverse atmospheric conditions.

Engine-driven vacuum pump. One source of vacuum for the gyros installed in light aircraft is the vane-type engine-driven pump that is mounted on the engine's accessory drive shaft and connected to the engine lubrication system to seal, cool, and lubricate the pump. Another type of pump is mounted on the side of the engine block, forward of the engine cylinders, and is driven from the engine crankshaft by a pulley and V-belt arrangement. Pump capacities and sizes vary in different aircraft, depending on the number of gyros to be operated.

A typical vacuum system (Fig. 4-5) consists of an engine-driven vacuum pump, an air/oil separator, a vacuum regulator, a relief valve, an air filter, and tubing and manifolds necessary to complete the connections. A suction gauge on the airplane instrument panel indicates the amount of vacuum in the system.

Air filters prevent foreign matter from entering the system. In some cases, individual filters are installed for each instrument, while in others, depending on the system design, a master air filter is used to screen foreign matter from the air flowing through all the gyro instruments. As with any such system, the master filter inevitably

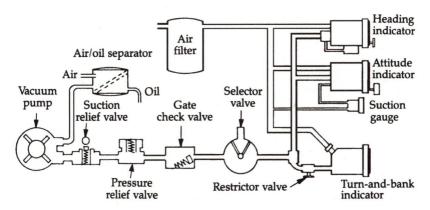

Fig. 4-5. *A schematic of a typical pump-driven vacuum system.*

becomes dirty and, as it does, the airflow is reduced, resulting in a lower reading on the vacuum gauge. With the individual filter system, a dirty filter does not necessarily show on the suction gauge.

Gyroscopic principles

Any spinning object exhibits gyroscopic properties; however, a wheel designed and mounted to utilize these properties is called a gyroscope. Two important design characteristics of an instrument gyro are: great weight or high density for size and rotation at high speeds with low friction bearings. The mountings of the gyro wheels are called *gimbals*, which might be circular rings, rectangular frames or, in flight instruments, a part of the instrument case itself.

There are two general types of mountings, with the type used depending on which property of the gyro is utilized. A *freely* or *universally mounted* gyroscope is free to rotate in any direction about its center of gravity. Such a wheel is said to have three planes of freedom. The wheel or rotor is free to rotate in any plane in relation to the base and is so balanced that, with the gyro wheel at rest, it remains in the position in which it is placed. *Restricted* or *semirigidly mounted* gyroscopes are those so mounted that one of the planes of freedom is held fixed in relation to the base.

Gyroscopic action has two fundamental properties: *rigidity in space* and *precession.*

Rigidity in space can best be explained by applying Newton's first law of motion that states: "A body at rest will remain at rest; or if in motion in a straight line, it will continue in a straight line unless acted upon by an outside force." An example of this law is the rotor of a universally mounted gyro. When the wheel is spinning, it exhibits the ability to remain in its original plane of rotation regardless of how the base is moved. However, because it is impossible to design bearings without some friction present, there will be a certain deflective force upon the wheel.

The flight instruments using the gyroscopic property of rigidity for their operation are the attitude indicator and the heading indicator. Their rotors, then, must be freely or universally mounted.

The second property of a gyroscope, precession, is the resultant action or deflection of a spinning wheel when a deflective force is applied to its rim (Fig. 4-6). When a deflective force is applied to the rim of a rotating wheel, the resultant force is 90° ahead in the direction of rotation and in the direction of the applied force. The rate at which the wheel precesses is inversely proportional to the speed of the rotor and proportional to the deflective force. The force with which the wheel precesses is the same as the deflective force applied (minus the friction in the bearings). If too great a deflective force is applied for the amount of rigidity in the wheel, the wheel precesses and topples over at the same time.

Gyroscopic instruments: what they are

The following describes the gyroscopic instruments found in most light aircraft.

Turn-and-slip indicator

The turn-and-slip indicator (also frequently referred to as the turn-and-bank indicator or "needle and ball") was one of the first instruments used to control an airplane without visual reference to the ground or horizon (Fig. 4-7). Its principal uses in airplanes are to indicate turns

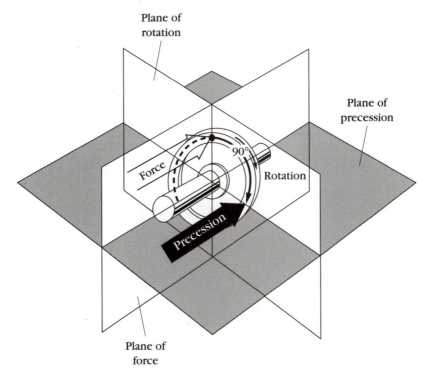

Fig. 4-6. *Precession of a gyroscope resulting from an applied deflective force.*

and to serve as an emergency source of bank information in the event the attitude indicator fails.

The turn-and-slip indicator is actually a combination of two instruments: the *turn needle* and the *ball*, or *inclinometer*. The needle shows rate of turn, and the ball reacts to gravity and/or centrifugal force to indicate the need for directional trim.

The turn needle is operated by a gyro, driven by either vacuum or electricity. Semirigid mounting of the gyro allows it to rotate freely about the lateral and longitudinal axes of the airplane, but it is restricted in rotation about the vertical axis. When the airplane is turned or rotated around the vertical axis, a deflective force is set up causing the gyro to precess, which results in tilting the gyro. This tilting is transmitted to the turn needle through linkage. As the rate of turn increases, the precession of the gyro increases, resulting in an increased rate of turn being indicated. A spring assembly attached to the gyro keeps the gyro upright when a deflective force is not applied. The spring is also adjustable to calibrate the instrument for a given rate or turn. In addition, a dampening mechanism prevents excessive oscillation of the turn needle.

The turn needle. The turn needle indicates the rate (number of degrees per second) at which the aircraft is turning about its vertical axis. Unlike the attitude indicator, which I'll discuss in a moment, it does not give a direct indication of the banked attitude of the aircraft. For any given airspeed, however, there is a specific angle of bank necessary to maintain a coordinated turn at a given rate. The faster the airspeed, the greater the angle of bank required to obtain a given rate of turn. Thus, the turn needle gives only an indirect indication of the aircraft's banking attitude or angle of bank.

Fig. 4-7. *The turn-and-slip (or needle-and-ball) indicator.*

Types of turn needles. There are two types of turn needles: the "two minute" turn needle and the "four minute" needle. When using a two-minute needle, a 360° turn made at a rate indicated by a one-needle width deflection would require two minutes to complete. In this case, the aircraft would be turning at a rate of 3° per second, which is considered a *standard rate* turn. When using a four-minute needle, a 360° turn made at a rate indicated by a one-needle width deflection would take four minutes to complete. In this case, the aircraft is turning at a rate of 1.5° per second. A standard rate turn of 3° per second would be indicated on this type of turn needle by a two-needle width deflection.

The ball. This part of the instrument is a simple inclinometer, consisting of a sealed, curved glass tube containing kerosene and a black agate or steel ball bearing that is free to move inside the tube. The fluid provides a dampening action that ensures a smooth and easy movement of the ball. The tube is curved so that when in a horizontal position the ball seeks the lowest point. Two reference markers are provided as an aid in determining when the ball is in the center of the tube. During coordinated straight-and-level flight, the force of gravity causes the ball to rest in the lowest part of the tube, centered between the reference lines. During a coordinated turn, turning forces are balanced, which cause the ball to remain centered in the tube. If the turning forces are unbalanced, as during a slip or a skid, the ball moves away from the center of the tube in the direction of the excessive force.

The ball, then, is actually a balance indicator and serves as a visual aid to determine coordinated use of the aileron and rudder control. During a turn, it indicates the relationship between the angle of bank and rate of turn. It further indicates the "quality" of the turn and whether the aircraft has the correct angle of bank for the rate of turn. For instance:

In a coordinated turn, the ball assumes a position between the reference markers (Fig. 4-8A).

In a slip, the rate of turn is too slow for the angle of bank, and the lack of centrifugal force moves the ball to the inside of the turn (Fig. 4-8B). To achieve coordinated flight from a slip, through aileron and/or rudder control, the bank must be decreased, the rate of turn increased, or a combination of both.

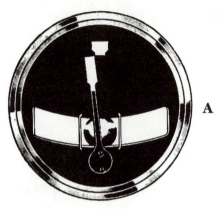

Coordinated single-needle-width turn

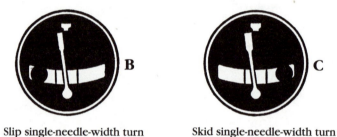

Slip single-needle-width turn   Skid single-needle-width turn

Fig. 4-8. *Examples of the ball in a coordinated turn, a slip, and a skid.* U.S. Air Force

In a skid, the rate of turn is too great for the angle of bank, and the excessive centrifugal force moves the ball to the outside of the turn (Fig. 4-8C). To attain coordinated flight from a skid, again, with rudder and/or aileron control, the bank must be increased, the rate of turn decreased, or a combination of both.

The important thing is to understand that the ball should be kept in the center at all times during flight except for certain maneuvers, such as intentional slips. If the ball is not centered, it means that abnormal forces are being created that have the potential of causing the airplane to stall or spin unexpectedly—something that could be a bit serious, especially close to the ground.

Turn coordinator

The turn-and-slip indicator is practically obsolete, having been replaced by the *turn coordinator* (Fig. 4-9). Instead of the turn needle indication, this instrument shows the movement of the aircraft about the longitudinal axis by displaying a miniature airplane on the instrument. The movement of this miniature is proportional to the roll rate of the real airplane. When the roll is reduced to zero (meaning that the bank is held constant), the instrument indicates the rate of turn.

This design features a realignment of the gyro in such a manner that it senses the airplane movements about the yaw and roll axes and thus displays the resultant motion as described above. The conventional inclinometer (ball) is also incorporated in this instrument.

The heading indicator

The heading indicator (or *directional gyro*) is fundamentally a mechanical instrument designed to facilitate the use of the magnetic compass. Temporary errors in the magnetic compass are numerous, making straight flight and precision turns to headings difficult to accomplish, particularly in turbulent air. Heading indicators (Figs. 4-10 and 4-11), however, are not affected by the forces that sometimes make the magnetic compass difficult to follow.

The operation of the heading indicator depends on the principle of rigidity in space. The rotor turns in a vertical plane, and fixed to the rotor is a compass card. Because the rotor remains rigid in space, the points on the card hold the same position in space relative to the vertical plane. As the instrument case and the airplane revolve around the vertical axis, the card provides clear and accurate heading information.

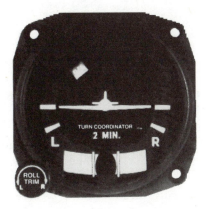

Fig. 4-9. *The more current turn coordinator.*

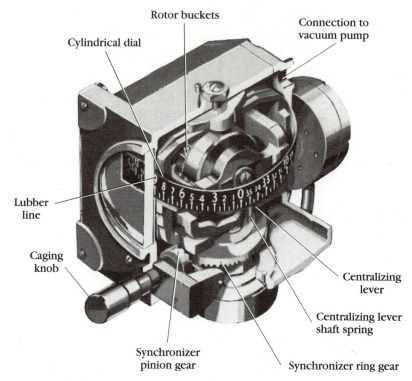

Fig. 4-10. *Cutaway view of the older suction-driven heading indicator (sometimes called "directional gyro").*

Fig. 4-11. *This is the more current version of the heading indicator.*

Heading information is displayed one of two ways: Fig. 4-10 is the older type that displays headings on a card mounted horizontally around the gyro mechanism. Figure 4-11 is the more current indicator that displays the headings on a dial that is mounted vertically to the instrument. As you can see, both types are calibrated in five-degree increments.

Because of precession, caused chiefly by bearing friction, the heading indicator will creep, or drift, from a selected heading. Among other factors, the amount of drift depends largely on the condition of the instrument. If its bearings are worn, dirty, or improperly lubricated, the drift could be excessive.

Keep in mind that this indicator is not direction-seeking, as is the magnetic compass. Because of that, and because of precession, you should check its readings frequently and realign it, as necessary, with the magnetic compass. The resetting should be done, though, only when the airplane is in straight-and-level, constant-speed flight. Otherwise, erroneous magnetic compass readings are probable.

The bank and pitch limits of the heading indicator vary with the particular design and make of the instrument. On some indicators found in light airplanes, the limits are approximately 55° of pitch and 55° of bank, which means that when either of these attitude limits is exceeded, the instrument may tumble, or spill, and no longer give the correct directional indication until it has been reset. Many of these instruments, however, have been so designed that they cannot tumble.

The attitude indicator

The older vacuum-driven or the newer electical *attitude indicator*, sometimes called the *artificial horizon*, with its miniature airplane and horizon bar, reflects the attitude of the real airplane (Fig. 4-12). The relationship of the miniature aircraft to the horizon bar is the

Fig. 4-12. *The attitude indicator (often called the "artificial horizon") imitates the altitude, or position relative to the horizon, of the real airplane.*

same as the relationship of the real aircraft to the actual horizon. The instrument gives an instantaneous indication of even the smallest changes in attitude.

The gyro in the attitude indicator is mounted on a horizontal plane and depends upon rigidity in space for its operation. The horizon bar, representing the true horizon, is fixed to the gyro and remains locked in a horizontal plane as the airplane pitches or banks about either its lateral or longitudinal axis. As it does so, the indicator moves about and reflects the attitude of the real airplane relative to the true horizon.

An adjustment knob is provided with which the pilot can move the miniature airplane up or down to align it with the horizon bar to suit his or her line of vision. Normally, the miniature is adjusted so that the wings overlap the horizon bar when the airplane is in straight-and-level cruise flight.

Some attitude indicators are equipped with a caging mechanism that locks the instrument so that it will not tumble or spill during unusual attitude maneuvers. If the plane you fly has an instrument so equipped, be sure to uncage it for normal operations. If you don't, it will remain locked in its caged position and will be completely useless.

The instrument's pitch-and-bank limits, and whether or not it will tumble, again depend on the make and model. Some won't tumble at all. Otherwise, the limits in the banking plane are usually around 100° and the pitch limits are between 60° and 70°. If either extreme is exceeded, the instrument will tumble and give incorrect indications until reset.

Interpreting the banking scale (Fig. 4-13) could be a bit confusing for the new pilot until he or she understands the instrument. The "problem" is that in many instruments the scale indicator at the top of the instrument moves in the opposite direction of the actual bank and thus, under instrument or instrument training conditions, might cause you to misinterpret the direction of that bank. This scale, then, should be used only to control the *degree* of bank. On the other hand, the relationship of the miniature airplane to the horizon bar indicates the direction of bank. Not all attitude indicators present this problem because there are available those with banking scale indicators that move in the same direction as the bank.

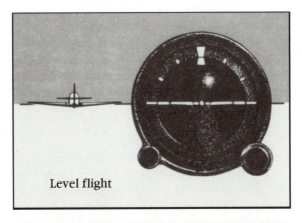

Level flight

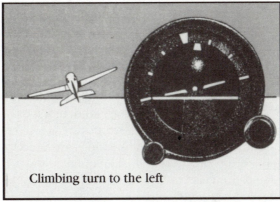

Climbing turn to the left

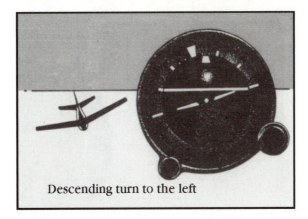

Descending turn to the left

Fig. 4-13. *Three examples of how an aittitude indicator imitates aircraft positions in relation to the "artificial horizon."*

This instrument, though, in living up to its name, is highly reliable as an "attitude indicator," and is one of the most realistic flight instruments on the panel. Its indications are very close approximations of the actual attitude of the airplane and are thus essential in instrument flight and in maintaining the desired attitudinal and directional control of the aircraft.

The magnetic compass

The magnetic compass, (Fig. 4-14), which is the only direction-seeking instrument in the airplane, is simple in construction. It contains two steel magnetized needles fastened to a float around which is mounted a compass card. The needles are parallel, with their north seeking ends pointed in the same direction. The compass card has letters for cardinal headings, and each 30 degree interval is represented by a number, the last zero of which is omitted. For example, 30° would appear as a "3" and 300° "30." Between these numbers, the card is graduated for each five degrees.

The float assembly is housed in a bowl filled with acid-free white kerosene. The purposes of the liquid are to dampen excessive compass card oscillations and to relieve, by buoyancy, part of the weight of the float from the bearings. Jewel bearings are used to mount the float assembly on top of a pedestal. A line (called the lubber line) is mounted behind the glass of the instrument for reference purposes when aligning the headings on the compass card.

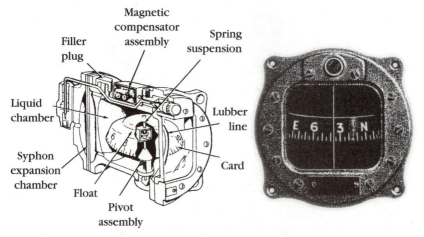

Fig. 4-14. *Magnetic compass and its components.*

Compass errors

Variation. Although the magnetic field of the earth lies roughly north and south, the earth's *magnetic* poles do not coincide with its *geographic* poles. Consequently, at most places on the earth's surface, the direction-sensitive steel needles that seek the earth's magnetic field do not point to *true north* but to *magnetic north.*

Another factor to be considered: Local magnetic fields from mineral deposits and other in-ground elements can further distort the reading on the compass card as far as its relationship to true north is concerned. These deposits are usually secondary, however, compared to the forces exerted by the magnetic poles.

The angular difference between true north and magnetic north is called *variation.* Variation, which is different at different points on the earth's surface, is shown on aeronautical charts as broken lines, called *isogonic lines,* which connect points of equal variation. The line where there is no variation between true and magnetic north is an *agonic line.*

Because of its importance in flight planning, this matter of variation I'll discuss further in the navigation section of the book.

Deviation. Actually, a compass is rarely influenced solely by the earth's magnetic lines of force. Disturbances from magnetic fields produced by metals and electrical accessories in an aircraft also affect the compass needles and produce an additional error. The difference between the direction indicated by a compass not installed in an airplane and one that is installed, is called "deviation." This, though, along with variation, is another subject for discussion later in the navigation chapter.

Using the magnetic compass

Although the magnetic compass is the only direction-seeking instrument in most airplanes, it has some peculiarities with which pilots have to be aware if they want to turn an airplane to a magnetic compass heading and maintain that heading. Keeping in mind the following characteristics of the compass may help:

    1. If on a northerly heading and you turn toward east or west, the compass initially lags or indicates a turn in the opposite direction. This lag diminishes as the turn progresses toward east or west where there is no turn error.

2. If on a southerly heading and you turn toward the east or west, the compass initially leads and indicates a greater amount of turn than is actually made. This lead also diminishes as the turn progresses toward east or west where there is no turn error.

3. If you turn to a northerly heading from any direction, the compass indication, when approaching the northerly heading, leads or is ahead of the turn. To avoid overshooting the desired heading, start rolling out of the turn about 30 degrees before the needle hits the "N," or 360°, mark. (The exact rollout point depends on the aircraft's degree of bank and rate of turn.)

   In a turn to a southerly heading from any direction, the compass indication, when approaching that heading, lags behind the turn. So, to avoid undershooting, start the rollout after that heading is passed—again, by about 30 degrees, depending on the degree of bank.

4. Turning to an east or west heading, there is no lead or lag, so you can begin a normal rollout when the compass needle approaches either the 90 or 270 degree mark. When on either heading, no error is apparent while starting a turn to the north or south. An increase in airspeed or acceleration will, however, cause the compass momentarily to indicate a turn toward north, while a decrease causes it to indicate a turn toward the south.

5. On a north or south heading, no error will be apparent because of acceleration or deceleration.

Remember that the magnetic compass is truly reliable only when you are flying straight and level at a constant speed. It's partly because of the compass's inherent characteristics that the gyroscopic heading indicator becomes so helpful in precision flying. But, if you understand its various characteristics, the magnetic compass can be a most reliable direction-indicating instrument.

Quickie quiz questions
Chapter 4

1. The pressure provided by the pitot tube and pitot system affects the reading of what cockpit instrument(s)?

2. What are the five "types" of altitude?

3. Which are the cockpit gyroscopic instruments?

4. The white and yellow arcs on the airspeed indicator reflect what operating limits. or warnings?

5. What are the three "kinds" of airspeed?

6. When turning toward a southerly or northerly heading, what are the characteristics of the magnetic compass?

7. What gyroscopic instruments are usually found in the typical light aircraft?

8. Describe briefly factors that produce changes in the airspeed indicator readings.

9. What are the meanings of these V velocities?

    Vy   Vx   Vso   Vne   Vfe

10. What are the two basic gyroscopic properties?

Answers in Appendix, pages 573-574.

5

Airplane performance

Airplane performance is really the ability of an aircraft to do what it was designed to do and to do it well. Some aircraft are destined to be trainers, others transports, others crop-dusters, military fighters or bombers, and so on. Whatever its intended mission, though, if the plane performs with excellence and dependability in accordance with its design potential, it has obviously fulfilled its purpose.

All of which is quite apparent, but a plane's ultimate performance is not solely the product of its design and construction. Much rests on the pilot and his or her understanding of what affects the potential or designed performance. Consequently, discussing the ". . . what affects . . ." is the purpose of this chapter, and it begins with one of a pilot's most critical considerations—aircraft weight control.

Weight control

Weight (in the context of this discussion) is the force with which gravity attracts a body toward the center of the earth. It is a product of the mass of a body and the acceleration acting on the body. Weight is thus a major factor in airplane construction and operation, and it demands respect from all pilots.

With gravity forever attempting to pull the airplane to earth, the force of lift is the only force that counteracts weight and keeps the aircraft aloft. The amount of lift produced by an airfoil, however, is limited by the airfoil design itself, the aircraft's angle of attack, its airspeed, and air density. Therefore, to assure that the lift generated is sufficient to counteract weight, loading the airplane within the manufacturer's recommended weight is critically important. Simply said, if the weight is greater than the lift generated, altitude can be neither attained nor maintained.

Effects of weight

Every pilot should always be aware of the consequences of over-loading. An overloaded airplane might not be able to get off the ground, but if it could struggle into the air, it would likely exhibit unexpected and unusually poor flight characteristics. Each airplane has limits. If exceeded, the results are inferior operation and possible disaster. Also, when not properly loaded, the initial indication of a problem is usually during takeoff—which is a very bad time for both plane and pilot to be in trouble.

Excessive weight reduces an airplane's flight performance in almost every respect, with the most important performance deficiencies showing up in:

- Higher takeoff speed
- Longer takeoff run
- Reduced rate or angle of climb
- Lower maximum altitude
- Shorter range
- Reduced cruising speed
- Reduced maneuverability
- Higher stalling speed
- Higher landing speed
- Longer landing roll
- Excessive weight on the nosewheel

The first step in avoiding overloading is, of course, knowing the weight limitations of the particular aircraft you are about to fly. Barring the short local flights where you know you'll be well within all limits, an early preflight planning step should include a check of performance charts to determine if the airplane's weight could contribute to a dangerous operation. For instance, what about performance-reducing factors such as high-density altitude, frost on the wings, low engine horsepower, the possibility of severe or uncoordinated maneuvers because of turbulence, strong cross-winds, and so on?

Excessive weight in itself reduces the available safety margins and becomes even more hazardous when combined with any of these other performance-reducing conditions. In the same context, you have to consider the consequences of overweight should an emergency arise. If an engine falters on takeoff or ice forms at a low altitude, keeping a properly loaded aircraft in the air is challenge enough; keeping one aloft that's overloaded is often next to impossible.

Weight changes

The weight of a plane can be changed by various actions, one of which is altering the fuel load. Gasoline has considerable weight— 6 pounds per gallon—so 30 gallons could weigh more than one passenger. If need be, one way to stay within the prescribed weight limits is to reduce the volume of fuel carried. Remember that reducing the amount of fuel shortens the plane's range, which might mean that you'll have to plan an undesired but necessary en route fuel stop. Changes in fixed equipment have a major effect on the aircraft weight. Installation of extra radios or instruments and repairs or modifications usually add weight. It's a rare exception when a structural or equipment change results in a weight reduction. Also, maybe like humans, as an airplane ages, it tends to get heavier.

The total effect of these changes is referred to as *service weight pickup*. Most such pickup is the known weight of actual parts installed during aircraft repair, overhaul, or modification. But then there's an unknown pickup resulting from the collection of trash, moisture absorption, the addition of miscellaneous hardware, and the almost inevitable accumulation of dirt and grease. The amount of weight accumulated in this overall category can be determined only by putting the aircraft on scales and weighing it.

Balance, stability, and center of gravity

Balance refers to the location of an airplane's *center of gravity* (CG), which, as you'll recall from Chapter 2, is the point at which an airplane would hang in perfect balance if it were tied to a rope and suspended at that point. Suffice it to say right now that no airplane should ever be flown if the pilot is dissatisfied with its loading, its weight, or how the load has been distributed relative to the aircraft's center of gravity and balance.

The prime concern of airplane balancing is the fore and aft location of the CG along the longitudinal axis. At the same time, don't overlook the location of the CG in terms of the lateral axis. For each item of weight existing to the left of the fuselage centerline, there is generally an equal weight existing at a corresponding location on the right. This might be upset, however, by unbalanced lateral loading.

The position of the lateral CG is not computed, but you should be aware of the adverse effects that can arise from a laterally unbalanced condition. One example is fuel mismanagement by almost draining dry the fuel from one wing tank while leaving the tank on the other wing full (Fig. 5-1).

You can, of course, compensate for the resulting wing-heavy condition by using a lot of aileron trim tab or by holding a constant aileron control pressure. Doing so, however, places the airplane controls in an out-of-streamline condition, increases drag, and results in decreased operating efficiency. Preventing this type of imbalance is easy by using fuel from, say, the left tank for one hour, then switching to the opposite wing tank for two hours, and then back to the first tank, and so on. But because lateral balance is relatively easy to control and longitudinal balance is more critical, further reference to balance here is in terms of the longitudinal location of the center of gravity.

The CG is not necessarily a fixed point, inasmuch as its location can vary according to how the weight is distributed. Depending on

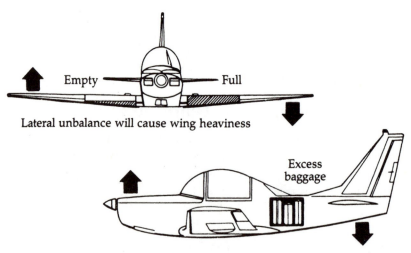

Fig. 5-1. *Examples of lateral and longitudinal unbalance.*

where baggage, cargo, or passengers are placed, there can be a resultant shift in the CG location. If the CG is displaced too far forward on the longitudinal axis, a nose-heavy condition results. Conversely, if it's displaced too far aft, the plane is tail-heavy (Fig. 5-1). Considering such displacements, it's entirely possible that an unfavorable location of the CG would produce such an unstable condition that you simply couldn't control the airplane.

Regardless of that potential, just flying an out-of-balance airplane can produce increased pilot fatigue with its obvious effects on the safety and efficiency of the flight. A pilot's natural correction for longitudinal unbalance is a change of trim to reduce the need for the continuing and tiring control pressure. Excessive trim, however, not only reduces aerodynamic efficiency but also reduces primary control travel distance in the direction the trim is applied. In other words, it's bad news all around.

Effects of adverse balance

There is more to this issue of counteracting overloading or improper balancing than the mere use of trim tabs. As already hinted, stability and control and the extent to which adverse balance affects them enter the picture.

For instance, nose-heavy loading causes problems in controlling and raising the nose, especially during takeoff and landing. A tail-heavy condition has a most serious effect on longitudinal stability and can reduce the airplane's ability to recover from stalls or spins. Another undesirable characteristic is that tail-heavy loading produces very light stick (control column) forces that make it easy for the pilot to inadvertently overcontrol or overstress the airplane.

As I said before, the limits for the location of the airplane's CG are established by the manufacturer. These are the fore and aft limits, beyond which the CG should not be located for flight. If, after loading, the CG is not within the allowable limits, passengers, baggage, and/or cargo must be relocated or offloaded before flight is attempted.

The forward CG limit is usually established at a location determined by the airplane's landing characteristics. It might be possible to maintain stable and safe cruising flight if the CG is located ahead of the prescribed forward limit, but during landing, a nose-heavy condition could cause serious problems. Manufacturers purposely try to place the forward CG limit as far rearward as possible to help pilots avoid landing accidents or incidents.

A restricted forward CG limit is also specified to assure that sufficient elevator deflection is available at minimum airspeed. When structural limitations or large stick forces do not limit it, the forward CG is located at the position where full-up elevator is required to obtain a high angle of attack for landing.

The aft CG limit is the most rearward position that still allows critical operating maneuvers. As the CG moves aft, it creates a less stable condition, which, in turn, decreases the airplane's ability to right itself after maneuvering or disturbances by wind gusts or turbulence.

The actual location of the CG can be altered by many variable factors almost always controlled by the pilot. Placement of baggage and cargo items determine the CG location. If they can't be moved, and there is still a weight or balance problem, something's got to give. A piece of baggage, a box, or a passenger must be unloaded until both the weight and the balance are within the aircraft's prescribed limits. Any pilot who takes off knowing that the limits have been exceeded is a very foolish pilot—to put it nicely. If it's not a matter of bags or cargo, passenger seat assignment is a logical balancing action. In a tail-heavy situation, a simple solution is to place a heavy passenger in a front seat.

Management of weight and balance control

The pilot is totally responsible for, and in control of, what is placed aboard his or her aircraft and where it is located. The aircraft owner, who may not be the pilot, also has weight and balance responsibilities. These include the proper placement of related placards, making airplane records and operating handbooks available, ensuring that appropriate entries are made in the airplane records when repairs or modifications have been made, and that weight changes, along with proper notations, are recorded in the weight and balance records.

Without such information, the pilot has no foundation upon which to base the necessary calculations and decisions.

Terms and definitions

Before getting into weight and balance problems, knowing and understanding the related terms are, of course, fundamental. The following definitions, which are fairly well standardized, are offered to contribute to a better understanding of the whole subject and the calculations that go with it. Some of the definitions may seem a little vague or confusing, but later examples should help clear the air.

Arm (moment arm) is the horizontal distance, in inches, from the reference datum line to the center of gravity of an item. The algebraic sign is plus (+) if measured aft of the datum and minus (–) if measured forward of the datum.

Center of gravity (CG) is the point about which an airplane would balance if it were possible to suspend it at that point. It is the mass center of the airplane, or the theoretical point at which the entire weight of the airplane is assumed to be concentrated. It might be expressed in percent of MAC (*mean aerodynamic chord*) or in inches from the reference datum.

Mean aerodynamic chord (MAC) is the average distance from the leading edge to the trailing edge of the wing.

Center of gravity limits are the specified forward and aft points within which the CG must be located during flight. These limits are indicated on pertinent airplane specifications.

Center of gravity range is the distance between the forward and aft CG limits indicated on pertinent airplane specifications.

Datum (reference datum) is an imaginary vertical plane or line from which all measurements of arm are taken. The datum is established by the manufacturer. Once established, all moment arms and the location of CG range are measured from this point.

Delta is the Greek letter expressed by the symbol Δ to indicate a change of values. As an example, Δ CG indicates a change (or movement) of the CG.

Fuel load is the expendable part of the load of the airplane. It includes only usable fuel, not fuel required to fill the lines or fuel trapped in the tank sumps.

Moment is the product of the weight of an item multiplied by its arm. Moments are expressed in *pound-inches* (lb-in.). Total moment is the weight of the airplane multiplied by the distance between the datum and the CG

Moment index (or index) is a moment divided by a constant such as 100, 1000, or 10,000. The purpose of using a moment index is to simplify weight and balance computations of airplanes where heavy items and long arms result in large, unmanageable numbers.

Standard weights have been established for numerous items involved in weight and balance computations. These weights, as follows, should not be used if actual weights are available:

   General aviation (crew and passenger), 170 pounds each

   Fuel, 6 pounds /U.S. gallon

   Oil, 7.5 pounds /U.S. gallon

   Water, 8.35 pounds/U.S. gallon

Station is a location in the airplane that is identified by a number that designates its distance in inches from the datum. The datum is, therefore, identified as station zero. An item located at station +50 would have an arm of 50 inches.

Useful load is the weight of the pilot, copilot, passengers, baggage, usable fuel, and drainable oil. It is the difference between the empty weight subtracted from the maximum allowable gross weight. This term applies to general aviation aircraft only.

Weight, empty consists of the airframe, engines, and all items of operating equipment that have fixed locations and are permanently installed in the airplane. It includes optional and special equipment, fixed ballast, hydraulic fluid, unusable (residual) fuel, and undrainable (residual) oil.

Control of loading

Before any flight, it's up to the pilot to determine the weight and balance condition of the airplane. Too frequently, airplanes are loaded by guess and intuition—with occasional grim results for which there are no excuses. The aircraft manufacturers have developed simple and orderly procedures, based on sound principles, to determine loading conditions. The pilot, however, must use these procedures and make decisions that are the results of careful analysis and good judgment. In many general aviation airplanes, you just can't always fill every seat, the baggage compartment, and the fuel tanks and still remain within the approved weight and balance limits. If you try to, and it's a hot day at a high elevation airport, you can be pretty sure that, whether you want the property or not, you're going to buy the farm.

Term	Aircraft weight nomenclature (General aviation aircraft) Example (pounds)	Notes
Empty weight	2,905	Includes airframe, engines, all fixed and permanent operating equipment, and unusable fuel and oil.*
+ Useful load	1,695	Includes pilot, copilot, passengers, baggage, fuel, and oil.
= Takeoff weight	4,600	
– Fuel used	460	Includes fuel burned.
= Landing weight	4,140*	

Note: The weights above are used for illustration only. The actual values vary for each aircraft and each flight.

* Some aircraft include all oil in empty weight.

Basic principles of weight and balance computations

By determining the weight of the empty airplane and adding the weight of everything loaded on it, you can easily compute the plane's total weight, as the example used above illustrates. This is simple, but to distribute that weight so that the entire mass of the loaded airplane is balanced around a point (CG) that must be located within specified limits is a more difficult assignment. This is especially true if the principles of weight and balance are not understood.

One of the first steps is to determine the location of the CG of the plane you are going to fly. To provide the necessary balance between longitudinal stability and elevator control, the CG is usually located slightly forward of the center of lift. This loading condition causes a slight nose-down tendency in flight, which is desirable when flying at a high angle of attack and slow speeds.

The safe zone within which the balance point (CG) must fall is called the *CG range.* The extremes of that range are the *forward CG limits* and *aft CG limits.* These limits usually are specified in inches, along the longitudinal axis of the airplane, measured from a datum reference. The *datum* is an arbitrary point (Fig. 5-2), established by airplane designers, which may vary in location between different airplanes.

The distance from the datum to any component part of the airplane, or any object loaded on the airplane, is called the *arm.* When the object or component is located aft of the datum, it is measured in positive inches; if located forward of the datum, it is measured as negative, or minus, inches (Fig. 5-2). The location of the object or part is often referred to as the *station.* If the weight of any object or component is multiplied by the distance from the datum (arm), the product is the *moment,* and it is expressed in pound-inches (lb-in.).

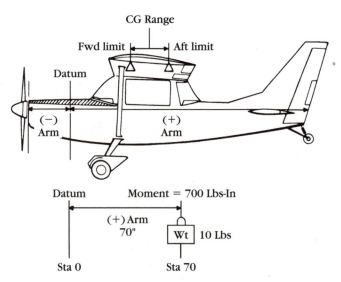

Fig. 5-2. *Weight and balance illustrated, along with some of the terms associated with weight and balance calculations.*

As a further illustration, assume a weight of 50 pounds is placed on a plank at a station, or point, 100 inches from the datum (Fig. 5-3). The downward force of the weight is then determined by multiplying 50 pounds by 100 inches, which produces a moment of 5000 pounds-inches.

To establish a balance, a total of 5000 pound-inches must be applied to the other end of the board. Any combination of weight and distance that, when multiplied, produces 5000 pound-inches moment, provides the balance. For example, as illustrated in Fig. 5-4, if a 100-pound weight is placed at a point (station) 25 inches from the datum, and a 50-pound weight is placed at a point (station) 50 inches from the datum, the sum of the product of the two weights and their distances total a moment of 5000 pound-inches, which balances the board.

The following is intended simply to show how this method of determining balance is applied to the airplane. Keep in mind, though, that the complexity of the problems increases to some extent in different types of airplanes, particularly in respect to size and the number of items that the airplane is designed to carry.

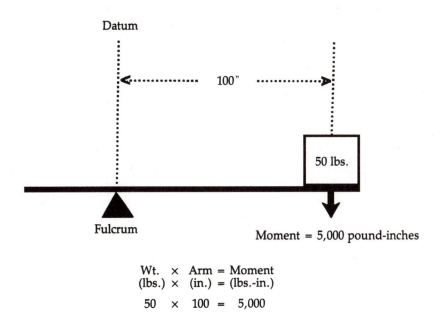

NOTE: The datum is assumed to be located at the fulcrum.

Fig. 5-3. *How to determine moments.*

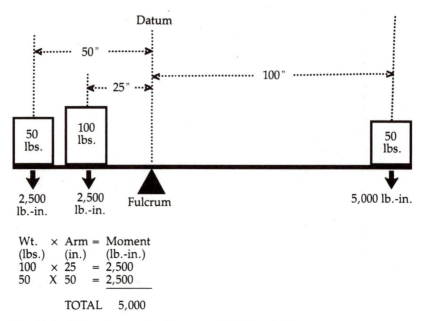

Wt. × Arm = Moment
(lbs.) (in.) (lb.-in.)
100 × 25 = 2,500
50 X 50 = 2,500
───────
TOTAL 5,000

Fig. 5-4. *What has to be done to establish a balance.*

In Fig. 5-5, the fulcrum is at the empty weight CG location, but the datum reference is moved to a convenient place to the left of the fulcrum. Also, in this example, the airplane's empty weight and empty center of gravity are included in the calculations, as required in all calculations of this nature.

Also in this example, if the maximum allowable gross weight is 1400 pounds the loaded weight is 82.5 pounds below the maximum (1400.0 minus 1317.5). Another 82.5 pounds could be added without exceeding the maximum allowable gross weight. Also, with this information, you can determine the loaded center of gravity—the balance point of the loaded airplane. This you do by dividing the total moments by the total weight as follows:

$$CG = \frac{\text{Total moments}}{\text{Total weight}} \quad \text{or} \quad CG = \frac{10,820.0}{1317.5}$$

$$CG = 8.21$$

As the center of gravity limit in this example ranges from 7.5" fore to 8.5" aft, the actual loaded center of gravity falls between these two limits. The loading on this plane, then, is both within the weight limits and the balance limits.

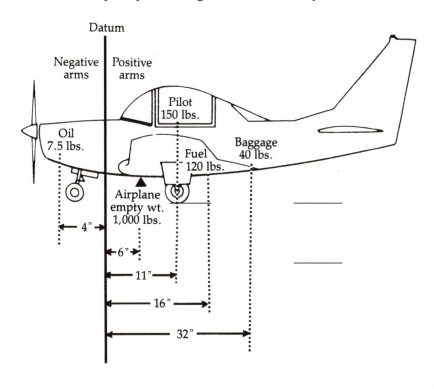

Item	Weight (pounds)	Arm (inches)	Positive moments	Negative moments
Airplane Empty Weight	1,000.0	6	6,000.0	
Pilot (Actual Weight)	150.0	11	1,650.0	
Baggage	40.0	32	1,280.0	
Oil—4 qts (7.5 pounds/gallon)	7.5	–4		–30.0
Fuel—20 gal (6 pounds/gallon)	120.0	16	1,920.0	
TOTAL WEIGHT	1,317.5		10,850.0	
				–30.0
TOTAL MOMENTS			10,820.0	

Note: Remember the positive moments must be added and the total negative moments must be subtracted from the total positive moments.

Fig. 5-5. *The factors to be considered in aircraft weight and balance computations.*

Useful load check

A simple weight check should always be made before flight to determine if the useful load is exceeded. The check might be a mental calculation if you are familiar with the airplane's limits and know that unusually heavy loads are not aboard. But when all seats are occupied, fuel tanks are full, and baggage is aboard, it's critical to calculate the weight and balance carefully.

In so doing, you need to know the useful load limit of the airplane. This you can find in the latest weight and balance report, in a logbook, or on a major repair and alterations form. If the load is not stated directly, subtract the empty weight from maximum takeoff weight.

The weight check is simple: Just add the weight of the items included in the useful load—then compare that total against the limit. The calculations might look like this example:

	Pounds
M.A. Jones (instructor)	175
Pilot	180
Fuel—30 gal (6 pounds/gallon)	180
Oil—8 qts (7.5 pounds/gallon)	15
Baggage	5
Total	555

Useful load limit is 575 pounds.
The calculations show that the useful load is not exceeded.

Now suppose that Mr. Jones is replaced by an instructor weighing 210 pounds. A new check shows that the useful load limit is exceeded, and the load must be reduced to or below the specified useful 575-pound limit. Depending on the aircraft, there may be no alternative but to reduce or remove some of the fuel load, even if all the baggage is removed.

Initial weight and balance calculations for airplanes often make the assumption that the pilot and passengers each weigh a standard 170 pounds. As you well know, that's not always the case, and heavy pilots or passengers can seriously overload a small airplane. A student and instructor might easily weigh 220 pounds each, and should that be the case, you have a potential overload of 100 pounds right off the bat.

Another thing: Don't overload the baggage compartment. Observe and abide by the placarded maximum baggage compartment weight limits. Also, watch out for rear-seat occupancy restrictions with the maximum baggage aboard. Restrictions like those are there for a purpose, so be sure to follow them.

Weight and balance (w & b) restrictions

In computing an aircraft's weight and balance (W&B), some conditions and restrictions have to be kept in mind. For instance, not all aircraft of the same make and model necessarily have the same CG or the same useful load weights. For example, two Cessna 150s sit side by side but one is freshly painted and has all sorts of fancy avionics and cockpit goodies that its next-tie-down neighbor lacks. Although not a comparison between two planes, Fig. 5-6 is an example of W&B data for N3248X. In sum, the weight difference, the CG, and the useful load restrictions between two same-make-and-model planes might differ considerably, so if you are planning to fly the dolled-up C150 and assume that its weight, CG, and all are the same as the sterile bird you've been flying, you might have a sad surprise awaiting you.

The obvious moral: Treat each plane individually and as one-of-a-kind.

There also are airport and atmospheric conditions to consider that could affect your loading plans. Your plane may be certificated for a specified maximum gross takeoff weight, but that's no guarantee that it will always take off safely with that load. Conditions that affect takeoff and climb performance, such as high elevations, high temperatures, and high humidity (high-density altitudes), could well require a reduction in weight before flight is attempted. There also is runway length, runway surface, runway slope, surface wind, or the presence of obstacles. Add up all these problem potentials and it's easy to see that serious calculations might have to be made before launching forth.

Other things to consider: Some planes are designed so that no matter how you load them, the CG load always falls within the fore

WEIGHT & BALANCE DATA

AIRCRAFT SERIAL NO. **15556480**   FAA REGISTRATION NO. **N3248X**

ITEM	WEIGHT	× ARM	= MOMENT
STANDARD AIRPLANE	975. 0	32. 0	31200. 0
OPTIONAL EQUIPMENT	89. 0	26. 1	2322. 9
PAINT	15. 5	85. 3	1322. 2
UNUSABLE FUEL	20. 0	43. 0	860. 0
LICENSED EMPTY WEIGHT	1099. 5	32. 5	35705. 1

(GROSS WT)−(LICENSED EMPTY WT) = USEFUL LOAD
(1800 LB)−(1099. 5 LB) = 700. 5 LBS

IT IS THE RESPONSIBILITY OF THE OWNER AND PILOT TO
ENSURE THAT THE AIRPLANE IS PROPERLY LOADED. THE
DATA ABOVE INDICATES THE EMPTY WEIGHT, C.G. AND USE-
FUL LOAD WHEN THE AIRPLANE WAS RELEASED FROM THE
FACTORY. REFER TO THE LATEST WEIGHT AND BALANCE
RECORD WHEN ALTERATIONS HAVE BEEN MADE.

SAMPLE LOADING PROBLEM

ITEM	WEIGHT (LBS)	ARM (IN)	MOMENT (LB-IN/1000)
LICENSED EMPTY WEIGHT	1099. 5		35. 7
OIL	12	-15. 0	-0. 2
PILOT & PASSENGER	340	40. 0	13. 6
FUEL	188. 5	43. 0	8. 1
BAGGAGE	160	65. 0	10. 4
TOTAL LOADED AIRPLANE	1800		67. 6

Fig. 5-6. *Examples of weight and balance data, along with a sample loading problem.*

or aft limits. These are usually small airplanes with the seats, fuel, and baggage compartments located very near the CG limits. Never-theless, even these can be overloaded weight-wise.

Others can be loaded so that the CG is beyond limits but the useful load is not exceeded. Here we have an out-of-balance condition that is serious from the standpoint of stability and control. As the pilot, though, you can determine if the load is within limits by using a loading schedule. This schedule usually is located in the weight and balance report, the aircraft logbook, the Aircraft Flight Manual, the Pilot's Operating Handbook, or posted in the airplane in the form of a placard. Figure 5-7 illustrates a typical placard.

The loading schedule should be used as a suggested loading plan only. If there's any question about the limitations being exceeded, go through the weight and balance calculations. Depending on the circumstances, the fact that the loading schedule, for instance, assumes that each passenger weighs 170 pounds could be an immediate indication that calculations are necessary.

Light single-engine loading problems

Assuming you have the manufacturer's data, the plane's logs, and/or other modification records, now comes the task of solving weight and balance problems—if "problems" is the right word. Hopefully, the following examples illustrate how to determine if the maximum weight limit is exceeded or if the CG is located beyond limits.

LOADING SCHEDULE

FUEL	PASSENGERS	BAGGAGE
FULL	2 REAR	100 LBS
39 GAL	1 FRONT AND 2 REAR	NONE
FULL	1 FRONT AND 1 REAR	FULL

INCLUDES PILOT AND FULL OIL

Fig. 5-7. *A typical loading schedule placard often posted in the cockpit.*

Let's say a flight is planned in a single-engine, four-place airplane. The load consists of the pilot, one front-seat passenger, two rear-seat passengers, full fuel and oil, and 60 pounds of baggage (Fig. 5-8).

Here is how this weight and balance problem is solved by using one of two different methods. One solution uses an index table, the other, graphs.

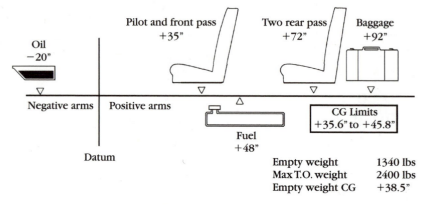

Fig. 5-8. *An aircraft weight and balance diagram.*

Using the index table:

1. From the manual or weight and balance report, determine the empty weight and empty weight CG (arm) of the airplane.
2. Determine the arms for all useful load items.
3. Determine the maximum weight and CG range. (For this problem the maximum takeoff gross weight is 2400 pounds and the CG range is Sta. 35.6 to 45.8.)

	Weight	×	**Arm**	=	**Moment (lb-in.)**
Airplane—empty	1,340		38.5		51,590
Oil—(8 quarts)	15		−20.0		−300
Pilot & front passenger	320		35.0		11,200
Fuel (40 gallon)	240		48.0		11,520
Rear passengers	300		72.0		21,600
Baggage	60		92.0		5,520
Total	2,275				101,130

Note: The oil tank for this airplane is located forward of the datum and has a negative value; therefore, subtract the oil moment when totaling the moment column.

4. Calculate the actual weights for the useful load items.

5. Construct a table as follows, and enter the appropriate values. Multiply each individual weight and arm to obtain moments.

6. Adding the weights produces a total of 2275 pounds and adding the moments produces a total of 101,130 lb-in. The CG is calculated by dividing the total moment by the total weight:

$$101,130 \div 2275 = 44.4 \text{ inches aft of datum}$$

7. The total weight of 2275 pounds does not exceed the maximum weight of 2400 pounds and the computed CG of 44.4 falls within the allowable CG range of 35.6 to 45.8 inches aft of datum.

Using graphic aids

Weight and balance computations are greatly simplified by two graphic aids: the *loading graph* and the *center of gravity moment envelope*. The loading graph (Fig. 5-9), is typical of those found in Pilot's Operating Handbooks.

This graph, in effect, multiplies weight by the arm, resulting in the moment. Note that the moment has been divided by a reduction fac-

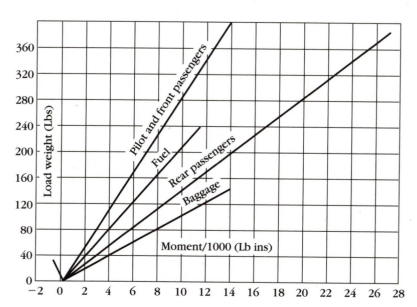

Fig. 5-9. *This loading graph simplifies weight and balance computations.*

tor (1000), resulting in an index number. Weight values appear along the left side of the graph. The moment/1000 or index numbers are along the bottom. In this example, each line representing a load item is labeled. To determine the moment of any item loaded, find the weight of the item along the left margin, then project a line to the right to intersect with the appropriate load item line. Now project a line vertically downward to the index number. For example, the index number of a pilot weighing 170 pounds is 6.1. The CG moment envelope (Fig. 5-10) eliminates the division to compute the CG. It gives an acceptable range of index numbers for any airplane weight from minimum to maximum.

If the lines from total weight and total moment intersect within the envelope, the airplane is within weight and balance limits. In solving the same sample problem, follow this procedure:

1. Determine the airplane empty weight and the empty weight index from the weight and balance report.

2. Construct a table such as the one that follows. In the left column, enter the actual weights of the empty airplane, oil, pilot and front seat passenger, fuel, rear seat passenger, and baggage. In the right column, enter the airplane empty weight index (moment/1000).

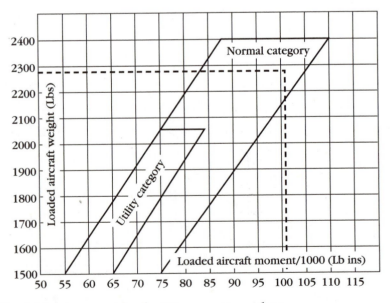

Fig. 5-10. *An example of a CG moment envelope.*

3. From the loading graph (Fig. 5-9) determine the index number (moment/1000) of each item and enter it in the table.

4. Add the two columns to determine the total weight and total moments.

5. Refer to the CG moment envelope (Fig. 5-10) and find the point of intersection of a line projected right from total weight (2275 pounds) and a line projected upward from total moment 1000 [101.2].

6. If the point of intersection falls within the envelope, as it does in this problem, the weight and CG are within limits.

Sample Loading Problem		
Item	Weight	Moment/1,000
1. Empty airplane weight	1,340	51.6
2. Oil	15	−0.3
3. Pilot and front passenger	320	11.2
4. Fuel	240	11.6
5. Rear seat passengers	300	21.6
6. Baggage	60	5.5
7. Total airplane weight	2,275	101.29

Change of weight. In many instances, the pilot must be able to solve problems that involve the shifting, addition, or removal of weight. For example, the airplane could be loaded within the allowable takeoff weight limit, but the CG limit is exceeded. The most satisfactory solution here is to relocate baggage, or passengers, or both. The pilot should be able to determine the minimum amount of load that needs to be shifted to make the airplane safe for flight and also be able to determine if shifting the load to a new location will correct an out-of-limit condition. There are some standardized and simple calculations that can help make these determinations.

Weight shifting. When weight is shifted from one location to another, the total weight of the airplane does not change. The total moments, however, do change in relation and proportion to the direction and distance the weight is moved. When weight is moved forward, the total moments decrease; when it is moved aft, they increase. The amount of moment change is proportional to the amount of weight moved. Because many airplanes, as in the following illustration, have forward and aft baggage compartments, weight is often shifted from one to the other to change the CG. If the aircraft weight, CG, and total moments are known, the new CG (after the weight shift) can be determined by dividing the new total moments by the total airplane weight.

Example:

To determine the new total moments, find out how many moments are gained or lost when the weight is shifted.

The weight shift conditions indicated for the airplane illustrated in Fig. 5-11 show that 100 pounds have been shifted from Sta. 30 to Sta. 150. This movement increases the total moments of the airplane by 12,000 lb-in.

Baggage moment when at Sta. 150 = 100 pounds × 150 inches
= 15,000 lb-in.

Baggage moment when at Sta.   30 = 100 pounds ×   30 inches
= 3000 lb-in.

Moment change   = 12,000 lb-in.

By adding the moment change to the original moment (or subtracting if the weight has been moved forward instead of aft), the new total moments are determined. The new CG is then calculated by dividing the new moments by the total weight.

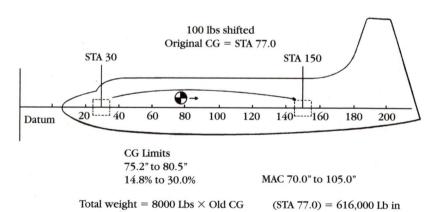

Fig. 5-11. *A weight-shifting problem and diagram.*

Total moments = 616,000 + 12,000 = 628,000

$$CG = \frac{628,000}{8000} = 78.5 \text{ inches}$$

The shift of the baggage has caused the CG to shift to Sta. 78.5.

A simple solution can be obtained by using the computer or electronic calculator. This can be done because the CG shifts a distance that is proportional to the distance the weight has shifted. The solution to the proportion problem is shown in Fig. 5-12.

Values needed:

Weight to be shifted	= 100 lbs.
Total weight	= 8000 lbs.

Change in CG	
(Unknown)	= ΔCG
Distance weight moved	= 120 in.
Old CG location	= 77 in.

Set up proportion:

$$\frac{\text{Weight to be shifted}}{\text{Total weight}} \; : \; \frac{\text{Change in CG}}{\text{Distance weight moved}}$$

$$\frac{100}{8,000} \; : \; \frac{\Delta CG}{120}$$

Cross multiply:

$$
\begin{aligned}
100 \times 120 &= 12,000 \\
8000 \times \Delta CG &= 8000 \Delta CG \\
8000\, \Delta CG &= 12,000
\end{aligned}
$$

Divide:

$$
\begin{aligned}
12,000 \div 8000 &= 1.5 \text{ in.} \\
\Delta CG &= 1.5 \text{ in.}
\end{aligned}
$$

(Add if weight shifted rearward. Subtract if weight shifted forward.) In this problem add:

$$
\begin{aligned}
\text{Old CG} &= 77.0 \text{ in.} \\
\Delta CG &= \underline{1.5} \text{ in.} \\
\text{New CG} &= 78.5 \text{ in.}
\end{aligned}
$$

Fig. 5-12. *The solution to the proportion problem.*

Example:

1. $\dfrac{\text{Weight shifted}}{\text{Total weight}} = \dfrac{\Delta \text{ CG (change of CG)}}{\text{Distance weight is shifted}}$

$$\frac{100}{8000} = \frac{\Delta \text{ CG}}{120}$$

Δ CG = 1.5 inches

2. The change of CG is added to (or subtracted from) the original CG to determine the new CG:

$$77 + 1.5 = 78.5 \text{ inches aft of datum}$$

Difficulty could arise in the computer-type solution when locating the decimal point in the answer. To make certain that Δ CG in the above problem is not .15 inches or 15.0 inches, insert the answer obtained into the formula, or, in other words, substitute the answer 1.5 for the unknown Δ CG, and cross multiply as follows:

$$1.5 \times 8000 = 12{,}000$$
$$100 \times \ \ 120 = 12{,}000$$

If the products are the same, the decimal is properly placed. If not the same, the wrong decimal location for the Δ CG has been selected and should be relocated accordingly.

The shifting weight proportion formula can also be used to determine how much weight must be shifted to achieve a desired shift of the CG. The following problem illustrates a solution to this type of problem.

Example:

Given—

Airplane total weight	7800 pounds
CG	Sta. 81.5 inches
Aft CG limit	80.5 inches

Find—

How much weight must be shifted from the aft cargo compartment at Sta. 150 to the forward cargo compartment at Sta. 30 to move the CG to exactly the aft limit?

Solution—

1. Use the shifting weight proportion:

$$\frac{\text{Weight to be shifted}}{\text{Total weight}} = \frac{\Delta \text{ CG}}{\text{Dist. wt. shifted}}$$

$$\frac{\text{Weight to be shifted}}{7800} = \frac{1.0 \text{ inches}}{120 \text{ inches}}$$

Weight to be shifted = 65 pounds

2. Cross multiply to check for correct location of decimal point.

$$7800 \times 1.0 = 7800$$
$$65 \times 120 = 7800$$

Similar to the previous problem, a computer or electronic calculator can be used to determine the solution.

Weight addition or removal. Very frequently, the weight and balance of an airplane changes when weight is added or removed. When this occurs, a new CG must be calculated and checked against the limitations to determine that the new CG is within limits.

This type of weight and balance problem is commonly encountered when the airplane burns fuel in flight, thereby reducing the fuel weight. Many planes are designed with the fuel tanks located close to the CG so that the CG is not affected to any major extent by the fuel consumption. The location of some tanks, though, requires careful planning to prevent the CG from shifting out of limits during flight.

If this weight condition is possible, it's advisable to calculate the weight and balance twice before flight. First to determine the weight and balance with all items loaded *except* fuel; and second, to determine the weight and balance, *including* the fuel. The contrast gives you a good indication of how fuel consumption affects balance.The addition or removal of cargo, of course, causes a CG change, which should be calculated before flight. Such problems can be solved by calculations involving total moments. However, this shortcut formula simplifies computations:

$$\frac{\text{Weight added (or removed)}}{\text{Total weight}} = \frac{\Delta \text{ CG}}{\text{Distance between wt. and old CG}}$$

In this formula, "new" and "old" refer to conditions before and after the weight change.

It might be more convenient to use another form of this formula to find the weight change needed to accomplish a particular CG change (Δ CG). In this case use:

$$\frac{\text{Weight added (or removed)}}{\text{Old total weight}} = \frac{\Delta\,\text{CG}}{\text{Distance between wt. and new CG}}$$

Notice that "new" and "old" are found on both sides of the equation in either of the above proportions. If the "new" total weight is used, the distance must be calculated from the "old" CG. Just the opposite is true if the "old" total weight is used.

A typical problem involves the calculation of a new CG for an airplane that has been loaded, is ready for flight, and receives additional cargo or passengers just before departure time:

Given—

Airplane total weight   6860 pounds

CG   Sta. 80.0

Find—

What is the location of the CG if 140 pounds of baggage are added to station 150?

Solution—

1. Use the added weight formula:

$$\frac{\text{Added weight}}{\text{New total weight}} = \frac{\Delta\,\text{CG}}{\text{Dist. between wt. and old CG}}$$

$$\frac{140}{6860 + 140} = \frac{\Delta\,\text{CG}}{150 - 80}$$

$$\frac{140}{7000} = \frac{\Delta\,\text{CG}}{70}$$

$$\text{CG} = 1.4 \text{ inches aft}$$

2. Add CG to the old CG:

New CG = 80.0 inches + 1.4 inches = 81.4

Example:

Given—

Airplane total weight   6100 pounds

CG   Sta. 78

Find—

What is the location of the CG if 100 pounds are removed from station 150?

Solution—

1. Use the removed weight formula:

$$\frac{\text{Weight removed}}{\text{New total weight}} = \frac{\Delta\,\text{CG}}{\text{Dist. between wt. and old CG}}$$

$$\frac{100}{6100 - 100} = \frac{\Delta\,\text{CG}}{150 - 78}$$

$$\frac{100}{6000} = \frac{\Delta\,\text{CG}}{72}$$

$$\Delta\text{CG} = 1.2 \text{ inches forward}$$

2. Subtract Δ CG from old CG:

New CG = 78 inches – 1.2 inches = 76.8 inches

Note: In the above two examples, the Δ CG is either added to or subtracted from the old CG. Deciding which to accomplish is best handled by mentally calculating which way the CG shifts for the particular weight change. If the CG is shifting aft, the Δ CG is added to the old CG; if it is shifting forward, the Δ CG is subtracted from the old CG.

To summarize CG movement:

Weight added forward of old CG

OR

Weight removed aft of old CG means CG moves forward

Weight added aft of old CG

OR

Weight removed fwd. of old CG means CG moves aft

Airplane performance

Many accidents have occurred because pilots failed to understand the effects that varying conditions can have on aircraft performance. In addition to those of weight and balance, others, such as density altitude, humidity, winds, runway gradient, and runway surface conditions, all can profoundly influence how an airplane performs. Some of the more critical elements include the following:

Density altitude. Air density can materially affect airplane performance because it has a direct bearing on the power output of the engine, the efficiency of the propeller, and the lift generated by the wings. As discussed earlier, when the air temperature increases, the density of the air decreases. And, as altitude increases, the density also decreases. From this combination of occurrences, then, comes the term, "density altitude."

Because it can get a little confusing, remember that a decrease in air density means a high density altitude. Or said another way, it means that because the air is thinner than standard, the air at a given altitude has the characteristics of air at some higher altitude. The thinner air, in turn, adversely affects lift, engine power, fuel consumption, and overall engine efficiency. Conversely, an increase in air density means a lower density altitude (the air is becoming thicker, heavier, more dense) and aircraft lift as well as engine performance is more efficient.

Until you get used to the term, "higher density altitude" is often thought to mean that the altitude, whatever it may be, has "higher density." That's not it. Saying it once again, it means that the altitude takes on the characteristics of a higher altitude because the density is lower, and thus the air is thinner. If there's still any confusion, the following may help:

Condition:	Means:	Produces Results/Effects of:
Lower density	= thinner air	= higher altitude, poorer aircraft performance
Higher density	= thicker air	= lower altitude, better aircraft performance

Humidity. Because of evaporation, the atmosphere always contains moisture in the form of water vapor. This water vapor replaces molecules of dry air, and, because water vapor weighs less than dry air, any given volume of moist air weighs less— is less dense—than an equal volume of dry air.

Density altitude effect on engine power and propeller efficiency. Said once more, even though it's repetitive, an increase in air temperature or humidity, or a decrease in air pressure that results in a higher density altitude, significantly decreases power output and propeller efficiency.

The engine produces power in proportion to the weight or density of the air. Therefore, as air density decreases, the power output of the engine decreases. This is true of all engines that are not equipped with a supercharger or turbocharger. At the same time, the propeller produces thrust in proportion to the mass of air being accelerated through the rotating blades. If the air is less dense, the mass of air is less, and propeller efficiency is decreased.

The problems associated with high density altitude operation are compounded by the fact that when the air is less dense, more engine power and increased propeller efficiency are needed to overcome the decreased lift efficiency of the airplane wing. This additional power and propeller efficiency are not available under high density altitude conditions, consequently, airplane performance decreases considerably.

Effect of wind on airplane performance. Surface winds during takeoffs and landings have, in a sense, an opposite effect on airplane performance to winds aloft during flight.

During takeoff, a headwind shortens the takeoff run and increases the angle of climb. This increases performance and, if the density altitude is high, helps to compensate for lost performance. A headwind during flight, however, has the opposite effect on performance, in that it decreases groundspeed and consequently increases the total amount of fuel consumed for that flight.

During takeoff, a tailwind increases the takeoff run and decreases the angle of climb. Because of the risks involved, a pilot should carefully consider this decrease in performance before attempting a downwind takeoff; the results, otherwise, could be disastrous. During flight, though, a tailwind is a great plus, as it increases groundspeed, conserves fuel, and saves time.

During landing, a headwind steepens the approach angle and shortens the landing roll, while a tailwind decreases the approach angle and increases the landing roll. In light of the dangers, downwind operations should be carefully evaluated before being attempted.

Runway surface condition and gradient. Takeoff distance can obviously be affected by the surface of the runway. With a runway that is muddy, wet, soft, rough, or covered with tall grass, you'll be fighting a condition that acts as a retarding force and increases the takeoff distance, while decreasing the landing roll. But then, on landing, factors such as runway ice or snow affect braking action and increase the landing roll considerably.

The upslope or downslope of the runway (runway gradient) is another important element when length and takeoff distance are critical. With an upslope, you have a retarding force that impedes acceleration and inevitably results in a longer takeoff ground run. Of course, landing uphill usually results in a shorter landing roll, but downhill operations have the reverse effect of shortening the takeoff distance and increasing the landing roll.

Ground effect. When an airplane is flown at about the equivalent of one wing span above the surface, maybe a little less, the vertical component of airflow is modified, and changes occur in the normal pattern of the airflow around the wing and from the wing tips. This change alters the direction of the relative wind so that it produces a smaller angle of attack. In turn, with the wing operating in ground effect at a given angle of attack, it generates less induced drag than a wing out of ground effect. Consequently, it's more efficient.

This phenomenon is useful in specific situations, but it can also trap the unwary into expecting greater climb performance than the airplane is capable of sustaining. In other words, an airplane can take off and, while in ground effect, establish an angle or rate of climb that the plane can't maintain once it reaches an altitude where ground effect can no longer influence performance. Conversely, on a landing, ground effect might cause the plane to float and overshoot, particularly at fast approach speeds.

Use of performance charts

Most aircraft manufacturers provide adequate information to help pilots familiarize themselves with their aircraft and its performance. This basic information is usually found in Aircraft Flight Manuals, Pilot's Operating Handbooks, or through other written materials.

Among the data provided or available are two common vehicles for performance determinations:

1. Tables, which are compact arrangements of conditions and performance values placed in an orderly sequence, usually arranged in rows and columns.

2. Graphs, which are pictorial presentations consisting of straight lines, curves, broken lines, or a series of bars representing the successive changes in the value of a variable quantity or quantities. Airplane performance graphs are usually the straight-line or curved-line types. The straight-line graph is a result of two values that vary at a constant rate, while the curved-line graph is a result of two values that vary at a changing rate.

Because all values are not listed on the tables or graphs, interpolation is often required to determine intermediate values for a particular flight condition or performance situation. Interpolation is discussed later in this chapter.

In talking about airplane performance, keep in mind that the data on the performance charts are based on flight tests conducted under normal operating conditions, using average piloting skills, with an airplane and engine in good operating condition. Any deviation from one or more of these conditions inevitably affects airplane performance and perhaps the significance of some of the data. Other than that, what is presented on the charts is accurate. It's a good idea to consider the performance of the plane you're going to fly to be somewhat less than that predicted by the performance charts. In other words, give yourself a little wiggle room.

Also keep in mind that standard atmospheric conditions (temperature 59° Fahrenheit [15° Celsius], zero relative humidity, and a pressure of 29.92 inches of mercury at sea level) are used in the development of performance charts. This "standard" provides a base from which to evaluate performance when actual atmospheric conditions change.

Interpolation

To "interpolate" means to compute intermediate values between a series of given values. In many instances when performance is critical, an accurate determination of the performance values is the only acceptable means to enhance safe flight. Guessing to determine these values is not the way to go.

Interpolation is simple to perform if the method is understood. The following are examples of three different ways to go through the process. Of these, the last seems the easiest and the most frequently used, but the other two are included to avoid reader confusion in case they are favored by either the reader or ground instructor personnel.

Starting with a simple example to illustrate interpolation, the numbers in column A range from 10 to 30 and the numbers in column B range from 50 to 100. The problem: Determine the intermediate numerical value in column B that would correspond to an intermediate value of 20 in column A.

A	B
10	50
20	X = unknown
30	100

The answer here is obvious at first glance. Twenty is halfway between 10 and 30, so the corresponding value of the unknown number in column B would be halfway between 50 and 100, or 75.

Since most interpolation problems are more difficult to visualize than this, a systematic method has to be used to determine intermediate values. The following is one method that can be used:

The numbers in column A range from 10 to 30 with intermediate values of 15, 20, and 25. The problem: Determine the intermediate numerical value in column B that would correspond with 15 in column A.

A	B
10	50
15	
20	
25	
30	100

First, in column A, determine the relationship of 15 to the range between 10 and 30 as follows:

$$\frac{15-10}{30-10} = \frac{5}{20}, \text{ or } 1/4$$

So 15 is ¼ of the range between 10 and 30. Now determine ¼ of the range of column B between 50 and 100 as follows:

$$100 - 50 = 50$$

$$¼ \text{ of } 50 = 12.5$$

The answer: 12.5, but to arrive at the correct value, 12.5 has to be added to the lower number in column B:

$$50 + 12.5 = 62.5$$

The interpolation has been completed, and 62.5 is the actual value, which is ¼ of the range of column B.

Here's the second method of interpolation:

Using the same numbers as in the previous example, a proportion problem based on the relationship of the numbers is set up:

$$\text{Proportion: } \frac{5}{20} = \frac{x}{50}$$

$$\text{Cross multiply: } \frac{5}{20} = \frac{x}{50}$$

$$20x = 250$$

$$x = 12.5$$

As before, 12.5 is added to 50 to arrive at the actual value of 62.5.

The third interpolation method eliminates the need for formulas and seems a little simpler. Using the same numbers as in the previous example, we have this situation:

Step 1: Set up the two columns:

A	B
10	50
15	
20	
25	
30	100

Step 2: Number each of the column A values, beginning with zero, the base value.

	A	B
0	10	50
1	15	
2	20	
3	25	
4	30	100

Step 3: Determine the difference in values between the numbers in column B:

$$100 - 50 = 50$$

Step 4: Divide 50 by 4 (the number of values in column A beyond the base value).

$$50 \div 4 = 12.5$$

Step 5: To find the value of 15 in column B, merely add 12.5 to 50, or 62.5.

That's simple enough, but suppose you wanted to find the value of 17 in column A. You have two alternatives: One, list all individual digits between 10 and 30 (11, 12, 13, 14, etc.) and then start with Step 2, above. That's a lengthy process, though, so the easier method is to determine the values of 15 and 20, which, as in the example, are 62.5 and 75. Now go back to Step 2, using only the 15 and 20 values:

	A	B
0	15	62.5
1	16	
2	17	
3	18	
4	19	
5	20	75

Step 3: Determine the difference between 62.5 and 75, which, of course, is 12.5.

Step 4: Divide 12.5 by 5, or 2.5.

Step 5: Add 2.5 to 62.5 and each succeeding total (or subtract from 75):

	A	B
0	15	62.5
1	16	65
2	17	67.5
3	18	70
4	19	72.5
5	20	75

The value of 17 is thus 67.5.

Moving the interpolation method to an aircraft performance problem, with the given temperatures and takeoff distances, what is the takeoff distance when the temperature is 77°F?

Temperature (°F)	Takeoff Distance (feet)
70	1,173
80	1,356

Again, two alternatives exist. One is to list all temperatures between 70 and 80 (71, 72, 73, etc.); the other (and in this case, the simpler) is first to determine the takeoff distance in a 75° temperature, which is obviously halfway between 1173 and 1356, or 1264 feet.

With that established, set up the two columns as before:

	Temperature	Takeoff Distance
0	75	1,264.5
1	76	
2	77	
3	78	
4	79	
5	80	1,356

Takeoff distance difference between 75° and 80° temperatures is 91.5 feet (1356 minus 1264.5). 91.5 divided by 5 = 18.3 feet; 18.3 feet added to 1264.5 and each succeeding temperature value (or subtracted from 1356) produces this:

	Temperature	Takeoff Distance (feet)
0	75	1264.5
1	76	1282.8
2	77	1301.1
3	78	1319.4
4	79	1337.7
5	80	1356

The takeoff distance with a 77°F temperature is thus 1301 feet.

While not essential, it's suggested that you continue the addition or subtraction in the B column for the entire series of values listed in the first column, rather than stopping when you have determined, as in this case, the 77°F takeoff distance. The reason: There's always the possibility of a small division, addition, or subtraction error that would produce an incorrect answer. Completing the addition or subtraction throughout the range of values and coming up with exactly the same known values in the second column (1356 if you start by adding to the lower number [1264.5]) will verify the correctness of your computations.

Performance charts and problems

Following are descriptions and examples of various performance charts. The information on these charts is not intended for operational use but rather for familiarization and study. Because charts like these are developed for each specific make, model, and type of airplane, you need to be careful that you're referencing the chart that pertains to the aircraft you are flying. That sounds obvious enough, but there sometimes is the tendency to believe that one size fits all. Not so, in this instance.

Density altitude charts

Several methods can be used to determine density altitude, one of which is the "Pressure Altitude and Density Chart," illustrated in Fig. 5-13, which includes a sample problem. Another chart used for

PRESSURE ALTITUDE AND DENSITY CHART

A practice problem - find the Density Altitude with these existing conditions:
Airport elevation 2,545 feet, OAT 70° F., and Altimeter Setting 29.70.

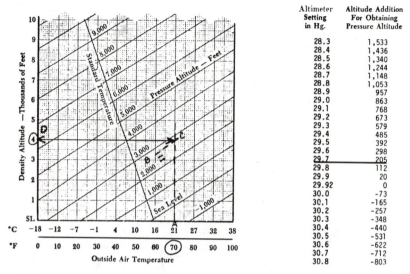

Altimeter Setting in Hg.	Altitude Addition For Obtaining Pressure Altitude
28.3	1,533
28.4	1,436
28.5	1,340
28.6	1,244
28.7	1,148
28.8	1,053
28.9	957
29.0	863
29.1	768
29.2	673
29.3	579
29.4	485
29.5	392
29.6	298
29.7	205
29.8	112
29.9	20
29.92	0
30.0	-73
30.1	-165
30.2	-257
30.3	-348
30.4	-440
30.5	-531
30.6	-622
30.7	-712
30.8	-803

SOLUTION: The chart requires Pressure Altitude which is determined from the conversion table at the right of the graph. 2,545 + 205 = 2,750 feet Pressure Altitude.

Step 1.   Draw a line parallel to the vertical lines from the 70° on the Fahrenheit Scale (A) to about the diagonal 3,000 feet Pressure Altitude line.

Step 2.   Draw line B representing a value of 2,750 feet (interpolate 3/4 of distance from 2,000 to 3,000) parallel to the pressure altitude lines so that it intersects the line drawn in step 1.

Step 3.   The intersection of these two lines (C) lies on the 4,000 foot value of the Density Altitude scale (D). THE DENSITY ALTITUDE IS 4,000 FEET.

Fig. 5-13. *A pressure altitude and density altitude graph.*

the same purpose is shown in Fig. 5-14 and also has a sample problem for study purposes.

Takeoff data chart

Takeoff data charts are found in many Aircraft Flight Manuals or Pilot's Operating Handbooks. From these charts, you can determine the length of the takeoff ground-run as well as the distance required to clear a 50-foot obstacle under various airplane weights, headwinds, pressure altitudes, and temperatures. While charts for different airplanes vary, Fig. 5-15 shows one that is typical.

The first column gives three possible gross weights (2100 pounds, 2400 pounds, and 2650 pounds). The second column lists three

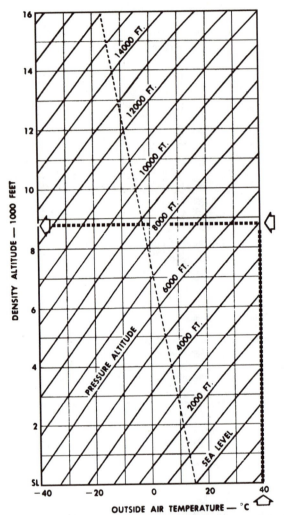

At an elevation of 5,000 ft. (assuming pressure altitude
and elevation are identical) and a temperature of 40° C
(104° F) the density altitude is approximately 8,800 ft.

Fig. 5-14. *Another type of graph to determine density altitude.*

windspeeds (0, 15, and 30 mph) opposite each gross weight. The
remainder of the chart consists of pairs of columns, each pair having
a main heading of a pressure altitude and temperature standard for
that altitude (sea level, 59°; 2500 feet, 50°F; 5000 feet, 41°F; and 7500
feet, 32°). The first column of each pair is headed "Ground-Run"; the
second, "To Clear a 50-foot Obstacle."

TAKEOFF DATA

TAKEOFF DISTANCE WITH 20° FLAPS FROM HARD SURFACE RUNWAY.

GROSS WEIGHT LBS.	HEAD WIND MPH	AT SEA LEVEL & 59°F		AT 2500 FT & 50°F		AT 5000 FT & 41°F		AT 7500 FT & 32°F	
		GROUND RUN	TO CLEAR 50' OBSTACLE	GROUND RUN	TO CLEAR 50' OBSTACLE	GROUND RUN	TO CLEAR 50' OBSTACLE	GROUND RUN	TO CLEAR 50' OBSTACLE
2100	0	335	715	390	810	465	935	560	1100
	15	185	465	225	540	270	625	330	745
	30	75	260	95	305	125	365	160	450
2400	0	440	895	525	1040	630	1210	770	1465
	15	255	600	310	700	380	835	475	1020
	30	115	350	150	420	190	510	245	640
2650	0	555	1080	665	1260	790	1500	965	1835
	15	330	735	405	865	490	1050	655	1345
	30	160	445	205	535	255	665	335	845

Note: Increase distances 10% for each 25°F above standard temperature for particular altitude.

Fig. 5-15. *Takeoff performance is more easily determined by this data chart.*

At the bottom of the chart is this note: "Increase distance 10 percent for each 25°F above standard temperature for particular altitude."

To determine the takeoff ground-run for a given set of conditions, these are the steps to follow, although the chart is rather self-explanatory:

1. Locate the computed gross weight in the first column.
2. Locate the existing headwind in the second column adjacent to the computed gross weight in (1).
3. Follow that line to the first "Ground-Run" column. The number at the intersection of this line and the column is the length of the ground-run in feet for the given set of conditions, provided the temperature is standard for the altitude.
4. Increase the number found in (3) by 10 percent for each 25°F of temperature above standard (for that altitude). The resulting figure is the length of the ground-run.

The same steps are followed to find the distance to clear a 50-foot obstacle except that in (3) the headwind line is extended to the second column (headed by "To Clear a 50-foot Obstacle").

So far, the chart is simple enough, but suppose you want to find takeoff runs when winds, temperatures, or pressures are not as clear-cut as on the chart? This is where close reading of the chart and/or interpolation enters the scene.

Sample Problem. What will be the takeoff ground-run distance with the following conditions?

Gross weight	2100 pounds
Pressure altitude	2500 feet
Temperature	75°F
Headwind	15 mph

Applying steps (1), (2), and (3) to the performance chart, the ground-run at an airport where this pressure altitude is 2500 feet is obviously 225 feet. But because the temperature is 25° above standard, step (4) must also be applied. Ten percent of 225 is 22.5, or approximately 23. Adding 23 to 225 gives a total of 248 feet for the takeoff ground-run. Putting this in tabular form, we have:

Basic distance exclusive of correction for above standard temperature	225 feet
Correction for above standard temperature (225 × 0.10)	23 feet
Approximate takeoff distance required	248 feet

Sample Problem: What will be the distance required to take off and clear a 50-foot obstacle with the same airplane and with the following conditions?

Gross weight	2650 pounds
Pressure altitude	5000 feet
Temperature	91°F
Headwind	Calm

Following the four-step procedure, except using the "To Clear a 50-foot Obstacle" column, the solution of this problem gives these results:

Basic distance exclusive of correction for above standard temperature	1500 feet
Correction for above standard temperature (1500 × 0.20)	300 feet
Approximate distance required to take off and clear a 50-foot obstacle	1800 feet

Exercises. Find the takeoff ground-run distance and the distance necessary to clear a 50-foot obstacle under each of the following sets of conditions:

Gross weight (pounds)	Headwind (mph)	Pressure altitude (feet)	Temperature (°F)
1. 2,100	30	Sea level	59
2. 2,650	Calm	7,500	57
3. 2,400	15	2,500	50
4. 2,650	Calm	Sea level	109
5. 2,250	15	5,000	41

Solving the first four problems is merely a matter of following the four-step procedure. The correct answers are:

Ground run (feet)	To clear 50-foot (feet)
1. 75	260
2. 1,062	2,019
3. 310	700
4. 666	1,296

The last exercise, however, with an aircraft gross weight of 2250 pounds, requires interpolation. Applying the third interpolation method discussed earlier, we have this result (keep in mind the conditions: 15 mph headwind; airport altitude, 5000 feet; temperature standard, 41°F:

Gross weight	Ground-run	To clear 50-foot obstacle
0. 2,100	270 feet	625 feet
1. 2,150		
2. 2,200		
3. 2,250		
4. 2,300		
5. 2,350		
6. 2,400	380 feet	835 feet

Ground-run difference between 2100 and 2400 gross weights is 110 feet; 110 divided by 6 = 18.3 feet; add 18.3 to 270, and each succeeding sum results in the following:

Gross weight	Ground run	To clear 50-foot obstacle
0. 2,100	270.0 feet	625 feet
1. 2,150	288.3	
2. 2,200	306.6	
3. 2,250	324.9	
4. 2,300	343.2	
5. 2,350	361.5	
6. 2,400	380.8 feet	835 feet

The correct answer is 324.9, or 325 feet. Following the same steps to determine the distance to clear a 50-foot obstacle, the difference between the 2100 and 2400 gross weight distance is 210 feet (835 – 625); 210 divided by 6 = 35; add 35 to 625 and each succeeding sum. The correct answer for an aircraft weighing 2250 pounds is 730 feet.

Climb performance

The rate of climb under various conditions can be determined by climb performance charts such as those illustrated in Figs. 5-16 and 5-17. The data available from these charts become particularly important should you be planning to fly over high terrain or mountain ranges relatively soon after takeoff. Some charts, such as Fig. 5-16, also give the best climb airspeed and fuel consumed during the climb.

CLIMB DATA

GROSS WEIGHT LBS.	AT SEA LEVEL & 59 °F.			AT 5000 FT. & 41 °F.			AT 10000 FT. & 23 F.		
	BEST CLIMB IAS MPH	RATE OF CLIMB FT/MIN	GAL. OF FUEL USED	BEST CLIMB IAS MPH	RATE OF CLIMB FT/MIN	From SL FUEL USED	BEST CLIMB IAS MPH	RATE OF CLIMB FT/MIN	From SL FUEL USED
2100	87	1470	1.5	82	1200	2.8	78	925	4.3
2400	88	1210	1.5	84	960	3.1	80	710	5.0
2650	90	1030	1.5	86	795	3.5	83	560	5.9

Note: Flaps up, full throttle and 2600 RPM. Mixture leaned for smooth operation above 5000 ft. Fuel used includes warmup and takeoff allowance.

Fig. 5-16. *The Climb Data chart helps determine aircraft performance under several different conditions.*

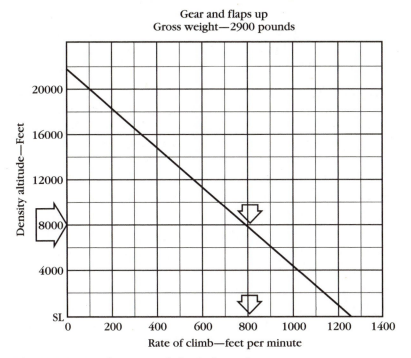

Fig. 5-17. *Another rate-of-climb data chart.*

With reference to Fig. 5-16, using this chart is a simple process. For example, if you have a plane with a 2100-pound gross weight and then follow that line across the chart to the 5000 feet, 41°F column, you'll see that the best angle of climb at that altitude is at 82 mph and the best rate of climb is 1200 feet per minute. At these speeds and rates, the fuel used to climb from sea level to 5000 feet would be 2.8 gallons. Under the same conditions, if your plane weighed 2650 pounds, the chart says that the rate of climb would be 795 feet per minute.

Another performance chart is illustrated in Fig. 5-17. The problem: With a pressure altitude of 5000 feet, a temperature of 86°F, and a 2900-pound gross weight aircraft, what would be the aircraft's rate of climb?

First, remember that the pressure altitude, based on the existing or forecast temperature, must be converted to a density altitude. To do that, convert the 86°F temperature to centigrade (30°), and then go back to Fig. 5-14. Next, on that performance chart, trace the 30°C vertical line up to where it intersects the 5000-foot pressure line. Finally, read across to the vertical scale on the left, where you'll see that the density altitude is approximately 7700 feet.

Now go to the rate-of-climb chart and locate the 7700-foot density altitude reading. Trace that across to the diagonal black line and then read down to the horizontal rate-of-climb scale, which, in this case of density altitude and aircraft gross weight, is 820 feet per minute.

Maximum glide

The type of chart illustrated in Fig. 5-18, available for some aircraft, reflects the ground distance that a plane would cover under the various conditions (speed, flaps, etc.) listed above the chart. As it stands, the chart has minimal value because it does not reflect the weight of the aircraft or its load. Also, a change in any of the conditions could have a major effect on the data the chart portrays. If designed for a given airplane, however, and if the pilot computed for loads, forecast winds, density altitude, and so on, the chart could then have considerable flight-planning merit.

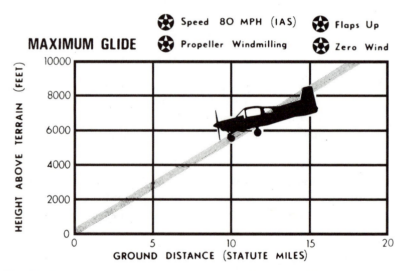

Fig. 5-18. *The maximum glide distance chart could heve merit when computed for a given aircraft and current operating conditions.*

Crosswind and headwind component charts

Takeoffs and landings in certain crosswind conditions are inadvisable or even dangerous. If the crosswind is strong enough to require an extreme drift correction, you can be reasonably sure you're venturing into a potentially threatening situation. Accordingly, and before finally committing yourself, it's suggested that you carefully evaluate:

1. The crosswind capabilities of the aircraft you're flying
2. Your own ability to handle crosswind takeoffs or landings
3. How much of a crosswind it is (meaning its direction in relation to the active runway)
4. The velocity of the crosswind

Before an airplane is type-certificated by the FAA, it must be flight tested to meet certain requirements. Among those is the demonstration of it being satisfactorily controllable, requiring no exceptional degree of skill or alertness on the part of the pilot, in 90° crosswinds up to a velocity equal to 0.2 V_{so}. The last means a windspeed of two-tenths of the airplane's stalling speed with power off and gear and flaps down. (If the stalling speed is 60 knots, then the airplane must be capable of being landed in a 12 knot 90 degree crosswind.) So that pilots know the capability of the aircraft they are flying, regulations require that the demonstrated crosswind velocity be made available.

In line with that, those manuals often contain a chart to help the pilot determine the maximum safe wind velocities for various degrees of crosswind for his or her particular airplane. The chart, Fig. 5-19, along with the example, should familiarize you with a method of determining crosswind components. The angle between the wind and nose is considered to be the same as the angle between the wind and the takeoff or landing runway.

Stall speed charts

Figure 5-20 is a typical example of a Stall Speed Chart. Note the wide variation in stall speeds between straight-and-level flight and various angles of bank. Note, too, that the stall speed in a 60° bank with flaps up and power off (102 mph) is almost double the stall speed in straight-and-level flight with flaps down and power on (55 mph). Even with power on in the 60° bank, the stall speed is reduced only 4 mph to 98 mph.

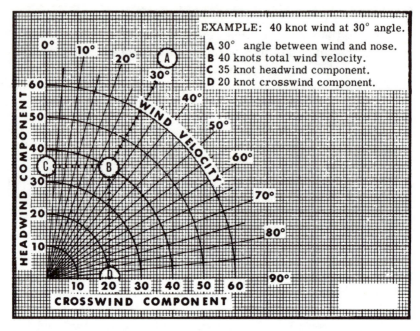

EXAMPLE: 40 knot wind at 30° angle.
A 30° angle between wind and nose.
B 40 knots total wind velocity.
C 35 knot headwind component.
D 20 knot crosswind component.

Fig. 5-19. *This is a helpful chart to detrmine crosswind and headwind components.*

CONFIGURATION		ANGLE OF BANK		
	0°	20°	40°	60°
Flaps Up — Power Off	72 mph	74 mph	82 mph	102 mph
Flaps Up — Power On	69 mph	71 mph	79 mph	98 mph
Flaps Down (30°) — Power Off	64 mph	66 mph	73 mph	91 mph
Flaps Down (30°) — Power On	55 mph	57 mph	63 mph	78 mph

Fig. 5-20. *This is an example of a typical stall speed chart.*

This is a worthwhile chart to study, both because of the data it contains and the fact that, in doing so, it is representative of the characteristics of a typical single-engine light plane. As such, it's a useful tool for a good number of general aviation pilots. It's further suggested that you be particularly attentive to what the chart is saying when landing and operating in the traffic pattern. Especially in that environment, aware-ness of the relationships between air speed, bank angle, power, and flaps, and their respective effects on stalling speed is critical.

If one chart on stalling speeds isn't enough, Fig. 5-21 is another ex-ample. Because of its simplicity, little explanation of it would seem necessary.

Landing performance data

Variables similar to those discussed under "Factors Affecting Takeoff Distance" also affect landing distances, although generally to a lesser extent. You should, however, consult your Aircraft Flight Manual or Pilot's Operating Handbook for landing distance data, recommended flap settings, and recommended approach airspeeds.

One chart that is helpful in determining probable landing distances and ground rolls under various conditions is reproduced in Fig. 5-22.

=Power Off= **STALLING SPEEDS** MPH ═ CAS				
┌Gross Weight┐ └ 1600 lbs. ┘ **CONDITION**	**ANGLE OF BANK**			
	0°	**20°**	**40°**	**60°**
Flaps UP	55	57	63	78
Flaps 20°	49	51	56	70
Flaps 40°	48	49	54	67

Fig. 5-21. *A variation of stall speed charts.*

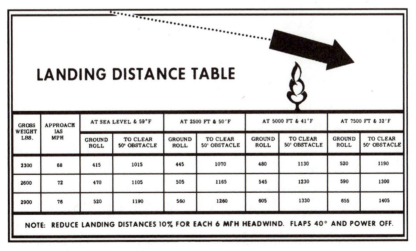

LANDING DISTANCE TABLE

GROSS WEIGHT LBS.	APPROACH IAS MPH	AT SEA LEVEL & 59°F		AT 2500 FT & 50°F		AT 5000 FT & 41°F		AT 7500 FT & 32°F	
		GROUND ROLL	TO CLEAR 50' OBSTACLE	GROUND ROLL	TO CLEAR 50' OBSTACLE	GROUND ROLL	TO CLEAR 50' OBSTACLE	GROUND ROLL	TO CLEAR 50' OBSTACLE
2300	68	415	1015	445	1070	480	1130	520	1190
2600	72	470	1105	505	1165	545	1230	590	1300
2900	76	520	1190	560	1280	605	1330	655	1405

NOTE: REDUCE LANDING DISTANCES 10% FOR EACH 6 MPH HEADWIND. FLAPS 40° AND POWER OFF.

Fig. 5-22. *Similar to the takeoff data chart (Fig. 5-15), this is its landing performance data counterpart.*

As a companion piece to the takeoff data chart (Fig. 5-15), the construction is the same and the information you want is derived the same way. So, using the chart, try a couple simple sample problems. The answers appear at the end of this chapter.

Sample Problem #1. With a power-off approach speed of 68 mph and 40 degrees of flap, approximately what ground roll will be required under the following conditions?

Elevation	Sea level
Gross weight	2300 pounds
Temperature	59°F
Headwind	Calm

Solution:

Approximately 415 feet

Sample Problem #2: With power-off approach speed of 72 mph, and 40 degrees of flaps, approximately what total landing distance (including ground roll) would be required to clear a 50-foot obstacle and land under the following conditions?

Elevation	2500 feet
Gross weight	2600 pounds
Temperature	50°F
Headwind	12 mph

Solution:

Basic landing distance before headwind correction	1165 feet
Correction for headwind (1165 × .20)	−233 feet
Approximate landing distance	932 feet

Combined graphs

Some Aircraft Performance Charts incorporate two or more graphs when an aircraft flight performance involves several conditions. For example, to determine the takeoff distance to clear a 50-foot object at the end of the runway involves several factors, including the airport temperature, its altitude, the aircraft weight, and the winds. Figure 5-23 illustrates how those elements—altitude/temperature,

NORMAL TAKEOFF

ASSOCIATED CONDITIONS:

POWER	TAKEOFF POWER SET BEFORE BRAKE RELEASE	
FLAPS	UP	
RUNWAY	PAVED, LEVEL, DRY SURFACE	
TAKEOFF SPEED	IAS AS TABULATED	

NOTE: GROUND ROLL IS APPROX. 59% OF TOTAL TAKEOFF DISTANCE OVER A 50 FT OBSTACLE.

EXAMPLE:

OAT	75°F
PRESSURE ALTITUDE	4000 FT
TAKEOFF WEIGHT	3200 LBS
HEAD WIND	10 KNOTS
TOTAL TAKEOFF DISTANCE OVER A 50 FT OBSTACLE	2190 FT
GROUND ROLL (59% OF 2190)	1292 FT
IAS TAKEOFF SPEED LIFTOFF	79 MPH
AT 50 FT	90 MPH

WEIGHT POUNDS	IAS TAKEOFF SPEED (ASSUMES ZERO INSTR. ERROR)			
	LIFT-OFF		50 FEET	
	MPH	KNOTS	MPH	KNOTS
3400	81	70	92	80
3200	79	69	90	78
3000	76	66	87	76
2800	73	63	84	73
2600	70	61	80	70
2400	67	58	77	67

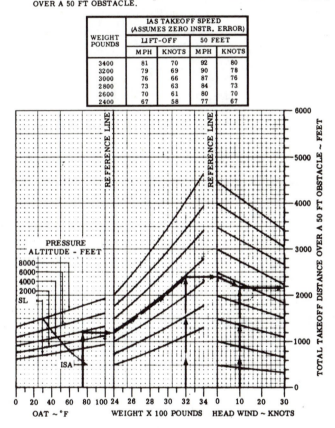

Fig. 5-23. *One chart that combines temperature, pressure altitude, aircraft weight, and winds to determine total takeoff distance in feet to clear a 50-foot obstacle.*

weight, and winds—are made part of one chart or graph and how the takeoff distance required to clear the 50-foot obstacle is then determined.

To walk through a problem using Fig. 5-23, refer first to the situations at the top of the figure—the conditions and the data under

"Example." The problem is, just as was said, to determine the total distance that is required to take off and clear a 50-foot obstacle under the conditions stated and at the takeoff speed indicated for an aircraft weighing 3200 pounds. Next, note the three "panels" that make up the chart—those identified as "OAT – °F," "Weight × 100 Pounds," and "Headwind-Knots."

To start out, the first thing is to determine the density altitude of, in this case, a 4000-foot airport at a 75 degree temperature. Accordingly, draw a heavy black line from the 75° mark until it meets the upward-curving 4000-foot pressure line. At the point of intersection, draw a heavy line at right angles to the vertical temperature line until it meets the Weight column.

Draw a heavy line over the abutting upward-sloping weight line until it meets the vertical drawn up from the "32," representing the 3200 pounds. At the point of meeting, draw another right angle off the vertical until it meets the wind panel. There, draw a line paralleling the down-sweeping wind line until it meets the vertical line from the "10," or 10 knots wind speed mark. One more right angle to the vertical is drawn until it meets the extreme right of the graph, ending at the almost-2200 foot mark—actually 2190.

The conclusion from the exercise? Under the conditions stated, the aircraft requires a takeoff run of 2190 feet to clear the 50-foot obstacle. And the calculations were all determined from one chart.

Quickie quiz questions
Chapter 5

1. For weight and balance (W&B) computations, what are the accepted standard weights for:

   Crew and passengers?

   Fuel?

   Oil?

   Water?

2. In terms of weight and balance, define:

Arm

Moment

Datum

3. What are some of the effects of high-density altitude on engine performance and propeller efficiency?

4. What effect can ground effect have on aircraft takeoffs and landings?

5. How can wind affect takeoffs and landings?

(No other questions about this chapter, as several problems are presented in the text materials.) Answers in Appendix, pages 574-575.

6

Weather

Despite the improvements in aircraft design, power plants, radio aids, and navigation techniques, safety in flight is still subject to conditions that broadly produce the three basic weather-related hazards: limited visibility, turbulence, and icing. It's thus obvious that to avoid such conditions, pilots must have a knowledge of the atmosphere and of weather behavior.

That, of course, raises the question of how *much* knowledge they need this day and age because of (1) the AFSSs (Automated Flight Service Stations), and (2) DUAT (Direct User Access Terminal). There was a time when pilots had to know the multitude of weather symbols, be able to decode the various weather reports and forecasts, and read as well as interpret surface analysis, weather depiction, radar summary, and other charts or maps that displayed the weather's current conditions and its probable tendencies.

Things have changed, though. With an AFSS within a toll-free phone call of almost every pilot, you can get all the information you need from a skilled and qualified briefer about an intended flight—and get it in plain English. No decoding necessary. The only thing you won't get over the phone is a weather map. So the question: How much do you need to know about the construction, the decoding, and the interpretation of the actual physical weather reports and maps? All of that the AFSS briefer does for you. It's then up to you to decide whether you go or don't go.

And then there's DUAT. If you have a computer, a modem, and hold a current FAA medical certificate, you can dial up one of the DUAT contractors and, as with an AFSS, ask for and receive any and all information you could want. With DUAT, though, you have the advantage over an AFSS phone briefing: a printout of everything you have requested in both code and plain English. Also, with a laser printer or certain types of dot matrix printers, you can reproduce the weather maps as well.

So, with these sources, plus the TV weather channel, as well as the frequent colored radar reports presented by local TV stations, how much knowledge is essential versus incidental? Considering your ability to make sound operational decisions based on current and forecast conditions, one answer is that you really can't know too much. To fly safely and intelligently, you *must* have a solid understanding of weather fronts, cloud formations, fog, wind, the affects of heat, humidity, and high altitudes on flight, and so on and on.

On the other hand, the extent to which you have to be able to read and interpret maps or translate into plain English coded weather reports is debatable—especially when briefers and DUAT do that for you anyway. Several highly qualified and experienced instructors have indicated that the need for such abilities is rare—a fact that seems to be borne out by the relatively few weather map and symbol interpretation questions that are on the private pilot written test.

Considering everything, though, this book would be remiss if it failed to introduce you to some of the coded/decoded reports and warnings, the more common symbols used, and samples of various weather charts and maps. If nothing else, you should be aware of the types of data that are fed into the weather processing system and that are ultimately reported to the flying users. The time might well come when you would need to be familiar with the coded reports or the symbolized weather maps. Also, there are a fair number of pilots who are served only by the few remaining nonautomated FSSs and might be so served for some time to come. Thus the need to be able to read and interpret the reports and forecasts could be rather important. Consequently, while this chapter cannot transform you into an interpretive expert, it does provide the basics for understanding what you are reading or seeing. In the process, it might also answer questions as to why the whole subject of weather is so critical to every pilot.

While nonflyers and the ground-bound usually need little more weather information than what a TV weather person reports, it's a different story for the pilot. He or she must be able to grasp the significance of what trained meteorologists are currently reporting and what they forecast will occur, based on the movements of large air masses and on local conditions at points where weather stations are located. Air masses, though, are sometimes unpredictable, and weather stations in some areas are spaced rather widely apart. Consequently, as a pilot, it's critical to understand what could cause unfavorable weather to develop along a route of flight and what to do should that occur.

The meteorologist, though, can only predict the weather conditions; it's then up to you to decide whether a given flight might be risky, considering the type of aircraft you're flying, the equipment used, your flying ability, experience, and physical limitations.

This chapter, then, is designed to help you acquire a general background of weather knowledge by discussing four broad areas:

1. Weather data sources
2. The nature of the atmosphere
3. Aviation weather forecasts
4. Aviation weather reports

Within these areas, the following basics are reviewed, although not necessarily in the sequence indicated:

- Services provided by the National Weather Service and FAA to give the pilot weather information
- Sources of available weather information
- Knowledge required to understand the weather terms commonly used by meteorologists and weather briefers
- A brief introduction to weather charts and maps, aviation weather reports and forecasts, and of other data
- Conditions of clouds, wind, and weather that are inconvenient or dangerous, and those that the pilot can use to advantage
- Suggested methods to use in avoiding dangerous weather conditions
- Significance of cloud formations and precipitation areas that might be encountered during flight

Under the National Airspace Plan (NASP), designed in 1980 to move aviation into the twenty-first century, a portion of the plan affecting weather forecasting and reporting was intended to produce faster, more automated, and more extensive systems. Some of the projects have been completed, while others are in the experimental or installation stages.

A partial listing of those projects includes:

- More accurate and real-time weather reporting
- Automated weather observing systems
- Increased use of color radar graphics that are similar to but more detailed than those in commercial TV weather broadcasts
- Enhanced Flight Service Station computer systems for instant weather reports over extended cross-country routes
- Expansion of the Low Level Wind Shear Alert System (LLWAS)
- Consolidation of all Flight Service Stations into 61 Automated Flight Service Stations (AFSSs)
- High-speed communications and automated data processing systems that have eliminated the slower teletype circuits

Although this chapter is not designed to discuss the details of weather data accumulation and how it is made available to the users, the following is a summary of the system and the principal National Oceanic and Atmospheric Administration (NOAA) and FAA agencies that are involved in the process. For more details, excellent references are the FAA's *Aviation Weather Services* (AC 00-45C) publication, the FAA/National Weather Service handbook, *Aviation Weather* (AC 00-6A), and *AIM (Airman's Information Manual)*, Chapter 7, Paragraphs 7-1 through 7-28.

Some of the key aviation weather data sources

In the process of obtaining, recording, analyzing, forecasting, and distributing weather data, a wide variety of sources as well as functions are involved. The sources range from a simple radio call to a Flight Service Station, in which a pilot reports a particular weather condition, up to sophisticated weather satellites. The functions, meanwhile, range from Flight Service Stations, airport Control Towers, and Air Route Traffic Control Centers, to various offices such as the National Meteorological Center, National Hurricane Center, National Severe Storms Center, and a few other organizational units that ensure the accurate and rapid distribution of weather data.

First, however, a few words about observations and the accumulation of that data.

Observations

Weather observations are measurements and estimates of existing weather both at the surface and aloft. When recorded and transmitted, an observation becomes a report, and these reports are the basis for all weather analyses and forecasts. It is then through high-speed communications and computers that the flow of weather reports reach the service outlets for dissemination to the user.

Surface observations. A network of airport stations provides routine surface observations at more than 600 airports. Most of the observations are produced by NWS (National Weather Service) or FAA personnel, although military services and contracted civilians also provide the service.

A major development in the surface weather observation network over the past few years has been the installation of automated weather reporting systems at Tower- and nontower airports. I'll review these later, but for identification, the two in question are called AWOS (Automated Weather Observing System) and ASOS (Automated Surface Observing System).

Radar observations. Another important source of weather data comes from radar and the Remote Radar Weather Display System (RRWDS), both of which reflect echoes of precipitation on the radar scopes. Particularly significant is RRWDS. This system provides real-time weather information from many different remoted radars and presents color video displays comparable to those of private enterprise. The display is routed to FSSs, the Air Route Traffic Control Center (ARTCC) meteorologist, and is connected to FAA and Air Force Air Route Surveillance Radars as well as NWS radars. Being remoted, RRWDS thus gives briefers real-time radar weather information from areas of the country where it was previously not available.

NWS radar covers nearly all of the United States east of the Rocky Mountains. Coverage of the rest of the country is provided by ARTCC radars.

Other observations. Additional sources of weather data come from radiosonde balloons, released twice daily at specific stations across the United States. These transmit temperature, humidity, barometric pressure, and winds from altitudes often in excess of 100,000 feet.

Two types of weather satellites are also in use: GOES, a Geostation-ary Operational Environmental Satellite, and NOAA (the National Oceanic and Atmospheric Administration), which is a near-polar orbiter satellite. Two GOES are used for picture-taking, with one sta-tioned over the equator at 75 degrees west and the other at 135 degrees west. Together, they cover North and South America and surrounding waters, normally transmitting a picture of the earth, pole to pole, each half hour. Being stationary, however, the pictures poleward become significantly distorted. Thus the NOAA near-polar orbiter satellite is employed to produce a high resolution picture about 800 miles either side of its track on its pole-to-pole journey.

The satellites transmit two types of images: The one produced by GOES is "visible imagery" (Fig. 6-1), which is a picture of clouds and the earth reflecting sunlight to the satellite sensor. The greater the reflection, the whiter the object is on the picture. As thick clouds produce more reflectivity, the picture makes it possible to determine

Fig. 6-1. *The visible imagery produced by the Geostationary Operational Environmental Satellite (GOES).*

the presence of clouds as well as the type of cloud from shape and texture.

The NOAA satellite, on the other hand, produces "infrared imagery" (IR) (Fig. 6-2). An IR picture shows temperature differences between cloud types and the ground, based on heat radiated from the clouds and the earth. Simply put, IR pictures are used to determine cloud top temperatures and thus their approximate heights.

Weather Forecast Offices and FSSs receive the satellite pictures every 30 minutes. With that frequency, meteorologists and specialists can monitor the development or dissipation of weather all over the country.

Another very important source of data is pilots and their pilot reports (PIREPs). Despite the technological advances, no one knows better what the actual weather conditions are than someone who is, or has just been, in them. Although PIREPs are discussed later, you are

Fig. 6-2. *An example of the infrared imagery produced by the National Oceanic and Atmospheric Administration's (NOAA) satellite.*

urged to keep FSS personnel, ARTCC controllers, or other appropriate ground personnel informed of conditions that vary from those
forecast or that might affect the flight plan strategies of others in the
general area.

Meteorological and forecast centers

Functioning under The National Oceanic and Atmospheric Administration (NOAA), meteorological centers collect and analyze the
weather data received and prepare forecasts on a national, hemispheric, or worldwide basis. Just so you can become familiar with
them, here are some of the prime contributors to the forecasting and
reporting process:

- The National Meteorological Center (NMC) of the National
  Weather Service (NWS), located in Maryland, is the hub of
  all weather processing. From worldwide weather reports, it
  provides guidance forecasts and charts of observed and
  forecast weather for use by the various forecast facilities
  described below.

- National Severe Storms Forecast Center (NSSFC), located in
  Oklahoma City, prepares forecasts of severe convective
  storms over the contiguous 48 states.

- National Hurricane Center (NHC) in Miami develops
  hurricane forecasting techniques and issues hurricane
  forecasts for the Atlantic, the Caribbean, the Gulf of
  Mexico, and adjacent land areas. The Hurricane Warning
  Center in Honolulu issue warnings for the eastern and
  central Pacific.

- National Environmental Satellite Data and Information Service
  (NESDIS), located in Washington, D.C., directs the weather
  satellite program and works in close cooperation with the
  NMC and the Satellite Field Service Stations.

Aviation Weather Center (AWC), located in Kansas City, originates
the centralized aviation forecast program. All inflight advisories
(SIGMETs, convective and nonconvective SIGMETs, and AIRMETs)
and all Area Forecasts for six areas in the conterminous United
States are issued by the AWC. These and all other aviation weather
forecasts are given wide distribution through the Weather Message
Switching Centers (WMSC), located in Atlanta and Salt Lake City.

Weather Forecast Offices (WFO) prepare and distribute various public and aviation-oriented forecasts and weather warnings for their areas of responsibility. Over 100 WFOs are located around the country, and among their products are approximately 500 terminal forecasts issued three times daily in the contiguous 48 states and the Caribbean (four times daily in Alaska and Hawaii), more than 300 route forecasts, and 39 synopses for Transcribed Weather Broadcasts (TWEBs) and the Pilot's Automatic Telephone Weather Answering Service (PATWAS) for briefing purposes.

Service outlets

Disregarding the various (and sometimes complex) internal processes, an almost continuous flow of weather data, beginning with observations, through the Meteorological and Forecast Centers, reaches the Service Outlets, either government or nongovernment, that provide aviation weather service. Only FAA and NWS outlets are discussed in this chapter.

Flight service stations (FSSs)

The 61 Automated Flight Service Stations across the country provide more aviation weather services than any other government service outlet. Included are preflight and inflight briefings, flight plan filing, scheduled and unscheduled weather broadcasts, and weather advisories to known flights in the FSS area.

Because of the high number of flight operations, these automated FSSs also provide transcribed briefings. A pilot, by listening to a recording, can assess the need for a more detailed in-person or telephone briefing by an FSS specialist. The principal recorded source, largely replacing the telephone access to the Transcribed Weather Broadcasts (TEL-TWEBs) and the Pilot's Automatic Telephone Weather Answering Service (PATWAS), is the Transcribed Information Briefing Service (TIBS). TIBS, however, is available only at the Automated Flight Service Stations, the AFSSs, while PATWAS is available at the relatively few nonautomated FSSs. (Because the AFSSs predominate throughout the United States, I'll refer to them simply as FSSs from this point on. Should a given service be provided solely by a nonautomated FSS, the FSS will be so identified.)

Another form of TWEB is a continuous en route weather broadcast on low to medium frequencies (200 to 415 kHz) and selected VORs (108.0 to 117.95 MHz). This service, however, is being replaced by HIWAS (Hazardous Inflight Weather Alert Service) VOR transmissions.

TIBS. In a bit more detail, TIBS is a continuous telephone recording of meteorological and/or aeronautical information provided by the Automated Flight Service Stations. Once accessed (a touch-tone phone is necessary for maximum use of the service), the caller has the ability to obtain weather information within a 50-mile radius of several locations in the FSS's area, as well as a weather synopsis for the area, thunderstorm activity, winds aloft, ATC delays, and information on how to get a good weather briefing.

TIBS thus assists in the preflight planning process and in determining whether flight to a given location should be considered. It should never serve, however, as a substitute for an FSS specialist's *standard* briefing, unless the reported conditions make the planned flight obviously impractical.

Computerized briefings. One of the computerized services available is Direct User Access Terminal, or DUAT, which allows you to obtain weather briefings and file flight plans from your home or office with a modem-equipped computer. Except for the telephone charge, the service is free, but it can be accessed only by a certificated pilot with a current medical. Two companies, under government contract, currently provide the DUAT service: GTE Federal Systems, in Chantilly, Virginia, and Data Transformation Corporation, of Turnerville, New Jersey. Both offer almost identical services, so which you contact is your choice.

One of DUAT's several advantages is that the weather information you want is usually immediately available and, if you request, it can be printed out for you in code along with the plain English translation. If you want a standard briefing, what you'll get is the same information an FSS briefer would give, in the same sequence. Then with NOTAMs (Notices to Airmen) added at the end, you'll have everything you need to know what conditions exist, or are forecast to exist, along your intended flight route. Even though you'll be given everything the FSS briefing specialist would give you over the phone, and more, the big plus DUAT offers is the printout of the entire briefing. With that in hand, you have the chance to study the current and forecast conditions more thoroughly and be better prepared to make a go/no-go decision.

Relative to a "go" decision, another DUAT plus is that you can file a flight plan with it, which means that you don't have to take the time to phone or make a radio call to an FSS. On a bad-weather day, trying to reach some FSSs could take time and maybe a few busy signals before you got a real-live briefer on the line.

One disadvantage of relying on DUAT at an airport is that several people might want weather information, at the same time, to widely different locations and/or to file flight plans. If the airport facility has only one computer, a phone call to the nearest FSS might be the most logical alternative.

Another DUAT disadvantage is the absence of human interaction. The data DUAT spews out are the same, and maybe more, than what a briefer would give, but DUAT offers no opportunity to question, discuss, evaluate, seek alternate routes, investigate the possibility of minor detours around bad-weather areas, or the like. This is where the live communication interchange between pilot and briefer can be so important and so much more meaningful than the cold printed word.

That said, though, the pluses of DUAT are unquestioned, and if the FAA doesn't decide to drop it (which it threatened to do a few years ago because of alleged costs), it will only increase in both value and pilot use.

En route flight advisory service (EFAS). Commonly called "Flight Watch," EFAS is a live (nonrecorded) service to pilots in flight who want weather reports along their route. All that's necessary is to contact an FSS on the common low-altitude Flight Watch frequency of 122.0 MHz and verbally address the call to the Air Route Traffic Control Center— repeat, the Air Route Traffic Control Center—responsible for the geographic area in which the FSS is located. Transmitting on 122.0, the call automatically goes to the appropriate FSS and the FSS weather specialist manning Flight Watch. After giving the aircraft call sign, identify the VOR that is closest to your current position. The specialist needs this information in order to select the best transmitter/receiver outlet for communication coverage.

To illustrate: You're flying near Albany, Georgia. The FSS Flight Watch is in Macon, and the ARTCC is located in Atlanta. The call on 122.0: "Atlanta Center, Cherokee 1234 Alpha, Albany VOR."

If you're not sure which ARTCC has jurisdiction over the area, the call, still on 122.0, then, is "Flight Watch, Cherokee 1234 Alpha at

(Blank) VOR (or identify some prominent geographic location)." The appropriate FSS then responds.

The Flight Watch specialist maintains a continuous weather watch, provides time-critical assistance to en route pilots facing hazardous or unknown weather, and may recommend alternate or diversionary routes. Additionally, Flight Watch is a focal point for rapid receipt and dissemination of pilot reports.

Other service outlets

Although FSSs are the most frequent source of weather data for pilots, other outlets such as these can be equally valuable:

Air Route Traffic Control Centers (ARTCC or "Center") advise traffic under their control of significant weather. The controller may also inform pilots of forecast weather conditions affecting airports that could cause a change in flight plans. Automatic Terminal Information Service (ATIS) is a recording, updated once an hour or more frequently if changing conditions warrant, that advises arriving and departing pilots of current weather conditions and other pertinent local airport information. The service is available at most (but not all) Tower-controlled airports and can be accessed by telephone or by tuning to the published radio frequency for the airport in question. Pilots are expected to monitor the ATIS before taxiing out for takeoff and before contacting the terminal controller for landing instructions.

Controllers in the terminal area (whether in the Tower cab itself or in Approach/Departure Control) communicate to arriving and departing aircraft rapidly changing local conditions, such as wind speeds or wind direction, that might differ from the last ATIS report.

Users of the service outlets

Many people use the Aviation Weather Service, but pilots are the primary customers. That being so, they should contribute to the completeness and accuracy of the service by communicating weather conditions encountered during flight. How to do this? By providing the nearest or most appropriate weather outlet with what are called *PIREPs*, or pilot reports. A PIREP reflects real-time data on conditions such as unexpected turbulence, precipitation, icing, cloud levels, visibility, and the like. As a major source of *current* information, the PIREP helps forecasters develop a more accurate picture of existing conditions and so inform other pilots—information that might cause them to alter their flight route, their altitude, or intended point of landing. PIREPS can be given on the ground by telephone or in the air by radio to terminal controllers, an FSS specialist, or to Flight Watch.

An important user responsibility is to obtain a complete weather briefing before each flight, particularly a flight of any distance from the departing point. Discussion of the types of briefings an FSS can give, what information the pilot should provide in what sequence, and what data the briefing contains is reserved for Chap. 10.

Suffice it to say, a weather briefing is complete only when you have a clear understanding of the conditions you can expect to encounter on the flight. Depending on what the briefing tells you, be sure to have an alternate plan in mind, especially if the weather is questionable. While en route, if conditions deteriorate to the extent that safe flight is questionable, make an immediate turn away from the adverse weather. Without proper planning, though, and knowing where the hazardous weather lies, you could divert the wrong way and head into even more serious problems. If it should be necessary, a planned rerouting (which may be a 180-degree turn) that will take you to an area of safer weather is obviously far superior to a panicky, spur-of-the-moment decision that could lead to disaster.

Before discussing the various kinds of aviation forecasts and reports available to pilots, some of the basics of weather with which pilots must be familiar are reviewed next. These include the nature of the atmosphere, atmospheric pressure, wind, moisture, temperature, condensation, and air masses and fronts. Once these basics are mastered, the forecasts and reports will be more meaningful and, hopefully, lead to better preflight planning.

The nature of the atmosphere

Life exists at the bottom of an ocean of air called the atmosphere. This ocean extends upward from the earth's surface for many miles, gradually thinning as it nears the top, although its exact upper limit has never been determined. Near the surface, the air is relatively warm from contact with the earth, with the temperature in the United States averaging about 15°C (59°F) the year round. As altitude increases, the temperature decreases by approximately 2°C (3.5°F) for every 1000 feet (the normal lapse rate) until it reaches about –55°C (–67°F) at seven miles above the earth.

For flight purposes, the atmosphere is divided into two layers: the upper layer, beginning at about 35,000 feet, where temperature remains practically constant, is the stratosphere; the lower layer, rising from the surface to approximately 35,000 feet, where the temperature changes, is the troposphere (Fig. 6-3). Although jets routinely fly in the stratosphere, the private pilot rarely has occasion to go that high, usually remaining in the troposphere. It's in this area where all weather occurs and practically all light airplane flying is done.

Obviously, a body of air as deep as the atmosphere has tremendous weight, and it's difficult to realize that the normal sea-level pressure

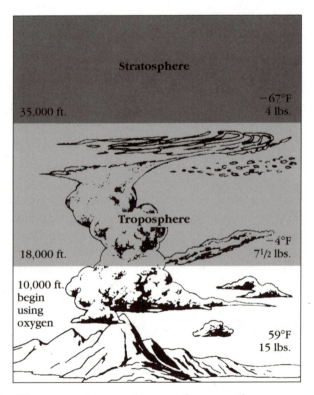

Fig. 6-3. *The troposphere and stratosphere are the upper realm of flight.*

on the body is about 15 pounds per square inch. This means that a column of air one inch square extending from sea level to the top of the atmosphere would weigh about 15 pounds, or roughly 20 tons on the average person. The body does not collapse because this pressure is balanced by an equal pressure within the body. In fact, if the external pressure were suddenly released, the human body would explode.

As altitude is gained, the air becomes thinner, meaning, of course, that there is less pressure. At first, pressure reduces rapidly up to about 18,000 feet, where it is only half as great as at sea level. And, as the pressure decreases, so does the air temperature, being almost always below the freezing level above 18,000 feet.

Oxygen and the human body

The atmosphere is composed of gases, about 78 percent of which is nitrogen, 21 percent oxygen, and 1 percent various other gases. Oxygen, of course, is essential to human life, but at 18,000 feet, with only half the normal atmospheric pressure, the oxygen intake would be only half the required amount. At that point, body reactions become definitely subnormal, and unconsciousness can easily follow—which means that unless the cabin or cockpit is pressurized, oxygen-breathing equipment becomes critical to life itself.

Measurement of atmospheric pressure

A barometer is generally used to measure the height of a column of mercury in a glass tube, sealed at one end and calibrated in inches. An increase in pressure forces the mercury higher in the tube, while a decrease allows some of the mercury to drain out, reducing the height of the column. In this way, changes of pressure are registered in inches of mercury. The standard sea-level pressure expressed in these terms is 29.92 inches at a standard temperature of 15°C (59°F).

The mercury barometer, however, is sometimes both cumbersome and difficult to read. A more compact, more easily read, and more mobile barometer is the aneroid, although not as accurate as the mercurial. The aneroid barometer is a partially evacuated cell that expands or contracts with pressure changes. The cell is then linked to an indicator that moves across a scale graduated in pressure units.

If all weather stations were at sea level, the barometer readings would give a correct record of the distribution of atmospheric pressure at a common level. Since that's not the case, to achieve a common level, each station translates its barometer reading into terms of sea-level pressure. A change of 1000 feet of elevation makes a change of about one inch on the barometer reading. Thus, if the reading was 25 inches high in the barometer tube at a station located 5000 feet above sea level, the station would translate and report this reading as 30 inches of mercury at sea level, or "30.00 inches msl" (mean sea level) (Fig. 6-4).

Because the rate of decrease in atmospheric pressure is fairly constant in the lower layers of the atmosphere, your approximate altitude can be determined by finding the difference between pressure at sea level and the pressure at the given atmospheric level, on the basis of the loss of about one inch of pressure per 1000 feet.

If you're on the ground at an airport that can't provide the current barometric pressure, you can determine it by reference to the aircraft altimeter. Since the altimeter is, in itself, an aneroid barometer, just turn the hands to the airport altitude and then refer to the reading in the little window on the face of the altimeter. That gives you the current sea level barometric pressure at that location.

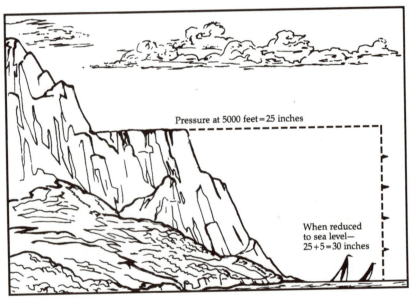

Pressure at 5000 feet = 25 inches

When reduced
to sea level—
25 + 5 = 30 inches

Fig. 6-4. *Barometric pressure at a weather station is expressed in terms of sea level pressure.*

The obvious conclusion from all of this is that as altitude increases, pressure becomes less as the weight of the air column decreases. Accordingly, you could conclude that the pressure decrease should have a pronounced effect on flight . . . which raises the matter of "density altitude."

The meaning of "density altitude"

Density altitude is so much a part of aviation weather that, despite an explanation of it in Chap. 5, I can't avoid a brief discussion of it at this point. So bear with me . . .

The higher the altitude, the less the air pressure. The less the pressure, the thinner the air becomes, or, said another way, the less dense it becomes. The less dense the air, the more it takes on the characteristics of a higher altitude. So when you say that an airport, for instance, has a "high density altitude," the word "high" is not describing the density but the fact that the airport possesses the characteristics of high *altitude* because the air is less dense. And, if the temperature at that airport is also high, the air is thinner yet, which produces the characteristics of an even higher altitude. So when you hear the phrase, "high density altitude," interpret it as "high altitude reading because of low (or lower) air density." Keep in mind that the "high" refers to the altitude, not the density.

Perhaps this is self-evident, but the meaning of "high density altitude" has confused more than one student pilot, so a brief explanation seemed appropriate at this point.

Effect of altitude on flight

The most noticeable effect of a decrease in pressure (increase in density altitude), due to an altitude increase, becomes evident in takeoffs, rates of climb, and landings. An airplane that requires a 1000-foot run for takeoff at a sea-level airport needs almost double that at an airport approximately 5000 feet above sea level (Fig. 6-5). The purpose of the takeoff run, of course, is to gain enough speed to generate lift from the passage of air over the wings. If the air is thin, more speed is needed to obtain enough lift for takeoff, hence, a longer ground run. At the same time, the engine is less efficient in thin air and the thrust of the propeller is less effective. The rate of climb is also slower at the higher elevation, requiring a greater distance to gain the altitude necessary to clear any obstructions. In landing, the difference is not as noticeable, except that the plane has greater groundspeed when it touches the ground.

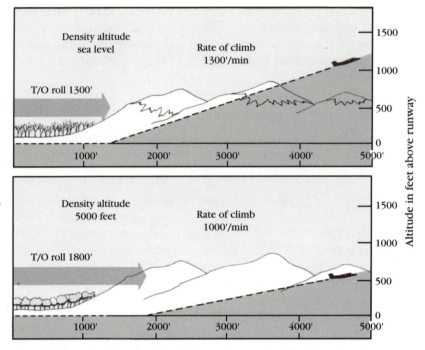

Fig. 6-5. *High density altitude lengthens takeoff roll and reduces rate of climb.*

Effect of differences in air density

Differences in air density caused by changes in temperature result in changes in pressure, which, in turn, creates motion in the atmosphere, both vertically and horizontally (currents and winds). That action, when mixed with moisture, produces clouds and precipitation, which, in fact, are all the phenomena making up this thing called "weather."

Millibars vs. mercury

The mercury barometer reading at the individual weather stations is converted to the equivalent sea-level pressure and then translated from terms of inches of mercury to a measure of pressure called *millibars* or "mbs," for short. One inch of mercury is equivalent to approximately 34 mbs; hence, the normal atmospheric pressure at sea level (29.92), expressed in millibars, is 1013.2 or roughly 1000 millibars. The usual pressure readings range from 950.0 to 1040.0 mbs, so for economy of space, the entry is shortened on some reports by omitting the initial 9 or 10 and the decimal point. On the hourly weather report, a number beginning with 5 or higher presupposes an initial "9," whereas a number beginning with a four or lower presupposes an initial "10." For example: 653 = 965.3; 346 = 1034.6; 999 = 999.9; 001 = 1000.1; etc. If the sea level pressure in an aviation weather report is coded "132," it is decoded as "1013.2 millibars."

Individually, these pressure readings are of no particular value to the pilot, but when pressures at different stations are compared, or when pressures at the same station show changes in successive readings, you have one of the many symptoms reflecting the trend of weather conditions. In general, a marked fall indicates the approach of bad weather and a marked rise is a sign of clearing weather.

Wind

The pressure and temperature changes discussed in the previous section produce two kinds of motion in the atmosphere: vertical movement of ascending and descending currents, and horizontal flow known as *wind*. Both of these motions are of primary interest to the pilot because they affect the flight of aircraft during takeoff, climb, cruise, and landing. This motion also brings about changes in weather, which might make the difference between a safe flight or a disastrous one.

Conditions of wind and weather occurring at any specific place and time are the result of the general circulation in the atmosphere. The atmosphere tends to maintain an equal pressure over the entire earth, just as the ocean tends to maintain a constant level. When the equilibrium is disturbed, air begins to flow from areas of higher pressure to areas of lower pressure—which leads to the next point:

The cause of atmospheric circulation

The factor that upsets the normal equilibrium is the uneven heating of the earth. At the equator, the earth receives more heat than in areas to the north and south. This heat is transferred to the atmosphere, warming the air and causing it to expand and become less dense. Colder air to the north and south, being more dense, moves toward the equator forcing the less dense air upward. The colder air, in turn, becomes warmer and less dense, thus establishing a constant circulation that might consist of two circular paths: the air rising at the equator, traveling aloft toward the poles, and returning along the earth's surface to the equator, as shown in Fig. 6-6.

This theoretical pattern, however, is greatly modified by many forces, an important one being the rotation of the earth. In the Northern Hemisphere, the rotation causes air to deflect to the right of its normal path and to the left of its path in the Southern Hemisphere. For simplicity, the discussion here is confined to the motion of air in the Northern Hemisphere (Fig. 6-7).

As the air rises and moves northward from the equator, it is deflected toward the east, and by the time it has traveled about a third of the distance to the pole, it is no longer moving northward, but eastward. This causes the air to accumulate in a belt at about latitude 30°, creating an area of high pressure. Some of the air is then forced down to the earth's surface, where part flows southwestward, returning to the equator, and part flows northeastward along the surface.

A portion of the air aloft continues its journey northward, being cooled en route, and finally settles down near the pole, where it begins a return trip toward the equator. Before it has progressed very far southward, it comes into conflict with the warmer surface air

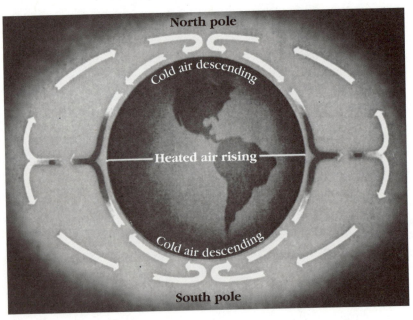

Fig. 6-6. *Heat at the equator would cause the air to circulate uniformly, as shown, if the earth did not rotate.*

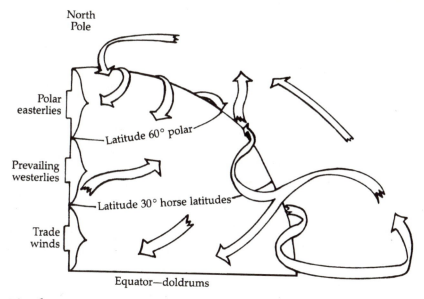

Fig. 6-7. *The arrows reflect the principal air currents in the Northern Hemisphere.*

flowing northward from latitude 30°. The warmer air moves up over a wedge of the colder air and continues northward, producing an accumulation of air in the upper latitudes.

Further complications in the general circulation of the air are brought about by the irregular distribution of oceans and continents, the relative effectiveness of different surfaces in transferring heat to the atmosphere, the daily variation in temperature, and the seasonal changes, to mention just a few of the factors.

Regions of low pressure, called lows, develop where air lies over land or water surfaces that are warmer than the surrounding areas. In India, for example, a low forms over the hot land during the summer months, but moves out over the warmer ocean when the land cools in winter. Lows of this type are semipermanent, however, and are less significant to the pilot than the *migratory cyclones* or *cyclonic depressions* that form when unlike air masses meet. These lows are discussed later in this chapter under *Occlusions.*

Wind patterns

The focus of attention here is on the wind patterns associated with areas of high and low pressure. As I just said, air flows from an area of high pressure to one of low pressure. In the Northern Hemisphere during this flow, the air is deflected to the right. Thus, as the air leaves the high-pressure area, it produces a clockwise circulation. But, as it flows toward the low-pressure area, it is again deflected and produces a counterclockwise flow around the low-pressure area.

Another important aspect is that movement out of a high-pressure area depletes the quantity of air. Consequently, highs are areas of descending air. Descending air tends to dissipate cloudiness, hence the association: high pressure equals good weather. By similar reasoning, when air converges into a low-pressure area, it can't go outward against the pressure gradient and it can't go downward into the ground. Its only path is upward. Rising air is conducive to cloudiness and precipitation, so, again, we have the general association that low pressure equals bad weather.

A knowledge of these patterns frequently enables pilots to plan a course that takes advantage of favorable winds, particularly during long flights. In flying from east to west, for example, you would find favorable winds to the south of a high or to the north of a low (Figs. 6-8 and 6-9). The patterns also give pilots a general idea of the type of weather to expect relative to the highs and lows.

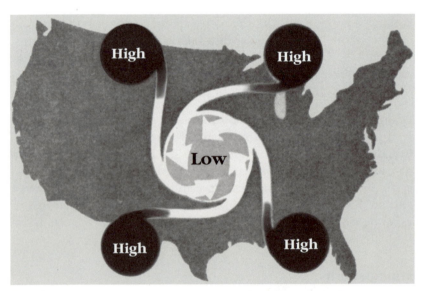

Fig. 6-8. *The wind circulates counterclockwise around a low-pressure area.*

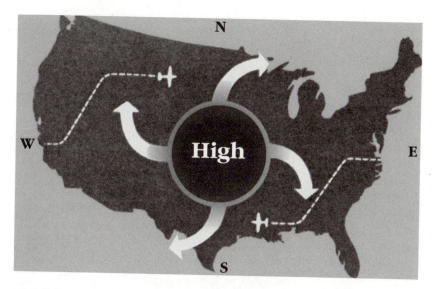

Fig. 6-9. *Winds flow clockwise around a high-pressure area—and how to take advantage of the flow in flight.*

So much for the "theory" of air circulation in the atmosphere and the formation of wind patterns. The theory explains the large-scale movements of the wind but does not take into account the effects of local conditions that frequently cause drastic modifications in wind direction and speed near the earth's surface. Hence the following review of some of those conditions.

Convection currents

Certain kinds of surfaces are more effective than others in heating the air directly above them. Plowed ground, sand, rocks, and barren land give off a great deal of heat, whereas water and vegetation tend to absorb and retain heat. The uneven heating of the air causes small local circulations, called convection currents, which are similar to the general circulation just described.

These circulations are particularly noticeable over land adjacent to a body of water. During the day, the air over land becomes heated and less dense and colder air over the water moves in to replace it, forcing the warm air aloft and causing an onshore wind. At night the land cools, and the water is relatively warmer. The cool air over the land, being heavier, then moves toward the water as an offshore wind, lifting the warmer air and reversing the circulation (Figs. 6-10 and 6-11).

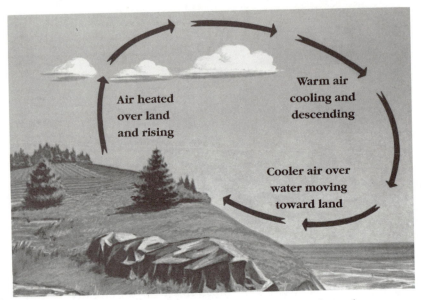

Fig. 6-10. *Convection currents form onshore winds in the daytime.*

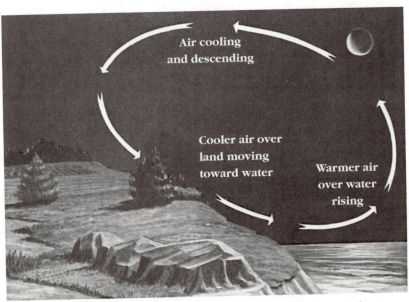

Fig. 6-11. *And convection currents produce offshore winds at night.*

Convection currents cause the bumpiness you often experience flying at low altitudes in warmer weather. On a low flight over varying surfaces, you'll encounter updrafts over pavement or barren places and downdrafts over vegetation or water. Ordinarily, this can be avoided by flying at higher altitudes. When the larger convection currents form cumulus clouds, you'll invariably find smooth air above the cloud level (Fig. 6-12).

Convection currents also cause difficulty in making landings, since they affect the rate of descent. For example, depending upon the presence and severity of convection currents, a pilot making a constant approach glide may tend to land short of or overshoot the intended landing spot, as illustrated in Figs. 6-13 and 6-14.

Effect of obstructions on wind

The effects of local convection in a landing or takeoff are, however, less dangerous than the turbulence caused by wind when it is forced to flow around or over obstructions. The only way for the pilot to avoid this invisible hazard is to be forewarned and to know where to expect unusual conditions.

Fig. 6-12. *For smoother flights, get above the clouds formed by convection currents.*

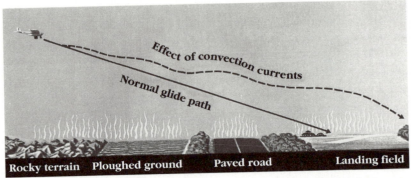

Fig. 6-13. *Varying surfaces affect the normal approach path. Some surfaces create rising currents that tend to cause the pilot to overshoot the field.*

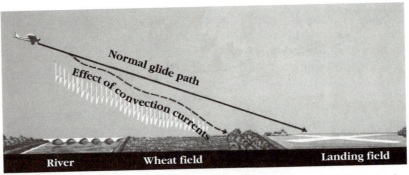

Fig. 6-14. *Descending currents prevail above certain surfaces and tend to cause the pilot to land short of the field.*

When the wind flows around an obstruction, it breaks into eddies or gusts with sudden changes in speed and direction that could be carried along some distance from the obstruction. A pilot flying through the potential of such turbulence should anticipate a bumpy and unsteady flight. The turbulence, the intensity of which depends on the size of the obstacle and the velocity of the wind, can present a serious hazard, particularly during takeoffs and landings. For example, in a landing, as Fig. 6-15 implies, it could cause severe turbulence just at a time when control of the aircraft is especially acute.

On a takeoff, the hazard is not quite as severe because you're presumably operating at full power and thus have better and more

Fig. 6-15. *Watch out for turbulence caused by obstructions when landing or taking off.*

instantaneous control of the plane. When first airborne and at initial lift-off airspeed, however, you're still at the mercy of the turbulence, so caution and preparedness are essential. Considering these phenomena, landings especially should be made at higher speeds under gusty conditions to be sure to maintain adequate control.

The same turbulent condition is even more noticeable when larger obstructions such as bluffs or mountains are involved. As shown in Fig. 6-16, the wind blowing up the slope on the windward side of a mountain is relatively smooth, and its upward current helps to carry the aircraft over the peak. The wind on the leeward side, however, following the terrain contour, flows sharply downward with considerable turbulence and would tend to force an aircraft into the mountainside. The stronger the wind, the greater the downward pressure and the accompanying turbulence. Consequently, if you're approaching a bluff or mountain from the leeward side, be sure to gain enough altitude well in advance to clear the obstacle. Because of these downdrafts, it's recommended that you be *at least* 2000 feet above mountain ridges and peaks. If there is any doubt about having adequate clearance, turn away at once and gain more altitude.

Between hills or mountains, where there is a canyon or narrow valley, the wind generally veers from its normal course and flows through the passage with increased velocity and turbulence. If you're flying over such terrain, be very much on the alert for wind shifts and be particularly cautious if you're coming in for a landing.

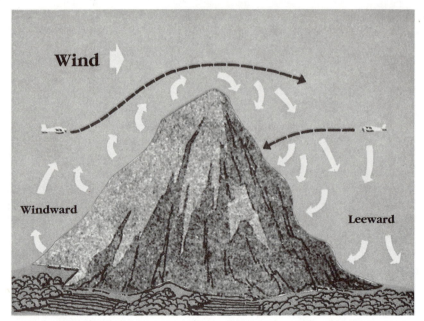

Fig. 6-16. *Airplanes approaching hills or mountains from the windward side are helped by rising currents. Those approaching from leeward encounter descending currents, which can be very powerful and dangerous.*

Low-level wind shear

Wind shear is best described as a change in wind direction and/or speed within a very short distance in the atmosphere. Under certain conditions, the atmosphere is capable of producing some dramatic shears very close to the ground. For example, wind direction changes of 180° and speed changes of 50 knots or more within 200 feet of the ground have been recorded. Although such shifts don't occur every day, it is their very rareness that makes them more of a problem.

Under normal conditions, wind doesn't have a major effect on an aircraft once it is flying, except for drift and groundspeed. This is true with steady winds or winds that change gradually, but it isn't true at all if the wind changes faster than the aircraft mass can be accelerated or decelerated—which is the major problem with wind shears.

The most prominent meteorological phenomena that cause significant low-level wind shear problems are thunderstorms and certain frontal systems at or near an airport. When those exist, red danger flags should wave prominently.

Basically, there are two potentially hazardous shear situations. First, a tailwind might suddenly shear to either a calm or headwind component. In this instance, the airspeed initially increases, the aircraft pitches up and the altitude increases. In the second situation, a headwind could shear to a calm or tailwind component. When that occurs, the airspeed initially decreases, the aircraft pitches down, and the altitude decreases. Aircraft speed, aerodynamic characteristics, power/weight ratio, powerplant response time, and pilot reactions, are among the other factors. that have a bearing on wind shear effects. What is important to remember, though, is that shear can cause problems for *any* aircraft and *any* pilot.

Two atmospheric conditions cause the type of low-level wind shear we're talking about. These are thunderstorms and fronts.

The winds around a thunderstorm are complex. Wind shear can be found on all sides of a cell, and the wind shift line or gust front associated with thunderstorms can precede the actual storm by as much as 15 nautical miles. Consequently, if a thunderstorm is near an airport of intended landing or takeoff, low-level wind shear hazards are very much a potential.

While the direction of the winds above and below a front can be accurately determined, existing hardware does not yet provide precise and current measurements of the height of the front above an airport. Regardless, the following is a method of estimating the approximate height of a front, keeping in mind that wind shear is most critical when it occurs close to the ground:

A cold front wind shear occurs just after the front passes the airport and for a short period thereafter. If the front is moving 30 knots or more, the frontal surface is usually 5000 feet above the airport about three hours after the frontal passage.

With a warm front, the most critical period is before the front passes the airport. Warm front shear can exist below 5000 feet for approximately six hours; the problem ceases after the front passes the airport. Data compiled on wind shear indicate that the amount of shear in warm fronts is much greater than that found in cold fronts.

Turbulence might or might not exist in wind shear conditions. If the surface wind under the front is strong and gusty there will be some turbulence associated with wind shear.

Suffice it to say that all pilots should be alert to the possibility of low-level wind shear any time the conditions stated are present.

Wind and pressure representation on surface weather maps

The excerpted portion of a surface weather map (Fig. 6-17) illustrates information about winds at the surface. The wind direction at each weather station (the "stations" are the large dots) is shown by an arrow that points in the direction towards which the wind is blowing. It's probably most apparent, but remember that winds are identified by the direction *from* which they blow—as a northwest wind is a wind blowing *from* the northwest.

Windspeed is indicated by the number of half feathers, full feathers, or pennants located on the end of the arrow. Each half feather represents approximately 5 knots, each full feather 10 knots, and each flag or pennant 50 knots. (**Note:** No pennants are visible in this Figure.) So, two full feathers plus a one-half feather indicate a 25-knot windspeed; a pennant, two feathers, and a one-half feather indicate a windspeed of approximately 75 knots, etc. Thus, at a glance, it's easy to determine the wind conditions prevailing at map time at any weather station.

The pressure at each station is recorded on the weather map, and lines (*isobars*) are drawn to connect points of equal pressure. Many

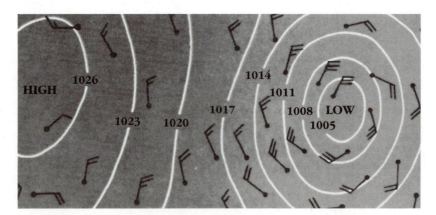

Fig. 6-17. *The speed and direction of the winds are shown on a weather map by wind arrows and isobars.*

of the lines make complete circles to surround pressure areas marked H (high) or L (low).

Isobars identify the amount of pressure and the steepness of pressure gradients. If the gradient (slope) is steep, the isobars are close together, and the wind is strong. If the gradient is gradual, the isobars are far apart, and the wind is gentle (Fig. 6-18).

Isobars furnish valuable information about winds in the first few thousand feet above the surface. Close to the earth, wind direction is modified by the contours over which it passes, and windspeed is reduced by friction with the surface. At levels 2000 or 3000 feet above the surface, however, the speed is greater and the direction is usually parallel to the isobars. Thus, while wind arrows on the weather map excerpt indicate wind near the surface, isobars indicate winds at slightly higher levels (Fig. 6-17 again).

In the absence of specific information on upper winds, you can often make a fairly reasonable estimate of conditions in the lower few thousand feet on the basis of the observed surface wind. As a general rule, winds at an altitude of 2000 feet above the surface are somewhere between 20° and 40° to the right of the surface direction and almost double in speed. The deviation is greatest over rough terrain and least over flat surfaces. Thus, a north wind of 20 knots at the airport is likely to change to a northeast wind of 40 knots at 2000 feet. More on this later in the chapter.

Moisture and temperature

The atmosphere always contains a certain amount of foreign matter, such as smoke, dust, salt particles, and particularly moisture in the form of invisible water vapor. The amount of moisture that can be present in the atmosphere depends upon the temperature of the air. For each increase of 20°F, the capacity of the air to hold moisture is about doubled; conversely, for each decrease of 20°F, the capacity becomes only half as much.

Relative humidity

Humidity is commonly referred to as the apparent dampness in the air. A similar term used by the National Weather Service is *relative*

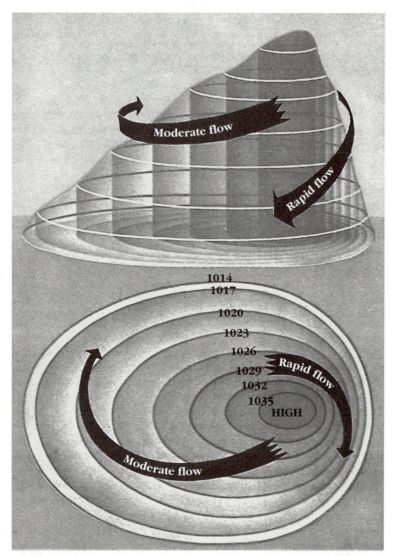

Fig. 6-18. *Above: Flow of air around a "high." Below: isobars on a weather map indicate various levels of pressure within a high.*

humidity, which is a ratio of the amount of moisture present in any given volume of air to the amount of moisture the air *could* hold in that volume of air at prevailing temperature and pressure. For in-stance, "75 percent relative humidity" means that the air contains three-fourths of the water vapor that it is capable of holding at the existing temperature and pressure.

Temperature-dewpoint relationship

For the pilot, relative humidity is expressed in terms of *temperature and dewpoint*. As indicated above, if a mass of air at 80°F has a relative humidity of 60 percent and the temperature is reduced 20° to 60°F, the air will then be saturated (100-percent relative humidity). In this example, the relationship would be stated as "temperature 80°F, dewpoint 60." In other words, dewpoint is the temperature to which air must be cooled to become saturated.

Dewpoint is of tremendous significance to the pilot because it represents a critical condition of the air. When a temperature reaches the dewpoint, water vapor can no longer remain invisible. Instead, it is forced to condense, becoming visible on the ground as dew or frost, appearing in the air as fog or clouds, or falling to the earth as rain, snow, or hail.

Note: This is how water can get into the fuel tanks when the tanks are left partially filled overnight. The temperature cools to the dewpoint and the water vapor contained in the fuel tank airspace condenses. This condensed moisture then sinks to the bottom of the fuel tank, because water is heavier than aviation fuel.

Methods by which air reaches the saturation point

Besides becoming saturated by precipitation, air can reach its saturation point by lowering the temperature under any of the following conditions: (1) Warm air moves over a cold surface; (2) cold air mixes with warm air; (3) air is cooled during the night by contact with the cold ground; or (4) air is forced upward. Some comments relative to the last . . . .

When air rises, it uses heat energy in expanding. Consequently, the rising air loses its heat rapidly. If the air is unsaturated, the loss is approximately 2.0°C for every 1000 feet of altitude.

Warm air can be lifted aloft by three methods: By becoming heated through contact with the earth's surface, resulting in convective currents; by moving up sloping terrain (as wind blowing up a mountainside); or by being forced to flow over another body of air (when air masses of different temperatures and densities meet). Under the last condition, the warmer, lighter air tends to flow over the cooler, denser air.

However it occurs, when temperature and dewpoint on the ground are close together, there is a good possibility for low clouds and fog to form.

(**Note:** While several of the above examples cite temperatures and dewpoint in both centigrade and Fahrenheit, they are reported in degrees Fahrenheit in the aviation weather report. When necessary or desirable to convert one reading to another, the chart in Fig. 6-19 can be useful. Here, as illustrated, 0°C equals 32°F. A ballpark method to convert centigrade to Fahrenheit is to double the centigrade figure and then add thirty degrees. For example, 25 degrees centigrade doubled is 50 degrees plus 30 equals 80 degrees Fahrenheit.

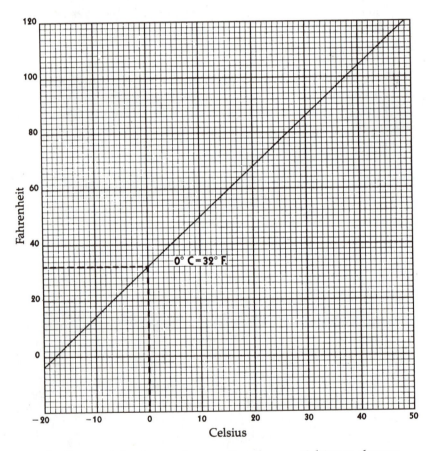

Fig. 6-19. *A quick means of converting degrees Celsius to degrees Fahrenheit, and vice versa.*

The accurate Fahrenheit temperature is 77 degrees, but the rule of thumb calculation is close enough for a rough approximation.)

Effect of temperature on air density

Atmospheric pressure not only varies with altitude, it varies also with temperature. When air is heated, it expands, contains fewer molecules, and therefore has less density. A cubic foot of warm air is less dense than a cubic foot of cold air. As you have undoubtedly already surmised after so many references to it, this decrease in air density, resulting in a higher density altitude, has a pronounced effect on flight.

Effect of temperature on flight

Because an increase in temperature makes the air less dense and increases density altitude, the takeoff run is longer on a hot day than on a cold day, the rate of climb slower, and the landing speed (groundspeed) faster. Thus, an increase in temperature has the same effect as an increase in altitude. An airplane that requires a ground run of 1000 feet on a winter day when the temperature is 0°F requires a much longer run on a summer day when the temperature is 100°F. In that respect, an airplane that requires the greater portion of a short runway for takeoff on a cold winter day might not be able to take off at all from the same runway on a hot summer day.

Effect of high humidity on air density

A common misconception is that water vapor weighs more than an equal volume of dry air. This is not true. Water vapor weighs approximately five-eighths or 62 percent of an equal volume of perfectly dry air. When the air contains moisture in the form of water vapor, it is not as heavy as dry air and so is less dense.

Assuming that temperature and pressure remain the same, the air density varies inversely with the humidity; that is, as the humidity increases, the air density decreases, (density altitude increases); and, as the humidity decreases, the air density increases (density altitude decreases).

The higher the temperature, the greater the moisture-carrying ability of the air. Therefore, air at a temperature of 100°F and a relative humidity of 80 percent contains a greater amount of moisture than air at a temperature of 60° and a relative humidity of 80 percent.

Effect of high humidity on flight

Because high humidity makes the air less dense, the takeoff roll will be longer, rate of climb slower, and landing speed higher.

It sounds like the same old song, but these various conditions make repetition inevitable. The effects of high altitude, high temperature, and high humidity on flight *must* be actively considered when these combinations of "highs" exist. Each can seriously affect flight characteristics, and when all three are present, the problem is aggravated. Therefore, beware of "high, hot, and humid" conditions that produce high density altitudes. Then take the necessary precautions by using performance charts to assure that the runway is long enough for takeoff.

Dew and frost

When the ground cools at night, the temperature of the air immediately adjacent to the ground is frequently lowered to the saturation point, causing condensation. This condensation takes place directly upon objects on the ground as dew if the temperature is above freezing, or as frost if the temperature is below freezing.

Dew is of no significance to aircraft, but frost creates friction that interferes with the smooth flow of air over the wing surfaces, resulting in a tendency to stall during takeoff. FROST SHOULD ALWAYS BE REMOVED BEFORE FLIGHT.

Fog

When the air near the ground is four or five degrees above the dewpoint, the water vapor condenses and becomes visible as fog. There are many types of fog, varying in degrees of intensity and classified according to the particular phenomena that cause them. One type, *ground fog*, which frequently forms at night in low places, is limited to a few feet in height and is usually dissipated by the heat of the sun shortly after sunrise. Other types, which can form any time conditions are favorable, might extend to greater heights and persist for days or even weeks. Along seacoasts, fog often forms over the ocean and is blown inland. All fogs produce low visibilities, with all the threats to aircraft that such conditions imply.

Clouds

There are two fundamental types of clouds. First, those formed by vertical currents carrying moist air upward to its condensation point are lumpy or billowy and are called *cumulus* (Fig. 6-20), which means an accumulation or a pile. Second, those that develop horizontally and lie in sheets or formless layers like fog are called *stratus* (Fig. 6-21), which means spread out.

When clouds are near the earth's surface they are generally designated as cumulus or stratus unless they are producing precipitation, in which case the word *nimbus* (meaning rain cloud) is added, as nimbostratus or cumulonimbus (Fig. 6-22).

If the clouds are ragged and broken, the word fracto (or "broken") is added, as fractostratus or fractocumulus.

The word *alto* ("high") is generally added to designate clouds at intermediate heights, usually appearing at levels of 5000 to 20,000 feet, as altostratus or altocumulus.

Clouds formed in the upper levels of the troposphere (commonly between 20,000 and 50,000 feet) are composed of ice crystals and

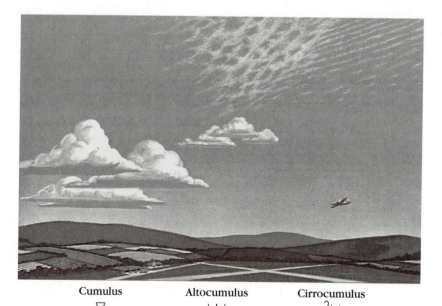

Cumulus   Altocumulus   Cirrocumulus

Fig. 6-20. *Cumulus clouds as they appear at low, intermediate, and high levels.*

Fog	Stratus	Altostratus	Cirrostratus	Cirrus
≡	⌄	╱╱	╱	2

Fig. 6-21. *Stratus-type clouds at various altitudes.*

Stratocumulus	Nimbostratus	Cumulonimbus	Fractocumulus
⌄	╱╱	⊟	– – –

Fig. 6-22. *Various types of bad weather clouds.*

generally have a delicate, curly appearance, somewhat similar to frost on a windowpane. For these clouds, the word *cirro* ("curly") is added, as cirrocumulus or cirrostratus. At these high altitudes, there is also a fibrous type of cloud appearing as curly wisps, bearing the single name *cirrus*.

In the upcoming section "Air Masses and Fronts," the relationship is shown between the various types of clouds and the kinds of weather expected. For now, though, the chief concern is the flying conditions directly associated with the different cloud formations.

The ice-crystal clouds (cirrus group) are well above ordinary flight levels of light aircraft and normally don't concern pilots of these aircraft, other than as indications of approaching changes in weather.

Clouds in the alto group are also not normally encountered by the smaller planes, but they sometimes do contain icing conditions that can affect commercial and military aircraft. Altostratus clouds usually indicate that unfavorable flying weather is near.

The low clouds are of greater importance to pilots because they create low ceilings and low visibilities. They change rapidly and frequently drop to the ground, forming a complete blanket over landmarks and landing fields. In temperatures near freezing, they are a constant threat because of the probability of icing. With low-level clouds in the area, you should be very much on the alert for any changes and be prepared to land before the terrain becomes totally obscured.

Cumulus clouds (Fig. 6-23) vary in size from light scud or fluffy powder puffs to towering masses rising thousands of feet in the sky. Usually they are somewhat scattered and you can fly around them without difficulty. Under some conditions, particularly in the late afternoon, they are likely to multiply, flatten out, and cover the sky. When this occurs, you could well have no choice other than to reverse course or find a safe spot to put the bird down.

As Fig. 6-24 implies, cumulonimbus clouds are very dangerous. When they appear individually or in small groups, they are usually of the type called air mass thunderstorms (caused by heating of the air at the earth's surface) or orographic thunderstorms (caused by the upslope motion of air in mountainous regions). On the other hand, when these clouds take the form of a continuous or almost continuous line, they are usually caused by a front or squall line. The

Fig. 6-23. *Examples of towering cumulus (tcu) formations.*

Fig. 6-24. *The cumulonimbus contains most of the hazards to planes and pilots: turbulence, ice, hail, and low-level wind shear.*

most common position for a squall line is in advance of a cold front, but one can form in air far removed from a front.

Because cumulonimbus clouds are created by rising air currents, they are extremely turbulent. If a pilot is foolish enough to intentionally enter one of these formations, he or she could encounter updrafts and downdrafts with velocities as great as 3000 feet a minute. Airplanes have been torn apart by the violence of these currents. In addition, the clouds frequently contain lightning, large hailstones capable of severely damaging aircraft, and great quantities of water at temperatures conducive to heavy icing.

Many "unexplained" crashes have undoubtedly been caused by the disabling effect of cumulonimbus clouds on aircraft that have been accidentally or intentionally flown into them. If you're ever caught in one, about all you can do is reduce airspeed to no more than the maneuvering speed for the airplane and maintain control of the aircraft any way you can.

Figure 6-25 shows the important characteristics of a typical cumulonimbus cloud. The top of the cloud flattens into an anvil shape

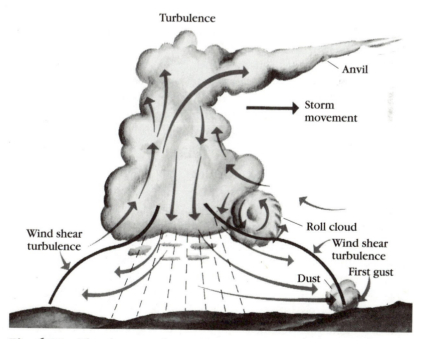

Fig. 6-25. *The elements that make these cumulonimbus clouds so dangerous.*

and points in the direction the cloud is moving, generally with the prevailing wind. Near the base, however, the winds blow directly toward the cloud and increase in speed, becoming violent updrafts as they reach the low rolls at the forward edge.

Within the cloud and directly beneath it are updrafts and down-drafts, while in the rear portion is a strong downdraft that becomes a wind blowing away from the cloud.

This cloud formation is a storm factory. The updrafts quickly lift the moist air to its saturation point, whereupon it condenses and rain-drops begin to fall. Before these have reached the bottom of the cloud, updrafts pick them up and carry them back aloft, where they may freeze and again start downward, only to repeat the process many times until they have become heavy enough to break through the updrafts and reach the ground as hail or very large raindrops. As the storm develops, more and more drops fall through the turbulence, until the rain becomes fairly steady. The lightning that accompanies such a storm is probably due to the breakup of raindrops. This pro-duces static electricity that discharges as lightning, thus causing sudden expansion of the air in its path, resulting in thunder.

It's impossible for a small plane to fly over these clouds because they frequently extend to 50,000 feet and are usually too low to fly under. If they're close together, there may be violent turbulence in the clear space between them. If they're just isolated thunderstorms, you can usually fly around them safely, but be sure to stay a good distance from them. If, however, they are "frontal" of squall line storms, they may extend for hundreds of miles, and the only safe procedure is to land immediately and wait until the line has passed.

Ceiling

A ceiling is defined as the height above the surface of the base of the lowest layer of clouds or obscuring phenomena that hide more than half of the sky. In such instances, the ceiling is reported as "broken" or "overcast." Clouds are reported as broken when they cover six-tenths to nine-tenths of the sky and as overcast when they cover more than nine-tenths. The ceiling is unlimited if the sky is cloudless or less than six-tenths covered as seen from the ground. The latest information on ceilings can be obtained from the various weather reports, Flight Service Stations, Air Traffic Controllers, AWOS or ASOS, other pilots at uncontrolled airports, and so on. Forecasts of expected changes in ceilings and other conditions are, of course, available also at weather stations and Flight Service Stations.

Visibility

Closely related to ceiling and cloud cover is visibility, defined as the greatest horizontal distance at which prominent objects can be distinguished with the naked eye. Visibility, like ceiling, is included in hourly weather reports and in aviation forecasts.

Precipitation

Along with possible damage by hail and the danger of icing, precipitation might be accompanied by low ceilings, and, in heavy precipitation, visibilities could suddenly be reduced to zero.

On the ground, pay particular attention to forms of precipitation other than rain. Snow is one example. No aircraft that has accumulated snow while on the ground should ever be flown until all traces of the snow have been removed, including the hard crust that frequently adheres to the surfaces. Ice is another obvious example. An aircraft that has been exposed to rain followed by freezing temperatures should be carefully cleared of all ice and thoroughly checked before takeoff to make certain that the controls operate freely.

Air masses and fronts

Large, high-pressure systems frequently stagnate over areas of land or water that have relatively uniform surface conditions. The systems take on the characteristics of these source regions, as the coldness of polar regions, the heat of the tropics, the moisture of oceans, or the dryness of continents.

As they move away from their source regions and pass over land or sea, the air masses are constantly being modified through heating or cooling from below, lifting or subsiding, absorbing or losing moisture. Actual temperature of the air mass is less important than its temperature in relation to the land or water surface over which it is passing. For instance, an air mass moving from polar regions usually is colder than the land and sea surfaces over which it passes. On the other hand, an air mass moving from the Gulf of Mexico in winter usually is warmer than the territory over which it passes.

If the air is colder than the surface, it is warmed from below and convection currents are set up, causing turbulence. Dust, smoke, and atmospheric pollution near the ground are carried upward by these currents and dissipated at higher levels, improving surface visibility. Such air is called unstable.

Conversely, if the air is warmer than the surface, there is no tendency for convection currents to form, and the air is smooth. Smoke, dust, etc., concentrate in lower levels with resulting poor visibility. Such air is called stable.

From these combinations of the source characteristics and the temperature relationship, air masses can be associated with certain types of weather. The following are general characteristics of cold and warm air masses, but the characteristics could vary considerably:

Characteristics of a cold (unstable) air mass

- Types of clouds: cumulus and cumulonimbus
- Ceilings: generally unlimited (except during precipitation)
- Visibilities: excellent (except during precipitation)
- Unstable air: pronounced turbulence in lower levels (because of convection currents)
- Types of precipitation: occasional local thunderstorms or showers: hail, sleet, snow flurries

Characteristics of a warm (stable) air mass

- Types of clouds: stratus and stratocumulus (fog, haze)
- Ceilings: generally low
- Visibilities: poor (smoke and dust held in lower levels)
- Stable air: smooth, with little or no turbulence
- Types of precipitation: drizzle

When two air masses meet, they won't mix readily unless their temperatures, pressures, and relative humidities are very similar. Instead, they set up boundaries called *frontal zones*, or *fronts*, the colder air mass projecting under the warmer air mass in the form of a wedge. This condition is known as a *stationary front* if the boundary is not moving.

Usually, however, the boundary moves along the earth's surface, and as one air mass withdraws from a given area, it is replaced by another air mass. This action creates a moving front. If warmer air is replacing colder air, the front is called *warm*; if colder air is replacing warmer air, it is a *cold front*.

Warm front

When a warm front moves forward, the warm air slides up over the wedge of colder air lying ahead of it.

Warm air usually has high humidity. As the air is lifted, its temperature is lowered, condensation occurs, low nimbostratus and stratus clouds form, and drizzle or rain develops. The rain then falls through the colder air below, increasing the moisture content of that air so that it, too, becomes saturated. Any reduction of temperature in the colder air, which might be caused by upslope motion or cooling of the ground after sunset, could result in extensive fog.

As the warm air progresses up the slope, with constantly falling temperature, clouds appear at increasing heights in the form of altostratus and cirrostratus, *if* the warm air is stable. If it is unstable, cumulonimbus clouds and altocumulus clouds form and frequently produce thunderstorms. Finally, the air is forced up near the stratosphere, and, in the freezing temperatures at that level, the condensation appears as thin wisps of cirrus clouds. The upslope movement is very gradual, rising about 1000 feet every 20 miles. Thus, the cirrus clouds, forming at perhaps 25,000 feet altitude, might appear as far as 500 miles in advance of the point on the ground that marks the position of the front (Fig. 6-26).

Flight toward an approaching warm front. A warm front is approaching your area. Although no two fronts are exactly alike, what sort of a weather pattern could you expect? Depending on where you were geographically or where you might be flying, the example of a front moving from St. Louis towards Pittsburgh in Fig. 6-26 would present these probable (but not guaranteed) city-by-city atmospheric conditions:

St. Louis: The weather would be very unpleasant, with drizzle and probably fog.

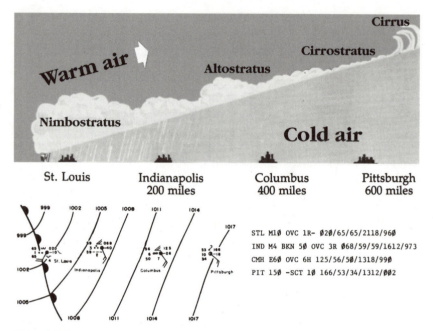

Fig. 6-26. *A warm front (Upper) cross-section; (Lower left) as shown on a weather map; (Lower right) as reported by computers or fax equipment.*

Indianapolis, Indiana: 200 miles in advance of the warm front, the sky would be overcast with nimbostratus clouds and continuous rain.

Columbus, Ohio: 400 miles in advance, the sky would be overcast with stratus and altostratus clouds predominating. The beginning of a steady rain would be probable.

Pittsburgh, Pennsylvania: 600 miles ahead of the front, there would probably be high cirrus and cirrostratus clouds.

If a westbound flight from Pittsburgh to St. Louis was made, the ceilings and visibility would decrease steadily. The start would be under clear skies, lowering stratus-type clouds would be noted near Columbus, and soon afterward precipitation would be encountered. After arriving at Indianapolis, the ceilings would be too low for further flight under visual flight rules, with precipitation reducing visibilities to practically zero. If you're a noninstrument-rated pilot, you really have only two choices at this point: one, land and stay in Indianapolis until the warm front passes, which might take a day or two; or two, do a 180 and head back east where you *know* the weather is still VFR-flyable.

If you do stop in Indianapolis and intend to return to Pittsburgh after the front passes, you'd probably be wise to wait until that same front had gone beyond Pittsburgh. This might take three or four days, though, because warm fronts generally move at the rate of only 10 to 25 miles an hour.

On the trip from Pittsburgh to Indianapolis, you would have noticed a gradual increase in temperature and a much faster increase in dew-point until the two coincided. At the same time, the atmospheric pressure would be gradually dropping because the warmer air aloft would have less weight than the colder air it was replacing. This condition illustrates the general principle that a falling barometer indicates the approach of stormy weather.

Cold front

When a cold front moves forward, it acts like a snow plow, sliding under the warmer air and forcing it aloft. This causes the warm air to cool suddenly and form cloud types that depend on the stability of the warm air.

Fast-moving cold fronts. In fast-moving cold fronts, friction retards the front near the ground, which produces a steeper frontal surface. This surface results in a more narrow band of weather concentrated along the forward edge of the front. If the warm air is stable, an overcast sky might occur for some distance ahead of the front, accompanied by general rain. If the warm air is conditionally unstable, scattered thunderstorms and showers might develop in the warm air. At times, an almost continuous line of thunderstorms can form along the front or ahead of it. These lines of thunderstorms (squall lines) contain some of the most turbulent weather pilots can encounter.

Behind the fast-moving cold front there is usually rapid clearing, with gusty and turbulent surface winds and colder temperatures.

Comparison of cold fronts with warm fronts. The slope of a cold front is much steeper than that of a warm front and the progress is generally more rapid—usually from 20 to 35 miles per hour, although in extreme cases, cold fronts have been known to move as much as 60 miles per hour. Weather activity is more violent and usually takes place immediately at the front instead of in advance of it. In late afternoon during the warm season, however, squall lines frequently develop as much as 50 to 200 miles ahead of the actual cold front. Whereas warm front dangers are low ceilings and visibilities, cold front dangers are chiefly sudden storms, high and gusty winds, and turbulence.

Unlike the warm front, the cold front rushes in almost unannounced, makes a complete change in the weather within a period of a few hours, and moves on. Altostratus clouds sometimes form slightly ahead of the front, but these are seldom more than 100 miles in advance. After the front has passed, the weather often clears rapidly, and cooler, drier air with usually unlimited ceilings and visibilities prevail.

Flight toward an approaching cold front. Back to a flight from Pittsburgh toward St. Louis with a cold front approaching from St. Louis (Fig. 6-27). In this instance, weather conditions quite different from those associated with a warm front would be experienced. The sky in Pittsburgh would probably be somewhat overcast with stratocumulus clouds typical of a warm air mass, the air smooth, and the ceilings and visibilities relatively low although suitable for flight.

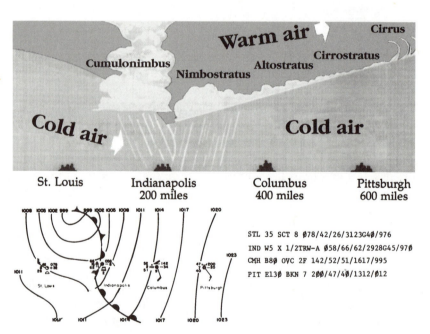

STL 35 SCT 8 Ø78/42/26/3123G4Ø/976
IND W5 X 1/2TRW-A Ø58/66/62/2928G45/97Ø
CMH B8Ø OVC 2F 142/52/51/1617/995
PIT E13Ø BKN 7 2ØØ/47/4Ø/1312/Ø12

Fig. 6-27. *A cold front cross-section (upper); as shown on a weather map (lower left); as reported by computers or fax equipment (lower right).*

As the flight progressed, those conditions would generally prevail until nearing Indianapolis. Somewhere east of Indianapolis, it would be wise to check the position of the front by contacting a Flight Watch, an FSS specialist, or an Air Route Traffic Control Center controller. If you did, you'd probably find that the front was now about 75 miles west of Indianapolis. Using sound judgment, based on your knowledge of frontal conditions, you'd undoubtedly land in Indianapolis and stay there until the front had passed—a matter of a few hours—and then continue to the destination under near perfect flying conditions.

If, however, you foolishly continued the flight toward the approaching cold front, you'd note a few altostratus clouds and a dark layer of nimbostratus lying low on the horizon, with perhaps cumulonimbus in the background. Two courses would now be open: (1) Either turn around and outrun the storm, or (2) make an immediate landing, which might be extremely dangerous because of gustiness and sudden wind shifts.

If you continued the flight, entrapment in a line of squalls and cumulonimbus clouds would likely occur. To fly below these clouds could prove disastrous; to fly above them in a small plane, impossible. At low altitudes, there are no safe passages through them and usually no possibility of flying around them because they often extend in a line for 300 to 500 miles. As you've undoubtedly gathered, these things are bad news, and the *only* advice is a simple STAY OUT OF THEM!

Wind shifts. Wind shifts perhaps require further explanation. The wind in a high blows in a clockwise spiral. When two highs are adjacent, the winds are in almost direct opposition at the point of contact as illustrated in Fig. 6-28.

Because fronts normally lie between two areas of higher pressure, wind shifts occur in all types of fronts, but they usually are more pronounced in cold fronts.

Occluded front

One other form of front with which pilots need to become familiar is the *occlusion* or *occluded front*. This is a condition in which one air mass is trapped between two colder air masses and forced aloft to higher and higher levels until it finally spreads out and loses its identity.

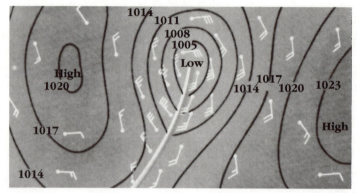

Fig. 6-28. *The weather map indication of a wind shift line (the center line leading to the low pressure area).*

Meteorologists divide occlusions into two types, but as far as the pilot is concerned, the weather in any occlusion is a combination of warm front and cold front conditions. As the occlusion approaches, the usual warm front indications prevail: lowering ceilings, lowering visibilities, and precipitation. Generally, the warm front weather is then followed almost immediately by the cold front type, with squalls, turbulence, and thunderstorms.

Figure 6-29 is a vertical cross section of an occlusion, while Fig. 6-30 shows the various stages as they might occur during development of a typical occlusion. Usually the development requires three or four days, during which the air mass might progress as indicated on the map.

The first stage (A in Fig. 6-30) represents a boundary between two air masses, the cold and warm air moving in opposite directions along a front. Soon, however, the cooler air, being more aggressive, thrusts a wedge under the warm air, breaking the continuity of the boundary, as shown in (B). Once begun, the process continues rapidly to the complete occlusion as shown in (C). As the warmer air is forced aloft, it cools quickly and its moisture condenses, often causing heavy precipitation. The air becomes extremely turbulent, with sudden changes in pressure and temperature.

Figure 6-31 illustrates the development of the occluded front in greater detail, while Fig. 6-32 is an enlarged view of (C) in Fig. 6-29, showing the cloud formations and the areas of precipitation.

Figure 6-33 is a section of a surface weather map showing a low pressure center with warm, cold, and occluded fronts.

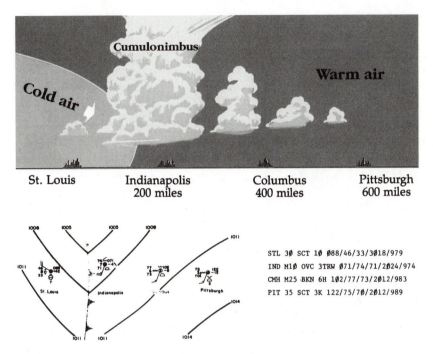

St. Louis   Indianapolis   Columbus   Pittsburgh
       200 miles   400 miles   600 miles

```
STL 3Ø SCT 1Ø Ø88/46/33/3Ø18/979
IND M1Ø OVC 3TRW Ø71/74/71/2Ø24/974
CMH M25 BKN 6H 1Ø2/77/73/2Ø12/983
PIT 35 SCT 3K 122/75/7Ø/2Ø12/989
```

Fig. 6-29. *An occluded front cross-section (upper); as shown on a weather map (lower left); as reported by computers or fax equipment (lower right).*

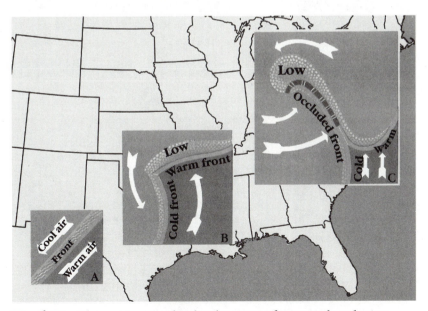

Fig. 6-30. *Three stages in the development of a typical occlusion moving northeastward.*

While the preceding categorizes weather according to types of fronts, weather associated with a front depends more on the characteristics of the conflicting air masses than on the type of front itself. As a pilot, don't attempt to determine expected weather from fronts and pressure centers on the surface map alone. Instead, should you have them available through DUAT or personal visits to an FSS, consult and rely heavily on other weather maps reports, and forecasts, many of which are discussed in the next section of this chapter.

Aviation weather forecasts and reports—in summary

Regardless of the vehicle used to obtain a weather briefing (by phone, in-person, or via a computer connection), it's essential to know what in-flight weather information and types of forecasts are available to you for flight planning purposes. Similarly, if you're talking with a briefer and are aware of the nature of the various forecasts, you'll be in a much better position to ask meaningful questions and glean more from what the briefer is telling you.

A. Air flowing along a front in equilibrium.

B. Increased cold-air pressure causes "bend."

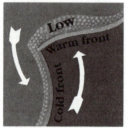

C. Cold air begins to surround warm air.

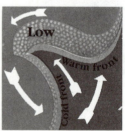

D. Precipitation becomes heavier.

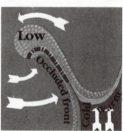

E. Warm air completely surrounded.

F. Warm air ends in mild whirl.

Fig. 6-31. *If you were high enough and looking toward the earth, this is how the various stages in the development of an occlusion would appear.*

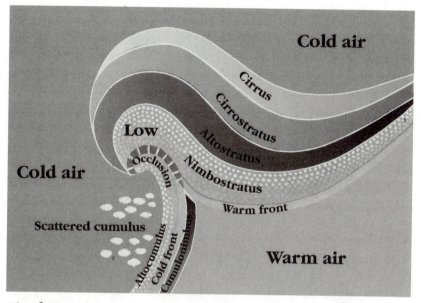

Fig. 6-32. *The cloud formations and precipitation accompanying a typical occlusion. (Details of the third stage of development series are shown in Fig. 6-30.)*

Among the many weather products and related data produced by NOAA and the FAA, the following are available to the various service outlets, such as FSSs and DUAT contractors, and are typically of primary concern to pilots:

- Area Forecasts (FA)
- Meteorological Reports-Aviation Routine (METARs)
- Terminal Area Forecasts (TAFs)
- In-Flight Weather Advisories as: SIGMETs (WS), CONVECTIVE SIGMETs (WST), AIRMETs (WA), HAZARDOUS INFLIGHT WEATHER ADVISORY SERVICE (HIWAS)
- Winds and Temperatures Aloft (FD)
- Pilot Reports (PIREPs)
- Radar Weather Reports (RAREPs)
- Weather Charts (Surface Analysis and Surface Weather Prognostication)
- Automated Weather and Surface Observation Systems (AWOS and ASOS)

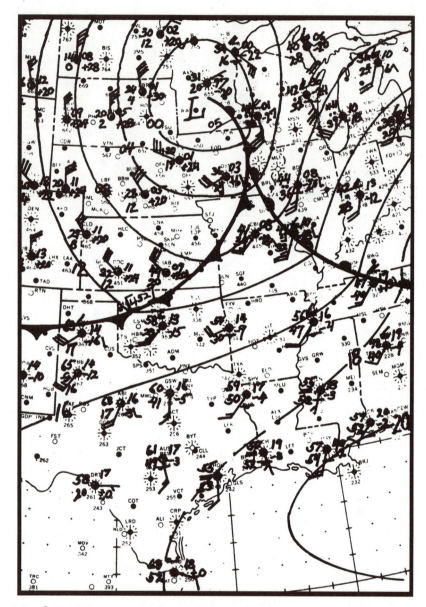

Fig. 6-33. *This section of a typical weather map shows a low pressure area, a cold and warm front, wind directions and velocities, station temperatures, and other meaningful pilot information.*

The principal aviation weather information sources

Basically, as AIM (Aeronautical Information Manual) puts it, the gathering and reporting of weather data are the responsibilities of the National Weather Service (NWS), the FAA, military weather services, and other similarly concerned groups or individuals. Although I touched on this early in the chapter, a few more words about these two sources are still in order.

The National Weather Service (NWS)

As the National Weather Service's manual, Aviation Weather Services, AC 00-45D, puts it, "The National Weather Service collects and analyzes meteorological and hydrological data, and subsequently prepares forecasts on a national, hemispheric, and global scale." Considering the scope of that charge, the following organizations within the NWS play necessary roles in the forecasting and reporting of aviation weather:

- National Meteorological Center (NMC), Washington, D.C.
- National Severe Storms Forecast Center (NSSFC), Oklahoma City, OK. (Formerly in Kansas City.)
- National Hurricane Center (NHC), Miami, FL. Issues hurricane advisories for the Atlantic, Caribbean, Gulf of Mexico, eastern Pacific, and adjacent land masses. A hurricane center in Honolulu issues advisories for the Central Pacific Ocean
- Aviation Weather Center (AWC), Kansas City, MO
- Weather Forecast Offices (WFOs). Approximately 100 outlets throughout all 50 states

Quoting AIM, "The NWS maintains an extensive surface, upper air, and radar weather observing program; a nationwide aviation weather forecasting service; and provides a limited pilot briefing service (interpretational)." The last means that, except for a very few WFOs, the NWS may interpret for a pilot the significance of certain weather conditions or patterns but does not conduct pilot briefings. That is the responsibility of Flight Service Station specialists.

Essentially, NOAA, through its 100-plus WFOs, prepares and issues some 500 airport forecasts four times a day in the 50 states, Puerto Rico, the Caribbean, and Pacific Islands, plus 300 route forecasts and 39 synopses for Transcribed Weather Broadcasts (TWEBs) and pilot briefing purposes.

To further enhance aviation safety, an AWC (Aviation Weather Center) is based in Kansas City, MO. This office is responsible for issuing warnings, forecasts, and analyses of weather hazards such as turbulence, icing, low clouds and reduced visibility from the earth's surface up to 24,000 feet. Above 24,000 feet, the AWC warns of dangerous wind shear, turbulence, thunderstorms, and icing that aircraft might encounter in the northern hemisphere from the middle of the Pacific Ocean eastward to the middle of the Atlantic. Also above that altitude, the AWC forecasts jet stream cores, thunderstorms, turbulence, and weather fronts, again in the northern hemisphere but from the east coast of Asia to the west coast of Europe and Africa. Citing AIM again, "In the conterminous U.S., all in-flight advisories, Significant Meteorological Information (SIGMETs), Convective SIGMETs, Airmen's Meteorological Information (AIRMETs), and all Area Forecasts (FAs) (six areas) are now issued by the AWC." These various in-flight advisories, of course, are issued only when existing or forecast conditions so warrant. Winds aloft forecasts (FDs) are prepared for some 175 locations in the lower 48 states and 21 locations in Alaska, while similar forecasts for Hawaii are prepared in Honolulu.

All weather advisory forecasts actually pass through the Weather Message Switching Center (WMSC) in Atlanta, Georgia, and Salt Lake City, Utah, for distribution. While the Georgia WMSC transmits the advisories, Salt Lake City serves as a backup in case of equipment failure in Atlanta.

The Federal Aviation Administration (FAA)

The FAA enters the weather side of the picture as the principal communicator of weather data via its FSS telephone or in-person pilot briefings and its transcribed services. In summary again, the aviation weather facilities and services offered by the FAA include:

- Flight Service Stations (FSSs). Sixty one automated FSSs, plus a handful that are nonautomated, now provide aviation weather information and pilot briefings in all 50 states.
- Transcribed Weather Broadcast (TWEB). A gradually disappearing continuous broadcast on selected navigation facilities and VORs, TWEBs provide weather data along specific local or short flight routes.

- Transcribed Information Briefing Service (TIBS) is available through phone contact with an FSS. This service provides weather briefings affecting airports located within the FSS's regional area of responsibility, plus any special announcements/information that could be of concern to the pilot.

- Hazardous In-flight Weather Advisory (HIWAS). A continuous broadcast over selected VORs of actual or forecasted severe or hazardous weather within a given geographic area.

- En route Flight Advisory Service (EFAS, also called "Flight Watch"). En route weather data available to pilots while in flight by contacting specifically designated FSSs on the common radio frequency of 122.0 MHz.

- ATIS (Automatic Terminal Information Service). This is a continuously transcribed and updated hourly weather and/or ground conditions at a given airport. All pilots are expected to monitor the ATIS before taking off or landing at any tower-controlled airport.

- Air Route Traffic Control Center (ARTCC). Twenty-four ARTCCs, or "Centers," control all IFR (instrument flight rules) traffic within the 50 states, plus Guam and Puerto Rico. Also, but only when the pilot initiates the radio contact, and if its work load permits, Center will help VFR aircraft with limited weather information, along with what is called "flight following," advisories of possible conflicting traffic, and the like. In an emergency, however, Center will do whatever it can to assist the endangered or perhaps lost pilot. The centers exist primarily, though, to control instrument flight operations. Help to VFR aircraft is on that "work load permitting" basis.

- DUAT (Direct User Access Terminal). Private companies contracted by the FAA to provide pilots computerized weather reports and briefings. The two organizations under present contract are GTE Federal Systems, Chantilly, VA, and Data Transformation Corporation, Turnersville, NJ.

When it comes to airports and the immediate airport vicinity, FAA personnel, contractors, qualified observers, and automated airport-based equipment compile and transmit current reports. Among such reports available to pilots, in addition to the locally prepared ATIS transcriptions, are METARs, TAFs, AWOS (Automated Weather Observation System), and ASOS (Automated Surface Observing System).

For the NWS, the FAA, and indeed the entire international aviation world, to compile, prepare, and transmit the many forecasts and current weather conditions, brevity is essential. That being somewhat obvious, all sorts of codings, contractions, abbreviations, and the like have come into being over the years. Some of these are easily distinguished, boiled-downs of the longer parent word or term. In other cases, the coding bears no resemblance to the meteorological condition being reported. For example, as you may have noted above, the code for "Winds and Temperatures Aloft Analysis" is "FD," "WA" stands for "Airmet," and "WST" represents a "Convective SIGMET," meaning severe weather with thunderstorms, turbulence, possible icing, or low-level wind shear. Until you've mastered the code and what it stands for, it would be hard to translate "FD," "WA," or "SIGMET" into anything meaningful.

As further examples of the various weather-related codings and abbreviations, Fig. 6-34 illustrates the symbols used to describe conditions of sky cover, while Fig. 6-35 explains the three ceiling designations. Figure 6-36 illustrates the symbols and meanings of the various weather conditions, primarily precipitation, and Fig. 6-37 lists the abbreviations for obstructions to visibility.

	Meanings	Spoken
CLR	CLEAR. (Less than 0.1 sky cover.)	Clear
SCT	SCATTERED LAYER ALOFT. (0.1 through 0.5 sky cover.)	Scattered
BKN*	BROKEN LAYER ALOFT. (0.6 through 0.9 sky cover.)	Broken
OVC*	OVERCAST LAYER ALOFT. (More than 0.9 or 1.0 sky cover.)	Overcast
−SCT	THIN SCATTERED. ⎫ At least ¹/₂ of the sky cover aloft	Thin scattered
−BKN	THIN BROKEN. ⎬ is transparent at and below the	Thin broken
−OVC	THIN OVERCAST. ⎭ level of the layer aloft.	Thin overcast
X*	SURFACE BASED OBSTRUCTION. (All of sky is hidden by surface based phenomena.)	Sky obscured
−X	SURFACE BASED PARTIAL OBSCURATION. (0.1 or more, but not all, of sky is hidden by surface based phenomena.)	Sky partially obscured

* Sky condition represented by the designator might constitute a ceiling layer.

Fig. 6-34. *These are the sky cover designators and their meanings.*

Coded	Meanings	Spoken
M	MEASURED. Heights determined by ceilometer, ceiling light, cloud detection radar, or by the unobscured portion of a landmark protruding into ceiling layer.	Measured ceiling
E	ESTIMATED. Heights determined from pilot reports, balloons, or other measurements not meeting criteria for measured ceiling.	Estimated ceiling
W	INDEFINITE. Vertical visibility into a surface based obstruction. Regardless of method of determination, vertical visibility is classified as an indefinite ceiling.	Indefinite ceiling

Fig. 6-35. *The symbols that indicate how ceilings are determined.*

Coded	Spoken
Tornado	Tornado
Funnel Cloud	Funnel cloud
Waterspout	Waterspout
T	Thunderstorm
T+	Severe thunderstorm
R	Rain
RW	Rain shower
L	Drizzle
ZR	Freezing rain
ZL	Freezing drizzle
A	Hail
IP	Ice pellets
IPW	Ice pellet showers
S	Snow
SW	Snow showers
SP	Snow pellets
SG	Snow grains
IC	Ice crystals

Fig. 6-36. *Some of the common weather symbols and meanings. "Weather" here means the existence of one or more forms of precipitation and their identifying coding(s).*

Coded	Spoken
BD	BLOWING DUST
BN	BLOWING SAND
BS	BLOWING SNOW
BY	BLOWING SPRAY
D	DUST
F	FOG
GF	GROUND FOG
H	HAZE
IF	ICE FOG
K	SMOKE
VOLCANIC ASH	WRITTEN OUT IN FULL

Fig. 6-37. *Other obstructions to vision and their symbols.*

Other contractions and symbols are used in the various reports, including city or location codes, as BOI for Boise, BNA for Nashville, CVG for Cincinnati, or DFW for Dallas/Ft. Worth. Then there are contractions, many of which when read in context are rather easily translatable. Examples: SLY (southerly); NEWD (northeastward); OCNL (occasional); VCNTY (vicinity); UDDW (updraft, downdraft)—and the examples could go on. Suffice it to say, however, that for those just starting to fly, be prepared to learn almost a second language—the language of aviation, with its various abbreviations, codes, acronyms, and verbal shorthand.

Area forecasts (FA)

Moving on, let's look at the structure and content of some of the principal weather advisories and warnings that emanate from the NOAA and FAA sources—beginning with the area forecast (FA).

An FA is a forecast of general weather conditions over the expanse of several states. It's used to determine anticipated en route weather and to interpolate conditions at airports that don't have terminal forecasts, formerly called FTs, but now known as TAFs. FAs are issued three times a day by the Kansas City AWC for each of the six areas in the contiguous United States (Fig. 6-38). In Alaska, the FAs are also issued three times a day by the WFOs in Anchorage, Fairbanks, and Juneau (Fig. 6-39), while the Honolulu WFO does the same for Hawaii four times a day.

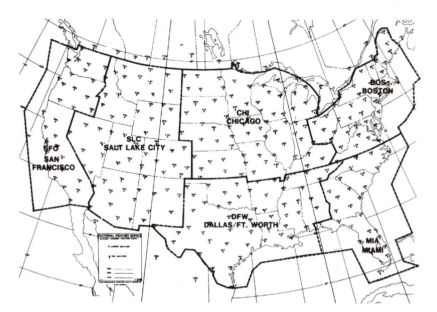

Fig. 6-38. *The six areas in the 48 contiguous states for which the Kansas City AWC prepares Area Forecasts (FAs) three-times-a-day.*

Each FA consists of a 12-hour forecast, plus a six-hour outlook. All times are UTC (Coordinated Universal Time), and all distances are in nautical miles, except visibility, which is stated in statute miles.

The FA's structure consists of the following four major sections:

- Heading, including the originating Weather Office, the type of report, and time of issuance
- Synopsis of conditions over the next 12 hours and times of the six-hour outlook
- Area Conditions anticipated over the next 12 hours
- Hazards and Flight Precautions that do or may exist, depending on the type of report, such as icing and the outlook, turbulence and low level wind shear and outlook, or significant clouds and weather and outlook.

To illustrate this structure as well as the message coding, refer to Fig. 6-40 and the following explanations:

MIAC FA 190945. The Miami WFO is the originating station; the "C" identifies the FA as a Cloud and Weather report. "FA'" of course,

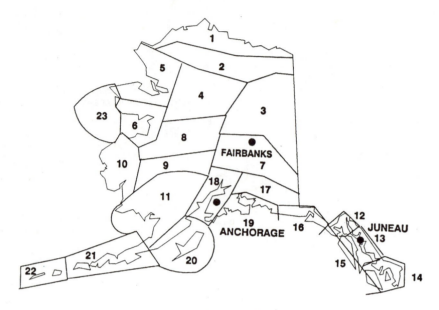

Prepared by WFO Fairbanks, AK
1-Arctic Slope, Coastal
2-North Slopes of Brooks Range
3-Upper Yukon Valley
4-Koyukuk and Upper Kobuk Valley
5-Northern Seward Peninsula and Lower Kubuk Valley
6-Southern Seward Peninsula and Eastern Norton Sound
7-Tanana Valley
8-Lower Yukon Valley
23-St. Lawrence Island and Western Norton Sound

Prepared by WFO Anchorage, AK
9-Kuskokwim Valley
10-Yukon Kuskokwim Delta
11-Bristol Bay
17-Copper River Basin
18-Cook Inlet and Susitna Valley
19-Central Gulf Coast
20-Kodiak Island
21-Alaska Peninsula-Port Heiden to Unimak Pass
22-Unimak Pass to Adak

Prepared by WFO Juneau, AK
12-Lynn Canal and Glacier Bay
13-Central Southeast Alaska
14-Southern Southeast Alaska
15-Coastal Waters
16-Eastern Gulf Coast

Fig. 6-39. *Sectors covered by the three Alaskan WFOs.*

```
MIAC FA 190945
SGFNT CLDS AND WX VALID UNTIL 192200...OTLK 192200-200400Z

IFR...NC SC GA FL AND CSTL WTRS
FROM SBY TO HAT TO VRB TO BRO TO 80W BRO TO DRT TO SPS TO BNA TO
LOZ TO SBY
OCNL CIGS BLO 10 AND OR OCNL VSBYS BLO 3F/PCPN. CONDS CONTG BYD
22Z. SEE BOS CHI AND DFW FA FOR DETAILS IN THOSE AREAS.

MTN OBSCN...NC SC GA
FROM CHO TO CLT TO ATL TO CHA TO LOZ TO CHO
MTNS OCNL OBSCD IN CLDS F/PCPN. CONDS CONTG BYD 22Z. SEE BOS CHI
AND DFW FA FOR DETAILS IN THOSE AREAS.
```

Fig. 6-40. *This is an example of an Area Forecast received in an Automated Flight Service Station.*

identifies the report as an Area Forecast, while "190945" is the date, the 19th, and the time of issuance. Times are always cited in terms of the 24-hour clock. "0945" is thus 9:45 AM. while 9:45 PM is "2145."

SGFNT CLDS AND WX VALID UNTIL 192200...OTLK 192200-200400Z. This is the general synopsis, stating that: "Significant clouds and weather will exist until 2200 hours on the 19th. The six-hour outlook is from 2200 hours on the 19th until 0400 hours Z time on the 20th." The forecast continues:

IFR...NC SC GA FL AND COASTAL WTRS

FROM SBY TO HAT TO VRB TO BRO to 80W BRO TO DRT TO SPS TO

BNA TO LOZ TO SBY. OCNL CIGS BLO 10 AND OR OCNL VSBYS

BLO 3F/PCPN. CONDS CONTG BYD 22Z. SEE BOS CHI DFW FA FOR

DETAILS IN THOSE AREAS.

"IFR conditions will exist in North Carolina, South Carolina, Georgia, Florida, and along the coastal waters from Salisbury, Maryland, to Hatteras, to Vero Beach, Florida, to Brownsville, Texas, to 80 miles west of Brownsville to Del Rio, Texas, to Wichita Falls, Texas, to Nashville, Tennessee, to London, Kentucky, to Salisbury. Occasional ceilings will exist below 1000 feet and or occasional visibilities below 3 miles in fog and precipitation. Conditions will continue beyond 2200 hours Z. See Boston, Chicago, and Dallas-Fort Worth FAs for details in those areas." ...And the FA concludes:

MTN OBSCN...NC SC GA

FROM CHO TO CLT TO ATL TO CHA TO LOZ TO CHO

MTNS OCNL OBSCD IN CLDS F/PCPN. CONDS CONTG BYD 22Z.

SEE BOS CHI AND DFW FA FOR DETAILS IN THOSE AREAS.

"There is mountain obscuration in North Carolina, South Carolina, and Georgia from Charlottesville, Virgina, to Charlotte, North Carolina, to Atlanta, Georgia, to Chattanooga, Tennessee, to London, Kentucky, to Charlottesville. Mountains are occasionally obscured in clouds with fog and precipitation. Conditions will continue beyond 2200Z. See Boston, Chicago, and Dallas-Fort Worth area forecasts for details in those areas."

If icing conditions existed in the same area, a second FA would be transmitted, with the heading of MIAI FA 190945—the "I" indicating that it is an icing forecast. Similarly, should turbulence exist or be anticipated, a third FA, headed MIAT FA 190945 is transmitted. Following each FA would be a synopsis and the prevailing or anticipated conditions, just as in the Clouds and Weather FA.

Amendments or corrections to previous FAs are issued as necessary and so identified in the heading by an AMD or a COR. Whichever the case, only the portion of the FA being corrected or amended is transmitted.

METARs and TAFs   Back in 1996, the United States introduced the most significant change since the early 1950s in its observing, reporting, and coding surface weather observations. Basically, two reports that had been around for years passed away—the hourly Surface Aviation Observation, or "SA" report, and the Terminal Forecast (FT). In place of the SA, the METAR, also prepared hourly, was adopted, or when conditions warrant, a SPECI, or Special report. At the same time, "TAF" became the substitute for the old FT, which had been the standard U.S. airport weather-reporting instrument.

The ICAO (International Civil Aviation Organization) METAR acronym, standing for a routine Meteorological Aviation Report, is a rough translation of the French Aviation Routine Weather Report. A SPECI is merely a METAR issued on a nonroutine basis because of changing meteorological conditions. "TAF" broadly translates to Aerodome Forecast.

The reason for the changes was simply the need to standardize these reports worldwide. In essence, the United States had been out of step with international aviation in coding and structure with its old SAs and FTs. But as NOAA put it, "The increase in international flights between the U.S. and other nations from more U.S. locations than ever before lends itself to developing a more 'seamless' international standard for aviation. Moreover, the standardization becomes vital for the general aviation community flying from the U.S. to Canada, the Caribbean area, and Mexico."

"Going international" is hardly a new trend in U.S. aviation. The airspace reclassification back in 1993 and the adoption of the international phonetic alphabet (see Chap. 8) several years before illustrate that. Despite the trend towards an aviation "one-worldism," however, each ICAO nation has the freedom to retain for its internal domestic use some of its long-held weather abbreviations and reporting practices. Consequently, many of the traditional U.S. reporting codes and units of measurement, including the following, have survived the internationalization:

- Winds continue to be reported in knots (as opposed to meters per second elsewhere);
- Cloud layer heights and runway visual range (RVR) are reported in feet (as opposed to meters);
- Visibility is reported in statute miles versus meters;
- Altimeter settings are still referred to in inches of mercury (as opposed to millibars).

Also, many of our long-familiar abbreviations remain, such as RA identifying rain and FG fog.

Some of the coding, however, stems from French words, as GR for hail or FU for smoke. If flying beyond the U.S. borders, just be alert to the measurement differences as indicated above between U.S. and international METAR/TAFs

The METAR: Its structure and elements   A METAR basically consists of two parts: the main body (entries 1–7 below) and a Remarks or trend forecast (entry 8) that is valid for a period of two hours from

the time of the METAR observation. Briefly described, the eight
entries are as follows:

1. Identification Grouping

   - METAR or SPECI The type of report.

   - Four-letter ICAO station identifier. In the 48 states, the
     identifiers start with "K," followed by the three-letter
     standard airport code, as "KPHL," "KLAX," "KMIA," and the
     like. For Alaska, the station identifiers start with "PA,"
     followed by a two-letter airport designation, as "PAFA" for
     Fairbanks, "PANC" for Anchorage, or "PAJN" for Juneau.
     Hawaiian identifiers begin with "PH," followed by the
     same two-letter station code system. "PHNL" is thus
     Honolulu, "PHLO" Hilo, and "PHMK" Malokai. In Canada,
     the identifiers begin with "CU," "CW," "CY," or "CZ," as
     "CYUL" for Montreal, "CYOW," Ottawa, or "CWJD," Grand
     Rapids, Manitoba. In Mexico, the introductory code is
     "MM," while it's "MU" for Cuba, and so on, with the same
     station identification system applying throughout the rest
     of the aviation world.

   - Time. Time is always transmitted in a four-digit grouping,
     followed by a Z to denote Coordinated Universal Time,
     often referred to as "Z time" or "Zed" (the French
     pronunciation of the letter "Z").

2. Surface Winds

   - Wind is a described in a five-digit group (six if the wind
     speed is greater than 99 knots). The first three digits reflect
     the direction from which the wind is blowing, followed by
     two digits indicating its speed in knots, as: "16020KT:"
     (Wind is blowing from 160 degrees at 20 knots). If the wind
     is variable, "VRB" replaces the direction: "VRB08KT"
     (Variable at 08 knots). If the wind were from 75 degrees and
     gusty (G) with speeds varying from 27 to 40 knots, the
     report would read, "07527G40KT."

3. Visibility

   Visibility is reported in statute miles in the United States, with
   "SM" appended to the reported or recorded distance, as
   "10SM," decoded as "ten statute miles."

   Runway Visual Range, when reported, appears in this format: Runway heading, "/", and then the visual range in feet

(in the United States, elsewhere in meters). Example: R32L/1200FT–Translation: Runway 32 left visual range 1200 feet.

4. Present Weather

Weather is reported in the format of: Intensity/Proximity/ Descriptor/Precipitation/Obstructions to visibility/Other. If two or more types of precipitation are being reported, intensity applies only to the first type. Light precipitation is identified with the minus sign, moderate precipitation has no sign or symbol, while a plus sign denotes heavy precipitation.

Proximity applies to and is reported only for weather between five and 10 miles of the center of the airport complex. The identifying code used here is "VC," for "vicinity."

Descriptors are the two-letter codes that describe the current types of precipitation, obstructions to visibility on or in the proximity of the airport, and "other" weather phenomena that could occur.

The symbols related to these various weather conditions are reproduced on Fig. 6-41.

5. Sky Conditions

This element of the METAR relates to clouds, the amount of sky coverage, cloud height, and type or vertical visibility. Amounts of sky cover in the METAR system are reported in eighths, as:

SCT - Scattered (1/8 to 4/8s of clouds)

BKN - Broken (5/8s to 7/8s of clouds)

OVC - Overcast (8/8s of clouds)

SKC - Sky clear, no clouds

The bases of cloud are reported with three digits in hundreds of feet, while the type of cloud—cumulus (CU) or cumulonimbus (CB), when either exists—is reported following the sky condition and the cloud base: Example:

- SCT025TCU BKN080 BKN250 Translated: Scattered towering cumulus at 2,500 feet, broken at 8,000 feet, broken at 25,000 feet.

- SCT008 OVC0125CB Translated: Scattered clouds at 800 feet, overcast cumulonimbus at 12,500 feet.

Proximity—applies to and reported <u>only</u> for weather occurring in the vicinity of the airport (between 5 and 10 miles of the center of the airport runway complex). It is denoted by the letters "VC."

Descriptor—these seven descriptors apply to the precipitation or obstructions to visibility.

TS—thunderstorm	DR—low drifting
SH—shower(s)	MI—shallow
FZ—freezing	BC—patches
BL—blowing	

Precipitation—there are eight types of precipitation in the METAR code:

RA—rain	GR—hail (> ¼")
DZ—drizzle	GS—small hail/snow pellets
SN—snow	PE—ice pellets
SG—snow grains	IC—ice crystals

Obstructions to visibility—there are eight types of obstructing phenomena in the METAR code:

FG—fog (vsby < ⅝ mi.)	PY—spray
BR—mist (vsby ⅝–6 mi)	SA—sand
FU—smoke	DU—dust
HZ—haze	VA—volcanic ash

Note: fog (FG) is reported <u>only</u> when the visibility is less than five eighths of mile otherwise mist (BR) is reported.

Other—there are five categories of other weather phenomena which are reported when they occur:

SQ—squall	SS—sandstorm
DS—duststorm	PO—dust/sand whirls
FC—funnel cloud/tornado/waterspout	

Examples:

TSRA—thunderstorm with moderate rain

+SN—heavy snow

−RA FG—light rain and fog

BRHZ—mist and haze (vsby > than ⅝ mi)

FZDZ—freezing drizzle

VCSHRA—rain shower in the vicinity

Fig. 6-41. *Some of the METAR weather condition symbols and codings.*

6. Temperature/Dewpoint

Temperature and dewpoint are each reported in two digits Celsius, as "15/08"—where the temperature is 15 degrees and the dewpoint is 8 degrees Celsius. When an "M" is prefixed to one of the elements, it indicates a below zero temperature. Example: "05/M07." Temperature is 5 degrees, dewpoint is 7 degrees below zero—again, both Celsius readings.

7. Altimeter Setting

Altimeter settings are reported in four digits in inches of mercury, prefixed by an "A." Example: "A2995." The altimeter setting is 29.95 inches of mercury.

8. Remarks

Significant weather conditions not otherwise reported are entered in this block, preceded by the contraction "RMK." "RE" denotes recent weather events, while "WS" indicates wind shear, followed by "TKO" or "LDG" for takeoff or landing.

An example and translation of a typical METAR:

METAR KSFO 1453Z VRB02KT 3SM MIBR SKC 15/12 A3012

Routine weather report; San Francisco, CA: time 1435 UTC (2:35 PM); wind variable at 2 knots: visibility 3 statute miles; visibility obstructed by shallow mist (MI) (ground fog) (BR); sky clear; temperature 15 degrees Celsius, dewpoint 12 degrees Celsius; altimeter setting three zero one two inches.

A SPECI, or Special report, follows the same basic format as a METAR, the only difference other than the conditions being reported, is the initial heading which identifies it as a Special. To complete the example, though, here is a SPECI and its decoding:

SPECI KCVG 2228Z 28024G36KT 3/4SM +TSRA BKN008 OVC020CB 28/23 A3000 RMK RETSB24RAB24

Special weather report; Cincinnati, OH; time 2228 UTC ("Z" time); wind from 28 degrees at 24 knots with gusts to 36 knots; visibility 3/4 of a statute mile; thunderstorm with heavy rain (the + or – refers to the intensity of the precipitation); broken clouds at 800 feet, overcast with cumulonimbus cloud at 2000 feet; temperature 28 degrees Celsius, dewpoint 23 degrees Celsius; altimeter setting three zero point zero zero inches; Remarks (RMK) to follow: recent (RE) weather event: thunderstorm began 24 past the hour, rain began 24 past the hour.

A TAF (terminal airport forecast):
Its structure and elements

The TAF station forecasts, which are very similar in structure and language to the METARs, are produced four times a day at approximately 0000Z, 0600Z, 1200Z, and 1800Z, thus covering a 24-hour period. When weather conditions change to the extent that the last-issued TAF is not, or will not be, representative of the forecast weather, a TAF amendment is issued and so identified in the message header, as "TAF AMD."

A routine TAF consists of the ICAO station identifier, the date and time the TAF was actually prepared, and its date and time of validity. Example:

TAF KPIT 091745 091818

This is the TAF for Pittsburgh. It was prepared on the 9th day of the month at 1745Z hours, and is valid from 1800Z on the 9th to the same time, 1800Z, the next day, the 10th.

Next, as with the METAR, comes the wind, with these possible conditions:

11012KT - wind from 110 degrees at 12 knots

27512G25KT - wind from 275 degrees at 12 knots gusting to 25 knots

VRB15G27KT - wind variable at 15 knots gusting to 27 knots

00000KT - wind calm

Then the visibility at the airport. In this example, the "P6SM" means that the airport visibility is better than 6 statute miles, with the letter "P" identifying conditions that are "better than...."

Weather conditions use the same METAR format, qualifiers, and contractions as illustrated in Fig. 6-41. If no significant weather is expected during the specific period of the forecast, the weather group is omitted.

Sky conditions also use the same METAR symbols (Fig. 6-41 again), but cumulonimbus (CB) clouds are the only type forecast in a TAF.

Also, TAFs do not designate ceiling layers, which, for aviation purposes, are considered to be the lowest level broken or overcast layer, or the altitude at which vertical visibility becomes completely obscured. When the sky is obscured by surface-based conditions, vertical visibility (VV) into obscuration is forecast. In such cases, the "VV" is followed by a three-digit height in hundreds of feet. Some examples of reported sky conditions:

- SKC—Sky clear
- SCT 005 BKN025CB BKN 250—Five hundred feet with scattered clouds, ceiling is 2500 feet broken with cumulonimbus clouds, and broken clouds at 25,000 feet.
- VV006—An indefinite ceiling of 600 feet.

Optional data (wind shear - WS) may be appended when low level wind shear (up to a 2000-foot altitude) is expected. The forecast includes the height of the wind shear, followed by the wind direction and speed. Example: WS15/22045KT. Translation: Low level wind shear at 1500 feet is expected, with wind from 220 degrees at 45 knots.

Probability forecast comes into play when the chance of precipitation and associated weather conditions are in the 30% to less than 50% range. When such conditions exist, the contraction "PROB40," is used, followed by a four-digit group designating the beginning and ending hours during which the expected weather conditions will occur. That PROB is not shown during the first six hours of the forecast, however.

A couple of examples:

- PROB40 1014 1SM RASN—Forty percent chance of rain and snow and 1-mile visibility between 1000Z and 1400Z.
- PROB40 2024 2SM FZRA—Forty percent chance of freezing rain and 2-miles visibility between 2000Z and 2400Z

The FROM (FM) Group appears in a TAF when a rapid change in conditions, usually within an hour, is expected. Comprising the FM group is the four-digit hour and minute at which the change is expected to begin and which is expected to continue until the next change group or until the end of the current forecast. An FM group always starts a new line and contains all the pertinent elements of wind, visibility, weather, and sky conditions. Conditions not significant to aviation are omitted from the group. Examples of FM reports:

- FM0700 SKC—Sky clear after 0700Z hours.
- FM1430 OVC020—A 2000-foot ceiling after 1430Z is expected.

The BECOMING (BECMG) Group comes into play when a gradual change is expected over a longer period, usually at least two hours. Following the BECMG indicator is the four-digit time group reflecting the beginning and ending hours of the change, as per this example:

- OVC09 BECMG 1416 BKN20—Ceiling is 900 feet overcast, becoming 2000 broken between 1400Z and 1600Z.

The TEMPORARY (TEMPO) Group is used when any condition is expected to last for generally less than an hour at a time and occurs during less than half the time period. The TEMPO indicator is followed by the typical four-digit group with the beginning and ending hour and minute, during which the temporary conditions are expected. Only the changing conditions are included in the TEMPO group as these two examples illustrate:

- SCT030 TEMPO 1923 BKN 030—Scattered clouds are at 3000 feet with occasional broken ceilings at 3000 between 1900Z and 2300Z.
- 4SM HZ TEMPO 0006 2SM BR HZ—Visibility four in haze with occasional visibility two in mist and haze between 0000Z and 0600Z

Automated weather observing system (AWOS) and automated surface observation system (ASOS)

If you glance at the airport data blocks on almost any sectional chart, you'll find a goodly number that are equipped with AWOS, (the Automated Weather Observing System), or ASOS, (the Automated Surface Observation System). A "goodly" number is probably not very descriptive, however, because estimates, including those from the National Weather Service ASOS Program Office in Silver Springs, Maryland, put the current installations at well in excess of 1000, with many additional systems under way or projected.

The advantages of an automated system are many, ranging from minute-to-minute real-time observations, to more consistent information, undiluted by human judgment, interpretation, vision-blocking obstructions or darkness, to more economic use around the clock of airport personnel. Going beyond these advantages is the obvious safety factor. Particularly with ASOS's more extensive observations and reports, pilots, when approaching an unattended Class E or G airport, will have a much clearer picture of the current conditions than would otherwise be possible or probable. And, in a similar vein, AWOS or ASOS on the unattended field opens the airport to increased local and transient traffic, ultimately resulting in a more profitable operation for the community.

Much has been written describing and justifying both AWOS and ASOS. For purposes here, however, a broad overview of the two systems and the data they transmit would seem more to the point. Consequently, what follows focuses on what the systems are, what they do, and what they don't do.

AWOS/ASOS: general

As the National Weather Service's *Tool Box* (a summary of automated surface observations for ASOS trainers) puts it, both the AWOS and ASOS systems are composed of "electronic sensors, connected to a computer, that measure, process, and create surface observations every minute. These systems provide 1-minute, 5-minute, hourly, and special observations 24 hours a day." Through computer-generated voice subsystems, the minute-by-minute observations are transmitted over discrete VHF radio frequencies and can be received up to 25 nautical miles from the airport as well as up to 10,000 feet AGL. Transmissions may also be over the voice portion of a local navaid. Whichever the vehicle, the weather message is 20 to 30 seconds long and is updated each minute. Consequently, if you monitor the reports from a given airport over a reasonable period of time, you can develop a picture of the prevailing conditions and whether they are degenerating, improving, or remaining static. Figure 6-42 compares the AWOS and ASOS observing programs and the elements reported.

Although AWOS and ASOS would seem to have a close-cousin relationship, there are differences that make ASOS the more complete system and the system that is in the gradual process of replacing AWOS. Neither system, however, is likely to eliminate entirely the need for human observations, if only for the reasons that the electronic systems are limited in their horizontal coverage and cannot forecast weather trends. They only report what *is* happening—not

WEATHER OBSERVING PROGRAMS

Element Reported	AWOS-A	AWOS-1	AWOS-2	AWOS-3	ASOS	Manual
Altimeter	X	X	X	X	X	X
Wind		X	X	X	X	X
Temperature/ Dew Point		X	X	X	X	X
Density Altitude		X	X	X	X	
Visibility			X	X	X	X
Clouds/Ceiling				X	X	X
Precipitation				X	X	X
Remarks					X	X

Fig. 6-42. *The weather observing programs matrix and the elements reported by the various automated systems.*

what *will* happen. Of course, as I said, if you listen to enough consecutive reports of what is going on now at an airport, you'll be able to detect or establish a weather pattern trend. That trend, though, is a product of deduction, not prognostication.

Another factor relative to human involvement: The automated systems report only the weather that exists directly above the sensors. They have no ability, as yet, to accumulate and digest conditions that might be surrounding or approaching the airport. For example, the observing system reports highly favorable conditions at a given airport in terms of ceiling, visibility, winds, temperature, density altitude, dewpoint, and the like. In essence, perfect flying weather. But only a couple of miles or so off the airport property, a raging thunderstorm has blackened the sky. The automated observing systems will not report that storm because other than short-range visibility reading, they're not capable of processing horizontal or diagonal weather. Despite all of their data-collecting capabilities, the current systems have a built-in vertical tunnel vision which, at times, requires human intervention, or "augmentation," to provide a more complete report of present and/or anticipated conditions. Whenever this augmentation by a qualified observer is considered necessary, it is, as *AIM* puts it, "identified in the observation as 'OBSERVER WEATHER.'"

Location of the sensors on the airport is important. Generally speaking, the chosen site is near the touchdown point of the principal instrument runway, but also to be considered in that decision are local conditions such as nearby lakes, rivers, an ocean, or terrain that could adversely affect accurate observations. If such potentially distorting elements exist, additional sensors could be installed to produce more accurate reports.

Of the two system, AWOS is the older, having been around in one form or another for over 30 years. Despite a continuing pattern of adding information to the system, AWOS does not produce the variety of observations provided by ASOS. Consequently, ASOS is gradually replacing AWOS, and AWOS will presumably disappear from the scene within the next few years.

The AWOS system, in brief

Four levels make up the AWOS system:

1. *AWOS-A:* only reports altimeter setting;

2. *AWOS-1:* reports altimeter setting, winds, temperature, dewpoint, and density altitude;

3. *AWOS-2:* reports the information provided in AWOS-1, plus visibility;

4. *AWOS-3:* reports the information provided in AWOS-2, plus cloud and ceiling data.

In addition to the radio transmissions, most AWOS messages can be monitored on the ground via telephone. For the level of AWOS system at a given airport, plus the radio frequency and telephone number, consult the appropriate *A/FD*. If AWOS or ASOS is on the field, you'll see in bold print an *A/FD* entry similar to this: WEATHER DATA SOURCES: AWOS-3 133.8 (814) 443-2114.

The ASOS system, in brief

The ASOS program, which is the primary surface weather observing system, is a joint effort of the National Weather Service, the Department of Defense, and the FAA. The system, as *AIM* puts it, provides "continuous minute-by-minute observations and performs the basic observing functions necessary to generate an aviation routine weather report (METAR) and other aviation weather information." Equipped with at least one sensor for each unit, (Fig. 6-42), a given ASOS, as the National Oceanic and Atmospheric Administration (NOAA) describes it, will be able to "observe" and report these conditions:

- Cloud height and amount (clear, scattered, broken, overcast) up to 12,000 feet
- Visibility (to at least 10 statute miles)
- Precipitation identification (type and intensity for rain, snow, and freezing rain)
- Barometric pressure and altimeter setting
- Ambient temperature/dewpoint temperature
- Wind direction, speed, and character (gusts, squalls)
- Rainfall accumulation
- Selected significant remarks as: variable cloud heights, variable visibility, precipitation beginning/ending times, rapid pressure changes, pressure change tendency, wind shift, peak wind

Figure 6-43 is an NOAA illustration of the principal elements and sensors of an ASOS installation. With all of its positive features, however, ASOS is *not* designed to report:

- Clouds above 12, 000 feet
- Tornadoes
- Funnel clouds
- Ice crystals
- Drizzle
- Freezing drizzle
- Blowing obstructions (snow, sand or dust, snow fall, and snow depth.

Paraphrasing NWS's *Toolbox*, data related to many of these latter conditions are, or can be, provided by other sources. Meanwhile, NWS notes that ". . . new sensors will be added to measure some of these weather elements."

As a reminder again, these automated systems provide 24-hour observations of weather conditions within two to three miles of the sensor site. Beyond those limits, barring visibility, lateral coverage is not possible. Keep in mind, though, that observing systems are really in their infancy, despite the fact that AWOS has been around quite a few years. As new sensors are developed and computer technology increases, improvements in the systems are inevitable.

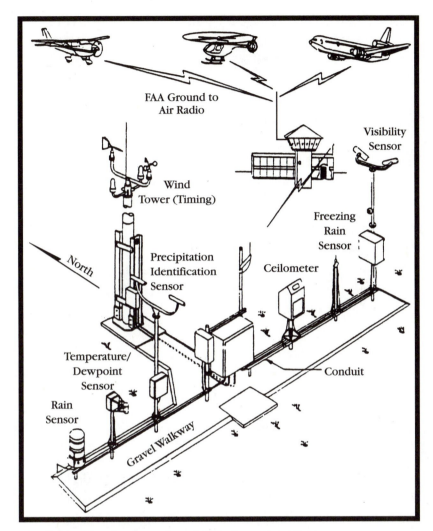

Fig. 6-43. *The elements of an ASOS airport installation.*

These, then, are some of the AWOS and ASOS basics, although there's more that could be said about this electronic weather data processsing system. I felt, however, that an overview of what the systems do and can't do would be more meaningful here than a technical discussion of their components, the application of mathematical logic (alogrithms), or why human augmentation is often an essential supplement to the automated report. But like so many other aspects of aviation, this is just one more subject or area in which the proficient pilot keeps him or herself informed. If you tend to do most of your flying in the Class E or G airport environments where 24-hour automated weather broadcasts may be available, knowledge of the system, what it's telling you, and its limitations could be especially important. There will be changes—mostly for the good—as time moves along, so staying on top of these safety-enhancing systems should be a high priority project for every pilot, whatever his or her rating or experience level.

In-flight weather advisories

Among its many products, the weather service provides five critical reports or advisories to pilots and forecasters:

- Severe Weather Forecast Alerts (AWW) and Bulletins (WW)
- Significant Meteorological Information, or SIGMETS (WS)
- Airman's Meteorological Information, or AIRMETS (WA)
- Convective Meteorological Information, or Convective SIGMETS (WST)
- Center Weather Advisories (CWA)

Each of these advisories primarily focuses on known or anticipated weather conditions that could affect flight. Being of obvious concern to the pilot, they are thus quite logically classified as "in-flight advisories." For the conterminous 48 states, the advisories are described, plotted, and issued by the Aviation Weather Center in Kansas City using VORs as reference points.. In Alaska, the three WFOs (Anchorage, Fairbanks, and Juneau) issue the advisories for their respective areas, using geographic references or latitude/longitude coordinates. The WFO in Honolulu does the same for Hawaii.

The first four advisories listed above are broadcast by Flight Service Stations during the periods of validity when they affect an area within 150 NMs of the FSS facility. If you're flying along and haven't heard the actual advisory but have been alerted to it by a ground agency, you should contact the nearest FSS to determine what the advisory is and if it pertains to your line of flight

A Center Weather Advisory is transmitted by the Air Route Traffic Control Centers, These CWAs are unscheduled advisories of adverse conditions expected to develop within the next two hours. Based on recently reported information, a CWA can be issued 1) to supplement an existing SIGMET, Convective SIGMET, or AIRMET; 2) when pilot reports or other sources of information indicate the probability of conditions that meet SIGMET or AIRMET criteria but no in-flight advisory has yet been issued; 3) when conditions within the Center's area of responsibility are below the SIGMET/AIRMET advisory criteria of intensity, turbulence, area coverage, and the like, but pilot reports or other information sources indicate flight safety could still be jeopardized by the developing weather situation.

To clarify these various advisories a bit more:

Severe Weather Forecast Alerts (AWW)

An AWW (meaning "Alert Weather Watch") is designed to alert the various weather offices, pilots, and other users of the potential of severe weather (tornadoes or thunderstorms) within a given area and the fact that a Severe Weather Bulletin (WW) will soon be forthcoming. AWWs are numbered sequentially, beginning with number 1 on January 1 of each year. As an example of an AWW, the following was issued by the MKC AWC on the 28th at 1909; it is the 56th severe weather bulletin of the year and warns of tornadoes in the southeast between 2000Z on the 28th to 0300Z on the 29th. The AWW thus simply reads:

OKC AWW 281909

WW 56 TORNADO GA SC NC VA ADJ CSTL WTRS 282000Z—29000Z

AXIS...70 STATUTE MILES EITHER SIDE OF LINE...30 W AGS (AUGUSTA GA) TO 30 NE ECG (ELIZABETH CITY NC) HAIL SURFACE AND ALOFT. .3 INCHES. WIND GUSTS...70 KNOTS. MAX TOPS TO 5000. MEAN WIND VECTOR 25060

Shortly after the AWW goes out, the more detailed weather bulletin (WW) itself is issued, a portion of which is as follows:

OKC WW 281914

A. BULLETIN—IMMEDIATE BROADCAST REQUESTED. TORNADO WATCH NUMBER 56 NATIONAL SEVERE STORM FORECAST CENTER OKC
214 PM EST WED MAR 28 19—

A. THE NATIONAL SEVERE STORM FORECAST CENTER HAS ISSUED A TORNADO WATCH FOR

MOST OF SOUTH CAROLINA
MOST OF CENTRAL AND EASTERN NORTH CAROLINA

PARTS OF SOUTHEAST VIRGINIA
PARTS OF EASTERN GEORGIA
ADJOINING COASTAL WATERS

FROM 3 PM EST UNTIL 10PM EST TODAY

B. TORNADOES. LARGE HAIL.DANGEROUS LIGHTNING AND DAMAG-
ING THUNDERSTORM WINDS ARE POSSIBLE IN THESE AREAS.

THE TORNADO WATCH AREA IS ALONG AND 70 STATUTE MILES EI-
THER SIDE OF A LINE FROM 30 MILES WEST OF AUGUSTA GEORGIA
TO 30 MILES NORTHEAST OF ELIZABETH NORTH CAROLINA

C. TORNADOS AND A FEW SVR TSTMS WITH HAIL TO 3 IN. EXTREME
TURBC AND SFC WND GUSTS TO 70 KT. A FEW CBS WITH MAX TOPS
TO 5000.

D. PARAMETERS IN CAROLINAS VERY STG WITH STG LOW LEVEL
FLOW AND CNVRGNC ALG WITH UNSTABLE AIRMASS. LOW MVG
RPDLY THRU ERN AL. WILL CONT ENE INTO CAROLINAS THIS EVENG.
MEANWHILE SVR TSTMS LIKELY DVLPG IN ADVANCE THIS AFTN DUE
TO ABOVE-MENTIONED CONDS.

Status reports are issued as needed to show progress of storms and
to identify areas no longer under the threat of severe storm activity.
When it becomes evident that a given area is no longer under threat
of severe storm activity, a cancellation bulletin is issued.

Sigmet (WS) A SIGMET (WS) (Significant Meteorological
Information) warns pilots of weather conditions considered
potentially hazardous to all aircraft, including severe turbulence,
severe icing, and dust storms or sandstorms that reduce visibility
below three miles. It does *not* report convective activity
(thunderstorms and the like). That is the function of the Convective
SIGMET.

SIGMETs are identified by the phonetic alphabet, Alpha through
November. If revisions or updates of a previous WS are required, the
sequential update number follows the original identification, as
ALPHA 2 or INDIA 6. Figure 6-44 illustrates the structure and content
of a SIGMET, with the following decoding:

SLCI WS 162200: The Salt Lake City WFO is issuing SIGMET India
(the "I") on the 16th at 2200.

```
. . . .
SLCI WS 162200
SIGMET INDIA 8 VALID UNTIL 170200
ID NV UT WY
FROM COD TO RKS TO PSP TO LAX TO 40W SBA TO 30SW UKI TO 90N PIH
TO COD
OCNL SVR TURBC BLO 160 DUE TO STG LOW AND MID LVL WINDS ACRS
RUFF TRRN. STG UDDFS VCNTY MINS. LLWS POTENTIAL BELOW 20 AGL.
CONDS CONTG BYD 0200Z.
```

Fig. 6-44. *The example illustrates the construction and wording of a SIGMET.*

SIGMET INDIA 8 indicates that this is the 8th revision or update of India and is valid until the 17th at 0200.

The WS affects conditions in Idaho, Nevada, Utah, and Wyoming within the boundaries from Cody to Rock Spring to Palm Springs to Los Angeles to 40 miles west of Santa Barbara to 30 miles west of Ukiah to 90 miles north of Pocatello back to Cody.

The advisory reads: "Occasional severe turbulence below 16,000 feet due to strong low and midlevel winds across rough terrain. Strong updrafts and downdrafts in the vicinity of mountains. Low-level wind shear potential below 2000 feet agl. Conditions continuing beyond 0200Z."

Convective SIGMET   Convective SIGMETs (WST), as illustrated in Fig. 6-45, are issued in the conterminous United States when any of the following conditions exist or are forecast:

- Severe thunderstorms due to (1) surface winds greater than or equal to 50 knots, or (2) hail at the surface greater than or equal to ¾ inch in diameter, or (3) tornadoes

- Embedded thunderstorms

- Lines of thunderstorms

- Thunderstorms greater than or equal to VIP Level 4 affecting 40 percent or more of an area at least 3000 square miles

- A WST implies severe or greater turbulence, severe icing, or low-level wind shear. In effect, a WST could be issued for any convective situation that the forecaster believes is hazardous to all categories of aircraft.

WST bulletins are issued for the Eastern (E), Central (C), and Western (W) United States. The areas separate at 87 and 107 degrees west

```
MKCE WST 191355
CONVECTIVE SIGMET 7E
VALID UNTIL 1555Z
NC CSTL WTRS
FROM 110E ORF-140ENE HAT-100SE ILM-110E ORF
AREA EMBDD TSTMS MOVG FROM 2520. TOPS TO 350.

*
MKCE WST 191355
CONVECTIVE SIGMET...OTLK
WST'S EXIST

OUTLOOK VALID UNTIL 1955Z
AREA 1...FROM FLO-JAX-140SSW TLH-ABY-FLO
A GSTRNY FNT FM NRN FL PEN EXTDS WWD TO A SFC LO PRES CNTR OVR
THE NE GLFMEX. A WRM MOIST SLY FLOW IS OVRRIDING THE SHALLOW
DOME OF CD AIR ALG CSTL SXNS. A SERIES OF UPR IMPULSES IS MOVG
NEWD FM MEX THRU THE GLF CST STATES. XPC OVRRNG CNVTN TO CONT BUT
MAINLY CONFINED TO CSTL AREAS AND ADJ WTRS.
```

Fig. 6-45. *The example from an Automated FSS illustrates how a convective SIGMET and an Outlook are worded.*

longitude, with sufficient overlap to cover most cases when the conditions cross the boundaries. A bulletin thus covers the area in which the bulk of the observed or forecast conditions are located.

Bulletins are issued hourly at H+55 (the hour plus 55 minutes), and special bulletins are issued at any time as required and updated at H+55. If no conditions meeting the WST criteria are observed or forecast, the message "Convective SIGMET...None" is issued at H+55.

Individual Convective SIGMETs for each area are numbered sequentially from 01 to 99 each day, beginning at 0000Z. A continuing WST condition is reissued every hour at H+55 with a new number. The text of the bulletin consists of either an observation and a forecast or just a forecast. The forecast is valid for up to two hours.

Figure 6-45 illustrates a Convective SIGMET for the eastern portion of the country, as identified by the "E" following "MKC" (Kansas City). The time of issue is the 19th at 1355. The type of bulletin is on the second line, and the "7E" identifies it as the seventh bulletin for the eastern area. Line three establishes the time of validity, while the fourth line identifies the North Carolina coastal waters as the specific area affected.

The first portion of the WST, decoded, reads: "From 110 miles east of Norfolk to 140 miles east northeast of Hatteras to 100 miles southeast of Wilmington, North Carolina, to 110 miles east of Norfolk, an area of embedded thunderstorms is moving from 250 degrees at 20 miles per hour. The tops are up to 35,000 feet."

The next section contains the Convective SIGMET Outlook, which is valid until 1955Z. The area involved extends from Florence, South Carolina, to Jacksonville to 140 miles south southwest of Tallahassee to Albany, Georgia, back to Florence.

The body of the WST starts with "A QSTRNY FNT...," which identifies a stationary front, but because no front is totally stationary, the "Q" denotes "Quasi," meaning "approximately" or "to some degree." The message then reads: "A quasi stationary front from the northern Florida peninsula extends westward to a surface low pressure center over the northeast Gulf of Mexico. A warm moist southerly flow is overriding the shallow dome of the cold air along coastal sections. A series of upper impulses is moving northeastward from Mexico through the Gulf Coast states. Expect overriding convection to continue but mainly confined to coastal areas and adjacent waters."

As they do with SIGMETs, FSSs broadcast the WSTs over VORs when they pertain to areas within 150 miles of the FSS or over a broadcast facility controlled by the FSS. WSTs and Severe Weather Forecast Alerts (AWW) are broadcast at 15 minute intervals—H+00, H+15, H+30, H+45—for the first hour after issuance. The other advisories— SIGMETs, AIRMETs, and Center Weather Advisories (CWA) are broadcast at 30-minute intervals at H+15 and H+45 for the first hour after issuance. The FSS message would be similar to this: "Aviation Broadcast. Weather Advisory. A Convective SIGMET is current for (area affected) (description of weather)."

ARTCCs also broadcast WSTs as well as SIGMETs, Severe Weather Forecast Alerts (AWW), AIRMETs (WA), and Center Weather Advisories (CWA), the last being an unscheduled advisory (generally a *Nowcast*) for conditions beginning within the next two hours. Depending on the type of advisory, the ARTCC transmission would read: "Attention all aircraft. Convective SIGMET Five Eastern. From the vicinity of Elmira to Phillipsburg, scattered embedded thunderstorms moving east at one zero knots. A few intense level five cells. Maximum tops four five zero."

Terminal control facilities (Tower and Approach Control) might or might not broadcast these weather advisories. They have the option of doing so only when the area of the advisory or alert is within 50 miles of the airspace under their jurisdiction. ATIS (Automatic Terminal Information Service) transmissions do not broadcast the advisory, but include in the message that "Convective SIGMET Five Central is in effect until (time)."

In that case, or in any other when the pilot has not received the advisory, whatever it might be, he or she should call the nearest FSS for the full details.

AIRMET   An AIRMET (WA) (Airman's Meteorological Information) advises of less severe weather conditions than a SIGMET, but conditions that could still be hazardous to light aircraft or inexperienced pilots, as:

- Moderate icing
- Moderate turbulence
- Sustained winds of 30 knots or greater at the surface
- Extensive areas of visibility below three miles and/or ceilings of less than 1000 feet
- Extensive mountain obscuration

AIRMETs also serve as amendments to area forecasts, meaning that if AIRMET conditions have been included in the area forecast, no AIRMET will be issued. One will be issued, however, if conditions develop that were not in the forecast.

As with SIGMETs, AIRMETs are alphanumerically identified. While the SIGMETs start with Alpha and go up to November, AIRMETs start with Oscar and conclude with Zulu. Each AIRMET is numbered sequentially, as Oscar 1 or Papa 3, etc.

An example of an AIRMET:

MKC AWC WA 291200

AIRMET ROMEO 1. FLT PRCTN OVR EXTRM NE OK. VSBYS BLO 3F. N OF PNC-TUL-FYV LN VSBYS FQTLY BLO 3F. CNDNS IPVG RPDLY AFT 13Z. CNL AT 14Z.

Translation: "Flight precautions over extreme northeast Oklahoma. Visibilities below 3 miles in fog. North of Ponca City-Tulsa-Fayetteville line visibilities frequently below 3 miles in fog. Conditions improving rapidly after 13Z. Cancel at 14Z."

Winds and temperatures aloft   The Winds and Temperatures Aloft (FD) are forecast for specific locations across the contiguous United States as well as for a network of locations in Alaska. Obviously, the winds and temperatures at a proposed altitude are important in the flight planning process. Accordingly, and where physically possible, you should study the current FD or the data requested when receiving a telephone FSS briefing. FDs are 12-, 18-, and 24-hour forecasts of wind direction (nearest 10° true north) and speed (knots) for each of nine flight levels: 3000, 6000, 9000, 12,000, 18,000, 24,000, 30,000, 34,000, and 39,000 feet. These levels are listed at the top of the report. A planned flight between any two of the levels, as 4500 or 5000 feet, would of course require an averaging of wind direction, speed, and temperature.

The following is an excerpt from an FD, coupled with explanations of the figures and their meanings.

FT	3000	6000	9000	12000	18000	24000	30000	34000	39000
ABI		2213+19	2315+14	2313+08	2208−07	9900−19	990034	090644	101155
ABQ			2605+17	9900+10	0710−05	0710−17	990033	990043	060655
AMA		2210	2409+16	2406+10	9900−	9900−18	010534	350543	021055
ATL	2611	2611+17	2612+13	2612+08	2713−06	2712−18	281134	291143	300754
BNA	2414	2617+17	2617+12	2718+07	2819−07	2721−19	272434	272543	262554

Forecast levels: The line labeled "FT" shows the nine standard levels in feet for which the winds and temperatures apply. The levels through 12,000 feet are based on true altitude, and the levels at 18,000 feet and above are based on pressure altitude. The station identifiers denoting the location for which the forecast applies are arranged in alphabetical order in a column along the left side of the data sheet. The coded wind and temperature information in digits is found in columns under each level and in the line to the right of the station identifier.

Note that at some of the lower levels the wind and temperature information is omitted. The reason for the omission is that winds aloft are not forecast for levels within 1500 feet of the station elevation. (The elevations at ABI [Abilene], ABQ [Albuquerque], and AMA [Amarillo] are: ABI—1790 feet msl; ABQ—5360 feet msl; AMA—3605 feet msl.) Also, note that no temperatures are forecast for the 3000-foot level or for a level within 2500 feet of the station elevation.

Decoding: A four-digit group shows the wind direction in reference to true north and the windspeed in knots. For an example, refer to the Atlanta (ATL) forecast for the 3000-foot level. The group "2611" means the wind is forecast to be from 260° true north at a speed of 11 knots. Note that to decode, a zero is added to the end of the first two digits giving the direction in increments of 10 degrees, and the second two digits give speed in knots.

A six-digit group includes the forecast temperature aloft. In the Abilene (ABI) forecast for the 6000-foot level, the group 2213 + 19 means that the wind is forecast to be from 220° at 13 knots and a temperature of +19° Celsius (C).

If the windspeed is forecast to be 100 to 199 knots, the forecaster adds 50 to the direction and subtracts 100 from the speed. To decode, the reverse must be done, i.e., subtract 50 from the direction and add 100 to the speed. For example, if the forecast for the 39,000-foot level appears as "731960," subtract 50 from 73, and add 100 to 19. The wind, then, would be from 230° at 119 knots, with a temperature of –60°C. Above 24,000 feet, the Celsius temperature is always below zero, so the minus sign is omitted in the FDs.

It's quite simple to recognize when the coded direction has been increased by 50. Direction (in tens of degrees) ranges from 01 (010°) to 36 (360°). Thus, any coded direction with a numerical value greater than "36" indicates a wind of 100 knots or greater.

If the windspeed is forecast to be 100 knots or greater, the wind group is coded as 199 knots, i.e., "7799," decoded, is 270° at 199 knots or greater. When the forecast speed is less than five knots, the coded group is "9900," which means "light and variable."

Pilot reports (PIREPs)

While pilots are the beneficiaries of all the forecasting facilities, they should also be major contributors to the currency of weather information communicated to others. Obviously, no one knows better than the pilot who is on the spot what conditions actually exist.

Not only that, but FAA air traffic facilities are required to solicit PIREPs when the following conditions have been reported or forecast: ceilings at or below 5000 feet; visibility at or below 5 miles; thunderstorms and related phenomena; icing of light degree or greater; turbulence of moderate degree or greater; wind shear, reported or forecast volcanic clouds.

Even if not solicited, pilots should initiate PIREPs whenever conditions arise that were not forecast or that are different (better or worse) than anticipated. These can be communicated to any of the FAA facilities, such as an FSS inflight specialist (the person who normally responds to radio calls), the FSS Flight Watch specialist (who provides the En route Flight Advisory Service), an ARTCC, Approach Control, or a Terminal Tower Controller.

If not practical to do so in the air, the reports should be made on the ground by phone to the nearest FSS or Weather Service Office. The pertinent PIREP data, as applicable to each, is then used by terminal controllers, FSSs, ARTCCs, and the National Weather Service to assist in the briefing of other pilots. It's also used to communicate to those in flight potentially hazardous conditions, as well as routes and altitudes that would avoid or minimize conflict with the reported conditions.

The contents and structure of a PIREP as transmitted to weather circuits, once the PIREP has been received, are as follows:

PIREP elements	PIREP code	Contents
1. 3-letter station identifier	ABC	Nearest weather reporting location to the reported condition
2. Report type	UA or UAA	Routine or Urgent PIREP
3. Location	/OV	Over, as in "above," or in relation to a VOR
4. Radial and nautical miles	No code	The radial and nautical miles from the location as applicable
5. Time	/TM	Coordinated Universal Time
6. Flight level (altitude)	/FL	Essential for turbulence and icing reports
7. Type aircraft	/TP	Essential for turbulence and icing reports
8. Sky cover	/SK	Cloud height and coverage (scattered, broken, or overcast)
9. Weather	/WX	Flight visibility, restrictions to visibility, precipitation, etc.
10. Temperature	/TA	Degrees Celsius
11. Wind	/WV	Direction in degrees magnetic, speed in knots
12. Turbulence	/TB	As defined later
13. Icing	/IC	As defined later
14. Remarks	/RM	For elements not included or to clarify previously reported items

Two examples of the construction of PIREPs as transmitted to weather circuits:

JXN UA /OV JXN24004/TM 1637/FL060/TP PA32/TB LGT-MDT

The pilot is over Jacksonville on the 240-degree radial, four miles from the VOR at 1637Z. He is flying at 6000 feet, the aircraft type is a PA32, and he is encountering light to moderate turbulence. Another example:

UA/OV BKW/TM 1815/FL120/TP BE99/SK OVC/WX R/TAM08/WV 290030/TB LT-MDT/IC LGT RM/MDT MXD ICG DURGC ROA NWBND FL080-100 1750

This pilot is over BKW (Raleigh County Memorial) at 1815Z. His altitude is 12,000 feet, and the aircraft is a BE-99. He is encountering an overcast sky with rain. The temperature is minus 8 degrees Celsius, and the wind is variable from 290 degrees at 30 knots. The turbulence is light to moderate. Icing is light rime. He encountered moderate mixed icing during a climb northwest bound from Roanoke between flight levels 8000 and 10,000 feet at 1750Z.

To ensure that conditions in PIREPs are properly interpreted, two elements in the report are important. First is the type of aircraft, and second is the pilot's use of the correct adjective to describe the condition he is reporting, particularly those related to turbulence and icing. The following perhaps explains rationale for this statement:

Turbulence. Figure 6-46 illustrates the turbulence-reporting criteria and the meanings of *light, moderate, severe,* and *extreme* turbulence. Since the degree of turbulence varies, the type of aircraft reporting the condition is critical to an accurate interpretation of a PIREP. What might be severe to a Piper Cherokee 140 could be only light or even nonexistent turbulence to a Boeing 747. Conversely, light turbulence in a 747 might be extreme for a Piper. Understanding the symptoms of each in terms of aircraft reaction and reaction inside the aircraft is thus essential when reporting turbulence or when hearing a PIREP from another aircraft.

Icing. When icing exists, it is reported by one of these four stages:

1. *Trace.* Ice is perceptible and the accumulation rate is slightly greater than the sublimation rate. It is not hazardous unless encountered over a one hour or longer period of time.

2. *Light.* The accumulation rate might create a problem if flight in the condition is more than one hour. The accumulation

Turbulence Reporting Criteria Table

INTENSITY	AIRCRAFT REACTION	REACTION INSIDE AIRCRAFT	REPORTING TERM-DEFINITION
	Turbulence that momentarily causes slight, erratic changes in altitude and/or attitude (pitch, roll, yaw). Report as **Light Turbulence;*** or	Occupants may feel a slight strain against seat belts or shoulder straps. Unsecured objects may be displaced slightly. Food service may be conducted and little or no difficulty is encountered in walking.	Occasional - Less than 1/3 of the time Intermittent - 1/3 to 2/3 Continuous - More than 2/3
Light	Turbulence that causes slight rapid and somewhat rhythmic bumpiness without appreciable changes in altitude or attitude. Report as **Light Chop.**		
	Turbulence that is similar to Light Turbulence but of greater intensity. Changes in altitude and/or attitude occur but the aircraft remains in positive control at all times. It usually causes variations in indicated airspeed. Report as **Moderate Turbulence;***	Occupants feel definite strains against seat belts or shoulder straps. Unsecured objects are dislodged. Food service and walking are difficult.	**NOTE** 1. Pilots should report location(s), time (UTC), intensity whether in or near clouds, altitude, type of aircraft and when applicable, duration of turbulence.
Moderate	or Turbulence that is similar to Light Chop but of greater intensity. It causes rapid bumps or jolts without appreciable changes in aircraft or attitude. **Report as Moderate Chop.***		2. Duration may be based on time between two locations or over a single location. All locations should be readily identifiable.
Severe	Turbulence that causes large, abrupt changes in altitude and/or attitude. It usually causes large variations in indicated airspeed. Aircraft may be momentarily out of control. Report as **Severe Turbulence.***	Occupants are forced violently against seat belts or shoulder straps. Unsecured objects are tossed about. Food service and walking are impossible.	EXAMPLES: a. Over Omaha, 1232Z, Moderate Turbulence, in cloud. Flight Level 310,B707. b. From 50 miles south of Albuquerque to 30 miles north of Phoenix, 1210Z to 1250Z, occasional Moderate Chop, Flight Level 330, DC8.
Extreme	Turbulence in which the aircraft is violently tossed about and is practically impossible to control. It may cause structural damage. Report at **Extreme Turbulence.***		

*High level turbulence (normally above 15,000 feet ASL) not associated with cumuliform cloudiness, including thunderstorms, should be reported as CAT (clear air turbulence) preceded by the appropriate intensity, or light or moderate chop.

Fig. 6-46. *The chart describes how an aircraft and those inside it react when encountering the various levels of turbulence intensity, and how the conditions should be reported.*

is removed or prevented and is not hazardous when using deicing/anti-icing equipment.

3. *Moderate.* The rate of accumulation is such that even short encounters become potentially hazardous, and the use of deicing/anti-icing equipment or flight diversion is necessary.

4. *Severe.* The rate of accumulation is such that deicing/anti-icing equipment fails to reduce or control the hazard. Immediate flight diversion is necessary.

Once again, light icing in a large aircraft with anti-icing equipment could be severe to a small Cherokee or Cessna. So understanding both the type of turbulence, the type of icing, and the type of aircraft reporting either phenomenum is essential, particularly for those flying the typical small general aviation aircraft.

Transcribed weather broadcasts (TWEBs)

TWEBs (Transcribed Weather Forecasts) have been long-time elements in the weather information system, but they are reportedly in the process of being gradually eliminated (for instance, in 1997, although 15 new routes were added, 134 were discontinued.) Despite their potential disappearance, however, a brief description of what they are is still in order.

Two types of TWEBs are issued. One is similar to an Area Forecast (FA), except that it is contained in a route format, meaning that the forecast sky cover, cloud tops, visibility, weather, and obstructions to vision are described for a corridor 25 miles either side of a given route. The second TWEB is a Synopsis, consisting of a brief statement of frontal and pressure systems affecting the route during the forecast period.

TWEBs are prepared by the WFOs and are broadcast over selected low-frequency VOR transmitters by flight service stations. The VORs that do transmit TWEBs are identified on the sectional charts by a small blue circle with a white T on it located in the upper right corner of the rectangular VOR identification box (Fig. 6-47).

At one time, the availability of TWEB service was indicated by a small square in the lower right corner of the VOR box. The symbology has changed, however, and the same small square now indicates the availability of HIWAS information.

Figure 6-48 illustrates the TWEB route structure and numbers for the western half of the continental United States—but don't rely on their accuracy today. Either might well have been changed or revised.

In addition to tuning to the VOR outlets, TWEBs for a given route can be accessed on the ground by telephone (TEL-TWEB). TEL-TWEB is not available everywhere, however, but the Airport/Facility Directory lists the numbers where the service can be obtained.

The TWEB Route Forecasts are prepared three times daily according to time zones. The early morning and midday forecasts are valid for 12 hours and the evening forecast for 18 hours.

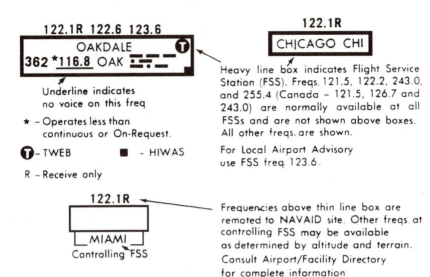

Fig. 6-47. *VORs that transmit TWEBs are identified on the sectional charts by a small blue circle with a white T on it located in the upper right corner of the rectangular VOR identification box.*

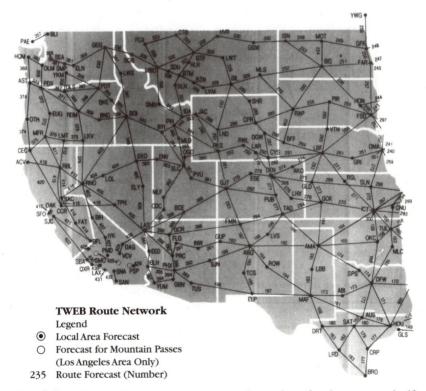

TWEB Route Network
Legend
⊙   Local Area Forecast
○   Forecast for Mountain Passes
(Los Angeles Area Only)
235   Route Forecast (Number)

Fig. 6-48. *The TWEB route structure and numbers for the western half of the continental United States.*

The following is an example of a general Synopsis TWEB:

BIS SYNS 252317. LO PRESSURE TROF MVG ACRS ND TDA AND TNGT. HI PRES MVG SEWD FM CANADA INTO NWRN ND BY TNGT AND OVR MST OF ND BY WED MRNG.

The Bismarck, North Dakota, WFO is issuing the Synopsis on the 25th at 2300Z and is valid until 1700Z on the 26th (18 hours). Low-pressure trough is moving across North Dakota today and tonight. High pressure is moving southeastward from Canada into northwestern North Dakota by tonight and over most of North Dakota by Wednesday morning.

A TWEB Route Forecast, prepared by the NWS, is more detailed, as this example illustrates:

249 TWEB 252317 GFK-MOT-ISN. GFK VCNTY CIGS AOA 5 THSD TIL 12Z OTRW OVR RTE CIGS 1 TO 3 THSDS. VSBY TO 3 TO 5 MI IN LGT SNW WITH CONDS BRFLY LWR IN HVYR SNW SHWRS.

"249" is the Route number. "TWEB" indicates a TWEB Route Forecast issued on the 25th at 2300Z that is valid until 1700Z on the 26th. The route being forecast is from Grand Forks to Minot to Williston. The balance of the message reads: "Grand Forks vicinity ceilings will be at or above (AOA) 5000 feet until 1200Z. Otherwise, over the route ceilings will be one to three thousand feet with a visibility of three to five miles in light snow, with conditions briefly lower in heavier snow showers."

Considering their varied accessibility and route format, TWEBs are important sources for flight planning and operational weather information. Pilots should thus become familiar with them and, where they are available, use them regularly.

HIWAS (Hazardous In-flight Weather Advisory Service)

As I indicated a moment ago, the Hazardous In-flight Weather Advisory Service is being implemented while TWEBs are dwindling. HIWAS is essentially a continuous, recorded broadcast transmitted by one or more flight service stations whose geographic area is expected to be affected by the HIWAS. The purpose of the transmission, of course, is to alert pilots to the fact that a weather advisory, such as a severe weather alert (AWW), an AIRMET, SIGMET, Convective SIGMET, PIREP, or the like, has been issued for all or a portion of the airspace controlled by one of the Air Route Traffic Control Centers. (A discussion of Centers and their areas of responsibility follows in Chap. 8). Included in the broadcast is the name and number of the advisory and what facility the pilot should contact for further information. If no weather advisories have been issued, an hourly statement to that effect is also recorded and broadcast over the selected VORs.

The HIWAS is provided 24 hours a day, and the responsible FSS completes the recording of the applicable data within 15 minutes of receipt. The actual message includes:

- Statement of introduction
- Summary of the reported conditions (AWW, SIGMET, AIRMET, etc.)
- Recommendations to contact the FSS for further details
- Request for PIREPs

An example of a typical HIWAS

HIWAS FOR JACKSONVILLE CENTER AREA AND PORTIONS OF ATLANTA AND MIAMI CENTER AREAS RECORDED AT ONE FOUR THREE ZERO ZULU. CONVECTIVE SIGMET ONE FIVE ECHO. FROM TWENTY SOUTH OF TAMPA TO ONE ZERO NORTH OF COLUMBUS, LINE OF THUNDERSTORMS FOUR ZERO MILES WIDE MOVING EAST AT TWO ZERO KNOTS. MAXIMUM TOPS FIVE FOUR THOUSAND. ISOLATED THUNDERSTORMS OBSERVED ON WEATHER RADAR TALLAHASSEE VICINITY. IFR CONDITIONS REPORTED AT ALBANY AND VALDOSTA. CONTACT FLIGHT WATCH FOR ADDITIONAL DETAILS. PILOT REPORTS ARE REQUESTED.

Inasmuch as HIWAS has not yet been completely implemented throughout the conterminous United States, you can determine where the service is available by checking the sectional chart(s) along your route of flight. If you find a VOR with a small box in the lower right corner of the VOR communications rectangle (Fig. 6-47), the box will indicate that the FSS transmits HIWAS messages over the VOR frequency. Should TWEBs still be available, the "T" in the upper right corner will indicate that. The frequencies above the rectangular box, by the way, are those over which you can contact the serving FSS and are in addition to the universal FSS frequencies such as 121.5 for emergencies, 122.0 to reach EFAS, 122.2, a common FSS frequency or, under certain circumstances, 123.6 for airport traffic advisories.

Since not all pilots are continually monitoring a VOR voice frequency and thus may not be aware that a weather alert has been issued, the centers and airport traffic control personnel also alert pilots to the existence of a HIWAS on all frequencies except 121.5, which again is the frequency reserved strictly for emergency calls. A typical alert call would be something like this:

ATTENTION ALL AIRCRAFT; MONITOR HIWAS OR CONTACT A FLIGHT SERVICE STATION ON FREQUENCY_____ MEGAHERTZ OR_____MEGAHERTZ FOR NEW CONVECTIVE SIGMET NUMBER ONE SIX INFORMATION

Weather charts

At the time of publication of this Handbook, the vehicle for transmission of the weather charts to be discussed is in a state of flux. The few nonautomated FSSs receive the charts prepared by the NWS, but the automated FSSs (AFSSs) are currently using private organizations contracted by the FAA for the actual preparation of the charts. (Presumably, one contractor was to be selected, but such has not been done yet.) The contractors receive the NWS data, prepare the charts themselves, and then have them available for display on color television receivers in the AFSSs. As just one example, the Columbia, Missouri, AFSS uses a contractor (Kavorus) for weather chart data and computers for other data.

Another thing about the charts is their relatively decreasing value as far as many pilots are concerned. What with a fewer number of FSSs on airport properties because of consolidation, there are fewer opportunities to get in-person flight briefings and to study, first-hand, the various charts or maps available. Admittedly, with the right type of printer, you can receive the charts via DUAT, but even then, there doesn't appear to be a heavy demand, or perhaps need, for them. Nonetheless, as part of the full weather picture, brief descriptions of Surface Analysis Charts, Weather Depiction Charts, Radar Summary Charts, and System Weather Prognostic Charts are essential.

Surface analysis charts

The Surface Analysis Chart, often referred to as a "surface weather map," is the basic weather chart, a small portion of which is depicted in Fig. 6-49 (which is a repeat of Fig. 6-33). The chart is prepared by the NWS from reports of existing weather conditions and is transmit-

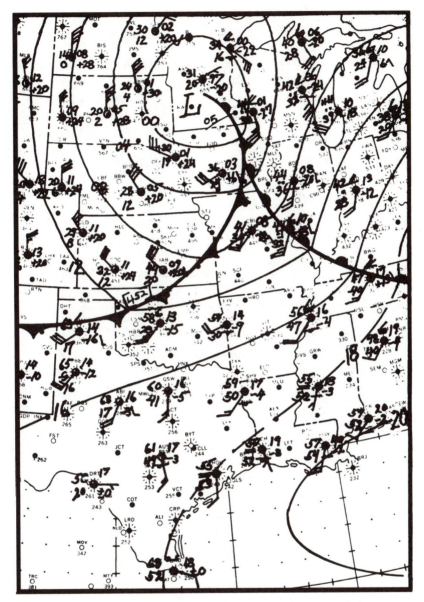

Fig. 6-49. *A portion of a surface weather map and its symbols.*

ted to many weather outlets every three hours. A date and UTC-time group indicate when the conditions portrayed on the chart were actually occurring. The charted weather information includes conditions such as surface wind direction and speed, temperature, dewpoint, cloud cover, cloud types, visibility, barometric pressure, and various other weather data. It also includes the position of fronts as well as areas of high or low pressure, as Fig. 6-49 partially illustrates.

The reporting station is depicted by a small circle. The weather data pertaining to that station is placed in a standard pattern around the circle, and the completed product is called a "station model." An example of a typical model, along with the symbols used, is shown in Fig. 6-50.

The types of fronts are characterized on Surface Analysis Charts by the symbols shown in Fig. 6-51.

If you'll refer back to Fig. 6-49 for a moment, look about in the middle of the figure and slightly to the left. There you'll see in brackets the number [452]. This is a three-digit code recorded along the frontal line

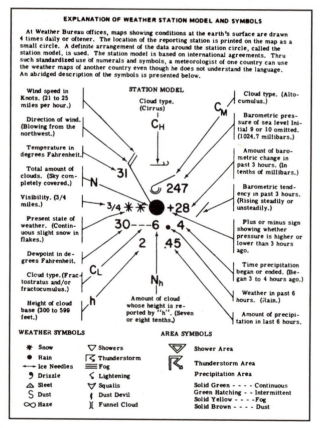

Fig. 6-50. *This figure provides a clearer picture of the "station model" in Fig. 6-49 and the symbols that could be found on the surface weather map.*

Many of the elements in the STATION MODEL are entered in values which can be interpreted directly. Some, however, require reference to coded tables and these STATION MODEL entries are described in the tables below:

C_L	Description (Abridged From W. M. O. Code)	C_M	Description (Abridged From W. M. O. Code)	C_H	Description (Abridged From W. M. O. Code)
	Cu of fair weather, little vertical development and seemingly flattened.		Thin As (most of cloud layer semi-transparent).		Filaments of Ci, or "mares tails", scattered and not increasing.
	Cu of considerable development, generally towering, with or without other Cu or Sc bases all at same level.		Thick As, greater part sufficiently dense to hide sun (or moon), or Ns.		Dense Ci in patches or twisted sheaves, usually not increasing, sometime like remains of Cb; or towers or tufts.
	Cb with tops lacking clear-cut outlines, but distinctly not cirriform or anvil-shaped; with or without Cu, Sc, or St.		Thin Ac, mostly semi-transparent; cloud elements not changing much and at a single level.		Dense Ci, often anvil-shaped, derived from or associated with Cb.
	Sc formed by spreading out of Cu; Cu often present also.		Thin Ac in patches; cloud elements continually changing and/or occurring at more than one level.		Ci, often hook-shaped, gradually spreading over the sky and usually thickening as a whole.
	Sc not formed by spreading out of Cu.		Thin Ac in bands or in a layer gradually spreading over sky and usually thickening as a whole.		Ci and Cs, often in converging bands, or Cs alone; overspreading and growing denser; the continuous layer not reaching 45° altitude.
	St or Fs or both, but no Fs of bad weather.		Ac formed by the spreading out of Cu.		Ci and Cs, often in converging bands, or Cs alone; generally overspreading and growing denser; the continuous layer exceeding 45° altitude.
	Fs and/or Fc of bad weather (scud).		Double-layered Ac, or a thick layer of Ac, not increasing; or Ac with As and/or Ns.		Veil of Cs covering the entire sky.
	Cu and Sc (not formed by spreading out of Cu) with bases at different levels.		Ac in the form of Cu-shaped tufts or Ac with turrets.		Cs not increasing and not covering entire sky.
	Cb having a clearly fibrous (cirriform) top, often anvil-shaped, with or without Cu, Sc, St, or scud.		Ac of a chaotic sky, usually at different levels; patches of dense Ci are usually present also.		Cc alone or Cc with some Ci or Cs, but the Cc being the main cirriform cloud.

Cloud Abbreviation		R_t Time of Precipitation		h Height in Feet (Rounded Off)		N N_h Sky Coverage	
St or Fs-Stratus or Fractostratus	0	No Precipitation.	0	0 - 149	0	No clouds.	0
Ci-Cirrus	1	Less than 1 hour ago	1	150 - 299	1	Less than one-tenth or one-tenth	1
Cs-Cirrostratus	2	1 to 2 hours ago	2	300 - 599	2	Two and three-tenths	2
Cc-Cirrocumulus	3	2 to 3 hours ago	3	600 - 999	3	Four-tenths	3
Ac-Altocumulus	4	3 to 4 hours ago	4	1,000 - 1,999	4	Five-tenths	4
As-Altostratus	5	4 to 5 hours ago	5	2,000 - 3,499	5	Six-tenths	5
Sc-Stratocumulus	6	5 to 6 hours ago	6	3,500 - 4,999	6	Seven and eight-tenths	6
Ns-Nimbostratus	7	6 to 12 hours ago	7	5,000 - 6,499	7	Nine-tenths or overcast with openings.	7
Cu or Fc-Cumulus or Fractocumulus	8	More than 12 hours ago	8	6,500 - 7,999	8	Completely overcast	8
Cb-Cumulonimbus	9	Unknown	9	At or above 8,000, or no clouds	9	Sky obscured	9

Fig. 6-50. *(Continued.)*

to classify the front as to type, intensity, and character. To understand the meaning of those numbers, refer now to Fig. 6-52. According to the various classifications, the "4" identifies the front as a cold front on the surface; "5" means that its intensity is moderate, showing little or no change; and "2" says there is frontal activity with little change.

Continuing with Fig. 6-49 the solid lines depicting the pressure pattern are the isobars denoting lines of equal pressure. You might think of these lines as being similar to terrain contour lines on many

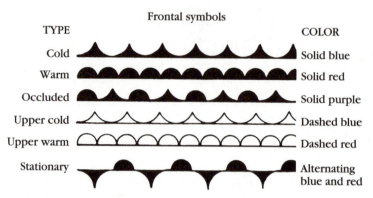

Fig. 6-51. *The various types of fronts are depicted on weather maps by these symbols.*

maps. Isobars are usually spaced at 4-millibar intervals and are labeled by a two-digit number that denotes the pressure. For example, 35 means 1035.0 MB; 04 means 1004.0 MB; and 93 means 993.0 MB. Isobars usually encircle a high- or low-pressure area. The actual pressure at each center is indicated on the station model by a two-digit number, which is decoded the same as the number along the isobars.

The large letter "L" on the chart marks the center of a low-pressure area, while an "H" would quite logically identify the center of a high-pressure area.

The Surface Analysis Chart gives a pictorial overview of the weather situation, but keep in mind that weather systems move and thus change the local weather. It's apparent, then, that the surface map should not be used alone but in conjunction with other available weather information.

Weather depiction chart

The weather depiction chart (Fig. 6-53) is computer-prepared from Surface Aviation Observations (SAC) which, in turn, is based on data from both manual and automated sources. The chart begins daily at 01Z and is transmitted at three-hour intervals.

While the chart shown in Fig. 6-53 does not contain examples of all the possible weather conditions and their related symbols, it does tell at a glance where clouds and weather might be a factor. It also shows the major fronts as well as the type of flight (IFR or VFR) that could be expected in various sections of the country. As the coding

Type of front		Intensity of front	
Code Figure	**Description**	**Code Figure**	**Description**
0	Quasi-stationary at surface	0	No specification
1	Quasi-stationary above surface	1	Weak, decreasing
2	Warm front at surface	2	Weak, little or no change
3	Warm front above surface	3	Weak, increasing
4	Cold front at surface	4	Moderate, decreasing
5	Cold front above surface	5	Moderate, little or no change
6	Occlusion	6	Moderate, increasing
7	Instability line	7	Strong, decreasing
8	Intertropical front	8	Strong, little or no change
9	Convergence line	9	Strong, increasing

Character of front

Code Figure	**Description**
0	No specification
1	Frontal area activity decreasing
2	Frontal area activity, little change
3	Frontal area activity increasing
4	Intertropical
5	Forming or existence expected
6	Quasi-stationary
7	With waves
8	Diffuse
9	Position doubtful

Fig. 6-52. *This chart decodes the numerical classifications of fronts illustrated in Fig. 6-49 in terms of a front's Description, Intensity, and Character.*

in the lower right corner of the chart says, a smooth outline of an area denotes "IFR ceilings <1000. feet and/or visibility <3 miles." A scalloped area represents marginal VFR: "MVFR ceiling _1000 to 3000 feet and or visibility _3 to _5 miles." Any area not outlined means VFR conditions with ceiling >3000 feet and visibility >5 miles.

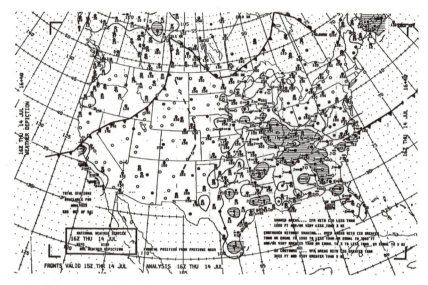

Fig. 6-53. *A weather depiction chart indicates at a glance where weather might be a factor.*

An enlarged station model (Fig. 6-54) illustrates the symbols that could be used at a given location to reflect the various sky cover possibilities, cloud heights or ceilings, weather conditions—fog, haze, smoke, etc.—as well as an overall analysis (not shown on the Fig. 6-54 chart) of favorable and unfavorable (for flying) conditions.

If you're in a position to get your hands on a current depiction chart, you have an excellent starting point for flight planning because it gives you a broad overview of probable weather conditions wherever you're going, at least at the time the chart was produced. But again, it's just a starting point; things could change dramatically between the issuance time of the chart and the estimated time of your departure or destination arrival time. So as NOAA's Aviation Weather Services publication, AC 00-45D, puts it, "After initially sizing up the general weather picture, final flight planning must consider forecasts, progs, and the latest pilot, radar, and surface weather reports."

Radar summary chart

Weather radar generally detects precipitation only, but ordinarily not small water droplets as found in fog and nonprecipitating

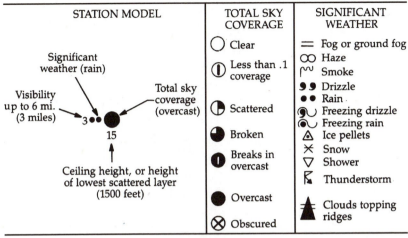

STATION MODEL	TOTAL SKY COVERAGE	SIGNIFICANT WEATHER
	◯ Clear	═ Fog or ground fog
Significant weather (rain)	⦶ Less than .1 coverage	∞ Haze
		⌇ Smoke
Visibility up to 6 mi. (3 miles) / Total sky coverage (overcast) 3•• ● 15	◐ Scattered	🢒🢒 Drizzle
		•• Rain
		🢒◡ Freezing drizzle
		◉◡ Freezing rain
	◓ Broken	⬠ Ice pellets
↑ Ceiling height, or height of lowest scattered layer (1500 feet)	◕ Breaks in overcast	✳ Snow
		▽ Shower
		⏚ Thunderstorm
	● Overcast	▲ Clouds topping ridges
	⊗ Obscured	

Analysis

IFR - Ceiling less than 1000 feet and/or visibility less than 3 miles

MVFR (Marginal VFR) - Ceiling 1000 to 3000 feet inclusive and/or visibility 3 to 5 miles inclusive

VFR - Ceiling greater than 3000 feet or unlimited and visibility greater than 5 miles, not outlined

Fig. 6-54. *The symbols and notations used on weather depiction charts and their meanings.*

clouds. The larger the drops, the more intense is the return to the radar screen.

Thunderstorms, tornadoes, and hurricanes contain very heavy concentrations of liquid moisture that reflect strong signals to the radarscope. These are called *echoes* and are analyzed and plotted on the computer-generated Radar Summary Chart to give a pictorial view of the storm locations, along with other significant information about the weather. It's for this reason that the Radar Summary Chart is an excellent aid in a weather briefing. A sample chart is shown in Fig. 6-55. Symbols used for echo intensity trend on the radar summary chart are shown in Fig. 6-56.

The information presented on this chart includes echo patterns and coverage, weather associated with echoes, intensity (contours) and trend (+ or −) of precipitation, height of the echo bases and their tops, and movement of echoes. A legend is located in the lower left corner of the chart (Fig. 6-55), along with additional decoding of chart symbols and weather symbols in Fig. 6-56.

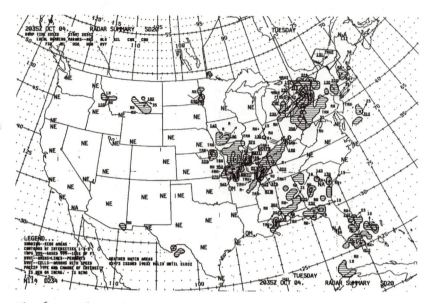

Fig. 6-55. *This radar summary chart shows storm areas based on radar returns.*

VIP LEVEL	ECHO INTENSITY	PRECIPITATION INTENSITY	RAINFALL RATE in/hr STRATIFORM	RAINFALL RATE in/hr CONVECTIVE
1	WEAK	LIGHT	LESS THAN 0.1	LESS THAN 0.2
2	MODERATE	MODERATE	0.1 - 0.5	0.2 - 1.1
3	STRONG	HEAVY	0.5 - 1.0	1.1 - 2.2
4	VERY STRONG	VERY HEAVY	1.0 - 2.0	2.2 - 4.5
5	INTENSE	INTENSE	2.0 - 5.0	4.5 - 7.1
6	EXTREME	EXTREME	MORE THAN 5.0	MORE THAN 7.1

450
Highest precipitation top in area in hundreds of feet MSL.
(45,000 FEET MSL)

* The numbers representing the intensity level do not appear on the chart. Beginning from the first contour line, bordering the area, the intensity level is 1-2, second contour is 3-4, and third contour is 5-6.

─────── SYMBOLS USED ON CHART ───────

SYMBOL MEANING

R RAIN
RW RAIN SHOWER
HAIL HAIL
S SNOW
IP ICE PELLETS
SW SNOW SHOWER
L DRIZZLE
T THUNDERSTORM
ZR,ZL FREEZING PRECIPITATION
NE NO ECHOES OBSERVED
NA OBSERVATIONS UNAVAILABLE
OM OUT FOR MAINTENANCE
STC STC ON – all precipitation may not be seen
ROBEPS RADAR OPERATING BELOW PERFORMANCE STANDARDS
RHINO RANGE HEIGHT INDICATOR NOT OPERATING
RAINFALL RATES SHOULD BE USED WITH CAUTION

SYMBOL MEANING

+ INTENSITY INCREASING OR NEW ECHO
− INTENSITY DECREASING
NO SYMBOL NO CHANGE IN INTENSITY
35 CELL MOVEMENT TO NE AT 35 KNOTS
 LINE OR AREA MOVEMENT TO EAST AT 20 KNOTS
LM LITTLE MOVEMENT
MA ECHOES MOSTLY ALOFT
PA ECHOES PARTLY ALOFT

SYMBOL MEANING

 LINE OF ECHOES
SLD 8/10 OR GREATER COVERAGE IN A LINE
WS999 SEVERE THUNDERSTORM WATCH
WT999 TORNADO WATCH
LEWP LINE ECHO WAVE PATTERN
HOOK HOOK ECHO

Fig. 6-56. *These are the symbols describing the radar echo intensity trend—plus a decoding of other chart symbols.*

The arrangement of echoes, as seen on the radarscope, form a certain pattern that is symbolized on the chart. This pattern of echoes may be a line, an area, or an isolated cell. A cell is a concentrated mass of convection that is normally 20 nautical miles or less in diameter. Echo coverage is the amount of space the echoes, or cells, occupy within an area or line. (Don't interpret these symbolized patterns to mean sky cover.) Radar can't specifically identify the type of precipitation associated with the echoes, but the weather observer, using other sources of weather information, can make that determination.

The height of the tops and bases of echoes are shown in hundreds of feet above mean sea level. A horizontal line is used with the heights shown above or below the line denoting the top height or base heights respectively. The absence of the number below the line indicates the echo base was not reported. Radar detects tops more readily than bases because, as distances increase between the radar antenna and the echo, the earth's curvature is such that the ground obstructs the signal and cloud bases can't be detected. Also, radar detects precipitation that reaches the ground and therefore obscures the base of the cloud on the radar screen.

The movement of individual storms as well as the movement of a line or area is also shown. The movement of the individual storms within a line or area, however, often differs from the movement of the overall storm pattern. The means of depicting these movements are as shown:

Individual echo movement to the northeast at 35 knots.

Line or area movement to the east to 20 knots. (**Note:** A half flag represents 5 knots and a full flag, 10 knots.)

Additional information included on the chart, when appropriate, shows areas that indicate a severe weather watch in effect. Such areas are depicted by a dashed-line rectangle or square. Also, if reports from a particular radar station do not appear on the chart, symbols explain the reason. Examples: **NE** means no echo (equipment operating but no echoes observed); **NA** means observation not available; and **OM** means equipment out for maintenance.

Remember that the radar summary chart is for preflight planning only and should be updated by hourly radar reports. But once you're in the air, watch out for those thunderheads, whether they were reported or not. Depending on the time of year (as spring or summer, especially), and whether storms were forecast or not, ask an FSS Flight Watch for a weather update, including a Radar Remote Weather Display (RRWDS). By whatever means, though, be it visual sighting or your own airborne radar stormscope, stay out of cumulus and cumulonimbus buildups. You've got to avoid them anyway if you're only VFR rated, but regardless, the types of storms we're talking about, particularly the cumulonimbus, can tear you apart—literally. So, be forewarned, if you haven't been already.

Significant weather prognostic charts

Significant Weather Prognostic Charts (commonly referred to as "progs" or "prog charts") portray forecasted weather to assist in weather briefing. The National Weather Service issues these in four panels (Fig. 6-57).

The two lower panels are the 12- and 24-hour surface progs, while the two upper panels are the 12- and 24-hour progs of significant weather from the surface up to 400 millibars (24,000 feet). Both show conditions as they are forecast to be at the validity time of the chart.

The two surface prog panels use the standard symbols to depict fronts and pressure centers. The movement of each pressure center is indicated by an arrow showing the direction and a number indicating speed in knots. Isobars depicting forecast pressure patterns are included on some 24-hour surface progs.

The surface prog outlines areas in which precipitation and/or thunderstorms are forecast. Smooth lines enclose areas of expected precipitation, either continuous or intermittent, while dashed lines enclose areas of expected showers or thunderstorms. The symbols indicate the type and character of the precipitation. The area is shaded if the precipitation is expected to cover half or more of the area and unshaded if less than half.

The upper panels depict forecasts of significant weather such as ceiling, visibility, turbulence, and freezing level. A legend between the panels explains the methods of depicting weather information on these prog charts.

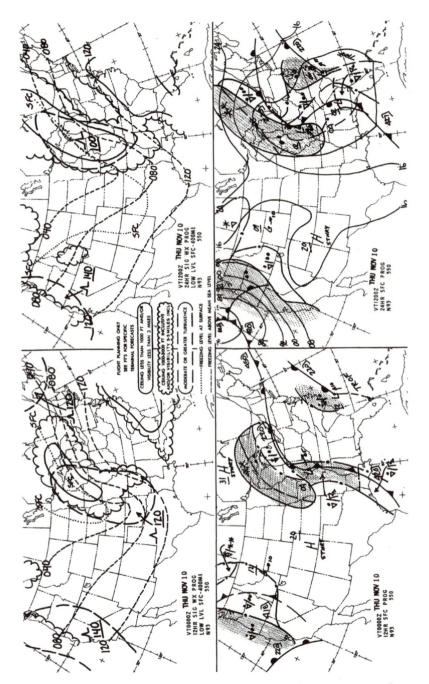

Fig. 6-57. *The four panels of the Significant Weather Prognostic charts are illustrated in this figure.*

This has been a lengthy chapter, but the subject of weather demands a minimum of a full book if it is to be discussed in any depth—to say nothing of the whole science of meteorology. Regardless of that, and within the space available, I've tried to focus on some of the important aspects related to aviation weather pilots must be aware of, understand, and consider before venturing much beyond the home airport's traffic pattern, even on a CAVOK day. At the same time, whether student or licensed pilot, please recognize that there is more to the subject—much more. There are more services available, more weather reports and analyses than those I've mentioned, and more knowledge that every pilot needs to acquire about operating in the various weather patterns Mother Nature can throw at us.

Said another way, I urge you not to leave home without knowing what meteorological conditions lie out there ready to help you along your way or present challenges you or your airplane might not be able to master. A few minutes studying computer charts or reports on your own before takeoff, or listening to a qualified briefer and asking questions, or getting weather updates while en route—these could be the most important minutes of your life. Weather can be beautiful, but it can also be a vicious killer. It's not wise to test Mother Nature.

Quickie quiz questions
Chapter 6

1. What are the two layers of atmosphere surrounding the earth and what are their altitudes?

2. The standard atmospheric pressure is _____inches of mercury, and the standard temperature is _____degrees Fahrenheit or _____ degrees Celsius.

3. Describe some of the effects convection currents can have on an aircraft in flight.

4. What are some of the significances of the temperature/dew-point relationship?

5. What are some of the common characteristics of cumulonimbus clouds?

6. List the characteristics of a cold front and a warm front.

7. What are the main elements that make up a METAR?

8. What weather information does an ASOS report?

9. What are five critical weather reports or advisories issued by the weather sources?

10. What is the name of the ground facility you should normally contact for en route weather information and on what radio frequency?

Answers in Appendix, pages 575-577.

7

Navigation

Now that you've got it all down—how an airplane flies, aircraft structure, engines, instruments, and all the rest, it's about time to go fly, isn't it? Well, yes, but maybe not quite. Oh, we do have to know how to take off and land (that's sort of important), but maybe even before mastering those skills, it might be well to know how to get from point A to B when you're a mile high in the sky with no roadside signs to guide you or gas stations to give you directions. What I'm talking about, of course, is navigation, which, in its broadest concept, is plotting the most direct course to a given destination, flying the route as plotted, and arriving at the destination within the established time parameter.

As I said, that's a very broad definition and doesn't take into consideration many such factors as current and forecast weather, winds, temperature, terrain, performance capabilities of the aircraft being flown, and the like. Still, that's what navigating is all about. Most pilots do—and all pilots should—take pride in their ability to satisfy the three basics of plotting the route, flying the plotted route, and arriving as planned. On the contrary, failure to master the fundamentals of navigation presents the possibility of running out of fuel, not having alternative plans if unexpected weather develops, becoming lost, having to make an off-airport landing, flying into restricted airspaces, or whatever.

Actually, if you haven't learned how to navigate, you're not likely to get a private pilot certificate anyway. The reason? Among other things, the FAA requires every applicant to have five solo hours of cross-country flight and one cross-country of 150 miles with at least three en route full-stop landings. Without those requirements logged and signed off by your instructor, the FAA regulations will not have been met and thus no certificate. So—the subject of this chapter has some importance for those who seriously want to become certificated pilots.

It wasn't too many years ago that navigation was considered quite a challenging art. Recent advancements, however, in instruments, aeronautical charts, pilot techniques, and navigation aids have greatly enhanced the ability of pilots to plan their flights more effectively and to arrive at their destinations according to the plan. And, of course, don't overlook the importance of loran (LOng RAnge Area Navigation) and especially GPS (Global Positioning System). The rapid development of these two systems, coupled with their continually lowering costs, have made navigation, even for the general aviation light-plane pilot, little more than reading and responding to computerized data. That's admittedly a bit of an exaggeration, but really, not too much so, particularly when the electronic marvels of GPS are concerned. I'll have a little more to say about those two systems at the end of this chapter.

All of that, however, does not alter the importance of learning and applying the principles and techniques of nonelectronic aerial navigation. The aircraft can always lose its electrical power, which could then force the pilot to rely on pilotage, dead reckoning, or navigation skills. Consequently, the primary purpose in this chapter is to provide information of practical value when flying under Visual Flight Rules (VFR) and without necessarily having the benefit of the latest scientific aids.

To navigate successfully, a pilot should be able to determine the aircraft's position relative to the earth's surface at any time. Ability to do so is accomplished by one or more of these methods:

1. Pilotage (by reference solely to visible landmarks)
2. Dead reckoning (by computing direction, distance, and time from a known position)
3. Radio navigation (by use of electronic aids)

The basic form of navigation for the beginning pilot is *pilotage*, which should be mastered first. The next step up, an understanding of *dead reckoning*, enables the pilot to make the necessary calculations of direction, heading, flight time, fuel consumption, and the effect of winds. Finally, the ever-increasing use of *electronic equipment* makes it essential to have a thorough knowledge of radio communications and the use of the available electronic aids.

While at first glance it may seem somewhat remote from the subject, and perhaps a bit rudimentary, a review of meridians of longitude and parallels of latitude, which are the bases of time, distance, and direction, is in order.

Meridians and parallels

The equator is an imaginary circle equidistant from the poles of the earth. Circles parallel to the equator (lines running east and west) are *parallels of latitude* and are used to measure degrees of latitude north or south of the equator. Because it's a little confusing, note that the arrows in Fig. 7-1 labeled "LATITUDE" point to the lines of latitude. The 48 conterminous states of the United States are located between 25° and 45° N latitude.

Fig. 7-1. *Meridians and parallels are the bases for measuring time, distance, and direction.*

Meridians of longitude are drawn from the north pole to the south pole and are at right angles to the equator. The *prime meridian*, which passes through Greenwich, England, is used as the zero line from which measurements are made in degrees east and west to 180°. The 48 conterminous states of the United States lie between 67° and 125° W longitude, and the arrows in Fig. 7-1 labeled "LONGITUDE" identify these lines.

Any specific geographical point can thus be located by reference to its longitude and latitude. Washington, D.C., for example, is approximately 39° N latitude, 77° W longitude. Chicago is approximately 42° N latitude, 88° W longitude (Fig. 7-1), and so on.

The meridians are also useful for designating time belts. A day is defined as the time required for the earth to make one complete revolution of 360°. Since the day is divided into 24 hours, the earth revolves at the rate of 15° an hour. Noon is the time when the sun is directly above a meridian; to the west of that meridian is forenoon, to the east is afternoon.

The standard practice is to establish a time belt for each 15° of longitude. This makes a difference of exactly one hour between each belt. In the United States there are four time belts—Eastern (75°), Central (90°), Mountain (105°), and Pacific (120°). The dividing lines are somewhat irregular because communities near the boundaries often find it more convenient to use time designations of neighboring communities or trade centers.

Figure 7-2 shows the time zones in the United States. When the sun is directly above the 90th meridian, it is noon Central Standard Time, 1 P.M. Eastern Standard Time, 11 A.M. Mountain Standard Time, and 10 A.M. Pacific Standard Time. When daylight saving time is in effect, generally between April and October, the sun is directly above the 75th meridian at noon, Central Daylight Time.

For the student or low-time pilot, these time zone differences should be considered during long flights eastward, especially if the flight must be completed before dark. Remember, an hour is lost when flying eastward from one time zone to another, or perhaps even when flying from the western edge to the eastern edge of the same time zone. Determine the time of sunset at the destination by consulting an FSS or a Weather Forecast Office and take this into account when planning an eastbound flight.

Fig. 7-2. *When the sun is directly above the meridian, the time at all points on that meridian is noon. This is the basis on which time zones are established.*

In most aviation operations, time is expressed in terms of the 24-hour clock. Air traffic control instructions, weather reports and broadcasts, and estimated times of arrival are all based on this system. For example: 9 A.M. is expressed as 0900; 1 P.M. is 1300; 10 P.M. is 2200, etc.

Measurement of direction

By using the meridians, direction from one point to another can be measured in degrees in a clockwise direction from true north. More specifically, to plot a course to be followed in flight, draw a line on an aeronautical chart, such as the sectional, from the point of departure to the destination and measure the angle from true north that this line forms with a meridian. Direction is expressed in degrees, as shown by the compass rose in Fig. 7-3.

Because meridians converge toward the poles, a course measurement should be taken at a meridian near the midpoint of the course rather than at the point of departure. The course plotted on the chart

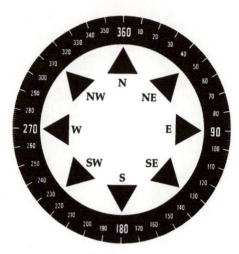

Fig. 7-3. *The compass rose enables the pilot to determine direction in terms of points on the compass.*

is known as the true course. This is the direction measured by reference to a meridian, or true north. It is the direction of intended flight in terms of degrees moving clockwise from true north. As shown in Fig. 7-4, the direction from A to B would be a true course of 065°, whereas the return trip (the reciprocal) would be a true course of 245°.

Variation and deviation

The *true heading* is the direction in which the nose of the airplane points during a flight when measured in degrees clockwise from true north. More often than not, however, you have to head the airplane in a direction slightly different from the true course to offset the effect of wind; consequently, the numerical value of the true heading might not correspond exactly with that of the true course. But I'll discuss this more fully later in the chapter.

Using the 65° course in the example above, assume that the flight is conducted under a no-wind condition. If that were the case, the true heading would also be 65°. But now, some other factors (besides wind) enter the picture. While mentioned briefly in Chapter 4, the matter of magnetic variation and compass deviation warrants further explanation and what you have to do to compensate for them in the navigation process.

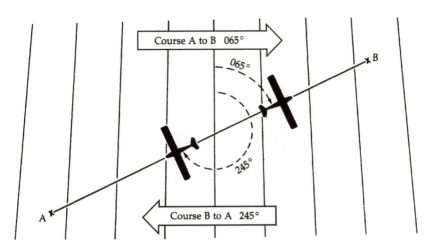

Fig. 7-4. *Courses headings are determined by references to meridians on aeronautical charts.*

Variation

Variation is the angle between true north and magnetic north. It is expressed as "east variation" or "west variation," depending on whether, relative to one's present geographical position, the magnetic north (MN) is to the east or the west of true north (TN).

To be more specific: The north magnetic pole is located close to latitude 71° N and longitude 96° W, about 1300 miles from the geographic or true north pole (Fig. 7-5). If the earth were uniformly magnetized, the compass needle would unerringly point to the magnetic pole, in which case the variation between true north (as shown by the geographical meridians) and magnetic north (as shown by the magnetic meridians) could be measured at any intersection of the meridians.

But the earth is not uniformly magnetized. In the United States, the compass needle usually points in the general direction of the magnetic pole but it could vary in certain geographical localities by many degrees.

Because of this, the exact amount of variation at thousands of selected locations in the United States has been carefully determined by the National Ocean Service. The amount and the direction of variation, both of which can change slightly from time to time, are shown on most aeronautical charts as broken red lines, called *isogonic* lines, which connect points of equal magnetic variation. (The line connect-

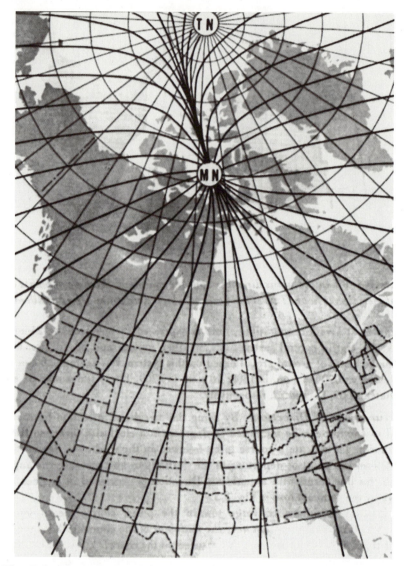

Fig. 7-5. *Magnetic meridians are based on magnetic north and geographic meridians on true north. Variation is the angle between a magnetic and a geographic meridian.*

ing points at which there is no variation between true north and magnetic north is the *agonic* line.) An isogonic chart is shown in Fig. 7-6. Minor bends and turns in the isogonic and agonic lines probably are caused by unusual geological conditions affecting magnetic forces in these areas.

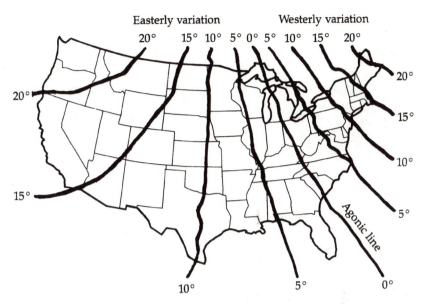

Fig. 7-6. *A typical isogonic chart. The heavy lines connect geographic points sharing identical magnetic variation.*

On the west coast of the United States, because of the position of the magnetic north, the compass needle points to the east of true north, while on the east coast, the needle points to the west of true north. Zero degree variation exists on the agonic line that runs roughly through Lake Superior, Michigan, the Appalachian Mountains, South Carolina, and off the coast of Florida. It is along this line where magnetic north and true north coincide. (Compare Figs. 7-7 and 7-8.)

Because courses are measured with reference to geographical meridians that point toward true north, not magnetic north, the actual heading must be converted into magnetic direction for the purpose of flight. This conversion is made by adding or subtracting the variation that is indicated by the nearest isogonic line on the chart. The true heading, when corrected for variation, is then known as the *magnetic heading.*

At Providence, Rhode Island, for instance, the charted variation is "14° W." This means that in Providence magnetic north is 14° west of true north. If a true heading of 360° is to be flown, 14° must be added to 360°, which results in a magnetic heading of 014°. The same correction for variation must be applied to the true heading to obtain any magnetic heading at Providence, or at any point close to the "14° W" isogonic line. Thus, to fly 90° east, a magnetic

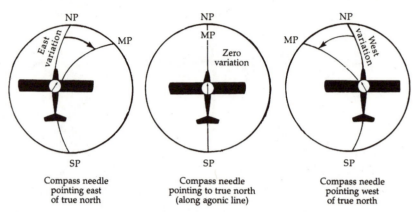

Fig. 7-7. *In an area of east variation, a compass needle points east of true north. In an area of zero variation, it points to true north, and in an area of west variation, it points west of true north.*

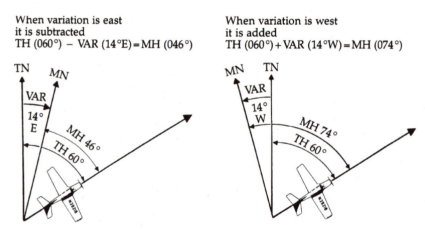

Fig. 7-8. *This illustrates the relationship between true heading, magnetic heading, and variation in areas of east and west variation.*

heading of 104° (090° + 14°) would be flown. To fly 180° due south, the magnetic heading would be 194°. Going west at 270°, it would be 284°. And so on.

Looking at it from a different perspective, suppose a flight is to take place near Denver, Colorado. The isogonic line shows the variation to be approximately "14° E." This means that magnetic north lies 14° to the east of true north. So, to fly a true heading of 360°, 14° is *subtracted* from 360°, resulting in a magnetic heading of 346°. Just as the 14 degrees are added in the Providence isogonic line area, so are 14 degrees subtracted from the appropriate true heading to obtain the magnetic heading at a point close to Denver's "14°E" isogonic line. (To fly 90°, the magnetic heading would be 76°, and so on.)

In summary, then, to convert the true course or heading to a magnetic course or heading, note the variation shown by the nearest isogonic line. If the variation is west, add; if east, subtract.

A simple method for remembering whether to add or subtract variation: West is best (add); East is least (subtract).

Deviation

Determining the magnetic heading is an intermediate step in obtaining the correct compass reading for the flight. To establish the compass heading in a no-wind condition, a further correction for something called *deviation* must be made. Because of magnetic influences within the airplane itself, such as electrical circuits, radio, lights, tools, engine, magnetized metal parts, etc., the compass needle is frequently deflected from its normal reading. This deflection is called *deviation*, and it is different for each airplane as well as possibly varying with different headings in the same airplane. For instance, if magnetism in the engine attracts the north end of the compass, there would be no effect when the plane is on a heading of magnetic north. On easterly or westerly headings, however, the compass indications would be in error, as shown in Fig. 7-9. Although magnetic attraction can come from many other parts of the airplane, the assumption of attraction in the engine is used here just to illustrate the point.

Some adjustment of the compass, referred to as *compensation*, can be made to reduce this error, but the remaining correction must be applied by the pilot.

Proper compass compensation is best performed by a competent technician, whether pilot or mechanic. Because the magnetic forces within the airplane change and because of landing shocks, vibration, mechanical work, or changes in equipment, the compass deviation should be checked periodically. The procedure to do so, called *swinging the compass*, is as follows:

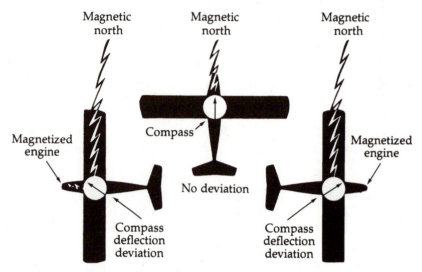

Fig. 7-9. *Magnetized portions of the airplane cause the compass to deviate from its normal indication.*

The airplane is placed on an outdoor magnetic compass rose, usually painted on the tarmac. The engine is started, and electrical devices normally used (such as radios) are turned on. (Tailwheel-type airplanes should be jacked up into flying position.) The plane is aligned with magnetic north, as indicated on the compass rose. If the aircraft compass reads other than 0° in this position, minor corrections can often be made in the cockpit by adjusting a small screw on the face of the compass with a demagnetized screwdriver until the compass reads the desired 0° heading. The airplane is then turned to 30-degree intervals around the compass rose, and each successive 30-degree reading is recorded on a small compass deviation card that is inserted in a bracket attached to the compass itself. If the airplane is to be flown at night, the lights are turned on and any significant changes in the readings are noted. If so, additional entries are made for use at night.

Brief accuracy checks can also be made by comparing the compass's reading with known runway headings. This is not the most reliable system, but it indicates any serious deviation that should either be corrected or recorded on the compass card.

On that card, as illustrated in Fig. 7-10, N, E, S, and W obviously identify north, east, south, and west. The card also reflects the

FOR (MAGNETIC)	N	30	60	E	120	150
STEER (COMPASS)	0	28	57	86	117	148
FOR (MAGNETIC)	S	210	240	W	300	330
STEER (COMPASS)	180	212	243	274	303	332

Fig. 7-10. *An example of the compass deviation card that is usually affixed to the compass for ease of reference.*

headings to steer, based on the latest compass-swinging check, when flying at the various 30-degree intervals.

For readings between the 30-degree intervals, you should be able to interpolate mentally with sufficient accuracy. For example, if you needed the correction for 195°, and noted the correction for 180° to be 0° and for 210° to be +2°, it could be assumed that the correction for 195° would be +1°. Once corrected for deviation, the *magnetic heading* is now known as *compass heading*.

To illustrate the application of these various compass corrections, assume that a flight is planned from Winston Field, southwest of Snyder, Texas, direct to Mineral Wells, Texas (Fig. 7-11). A line is first drawn between the centers of the two airports. The midmeridian for this course is 99°30' W. Measuring the direction of the course line at this meridian with a protractor gives a true course (TC) of 088°. If there were no wind, the true heading (TH) would be the same as the true course, or 88°. Magnetic variation, however, enters the picture at this point.

Magnetic variation over comparatively short distances is obtained from the isogonic line on the navigational chart nearest the midpoint of the planned route. If the flight distance and direction are such that several isogonic lines will be crossed, the number of degrees of variation added or subtracted must be computed to allow for significant changes in variation.

Variation (VAR) for this course is shown on the sectional as 8° E. Subtracting 8° from 088° gives a magnetic heading (MH) of 080°. Checking the deviation card for the airplane (Fig. 7-10), the instructions say that for "E STEER 86°." This means that 4° must be subtracted from the magnetic heading, resulting in a compass heading (CH) of 076°. If that compass heading is maintained (assuming no

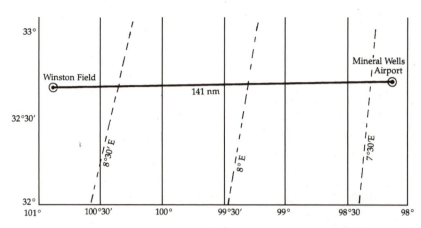

Fig. 7-11. *This drawing illustrates the route, mileage, and degrees of variation in the Winston Field to Mineral Wells flight.*

wind), the pilot should proceed directly on course from Winston Field to Mineral Wells.

As just an example, Fig. 7-12 shows the relationship between true heading, magnetic heading, and compass heading. A simple formula to determine compass heading is this: After the True Course (TC) is measured and wind correction applied, which results in a True Heading (TH), the calculating sequence is: TH [PLUS/MINUS] VAR = MH [PLUS/MINUS] DEV = CH.

Aeronautical charts

The National Oceanic and Atmospheric Administration (NOAA) publishes a number of aeronautical charts of the United States and foreign areas designed for low (up to but not including 18,000 feet) and high (18,000 feet and above) altitude flight. Those of the most concern to the VFR pilot are the sectional chart, the VFR terminal area chart for operations in or near Class B (airport) airspaces, the VFR/IFR planning chart (often referred to as a Wall Planning chart), the en route low altitude chart for radio navigation purposes, and a related publication, the *Airport/Facility Directory*.

While studying this chapter, it would be helpful to have current copies of these publications at hand to make the brief description of each that follows more understandable.

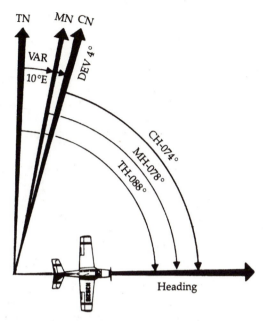

Fig. 7-12. *An example of the relationship between true, magnetic, and compass headings for a theoretical flight.*

Sectional chart

Thirty-seven sectional charts (and by the way, these are called "charts," not maps) cover the conterminous United States (Fig. 7-13). Each is identified by the name of the principal city in the geographic area represented by the chart, as "Seattle," "Great Falls," "Phoenix," "Atlanta," and so on. The scale is 1:500,000 (1 inch = 6.86 nm), and the charts are updated semiannually. Their basic purpose is to provide a source of visual navigation for slow and medium speed aircraft.

There should be little difficulty in reading these charts because, in many ways, they are similar to automobile road maps. In addition, a legend on the chart flap explains the color-coding and the various symbols used to identify ground features and navigational aids.

As just a few examples, many landmarks that are easily recognizable from the air, such as stadiums, race tracks, pumping stations, or refineries, are identified either by symbols or brief descriptions adjacent to the landmark. The symbol for obstructions is another important feature. The elevation of the top of obstructions above sea level is given in blue figures (without parentheses) adjacent to the

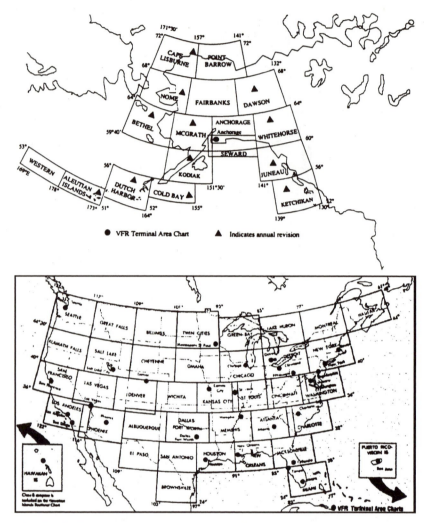

Fig. 7-13. *The sectional charts for Alaska, the conterminous United States, Hawaii, Puerto Rico, and the Virgin Islands. The black circles identify the Class B airports for which VFR Terminal Area charts are available.*

obstruction symbol. Immediately below this set of figures is another set of lighter blue figures enclosed in parentheses that represents the height of the top of the obstruction above ground level. Obstructions that extend less than 1000 feet above the terrain are shown by one type of symbol and those that extend 1000 feet or higher above ground level are indicated by a different symbol. Specific elevations of certain high points in terrain are shown on charts by dots accompanied by small black figures indicating the number of feet above sea level.

Additionally, in larger bold face blue numbers, the chart identifies Maximum Elevation Figures (MEF). These figures indicate the height of the terrain above mean sea level, doing so in terms of thousands (large numbers) and hundreds (in smaller numbers). An explanation of symbols used on the sectional charts appears on the exterior flap of the chart, with radio frequencies and other special information on the inside of that flap.

At the same time, and again through symbols and color-coding, the sectional identifies:

1. The location of airports in relation to cities or towns and whether the airport is controlled or uncontrolled, private, or military

2. Airport data, including runway layout, length of the longest runway, communication frequencies, field elevation, and runway lighting information

3. Navigation radio aids and communication frequencies

4. Airport traffic service and airspace information, such as federal airways, Special Use Airspace, the floors of controlled airspace, controlled airport areas (Classes B, C, and D), and Military Training Routes

5. Topographical information, as mentioned above, plus highways, railroad tracks, bridges, power lines, lakes, rivers, water tanks, and other prominent surface features

6. Miscellaneous, including isogonic lines, areas of glider operations, ultralight activity, flashing lights, and marine lights.

As with all charts, the sectional becomes obsolete and should be discarded as soon as the next updated version is published. The date of obsolescence is printed in magenta on the cover flap, stating that "This chart will become OBSOLETE FOR USE IN NAVIGATION upon publication of the next edition scheduled for (month, date, year)." As a rule, a given sectional is valid for about six months. And something to keep in mind about that: Should you be subject to a random ramp check by an FAA inspector, *don't* be caught with an outdated chart in your airplane. You'll be written up if you are. It's okay to fly with *no* chart on board, but it's not okay to fly with one that's obsolete.

Terminal area chart

The VFR Terminal Area charts are similar in design to the sectional—except that they detail the area within a 30 to 40 mile radius around the 23 busiest airports where the volume of activity warrants the establishment of a Class B airspace. The purpose of this chart is to provide enlarged details of the area for the VFR pilot entering or operating in the vicinity of one of these major terminals. Its scale is twice that of the sectional, or 1:250,000 (1 inch = 3.43 nm), and, as the sectional, is revised semiannually.

VFR/IFR planning chart

This chart is designed to assist in planning long flights that might otherwise require the use of several sectionals. The scale is thus 1:2,333,232 (1 inch = 32 nm). These are large charts, measuring 41 × 52 inches, which makes them impractical for navigational use in a confined cockpit. Because of their size, they are usually mounted on airport office walls for extended cross-country flight planning. Thus the common term, "wall planning charts" often given them.

In effect, two charts cover the entire United States, parts of Canada, and offshore areas. Each of the two charts has data for IFR planning on one side and data for VFR planning on the other. More specifically, the IFR planning chart for the eastern half of the country has VFR planning for the western half on the reverse side. Similarly, the western IFR chart is combined with the eastern VFR chart. Consequently, to display the entire country for either VFR or IFR flight planning, two charts are required.

For VFR purposes, such data as airports, VORs, Special Use Airspace, cities, bodies of water, military training routes, isogonic lines, and spot elevations are depicted. The VFR side, however, does not show federal airways and omits much of the detail found on the sectional. It is thus a long-flight planning chart but not satisfactory for VFR navigating.

En route low altitude chart

Although primarily designed for low-level IFR flight (below 18,000 feet), the en route chart is very useful for the VFR pilot who is knowledgeable in radio navigation. As the legend flap indicates, the data presented includes, among others, limited airport information, radio aids to navigation data boxes, Flight Service Station frequencies,

VOR airways, mileages between VORs, Special Use Airspace, and data essential to IFR operations.

Unlike the sectional, the en route chart does not depict cities, highways, rivers, ground terrain, ground obstacles, and similar details. Used in conjunction with the sectional, however, the en route simplifies cross-country flying for the VFR pilot skilled in dead reckoning and radio navigation.

Twenty-eight charts cover the conterminous United States, each labeled numerically, as "L-1," "L-2," up to "L-28" (Fig. 7-14). More accurately, there are 14 individual publications, but each consists of two separate charts printed back-to-back. The chart is revised every 56 days, effective with the date of airspace changes. The scale is 1 inch = 12 nm.

Airport/facility directory

The Airport/Facility Directory (A/FD) is not a navigation publication, but it is an essential reference source for determining details not

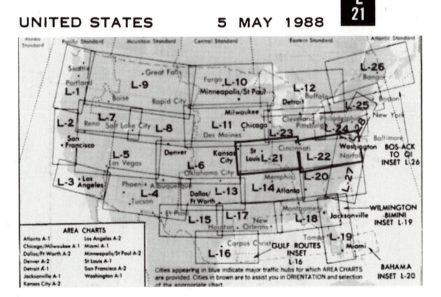

Fig. 7-14. *The 28 en route low altitude charts are identified by number and geographic area, as this excerpt from L-21 and L-22, extending from Kansas City to the Washington area, illustrates.*

found on any aeronautical chart about a specific airport. Such details include, but are not limited to, airport location and mileage from the airport's city, runway and lighting data, services available, as grades of fuel and repair capabilities, traffic pattern altitude, weather data sources, airport communication frequencies, and radio aids to navigation.

Seven directories cover the United States, Puerto Rico, and the Virgin Islands, providing data on all airports, seaplane bases, and heliports open to the public. As Fig. 7-15 indicates, the geographic areas for which individual directories are published are: northeast, southeast, east central, north central, south central, northwest, and southwest. Like the aeronautical charts, the A/FD is published by the National Ocean Service and is updated every eight weeks.

Navigation by dead reckoning

Earlier in this chapter, an example of determining a course heading after correcting for variation and deviation was illustrated. That example, however, assumed a no-wind condition—a condition that is possible but very rare in real life. Consequently, understanding how winds can affect an aircraft's ground track and how to correct for them are essential ingredients in the flight planning and navigating process. (**Note:** While most of the discussion and calculations in this section use miles and miles per hour, it should be pointed out that there is an increasing trend toward knots and nautical miles per hour. One statute mile = .87 knots; one knot = 1.15 statute miles.)

Fig. 7-15. *The Airport/Facility Directory provides detailed data for all airports located in the seven geographic areas.*

Effect of wind

As discussed in the study of the atmosphere, wind is a mass of air moving over the surface of the earth in a definite direction. When blowing from the north at 25 knots, it simply means that the air is moving southward over the earth's surface at a rate of 25 nautical miles in one hour.

Under these conditions, any inert object free from contact with the earth will be carried 25 nautical miles southward in one hour. This effect becomes apparent when clouds, dust, toy balloons, etc., are observed being blown along by the wind. Obviously, an airplane flying within the moving mass of air will be similarly affected. Even though the airplane does not float freely with the wind, it moves through the air at the same time the air is moving over the ground, and is thus affected by the wind. Consequently, at the end of one hour of flight, the airplane will be in a position that results from a combination of these two motions: the movement of the air mass in reference to the ground, and the forward movement of the airplane through the air mass.

Actually, these two motions are independent. So far as the airplane's flight through the air is concerned, it makes no difference whether the mass of air through which the airplane is flying is moving or is stationary. A pilot flying in a 70-knot gale would be totally unaware of any wind (except for possible turbulence) unless he or she could see the ground. In reference to the ground, however, the airplane would appear to fly faster with a tailwind or slower with a head-wind, or to drift right or left with a crosswind.

As shown in Fig. 7-16, an airplane flying eastward at an airspeed of 120 mph in calm wind has a groundspeed exactly the same—120 mph. If the mass of air is also moving eastward at 20 mph, the *airspeed* of the airplane is still 120 mph, but its progress over the ground is 120 plus 20, or a *groundspeed* of 140 mph. Conversely, if the mass of air is moving westward at 20 mph, the airspeed of the airplane still remains the same, but groundspeed becomes 120 minus 20, or 100 mph.

Assuming no correction is made for wind effect, if the airplane is heading eastward at 120 mph and the air mass is moving southward at 20 mph, the airplane at the end of one hour will be 120 miles east of its point of departure, because of its progress through the air but 20 miles south because of the motion of the air (Fig. 7-17).

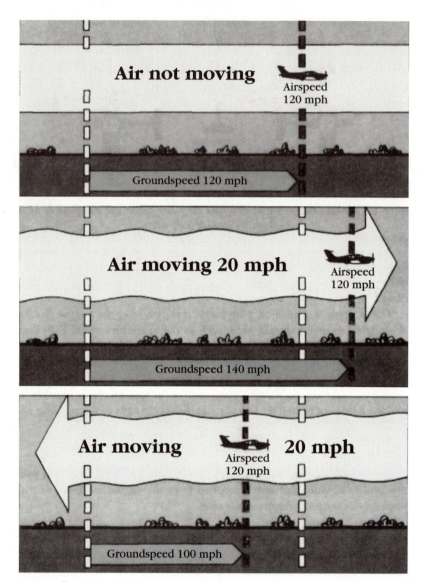

Fig. 7-16. *Motion of the air affects the speed with which airplanes move over the earth's surface, but not the plane's airspeed, meaning the rate at which the aircraft moves through the air.*

Under these circumstances, the airspeed remains 120 mph, but the groundspeed is determined by combining the movement of the airplane with that of the air mass. Groundspeed can be measured as the distance from the point of departure to the position of the airplane at the end of one hour and can be computed by determining

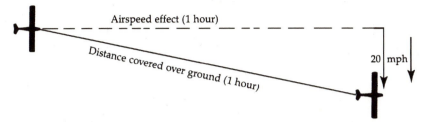

Fig. 7-17. *An example of how a plane's flight path can be affected by the direction and speed of the wind—if no corrective actions are taken to compensate for the wind.*

the time required to fly between two points a known distance apart. It also can be determined before flight by constructing a wind triangle, which is explained later in this chapter.

The direction in which the plane is pointing as it flies is *heading*. Its actual path over the ground, which is a combination of the motion of the airplane and the motion of the air, is *track*. The angle between the heading and the track is *drift angle*. If the airplane's heading coincides with the true course and the wind is blowing from the left, the track does not coincide with the true course. The wind drifts the airplane to the right, so the track falls to the right of the desired or true course (Fig. 7-18).

By determining the amount of drift, the pilot can counteract the effect of the wind and make the track of the airplane coincide with the desired course. If the mass of air is moving across the course from the left, the airplane naturally drifts to the right. Consequently, a correction must be made by heading the airplane a certain number of degrees to the left to offset the drift. This is called *wind correction angle* and is expressed in terms of degrees right or left of the true course (Fig. 7-19).

To summarize:

- *Course* is the intended path of an aircraft over the earth, reading clockwise from 0° through 360°.
- *Heading* is the direction in which the nose of the airplane points during flight.
- *Track* is the actual path made over the ground in flight. (If proper correction has been made for the wind, track and course are identical.)

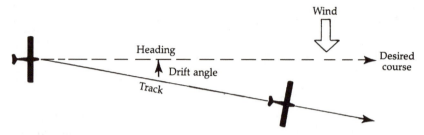

Fig. 7-18. *Effects of wind drift on maintaining a desired course.*

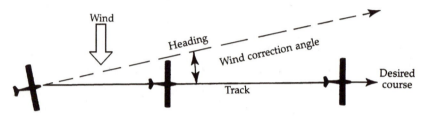

Fig. 7-19. *These planes should be angled into the wing just as the first one is. To maintain the desired course means establishing a wind correction angle to counteract the wind drift.*

- *Drift angle* is the angle between heading and track.
- *Wind correction angle* is correction applied to the course to establish a heading so that track coincides with course.
- *Airspeed* is the rate of the airplane's progress through the air.
- *Groundspeed* is the rate of the airplane's inflight progress over the ground.

The wind triangle

The wind triangle is a graphic explanation of the effect of wind upon flight. Groundspeed, heading, and time for any flight can be determined by using the wind triangle, which is applicable to the simplest kind of cross-country as well as the most complicated instrument flight. The experienced pilot becomes so familiar with the fundamental principles that he or she can make adequate estimates for visual flight without actually drawing the diagrams. The student pilot, however, needs to develop skill in constructing these diagrams as an aid to the complete understanding wind effect.

Let's say you're planning on a flight to a point due east of your present location, and you learn that you will face a 40-knot wind blowing from the northeast at 45 degrees. This means, of course, that you'll have to point the aircraft nose slightly towards the 45-degree heading to compensate for the wind and that your trip will be slowed down by a fairly stiff partial headwind. For purposes of visualizing the situation and to establish the principle of the wind triangle, refer to Fig. 7-20. The solid line represents the direction of the track (due east at 90 degrees), the short dashed line the direction of the wind, and the long dashed line the approximate heading you would have to fly to avoid drifting to the right of your course. Again, just look at Fig.7-20 so that you can picture the route and the conditions, because the next series of figures will illustrate the construction of the wind triangle as it would appear on paper. All you need for this plotting is a protractor, a ruler, and a sectional chart to determine the magnetic variation that would affect the ultimate compass reading. The purpose of the exercise is to compute your groundspeed at, let's say, a 120-knot-per-hour airspeed in a 40-knot wind coming at you from a 45-degree angle off the nose.

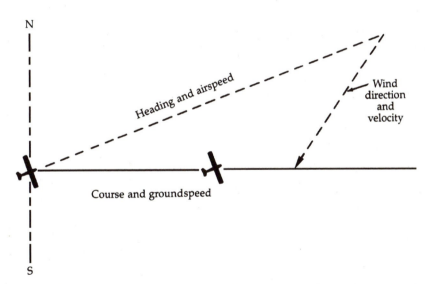

Fig. 7-20. *This diagram is simply to help you get a mental picture of the flight and wind conditions prior to outlining the steps of constructing a wind triangle.*

Step 1: Draw a vertical north-south line (Fig. 7-21). Place a protractor on that line, with the curved edge facing east. At the center point of the base, make a dot labeled "E," your departure point. Then at the curved edge, make another dot at 90 degrees for the true course and the same at the 45-degree point to represent wind direction. Before drawing any more lines, decide on some convenient unit or scale (such as 1" = 20 knots) that will represent distance, airspeed, and wind velocity. Just be sure to use the same unit for each of the linear measurements, and use either "knots" throughout the exercise or statute "miles." It's essential that all measurement units are consistent.

Step 2: Draw a straight 90-degree line east from E (Fig. 7-22). extending it several inches out from E. Label it the true course line: "TC 090."

Step 3: Next, (Fig. 7-23) align the ruler with E and the dot at 45 degrees. Then draw the wind arrow from E, not toward 045 degrees but downward in the direction the wind is blowing. Make the line 40 units long to correspond with the 40-knot wind velocity. Finally, measure 120 units on the ruler to represent your airspeed and put a mark on a ruler to identify that "120" point.

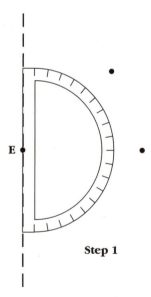

Step 1

Fig. 7-21. *Preparing the wind triangle.*

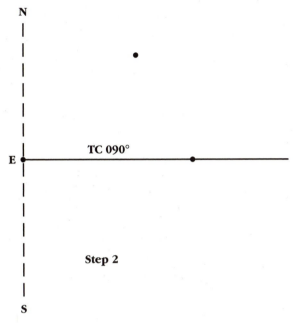

Fig. 7-22. *Establishing the course line.*

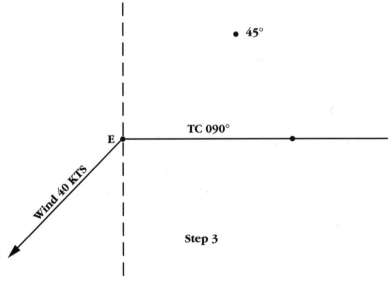

Fig. 7-23. *Plotting the wind direction and velocity.*

Step 4: Place the ruler (Fig. 7-24) so that the end is on the wind arrowhead and the 120-knot dot intercepts the TC line. Identify the intercept point with the letter "P." That represents the position of the aircraft on the TC at the end of one hour. Now put the ruler on the E–P line and, using the same unit scale, determine the groundspeed between E and P, which, in this case, turns out to be 88 nautical miles per hour (88 knots) versus a 120-knot airspeed.

The true heading to fly is easily established by one of two ways:

One (Fig. 7-25) is by placing the straight side of the protractor along the north-south line, with its center point at the intersection of the airspeed line and north-south line and reading the true heading directly in degrees (076°).

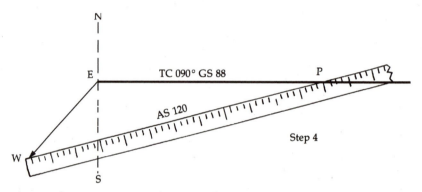

Fig. 7-24. *Determining the aircraft position and groundspeed after one hour of flight.*

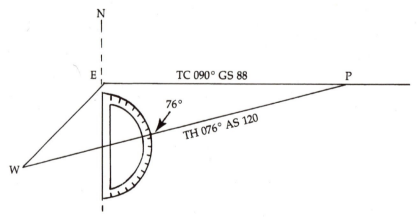

Fig. 7-25. *Finding the true heading by direct measurement.*

The second way (Fig. 7-26) is by placing the straight side of the protractor along the true course line, with its center at P and reading the angle between the true course and the airspeed line. This is the wind correction angle (WCA) that must be applied to the true course to obtain the true heading. If the wind blows from the right of true course, the angle is added; if from the left, it is subtracted. In the example given, the WCA is 14° and the wind is from left; therefore, subtract 14° from true course of 090°, making the true heading 076°.

After obtaining the true heading, apply the correction for magnetic variation to obtain magnetic heading, and the correction for compass deviation to obtain a compass heading. The compass heading can then be used to fly to the destination by dead reckoning.

To determine the time and fuel required for the flight, first find the distance to the destination by measuring the length of the course line drawn on the sectional chart (using the appropriate scale at the bottom of the chart or navigation flight plotter). If the distance measures 220 miles, divide 220 by the groundspeed of 88 mph, which gives a flight time of 2.5 hours (or 2:30). If fuel consumption is eight gallons an hour, 8 × 2.5, or about 20 gallons will be used.

Briefly summarized, then, the steps, or elements, in planning a VFR flight are:

True course. Direction of the line connecting two desired points, drawn on the chart and measured clockwise in degrees from true north on the midmeridian.

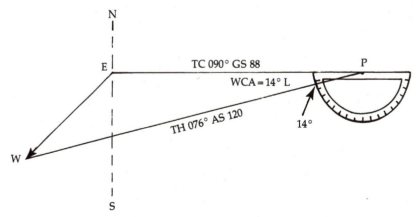

Fig. 7-26. *Finding the true heading by the wind correction angle.*

Wind correction angle. Determined from wind triangle. (Added to TC if the wind is from the right, subtracted if wind is from the left.)

True heading. The direction, measured in degrees clockwise from true north, in which the nose of the plane should point to make good the desired course.

Variation. Obtained from the isogonic line on the chart. (Added to TH if west; subtracted if east.)

Magnetic heading. An intermediate step in the conversion. (Obtained by applying variation to true heading.)

Deviation. Obtained from the compass deviation card in the airplane. (Added to MH or subtracted from, as indicated.)

Compass heading. The reading on the compass (found by applying deviation to MH) that is followed to make good the desired course.

Total distance. Obtained by measuring the length of the TC line on the chart (using the scale at the bottom of the sectional chart or flight plotter).

Groundspeed. Obtained by measuring the length of the TC line on the wind triangle (using the scale employed for drawing the diagram).

Time for flight. Total distance divided by groundspeed.

Fuel rate. Predetermined gallons per hour used at cruising speed. (Additional fuel for an adequate reserve should be added as a safety measure.)

A useful combination Planning Sheet and Flight Log form is shown in Fig. 7-27.

The true course for the return trip is the reciprocal of the outbound course. This can be measured on the chart, or found more easily by adding 180° to the outbound true course (090° + 180° = 270°). This assumes that the outbound course is less than 180°. If it is greater than 180°, the 180° should be subtracted instead of added. For example, if the outbound course is 200°, the reciprocal is 200°–180° = 020°. The wind correction angle is the same number of degrees as for the outbound course, but because the wind is on the opposite side (right) of the airplane, the correction must be added to the true

PILOT'S PLANNING SHEET

PLANE IDENTIFICATION   DATE

CRUISING AIRSPEED	TC	WIND		W/CA R+ L–	TH	VAR W+ E–	MH	DEV	CH	TOTAL MILES	GS	TOTAL TIME	FUEL RATE	TOTAL FUEL
		MPH	FROM											
From:														
To:														
From:														
To:														

VISUAL FLIGHT LOG

	RADIO FREQUENCIES	DISTANCE		ELAPSED TIME		CLOCK TIME		GS		CH		REMARKS
		POINT TO POINT	CUMULATIVE	ESTIMATED	ACTUAL	ESTIMATED	ACTUAL	ESTIMATED	ACTUAL	ESTIMATED	ACTUAL	BRACKETS, WEATHER, ETC.
TIME OF DEPARTURE												
POINT OF DEPARTURE												
CHECKPOINTS												
1.												
2.												
3.												
4.												
5.												
DESTINATION												
6.												

Fig. 7-27. *A sample planning sheet and visual flight log.*

course instead of subtracted (270° + 14° = 284°). Thus, the true heading for the return trip is 284°.

To find the groundspeed, construct a new wind triangle as shown in Fig. 7-28. Instead of drawing another complete diagram, however, consider point E on the previous diagram as the starting point for the return trip and extend the true course line in the direction opposite to the outbound course. The wind line is then in the proper relationship and does not need to be redrawn. The airspeed line (120 units long) can be drawn from the point of the wind arrow (W) to intersect the return-trip true course line. The distance measured on this course line from the north-south line to the intersection gives the groundspeed for the return trip (147 knots).

Figure 7-29 shows the various steps for constructing the wind triangle and measuring the true heading and the wind correction angle for the problem in which the true course is 110°, the wind is 20 knots from the southwest (225°), and the airspeed is 100 knots. Notice that the true heading line has to be extended to intersect the north-south line to measure the true heading directly.

Before attempting to use a manual or electronic computer, I highly recommend every pilot understand the relationships involved in constructing wind triangles for various airspeeds, winds, and true courses. These are fundamentals that will always stand you in good stead.

Basic calculations

Today's computers, either manual or electronic, greatly simplify calculating time, speed, heading, fuel flow, fuel consumption, density altitude, and similar pertinent data. Nonetheless, the pilot should be able to make certain basic calculations, such as the following, either mentally or with just a scratch pad and a pencil.

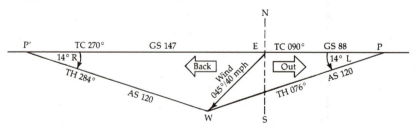

Fig. 7-28. *Making the computations for a round-trip flight.*

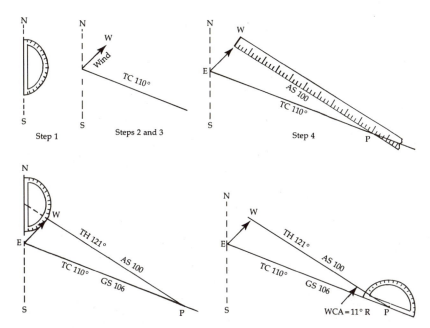

Fig. 7-29. *Another example of constructing a wind triangle with different conditions;: True course of 100 degrees, wind 90 mph from 225 degrees, airspeed 100 mph.*

Converting minutes to equivalent hours

Because speed is usually expressed in miles per hour or knots, it's frequently necessary to convert minutes into equivalent hours when solving speed, time, and distance problems. For example, to convert minutes to hours, divide the minutes by 60 (60 minutes = one hour). Thus, 30 minutes equals 30/60 = 0.5 hour. To convert hours to minutes, multiply by 60, or 0.75 × 60 = 45 minutes.

Time: T = D/GS. To find the time (T) in flight, divide the distance (D) by the groundspeed (GS). The time to fly 210 miles at a ground-speed of 140 mph is 210 divided by 140, or 1.5 hours. (The 0.5 hour multiplied by 60 minutes equals 30 minutes.) Answer: 1:30.

Distance: D = GS × T. To find the distance flown in a given time, multiply groundspeed by time. The distance flown in 1 hour 45 minutes at a groundspeed of 120 mph is 120 × 1.75, or 210 miles.

Groundspeed: GS = D/T. To find the groundspeed, divide the distance flown by the time required. If an airplane flies 270 miles in 3 hours, the groundspeed is 270 divided by 3 = 90 mph.

Converting knots to miles per hour

Another conversion is changing knots to miles per hour. The aviation industry uses knots more frequently than miles per hour, but it might be well to discuss the conversion for those who do use miles when working speed problems. The National Weather Service reports surface winds and winds aloft in knots. However, airspeed indicators in certain personal-type airplanes are calibrated in miles per hour (although many are calibrated in both miles and knots). It's almost essential, then, that you know how to make the conversion.

A knot is one nautical mile per hour. Because there are 6076.1 feet in a nautical mile and 5280 feet in a statute mile, the conversion factor is 1.15. Thus to convert knots to miles, multiply knots by 1.15. For example, a windspeed of 20 knots is equivalent to 23 mph.

Fortunately, most navigational or electronic computers have a simple means of making these conversions so that manual calculations aren't necessary. Another quick conversion method, though, is to use the scales of nautical and statute miles at the bottom of aeronautical charts.

Fuel consumption

Airplane fuel consumption rate is computed in gallons per hour. Obviously, then, to determine the fuel required for a given flight, the time for the flight must be known. Time in flight multiplied by rate of consumption gives the quantity of fuel required. A flight of 400 miles, for instance, at a groundspeed of 100 mph requires four hours. If the plane consumes five gallons an hour, the total consumption will be 4×5, or 20 gallons.

The rate of fuel consumption depends on many factors, such as the condition of the engine, the propeller pitch, propeller rpms, richness of the fuel/air mixture, the percentage of horsepower used for flight at cruising speed, altitude to be flown, and so on. You should have a reasonably accurate idea of the approximate consumption rate of a given airplane from its performance charts or personal experience, but keep in mind, whatever the rate, that there must be sufficient fuel for an adequate reserve, usually at least 30 minutes, over that required for just the intended flight itself.

Navigation problems

Almost any type of navigation requires the solution of simple arithmetical problems involving time, speed, distance, and fuel consumption. Also of concern only in aviation is the pressure altitude at which the flight is to be flown, the temperature at that altitude, the consequent density altitude and its impact on the aircraft's true airspeed. Further complicating what would otherwise be simple problems is the effect of wind on the airplane's course and performance. With those many variables, computers enter the picture.

A word about computers

As mentioned earlier, a number of small, pocket-type navigational computers are available to solve quickly the simple as well as the more complex problems. Suffice it to say that without the aid of a manual computer, such as the long-established E6-B, or one of the electronic flight computers, the task of performing many of the essential, calculations would be considerably greater. Neither type of computer is particularly difficult to master, and the manufacturers furnish instructional booklets explaining how the computer is to be used.

Of the two types, manual or electronic, the latter has certain advantages. For one, it is faster, a little more accurate, and performs a wide variety of functions. Another, it is compact and can be operated in flight with one hand, which is difficult with an E6-B. These are more expensive computers, however, varying from about $50 up to the $200 range for those of greater sophistication. Both types—manual and electronic—are approved by the FAA for written tests, so the choice is a matter of personal preference.

Practice problems

Relative to the practice problems, the answers derived from different computers might vary slightly from those given in this handbook. If the procedure used to solve the problem is correct, the variation should be negligible. An important point is always to use consistent values in the same problem. Don't use miles per hour in one instance and knots in another or switch from Celsius to Fahrenheit temperatures. Practically all computations use knots (nautical miles) and Celsius temperatures as common values, so conversion is usually necessary to determine statute miles or Fahrenheit temperatures.

Conversion problems

The correct answers to these problems are given at the end of the book, but don't accept them at face value. Make the conversions or work out the problems for yourself to see if your computation processes are on the right track.

If the following windspeeds are given in knots, find the speed in statute miles per hour.

A1. 20 knots

A2. 16 knots

A3. 26 knots

A4. 40 knots

A5. 47 knots

With these indicated airspeeds in miles per hour, determine the air-speed in knots.

B1. 130 mph

B2. 156 mph

B3. 95 mph

B4. 110 mph

B5. 121 mph

Convert the following Fahrenheit temperatures to Celsius.

C1. 82°

C2. 38°

C3. 97°

C4. 18°

C5. 0°

Convert these Celsius temperatures to Fahrenheit.

D1. 12°

D2. –7°

D3. 22°

D4. 15°
D5. 27°

Determining density altitudes

E1. If the pressure altitude at an airport is 3500 feet and the temperature is 18°C, what is the density altitude?

E2. You are planning to cruise at 6500 feet, and you learn from a Flight Service Station that the temperature at 6000 feet is 3°C. What is the density altitude?

E3. The field elevation of an airport is 950 feet and the current temperature is 97°F. What is the density altitude?

Determining true airspeed

F1. In planning a flight, you intend to cruise at 5500 feet, with an indicated airspeed of 125 knots. The temperature at that altitude is 12°C. What will your true airspeed be?

F2. While in flight at 7500 feet, the outside air temperature is 25°F. The indicated airspeed is 110 knots. What is the true airspeed?

F3. If you are cruising at 4000 feet at 145 knots and the temperature is 10°C, what is the true airspeed in knots and mph?

Determining total flight times available

G1. Your aircraft has a maximum capacity of 48 usable gallons, with a fuel flow of 9 gallons per hour. What is the total flight time available?

G2. What is the flight time available with 55 usable gallons and a fuel flow of 13 gph?

Determining total fuel to be used

How much fuel will be used during a flight of (a)_____ hours if the rate of fuel consumption is (b)_____ gallons per hour? Substitute the following in blanks (a) and (b) and solve.

(a) (time)	(b) (gph)
H1. 3:00	7.0
H2. 3:30	11.0
H3. 2:20	9.5
H4. 4:15	10.3
H5. 5:10	13.7

Determining wind correction angle, true heading, and ground speed

With the true airspeed, true course, wind direction, and wind speed known, determine the wind correction angle, true heading, and groundspeed.

TAS	TC	Wind speed (knots)	From	WCA R+	WCA L–	TH	GS (knots)
I125	010°	35	150°	___	___	___	___
I122	267°	42	087°	___	___	___	___
I144	045°	15	315°	___	___	___	___

J1. While in flight, true course is 175°, a true heading is 165°, a true airspeed is 165 knots, and groundspeed is 150 knots. What is the wind direction and speed?

Answers to these questions are in the Appendix, pages 577-578.

Radio navigation

With only a few exceptions, general aviation aircraft are equipped with radios that provide a means of navigation and communication with ground stations. At the same time, advances in navigational radio receivers, aeronautical charts that show the exact location of ground transmitting stations and their frequencies, along with refined cockpit instrumentation, make it possible for pilots to navigate with precision to almost any point desired.

Although such precision is obtainable through the proper use of this electronic-age equipment, beginning pilots should use that equipment to supplement navigation by visual reference to the ground (pilotage) and dead reckoning. If this principle is followed, he or she has an effective safeguard against disorientation in the event of radio malfunction. Despite the precision of Loran and, more recently, the marvels and even greater precision of GPS (Global Positioning System), the radio navigation systems most commonly used in VFR navigation are the *VHF Omnidirectional Range* (VOR) and the *Nondirectional Radiobeacon* (NDB). That will undoubtedly change within the next few years, but, for now, the prevalence of those two systems suggests that the focus be placed on those systems in this chapter.

VHF omnidirectional range (VOR)

Omni means *all.* Thus an omnidirectional range is a very high frequency (VHF) radio transmitting ground station, referred to as a VOR, that projects straight line courses (radials) that *radiate* out from the station in all directions. From a top view, a VOR might be visualized as similar to spokes from the hub of a wheel, except that there really is no space between the spokes. The distance that VOR radials are projected (can be received) from the station depends on the power output of the transmitter.

VORs, VORTACs, and VOR/DMEs

For purposes here, the acronym VOR is used to include VORs, VORTACs, and VOR/DMEs. A word about VORTACs and DMEs, however, is in order. TAC is short for TACAN, the acronym for Tactical Air Navigation, while DME means Distance Measuring Equipment. A plain VOR station transmits only the radials from the station, while a VOR/DME transmits the radials as well as the nautical mile distance of the aircraft from the station. To take advantage of the latter feature, however, the VOR receiver-equipped aircraft must also have a separate airborne DME unit.

For reasons peculiar to military or naval operations, the civil VOR/DME system was considered unsuitable. Consequently, a navigational system, TACAN, was developed for military use. Although the TACAN equipment technical principles are different from those of VOR/DME facilities, the FAA has integrated TACAN equipment into the civil VOR/DME program. Thus the term, VORTAC.

For the general aviation pilot, however, the end result of tuning to a VORTAC or a VOR/DME is the same. If the aircraft is equipped with a DME unit, the pilot receives azimuth data on the VOR omnihead, and a visual display of the distance from the station on the DME, plus, depending on the unit, current groundspeed in knots and projected time to the station at that speed. VORs, VORTACs, and VOR/DMEs are identified as such on sectional charts. Again, however, VOR is used here, unless otherwise necessary, to include all three types of navigational aids.

The VOR aircraft instrument

The following discussions will perhaps be clearer if reference is first made to Fig. 7-30, which illustrates parts of a basic aircraft VOR omnihead:

1. An *omnibearing selector* (OBS), sometimes referred to as the course selector.

2. A hinged course deviation indicator (CDI) needle points to the direction of the VOR radial being tracked. For instance, the needle deviates to the left when the radial is to the left of the aircraft. When the needle is centered, the aircraft is flying on the desired radial.

Fig. 7-30. *An example of an aircraft VOR omnihead.*

3. A "TO-FROM" indicator, indicating whether the identified radial is showing TO the VOR transmitter or FROM it.

4. A series of dots, each representing a left or right deviation of two degrees from the radial set in the course selector.

5. An *alarm flag*, not visible in this photograph, that indicates the signal strength from the transmitting station is inadequate to record a meaningful reading in the unit. This occurs when the aircraft is too low or too far from the station.

VOR classifications

VORs are classified according to operational use: T, (terminal); L, (low altitude); and H, (high altitude).

The normal usable altitude and radius of each classification is: T—12,000 feet and below, 25 miles; L—below 18,000 feet, 40 miles; H—below 18,000 feet, 40 miles; within the conterminous 48 states only, between 14,500 and 17,999 feet, 100 miles; 18,000 feet to FL450, 130 miles. The useful range of certain facilities might be less than 50 miles, or unusable between certain magnetic degrees or below certain altitudes. For information on possible restrictions, refer to the RADIO AIDS TO NAVIGATION section in the Airport/Facility Directory for the airport in question, as Fig. 7-31 indicates.

The course or radials projected from the station are referenced to magnetic north. Therefore, a radial is a line of magnetic bearing extending outward from the VOR station. Radials are identified by numbers beginning with 001, which is one degree east of magnetic north, and progress in sequence through all the degrees of a circle

---

BATTLE MOUNTAIN (BAM)   3 SE   UTC–8(–7DT)   N40°35.94′ W116°52.46′   SALT LAKE CITY
4532   B   FUEL 100LL, JET A   H–1B, L–7B
RWY 12–30: H7302X150 (ASPH)   S–30, D–45   IAP
RWY 03–21: H7299X150 (ASPH)   S–30, D–155   MIRL(NSTD)
   RWY 03: VASI(V4R)—GA 3.0° TCH 26′.
AIRPORT REMARKS: Attended 1600–0100Z‡. For svc after hours call 702–635–2245 on call 24 hours. Rwy 12–30
   extensive cracking. Rwy 03–21 NSTD MIRL, last 2000′ are white. ACTIVATE lgts Rwy 03–21—CTAF.
COMMUNICATIONS: CTAF/UNICOM 122.8
   RENO FSS (RNO) TF 1–800–WX–BRIEF. NOTAM FILE RNO.
   MT LEWIS RCO 122.65 (RENO FSS)
RADIO AIDS TO NAVIGATION: NOTAM FILE RNO.
   (H) VORTACW 112.2   BAM   Chan 59   N40°34.15′ W116°55.34′   033° 2.8 NM to fld. 4536/18E.
   VOR unusable:
   050°–060° byd 30 NM blo 12,000′   255°–290° byd 15 NM blo 12,000′
   115°–165° byd 15 NM blo 12,000′
   DME unusable 246°–255° byd 34 NM blo 14,000′

Fig. 7-31. *This excerpt from an Airport/Facility Directory provides essential VOR information.*

until reaching 360. To aid in orientation, a compass rose reference to magnetic north is superimposed on aeronautical charts at the station location (Fig. 7-32).

VORs operate within the 108.0-117.95 MHz frequency band and have a power output necessary to provide coverage within their assigned operational service volume. The equipment is VHF, thus subject to line-of-sight restrictions (Fig. 7-33), and its range varies proportionally with the altitude of the receiving equipment. There is some "spillover," however, and reception at an altitude of 1000 feet agl is about 40 to 45 miles. This distance increases, of course, with altitude.

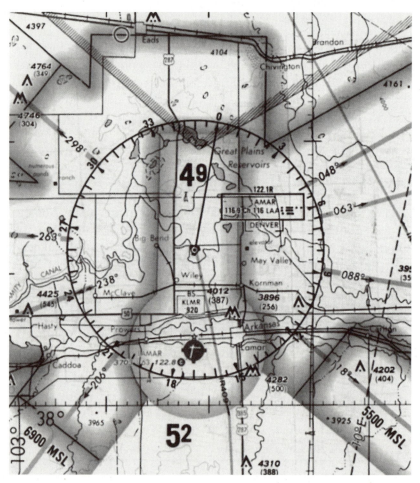

Fig. 7-32. *The sectional chart clearly locates the Lamar VOR, its radio frequencies, and the transmitted Morse code identification.*

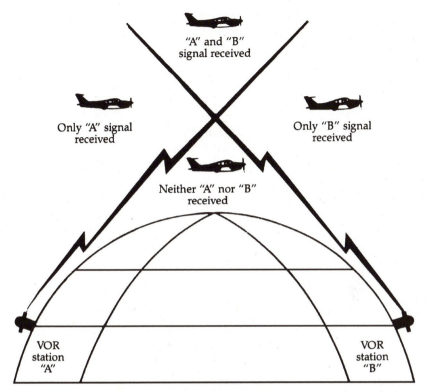

"A" and "B"
signal received

Only "A" signal
received

Only "B" signal
received

Neither "A" nor "B"
received

VOR
station
"A"

VOR
station
"B"

Fig. 7-33. *VHF transmissions follow a line-of-sight course.*

Identifying a VOR

The only positive means of identifying a given VOR station is by the Morse code signal it transmits. For example, as the rectangular box in the upper right quadrant of the compass rose illustrates (Fig. 7-32), the frequency of the Lamar VOR is 116.9, the identification is "LAA," and the transmitted code is dot-dash-dot-dot, dot-dash, dot-dash.

Also, a recorded voice identification has been added to many VHF omniranges. The transmission consists of the name of the station followed by the word "V-O-R," as "AIRVILLE V-O-R," alternating with the usual Morse code identification. Despite any voice transmissions, though, the Morse code signal is the only 100 percent sure way to identify a particular VOR, so listen for it and compare it with the code printed on the sectional.

When the VOR is down for maintenance, the code might be removed or the T-E-S-T code is transmitted (dash, dot, dot-dot-dot,

dash). Whichever the case, the VOR is useless for navigation purposes. A preflight briefing of NOTAMs or an en route call to an FSS,
however, will reveal whether a given VOR station is currently operational. Consequently, there is no reason for any pilot to be caught
unaware of interrupted or discontinued VOR services.

VOR dependability

The accuracy of the VOR's course alignment is excellent, being generally plus or minus one degree. On some VORs, however, minor
course "roughness" might be observed, as evidenced by the course
needle or brief alarm flag activity (some receivers are more sensitive
to these irregularities than others). At a few stations, usually in
mountainous terrain, the pilot might occasionally observe a temporary needle oscillation, similar to the indication that the aircraft is
close to the transmitting station. Pilots flying over unfamiliar routes
are cautioned to be on the alert for these vagaries, and, in particular, to use the "TO-FROM" indicator to determine positive station
passage.

Also, certain propeller rpm settings can cause the needle to fluctuate
as much as plus or minus six degrees. Slight changes in the rpm
setting normally smooth out this roughness. You're urged to check
for this propeller modulation phenomenon before reporting a VOR
station or aircraft equipment as operating unsatisfactorily.

VOR receiver checks

Periodic VOR receiver calibration is most important. If a receiver's automatic gain control or modulation circuit deteriorates, it is possible
for the instrument to display acceptable accuracy when close to a
VOR or an FAA VOR test facility (a VOT) but display out-of-tolerance
readings when located at greater distances where weaker signal areas
exist. The likelihood of this deterioration is considered a function of
time. The best assurance of having an accurate receiver is thus periodic calibrations. Yearly intervals are recommended, at which time
an authorized repair station should recalibrate the receiver to the
manufacturer's specifications.

Part 91.171 of the Federal Aviation Regulations (FARs) stipulates certain procedures for conducting VOR equipment accuracy checks prior
to flight under instrument flight rules. To comply with the requirement and to ensure satisfactory operation of the airborne system, the
FAA has provided pilots with these means of checking the VOR
receiver accuracy:

1. A VOR test facility (VOT) or a radiated test signal from an appropriately rated radio repair station

2. Certified airborne check points

3. Certified check points on the airport surface.

As Fig. 7-34 illustrates, these are listed by state and location in the *Airport/Facility Directory.*

The FAA VOT facility transmits a test signal for VOR receivers that provides a convenient method of determining the accuracy of a VOR receiver while the aircraft is on the ground. The radiated test signal is used by tuning the receiver to the published frequency of the test facility. When the Course Deviation Indicator (CDI) is centered, the omnibearing selector should read 0° with the TO-FROM indication

VOR RECEIVER CHECK
VOR RECEIVER CHECK POINTS
AND
VOR TEST FACILITIES (VOT)

The use of VOR airborne and ground check points is explained in Aeronautical Information Manual, Basic Flight Information and ATC Procedures.

NOTE: Under columns headed "Type of Check Point" & "Type of VOT Facility" G stands for ground. A/ stands for airborne followed by figures (2300) or (1000–3000) indicating the altitudes above mean sea level at which the check should be conducted. Facilities are listed in alphabetical order, in the state where the check points or VOTs are located.

ARKANSAS
VOR RECEIVER CHECK POINTS

Facility Name (Arpt Name)	Freq/Ident	Type Check Pt. Gnd. AB/ALT	Azimuth from Fac. Mag	Dist. from Fac. N.M.	Check Point Description
El Dorado (South Arkansas Regional at					On parking ramp at center
Goodwin Field)	115.5/ELD	G	228	4.0	twy.
Flippin	112.8/FLP	A/1900	053	6.0	Over water tower at Mountain Home.
Fort Smith (Fort Smith Regional)	110.4/FSM	G	226	5.2	On runup area on twy to Rwy 25.
	110.4/FSM	G	232	6.2	On runup area on twy to Rwy 07.
	110.4/FSM	A/1500	233	5.6	Over water tank N edge of arpt.
Gosnell	111.8/GOJ	A/1700	105	7.3	Over railroad bridge at Armorel.
Harrison (Boone County)	112.5/HRO	G	131	4.3	At int of N/S and E/W twys In front of trmI bldg.
Jonesboro (Jonesboro Muni)	108.6/JBR	G	224	3.9	On SE corner of terminal ramp.
Little Rock (Adams Field)	113.9/LIT	G	312	3.8	At intersection of Twys G and F
Monticello	111.6/MON	A/1500	307	5.7	Over white water tower.
Pine Bluff (Grider Field)	116.0/PBF	G	183	4.5	Center E/W twys front of twr.

Fig. 7-34. *The location of and data pertaining to VOR test facilities (VOT) are determined from the Airport/Facility Directory, as this excerpt illustrates.*

being "FROM." Conversely, the omnibearing selector should read 180° with the TO-FROM indication reading "TO." Two means of identification are used with the VOR radiated test signal. In some cases, it is a continuous series of dots, while in others a continuous 1020 Hz tone identifies the test signal. A radiated VOR test signal from an appropriately rated radio repair station serves the same purpose as an FAA VOT signal, and the check is made in much the same manner, with the following differences:

1. The frequency normally approved by the FCC is 108.0 MHz.

2. The repair stations are not permitted to radiate the VOR test signal continuously; consequently the aircraft owner/operator must make arrangements with the repair station to have the test signal transmitted.

This service is not available at all radio repair stations, so the aircraft owner/operator must determine where in the local area the test can be made. When conducting the test, a repair station representative must make an entry into the aircraft logbook or other permanent record certifying to the radial accuracy that was transmitted and the date of transmission.

VOR airborne and ground test checkpoints consist of certified radials that should be received at specific points on the airport surface or over specific landmarks while airborne in the immediate vicinity of the airport. Should an error of plus or minus four degrees be indicated in a ground check, or plus or minus six degrees using the airborne check, IFR flight is not be attempted without first correcting the source of the error.

If dual system VOR units (independent of each other except for the antenna) are installed in the aircraft, one system can be checked against the other. This is done by tuning both systems to the same VOR ground facility and noting the indicated bearings to that station. The maximum permissible variation between the two indicated bearings is four degrees.

It should be noted that VOR accuracy checks are not a regulatory requirement for VFR flight. To assure accuracy of the equipment, however, the checks should be made frequently, along with a complete calibration each year. Depending solely on VORs for VFR navigation purposes could result in a considerable course deviation if the aircraft receiver is not properly calibrated.

Using the VOR

Using the VOR receiver is simple, once the basic concept is understood. What follows, coupled with actual inflight practice, should erase all mysteries and provide a sense of security in navigating with the VOR.

As you'll recall, VOR radio navigation requires two components: the ground transmitter and the aircraft receiver. The ground transmitter is located at a specific geographical position, is easily identified on the sectional chart by the compass rose surrounding it (Fig. 7-32), and transmits on the assigned frequency printed in the rectangular identification box that is in or adjacent to the compass rose. The design of the symbol that locates the exact ground position of the station also identifies the VOR as a VHF Omni Range (VOR), a VORTAC, or a VOR/DME. The symbols are decoded on the legend flap of the sectional chart.

The aircraft equipment includes a receiver and navigation instrument. Referring to Fig. 7-30 again, the navigation instrument basically consists of an omnibearing selector (OBS), sometimes called a course selector, a course deviation indicator needle that points to the radial, and a TO-FROM indicator.

The course selector is an azimuth dial that can be rotated to select a desired radial or to determine the radial over which the aircraft is flying. The aircraft could be flying in *any direction* over this radial and a cross-check with the compass is necessary to determine the aircraft's direction of flight in relation to the VOR station. In addition, the magnetic course "TO" or "FROM" the station can be determined.

When the course selector is rotated, it moves the course deviation indicator, or needle, to indicate the position of the radial relative to the aircraft. If the course selector is rotated until the deviation needle is centered, the radial (magnetic course from the station) or its reciprocal (magnetic course to the station) can be determined. The course deviation needle also moves to the left or right if the aircraft is flown or drifting away from the radial that is set in the course selector.

By centering the needle, the course selector indicates either the course "FROM" the station or the course "TO" the station. Quite logically, if the flag displays a "TO," the course shown on the course selector should be flown to the station. If "FROM" is displayed and the course shown is followed, the aircraft is flying away from the station.

Tracking with omni

The following, with the help of Fig. 7-35, describes a step-by-step procedure when tracking to and from a VOR station.

1. First, tune the VOR receiver to the frequency of the selected VOR station—as 115.0 to receive the Bravo VOR. Next, check the BRA code to verify that you are indeed receiving that VOR. As soon as the VOR is properly tuned, the course deviation needle deflects either left or right; then rotate the azimuth dial of the course selector until the course deviation needle centers and the TO-FROM indicates TO. If the needle centers with a FROM indication, the azimuth should be rotated 180 degrees because, in this case, you want to fly TO the station. Now, turn the aircraft to the heading indicated on the omni azimuth dial or course selector. In this example, it's 350°.

2. If a heading of 350° is maintained with a wind from the right as shown, the airplane drifts to the left of the intended track. As it drifts off course, the VOR course deviation needle gradually moves to the right of center, indicating that the VOR transmitter is to the right of the aircraft.

3. To get back on the desired radial, the aircraft heading must be altered approximately 20° to the right. As the aircraft approaches the 350° radial, or track, the needle slowly returns to center. When centered, the aircraft is back on the desired radial and a left turn must be made toward, but not to, the original 350° heading, because a wind drift correction must be established. The amount of correction, of course, depends upon the strength of the wind. If the wind velocity is unknown, a trial-and-error method must be used to find the correct heading. For this example, let's say that a 10° correction, or a heading of 360° is established.

4. While maintaining this heading, you notice that the course deviation begins to move to the left. This means that the 10° wind correction was too much and that you're flying to the right of course. A slight left turn should be made at this point to return to the 350° radial.

5. When the needle centers, a smaller wind drift correction of 5°, or a heading correction of 355°, should be flown. If this

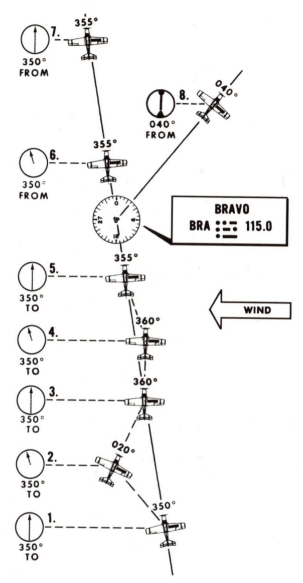

Fig. 7-35. *Tracking a VOR radial in a crosswind.*

correction is adequate, the airplane remains on the radial. If not, then make small heading variations to keep the needle centered and the airplane headed straight for the station.

6. When you are within a couple of miles of the VOR station, the needle fluctuates from side to side. Just don't try to chase it. If the needle has remained centered up to now, maintain

the same heading; you will shortly pass over the station, at which point the TO indicator will disappear and FROM will replace it.

7. The same techniques apply when tracking outbound as those for tracking inbound. If you intend to fly over the station and track outbound on the reciprocal of the inbound radial, don't change the course selector, and make corrections in the same manner to keep the needle centered. The only difference is that the omni reflects a FROM indication.

8. If tracking outbound on a course other than the reciprocal of the inbound radial, the new course or radial must be tuned in and a turn made to intercept the radial. Once on the outbound heading, tracking procedures are the same as when flying inbound.

Tips on using the VOR

In summary, these few tips might help in using and navigating with the VOR:

1. Positively identify the station by its code or voice identification.

2. Keep in mind that VOR signals are "line-of-sight." You'll receive a weak signal or no signal at all if the aircraft is too low or too far from the station.

3. When navigating to a station, determine the inbound radial and stay on it. If the aircraft drifts, don't reset the course selector. Instead, correct for wind drift and fly a heading that compensates for that drift.

4. If minor needle fluctuations occur, avoid changing headings immediately. Wait momentarily to see if the needle recenters. If it doesn't, then correct.

5. When close to the station, the needle tends to fluctuate more and more radically. Don't try to chase it with drastic heading changes. Merely turn slightly, a degree or two, towards the needle, using ailerons only. When the needle starts to return to the center position, again turn back slightly to the original heading. When the "TO" flag changes to "FROM," you have passed the station.

6. When flying to a station, always fly the selected course with a TO indication. Conversely, when flying away from a station, fly the selected course with a FROM indication. If you don't do this, the action of the course deviation needle will be reversed.

To explain: If you fly the aircraft toward a station with a FROM indication or away from a station with a TO indication, the course deviation needle will point in the opposite direction of what you want. More specifically, if the aircraft drifts to the right of the radial being flown, the needle will move to the right and point away from the radial and away from the VOR transmitter. Should you then try to center the needle by turning right, you'd only get farther and farther off course. Similarly, of course, if the plane drifts to the left of the radial, the needle will move left and away from the radial.

7. Finally, and in line with Tip #6, when flying to a station with a TO indication, always turn the aircraft toward the needle if it deflects from dead center. The same principle applies if flying from a station with a FROM indication. In effect, "chase" the course deviation needle. But, as stated in #6, the reverse is the case if flying to a station with a FROM indication or away from the station with a TO indication.

Nondirectional radio beacon and automatic direction finder

Another valuable aid to navigation is the ground-bound Nondirectional Radio Beacon (NDB) and its airborne receiver, the Automatic Direction Finder (ADF).

NDB stations normally operate in the low or medium frequency band of 190 to 535 kHz, and, except for those used in conjunction with the Instrument Landing System (ILS), transmit a continuous three-letter identification code. The only time the code is interrupted is when the station also has voice transmission. Where there is no voice, the letter "W" ("without voice") is included in the class description.

The following illustrates the classes of NDB stations, their power, and usable range:

Class	Power	Distance
Compass Locator	Under 25 watts	15 miles
MH	Under 50 watts	25 miles
H	50–1999 watts	*50 miles
HH	2000 or more watts	75 miles

*Service range of individual facilities might be fewer than 50 miles.

Identifying an NDB

Nondirectional Radio Beacons are easily spotted on sectional charts, with further details given in the *Airport/Facility Directory*. Figure 7-36 illustrates the sectional depiction—the circular series of small, magenta-colored dots surrounding Trenton's airport and the rectangular box with the station's frequency (400), plus the transmitted code, "TRX."

An important benefit of the NDB is that many are located on the smaller, uncontrolled airports that are off the VOR airways, thus simplifying navigation to such fields or being able to use NDBs as en route checkpoints. This on-airport location is not always true, however, as in Fig. 7-37. Here there are two NDBs, indicated by our arrows: Shaw, which is directly south of the Beatrice airport, and Big Blue to the northwest.

For further details, using Trenton as the example, the A/FD, under the Radio Aids to Navigation section (Fig. 7-38), lists the NDB as an MH Class without voice (the "W"), the frequency (400), the three-letter code (TRX), its latitude/longitude position, the fact that the station is located on the field ("at fld"), and that NOTAMs can be obtained through the Columbia, Missouri, Flight Service Station. If the NDB is not on the field, the heading and miles to the airport are added.

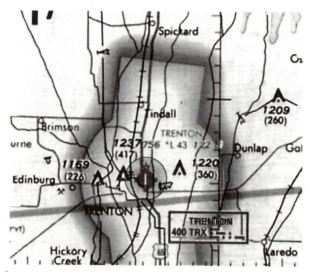

Fig. 7-36. *The Trenton example shows how NDBs are identified on sectional charts.*

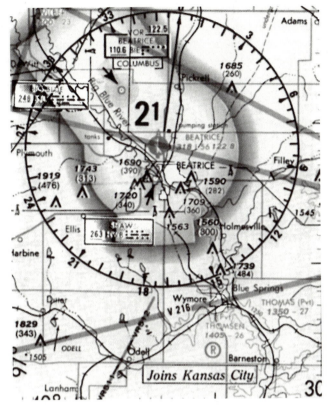

Fig. 7-37. *Not all NDBs are located on airports, as the two in the Beatrice area illustrate.*

TRENTON MUNI (TRX) 1 E UTC−6(−5DT) N40°05.01′ W93°35.44′   OMAHA
757 B S4 **FUEL** 100LL, JET A   L−11C
RWY 18−36: H4310X50 (ASPH−RFSC) S−4 RWY LGTS (NSTD)   IAP
    RWY 18: REIL. Thld dpslcd 272′. Road.   **RWY 36:** REIL. Thld dsplcd 396′. Tree.
AIRPORT REMARKS: Attended Mon−Fri 1400−2300Z‡. For fuel after hrs call 816−789−2128. Be alert for birds on and
    invof arpt spring and fall. Rwy 18−36 NSTD MIRL, thld lgts 12′ S of Rwy 36. MIRL Rwy 18−36 preset on low ints,
    to increase ints and ACTIVATE REIL Rwy 18 and Rwy 36—CTAF.
COMMUNICATIONS: CTAF/UNICOM 122.8
    COLUMBIA FSS (COU) 122.2 TF 1−800−WX−BRIEF. NOTAM FILE COU.
RADIO AIDS TO NAVIGATION: NOTAM FILE FOD.
    LAMONI (H) VORTAC 116.7 LMN Chan 114 N40°35.81′ W93°58.06′ 144° 35.3 NM to fld. 1140/7E.
    HIWAS.
    NDB (MHW) 400 TRX N40°04.82′ W93°35.58′ at fld. NOTAM FILE COU.

Fig. 7-38. *The Airport/Facility Directory is another source for determining NDB data.*

Nondirectional Radio Beacons have one advantage over the VOR in that low or medium frequencies are not affected by line-of-sight. The signals follow the curvature of the earth. Consequently, if the aircraft is within the power range of the station, the signals can be received regardless of altitude.

On the other hand, one of the disadvantages of using low frequency for navigation is that the signals are very susceptible to electrical disturbances, such as lightning. These disturbances create excessive static, needle deviations, and signal fades. There also might be interference from distant stations. You should know the conditions under which these disturbances can occur so you can be more alert to possible reception problems when using the ADF.

The automatic direction finding (ADF) equipment

Basically, the ADF aircraft equipment consists of a tuner, which is used to select the desired station frequency, a volume control, the navigational display, and an externally-mounted antenna.

The navigational display consists of a dial with an azimuth and a needle that rotates around the dial and points to the station to which the receiver is tuned.

Some of the ADF dials can be rotated to align the azimuth with the aircraft heading. Others, the type this handbook addresses, are fixed, with the 0°-180° points on the azimuth aligned with the longitudinal axis of the aircraft and the zero degree position representing the nose of the aircraft (Fig. 7-39).

Figure 7-40 helps illustrate some of the terms used in association with the ADF:

Relative Bearing is the value to which the indicator (needle) points on the azimuth dial. When using a fixed dial, this number is relative to the nose of the aircraft and is the angle measured clockwise from the nose of the aircraft to a line drawn from the aircraft to the station.

To determine the magnetic bearing *from* the station, 180° is added to or subtracted from the magnetic bearing *to* the station. This is the reciprocal bearing and is used when plotting position fixes.

Keep in mind that the needle of a fixed azimuth points to the station *in relation* to the nose of the aircraft. If the needle is deflected 30°

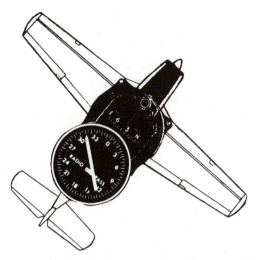

Fig. 7-39. *An ADF with a fixed azimuth and how its 0° reading relates to the magnetic compass heading.*

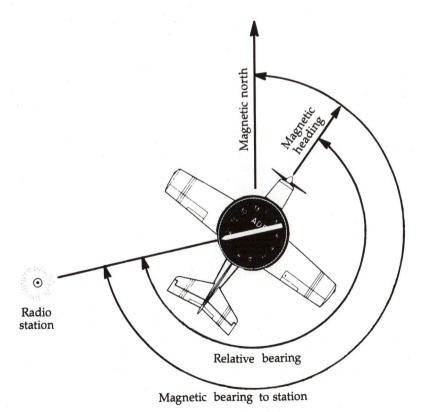

Fig. 7-40. *These are the terms associated with the ADF.*

to the left, it quite logically means that the station is located 30° off the nose to the left. If the aircraft is turned left 30°, the needle will begin to move to the right. When it reaches the 0° reading, the aircraft is pointing toward the station. If the pilot continues to fly toward the station, keeping the needle on 0°, the procedure being followed is called "homing." Should a crosswind exist, the ADF needle would continue to drift away from zero, so to keep the needle on zero the aircraft must be turned slightly, resulting in a curved flight path to the station. Homing to the station is a common procedure but can result in drifting downwind, thus lengthening the distance to the station.

To overcome this downwind drift, the common correction technique of turning into the wind, or "crabbing," comes into play again. The intent, of course, is to establish and maintain flight along a straight track, or bearing, to the station. Once the wind drift correction is established, the ADF needle, instead of pointing to the 0° heading, indicates the amount of correction to the right or left. For instance, referring to Fig. 7-41, if the magnetic bearing to the station is 340°, but to correct for a left crosswind the aircraft is turned to a heading of 330°, the ADF needle would read 10° to the right, for a relative bearing of 010°.

When tracking away from the station, wind corrections are similar to tracking to the station but the ADF needle points toward the tail of the aircraft on the 180° position on the azimuth dial. Just as when approaching a station, attempting to keep the ADF needle on the 180° position when encountering winds results in the aircraft flying a curved flight leading further and further from the desired track.

Another advantage of ADF is that in addition to receiving NDBs, you can tune to commercial AM radio broadcast stations for direction-finding as well as entertainment aloft. When using a commercial station, the principles of tracking inbound or outbound are the same as with an NDB.

Distance measuring equipment

A very useful navigation aid is Distance Measuring Equipment (DME). As mentioned earlier, the DME is a separate airborne instrument that sends and receives "signals" or pulses to and from VOR/DME, VORTAC, ILS/DME, and LOC/DME ground navigation facilities. ("ILS" = "Instrument Landing System;" "LOC" = "Localizer".)

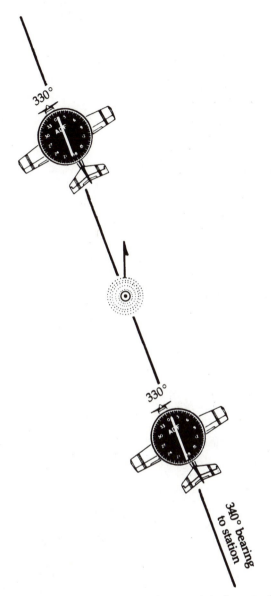

Fig. 7-41. *ADF tracking requires compensating for winds.*

When tuned to a DME-equipped ground facility, the airborne DME sends out paired pulses at a specific spacing. This is the *interrogation*. The ground facility receives the pulses and then transmits back to the interrogating aircraft a second pair of pulses with the same spacing but on a different frequency. The airborne DME measures the elapsed time required for the roundtrip signal exchange and translates that time into nautical miles and time to the station as well as the aircraft's current ground speed. The distance and time are constantly updated as the aircraft moves toward the station and records any changes in ground speed that might be taking place.

Operating on the line-of-sight principle, the mileage measurement is based on the direct distance of the aircraft from the transmitting station. This is commonly called the *slant-range* distance and is not exactly the same as the horizontal distance. The difference between the two, however, is negligible, especially when the aircraft is one mile or more from the station for each 1000 feet of altitude above the facility.

Barring this minor "slant-range error," the DME is highly accurate. Reliable signals can be received up to 199 nm at line-of-sight altitudes with an accuracy of one-half mile, or three percent of the distance, whichever is the greater. In conjunction with a VOR, the pilot now has instrument panel indications of azimuth, distance, groundspeed, and time to or from a selected VOR/DME, VORTAC, ILS/DME facility.

Aircraft equipment

The airborne DME equipment is simple to use. Depending, of course, on the design of the unit, it's merely a matter of tuning to the desired VOR facility and then watching the simultaneous but ever-changing mileage and time readouts, plus whatever groundspeed changes might be occurring because of winds or power adjustments.

Not only is the information displayed helpful in navigation, but it assists in determining when initial radio contacts should be established with Approach Control or Tower facilities. Small red flags on sectional charts indicate locations where the first contact should be made—as a rule, 10 to 15 miles out (excluding certain conditions when entering a Class B or C airspace, which are discussed later).

Not always, however, are those flags easy to spot and not always is a pilot entering an area for the first time certain of what landmark the plane is over when making the first call. With DME, however, pilots can report the exact DME-mileage from the VOR, whether the VOR is located on or off airport. The initial contact with Approach Control or a Tower is thus a much more accurate position report, especially for those unfamiliar with the area, and contributes to better control of arriving and departing traffic.

Radar: categories of

One form of radar (Radio Detection and Ranging) or another has been in use by military and civil aviation since the early 1940s. From relatively crude beginnings, constant advancements in ground and air equipment have greatly improved the control of traffic, and thus its safety, in the vicinity of busy airports as well as in the en route environment. While the basic principles apply in all cases, there are five broad categories of radar in use, with the first three referred to as *surveillance radar.*

ASR (airport surveillance radar). An approach control system whereby a controller orally provides range and azimuth data of an aircraft but not altitude to its pilot. ASRs are found in many of the military airports. The reverse side of the sectional chart legend identifies those airports where ASR service is available.

PAR (precision approach radar). A landing aid used by the military. With PAR, a controller orally advises the pilot of his aircraft range, azimuth, and altitude, but because range is limited to 10 miles, azimuth to 20 degrees, and elevation to 7 degrees, only the final approach area to a runway is covered. PAR is thus not adequate for separating and sequencing aircraft. The sectional also lists the airports where PAR or ASR/PAR is available.

ASDE (airport surface detection equipment). A radar system that displays the surface of the airport, including aircraft on the ground and motorized vehicles. ASDE is valuable to Tower cab controllers in conditions of reduced visibility or at large airports where distance makes visual scanning of the surface difficult or impossible.

ARTS (automated radar tracking system). The generic term for four systems (ARTS II, ARTS IIA, ARTS III, ARTS IIIA), each more sophisticated than its predecessor but all using computer-generated data. ARTS II and IIA provide automated traffic control capabilities at terminals with low to medium activity, while ARTS III and IIIA are used in the medium to high density terminals.

NAS Stage A (national airspace system). The system used in the Air Route Traffic Control Centers (ARTCCs) to control en route IFR traffic and provide advisories to participating VFR aircraft. Somewhat similar to ARTS, the data is computer-generated, producing alphanumeric readouts on the controller's screen. The symbols are different, however, and the system doesn't have the ARTS capability of displaying cloud formations, other than areas of heavy precipitation density. (ARTS and NAS Stage A are briefly described later.)

Primary radar is fundamentally a system whereby radio wave pulses are transmitted from a rotating ground antenna. The pulses strike an object or target in space and are reflected back to the receiver, which then displays the target on the controller's radarscope as a "blip." The distance, or range, of the target is determined by measuring the time (at the speed of light) required for the radio wave to reach the target and return to the receiving antenna.

The direction of the target from the radar site is established by the position of the rotating antenna when the reflected image, or echo, is received. An electron beam emanating from the center of the radarscope moves in a clockwise direction, coinciding with the rotation of the radar antenna. When the beam, or sweep, reaches a point corresponding to the target, the echo is intensified and appears as a blip of light on the scope. The blip fades away as the sweep passes the position of the target but reappears, when the beam completes its 360° sweep and again detects the target.

With the help of a series of concentric circles displayed on the radarscope, the controller can determine the bearing and range of a target from the radar facility as well as from other targets. In the airport environment, a "video map" overlaying the scope shows the position of runways, navigation aids, ground obstructions, and satellite airports. The map is thus a further aid in directing arriving or departing traffic.

Primary radar limitations

Some of the limitations of primary radar include:

1. Radio waves normally travel in a continuous straight line, unless they are (a) bent by abnormal atmospheric phenomena such as temperature inversion; (b) reflected or attenuated (weakened) by dense objects as ground obstacles, mountains, heavy clouds, precipitation, and the like; or (c) screened by high terrain features.

2. The amount of reflective surface of an aircraft determines the size of the radar return. A general aviation aircraft or a highly streamlined jet fighter is more difficult to see on radar than a Boeing 747 or a military bomber.

3. Primary radar can establish the range and azimuth of an aircraft but not its altitude.

4. In periods of heavy traffic volume, controllers could find it difficult to identify one aircraft from another.

"Secondary" radar

Some of the limitations of primary radar are overcome by what is called *secondary radar*, or the Air Traffic Control Radar Beacon System (ATCRBS). This system addresses the problem of specific aircraft identification and, with a Mode C airborne transponder, altitude determination. Three additional components to the basic radar system are required:

1. An *interrogator*
2. A *transponder*
3. A *decoder*

The interrogator, which is mounted on the primary radar antenna, rotates in unison with that antenna and scans the same area. As the two make their 360° sweep, the secondary antenna transmits a coded pulse sequence on 1030 MHz that "interrogates" each transponder-equipped aircraft and "asks" the transponder to "reply." The transponder replies on 1090 MHz, and the synchronized primary and secondary signals produce a distinctly shaped image on the controller's radarscope.

The image, however, indicates only that the aircraft has a transponder, that it has been turned to the ON, or ALT (for "Altitude," if the transponder is in Mode C) position, and, unless the pilot has been otherwise directed, is set to the standard VFR transmitting code of 1200. For further and more specific identification, the transponder is equipped with a small button, the ident feature. When, at a controller's request, the pilot presses the button, the radarscope image of his aircraft changes and "blossoms," thus identifying that aircraft among the others in the area.

The transponder

The transponder, as illustrated in Fig. 7-42, is a small receiver-transmitter installed in the aircraft instrument panel. The typical unit has a five-position function selector: OFF, SBY (Standby), ON, ALT (Altitude), and TST (Test), plus four rotating control knobs that are used to dial in any combination of four-number discrete codes assigned by a controller or pilot-selected emergency codes. Each knob can enter eight digits, 0 to 7, for a maximum combination of 4096 codes (8 × 8 × 8 × 8).

Finally, the set has the ident pushbutton (not identifiable in Fig. 7-42), which the pilot activates when directed to do so by a controller. Incorporated within the ident button is a reply light that blinks each time the set responds to the 10- to 15-second interval ground radar interrogations. If the light blinks almost continuously, it means that the transponder is replying to several different radar interrogations. The blinking also indicates that the transponder is functioning properly.

A decoder is part of the ATCRBS ground equipment that enables the controller to assign a different transponder code to each IFR aircraft under that person's control. Assignments might also be made to VFR aircraft when the pilot requests en route flight (traffic) advisories from an Air Route Traffic Control Center (ARTCC) or when operating into or out of a Class B terminal airspace. Code assignments, which the controller orally communicates to the pilot, are automatically made by the ARTCC computer, based on the National Beacon Code Allocation Plan. The common controller or pilot terminology, when referring to transponder codes, always includes the word "Squawk" or "Squawking," as: "Squawk One Two Zero Zero," "Squawk VFR," "Squawk Two Five Three Four" (a discrete code), "Squawking Two Four Two Three," or any other assigned four-digit combination.

Fig. 7-42. *This is a typical 4096 transponder with altitude-reporting (Mode C) capability.*

The use and operation of a transponder

A few hints on the use and operation of a transponder are in order at this point:

1. Transponder coverage is limited to "line of sight." Low altitude or antenna shielding by the aircraft might result in reduced range. The range can be increased by climbing to a higher altitude and/or minimizing antenna shield by placing the antenna where dead spots are noticed only during abnormal flight attitudes.

2. Transponders should be placed in the SBY position after engine start to allow the set to warm up. It then must be turned to ON or ALT (if equipped with Mode C altitude-reporting capability) before takeoff, unless directed otherwise by ATC. As soon as possible after landing, turn the set to OFF or SBY.

3. If Mode C equipped, pilots should report their exact altitude to the nearest one hundred foot increment when establishing initial contact with an ATC facility. This confirms that the stated altitude is the same as the Mode C readout. ATC requires this information before relying on Mode C altitudes for traffic separation purposes. The information also further reduces the need for altitude verification requests.

4. The IDENT feature is never to be activated unless or until requested by an ATC controller.

5. When making routine code changes in accordance with ATC requests, take care to avoid inadvertent selection of codes 7500, 7600, or 7700, thereby causing momentary false alarms at automated ground facilities. For example, when changing from 2700 to 7200, switch first to 2200 then 7200, not to 7700 and then 7200.

6. Unless ATC specifically directs otherwise, the last two digits of the transponder code should always read "00." Similarly, and barring an emergency or radio failure, the code for VFR operations should always be 1200, unless ATC advises otherwise.

Transponder codes

The various standard transponder codes are listed in Fig. 7-43. The most common, of course, is 1-2-0-0, the code for all VFR operations that should always be entered in the transponder *unless:* (1) directed

Transponder Code	Type of Flight	When Used
0000*	Military	North American Air Defense
1200	VFR	All altitudes, unless instructed otherwise by ATC
4000*	Military VFR/IFR	In Warning and Restricted Areas
7500	VFR/IFR	Hijacking
7700	VFR/IFR	In an emergency—"Mayday"
7600	VFR/IFR	Loss of radio communications
7777*	Military	Intercept operations
Any code	VFR/IFR	When using Center or Approach Control and ATC assigns a specific, or "discrete" code

Note: The starred (*) codes are for military operations only, and are never to be used by civilian pilots.

Fig. 7-43. *This figure lists the various transponder codes and uses with which pilots should be familiar and are summarized on this chart.*

otherwise by ATC; (2) you have a loss of radio communications and voluntarily squawk the 7600 radio failure code; or (3) you have an emergency and squawk 7700 to draw ATC attention to that fact and that help is needed.

Transponder modes

Transponders are usually referred to in terms of types of modes, of which seven are either in use or available:

- Modes 1 and 2 are assigned to the military.
- Mode 3/A is used by both military and civilian aircraft.
- Mode B is reserved for use in foreign countries.
- Mode C is a Mode 3/A transponder-equipped with altitude-reporting capabilities.
- Mode D is not presently in use.
- Mode S is relatively new and was originally intended to come into common use in the late 1990s; S stands for *selective address.*

A Mode 3/A transponder, the most common of all, is converted to a Mode C by one of two methods:

1. Replacing the existing altimeter with an *encoding* altimeter that is electronically connected to the transponder. The altimeter aneroid bellows expand and contract with altitude changes, and the changes are converted to coded responses by the transponder. When interrogated by the sweeping radar beacon, the transponder transmits those responses, which are then decoded on the ground. The process concludes when the aircraft's altitude appears on the radarscope.

2. Installing a *blind encoder*, which is usually located under the instrument panel on the firewall and is not normally visible to the pilot. The blind encoder performs the same function as an encoding altimeter and does not require replacement of the original, and probably perfectly satisfactory, altimeter.

To repeat one important regulation: When operating in any controlled airspace, if the aircraft has a Mode 3/A transponder, it *must* be turned to the ON position. If the unit is a Mode C, it *must* be turned to ALT altitude-reporting position. With only certain ATC authorized deviations, the FAA mandates this in FAR Part 91.215.

Transponder phraseology

Following is the common terminology or phraseology associated with Mode 3/A and Mode C transponder operation:

SQUAWK (number): Insert the four-number code given by ATC.

IDENT: Depress the "Ident" button—but only once.

SQUAWK (number) AND IDENT: Insert the four-number code given by ATC and depress the "Ident" button.

SQUAWK STANDBY: Switch the transponder from ON (in some units, NORMAL) or ALT to the STANDBY position.

STOP ALTITUDE SQUAWK: With Mode C, switch from ALT to ON or NORMAL.

STOP SQUAWK: Turn the transponder off or switch to SBY.

SQUAWK VFR: Dial in the VFR code of 1200 in the transponder.

SQUAWK MAYDAY: You have reported an emergency, and ATC wants you to insert the emergency code of 7700 for positive aircraft identification.

Mode C Transponders are required in certain airspace areas, including the following:

- At or above 10,000 feet msl over the contiguous 48 states or District of Columbia, excluding the airspace below 2500 feet agl
- Within 30 nautical miles of a Class B primary airport below 10,000 feet msl, with certain exceptions for balloons, gliders, and aircraft without an engine-driven electrical system
- Within and above a Class C airspace, up to and including 10,000 feet msl
- Within 10 miles of certain designated airports, excluding that airspace that is both outside the Class D surface area and below 1200 feet agl. Balloons, gliders, and aircraft not equipped with an engine-driven electrical system are also excluded from this requirement

Automated radar terminal system

ARTS, is the generic term for several automation systems, each differing in equipment and functional capabilities as denoted by suffix roman numerals and/or letters. ARTS II is the least sophisticated system, while ARTS IIIA is, right now, the most advanced. Whatever the designation, the system is used to control arriving and departing traffic, primarily but not exclusively IFR traffic, in the 35 Class B airport terminal areas in 31 cities.

In general, ARTS displays on the controller's radarscope the identification (N-number) of each aircraft, its flight plan data, its altitude, groundspeed, and position symbols. ARTS IIIA, for example, detects, tracks, and predicts primary and secondary radar-derived aircraft targets, as well as the altitude of secondary targets equipped with Mode C transponders.

All data, except computer-generated symbols representing the status of aircraft in the area, are presented alphanumerically in data blocks. Additionally, each level of ARTS has the capability of communicating, or interfacing electronically, with ARTCCs and other ARTS facilities, thus simplifying and expediting the transfer and coordination of flight information. The various images are illustrated in Fig. 7-44 and identified in Fig. 7-45.

All of this is accomplished with primary and secondary radar, transponders, automation, and programmable computer-aided subsystems.

ARTS III Radar Scope with Alphanumeric Data

Note: "ARTS" radar scope continue "broadband" (primary/secondary) radar targets with alphanumeric data. Lower right hand subset displays "broadband" (primary/secondary) radar and ARTS III when operating without automation.

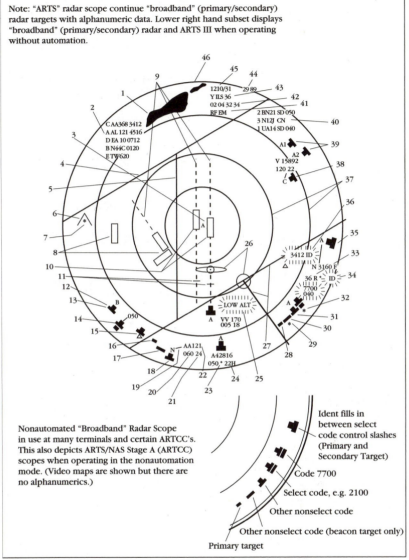

Nonautomated "Broadband" Radar Scope in use at many terminals and certain ARTCC's. This also depicts ARTS/NAS Stage A (ARTCC) scopes when operating in the nonautomation mode. (Video maps are shown but there are no alphanumerics.)

Ident fills in between select code control slashes (Primary and Secondary Target)

Code 7700

Select code, e.g. 2100

Other nonselect code

Other nonselect code (beacon target only)

Primary target

Note: A number of radar terminals do not have ARTS equipment. Those facilities and certain ARTCC's outside the contiguous U.S. would have radar displays similar to the lower right hand subset. ARTS facilities and NAS Stage A ARTCC's, when operating in the non-automation mode, would also have similar displays and certain services based on automation may not be available.

Fig. 7-44. *These are the typical ARTS III symbols as they appear on Approach and Departure Control radar screens. See Fig. 7-45 for the meaning of the symbols.*

1. AREAS OF PRECIPITATION (CAN BE REDUCED BY CP)
2. ARRIVAL/DEPARTURE TABULAR LIST
3. TRACKBALL (CONTROL) POSITION SYMBOL (A)
4. AIRWAY (LINES ARE SOMETIMES DELEATED IN PART)
5. RADAR LIMIT LINE FOR CONTROL
6. OBSTRUCTION (VIDEO MAP)
7. PRIMARY RADAR RETURNS OF OBSTACLES OR TERRAIN (CAN BE REMOVED BY MTI)
8. SATELLITE AIRPORTS
9. RUNWAY CENTERLINES (MARKS AND SPACES INDICATE MILES)
0. PRIMARY AIRPORT WITH PARALLEL RUNWAYS
.1. APPROACH GATES
.2. TRACKED TARGET (PRIMARY AND BEACON TARGET)
.3. CONTROL POSITION SYMBOL
.4. UNTRACKED TARGET SELECT CODE (MONITORED) WITH MODE C READOUT OF 5000'
.5. UNTRACKED TARGET WITHOUT MODE C
.6. PRIMARY TARGET
.7. BEACON TARGET ONLY (SECONDARY RADAR) (TRANSPONDER)
.8. PRIMARY AND BEACON TARGET
.9. LEADER LINE
!0. ALTITUDE MODE C READOUT IS 6000' (NOTE: READOUTS MAY NOT BE DISPLAYED BECAUSE OF NONRECEIPT OF BEACON INFORMATION, GARBLED BEACON SIGNALS, AND FLIGHT PLAN DATA WHICH IS DISPLAYED ALTERNATELY WITH THE ALTITUDE READOUT)
!1. GROUND SPEED READOUT IS 240 KNOTS (NOTE: READOUTS MAY NOT BE DISPLAYED BECAUSE OF A LOSS OF BEACON SIGNAL, A CONTROLLER ALERT THAT A PILOT WAS SQUAWKING EMERGENCY, RADIO FAILURE, ETC)
!2. AIRCRAFT ID
!3. ASTERISK INDICATES A CONTROLLER ENTRY IN MODE C BLOCK. IN THIS CASE 5000' IS ENTERED AND "05" WOULD ALTERNATE WITH MODE C READOUT.
!4. INDICATES "HEAVY" CP

25. "LOW ALT" FLASHES TO INDICATE WHEN AN AIRCRAFT'S PREDICTED DESCENT PLACES THE AIRCRAFT IN AN UNSAFE PROXIMITY TO TERRAIN. (NOTE: THIS FEATURE DOES NOT FUNCTION IF THE AIRCRAFT IS NOT SQUAWKING MODE C. WHEN A HELICOPTER OR AIRCRAFT IS KNOWN TO BE OPERATING BELOW THE LOWER SAFE LIMIT, THE "LOW ALT" CAN BE CHANGED TO "INHIBIT" AND FLASHING CEASES.)
26. NAVAIDS
27. AIRWAYS
28. PRIMARY TARGET ONLY
29. NONMONITORED, NO MODE C (AN ASTERISK WOULD INDICATE NONMONITORED WITH MODE C)
30. BEACON TARGET ONLY (SECONDARY RADAR BASED ON AIRCRAFT TRANSPONDER)
31. TRACKED TARGET (PRIMARY AND BEACON TARGET) CONTROL POSITION A
32. AIRCRAFT IS SQUAWKING EMERGENCY CODE 7700 AND IS NONMONITORED, UNTRACKED, MODE C
33. CONTROLLER ASSIGNED RUNWAY 36 RIGHT ALTERNATES WITH MODE C READOUT (NOTE: A THREE LETTER IDENTIFIER COULD ALSO INDICATE THE ARRIVAL IS AT SPECIFIC AIRPORT)
34. IDENT FLASHES
35. IDENTING TARGET BLOSSOMS
36. UNTRACKED TARGET IDENTING ON A SELECTED CODE
37. RANGE MARKS (10 AND 15 MILE) (CAN BE CHANGED/OFFSET)
38. AIRCRAFT CONTROLLED BY CENTER
39. TARGETS IN SUSPEND STATUS
40. COAST/SUSPEND LIST (AIRCRAFT HOLDING, TEMPORARY LOSS OF BEACON/TARGET, ETC.)
41. RADIO FAILURE, EMERGENCY INFORMATION
42. SELECT BEACON CODES (BEING MONITORED)
43. GENERAL INFORMATION (ATIS, RUNWAY, APPROACH IN USE)
44. ALTIMETER SETTING
45. TIME
46. SYSTEM DATA AREA

Fig. 7-45. *The meanings of the various Arts III symbols in Fig. 7-44*

The air route traffic control radar system

Unlike ARTS, which is used to sequence and separate departing and arriving aircraft in the airport environment, the various Centers (ARTCCs) are equipped with what is called "National Airspace Plan Stage A" for en route traffic control. And, while ARTS relies on primary (broadband) and secondary (narrowband) radar, Stage A uses only narrowband radar. In narrowband, the signal goes out, hits the target, and the reply is processed through a computer, which then produces only an alphanumeric data block of the pertinent aircraft data.

Comparing the Stage A figure (Fig. 7-46) with the ARTS illustration in Fig. 7-44, you'll see that there are no ARTS III-type symbols, except for a small blip representing the aircraft. Instead, there is a triangle over a target when the aircraft is off course, a diamond when it's on course and on time, a square for a major airport, a right angle for a small airport, and a few other symbols that identify types of targets and the current status of aircraft being tracked. Weather is depicted by solid areas with superimposed "Hs" representing high density precipitation. Thin radial lines indicate less dense precipitation.

Long-Range Navigation (LORAN)

With the help of and review by Col. John Schmidt (Ret.), of Leavenworth, Kansas, a Loran and GPS authority as well as an experienced flight instructor, the following is an effort to provide only a simplified overview of these two much more precise electronic navigating systems.

So let's begin with Loran, the acronym for LOng RAnge Navigation. Loran and its land-based network of radio transmitters was initially developed in World War II to provide a reliable, accurate system for ships to navigate the Great Lakes and the coastal waters of the United States.

What we have today is known as Loran-C, the third of four versions developed since the war. Because of its success as a navigation tool, the aviation world soon began to adopt the Loran concept, but it did take several years for the United States to complete the national installation and activation of what are called "chains." By

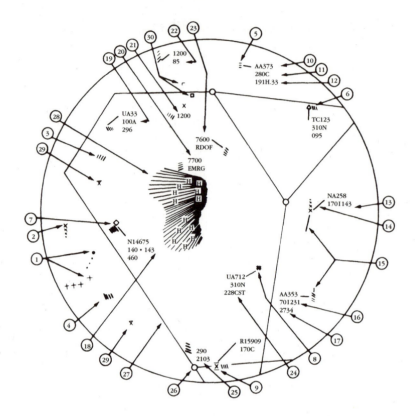

Target Symbols

1 Uncorrelated primar; radar targe +•

2 *Correlated primary radar target ×

3 Uncorrelated beacon target /

4 Correlated beacon target \

5 Identing beacon target ≡

(*Correlated means the association of radar data with the computer projected track of an identified aircraft)

Position Symbols

6 Free track (No flight plan tracking)Δ

7 Flat track (flight plan tracking) ◊

8 Coast (Beacon target lost) #

9 Present Position Hold x

Data Block Information

10 *Aircraft Identification

11 *Assigned Altitude FL280, mode C altitude same or within ±200' of assigned altitude

12 *Computer ID #191, Handoff is to Sector 33 (0-33 would mean handoff accepted) (*Nr's 10, 11, 12 constitute a "full data block")

13 Assigned altitude 17,000', aircraft is climbing, mode C readout was 14,300 when last beacon interrogation was received

14 Leader line connecting target symbol and data block

15 Track velocity and direction vector line (Projected ahead of target)

16 Assigned altitude 7000, aircraft is descending, last mode C readout (or last reported altitude was 100' above FL230)

17 Transponder code shows in full data block only when different than assigned code

18 Aircraft is 300' above assigned altitude

19 Reported altitude (No mode C readout) same as assigned. An "N" would indicate no reported altitude

20 Transponder set on emergency code 7700 (EMRG flashes to attract attention)

21 Transponder code 1200 (VFR) with no mode C

22 Code 1200 (VFR) with mode C an⌐ last altitude readout

23 Transponder set on Radio Failure code 7600, (RDOF flashes)

24 Computer ID #228, CST indicates target is in Coast status

25 Assigned altitude FL290, transponder code (These two items constitute a "limited data block")

Other Symbols

26 Navigational Aid

27 Airway or jet route

28 Outline of weather returns based on primary radar. H's represent ar eas of high density precipitation which might be thunderstorms. Radial lines indicate lower density precipitation.

29 Obstruction

30 Airports   Major: ☐, Small: ⌐

Fig. 7-46. *Using only narrow band radar, the images received on the Air Route Traffic Control Centers, as this figure shows, differ considerably from those produced by ARTS III.*

1991, however, the entire country was covered by this system—a system that has so greatly enhanced the whole spectrum of aerial navigation.

The basics of Loran—in brief

The United States Coast Guard maintains the Loran system and is responsible for the operation of 27 "stations" that comprise the 8 "chains" used in the National Airspace (there are actually 15 chains around the world). Before a Loran-C receiver on the ground or in the air can provide navigational aid, it must receive signals from at least three stations in a given chain. Each chain consists of four to six transmitter-equipped stations, with one station designated as the "Master" (M) and the others as "secondary," or substations, identified by the letters V, W, X, Y, or Z.

Once the aircraft receiver has been activated and the chain in which it will operate is entered, it maintains a database that precisely locates the Master and secondary station transmitters within the chain. From this point on, the navigation operation depends on the user receiver measuring a value called "time difference," or TD. To clarify that: The Master station transmits a pulse group signal that is followed sequentially at precise time intervals by similar pulse-group transmissions from the secondary stations in the chain. The only difference between the Master signal and those of the secondaries is that the latter radiates pulses in groups of eight, while the Master does the same but adds a ninth group for identification.

This is where TD enters the scene. TD is the time interval, measured in microseconds, between the transmission of one Master pulse group and the next Master pulse group That time interval, again in microseconds, falls somewhere in the five-digit range, such as 99,999, which, for ease of reference, is shortened to "9999." That figure—9999 (or whatever it might really be)—then becomes the chain's *Group Repetition Interval,* or GRI.

The GRI is the same for all stations in a given chain but is different for each of the eight U.S. chains, with each chain identified by its own GRI, as the following illustrates:

GRI	Chain Location	Master Station
7960	Gulf of Alaska	Kodiak, AK
7980	Southeast U.S.	Malone, FL
8290	North Central U.S.	Middletown, CA
8970	Great Lakes	Seneca, NY
9610	South Central U.S.	Malone, FL
9940	West Coast U.S.	Middletown, CA
9960	Northeast U.S.	Seneca NY
9970	Northwest Pacific	San Francisco, CA

The geography covered by one of these Loran chains is considerable. The Northeast chain, for instance, with its Master station in Seneca, NY, extends northeast from Seneca to Caribu, ME, east to Nantucket Island, south to Carolina Beach (on the NC/SC border), and west to Dana, IN. There's a lot of geography in that chain, which means that if you were anywhere in the general area identified by those secondaries, you could get Loran-produced navigational aid simply by entering the 9960 GRI in your receiver. With that entry, plus your destination or an en route VOR, the Loran-C receiver/computer will calculate your position in the chain area with intersecting Lines Of Position (LOPs), or triangulation, as determined by radio responses from the chain stations. This position is then presented to you in whatever format you wish, as latitude/longtitude, bearing and distance from a known point or position, groundspeed, estimated time of arrival, and the like. In terms of accuracy, most current Loran units provide an en route, point-to-point, position accuracy of about 2,000 feet, or .25 nautical miles. Another feature is that with Loran, being a dynamic process, the receiver continues to calculate multiple positions as you proceed along your route, including projections of future positionings based on present groundspeed and direction. Then when you near the area of another chain, you merely enter that chain's GRI in your receiver, and the process starts again.

Now what do we do with all this potential? Massive amounts of memory can be placed in a very small space (meaning in your receiver), including, if you wish, the precise location of all Master and Secondary transmitters, the locations of airports, VORs, NDBs, intersections, waypoints, and final approach fixes. Each of these bits of information will be in a database that is updated every 50 days, along with an identifying label that matches the approved or standard identifications you find on sectional charts, en route low altitude charts, instrument approach procedure charts, or the *Airport/Facility Directory*. Now, instant recall of key information or procedures is as simple as inputting the desired facility ICAO identifier.

Despite the availability of this information, most Loran installations in use today are not certified for stand-alone navigation in IFR conditions, including precision instrument approaches. And it appears that such certification will never come, because a great electronic navigating aid is destined to be replaced by our next subject of discussion, GPS, or the Global Positioning System. As of the date of writing, the FAA plans to close down the Loran operations on December 31, 2000.

Global Positioning System (GPS)

The Global Positioning System (GPS) is the future of air navigation, possessing advantages and accuracies unavailable in any other current system. Simply said, the system operates on the concept of triangulation based on information transmitted from orbiting satellites to a panel-mounted or hand-held GPS receiver The quality and quantity of that information is indicative of the technical advances being made to move us into the 21st century. In studying the system, even as it stands today, one wonders if this GPS concept marks the end state of air navigation. Are we finally reaching some sort of theoretical limit, beyond which new horizons seem unlikely? The temptation is to suggest that the only answer maybe just "yes."

As in the Loran discussion, the few words that follow are designed merely to present a broad overview of this almost magical system and the basics on which it is structured. For those interested, *AIM* devotes 15 or so pages to the subject, and then there are always libraries and the Internet. Meanwhile, though, the fundamentals of the system, in nontechnical terms, could be summed up this way:

The system, developed by the Department of Defense and managed by the U.S. Air Force from its Falcon Air Force Base near Colorado Springs, consists primarily of a constellation of 24 satellites that produces position signals to hand-held or panel-mounted GPS receivers. Those receivers interpret the incoming signals and translate the data into visual displays that report the aircraft's position, velocity, time, and altitude. Actually, two different "signals" for the user community are produced, each with significantly different degrees of accuracy. One, the "Standard Positioning Service" (SPS), is unprotected and available to all users. This system provides 100-meter (330 feet) or better accuracy 95 percent of the time and 300-meter or better accuracy 99.99 percent of the time. The second signal, "Precise Positioning Service" (PPS), produces much greater accuracy (20 meters, or 66 feet) than SPS but is currently limited to authorized U.S. and allied military, the federal government, and "civil users who can satisfy specific U.S. requirements," as *AIM* states it.

What makes the GPS system work is, of course, the receiver and the 24 satellites that orbit the earth every 12 hours, with five satellites always "observable" at any one time by a user or receiver anywhere on earth. The satellites repeat the same track configuration over any point every 24 hours, but arrive at that point 4 minutes earlier each day.

For a three-dimensional computation of position, velocity, and altitude, plus precise time, the system must have four satellites "in view," as well as a fifth that verifies the health of the GPS system through what is called "Receiver Autonomous Integrity Monitoring," or RAIM. This is the process by which the "integrity" (usability) of a satellite's signal can be determined and reported to the pilot's GPS receiver. Should the system be corrupted in any way, that information to the pilot will allow him or her time to revert to alternate navigation options in the event the extent of GPS corruption goes beyond predetermined safe limits.

From the pilot's point of view, all you have to do while you're still on the ground is turn on the receiver and enter the three- or four-letter alphanumeric code of your destination airport or of a VOR, NDB, or intrasection in the receiver, The system will take it from there by initially "drawing" a line in the receiver from where you are to where you're going. Once airborne, most receivers, become moving maps with a small airplane indicating whether you're on or off course. Then as you proceed along your flight route, towns, airports, the outward limits of Class B and C airspaces, or other identifying surface features will appear in the receiver's window. Coupled with on-going readings of distance and flying time to your destination (the flying time being based on your actual ground speed), you have a three-dimensional system that reports position, velocity, and altitude with a high degree of precision.

A caveat, though: As one experienced pilot put it, the temptation to keep your head in the cockpit and play with or cross-check the GPS against other navigating aids such as Loran, an NDB, a VOR, a DME, or your plotted course on a sectional can be almost overwhelming. With all your attention on the inside of the airplane, do you know what's going on outside? Are you aware of other traffic that might be in your immediate area, or of flocks of migrating birds seeking new homes in better climes, or isolated clouds that might lie dead ahead of you? The electronic navigating aids are marvelous pieces of equipment, but if you're flying VFR, that means your attention should be directed to what you can see outside the cockpit. If I haven't said it before, I'll say it now: If you keep your head in the cockpit more that 15 seconds at a time, you ought to be getting a little nervous. That's too long not to be alert to the skies about you!

Future GPS advances, such as Local Area Augmentation Systems (LAAS) and Wide Area Augmentation Systems (WAAS), are going to provide the vertical accuracy and resolution required for precise instrument approaches—but without the high cost of maintaining the ground equipment currently required for VORs, LORANs, TACANs, and NDBs. These long-time friends have all received their termination notices, even though the dates of their unemployment remain moving targets. Just as we've seen over the years in more and more dual VOR/ILS installations in general aviation aircraft, we're seeing more dual GPS installations in even the smaller aircraft.

But lest we get too carried away, *AIM* states that, "Aircraft using GPS navigation under IFR must be equipped with an approved and operational alternate means of navigation appropriate to the flight"— meaning a backup system. So even those authorized for the Precise Positioning Service (PPS) have limits placed upon them. That said, though, a sign of the times is the fact that the Instrument Pilot Test Standards now allow the practical test examiner to substitute a GPS approach for the traditional NDB approach. Yes, GPS is the future!

Quickie Quiz Questions
Chapter 7

(Questions for this chapter have been incorporated in text.)

8

The airspace system

The volume of general and commercial aviation is such that more and more regulations affecting flight operations have become essential in the interest of safety. Freedoms that the VFR pilot once enjoyed are being increasingly limited by regulations that demand current pilot familiarity if he or she is to operate within the various airspace segments. "Current" familiarity is emphasized because of the FAA changes being mandated that affect aircraft equipment as well as pilot requirements.

Regardless of the regulations, the VFR pilot can still operate with considerable freedom throughout most of the airspace and in all but the major terminals and tower airports without literally being controlled by ATC. Exercising that freedom, however, requires a knowledge of uncontrolled and controlled airspace, uncontrolled and controlled airports, and the operating regulations pertaining to each.

Airspace descriptions and definitions

Until 1993, the U.S. airspace system, in several respects, had historically been out of step with the rest of the aviation world. This was particularly true in terms of the system's nomenclature and structure. Where the United States had the Positive Control Area, the Continental Control Area, Terminal Control Areas, Airport Radar Service Areas, Terminal Radar Service Areas, Control Zones, and several other areas of control, the rest of the world had a simpler system. It structured the airspace alphabetically into Classes A, B, C, D, E, F, and G.

Effective September 16, 1993, the United States. adopted the International Civil Aviation Organization (ICAO) system and reclassified its airspaces to coincide with the common nomenclature and structure. Consequently, *Controlled* and *Uncontrolled* airspaces are now defined thusly:

Controlled airspace: A generic term that covers the different classifications of airspace (Classes A, B, C, D, and E) and defined dimensions within which air traffic control is provided to IFR flights and to VFR flights in accordance with the airspace classification. (Note: The United States has no airspace comparable to ICAO's Class F.)

Uncontrolled Airspace: The airspace that has not been designated as Class A, B, C, D, or E. In other words, the Class G airspace.

The airspace briefly described

Figure 8-1 illustrates graphically the six classifications of the U.S. airspace system. The basic characteristics of each are reviewed first in this chapter, followed by a discussion of the Class E airspace and some of the important operating regulations pertaining to it. Chapter 9 covers more on the structure and rules of airport operations in Classes B, C, and D.

Class A airspace. As Fig. 8-1 shows, Class A airspace, in which only IFR traffic is permitted, rises from 18,000 feet to 60,000 feet msl (FL600). It includes the airspace over ocean waters within 12 nautical miles of the coasts of the 48 contiguous states and Alaska, as well as designated

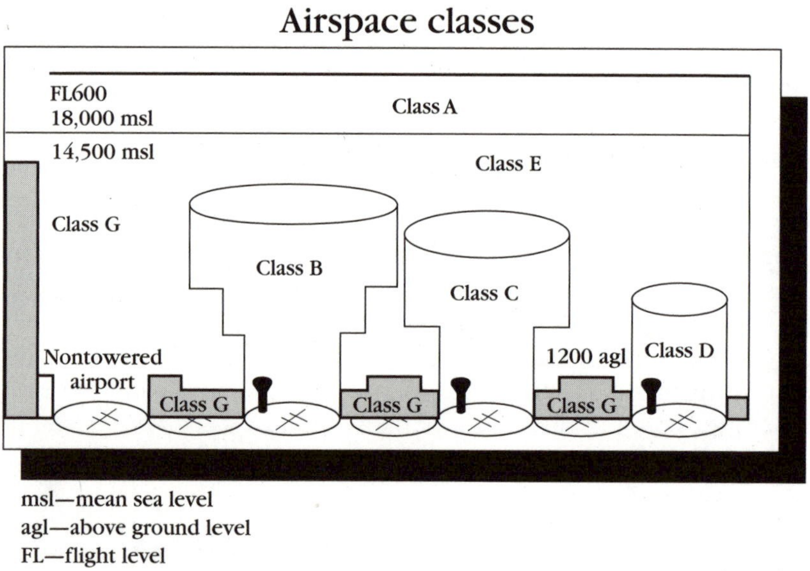

Airspace classes

msl—mean sea level
agl—above ground level
FL—flight level

Fig. 8-1. *This represents the basic structure of the controlled and uncontrolled airspace.*

airspace beyond the 12 mile limit within which domestic radio navigational signals or ATC (Air Traffic Control) radar coverage is possible and domestic procedures are applied.

Class B airspace. Class B is the airspace surrounding the 33 busiest airports, based on IFR operations and passenger enplanements. Each Class B airspace is structured to meet the needs of the individual airport, so the designs and sizes vary. All, however, are basically circular and shaped like an upside-down wedding cake (the traditional description). The core of the airspace, measured out from the center of the airport, generally has a radius of five to 15 nautical miles, depending on the airport, while the highest layer may extend out 20 or 30 nautical miles or more. The ceilings of the various Class Bs also vary, but the most common maximum is 8000 feet msl.

These airspaces are easy to spot on the sectional charts because the rings, identifying the various layers surrounding the primary airport, are printed in blue and are boxed in by a large blue square that also represents the geography covered by a VFR *Terminal Area Chart* (TAC). This is a chart that explodes the area within the square, thus making landmarks, names, and symbols more distinguishable and legible. The TAC should always be used when operating in any Class B environment, and radio contact with Approach Control to obtain permission to enter the Class B airspace is mandatory.

Class C airspace. This airspace is associated with 120 of the less busy airports but airports still active enough to warrant communication and radar control of all air traffic. A Class C is easily spotted on the sectional by the magenta circles that define its structure.

Fairly consistent in design, the core, or "inner circle," surrounding the primary airport has a 5 nautical miles radius. The second level, called the "outer circle," starts at 1200 feet agl and has a 10 nautical mile radius. The ceiling of a Class C is about 4000 agl, although that can vary somewhat from airport to airport. Establishing radio contact with Approach Control is mandatory before entering a Class C.

The Class C also has a circular "outer area" that extends 20 nautical miles out from the primary airport. This airspace, however is not charted on the sectional and pilot participation in the area (meaning establishing radio contact with Approach Control and receiving advisories of other aircraft traffic) is optional.

Class D airspace. Formerly referred to as an "Airport Traffic Area" or "ATA," Class D airspace now identifies all other tower-operated airports that are not large enough or busy enough to justify a Class C rating. Generally speaking, this airspace is cylindrical in shape with a 5 nautical miles radius from the airport center and rises to 2500 feet above the ground. It can be identified on the sectional by the five-mile-radius broken circle that surrounds the airport and the fact that the airport itself is colored blue (as are all tower-controlled airports). Radio contact with the Tower before entering the airspace is required and must be maintained while in it.

Radar coverage in a Class D, however, is unlikely unless the airport is located near a Class B or C Approach Control facility and the D tower is equipped with a receiver called BRITE (Bright Radar Tower Equipment). What happens is that the Approach Control receives the radar images within its scope of coverage and automatically transmits the same images to the nearby Class D airport tower via phone line. These second-generation images then appear on the BRITE receiver, permitting the Tower controller to provide radar-determined traffic advisories to all transponder-equipped aircraft operating within the five-mile Class D area.

Terminal radar service areas (TRSAs). The Terminal Radar Service Area, or TRSA, is a type of airport designation that may soon pass from the picture. TRSAs, as they currently exist, appear on the sectionals as airports surrounded by black circles (similar in shape to a Class B) that establish the horizontal and vertical limits of the TRSA airspace. The airport itself, with a control tower, is a Class D, and radar approach control service is *available* in the areas lying within the circles.

So far, descriptively, the TRSA has all the earmarks of a Class C or even a Class B. The difference lies in the fact that VFR pilots can enter the TRSA area (but not this 5-mile radius of the Class D air-space) without obtaining permission from approach control, or, in fact, even contacting approach at all, unless they want to. The only requirement at all is to call the Tower when about to enter the 5-mile airport airspace for landing or takeoff instructions.

The voluntary use of the approach control service makes the TRSA something between a Class C and Class D airspace.

When contacted for "TRSA service" (once called "Stage III service"), Approach provides safety alerts within the airspace, traffic advisories (of other aircraft), limited radar vectoring, and, at locations where the procedures have been established, sequencing of aircraft prior to turning the aircraft over to the control tower for traffic pattern and landing instructions.

Again, though, this service is voluntary as far as the VFR pilot is concerned. But the question always is: As long as such a service is there for the asking, why not use it? It's just another feature available to those who like the idea of added safety.

The reason that the TRSA airspace is undesignated is that when the Class C, was established, it was expected that the TRSAs would either move up to a Class C or down to a Class D. From a regulatory point of view, the TRSAs were never controlled because they were never subject to rulemaking. As a result, according to the *Airman's Information Manual* (AIM), they "are not contained in FAR Part 71 nor are there any TRSA operating rules in Part 91."

So the TRSA is somewhat of an anomaly and may or may not remain a part of the airspace program.

Class E airspace. Said simply, the Class E airspace is just about everything in the controlled airspace category except Classes A, B, C, and D. Generally ranging from a floor of 700 or 1200 feet agl, the ceiling of this airspace is 18,000 feet msl.

Included in Class E are nontowered airports, areas reserved for IFR aircraft making the transition from a terminal to an en route environment or vice versa, the federal airways from 1200 feet agl to 18,000 feet msl, and the off-shore areas mentioned above as part of the Class A airspace. In this last instance, however, the Class E goes from the surface up to but not including 18,000 feet agl. Also included are Class D airports that have part-time control towers. When the tower is closed, say between midnight and 6:00 AM, the airport becomes Class E during the down period.

Class G. All airspace extending from the surface to 700 or 1200 feet agl that is not included in a Class A, B, C, D, or E airspace is classified as uncontrolled and thus Class G. Nontowered airports are also part of the Class G airspace.

Operating VFR in the Class E controlled airspaces

Keeping in mind that Chap. 9 focuses on the Class B, C, D airports, some discussion here about operating in the Class E airspace is in order.

Understandably confusing, especially to new pilots, is the term "controlled airspace" and what operating freedoms are permitted or what limits are imposed in that environment. Perhaps the following can help clear the air:

VFR aircraft, whether on a VFR flight plan or no flight plan at all, may operate freely in the controlled Class E airspace without ever having to be in contact with any air traffic controlling agency. The *only* requirement is that the pilot strictly abide by all VFR regulations. Such operating freedoms do not exist, however, in the Class B, Class C, and Class D airspaces.

Barring the VFR regulation-abidance, VFR pilots may operate as they wish in the E-airspace. Should they choose, they could even fly coast-to-coast along VOR airways, perhaps receiving continuous traffic advisories from Centers, and land at nontowered Class G airports, without ever once being "controlled" by a Center or any other ATC (air traffic control) agency. If such pilots have been receiving traffic advisories, they *are* responsible for advising the controller of route deviations or altitude changes they may want to make or if they intend to leave the controller's frequency for any reason (as a call to a Flight Service Station's Flight Watch). Most important, though: they *must* remain VFR at all times and be constantly on the alert for other aircraft.

As said above, those freedoms end when it comes time to landing or taking off from a Class B, C, or D controlled airport. And they don't even exist when you're flying on an IFR flight plan. On IFR, you are in a strictly controlled environment and subject to ATC clearances, instructions, and approvals.

If this last is true, why fly IFR (assuming you are qualified)? Primarily for added safety in VFR weather conditions and to be able to operate in bad weather that would ground a noninstrument-rated pilot. Pilots flying on an IFR flight plan, even in perfect conditions, are constantly in contact with ATC controllers who clear them to certain altitudes and headings, advise them of potential conflicting traffic, approve or deny route deviations, monitor their progress, transfer them from controller to controller as they move across the country, coordinate their arrival with Approach Control as they near their destination, and generally watch over and assist them from flight departure to termination. With only a very few exceptions, these are not services available to the pilot on a VFR flight plan.

So VFR freedoms given up by those who fly IFR are more than off-set by the increased safety and flight assistance provided by the eyes and ears of the ground-bound controllers.

Identifying controlled and uncontrolled airspaces

Figure 8-1 indicates three levels of uncontrolled airspace: surface to 700 feet agl, surface to 1200 feet agl, and surface to 14,500 feet msl. Identifying which is which is most easily accomplished by referring to a sectional chart.

Surrounding many tower and nontower airports are circular or irregular-shaped magenta designs. These designs identify *transition areas*, which are defined later, and exist to expedite IFR arrivals and departures. If you check a sectional, you'll see that the magenta becomes fuzzy or fades inward towards the airport. This indicates that all of the airspace within the magenta design, up to any airport traffic control area, is uncontrolled from the surface to 700 feet agl.

Unless indicated otherwise, the airspace *away* from the sharply defined outer edge of the magenta coloring and between any other similarly marked airport is Class E, rising from 1200 feet agl to 18,000 feet msl. Accordingly, in the open country, except for certain special use airspaces and the mountainous areas of the West, the airspace between any two airports, or "between the magentas," is generally uncontrolled up to the 1200 foot agl.

That's fine, but it doesn't explain the extreme left of Fig. 8-1, which shows the Class G airspace rising to 14,500 feet. As a general rule, the 1200-foot ceiling/floor exists over most of the United States, but not in the Rocky Mountain regions. For example, Fig. 8-2 is an excerpt from the Phoenix sectional showing a segment of a Victor airway. Here, the outside of the blue (not magenta) lines along the airway fade in towards the airway center. This fading means that the controlled airspace (Class E) starts at 1200 above the ground everywhere *within* the eight nautical mile width of the airway. Outside the airway, however, outside of the sharp edge of the blue demarcation lines, the airspace is uncontrolled up to the 14,500-foot level, where once again, Class E takes over.

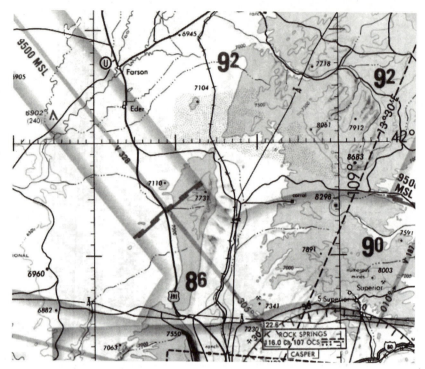

Fig. 8-2. *The area along an airway between the blue (on the sectional chart) lines is controlled airspace, while the area outside the line is uncontrolled.*

VFR requirements

Rules governing VFR flight have been adopted to assist the pilot in meeting the responsibility to see and avoid other aircraft. There are two basic requirements:

  1. Those related to flight visibility and distance from clouds
  2. Those that designate VFR altitudes and flight levels.

VFR visibility and cloud distance

These requirements are stated in FAR 91.155. Fig. 8-3 outlines in chart form the visibility and cloud separation minima in the uncontrolled and controlled airspaces. As the majority of VFR flying is in controlled airspace and in the 1200 foot agl to 10,000-foot msl range, an easy way to remember cloud separation is to start with 500 feet *below*, then double the distance to 1000 feet *above*, and double it once again for 2000 feet *horizontally*. In all cases, the visibility between 1200 agl

Basic VFR weather minimums

Airspace	Flight visibility (statute miles)	Distance from clouds
Class A	Not applicable	Not applicable
Class B	3	Clear of clouds
Class C	3	500 feet below 1000 feet above 2000 feet horizontal
Class D	3	500 feet below 1000 feet above 2000 feet horizontal
Class E Less than 10,000 feet msl	3	500 feet below 1000 feet above 2000 feet horizontal
At or above 10,000 feet msl	5	1000 feet below 1000 feet above 1 statue mile horizontal
Class G 1,200 feet or less above the surface (regardless of msl altitude): Day, except as provided in section 91.155(b)	1	Clear of clouds
Night, except as provided in section 91.155(b)	3	500 feet below 1000 feet above 2000 feet horizontal
More than 1,200 feet above the surface but less than 10,000 feet msl Day	1	500 feet below 1000 feet above 2000 feet horizontal
Night	3	500 feet below 1000 feet above 2000 feet horizontal
More than 1200 feet above the surface and at or above 10,000 feet	5	1000 feet below 1000 feet above 1 statue mile horizontal

Fig. 8-3. *This chart spells out the VFR weather minimums in each of the airspace classes.*

and 10,000 feet msl is 3 miles. Above 10,000 feet, cloud distance is a simple "1-1-1": "1000 below, 1000 above, 1 (mile) horizontal." Note, however, that flight visibility jumps to 5 statute miles.

VFR altitudes

Figure 8-4 summarizes the regulations pertaining to east and west VFR flight altitudes between 3000 feet agl and 18,000 feet msl. The

VFR flight altitudes

If your magnetic course (ground track) is	More than 3,000' above the surface but below 18,000 msl, fly
0° to 179° .... 180° to 359°	Odd thousands msl, plus 500' (3,500, 5,500, 7,500, etc.) Even thousands msl plus 500' (4,500, 6,500, 8,500, etc.)

West even, east odd : plus 500'

Fig. 8-4. *The VFR altitudes to fly, depending on your magnetic course.*

altitudes above 18,000 feet are not listed because that airspace is available only to IFR operations.

In essence, Fig. 8-4 says that going east, VFR altitudes above 3000 feet are at odd thousands, i.e., 3000, 5000, etc., *plus* 500 feet; going west, the altitudes are flown at even thousands of feet, plus 500. The acronym WEEO (West Even, East Odd) can help in remembering the regulation.

The airspace summarized

Figure 8-5 summarizes, in chart form, the features and requirements of each of the airspaces. Keep in mind, though, that this chapter only introduces the current airspace structure. Chapter 9 considers Classes B, C, and D in more detail, particularly the operating regulations pertaining to each.

Special use airspace

Another feature of the airspace system that can't be overlooked is Special Use Airspace (SUA). This is composed of a variety of airspaces in which activities, largely but not exclusively military, are confined because of their nature. It's also an airspace that can prohibit or limit aircraft that are not a part of those military activities. In all cases, SUAs are blocks of space established for purposes of national security, welfare, or environmental protection, as well as military training, research, development, testing, and evaluation

Airspace operating requirements

Airspace features	Class A airspace	Class B airspace	Class C airspace	Class D airspace	Class E airspace	Class G airspace
Operations permitted	IFR	IFR and VFR	IFR and VFR	IFR and VFR	IFR and VFR	IFR and VFR
Entry requirements	ATC clearance	ATC clearance	ATC clearance for IFR.All require radio contact.	ATC clearance for IFR.All require radio contact.	ATC clearance for IFR.All require radio contact.	None
Minimum pilot qualifications	Instrument rating	Private or student certificate	Student certificate	Student certificate	Student certificate	Student certificate
Two-way radio communications	Yes	Yes	Yes	Yes	Yes for VFR	No
VFR minimum visibility	NA	3 statute miles	3 statute miles	3 statute miles	3 statute miles	1 statute mile
VFR minimum distance from clouds	NA	Clear of clouds	500 feet below, 1,000 feet above, and 2,000 feet horizontal	500 feet below, 1,000 feet above, and 2,000 feet horizontal	500 feet below 1,000 feet above, and 2,000 feet horizontal	Clear of clouds
Aircraft separation	All	All	IFR, SVFR, and runway operations	IFR, SVFR, and runway operations	IFR, SVFR	None
Conflict resolution	NA	NA	Between IFR and VFR operations	No	No	No
Traffic advisories	NA	NA	YES	Workload permitting	Workload permitting	Workload permitting
Safety Advisories	Yes	Yes	Yes	Yes	Yes	Yes
Differers from ICAO	No	Yes	Yes	Yes for VFR	No	Yes VFR

Fig. 8-5. *The operating requirements in each of the airspace classes are summarized in this chart.*

(military training/RDT&E). All of these areas, except Controlled Firing Areas (CFAs) are depicted on aeronautical charts.

While most of the airspaces reserved for security, welfare, and the environment might require flight detours or altitude changes, they are usually small enough and infrequent enough to be relatively minor obstacles. Such is not the case, however, with the space set aside for military training/RDT&E. It is within these areas, some quite large geographically, where all sorts of training maneuvers, bombing runs, missile launchings, aerial gunnery, and artillery practice can take place. Considering the potential activities, careless or unauthorized penetration of a special-use area when that area is active (or "hot") could be very hazardous.

Consequently, VFR pilots have to know what these SUAs are, how they're identified on the aeronautical charts, and what regulations apply to operating within them. The following briefly describes the various types of SUAs, including military training routes (MTRs).

Prohibited areas

Prohibited areas contain airspace of defined dimensions, identified by an area on the surface of the earth, within which the aircraft flight is prohibited. Such areas are established for security or other reasons associated with the national welfare. Examples are Camp David, near Washington, D.C., the capitol in Washington, presidential residences or retreats, atomic or nuclear testing areas, and similar critical military or government facilities.

These areas are published in the Federal Register and depicted on aeronautical charts by varying shaped designs composed of short inward-pointing blue lines. The designs thus identify the area over which flight below a specified altitude is prohibited. The areas are also listed on the reverse of the sectional chart legend flap by location, minimum flight altitude, times in which the ban exists, usually "continuous."

Keep in mind that "Prohibited" means *prohibited*—no ifs, ands, or buts. Prior approval to enter the area is required and must be obtained through the proper channels.

Restricted areas

More common are *restricted* areas in which flight, while not wholly prohibited, is subject to restrictions. These areas contain unusual, often invisible, hazards to nonparticipating aircraft (those not authorized to be in the area), such as artillery firing, aerial gunnery, or guided missiles. Penetration of restricted areas, without authorization from the using or controlling agency, obviously could be extremely hazardous to the aircraft and its occupants. Figure 8-6 illustrates three such areas, located southeast of Gainesville, Florida. Restricted areas are also published in FAR Part 73 and typically on the reverse side of sectional legend flaps.

Warning area

This type of SUA should be of little concern to the average VFR pilot because the Warning Areas are located in offshore airspace. For those tempted, however, the area could well contain hazards to nonparticipating aircraft over those waters. The two types of warning areas are:

Nonregulatory Warning: These are areas over international waters in international airspace beyond 12 nautical miles from the United States coast and thus cannot be regulated by the FAA. For any nonparticipating pilot, however, the admonition that applies to prohibited or restricted areas is the same: Stay out!

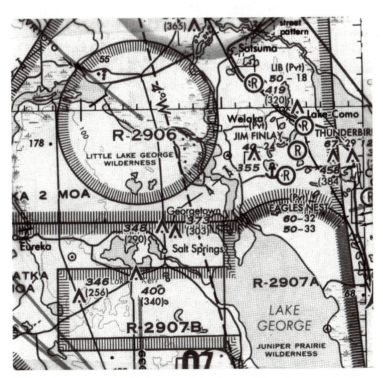

Fig. 8-6. *One of the elements of the Special Use Airspace is the Restricted Area, which really is saying, "Do not enter!"*

Regulatory Warning Area: This area extends from 3 to 12 nautical miles from the United States coast in U.S. territorial waters and contain the same hazardous activity as in the nonregulatory areas. Since they lie within U.S. waters, they are regulated by the FAA, and pilots must abide by the operating rules of FAR Part 91.

Military operations areas (MOAs)

Military Operations Areas (MOAs) represent chunks of airspace that, when active, pose the biggest obstacle to straight-line VFR flight because of their relative size and number. One example is illustrated in Fig. 8-7—the Bruneau and Sheep Creek MOAs, located about 175 nautical miles northwest of Salt Lake City.

In essence, a MOA is an airspace of defined vertical and lateral limits established for the purpose of separating certain military flight training activities from nonmilitary IFR traffic. Whenever a MOA is being used, the nonparticipating IFR traffic could be cleared through the area, if IFR separation can be provided by ATC (Air Traffic Control). Otherwise, ATC reroutes or restricts that IFR traffic.

The various flight training activities in the MOA often involve acrobatic maneuvers, and the using agency, principally the air force, is exempt from the regulation that prohibits acrobatic flight on airways that lie within a MOA. Unlike in restricted areas, VFR pilots are not prohibited from entering an MOA at any time, but they should exer-

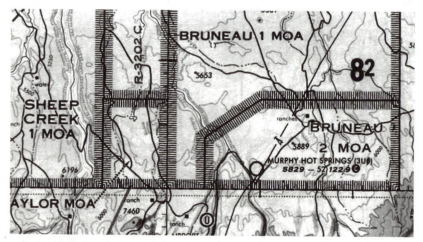

Fig. 8-7. *Military Operations Areas (MOAs) take up large chunks of airspace, as do these, located northwest of Salt Lake City.*

cise extreme caution if they venture into one when military activity is being conducted.

MOAs are depicted on the sectional chart by the vertically striped magenta bands that block off those chunks of terrain and the airspace above them. The reverse side of the sectional's legend (Fig. 8-8) also provides a table with the names of the MOAs covered by that sectional, the altitudes of use for each MOA, the time of use, and the controlling agency, which is the Air Route Traffic Control Center in whose geographical area the MOA lies.

A word of warning: Just because the time of use for a given MOA is listed as "0500-2000 MON-SAT," as the Gandy MOA in Fig. 8-8, don't believe what you read. The using agency, say the air force, can schedule a mission at any time, as long as it notifies the controlling ARTCC, which then coordinates the information with the appropriate Flight Service Station. Presumably Gandy is inactive on Sundays and you'd like to go though it at 1100 hours. To determine if it *is* inactive, ask the FSS specialist when you're getting your weather briefing if there are any NOTAMs about Gandy and if it will be inactive when you want to enter it.

By the same token, the times listed for the MOA to be in use are only the times when the using agency is free to schedule whatever activity it wishes. If one hour or more of that time is not to be scheduled, the agency releases the space back to the ARTCC for public use.

MOA NAME	ALTITUDE OF USE·	TIME OF USE†	CONTROLLING AGENCY··
AUSTIN 1	200 AGL	0800-2100 MON-FRI	ZLC CNTR
BRUNEAU 1	100 AGL TO 14,500	0600-0200	ZLC CNTR
BRUNEAU 2	2000 AGL TO 14,500	0600-0200	ZLC CNTR
GANDY	100 AGL	0500-2000 MON-SAT	ZLC CNTR
LUCIN A	100 AGL TO 9000	0500-2000 MON-SAT	ZLC CNTR
LUCIN B	100 AGL TO 7500	0500-2000 MON-SAT	ZLC CNTR
LUCIN C	100 AGL TO 6500	0500-2000 MON-SAT	ZLC CNTR
OWYHEE	100 AGL TO BUT NOT INCL 14,500	0600-0200	ZLC CNTR
PARADISE	14,500	0500-2100	ZLC CNTR
SAYLOR	100 AGL TO 14,500	0600-0200	ZLC CNTR
SEVIER B	100 AGL TO 9500	0500-2000 MON-SAT	ZLC CNTR
SEVIER D	9500	BY NOTAM 6 HRS IN ADVANCE	ZLC CNTR
SHEEP CREEK 1	100 AGL TO 11,000	0600-0200	ZLC CNTR
SHEEP CREEK 2	100 AGL TO 8500	0600-0200	ZLC CNTR
SHEEP CREEK 3	100 AGL TO BUT NOT INCL 7000	SR-SS MON-FRI O/T BY NOTAM 6 HRS IN ADVANCE	MOUNTAIN HOME RAPCON

Fig. 8-8. *Times and days MOAs are active are listed in the area's sectional chart.*

As to listed altitudes on the sectional: If a given MOA shows, for example, only an altitude of 6000 feet, that means that the altitude of use is from 6000 to 18,000 feet—the base of the Class A airspace. When only one altitude is listed, that is the floor of the MOA. If another MOA lists its altitudes as "500 to 6000," those represent the floor and ceiling of the MOA—meaning to VFR pilots that flight through the MOA above 6000 feet is risk-free from military activity.

Some points, in summary:

- VFR operations in an MOA are neither prohibited nor restricted.
- Entry into an MOA requires no permission.
- The status of an MOA can be determined by contacting the ARTCC responsible for the area in which the MOA is located or the appropriate FSS. (Use the FSS for preflight briefing and, preferably because it would have the most up-to-date information, the ARTCC while en route.)
- Seriously consider detouring around an MOA if it is reported hot. Either that or fly below or above the listed altitudes of use.
- Don't play Russian roulette by penetrating a hot MOA!

Military training routes

Military Training Routes (MTRs) (Fig. 8-9) are established by the FAA and the Department of Defense because of the recognized need for high-speed, low-altitude pilot training in the interests of national security. MTRs are identified by thin gray lines on the sectional charts, brown lines on the en route low altitude charts, and pink on VFR wall planning charts.

As Fig. 8-9 reflects, the type of route is further identified by "IR," for IFR flights, and "VR" for VFR operations. All routes flown below 1500 feet agl are assigned a four digit number, as "IR-1221" or "VR-1017" in Fig. 8-9 (artist circled to simplify location of same). Routes with one or more segments above 1500 feet have three digits, such as "VR105," again in Fig. 8-9.

Another element of the MTR structure is the small arrow adjacent to the route number. This indicates the direction of flight along the route. In other words, a given numbered route is always one-way. There might, however, be traffic in the opposite direction along the same route line. If so, and unlike the VOR airways, that reciprocal route would be designated by a different MTR number.

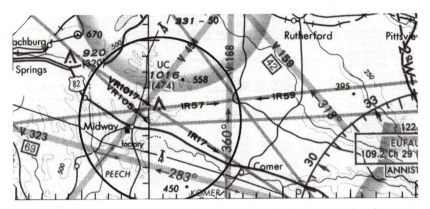

Fig. 8-9. *Those thin lines on the sectional look innocent, but be on guard. They're the highways of some rather rapid moving airborne vehicles.*

Another VOR-MTR difference is the route width. A VOR airway is generally 8 miles wide (4 miles either side of the center line). MTRs, however, can vary considerably. While 5/5 (5 miles either side of the center line) is a general standard, variations from 7.5/7.5, 10/10, or even 16/25 are not unusual. The thinness of the MTR lines on the aeronautical charts is thus not indicative of the width of the MTRs or the areas within which high-speed training operations could be in progress.

In planning cross-country flights, VFR you should note what MTRs cross or parallel your line of flight and then determine from the Flight Service Station the scheduled military activity at the approximate time you will be on or crossing a given MTR. As military schedules can change, you should obtain updated activity reports en route from the nearest FSS or from the appropriate Air Route Traffic Control Center when within 100 miles of an MTR. Be sure to exercise special alertness when near or on an MTR. Camouflaged aircraft traveling at high speeds are not easy to see. As the *Airman's Information Manual* states, "Nonparticipating aircraft are not prohibited from flying within an MTR; however, extreme vigilance should be exercised when conducting flight through or near these routes . . . ."

Air defense identification zones

Identified on aeronautical charts, Air Defense Identification Zones exist for the purpose of national security, as opposed to the Special

Use Airspaces, which, barring prohibited airspaces, are for military training, research, development, testing, and evaluation. As defined in FAR 99.3(a):

> The Air Defense Identification Zone (ADIZ) is an area of airspace over land or water in which the ready identification, location, and control of civil aircraft is required in the interest of national security.

FAR Part 99 establishes the rules pertaining to operations within an ADIZ, including special security instructions, radio requirements, flight plan requirements, transponder requirements, arrival or completion notices, position reports, radio failure—plus other pilot regulations. Pilots should refer to Part 99 before even considering operating in an ADIZ, which are located along the Atlantic, Gulf, and Pacific coasts.

Alert area

Alert areas are a little different breed of SUA, in that, except for Prohibited areas and Air Defense Identification Zones, they are the only areas that exist for other than purely military purposes. They are there solely to alert nonparticipating pilots that they are entering an area that might contain a high level of pilot training—civilian or military—or unusual types of aerial activity, neither of which, in itself, is classified as hazardous to aircraft. The activity, however, can be of such intensity that all pilots should be particularly alert.

As with the other SUAs, the alerts are charted on the sectional by the familiar vertically striped blue bands that define the perimeters of the area and are also included in the "Special Use" table on the reverse side of the sectional legend (Figs. 8-10 and 8-11).

Note the "No A/G" under the "Controlling Agency" column in Fig. 8-11. Defined as "No air/ground communications," this means that within the alert area there are no radio communications controlling traffic, issuing traffic advisories, or radar control. Yes, there could well be radio communications, but whatever there is would be unrelated to any activity in the alert area itself. Consequently, because of the potential hazards, all pilots operating in the area must abide by the Federal Aviation Regulations. Participating aircraft as well as those transiting the area are equally responsible for collision-avoidance.

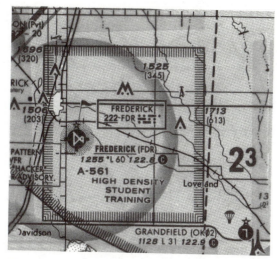

Fig. 8-10. *The way Alert Areas are depicted on the sectionals. Note the reason for the "alert:" high-density student training.*

SPECIAL USE AIRSPACE ON DALLAS-FT. WORTH SECTIONAL CHART

Unless otherwise noted altitudes are MSL and in feet; time is local.
Contact nearest FSS for information.
†Other time by NOTAM contact FSS

The word "TO" an altitude means "To and including."
"MON-FRI" indicates "Monday thru Friday"
FL – Flight Level
NO A/G – No air to ground communications

U.S. P–PROHIBITED, R–RESTRICTED, A–ALERT, W–WARNING, MOA–MILITARY OPERATIONS AREA

NUMBER	LOCATION	ALTITUDE	TIME OF USE	CONTROLLING AGENCY**
P-47	AMARILLO, TX	TO 4800	CONTINUOUS	NO A/G
R-5601 A	FORT SILL, OK	TO 40,000	CONTINUOUS	ZFW CNTR
R-5601 B	FORT SILL, OK	TO 40,000	CONTINUOUS	ZFW CNTR
R-5601 C	FORT SILL, OK	TO 40,000	CONTINUOUS	ZFW CNTR
R-5601 D	FORT SILL, OK	500 AGL TO 16,500	SR-SS TUE-SAT†	ZFW CNTR
R-5601 E	FORT SILL, OK	500 AGL TO 6000	SR-SS TUE-SAT†	ZFW CNTR
A-561	FREDERICK, OK	TO 4000	SR-SS MON-FRI	NO A/G
A-562 A	ENID, OK	TO 10,000	SR TO 3 HRS AFTER SS MON-FRI	NO A/G
A-636	WICHITA FALLS, TX	TO 4000	1 HR BEFORE SR- 1 HR AFTER SS MON-FRI	NO A/G
A-637	LUBBOCK, TX	TO 6000	SR TO 3 HRS AFTER SS MON-FRI, WEEKENDS BY NOTAM	NO A/G

**ZFW–Fort Worth

Fig. 8-11. *The altitude and time of use of A562B are on the reverse side of the sectional's legend.*

Temporary flight restrictions

A major fire, an explosion, an earthquake, an accident occurs. People flock to sight-see, planes circle overhead, and the volume of airborne traffic is such that it creates a hazardous congestion aloft.

To prevent such situations, FAR 91.137 requires the imposition of temporary flight restrictions in the vicinity of the event, which is then publicized to pilots by a NOTAM. Such NOTAMs also contain a description of the area in which the restrictions apply. Normally the area includes the airspace below 2000 feet agl within 5 miles of the site of the incident. The exact dimensions, however, are included in the NOTAM.

The rule is implemented in the case of disasters of substantial magnitude. It is also implemented, as necessary, in the case of demonstrations, riots, other civil disturbances, major sporting events, parades, pageants, and similar functions that are likely to attract large crowds and encourage viewing from the air.

Once the NOTAM has been issued, pilots are not to operate aircraft within the area described in the NOTAM unless one of the following conditions exists:

1. The aircraft is participating in disaster relief activities and is being operated under the direction of the agency responsible for relief activities.

2. The aircraft is operating to or from an airport within the area and such operation will not hamper or endanger relief activities.

3. The operation is authorized under an IFR ATC clearance.

4. Flight around the area is (a) impracticable because of weather or other considerations, (b) advance notice is given to the air traffic facility specified in the NOTAM, and (c) en route flight through the area will not hamper or endanger relief activities.

5. The pilot is carrying accredited news representatives or persons on official business concerning the incident, the flight is conducted in accordance with FAR 91, and a flight plan is filed with the air traffic facility specified in the NOTAM.

Considering the strictness of 91.137, it is not advisable for unauthorized pilots to venture forth just to gawk or photograph the event down below.

Some radio principles and techniques

Operating in the controlled airspaces and airport environments— whether the airport is controlled or not—requires a certain level of radio communicating ability. The following discussion outlines the principles, some of the techniques, and a few examples of the accepted phraseology.

Clarity and brevity

The single, most important element in pilot-controller communications is *understanding*. Brevity is important, but controllers must know what you want to do before they can effectively exercise their control responsibilities. And similarly, you must know exactly what the controller wants you to do. Because conciseness might not be adequate in every single case, use whatever words are necessary to get your message across—but say it briefly and to the point. A fitting acronym is the navy's admonition: KISS. "Keep it Simple, Stupid!"

Listen before transmitting

A basic principle: Always listen before transmitting. If you hear someone talking, trying to interrupt is futile. All you'll do is jam the other party's transmission and force them to repeat their call. Remember that a radio frequency is open to only one speaker at a time. If a second party tries to barge in, the result is no more than annoying squawks and screeches.

Another reason for listening first is that there might be a momentary silence over the air because the pilot is recording information or instructions just issued by the controller. Example: A controller has given an IFR pilot his departure clearance and the pilot is recording the instructions before reading them back. The air is momentarily silent, but that doesn't mean that the communication between the two is over. Give the parties a chance to finish their business.

A third reason for listening is that you might learn from other dialogues just what you want to know—as the active runway, what traffic pattern is used, weather conditions from a controller whom you've been monitoring on a cross-country flight, weather conditions at a tower airport that doesn't have the hourly-recorded ATIS (Automatic Terminal Information Service), and so on. Getting the information you wanted by listening just saves one more call that would otherwise needlessly consume air time. Plus that, it enables you to plan your next few actions, particularly in the approach-for-landing environment.

Think before transmitting

Yes, do think before transmitting. Know what you want to say and mentally rehearse how you're going to say it. This should be an obvious principle, but you'd be amazed at how many pilots get on the air and ramble through a disorganized, wordy transmission that only ties up the frequency and blocks others from using it.

For the actual transmission, hold the microphone close to your lips. Listen, and then after pressing the mike button, pause just a second to be sure that your first word is transmitted. Then speak in a normal conversational tone.

Procedural words and phrases

Mastering the words and phrases of the various pilot/controller exchanges isn't a major challenge; being able to use them with confidence in real-life, airborne situations does, however, take time and practice. The important thing, once you have the structure of the calls clearly in mind, is to know what to expect the controller to say in response to your call and in what order he or she is likely to say it.

Proficiency over the air is a learned skill because one has to know what to say, how to say it, when to say it, and then, if the situation requires, how to respond quickly to the directions controllers give. And all of this is done over a frequency to which every other pilot in the area is tuned. A little frightening? Sure. But, again, with practice based on knowledge, initial uneasiness disappears, just as it does with all things that are new to us.

One step towards professionalism is to avoid, even if tempted, slang, jargon, and "Hi, good buddy" CB chatter. Add to the no-nos even the mildest profanity. You might get away with a "darn" but you won't with a "damn." Remember, every communication exchange is being taped, and the use of profanity could well come back to haunt you.

Unless you have another source, you might consider *The Pilot's Radio Communications Handbook*, Fifth Edition (1998 McGraw-Hill). This covers all of the radio and communication principles, starting with calls at uncontrolled, no-tower airports up through cross-country exchanges, to operating in the Class B major airport airspaces.

The phonetic alphabet and aircraft call signs

The International Civil Aviation Organization (ICAO) phonetic alphabet frequently comes into play in radio communications, such as when stating your aircraft call sign (N-number) or spelling out difficult words or groups of letters during adverse communications conditions (distance, fading, radio problems, faulty transmitter, or the like). Figure 8-12 lists the Morse codes for the alphabet and the numbers 1 through 0. It further cites the phonetic alphabet and how each letter and number should be pronounced.

The main point to stress here is that you should always include the phonetic alphabet letter(s) assigned your aircraft in every radio transmission. Example: "Atlanta Center, Cherokee 1234 *Alpha* . . . ;" "Albany Tower, Cessna 5678 *Romeo* . . . ;" "Wichita Approach, Beech 9100 *November* . . . ." And, by the way, those digits are read one by one. The last example is "Beech niner one zero zero November"—not "ninety one hundred," and its "one two three four Alpha," not "twelve thirty four," or any other combination. After the first call to a controller and his or her response, succeeding contacts are frequently reduced to just the last two numbers and the phonetic letter, as "Cherokee 34 Alpha," or "Beech zero zero November."

When operating in a controlled environment, as in the airport vicinity or on an airway, keep an active ear out for calls to you from ATC as well as to the other aircraft call signs. Let's say that in a traffic pattern, another plane has a call sign very similar to yours, with only the difference of one digit. For instance, you are Cherokee 1234 Alpha, but there's also a Cherokee in the pattern with a "1243 Alpha" call sign. Another possibility: You are still Cherokee 1234 Alpha and another is "1234 Hotel." Unless you're listening carefully to the Tower, you might well assume that instructions to "43 Alpha" were meant for "34 Alpha"—which then might lead to complications.

No two FAA registered N-numbers are the same (like license plates), but close similarities do exist, so listen carefully when you hear an aircraft being addressed. Then if you're not sure whether the call is addressed to you, go back and question the controller. Don't worry about a repercussion: that controller wants to know that his or her message is going to the right party and that there is no confusion as to who is to do what!

Time and the 24-hour clock

As I mentioned in earlier chapters, international time is based on the time in Greenwich, England, which is located in the zero longitudinal meridian. As more rapid sea travel developed in the 1800s, navigational requirements, along with many different and uncoordinated times around the world, each based on an area's own meridian, the need for one accurate time reference became evident. Consequently,

Character	Morse code	Telephony	Phonic (pronunciation)
A	•–	Alfa	(AL-FAH)
B	–•••	Bravo	(BRAH-VOH)
C	–•–•	Charlie	(CHAR-LEE) (or SHAR-LEE)
D	–••	Delta	(DELL-TAH)
E	•	Echo	(ECK-OH)
F	••–•	Foxtrot	(FOKS-TROT)
G	––•	Golf	(GOLF)
H	••••	Hotel	(HOH-TEL)
I	••	India	(IN-DEE-AH)
J	•–––	Juliett	(JEW-LEE-ETT)
K	–•–	Kilo	(KEY-LOH)
L	•–••	Lima	(LEE-MAH)
M	––	Mike	(MIKE)
N	–•	November	(NO-VEM-BER)
O	–––	Oscar	(OSS-CAH)
P	•––•	Papa	(PAH-PAH)
Q	––•–	Quebec	(KEH-BECK)
R	•–•	Romeo	(ROW-ME-OH)
S	•••	Sierra	(SEE-AIR-RAH)
T	–	Tango	(TANG-GO)
U	••–	Uniform	(YOU-NEE-FORM) or (OO-NEE-FORM)
V	•••–	Victor	(VIK-TAH)
W	•––	Whiskey	(WISS-KEY)
X	–••–	Xray	(ECKS-RAY)
Y	–•––	Yankee	(YANG-KEY)
Z	––••	Zulu	(ZOO-LOO)
1	•––––	One	(WUN)
2	••–––	Two	(TOO)
3	•••––	Three	(TREE)
4	••••–	Four	(FOW-ER)
5	•••••	Five	(FIFE)
6	–••••	Six	(SIX)
7	––•••	Seven	(SEV-EN)
8	–––••	Eight	(AIT)
9	––––•	Nine	(NIN-ER)
0	–––––	Zero	(ZEE-RO)

Fig. 8-12. *The international phonetic alphabet, and number pronunciation, as established by ICAO, and the related Morse code transmissions.*

the earth was divided into 24 equal north-south time zones lying between two meridians. Each zone represented one hour, with the zero
longitudinal meridian—the meridian in which Greenwich fell—established as the base point. Once called Greenwich Mean Time, or GMT,
it is now referred to as Coordinated Universal Time (UTC) or Zulu (for
"zero") time and is variously stated as "Zulu," " Z," or "Zed" time, the
last the French pronunciation of the letter "Z."

Simple subtraction converts UTC to local times west of Greenwich
and local times to UTC by addition. For example, the U.S. Eastern
Standard Time (EST) zone is 5 hours earlier than UTC, so if the UTC
time is noon (1200 hours), it is 12:00 minus 5:00 hours, or 7:00 AM
(0700) generally along the Atlantic coast line. In reverse, if it's 3:00
PM EST (1500 hours) in Boston, to find UTC time, add five hours for
an 8:00 PM (2000 hours) time in the Greenwich zone. When it's Eastern Daylight Time, the UTC/EDT difference is 4:00 hours....and so
on across the country going east to west. The same subtract or add
principle applies in the other time zones.

The Central Standard Time Zone is 6 hours behind UTC, so when it's
noon in, say Chicago, the UTC time is 6:00 PM (1800 hours), or when
it's 1200 Central Daylight time in Chicago, the difference is 5 hours,
thus making it 5:00 PM UTC in Greenwich time. The Mountain Standard Time difference is 7 hours and 6 hours Daylight, while the Pacific Standard is 8 hours and Daylight 7 hours. Alaska has two time
zones—9 and 10 hours, and Hawaii 10 hours. Neither Alaska nor
Hawaii, however, observes Daylight time.)

Just remember: To convert U.S. time to UTC, add the U.S. time zone
hour difference; to convert UTC to U.S. time, subtract the difference.

The 24-hour clock system is used in flight plans, radio transmissions,
weather maps, and many other flight-related documents or references. Hours are indicated by the first two digits and minutes by the
last two: 0920 (9:20 AM is thus quoted as "zero niner two zero," while
9:20 P.M. is 2120 hours ("twenty one twenty hours"). Times are also
often stated in minutes only (two figures) when no misunderstanding
is likely to occur. Figure 8-13 might help in clarifying the conversion.

Numbers

Some other practices when citing figures or numbers:

Numbers involving elements such as ceiling heights, winds aloft, altitudes, and the like, are orally reported or spoken in thousands and

Morning		Afternoon	
AM/PM Times	24-Hour Clock	AM/PM Times	24-Hour Clock
1:00 AM	0100 Hours	1:00 PM	1300 Hours
2:00 :AM	0200 Hours	2:00 PM	1400 Hours
3:00 AM	0300 Hours	3:00 PM	1500 Hours
4:00 AM	0400 Hours	4:00 PM	1600 Hours
5:00 AM	0500 Hours	5:00 PM	1700 Hours
6:00 AM	0600 Hours	6:00 PM	1800 Hours
7:00 AM	0700 Hours	7:00 PM	1900 Hours
8:00 AM	0800 Hours	8:00 PM	2000 Hours
9:00 AM	0900 Hours	9:00 PM	2100 Hours
10:00 AM	1000 Hours	10:00 PM	2200 Hours
11:00 AM	1100 Hours	11:00 PM	2300 Hours
12:00 Noon	1200 Hours	12:00 Midnight	2400 Hours

Fig. 8-13. *Converting times from the 12-hour to the 24-hour clock.*

hundreds. For example, "5500 feet" is spoken as "five thousand five hundred . . .", not "fifty five hundred." Above 9900 feet, the first two digits are stated separately: "13,500" is "one three thousand five hundred," and so on. At and above 18,000 feet msl (FL180) the verbal thousands and hundreds are eliminated and a 19,000 foot altitude is cited as "Flight level one niner zero" (FL190)—the words "flight level," followed by the first three digits of the msl altitude. Airway route numbers are stated in the normal way, as "V12" becoming "Victor twelve," not "Victor one two." All other numbers are spoken by pronouncing each digit: "Runway 13," for example, is "Runway one three."

In the cases of radio frequencies with their decimal points, the decimal is included and stated as "point:" "122.9" is "one two two point niner," not, as a rule, "one twenty two point nine." You're likely, however, to hear shortened variations of frequency quotations, such as "Contact the Tower on 33.3." Because the "one" of 133.3 is understood to be part of the frequency, it is often omitted in busy airport environments. In the same vein, ground control frequencies are almost always 121.7, 121.8, or 121.9. You thus may hear the controller's abbreviated direction after landing to "Contact ground point niner." The Tower's assumption is that pilots know and understand that "121" is the ground control prefix, and to say it time after time to every landing aircraft would be both time-consuming and frequency-clogging. Hence the verbal shorthand.

Speeds

Airspeed is another element that is spoken in separate digits, as "niner five" for "95," then sometimes followed by the word "knots." Including "knots" is not always done, however, and the controller may omit it entirely when, for example, directing a speed adjustment. He or she might simply say, "Reduce speed to one five zero." "Knots" is taken for granted. The whole point, again, is terseness and to-the-point communications.

Directions

The three digits of a course—bearing, heading, or wind direction—should always be spoken and understood to be magnetic readings. "Magnetic" being assumed, the word "true" must be added on those occasions when it applies: a true course of 050 degrees is cited as "zero five zero true."

Ground station call signs

Addressing many facilities is straightforward and logical, as the examples in Fig. 8-14 illustrate: "Shannon unicom" (a call to a no-tower, uncontrolled airport where only a Fixed Base Operator [FBO] runs the facility); "Shannon Radio" (a call to a Flight Service Station. It's always "Radio" when calling any FSS)—except when you want to contact flight watch. In that case, if you are below 17,500 feet, dial in 122.0, the flight watch (a.k.a., the "EFAS") frequency, and address the call to the air route traffic control *center* in whose area you are flying. The call is simply, "Atlanta flight watch, Cherokee 1234 Alpha." Flight watch, in this case located in Macon, GA, will then respond. Other examples of correct phrasing are such as, "Augusta Tower;" "Dallas Clearance Delivery;" "Norman Ground (Control);" "Oklahoma City Approach;" "Tulsa Departure;" "Fort Worth Center;" and so on.

Facility	Call sign
Airport unicom	"Shannon Unicom"
FAA Flight Service Station	"Chicago Radio"
FAA Flight Service Station	"Seattle Flight Watch"
(En Route Flight Advisory	
Service (Weather))	
Airport Traffic Control	"Augusta Tower"
Tower	
Clearance Delivery Position	"Dallas Clearance Delivery"
(IFR)	
Ground Control Position in	"Miami Ground"
Tower	
Radar or Nonradar Approach	"Oklahoma City Approach"
Control Position	
Radar Departure Control	"St. Louis Departure"
Position	
FAA Air Route Traffic	"Washington Center"
Control Center	

Fig. 8-14. *How to initially address or contact the various air traffic control ground agencies and Flight Service Stations.*

If you're contacting a Center or an Approach Control facility, be sure that you have actually established contact with the controller before starting your message. More specifically, after determining that the frequency is clear, merely address the call to the facility you want to reach, as "Atlanta Center, Cherokee 1234 Alpha." Say no more at this point. Instead, wait for the controller to acknowledge your call with something like: "Cherokee 1234 Alpha, Atlanta Center." Now go ahead with what you want to say, but start by again re-identifying yourself, as: "Center, Cherokee 34 Alpha requests (or whatever) . . . etc."

The reason for this sequence is that the controller may be talking on another of his or her frequencies (the controller may have as many as six to monitor), or is otherwise momentarily occupied. So give the controller a chance to acknowledge your initial call before you deliver your message or make your request.

In case of radio silence . . .

Finally, be alert to the sounds or lack thereof in your receiver. If there has been an unusually long period of radio silence, adjust the squelch or turn up the volume. If you get the characteristic static, the radio is working. If there is no static sound, push the set in a little. Vibration might have caused it to slip out of its rack just enough to break electrical contact. If you're apparently not transmitting, is the mike plugged in? If you are using a headset, is it plugged in? Little things can happen in normal operations that produce all the symptoms of radio failure but which can be corrected by only a minor adjustment.

Another thing: If you hear a screeching in the radio, check the mike button to be sure that it's not stuck in the transmit position. This occasionally happens, and when it does, it causes a frequency blockage until the mike is "unstuck."

Of course, an obvious principle in establishing contact with ground stations is to be sure that you're within the performance range of your equipment and the station you're trying to reach. Remember that a higher altitude increases the range of VHF line of sight communications.

Some additional radio procedures

Along with those comments on radio principles and techniques, further discussion of certain basic procedures is in order. These are reviewed for the sole purpose of helping you master the various radio techniques more rapidly and thus increase your confidence about picking up the mike and being heard by a rather large unseen audience.

The initial contacts

The term *initial contact* or *initial callup* quite logically refers to the first radio call you make to a given ground facility. When doing so, use the following format:

1. The name of the facility you are calling, as "Nashville Approach," "Downtown Tower," "Wichita Departure."
2. Your *full* aircraft identification, meaning aircraft type and N-number: "Cherokee 1234 Alpha."

At this point, you have two options. The first, as discussed earlier, is to stop after the aircraft identification [2] above, and wait for the ground agency to acknowledge your call. This is the preferred technique when airborne and trying for the first time to contact a Center, a Class B or C approach control, or a Flight Service Station.

The second option, more fitting in the immediate airport vicinity is to follow the aircraft N-number with a very brief message. Just a couple of examples: You're planning to land at Alpha Airport and you've monitored the recorded ATIS, which gives, among other information, the current altimeter setting, winds, and active runway. With that, you can plan your approach and traffic pattern before talking with anyone. The call, then, is simply, "Alpha Tower, Cessna 5678 Uniform, 10 miles west with Hotel (the current ATIS information) for landing." That's all you need say. The Tower's reply would then be something like, "Cessna 5678 Uniform, left traffic for runway one niner."

A second example: You're on the ramp at Alpha, ready to taxi to the runway. You contact Alpha Ground Control (a controller position located in the tower cab) with this: "Alpha ground, Cessna 5678 Uniform, Hangar Four (where you are now) with Delta (the latest ATIS), VFR Memphis." With that, the controller has all the information needed to clear you to taxi to the active runway.

Note that is TO, not ON, the active runway. In the Tower, ground controllers handle traffic on the airport *except* for active runways, and the local controller is responsible for traffic on the active runways and within the 5 mile radius of the airport. Ground Control can authorize traffic to *cross* an active runway, but only the local controller can clear traffic *on* that runway for takeoff or landing purposes. More broadly, Ground Control supervises all traffic on the airport surface, meaning automobiles, trucks, personnel movements, as well as airplanes, but not on the active runway(s).

As I've strongly recommended, use discretion in your calls and don't overload a controller with information he or she doesn't need. Again keep KISS in mind. Those on the ground will greatly appreciate your preparation and your thoughtfulness.

Contacts in flight

If you are attempting to establish contact with a ground station and are receiving on one frequency while transmitting on another, as in the case of a VOR and a call to a Flight Service Station, indicate in your first call the VOR name or the frequency on which you expect a reply. Most FSSs and control facilities can transmit on several VOR stations in the area. Of course, use the appropriate FSS call sign as indicated on charts.

If the chart indicates FSS frequencies above the VORTAC or in FSS communications boxes, transmit or receive on those frequencies nearest your location.

For subsequent calls to any ground station, use the same basic format as in the initial contact, except state your message or request in one transmission. Don't pause for an acknowledgment. Also, in this type of call, since you've been in contact with the ground station, you can usually omit the station's name. Instead of addressing a subsequent call to "Downtown Tower," simply start the message with "Tower." Example: It's a gusty day, you're on the base leg for landing, and would like an update on the current wind. The Tower knows your N-number and it's obvious the call is addressed to Downtown, so all there is to it is this: "Tower, 34 Alpha, wind check."

Meanwhile, be sure to acknowledge all calls, advisories, or directions, unless the controller advises otherwise. For instance, you're on final about ready to flare prior to touchdown. The Tower contacts you with, "34 Alpha do not acknowledge. Clear the runway as soon as possible. Learjet behind you on one mile final."

Required acknowledgments should be made as tersely as possible, maybe in only one or two words, such as "Wilco," ("Will comply.") "Roger," "Affirmative," "Negative," or other appropriate remarks. While brevity is essential, it's equally important that you confirm your understanding of what the controller wants you to do. For example, the Tower calls and says: "Cherokee 34 Alpha, extend your downwind one mile and follow the twin Commander on four mile final." You reply: "Roger, extending one mile. Now contact the Commander (or have the Commander). 34 Alpha." In this case, a plain "Roger" doesn't confirm that you know what you're supposed to do. The "extending one mile" does.

There are some occasions when the controller must issue time-critical instructions and then observe your response, either visually or on radar. If the situation demands your response, take appropriate action or immediately advise the facility why you can't comply. Example of the last: An instruction to climb, descend, or turn might put you in a cloud bank—a no-no if you're flying VFR.

On the other hand, a controller calls you with this: "Cherokee 34 Alpha, turn right NOW 90 degrees. Target approaching dead ahead." As soon as you hear "NOW," start turning. Don't continue on until you've heard the full message and then begin your turn. The controller wants immediate action, so let your turn, which he can see on the radar screen, be your first acknowledgment. Then respond orally when the controller has completed the call, with "Roger, right to 90."

When advised by ATC to change frequencies, acknowledge the instruction with something like this: "Roger, Center, one two five point five five (the new frequency). Good day. 34 Alpha." If you tune to the new frequency without an acknowledgment, the controller's workload is increased because he has no way of knowing whether you received the instruction, lost your radio, decided to turn your radio off, or switched to some other frequency all on your own. Don't keep controllers in the dark!

Flying VFR, you do, of course, have the right to change frequencies any time you wish. But if you do, *always* tell the controller you've been talking with before you make the change. Otherwise, he'll miss you and wonder about you.

Aircraft call signs—in general

Perhaps enough has been said about the call signs, or N-numbers, associated with the typical small general aviation aircraft and how the call signs should be stated. Not previously noted, however, is the fact that the prefix "N" is dropped in radio transmissions. Occasionally, you might hear, "Alpha Tower, November 2468 Whiskey . . .," but the inclusion of "November" is unnecessary and only consumes brief but precious air time.

As to other types of aviation, air taxi or other commercial operators *not* having FAA authorized call signs prefix their normal identification with the phonetic word "Tango."

Air carriers and commuter air carriers having FAA authorized call signs use a group form for the numbers, such as "TWA Forty Five," and, if applicable, adding the word "Heavy" for the larger passenger jets.

Military aircraft have a variety of systems including serial numbers, word call signs, and combinations of letters/numbers.

Civilian airborne ambulance flights (aircraft carrying ambulatory or litter patients, organ donors, or organs for transplant) will be expedited and necessary notification will be made when or if the pilot so requests. When filing flight plans for such flights, the word "lifeguard" is added in the remarks section. In radio communications, the call sign "lifeguard" is inserted, followed by the aircraft type and the digits and letters of the registration number. The "lifeguard" designation is used *only* for those missions of an urgent nature.

In the event of radio problems

A full discussion of what to do should you have radio failure is not practical at this point. Nonetheless, the following procedures can generally apply. Primary to the overview, though, is the observation that if you have problems with either your transmitter or receiver, or both, stay out of and away from Class B and C terminal areas. Operable two-way radios are mandatory in both airspaces. If it is a Class D airport, however, these procedures are in order:

On arrival . . . Class D airports

If you have reason to believe your receiver is inoperative but that you still can transmit, remain outside or above the airport traffic area until the direction and flow of traffic has been determined. Then advise the Class D tower of your type aircraft, position, altitude, intention to land, and request that you be controlled with light signals (Fig. 8-15). When you're approximately 3 to 5 miles from the airport, again advise the Tower of your position and join the airport traffic pattern. From this point on, watch the Tower for light signals. As usual, continue to transmit your position when downwind, turning base leg, and when turning to the final approach.

If the transmitter is inoperative but your receiver is functioning, again remain outside or above the airport area until the direction and flow of traffic has been determined, then join the airport traffic pattern. Monitor the local control tower frequency as depicted on sectional charts for landing or traffic information, and look for a light signal that might be addressed to your aircraft. During hours of daylight, acknowledge Tower transmissions or light signals by rocking the wings. At night, acknowledge by blinking the landing or navigation lights.

If both transmitter and receiver are inoperative, remain outside or above the airport traffic area until the direction and flow of traffic has been determined, then join the airport traffic pattern and maintain visual contact with the Tower to receive light signals. Acknowledge light signals as previously described.

ATCT Light Gun Signals

Color and type of signal	Movement of vehicles, equipment, and personnel	Aircraft on the ground	Aircraft in flight
	Meaning		
Steady green	Cleared to cross, proceed or go	Cleared for takeoff	Cleared to land
Flashing green	Not applicable	Cleared for taxi	Return for landing (to be followed by steady green at the proper time)
Steady red	STOP	STOP	Give way to other aircraft and continue circling
Flashing red	Clear the taxiway/runway	Taxi clear of the runway in use	Airport unsafe, do not land
Flashing white	Return to starting point on airport	Return to starting point on airport	Not applicable
Alternating red and green	Exercise extreme caution	Exercise extreme caution	Exercise extreme caution

Fig. 8-15. *Familiarity with the light signal system could be important if you had to land at a controlled airport with a sick or dead radio.*

Departures . . . Class D airports

Should you experience radio failure prior to leaving the parking area, make every effort to have the equipment repaired. If this isn't possible and you *must* make the flight, telephone the Tower and request authorization to depart without an operable two-way radio. If the Tower so authorizes, you'll be given departure information and requested to monitor the tower frequency or to watch for light signals—whichever is appropriate. During daylight hours, acknowledge Tower transmissions or light signals by moving the ailerons or rudder. At night, acknowledge by blinking the landing or navigation lights. If radio malfunction occurs after departing the parking area, watch the Tower for light signals or monitor tower frequency, return to the ramp, and phone the Tower for instructions about operating in the Class D airspace.

Note: Chapter 11 has additional information regarding communications difficulties.

The air route traffic control centers—and operating VFR in controlled airspace

As you know from earlier discussions, excluding the Class A, B, C, and D airspaces, and certain Special Use Airspaces, VFR pilots can operate in controlled airspace and yet not be under the control of any ATC facility. The only requirement is to adhere to the VFR visibility, cloud separation, and east-west altitude requirements.

This freedom applies even when flying along a VOR airway on a cross-country flight and you have requested and are receiving en route traffic advisories from one of the nation's Air Route Traffic Control Centers. In this environment, you have the freedom to climb, descend, or deviate from your route as you wish (as long as you comply with the VFR requirements). In the process of so doing, however, you have certain communication responsibilities while you're in contact with a Center. Before reviewing those responsibilities, a brief discussion of these Centers might help in understanding what they are and the services they can provide.

ARTCCs' basic responsibilities

The Air Route Traffic Control Centers exist primarily to control IFR flight plan aircraft, which includes ensuring proper traffic separations, issuing traffic advisories, warnings, or alerts, monitoring the IFR aircraft's fix-to-fix, point-to-point progress, and sequencing the aircraft both en route and into the terminal environment. This is all done through radio communications and the Centers' radar system.

Additionally, when requested and workload permitting, a Center will provide traffic advisories to VFR aircraft. This simply means that the Center controller alerts the pilot to other traffic that might be in his or her line of flight and that could present a potential conflict situation. Also, but only if the pilot has established contact with Center and an emergency arises, the controller can be very helpful by guiding the pilot to the nearest airport, advising other ground agencies in the event of radio failure, reorienting pilots who are lost, alerting them to active Military Operations Areas, and providing other safety-enhancing services.

Those services, however, are available only if:

1. The VFR pilot has established radio contact with a Center controller;

2. The pilot has requested the service generally called "flight fol-

lowing";

3. The controller has agreed to provide the service;

4. The pilot remains in radio contact with the Center until that contact is terminated by mutual agreement.

Center locations

Twenty Centers cover the continental United States, plus one each in Alaska, Honolulu, San Juan, and Guam. Figure 8-16 illustrates the geographical areas for which each is responsible. Those in the 48 states are located in or near the cities of:

Albuquerque	Kansas City
Atlanta	Los Angeles
Boston	Memphis
Chicago	Miami
Cleveland	Minneapolis
Denver	New York
Fort Worth	Oakland
Houston	Salt Lake City
Indianapolis	Seattle
Jacksonville	Washington

Each Center has many remoted air-ground radio outlets and a smaller number of remoted radar antennas that are connected to the Center by microwave links and landlines. It's through these means that radio contact and radar coverage are maintained, even though the aircraft might be several hundred miles from the physical location of the Center.

The organization of a Center and the various functions within it are beyond the scope of this discussion. For those who have the opportunity, however, the FAA urges pilots to visit the nearest Center and/or attend one of the nationwide FAA "Operation Raincheck" programs. A tour of the Center, listening in on radio communications, observing the radar screen, and learning about the services the controllers can provide the VFR pilot should allay any concerns or fears you might have about using those services on cross-country flights and flying the VOR airways.

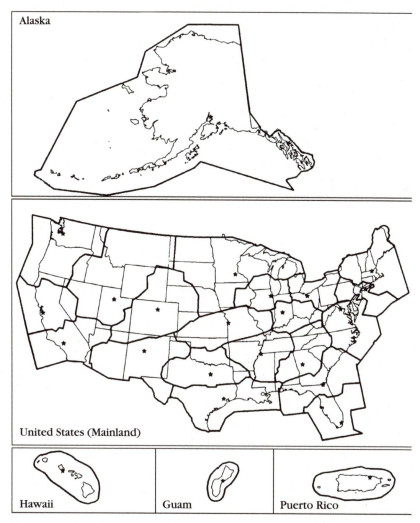

Fig. 8-16. *The locations of the Air Route Traffic Control Centers and the extensive geography over which each exercises traffic control.*

Establishing radio contact with a Center. Because of the many radio frequencies needed to provide service throughout a Center's geographical area of responsibility, it's not always easy to determine what frequency should be used to establish the initial contact. It just depends on the pilot's location within the Center's area.

One source for this information is the FSS while you're receiving a weather briefing. Others are Ground Control, Clearance Delivery, or the Tower at a controlled airport, and a third is Departure Control at a Class B or C airport.

While in flight, if contact had not been previously established, a radio call to the nearest FSS will give the frequency for the area in which you are currently flying. On the other hand, if you have made contact and Center, at your request, is tracking your progress on radar, the controller will advise when you're leaving that particular sector and what new frequency you should tune to for advisories from the next sector. Usually, but not always, the controller will do the same when you're approaching the boundary between the Center with which you have been in contact and the next Center in line of flight.

Pilot responsibilities when in contact with a Center. Although not literally controlled by ATC, the VFR pilot has certain responsibilities when requesting and receiving traffic advisories.

For re-emphasis, be sure the controller responds to your initial call before you announce your position and request traffic advisories. With up to perhaps six different frequencies to monitor, he or she could well be talking and listening on any of these, other than yours, when you made that first contact.

After the controller acknowledges your call, then state your present position, present and/or intended cruising altitude, the first point of landing, route of flight, and your request for en route advisories. Above all, keep your communications brief and to the point. The controller has no time to listen to disorganized ramblings.

Some dos and don'ts to keep in mind when using a Center's services on a VFR flight:

- Write down and repeat back the transponder code the controller gives you. It's easy to confuse "2435" with "2345," or any other combination.
- Continue to listen carefully for calls addressed to your N-number, and then respond promptly.
- *Do not* leave the controller's frequency without advising him or her in advance. Then be sure to recontact when you are back on that frequency.
- *Do not* change altitudes or deviate from your announced route of flight without telling the controller of your intentions. You have the right to do either or both, but unannounced deviations could put you or others in jeopardy.

- Remember that you *must* remain VFR at all times, regardless of altitude or flight route. If you have to climb or descend to do so, advise the Center controller accordingly before making any changes.

When being transferred (or "handed off") from one controller to another, or from one Center to another, the full contents of the your initial call are not necessary. The receiving controller knows your altitude, first landing point, etc. All that's necessary to give is your N-number, the phrase "with you," and confirmation of your present altitude. As with the transponder code, however, write down the new frequency you are to contact and repeat it back to the issuing controller. It's easy to forget or become confused.

If you get in trouble because of an inflight emergency, bad weather, you're lost, or whatever, don't hesitate to report the problem immediately. No matter what the ATC facility, controllers continually stress this. Their ability to assist is much greater at the beginning of a problem than later when the problem has become serious.

If you have requested traffic advisories from a Center and the controller tells you he is unable to provide them, don't argue or ask for an explanation. He or she is there primarily to serve IFR aircraft and, secondarily, workload permitting, VFR traffic—except, of course, in an emergency situation. If, in the controller's opinion, the current workload is too heavy to handle VFR aircraft, then that's that. Whatever the reason, the denial of the service is final, not subject to appeal, and the controller is under no obligation to explain.

Communications examples

With all of the previous references to radio communications, a few examples of typical exchanges with a Center controller might be of assistance. Keep in mind that these are exchanges while the pilot is en route and has requested traffic advisories. Examples of communications in the airport environment are given in the next chapter.

The first call to a center.

Pilot: Memphis Center, Cherokee 1234 Alpha.

Center: Cherokee 1234 Alpha, Memphis Center.

Pilot: Center, Cherokee 34 Alpha is over Holly Springs VOR at seven thousand five hundred, VFR Atlanta Fulton County via Victors 54 and 325. Request traffic advisories.

Center: Cherokee 34 Alpha, squawk 2-5-6-2 and ident.
(**Note:** "2562" is the code the pilot is to enter in the transponder. "Squawk" means the same as "enter" and "ident" means to push a small button on the transponder that specifically identifies Cherokee 1234 Alpha on the controller's radar screen.)

Pilot: Roger, 2-5-6-2. 34 Alpha.

Center: Cherokee 34 Alpha, radar contact. Holly Springs altimeter 2930. (**Note:** The decimal is omitted when quoting barometric pressure, and is stated as "two-niner three zero.")

Pilot: 2930. 34 Alpha.

En route advisories.

Center: Cherokee 34 Alpha, traffic at 11 o'clock, type and altitude unknown.

Pilot: Roger, Center. Negative contact. (Or, "Have traffic.") 34 Alpha.

Note: When ATC advises that traffic is at one of the clock positions, as "11 o'clock," the controller is basing that position on the track of your aircraft—not its heading.

For example: You are flying east at 90 degrees. The wind is from the north, so to maintain the 90-degree track over the ground, you crab 10 degrees to the left. Your compass heading is now 80 degrees. ATC's radar, however, can't detect the relative position of the aircraft to the track. It can record only the direction in which the aircraft is moving over the surface. Consequently, using this illustration, a target reported at your 11 o'clock position would, because of the 10-degree crab, be approximately dead ahead of you at 12 o'clock. If you scanned the skies to the left of the aircraft nose at 11 o'clock, you might not see the target at all.

Changing altitude.

Pilot: Center, Cherokee 34 Alpha leaving seven thousand five hundred for niner thousand five hundred account turbulence.

Center: Roger, Cherokee 34 Alpha. Advise when level at niner thousand five hundred.

Pilot: Will do. Cherokee 34 Alpha.

Pilot: Center, Cherokee 34 Alpha level at niner thousand five hundred.

Center: Roger, 34 Alpha.

A "handoff" to another controller and another Center.

Center: Cherokee 1234 Alpha, contact Memphis Center on 126.25.

Pilot: Roger, 126.25. 34 Alpha.

Pilot: Memphis Center, Cherokee 1234 Alpha is with you, level at niner thousand five hundred.

Center: Roger, Cherokee 34 Alpha. Radar contact. Huntsville altimeter 3005.

Pilot: 3005. Thank you. 34 Alpha.
(Later . . .)

Center: Cherokee 34 Alpha, contact Atlanta Center on 119.35.

Pilot: Roger, 119.35. Thank you. 34 Alpha.

Pilot: Atlanta Center, Cherokee 1234 Alpha is with you, level at niner thousand five hundred.

Center: Roger, Cherokee 1234 Alpha. Radar contact. Atlanta altimeter 2930.

Pilot: Roger, 2930. Cherokee 34 Alpha.

Radar service terminated.

Center: Cherokee 1234 Alpha. Radar service terminated. Frequency change approved. Squawk 1-2-0-0. (or "Squawk VFR.")

Pilot: Roger, Center. Thank you for your help. Cherokee 34 Alpha.

These are only samples of the types of communications that might take place when using a Center for en route advisories. Key points here and in all radio communications are:

- Know what you are going to say and rehearse it before getting on the air.
- Know what to expect to hear and the probable sequence in which it will be transmitted.
- Listen continuously for your aircraft call sign.
- Acknowledge instructions and tersely repeat them back to be sure the controller knows you have understood.
- Keep all communications short and to the point. Don't ramble.

Quickie quiz questions
Chapter 8

1. In which of the controlled airport area airspaces is the VFR pilot required to remain clear of clouds versus adhering to the standard cloud separation minimums?

2. What are the types of Special Use Airspaces (SUAs)?

3. What ground agency should you contact to determine when and whether a given SUA will be active?

4. If it's   The UTC time is:

3:00PM PST   _____

10:30AM EDT   _____

8:00PM CST   _____

5. Convert these times to or from the 24-hour clock:

4:00PM converted is:_____

7:30PM converted is _____

1:48AM converted is _____

1:48PM converted is _____

1650 converted is _____

2130 converted is _____

1200 converted is _____

0001 converted is _____

6. In contacting a ground facility, under what circumstances should you always give your full N-number and when can you eliminate some of the digits in the interest of brevity?

7. You want to land at a class D airport, but you are having receiver difficulties, you believe, however, that your transmitter is operable. What should you do?? (421)

8. What are the basic responsibilities of an Air Route Traffic Control Center?

9. What sort of military action usually takes place in a Restricted Area?

10. What does "TRSA" stand for, and what is its main difference from a Class B or C airspace?

Answers in Appendix, pages 578-579.

9

Airports

Similar to the airspace, airports are either controlled or uncontrolled. The difference (other than flight and communications procedures) is basically the existence or nonexistence of an operating control tower. Uncontrolled airports have no tower on the premises, or, if one does exist, it is open part-time, say from 0700 to 2100 hours. When closed, the airport is uncontrolled, and essentially reverts to a Class G, but pilots are still subject to FAA visibility and cloud separation minimums as well as certain radio communication responsibilities. In a controlled airport environment, radio communications with the Tower must be established before entering the area and pilots are subject to ATC instructions.

Before reviewing the specifics relative to controlled and uncontrolled airports, it seems appropriate to summarize some of the general procedures that govern flight operations in these environments.

Airport traffic patterns

Increased traffic congestion, aircraft in climb and descent attitudes, and preoccupation with cockpit duties are factors that increase the serious accident potential near airports, whether they are controlled or uncontrolled. The situation is further compounded when the weather is marginal, just meeting VFR requirements. This chapter, among other things, outlines certain rules and practices with which all pilots should be familiar and adhere to for safe airport operations.

Standard traffic patterns

Whether an airport is controlled or uncontrolled makes little difference: a standard traffic pattern and a standard terminology exist for all. Admittedly, if the airport is controlled, the controller can authorize exceptions to the usual rules to meet specific needs. Those variations, however, don't alter the basic and time-honored pattern that pilots have been taught for decades.

First, then, is an overview of this pattern and definitions of the elements that comprise it.

As Fig. 9-1 indicates, traffic in the airport area normally follows a left-hand pattern so that the airport is always easily visible to the pilot who usually sits in the cockpit's left seat. The various legs of the pattern are defined this way:

- **Upwind leg:** A flight path generally against the wind and parallel to the landing runway in the direction of landing.
- **Crosswind leg:** A flight path at right angles to the landing runway off its takeoff end.
- **Downwind leg:** A flight path with the wind and parallel to the landing runway in the direction opposite to landing.
- **Base leg:** A flight path at right angles to the landing runway off its approach end and extending from the downwind leg to the intersection of the extended runway centerline.
- **Final approach:** A flight path in the direction of landing along the extended runway centerline from the base leg to the runway.

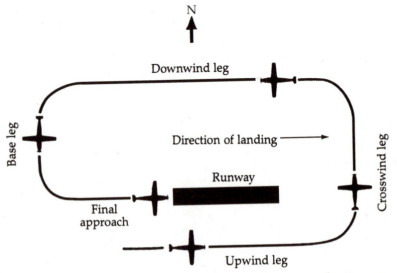

Fig. 9-1. *The nomenclature and design of the typical traffic pattern.*

Not always is a left pattern desirable or even legal, however. Refer to Fig. 9-2 for a moment. Let's assume that a well-developed shopping, business, or housing area lies just to the south of the airport. (These always seem to crop up shortly after an airport is built and the complaints about noise, etc., start pouring in) Anyway, being a good neighbor, the traffic pattern here would be routed to the north of the airport, regardless of the wind, thus avoiding flight over the populated area at the low altitude of 800 or 1,000 feet. As opposed to Fig. 9-1, if the wind is from the west and runway 27 is in use, the pattern will be right hand for all take-offs and landing. Conversely, with a wind from the east and runway 9 the active runway, the normal left-hand pattern pictured in Fig. 9-1 would prevail.

Variations like this aren't that rare—which should be another warning to pilots to study charts and references, such as sectionals and the *Airport/Facility Directory*, before launching forth into new territories.

Very often, those airports not having a Tower, a Flight Service Station, or unicom (to be defined shortly), may have installed a visual indicator on the field—a "segmented circle"—that is large enough to be seen from the air and consists of the following components, as in Fig. 9-3.

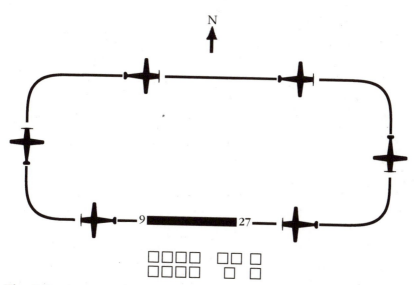

Fig. 9-2. *An example of a situation that might require a right-hand pattern.*

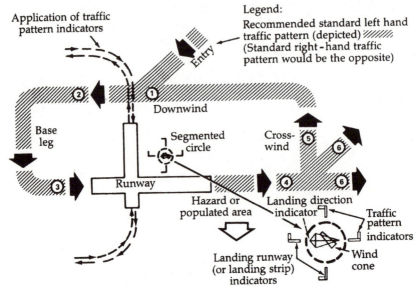

1. Enter pattern in level flight, abeam the midpoint of the runway, at pattern altitude. (1000' AGL is recommended pattern altitude unless established otherwise.)

2. Maintain pattern altitude until just beyond approach end of the landing runway, on downwind leg, then turn to base leg.

3. Complete turn to final at least 1/4 mile from the runway.

4. Continue straight ahead until beyond departure end of runway.

5. If remaining in the traffic pattern, commence turn to crosswind leg beyond the departure end of the runway, within 300 feet of pattern altitude.

6. If departing the traffic pattern, continue straight out, or exit with a 45° left turn beyond the departure end of the runway, after reaching pattern altitude.

Fig. 9-3. *The airport runway indicators and traffic patterns that are especially important at uncontrolled airports.*

- **Segmented circle.** Located in a position affording maximum visibility to pilots in the air and on the ground and providing a centralized location for other elements of the system.

- **Wind direction indicator.** A wind cone installed at the center of the circle used to indicate wind direction and velocity. The cone points into the wind.

- **Landing direction indicator.** A tetrahedron or a tee installed when conditions at the airport warrant its use, located at the center of the circle, and used to indicate the direction in which landings and takeoffs should be made. The large end (cross bar) of a tee is in the direction of landing. The small end of a tetrahedron points in the direction of the pattern.

- **Landing strip indicators.** Installed in pairs as shown in the segmented circle diagram and used to show the alignment of landing strips.

- **Traffic pattern indicators.** Arranged in pairs in conjunction with landing strip indicators and used to indicate the direction of turns when there is a variation from the normal left traffic pattern. (If there is no segmented circle installed at the airport, traffic pattern indicators might be installed on or near the end of the runway.)

Where installed, a flashing amber light near the center of the segmented circle (or on top of the control tower or adjoining building) indicates that a *right* traffic pattern is in effect at the time.

En route operations and traffic pattern altitudes

At most uncontrolled airports, traffic pattern altitudes generally extend from 600 feet to as high as 1500 feet agl. Consequently, if you're flying at a low altitude and just want to pass over an uncontrolled airport—not land— always (1) announce your position and altitude over the airport's CTAF (Common Traffic Advisory Frequency found on the sectional chart or in the A/FD) at least five miles out from the airport; example: "Eureka traffic, Cherokee 1234 Ten East, will cross Eureka at 2,500 to the west"; (2) cross the airport area at least 500 feet above the published pattern altitude; (3) announce over the CTAF when you are clear of the area; and (4) be constantly on the alert for other aircraft.

Unexpected maneuvers in controlled or uncontrolled airports

Unexpected maneuvers in either controlled or uncontrolled airport areas can obviously have serious repercussions. The safe flow of traffic is based on pilot knowledge of and conformance to the rules set up for each airport. In an uncontrolled environment, conformance is a matter of pilot self-discipline and willing compliance with the published practices for a given field. At a controlled airport, the basic responsibility for maintaining proper traffic flow within the airport area lies with the controller, but once again, the burden for knowing what to do and for complying with the regulations is on the shoulders of the pilot.

Controllers establish the sequence of arriving and departing aircraft by requiring them to adjust flight as necessary to achieve proper spacing. These adjustments can be based only on observed traffic, accurate pilot reports, and anticipated aircraft maneuvers. Pilots are expected to cooperate to preclude any disruption of traffic flow or creation of conflicting patterns.

As the pilot in command of an aircraft, you are directly responsible for and are the final authority as to the operation of that aircraft. On occasions, you may have to maneuver your aircraft to maintain spacing with the traffic you've been sequenced to follow. The controller can anticipate, and probably live with, minor maneuvering, such as shallow "S" turns, but he or she can't anticipate a major maneuver, such as a sudden 360-degree turn on the downwind leg of a busy traffic pattern.

If a pilot embarks on such a maneuver after he has obtained a landing sequence, the result is usually a gap in the landing interval. More important, though, it causes a chain reaction that might result in a conflict with following traffic and an interruption of the sequence the controller has established. If you decide that you need to make maneuvering turns to maintain spacing behind a preceding aircraft, always advise the controller first—unless there is a sudden emergency that demands action now and an explanation later.

Said simply, except when requested by the controller or in emergency situations, major directional changes should never be made in the traffic pattern or when receiving radar service without first advising ATC.

Runway operations

Runways are numbered to correspond to their magnetic bearing. Runway 27, for example, has a bearing of 270 degrees, and wind directions quoted by the Tower are also in magnetic degrees. Logically, of course, controllers always try to use the runway most closely aligned with the prevailing wind when that wind is five knots or more. If the wind is less than that, or, in effect, "calm," any runway more operationally advantageous would be selected.

Should you want to use a different runway than the one specified by ATC, you must first get the controller's approval. An example of such a situation might be this: The runway in use, with its 7000-foot length, is 36 and the wind today is from 20 degrees at 20 knots, gusting to 25. Another runway, 03, is only 3000 feet long, but is ample in length for the typical light single-engine aircraft. A Cessna pilot, wanting more of an into-the-wind takeoff, requests clearance on 03. It's now up to the tower to grant or refuse the request, with the final decision depending on the volume and type of traffic in the pattern or in the area.

The same scenario could apply in landing. The Cessna pilot, not relishing a fairly strong crosswind if landing on 36, can request approval to use 03. If the controller can fit the Cessna into the pattern without upsetting the existing traffic, the request will undoubtedly be granted.

Controllers *do* want to help, when it is feasible to do so.

Intersection takeoffs

In order to enhance airport capacities, reduce taxiing distances, minimize departure delays, and provide for more efficient movement of air traffic, controllers can initiate intersection takeoffs as well as approve them when the pilot requests. If, for any reason, you would prefer to use a different intersection or the full length of a runway, or want to know the distance between the intersection and the runway end, you are expected to inform ATC accordingly.

Because of wake turbulence, controllers are required to separate small propeller aircraft (less than 12,500 pounds) taking off from an intersection on the same runway following a large jet aircraft. The separation is accomplished by ensuring that at least a three-minute interval exists between the time the preceding large aircraft has departed and the small aircraft begins its takeoff roll.

Applying this rule, the controller advises the light-plane pilot of the required three-minute wait and states, "Hold for wake turbulence." If the pilot feels that the full three-minute interval is longer than necessary, he or she can request a waiver. The pilot must initiate such a request by stating something akin to: "Request waiver of three-minute interval." ATC can then issue the takeoff clearance, if other traffic permits, because the pilot has accepted responsibility for his own wake turbulence separation.

The exception to this: ATC cannot waive the three-minute interval when the small aircraft is departing behind a heavy jet. As indicated in the wake turbulence discussion in Chapter 12, the dangers of this phenomenon are too great to cut corners on something as insignificant as the saving of 60 or 90 seconds.

Simultaneous landings on intersecting runways

Despite the many additions made to the nation's airports in recent years, limited runway availability remains a major contributing factor to airport congestion. To help alleviate the problem, many high-density airports have gained a level of operational experience with intersecting runways that clearly indicate the safety and feasibility of simultaneous landings. Tower controllers can thus authorize simultaneous landings on intersecting runways when the following conditions are met:

1. The controller has received no reports that braking action is less than good.

2. Operations are conducted in VFR conditions unless visual separation is applied.

3. Instructions are issued to restrict one aircraft from entering the intersecting runway being used by another aircraft.

4. Traffic information is issued to and an acknowledgment received from one or both pilots as appropriate to the situation.

5. The measured distance from runway threshold to intersection is issued if the pilot requests it.

6. The conditions specified in 3, 4, and 5 are met at or before issuance of the landing clearance.

7. The distance from landing threshold to the intersection is adequate for the category of aircraft being held short. Controllers are provided a general table of aircraft category/minimum runway length requirements as a guide. It is incumbent on the pilot to determine the ability to hold short of an intersection after landing, when so instructed.

The safety and operation of an aircraft remain the responsibility of the pilot. If for any reason (difficulty in discerning location of an intersection at night, inability to hold short of an intersection, wind factors, etc.) a choice is made to use the full length of the runway, a different runway, or desires to obtain the distance from the landing threshold to the intersection, the pilot is expected to promptly inform ATC accordingly.

Light signals

The following procedures are used by tower personnel in the control of aircraft without radio equipment. These same procedures apply with a radio-equipped aircraft when radio contact cannot be established. In either instance, the Tower uses a light gun that projects an intense narrow light beam of a selected color (either red, white, or green). As Fig. 8-15, back in Chapter 8, illustrates, each color, or combination of colors, has a certain meaning, a certain instruction to the pilot. Although these signal lights have some definite advantages in a no-radio or radio-out situation, there are also disadvantages:

1. The pilot might not be looking at the Control Tower at the time a signal is directed toward him or her.

2. The directions transmitted by a light signal are very limited because only approval or disapproval of a pilot's anticipated actions can be transmitted. No supplementary or explanatory information can be transmitted except by the use of the "General Warning Signal," which advises the pilot to be on the alert.

As I said earlier, if your plane has no radio or the radio is currently inoperative, don't try to depart a controlled airport without first telephoning the Tower to explain your situation and to secure the Tower's approval of your intentions. The same applies in landing, except, of course, when you have a radio failure in flight. Even then, though, you would be much wiser to land at an uncontrolled field and either get the radio fixed or phone the Tower from there and request permission to enter the airspace. You can be almost certain, though, that such a request to a Class B or C airport would be denied. Two-way communications are required in these airspaces.

If prior approval to takeoff has been issued, the pilot should follow these procedures:

At night: Between sunset and sunrise, to attract the Control Tower's attention, turn on a landing light and taxi the aircraft into a position, clear of the active runway, so that light is visible to the Tower. The landing light should remain on until appropriate signals are received from the Tower.

Then acknowledge the light signals by blinking the landing or navigation lights.

Daylight: Move the ailerons or rudder. If airborne, rock the wings to acknowledge light gun instructions.

Uncontrolled airports

Approximately 12,000 out of 12,500 (95 percent) of the airports in the United States (not including heliports) are uncontrolled. That means that they have no Tower at all and are thus available for unrestricted public use. Of these, there are two general types: *Class G* and *Class E*, each sometimes referred to as *"multicom"* and *"unicom."* Those are not very good references because they classify an airport by the means of radio communications, but that isn't entirely out of place. It at least defines the type of communications that come into play in the two airport classes.

Multicom Class G airports

Multicom airports are those that have no air-ground radio communication whatsoever. They are identified on the sectional charts by their magenta coloring and only the airport msl field elevation, the length of the longest runway, and an "L," if the runway is lighted, are indicated.

Radio communication at these airports is strictly air-to-air between aircraft. All calls, generally referred to as "self-announce," or "blind," broadcasts, are thus made over the FAA's Common Traffic Advisory Frequency (CTAF), which, at multicom fields, is always 122.9, and the calls are always addressed to "(Airport or city name) Traffic."

When approaching the airport, approximately 10 to 15 miles out, tune to 122.9 and listen to determine if other aircraft are in the pattern and, if so, the runway in use. That information will help you plan the approach to the field. Regardless of what is or isn't learned, the call should include the aircraft type, call sign, present position, altitude, and intentions: to land, practice touch-and-goes, or transit the area.

If landing or doing touch-and-goes, subsequent reports are made on the downwind leg, base leg, final approach, and when clear of the runway. If transiting the area below 3000 feet agl, position reports are made over the field and when clear of the area. Examples:

"Parker Traffic, Cherokee 1234 Alpha is 10 west at two thousand five hundred. Will enter left downwind for landing one-three, Parker." ". . . landing one-three . . ." means I am landing on runway one-three (13). There's no need to state "runway." That's obvious.

Note: Always conclude multicom or unicom intention and position reports by repeating the name of the airport. The repetition helps others in the area who might not have heard or understood to whom the call was originally addressed. Repeating the name is particularly important when several airports in the same geographic vicinity often have the same multicom or unicom CTAF. (More on that in the unicom airport discussion.)

If you haven't been able to determine the active runway by just listening over 122.9, the first call is this: "Parker Traffic, Cherokee 1234 Alpha is 10 west at two thousand five hundred. Will cross over the field at two thousand for wind tee check, landing Parker."

Once in the traffic pattern, if landing, this series of calls is essential for a safe operation:

1. "Parker Traffic, Cherokee 34 Alpha left downwind, landing one-three, Parker."

2. "Parker Traffic, Cherokee 34 Alpha turning left base, landing one-three, Parker."

3. "Parker Traffic, Cherokee 34 Alpha turning final, landing one-three, Parker."

4. "Parker Traffic, Cherokee 34 Alpha clear of one-three, Parker."

If you're planning to practice touch-and-goes, merely substitute "touch-and-go" for "landing" in these examples.

Departure reports should start prior to taxi, as:

1. "Parker Traffic, Cherokee 1234 Alpha at the ramp, taxiing to one-three, west departure, Parker." (After engine start on the ramp.)

2. "Parker Traffic, Cherokee 34 Alpha taking one-three, west departure, Parker." (After pretakeoff check at runup area.)

3. "Parker Traffic, Cherokee 34 Alpha clear of the area to the west, Parker." (After takeoff and five miles out from the airport.)

The various calls are designed simply to keep other aircraft in the area informed of who you are, where you are, and your intentions. Above all, though, extreme vigilance is essential. These are uncontrolled airports where pilots are responsible for seeing, avoiding, and informing others who might be in the same airspace—and too often they don't do enough of one or more of these fundamental basics of safe VFR flight.

Unicom or Class E airports

The principal difference between multicom and unicom airports is the existence on the airport of a nongovernment radio facility (the unicom), usually manned by the local fixed-base operator (FBO). The sectional identifies unicom airports by the magenta coloring, the same airport data as for a multicom field, plus the unicom radio frequency, which is printed on the chart in italicized numerals, as *122.8.*

At airports such as these that have no Tower and no Flight Service Station on the property, the CTAF frequencies are almost universally 122.7, 122.8, or 123.0. The appropriate sectional or *Airport/Facility Directory* (A/FD) tells what that frequency is at a given airport.

The information the unicom operator provides is the current wind direction and velocity, possibly the altimeter setting, the favored runway in use, and any *reported* traffic in the pattern or area. All the operator does is give a "field advisory" to pilots who have called in and requested same. In no respect, however, is the person transmitting over unicom a traffic controlling agency. He or she may also be responsible for answering the phone, pumping gas, selling candy or sectional charts and is simply a source of basic airport information provided as a service by the local FBO.

Unicom can help in other ways, though, even at airports that have operating Control Towers. For instance, it can be contacted to request a taxi, make phone calls for you, alert the FBO to needed mechanical repairs, advise friends of your arrival time, arrange rental cars, and the like. In those cases, calls are addressed to "(Airport Name) unicom."

When approaching a nontower unicom field and you want a field advisory, (again, that means you want to know the favored runway, winds, altimeter setting, if possible, and what traffic is in the pattern), the initial contact is addressed to "(Airport Name) unicom" and includes aircraft type, position, altitude, intentions, concluding with "Request field advisory." From then on, all position reports are similar to those at a multicom airport. The only major difference is that these reports are now addressed to "(Airport Name) *Traffic,*" not "(Airport Name) unicom." To illustrate that type of call and a request for service:

> **Pilot:** "Ottawa unicom, Cherokee 1234 Alpha 10 miles north at three thousand, landing Ottawa. Request field advisory."
>
> **Unicom:** "Cherokee 1234 Alpha, Ottawa unicom. Winds one niner zero at five. Favored runway one-seven. Reported traffic two Cessnas making touch-and-goes."
>
> **Pilot:** "Roger, Ottawa. Cherokee 34 Alpha and would you order a taxi for me?"
>
> **Unicom:** "Will do, 34 Alpha."
>
> (When closer to the airport:)

Pilot: "Ottawa Traffic, Cherokee 34 Alpha will enter left downwind for landing one-seven Ottawa."

The balance of the position reports and intentions are the same as at a multicom field—position reports on downwind, base leg, when turning to the final approach, and when clear of the runway after landing.

Uncontrolled airport with a closed tower

Many of the smaller airports have Control Towers that operate part-time. When closed, the airport is uncontrolled and field advisory information is provided by unicom (if the FBO is open) over the unicom frequency. Once the advisory has been received, however, all calls are then addressed to "(Airport Name) Traffic" but on the *Tower* frequency, not the unicom CTAF, and the structure of those calls is exactly the same as at any uncontrolled airport. Whether the Tower is part- or full-time is determined by reference to the sectional chart of the *Airport/Facility Directory.*

Airport advisory service (AAS)

Another uncontrolled airport possibility is where an FSS is located on the field but there is no Tower. Or, if there is a Tower, it's only part-time. When it closes for its scheduled X-number of hours per day, the field becomes uncontrolled. (This situation is becoming increasingly less common as most of the FSSs have been consolidated into the 61 regional Automated Flight Service Stations.) An important point, though: Even if there is an FSS, the airport is still uncontrolled. This is because no Flight Service Station is ever a controlling agency. It can recommend, suggest, advise, but, unlike a Tower, a Center, or approach control, it cannot require that a pilot take this action or not take that.

Assuming a no-tower situation, the FSS provides an Airport Advisory Service (AAS) on the 123.6 frequency. Included in the Advisory are wind direction and velocity, the favored or designated runway, current altimeter setting, known traffic (it's classified as "known" because, as the field is uncontrolled, not all traffic in the vicinity might be communicating with the FSS), notices to airmen (NOTAMs), airport taxiways, airport traffic patterns, and instrument approach procedures.

These elements vary, of course, depending on the individual pilot's needs, and they do include information that best meets the current traffic situation. Some airport managers have specified that under certain wind or other conditions, only specific or designated runways are to be used. Pilots choosing to use other than the favored or designated runway should advise the FSS before so doing.

Unlike unicom, the FSS does not order ground transportation, make phone calls for pilots, or the like. Similar to unicom, though, the FSS, again, is not a traffic controlling agency. Consequently, you are not required to contact it to land, take off, or participate in the service in any way. That participation, though, is strongly recommended.

Whether the FSS at a nontower airport is open or closed, the CTAF for position reporting is 123.6, and calls are addressed to "(Airport Name) Traffic," not the Flight Service Station. Only when requesting an airport advisory or opening, closing, or filing a flight plan are the calls addressed to "(Airport Name) Radio." "*Radio*" is the term *always* used when in contact with any FSS for whatever purpose. The only exception is a call to Flight Watch.

At an airport where there is both an FSS and a Tower, but the Tower is closed, all radio contacts, including the request for advisories, making position reports, and so on, are made over the Tower frequency, which the FSS monitors and on which it replies.

Several other combinations of open and closed facilities, as well as the existence of Remote Communication Outlets (RCOs), are possible—all of which can become confusing. To clarify matters a little, Fig. 9-4 summarizes the alternatives and the frequencies or facilities that should be used.

Controlled airports

Every airport that has an operating Control Tower is considered a controlled airport. This means that radio contact with the Tower must be established before operating in the airport area. While that statement is true, there are variations and other requirements, such as Class B and C airports with their approach and departure control in addition to the Towers.

To keep a semblance of sequence in this chapter, the first airports discussed were the completely uncontrolled with no radio communications (the multicoms). Then came those with unicom service (both either Class G or E), followed by the airports with part time Towers and/or a Flight Service Station on the property (Class D

Tower status	On-site FSS status	On-site RCO	FBO status	Field advisories type/freq	Radio freq for position reports (CTAF)	ATC radio freq
Open						Tower
Closed	Open			AAS/Tower[5]	Tower	
Closed	Closed	RCO	Open	UFA/unicom[1]	Tower	
Closed	Closed	RCO	Closed	FFA/RCO	Tower	
Closed	Closed	RCO	No FBO	FFA/RCO	Tower	
Closed	Closed	No RCO	Open	UFA/unicom	Tower	
Closed	Closed	No RCO	No FBO	N/A	Tower	
Closed	No FSS	RCO	Open	UFA/unicom[1]	Tower	
Closed	No FSS	RCO	Closed	FFA/RCO	Tower	
Closed	No FSS	RCO	No FBO	FFA/RCO	Tower	
Closed	No FSS	No RCO	Open	UFA/unicom	Tower	
Closed	No FSS	No RCO	Closed	N/A	Tower	
Closed	No FSS	No RCO	No FBO	N/A	Tower	
None	FSS Open			AAS/123.6[3]	123.6[2]	
None	Closed	RCO	Open	UFA/unicom[1]	123.6[2]	
None	Closed	RCO	Closed	FFA/RCO	123.6[2]	
None	Closed	RCO	None	FFA/RCO	123.6[2]	
None	Closed	No RCO	Open	UFA/unicom	123.6[2]	
None	Closed	No RCO	Closed	N/A	123.6[2]	
None	Closed	No RCO	No FBO	N/A	123.6[2]	
None	No FSS	RCO	Open	UFA/unicom	unicom	
None	No FSS	RCO	Closed	FFA/RCO	unicom	
None	No FSS	RCO	No FBO	FFA/RCO	122.9[4]	
None	No FSS	No RCO	Open	UFA/unicom	unicom	
None	No FSS	No RCO	Closed	N/A	unicom	
None	No FSS	No RCO	No FBO	N/A	122.9[4]	

1 Last hour's official weather observation from FSS over RCO, if weather observer on duty.
2 Or as listed in A/FD.
3 Where available. Some AFSSs may not offer this service.
4 Multicom.
5 FSS will reply on tower frequency.

AFSS — Automated Flight Service Station (all AFSSs are open 24 hours)
ATC — Air Traffic Control
FBO — Fixed Base Operator with unicom
FSS — Flight Service Station
RCO — Remote Communications Outlet
ASS — FSS Airport Advisory Service (winds, weather, favored runway, altimeter setting, reported traffic within 10 miles of airport)
FFA — FSS Field Advisories (last hour's winds, weather, and altimeter setting, if observer is on duty at airport)
UFA — Unicom Field Advisories (winds, favored runway, known traffic, altimeter setting [at some locations])

Fig. 9-4. *This figure summarizes the facility and the radio frequency you should use at a Class E airport, depending on what facility exists and is open.*

Towers and/or a Flight Service Station on the property (Class D when the Tower is open, Class E when it's closed).

To build on this foundation, more needs to be said about the Class Ds before moving up to the Class Bs and Class Cs. To round things out, some of the operating rules and procedures pertaining to each Class are summarized, along with sample radio communication exchanges. While it's impossible in this chapter to discuss these three airspaces in the detail they deserve, an overview of their structure and their operating regulations should answer many questions about what they are and the pilot's responsibilities when entering and flying within them.

Class D airports—their design and basic regulations

There are many Class D airports around the country where the only source of traffic control is the Tower itself. There is no approach or departure control, and probably no radar, unless the Tower is near an approach control facility and is equipped with the BRITE monitor discussed in Chapter 8.

These airports are easily identified on sectional charts by their blue coloring and the segmented blue circles that surround them (Fig. 9-5). As is typical, the circle here represents the outward limit of the D airspace, which is 4.3 nautical miles from the center of the airport. The upper limit of the airspace is depicted by the "33" (meaning 3300 feet msl) in the segmented box just to the left of the airport symbol. (The typical Class D ceiling is 2500 feet agl.)

In effect, the area within the circle is the ATA—the airport traffic area, although not literally referred to as such. This is the area in which: (1) all traffic is controlled; (2) two-way radio communication with the Tower must exist; and (3) clearance from the Tower to operate in the area is required.

As a side note, the same type of area exists at all Class B and C airports but is not depicted on the sectional. The reason for the omission is that approach control must clear all arriving aircraft before they can even enter the B or C airspace— airspaces that extend out much farther than the so-called ATA itself. When nearing the airport's undesignated ATA, approach then turns the aircraft over to the Tower for any further instructions and landing clearance.

Since Class D airports have no approach control, the circle alerts arriving or transiting pilots to the outer limits of the airspace and by what point they should contact the Tower.

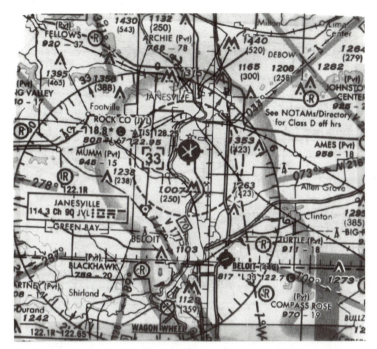

Fig. 9-5. *Class D airports are always depicted in blue on the sectional and are surrounded by a segmented blue circle or similar segmented design.*

One other feature on the sectional of some Class D airports: The blue circle might be a complete circle but have a segmented magenta design attached to it. (Figure 9-5 does not have this feature.) The design depicts an area that has been established to protect and expedite IFR arriving and departing traffic in IMC (Instrument Meteorological Conditions).

Generally speaking, if the extension is two nautical miles or less, it appears as a small irregularity on the otherwise circular design and is included in the segmented design. More than two miles, it becomes part of Class E, with its ceiling rising to the Class E floor of 700 or 1200 feet agl. Wherever the magenta extensions exist, however, they represent Class E airspace and, being Class E, radio communications *within* the magenta areas are not required for VFR flight.

Operating in a Class D airspace Unlike multicom or unicom airports, more operating and communication procedures exist in the controlled airport environment. Depending on the type of airport, meaning a Class B, C, or D, there can, of course, be certain procedural variations. Many general commonalties exist, however—commonalties with which all pilots flying into or out of these airports must be familiar. FAR 91 and sections of FAR 61 emphasize this point.

The reason for starting with the Class D airspace is that it is the least complex of the three, and yet the operating procedures and regulations within the ATA or its equivalent are very similar to those in the Class B and C airport environment. It's thus a matter of starting with the relatively simple and then proceeding to the slightly more involved.

Automatic terminal information service (ATIS).

Considering the airport itself first, many, but not all, Class D Towers have an airport weather and advisory service called *ATIS* (Automatic Terminal Weather Service). Although mentioned briefly in earlier chapters, more details about it are necessary at this point.

ATIS is a continuously repeated recorded message that provides current (or no more than 59 minutes old) data relative to airport operating conditions. Identified by the phonetic alphabet, an updated ATIS report is issued at least every hour, but not necessarily on the hour—or more frequently if weather changes occur—and, in sequence, includes the following:

- Location (airport name)
- Information code (phonetic alphabet)
- Time (Coordinated Universal Time [UTC]), stated as "Zulu"
- Sky condition (often omitted if the ceiling is higher than 5000 feet, or is stated as "Better than 5000")
- Visibility (often omitted if visibility is greater than five miles, or is stated as "Better than five miles")
- Temperature and dewpoint
- Wind direction (magnetic) and velocity
- Altimeter setting
- Instrument approach in use
- Current runway in use
- NOTAMs (if any)
- Information code (repeated)

Purpose of ATIS. The purpose of an ATIS is to relieve Tower personnel of having to advise departing and arriving aircraft of local conditions in the airport area. The ATIS, which is recorded in, and transmitted on, its own assigned frequency from the Tower, saves innumerable radio communications, thus making frequencies and controllers available for flight operation matters.

ATIS broadcast example. This is an example of a typical ATIS transmission: "Albany Information Bravo. One five four five Zulu weather. Four thousand three hundred broken, visibility five miles. Temperature six seven, dew point four five. Wind one four zero at ten, gusting to eighteen. Altimeter two niner niner five. ILS runway one six in use, land and depart one six. Notice to airmen: Numerous flocks of birds reported in area. Advise on initial contact you have Bravo."

When to listen to the ATIS. On departure: Either just before or immediately after starting the engine, tune to the ATIS frequency, which is printed on the sectional chart and in the Airport/Facility Directory. Listen as many times as necessary to be sure you have understood the information. On arrival, tune to the ATIS 15 or 20 miles out. This allows time to plan the approach and traffic pattern, based on the active runway.

When departing advise ATC that you have monitored the ATIS when you contact Ground Control for taxi instructions and when you first contact the Tower for landing instructions. Example: "Albany Ground, Cherokee 1234 Alpha at the terminal with Bravo." No need to add more. Ground Control knows from your call that you're ready to taxi out for takeoff.

If you neglect to include in the call the fact that you have monitored the latest ATIS, the controller is likely to ask if you have . . ." received Bravo," or whatever the phonetic alphabet. To report, as some pilots do, that you ". . . have the numbers," means only that you know the wind, runway, and altimeter setting. As *AIM* puts it, "It does not indicate receipt of the ATIS broadcast and "have the numbers" should never be used for this purpose."

Ground Control. Ground Control is a position in the Tower cab that is responsible for directing and approving the movement of aircraft and ground vehicles on the airport surface. The only exceptions to this are movements on ramp or parking areas and authorizing aircraft to go on an active runway. Remember that Ground can authorize an aircraft to cross such a runway, but that is all. What happens on the active runway is the Tower controller's responsibility. Before an aircraft can touch a taxiway, however, it must be cleared by Ground Control. This applies whether departing from a ramp or turning off the runway after landing. Otherwise, you can taxi your plane around the ramp and parking areas all you want without any contact with Ground Control.

Ground Control frequencies. Ground Control frequencies are almost always in the 121.6-121.9 MHz band (there are a few exceptions). Reserved only for communications between the Tower and aircraft on the ground and between the Tower and airport utility vehicles, these frequencies provide a clear VHF channel for arriving and departing aircraft.

As such, the assigned frequency is used to control ground taxi movements, provide ground-related information (such as where a given FBO or fueling facilities are located, how to taxi to a certain location, and the like), in some cases issue departure clearances, and generally maintain other necessary contacts between the Tower and aircraft or ground vehicles operating on the airport.

After landing, never change from the Tower frequency to the Ground Control frequency until directed to do so by the Tower controller. The pilot's responsibility is to clear the active runway as soon as possible, stop beyond the yellow line on the taxiway, and then call Ground for approval to continue. Example: "Albany Ground, Cherokee 1234 Alpha clear of two one. Taxi to the terminal." Ground then comes back with something like: "Roger 34 Alpha. Taxi to the terminal."

Normally, there is only one Ground Control frequency at an airport. At some locations, though, where the volume of traffic so warrants, as a Class B airport, a second frequency is assigned. Miami International is an example with two frequencies—one for Runway 09 Left–27 Right and one for a second runway, 09 Right–27 Left. This addition is rare at Class D airports, however, where the traffic doesn't justify such an added cost.

As I said previously, the Tower controller may omit the numbers that precede the frequency decimal point when directing the pilot to change to the Ground Control frequency after landing. This is often done when, in the controller's opinion, the pilot will clearly understand the abbreviation. Instead of quoting the whole frequency, he or she would boil it down to no more than: "Cherokee 34 Alpha, contact Ground point niner." (Remember that the frequencies are almost always 121.6 to 121.9.)

Taxiing. To reinforce some taxiing points already mentioned and to raise a couple of new ones:

- Approval must be obtained from Ground Control before taxiing an aircraft onto the airport movement areas. These "movement" areas are generally the taxiways and runways and *do not* include areas such as ramps or tarmacs, parking areas, space associated with hangars, fueling, terminal building facilities, and the like. You can move your aircraft in such areas all day long without permission as long as there is no intrusion on any taxiway or runway;

- Always state your position on the airport when calling Ground Control for taxi clearance;

- Never taxi on any taxiway or runway without Ground Control's permission;

- Authority to taxi "to" a runway constitutes approval to cross runways that intersect the taxi route *unless* Ground Control instructs otherwise, as ". . . hold short of runway one five."

- Authority to taxi *to* the active runway does *not* constitute permission to taxi *on* that runway;

- Taxi clearances or instructions are based on known traffic and known physical airport conditions. Therefore, it is important to understand the instructions. Even though a taxi clearance has been issued, it is the pilot's responsibility to avoid collisions with other aircraft;

- If in doubt about a taxi instruction or warning, immediately ask Ground Control for further details, clarification, or whatever is necessary to eliminate any confusion;

- Continue to monitor the Ground Control frequency while taxiing and conform to any requests or instructions the controller issues;

- If ATC has approved noncompliance with two-way radio communications at the airport, obtain taxi clearance via visual light gun signals.

Taxiing during low visibility. Pilots should be constantly aware that during certain low visibility conditions the Tower controller may not be able to see the movement of aircraft and vehicles on airports. Which means, of course, that you should be particularly vigilant under such conditions. It's vitally important that you immediately notify a controller when visibility difficulties are encountered and to inform the controller at the first indication of becoming disoriented.

In somewhat the same vein, be very careful when taxiing into the sun. If you encounter vision difficulties, inform the controller immediately.

Clearing the runway after landing. After landing, unless otherwise instructed by the control Tower, continue to taxi in the landing direction, proceed to the nearest turnoff, and exit the runway without delay. *Do not* change to the Ground Control frequency while on an active runway, and do not make a 180-degree turn to taxi back on the active runway without authorization from the control Tower.

"Progressive" taxi instructions. Pilots arriving at strange airports are often uncertain after landing as to the location of a given FBO on the airport, where their desired type of fuel can be obtained, where the restaurant is, or the like. In such cases, after establishing contact with Ground Control, request ". . . progressive taxi instructions to (Jet Air Center, a Phillips supplier, parking near the restaurant, etc.)." Ground then progressively directs you, step by step, to whatever facility you have requested.

Sample ground control radio calls

Departing

Pilot: Albany Ground, Cherokee 1234 Alpha at Hangar 2 with Bravo.

Ground: Cherokee 1234 Alpha, taxi to runway one six. Hold short of runway four.

Pilot: Roger, hold short of four. Cherokee 34 Alpha.
(Later . . .)

Ground: Cherokee 1234 Alpha, clear to cross runway four.

Pilot: Roger, clear to cross.

Now taxi to the runup area, well behind the hold line. Once the pre-takeoff check has been completed, move up to the hold line, come to a complete stop, change to the Tower frequency, and call the Tower when the frequency is clear. There is no need to contact ground again for approval to make this position change.

After landing

Tower: Cherokee 34 Alpha, turn right or left next intersection. Contact Ground 121.9 (or simply, "Contact ground point niner").

Pilot: Will do. 34 Alpha.

When clear of the active runway, come to a stop past the hold line, and then initiate the call to Ground Control.

Pilot: Fulton ground, Cherokee 1234 Alpha clear of two six. Request progressive taxi to Hangar One FBO.

Ground: Roger, 34 Alpha. Taxi straight ahead to the ramp area, and then 45 degrees right. Hangar One will be the white terminal dead ahead.

Pilot: Roger, I have it. Thank you.

Class B airspaces—their design and basic regulations

The Tower exercises control of traffic only within the approximate five-mile radius of the airport itself. At the 34 busiest commercial airports (the Class B airports), however, control areas have been established to ensure the orderly flow of traffic into and out of the terminal area beyond the 5 mile limits. Control of this traffic is the responsibility of Approach and Departure Control, which is typically housed in the Control Tower structure but in a windowless, dimly-lit room some floors below the Tower cab itself. Here, control of arriving and departing traffic in the airspace is accomplished through ARTS II or ARTS III radar.

The locations of these Class B airspaces are:

Atlanta*	Kansas City	Philadelphia
Baltimore	Las Vegas	Phoenix
Boston*	Los Angeles*	Pittsburgh
Charlotte	Memphis	St. Louis
Chicago*	Miami*	Salt Lake City
Cleveland	Minneapolis	San Diego
Dallas/Ft. Worth*	Newark*	San Francisco*
Denver	New Orleans	Seattle
Detroit	LaGuardia (New York)*	Tampa
Honolulu	John F. Kennedy (New York)*	Dulles (Washington, D.C.)
Houston	Orlando	National (Washington, D.C.)*
		Andrews AFB

*The 11 busiest airports, with stricter pilot requirements.

Class B description. The typical Class B structure resembles an upside-down wedding cake, with a core rising from the surface of the airport area to roughly 8000 feet msl (this ceiling can vary somewhat, depending on the airport). The core, in effect representing the airport area, typically has a five-nautical mile radius. A series of layers then extends horizontally from the core, each having a progressively higher altitude floor. All layers, however, rise upward to the same altitude as the core. Figure 9-6 illustrates the structure of a typical Class B.

On the sectional chart, the msl altitudes of each floor are indicated by two numbers specifying the ceiling/floor of that layer, as 80/30, meaning the ceiling is 8000 feet and the floor 3000 feet. Finally, 30 nautical miles out from the primary airport, a thin blue band circles the entire Class B airspace and defines the area within which Mode C transponders are required from the surface up to 10,000 feet msl. This is called the "Mode C Veil," which I'll explain in a moment.

Purposes of the Class B airspace. Class Bs exist primarily to separate, sequence, and vector, via radar, IFR traffic into and out of the airport area, and, in the process, to expedite arriving and departing aircraft. Service to VFR aircraft is also provided, but it is on a "workload permitting" basis.

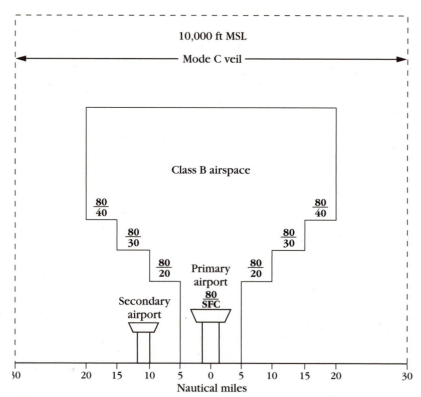

Fig. 9-6. *Class B airspaces are typically described as shaped like upside-down wedding cakes, with the primary airport in the center of core.*

Penetration of a Class B without specific approval from approach or departure control is strictly prohibited. Until radio contact is established and you hear ". . . cleared into the Class B airspace," or words to that effect, you *must* remain outside of the area. If you don't, violations subject you to an FAA citation and appropriate disciplinary action.

Pilot qualifications. To land or take off at a Class B primary airport, you must have at least a private license. However, if a student pilot has received ground and flight instruction for, and in, a Class B, and has obtained the proper instructor logbook endorsement(s) within the preceding 90 days, the student may fly solo through that specific Class B, and take off and land at an airport within the Class B, if instruction had taken place at that specific airport.

An exception: Student pilots are prohibited from landing or taking off from the 12 busiest Class B airports unless the pilot-in-command holds at least a private pilot certificate (FAR 61 and FAR 91). Those airports are:

Atlanta Hartsfield	Newark International
Boston Logan	New York Kennedy
Chicago O'Hare	New York LaGuardia
Dallas/Ft. Worth International	San Francisco International
Los Angeles International	Washington National
Miami International	Andrews AFB, Maryland

Aircraft equipment. Unless otherwise authorized by ATC, all aircraft operating in a Class B airspace must have an operable VOR or TACAN (Tactical Air Navigation) receiver, an operable two-way radio capable of communicating with ATC on the terminal frequencies, and an operable transponder with altitude-reporting capabilities (Mode C or Mode S) (FAR 91).

The Mode C veil. In 1989, the FAA established the veil rule requiring all aircraft operating within the veil to be Mode C-equipped. (There were certain exceptions, such as aircraft designed and built without electrical systems.) Because of the volume of pilot and FBO objections to the concept, particularly from those operating out of airports—right on the outer fringe of the veil—say just a mile or two in it—the FAA modified the ruling and issued Special Federal Aviation Regulation (SFAR) No. 62.

The SFAR meant that all aircraft flying into or out of airports located *under* any portion of the Class B airspace still had to be Mode C-equipped. However, those operating into or out of airports *not* under the outermost Class B level but still under the 30-mile veil would be exempt—but with the restrictions that operations:

1. Are conducted at or below the maximum altitude established for those airports listed (the altitudes vary from 1000 to 2500 feet agl, depending on the Class B);

2. Are conducted within a two-nautical mile radius of the listed Mode C-exempt airport (meaning for traffic patterns, touch-and-gos, etc.);

3. Can be conducted along a direct route between that airport and the outer boundary of the Mode C veil.

The many airports to which the exclusion applies are listed under the names of the Class B airports in FAR Part 91, SFAR-62.

The SFAR went into effect in 1990, as a temporary provision and theoretically expired December 31, 1993. The FAA retained it, however, and at the time of writing, the ultimate future of SFAR-62 remains unresolved.

Class C airspaces—their design and basic regulations

Approximately 135 of the less busy but still high volume airports fall into the "Class C" airspace category. Formerly known as "Airport Radar Service Areas" (ARSAs), the Class C is structured to provide radar separation, sequencing, and vectoring to *all* aircraft entering or departing these moderately busy terminal areas. In effect, and more than just alphabetically, the Class C lies between the B and D: it has a structure somewhat similar to a Class B but is smaller and the operating rules are less stringent. At the same time, it is larger than a Class D and has more stringent regulations.

Class C description. As Fig. 9-7, illustrates, Class C airspace is generally circular in structure, with a five nautical mile radius core. This is called the inner circle, and it rises from the surface of the primary airport to approximately 4000 feet agl. Then there is an outer circle with a 10 nautical mile radius from the primary airport. Typically, the outer circle floor starts at 1200 feet agl and has the same 4000 foot agl ceiling as the inner circle. Similar to the Class B, to enter either the inner or outer circle, radio communications with approach control must be established first.

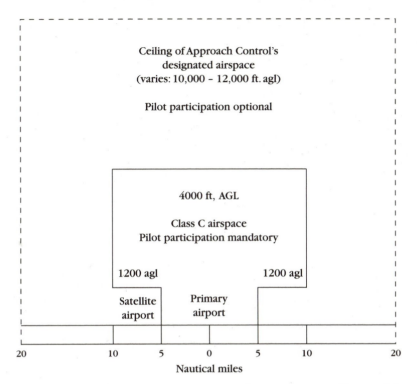

Fig. 9-7. *The Class C structure is similar to, but smaller and less complicated than the Class B airspace.*

Beyond the outer circle is the *outer area*, which is not depicted on any aeronautical chart, but is there, nonetheless. This area has a 20 nautical mile radius from the primary airport and rises from the surface to approximately 10,000 feet msl, the airport's approach control vertical limits. Radio communications with approach for traffic advisories while in the outer area, however, is optional. If the pilot requests them, ATC is required to provide the service.

Class C identification. Class C airspaces are depicted on sectional charts by two heavy magenta circles that surround the primary airport, but the outer area is not shown. Class Cs can be identified also by referring to the appropriate *Airport/Facility Directory*.

Pilot requirements. Class C airspaces have no minimum pilot requirements.

Aircraft equipment requirements. An operating two-way radio is required to operate in a Class C, *plus* an operable transponder with automatic altitude reporting equipment (a Mode C transponder).

A word about radio contact: You're approaching a Class C airport and want to land. Fifteen or so miles out, you call the airport's approach control. One of three situations could occur:

1. Approach responds to your call and, by whatever words he or she chooses, authorizes your entry into the Class C area.

2. You make your call and approach replies with, "Cherokee 1234 Bravo, stand by." The controller can't respond at the moment with more than that brief acknowledgment. Are you cleared into the area? Yes. Whether the controller has time to do more than transmit the standby message, he or she has responded to your call with your aircraft identification. That signifies approval to proceed, so continue on your way. Approach will recontact you when time permits.

3. You make your call and approach replies with "Aircraft calling Jonestown Approach, stand by." Are you cleared into the area in this instance? No. The controller did not mention your aircraft ID, so there's no way he or she could recontact you and approve entry. Consequently, do a couple of 360-degree turns to stay clear of the Class C Outer and Inner Circles. Then call approach again.

Terminal radar service areas (TRSAs)—their design and basic regulations

The Terminal Radar Service Area (TRSA) is an anomaly in the family of airports in that (1) it is identified by a name versus a letter, and (2) ICAO has no such type of airport (meaning operating procedures and regulations), hence there is no letter designation available that would have an international counterpart. In effect, as described earlier, the TRSA is "...something between a Class C and Class D," which, indeed, it is.

Identified on the sectional by large dark gray (almost black) circles or irregular circles, the TRSA completely fits the description of a Class D, with all of the operating regulations of a Tower-controlled airport. At the same time, it resembles a Class C, or even a Class B, in design. And, as with a B or a C, the TRSA approach control provides safety alerts, traffic advisories, limited radar vectoring, and, at locations where the procedures have been established, sequencing of aircraft prior to turning them over to the Control Tower for landing instructions.

The uniqueness of the TRSA, though, is that these services are voluntary on the part of the pilot. You do not have to contact approach control to enter the TRSA airspace, nor are you required to ask for "TRSA service" (which used to be called "Stage Three Service"). The only requirement is to contact the airport Tower for approval to enter the airport area and to obtain landing instructions—just as at a Class D field.

How long the TRSAs will exist is unknown. It's likely, though, that their airports will either be upgraded to a Class C designation or downgraded to a Class D. It will all depend on traffic volume and the number of instrument flight handlings over a period of time.

The tower at Class D airports

While much of what I'm saying here about Class D towers applies equally in the Class B and C environments, there are a few elements that pertain particularly to the Class Ds. In all cases, however, control of traffic within the airport traffic area (I'm using "ATA" for ease of reference), whether it is a Class B, C, or D airport, is the responsibility of ATC specialists often referred to as "local controllers," who function in the Tower cab. These controllers visually sequence departing and arriving aircraft and ensure the orderly flow of traffic into and out of the airport area.

At some Class D locations, particularly those near a Class B or Class C airport, the controller might also have the aid of BRITE (Bright Radar Indicator Tower Equipment). This is not a common addition, however, to the typical Class D Tower equipment.

The basics of operating in an ATA.

While some of the following have already been mentioned, they, plus a few additional points about operating in a Class D environment, should be raised.

- Unless otherwise authorized by ATC, two-way radio communications must be established before entering the ATA and maintained within it.

- VFR pilots are expected to comply with Tower instructions, UNLESS doing so would cause them to violate a VFR regulation or create a potentially hazardous situation.

- Controller instructions are to be tersely acknowledged in a few words that tell the controller you have received and understood what is expected of you. A mere "Roger" does not communicate understanding except in response to the simplest of instructions.

- Position reports on the downwind leg, base leg, and final approach, as at uncontrolled airports, are superfluous and unnecessary—unless the Tower so requests. The controller knows where you are, and such calls only consume air time and the controller's attention.

- The Tower has direct control over only the traffic that is within the 4.3 nautical miles radius of the ATA. In the Class D environment, the controller *might* issue traffic advisories to pilots who have left the limits of the ATA, but that is a secondary responsibility. His or her primary job is to keep track of the types and N-numbers of aircraft that have called in and to visually scan the skies surrounding the airport in order to sequence and/or separate departing, landing, and transiting aircraft.

- Despite the fact that they are operating in a controlled environment, VFR pilots MUST remain VFR at all times and be constantly alert for other traffic. If necessary to deviate from a previous Tower instruction, the controller is to be so notified as soon as possible.

- Tower instructions are to be followed, to the extent feasible, as:

"Make close-in pattern."

"Extend your downwind one mile."

"Make short approach."

"Enter downwind at midfield."

"Report over (a certain landmark)."

"Advise when you have the field in sight."

"Reduce your speed."

"You are number two to land. Follow the Mooney on one mile final."

"Cleared to land."

"Extend your downwind to (a certain landmark) before turning base."

"Cleared for immediate takeoff. Tomahawk on short final."

"Taxi in position and hold."

"Cleared for immediate takeoff or hold short."

- If any instruction is not clear, it is the pilot's responsibility to advise the controller immediately:

  "Tower, say again. Your transmission was garbled."

  "Am unfamiliar with (a certain landmark)."

  "Please repeat instructions. Did not understand."

  "Did you say *right* downwind?"

  "Your transmission was blocked. Say again, please."

  "Will you call my base?" (The Tower has asked you to extend your downwind, but did not say how far.)

  "Please say again, more slowly."

- Don't be afraid to ask for messages to be repeated or clarified. Controllers want to know that you have received and understood their instructions!

Radio call examples

Departing. You've taxied out to the runup area, have completed the final preflight checks, and are ready to go. At his point, taxi to the yellow hold lines on the taxiway, come to a full stop, and then call the Tower for takeoff clearance. Don't call the Tower when you're back in the runup area. Depending on the airport, this could be a couple of hundred feet or more from the active runway, and you're not ready to go now when you're that far back.

Once you're really ready to go, be sure the transponder is switched to the ON position, or, if you have Mode C, to ALT. Now call the Tower along the lines of these brief examples:

> **Pilot:** Albany Tower, Cherokee 1234 Alpha ready to go on one six. West departure.
>
> **Tower:** Cherokee 1234 Alpha, cleared for takeoff. West departure approved.
>
> **Pilot:** Roger, 34 Alpha.

For touch-and goes

> **Pilot:** Albany Tower, Cherokee 1234 Alpha ready to go on one six. Request closed traffic.
>
> **Tower:** Cherokee 1234 Alpha, cleared for takeoff. Closed traffic approved.
>
> **Pilot:** Roger, 34 Alpha.
>
> (When aircraft is in the pattern)

Tower: Cherokee 34 Alpha, cleared for touch-and-go, one six.

Pilot: Cleared for touch-and-go. 34 Alpha.

Pilot: Albany Tower, Cherokee 1234 Alpha ready to go on one six. West departure.

Tower: Cherokee 1234 Alpha, cleared for immediate takeoff or hold short.

If you're really ready to go, taxi as rapidly as possible to the runway and apply takeoff power immediately. If not ready, advise the Tower, "Holding short." You shouldn't have to do that, though, if you've told the Tower that you were "ready to go."

You have requested a west departure, the Tower has cleared you for takeoff, but has not verbally approved that departure. Get that approval before heading out and taking up a westerly heading!

Tower: Cherokee 1234 Alpha, cleared for takeoff.

Pilot: Tower, is west departure approved?

Tower: Affirmative, 34 Alpha. West approved.

Pilot: Roger, 34 Alpha.

Arriving

Pilot: Downtown Tower, Cherokee 1234 Alpha is over the stadium at three thousand for landing with India (the current ATIS).

Tower: Cherokee 1234 Alpha, ident.

Pilot: (Do not make any oral response. Merely depress the transponder IDENT button.)

Tower: Cherokee 34 Alpha, ident received. Enter left downwind for runway one niner.

Pilot: Roger, left for one niner. 34 Alpha.
(Later . . .)

Tower: Cherokee 1234 Alpha, traffic is a Sundowner at 10 o'clock to the northeast, indicating two thousand three hundred.

Pilot: Roger, 34 Alpha has traffic.
(Later . . .)

Tower: Cherokee 34 Alpha, cleared to land.

Pilot: Cleared to land. 34 Alpha.

Note: Never make a touch-and-go or a full-stop landing until specifically cleared to do so by the Tower. If the controller has omitted this clearance, the following is in order when on the base leg or final approach:

Pilot: Tower, is 34 Alpha cleared to land?

Tower: Affirmative. 34 Alpha is cleared to land.
(After landing . . .)

Tower: Cherokee 34 Alpha, turn left or right next intersection. Contact ground point niner.

Pilot: Will do. 34 Alpha.

There may be several other communication exchanges when departing or landing at a Tower-controlled airport. Those illustrated, however, represent the basic and typical calls.

Transiting an ATA

Pilot: Executive Tower, Cherokee 1234 Alpha is 10 south at two thousand. Request approval to transit your area to the north.

Tower: Cherokee 1234 Alpha, transit approved. Maintain two thousand and report when clear of the area. Executive altimeter three zero two four.

Pilot: Roger, two thousand, report when clear. Cherokee 34 Alpha. (Later . . .)

Pilot: Executive Tower, Cherokee 34 Alpha is clear of the area to the north. Request frequency change.

Tower: Roger, 34 Alpha. Frequency change approved. Good day.

Pilot: Thank you. Good day.

Those again are the basics of operating in and around a Class D airport and airspace. Now, with some of the fundamentals established, it's time to look at the rules and procedures involved in Class B and Class C airspaces.

Class B and C airspace operations

Many of the principles that govern operations within an ATA apply when departing or landing at a primary airport in a Class B airspace. The major difference that affects both departures and landings is, of course, the existence of Approach/Departure Control. Also, a couple of new elements enter the picture, as the following discussion of departures and arrivals illustrates:

Departing a Class B airport and airspace

Assuming no B or C airspace in the vicinity, the VFR pilot departing a Tower-only airport is free from any controlling agency once beyond the five-mile ATA. At a primary Class B airport, however, that freedom doesn't exist. When so instructed by the Tower, the pilot must change radio frequencies, contact Departure Control, and then be subject to vectors and altitude assignments while in the limits of the airspace and until released by departure. Conversely, an arrival requires contact with approach control *before* entering the B airspace and submits the pilot to the same vectoring and altitude changes as in a departure. At all times, however, the VFR pilot must remain VFR, regardless of instructions, and must advise the controller if a given instruction, other than a non-VFR altitude assignment while in the airspace, would result in a VFR violation.

One other new agency exists at Class B airports: Clearance delivery (CD), or sometimes referred to as "Pretaxi Clearance." On its own assigned frequency, CD communicates clearances to departing VFR and IFR aircraft in order to reduce congestion on the Ground Control frequency. Its existence and frequency at a given airport are listed in the "Communications" portion of the *Airport/Facility Directory*. What CD does is clear the pilot to depart the airport, establish the initial post-takeoff heading and altitude, give the pilot the appropriate departure control frequency and the transponder squawk code. All pertinent data is then communicated to the Tower controller and departure control before the pilot calls for takeoff clearance.

Barring these two elements, the basics of the Tower-only airport are the same: ATIS, Ground Control, and the Tower. The sequence of contacts for the departing VFR or IFR pilot, then, is:

1. ATIS.
2. Clearance Delivery.
3. Ground Control.
4. Tower.
5. Departure Control.
6. Center (if the VFR pilot desires en route traffic advisories).

Arriving at a Class B airspace and airport

When arriving at a Class B primary airport, one strict regulation exists: The VFR pilot *must* be cleared by approach control to enter any portion of the airspace. Once that clearance is issued, approach vectors and directs altitude changes through the airspace until the aircraft is properly sequenced with others for landing. When near the ATA, Approach tells the pilot to contact the Tower on its published frequency for landing instructions.

In the same manner, a transiting pilot must establish contact with Approach and receive clearance to enter the airspace. The pilot is then vectored through the area, but not necessarily in a direct line. The headings given depend on arriving and departing IFR aircraft and their route of flight into or out of the airspace.

One important VFR regulation should be noted: Only in the Class B airspace is the VFR pilot merely required to "remain clear of clouds." Elsewhere in controlled airspaces, the "500 feet below, 1000 feet above, 2000 feet horizontal" minimum separation rule applies. The reason for the exception in the busy Class Bs is that VFR pilots could disrupt the always heavy IFR traffic flow as they (the VFRs) climb, descend, or deviate horizontally in order to comply with the standard cloud separation regulation.

Finally, it must be stressed that Approach Control is not obligated to handle VFR aircraft that want to transit any portion of the airspace. As with Center, the controller has the authority to deny VFR aircraft entrance into a Class B for whatever reason he or she chooses: workload, pilot incompetence, lack of pilot communication skills, no Mode C transponder, or whatever. (A bona fide emergency, of course, is always the exception to this.) Also, as with Center, the controller has no obligation to explain the denial, nor is the decision subject to appeal by the pilot. Most controllers, however, clear VFR pilots into the airspace whenever they can do so without affecting their ability to handle the IFR traffic.

Typical Class B VFR radio call examples —in sequence

Departing

First, monitor ATIS and then contact Clearance Delivery:

Pilot: International Clearance, Cherokee 1234 Alpha.

C/D: Cherokee 1234 Alpha, Clearance.

Pilot: Clearance, Cherokee 34 Alpha is at the general aviation ramp, VFR to Des Moines. Request seven thousand five hundred.

C/D: Cherokee 1234 Alpha, roger. Cleared to depart the Kansas City Class B. Fly one three zero heading after takeoff, maintain three thousand, expect seven thousand five hundred ten minutes after departure. Departure frequency one two six point six. Squawk two five five two.

Pilot: Cherokee 1234 Alpha cleared to depart the Class B, one three zero heading, three thousand, seven thousand five hundred in ten, one two six point six, and two five five two.

C/D: Readback correct, 34 Alpha. Contact Ground Control.

Pilot: Will do. 34 Alpha.

Reading back the clearance is required to ensure the pilot has understood it and copied it correctly.

Ground control

Pilot: International Ground, Cherokee 1234 Alpha at the general aviation ramp with clearance and information Lima.

G/C: Cherokee 1234 Alpha, taxi to runway one eight.

Pilot: Roger, Cherokee 34 Alpha.

After the pretakeoff check, taxi to the hold line before calling the Tower.

Pilot: International Tower, Cherokee 1234 Alpha ready to go.

Tower: Cherokee 1234 Alpha, cleared for takeoff. Turn to one three zero heading.

Pilot: Will do, 34 Alpha. (Now switch the transponder from SBY to ALT and take off.)
(When airborne . . .)

Tower: Cherokee 1234 Alpha, contact departure.

Pilot: Will do. Cherokee 34 Alpha.

Departure control

Pilot: Kansas City Departure, Cherokee 1234 Alpha is with you, out of one thousand four hundred for three thousand.

D/C: Roger, Cherokee 1234 Alpha. Report when level at three thousand.

Pilot: Will do, 34 Alpha.

Pilot: Departure, Cherokee 34 Alpha level at three thousand.

D/C: Roger, 34 Alpha. Turn left heading zero three zero. Climb and maintain seven thousand five hundred.

Pilot: 34 Alpha to zero three zero, out of one thousand four hundred for seven thousand five hundred.

Pilot: Departure, Cherokee 34 Alpha level at seven thousand five hundred.

D/C: Roger, Cherokee 34 Alpha.

(Later . . .)

D/C: Cherokee 1234 Alpha, you are two zero miles northeast of International, departing the Class B. Stand by for advisories.

(34 Alpha is leaving the airspace limits but is still within departure's radar coverage range [approximately 35 miles]. The controller is thus asking the pilot to stay on his frequency for possible traffic in the area.)

(Later . . .)

D/C: Cherokee 1234 Alpha, radar service terminated. Squawk one two zero zero. Frequency change approved.

Pilot: Roger, 34 Alpha. Good day.

If you want further advisories from Center, you can ask departure for a "handoff" to Center. In this case, don't change the squawk, despite what the controller has just instructed. Departure now contacts the appropriate Center controller by direct phone to determine if the latter can accept a VFR aircraft. If so, departure recontacts 34 Alpha:

D/C: Cherokee 1234 Alpha, contact Kansas City Center on one two five point two five.

Pilot: Roger, one two five point two five. Thank you. 34 Alpha.

Pilot: Kansas City Center, Cherokee 1234 Alpha is with you, level at seven thousand five hundred.

Center: Roger, Cherokee 1234 Alpha. International altimeter two niner two four.

No additional information has to be relayed to Center. Departure has informed the controller of your position, altitude, destination, and squawk. All you have to do is establish contact and confirm your altitude.

Arriving

The main issue here, as emphasized before, is that specific clearance is mandatory before a VFR pilot may enter any portion of a Class B airspace. Consequently, radio contact with approach control should be established at least 10 miles out from the floor or level of the airspace that you want to penetrate.

Pilot: Kansas City Approach, Cherokee 1234 Alpha.

A/C: Cherokee 1234 Alpha, Kansas City Approach.

Pilot: Approach, Cherokee 34 Alpha is over Lake Perry at four thousand five hundred, VFR to International with foxtrot.

A/C: Cherokee 34 Alpha, squawk two three five four and ident. Remain clear of the Class B.

Pilot: Two three five four. Will remain clear.

A/C: Cherokee 1234 Alpha, radar contact. Cleared to enter the Class B airspace. Descend and maintain three thousand five hundred.

Pilot: Roger, understand Cherokee 1234 Alpha cleared into the Class B. Out of four thousand five hundred for three thousand five hundred. (Later . . .)

Pilot: Approach, Cherokee 34 Alpha level at three thousand five hundred.

From this point on, approach may request heading and altitude changes, until:

A/C: Cherokee 1234 Alpha, contact International Tower on one two eight point two.

Pilot: Roger, one two eight point two. 34 Alpha.

Pilot: International Tower, Cherokee 1234 Alpha is with you at two thousand.

After Tower contact is made, the subsequent transmissions with the Tower and Ground Control are the same as in any ATA.

Transiting a Class B airspace

The process of transiting or entering any portion of a Class B airspace is the same as when landing at the primary airport:

1. Establish radio contact with Approach.
2. Report position, altitude, and intentions.
3. Await clearance from Approach.
4. Follow instructions until out of the airspace and Approach advises, "Radar service terminated."
5. Request a handoff to Center, if desired.

Steps 1, 2, and 3 also apply when landing at a Class D airport that is *under*, but not in, the Class B airspace, and you want to transit a portion of the airspace to save time and fuel. Step 4 then becomes: Follow instructions until approach advises you to "Contact (Blank) Tower on (the Tower frequency)." From this point on, the procedures are the same as for landing at any Tower-controlled airport.

Just one more word for reemphasis about entering the Class B airspace: *Never* penetrate that airspace until you have distinctly heard approach control call *your* aircraft and specifically advise you that you have been cleared into the Class B area. The FAA is very firm about this regulation—and rightly so. With all of the traffic converging on and departing these super-busy terminals, tight control in their designated airspaces is absolutely essential.

Should you venture into one unannounced and then hear from the FAA, remember—you have been warned!

Class C airspace

Almost everything that has been said about operating in Class B and D airspaces applies to the Class Cs—with only one major difference. That difference relates to obtaining clearance into the outer circle (not "outer area") of the Class C airspace and the wording approach controllers use in response to the pilot's initial radio call.

Admittedly, this is a repeat of some things I said earlier in the chapter, but I do it for further emphasis of key radio communications regulations. Specifically, the regulation states that: "Two-way communication must be established with the ATC facility providing ATC services prior to entry and thereafter maintain those communications while in Class C airspace." That seems clear enough, but you're nearing a Class C airport, intending to land and make the initial call to approach control:

> **You:** Macon Approach, Cherokee 1234 Alpha is 15 north at three thousand, landing Macon, with Charlie.

Approach replies with:

> Cherokee 1234 Alpha, Macon Approach. Stand by.

That's the only response, but the fact that Approach acknowledged your call establishes communications and you are now clear to enter the airspace.

In another scenario, Approach responds to your initial call with: *"Aircraft calling Macon Approach, stand by."*

Does this clear you into the airspace? *No.* As *AIM* puts it, "If the controller responds to the initial call WITHOUT using the aircraft identification, radio communications have not been established and the pilot may not enter the Class C airspace."

In addition to this situation, it is also illegal to enter the airspace when there is no response by Approach to your call, or when the controller specifically tells you to "Remain clear (or outside) of the Class C airspace."

Relative to the last, although the occasions are becoming increasingly infrequent, Approach sometimes has to temporarily deny entry because of excessive workload and traffic area saturation. Also the fact that Approach must give traffic advisories to aircraft flying in the outer area that request them has contributed to occasional work overload. As I said before, pilots, do not have to contact Approach when intending to fly only in that outer area, but if they do request traffic advisories Approach is required to honor the requests.

Barring the initial contact requirement, and, of course, the dimensions of a Class C, radio communications and operating procedures are essentially the same as in the Class B environment. Pilot requirements are less stringent, but even Mode C transponders from the surface to 10,000 feet within the airspace are mandated, as is the standard VFR cloud separation regulation.

Airport lighting aids

An aeronautical light beacon is a visual NAVAID displaying flashes of white and/or colored lights to indicate the location of an airport, a heliport, a landmark, a certain point of a federal airway in mountainous terrain, or a hazard. The light used might be a rotating beacon or one or more flashing lights, and the flashing lights might be supplemented by steady burning lights of lesser intensity.

The color or color combination displayed by a particular beacon and/or its auxiliary lights tells whether the beacon is indicating a landing place, a landmark, a point of the federal airways, or a hazard. Coded flashes of the auxiliary lights, if employed, further identify the beacon site.

Airport rotating beacons

The airport beacon system that identifies airports has a vertical light distribution to make it most effective from one to 10 degrees above the horizon, although it can be seen well above or below that peak spread. The beacon might be an omnidirectional capacitor-discharge device or it might rotate at a constant speed that produces the visual effect of flashes at regular intervals. The flashes may be of one or two colors alternately. The number of flashes per minute is 12 to 30 for beacons marking airports, landmarks, and points on federal airways, and 30 to 60 for beacons marking heliports.

The beacon colors and color combinations are:

- White and green or green for lighted land airports.
- White and yellow or yellow for lighted water airports.
- Green, yellow, and white for lighted heliports.

Military airport beacons flash alternately white and green, but are differentiated from civil beacons by dual-peaked (two quick) white flashes between the green flashes.

In Classes B, C, D, and E surface areas, operation of the airport beacon during the daylight hours often indicates that the visibility is less than three miles and/or the ceiling is less than 1000 feet.

You should not, however, rely solely on the beacon to indicate if weather conditions are IFR or VFR. At certain locations with operating Control Towers, ATC personnel might turn the beacon on or off when the switch is in the Tower. At many airports, the beacon is activated by a photoelectric cell or time clocks that ATC personnel can't control. As there is no regulatory requirement for daylight beacon operation, it is the pilot's responsibility to comply with proper preflight planning as per by FAR 91.

Obstructions

Obstructions are marked or lighted to warn pilots during daytime and nighttime conditions. Those obstruction areas can be identified or lighted in any of the following combinations:

Aviation red obstruction lights: Flashing aviation red beacons and steady burning aviation red lights during nighttime operation. Aviation orange and white paint is used for daytime marking.

High-intensity white obstruction lights: Flashing high intensity white lights during daytime with reduced intensity for twilight and nighttime operation. When this system is used, the marking of structures with red obstruction lights and aviation orange and white paint might be omitted.

Dual lighting: A combination of flashing aviation red beacons and steady-burning aviation red lights for nighttime operation, and flashing high-intensity white lights for daytime operation. Aviation orange and white paint may be omitted.

High-intensity flashing white lights are used to identify some supporting structures of overhead transmission lines located across rivers, chasms, gorges, etc. These lights flash in a middle, top, lower light sequence at approximately 60 flashes per minute. The top light is normally installed near the top of the supporting structure, while the lower light indicates the approximate lower portion of the wire span. The lights are beamed towards the companion structure and identify the area of the wire span.

High-intensity flashing white lights are also employed to identify tall structures, such as chimneys and towers, as obstructions to air navigation. The lights provide a 360-degree coverage about the structure at 40 flashes per minute and consist of from one to seven levels of lights depending upon the height of the structure. Where more than one level is used the vertical banks flash simultaneously.

Airport approach lights

Airport approach lights have the sole purpose of guiding the IFR or VFR pilot to the runway and providing certain visual signals that indicate a safe or unsafe final landing approach or glide path. The two systems of concern here are the Approach Light System (ALS) and the Visual Approach Slope Indicator (VASI).

Approach light system. The Approach Light System (ALS) is primarily designed to assist IFR pilots in making the transition from instrument to visual flight for landing. The degree of sophistication of an ALS depends on the operational requirements of a particular runway. With several possible configurations, the system starts at the runway threshold and, for precision instrument runways, extends backwards 2400–3000 feet into the landing approach path. For nonprecision runways, the ALS extends back 1400–1500 from the threshold. A combination of flashing and steady burning lights provides direction to the runway in use.

Visual approach slope indicator (VASI). The VASI is a system of lights arranged to provide visual descent guidance information during the approach to a runway. These lights are visible for three to five miles away during the day and up to 20 miles or more at night.

The visual glide path of the VASI is designed to ensure safe obstruction clearance within plus or minus 10 degrees of the extended runway centerline and to four nautical miles from the runway threshold. Descent using the VASI, however, should not be initiated until the aircraft is visually aligned with the runway. Lateral course guidance is then maintained by reference to the runway or runway lights.

VASI installations can consist of 2-, 4-, 6-, 12-, or 16-light units, arranged in bars, referred to as "near," "middle," and "far" bars. Most VASI installations have two bars: near and far, and might be 2-, 4-, or 12-light units. Some airports have three bars, near, middle, and far, that provide an additional glide path for high-cockpit aircraft. Those consisting of 2-, 4-, or 6-light units are located on one side of the runway, usually the left. The 12- or 16-light units are placed on both sides of the runway.

Two-bar VASI units (Fig. 9-8) provide a visual glide path that is normally set at three degrees. The three-bar units (Fig. 9-9) produce two visual glide paths. The lower path is generated by the near and middle bars and the upper path by the middle and far bars, with the upper path normally four degrees. This higher path is intended for use only by high cockpit aircraft to ensure a sufficient threshold crossing altitude.

The basic principle of the VASI is that of color differentiation between red and white. Each light unit projects a beam having a white segment in the upper part of the beam and red segment in the lower part of the beam. The light units are arranged so that the pilot using the VASIs during an approach see the combination of lights in Fig. 9-10.

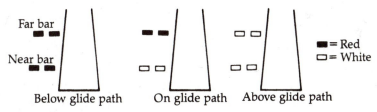

Fig. 9-8. *The two-bar VASI system.*

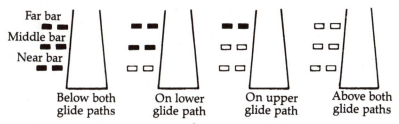

Fig. 9-9. *The three-bar VASI system.*

2-BAR VASI

	Light bar	Color
(a) Below glide path	Far	Red
	Near	Red
(b) On glide path	Far	Red
	Near	White
(c) Above glide path	Far	White
	Near	White

3-BAR VASI

	Light bar	Color
(a) Below both glide paths	Far	Red
	Middle	Red
	Near	Red
(b) On lower glide path	Far	Red
	Middle	Red
	Near	White
(c) On upper glide path	Far	Red
	Middle	White
	Near	White
(d) Above both glide paths	Far	White
	Middle	White
	Near	White

Fig. 9-10. *In one diagram, what the two- and three-bar light combinations mean.*

When on the proper glide path of a two-bar VASI, you see the near bar as white and the far bar as red. From a position below the glide path, you'll see both bars as red. In moving up to the glide path, the color of the near bar changes from red to pink to white. Above the glide slope, both bars are white, but as the aircraft moves down but still above the glide path, the color of the far bar changes from white to pink to red. When below the glide path, the red bars tend to merge into one distinct red signal, and a safe obstruction clearance might not exist under this condition.

A simple rule of thumb when using a two-bar VASI: All red—too low; all white—too high; red and white—just right.

With a three-bar VASI, it's not necessary to use all three bars (Figs. 9-9 and 9-10). The near and middle bars constitute a two-bar VASI for using the lower glide path, while the middle and far bars constitute a two-bar VASI for using the upper glide path.

In haze or dust conditions or when the approach is made into the sun, the white lights might appear yellowish. This is also true at night when the VASI is operated at a low intensity. Certain atmospheric debris may give the white lights an orange or brownish tint. The red lights, however, are not affected and the principle of color differentiation is still applicable.

Tricolor visual approach slope indicator. The Tricolor Approach Slope Indicator (Fig. 9-11) normally consists of a single light unit, projecting a three-color visual approach path. In this system, a below-glide path indication is red, the above-glide path indication is amber, and the on-path indication is green.

This system has a daytime useful range of approximately one-half to one mile. The nighttime range, depending upon visibility conditions, varies from one to five miles.

Some degree of difficulty might exist when trying to locate this type of indicator because of its small light source. Once the light source is acquired, however, it provides accurate guidance to the runway.

Precision approach path indicator (PAPI). The Precision Approach Path Indicator (Fig. 9-12) has light units similar to VASI, but they are installed in a single row of either two or four light units. This system has an effective visual range of about five miles during the day and up to 20 miles at night. The row of lights is normally installed on the left side of the runway and provides the glide path indications.

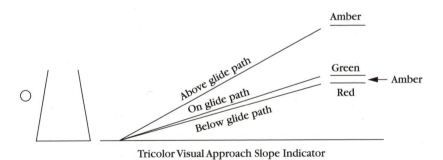

Tricolor Visual Approach Slope Indicator

Caution: When the aircraft descends from green to red, the pilot may see a dark amber color during the transition from green to red.

Fig. 9-11. *Another visual approach system: the tricolor VASI.*

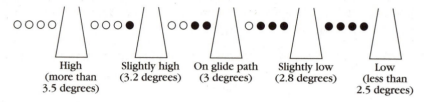

O White
● Red   PAPI

Fig. 9-12. *Precision Approach Path Indicators (PAPI) are four lights to the left of the runway. The trick: Keep two lights red, two lights white.*

Pulsating systems. A pulsating VASI (Fig. 9-13) normally consists of a single light unit projecting a two-color visual approach path. The below-glide path indication is usually a pulsating red and the above-glide path a pulsating white. When on the glide path, one system projects a steady white light, while another type shows an alternating red and white light. The range of these systems is about four miles during the day and up to 10 miles at night.

Runway lightings

Several types of runway lighting systems are common at both tower and nontower airports. Among the systems are Runway End Identifier Lights, Runway Edge Lights, and In-Runway Lighting. Although not all types exist at all airports or on all runways, the following is a brief description of each.

Runway end identifier lights (REILs)

REILs are installed at many airports for providing rapid and positive identification of the approach end of a runway. Simply designed, a REIL system consists of a pair of synchronized flashing lights that are located laterally on either side of the runway threshold.

Quite obviously, their value is that they: (1) identify the beginning of a runway that may be surrounded by a preponderance of other lighting; (2) identify a runway that lacks contrast from the surrounding airport complex; and (3) identify a runway during periods of reduced visibility.

Runway edge light systems

These are the lights that outline the edges of runways and are classified according to their intensity or brightness, as High-Intensity

Runway Lights (HIRL), Medium Intensity Runway Lights (MIRL), and Low-Intensity Runway Lights (LIRL). The MIRL and HIRL systems have a variable intensity control system, whereas the LIRL has only one setting.

The lights in this system are white, except on instrument runways where yellow replaces the white on the last 2000 feet, or half the runway length, whichever is less, to mark a warning zone for landings.

The far end of the runway is identified by red lights to alert departing aircraft that the end is near. These same lights project green away from the runway to mark the threshold for landing aircraft on that runway.

In-runway lighting systems

A variety of in-runway lights are installed at some precision approach runways to assist landings in low visibility weather conditions. The various systems include:

- *Runway Centerline Light System (RCLS).* These lights are located along the runway centerline, spaced at 50-foot intervals. Looking at them from the landing threshold, they are white until the last 3000 feet, at which point they begin to flash alternately with red for the next 2000 feet. For the last 1000 feet, they burn a constant red.

- *Touchdown zone lights (TDZL)* are steady-burning white lights spaced across the runway centerline and establish the zone in which the aircraft should touch down. Where installed, the lighting starts 100 feet beyond the landing threshold and extends 3000 feet down the runway past the landing threshold or to the midpoint of the runway, whichever is less.

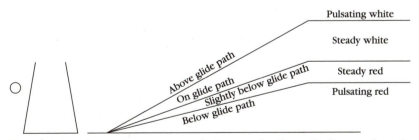

Fig. 9-13. *The Pulsating Visual Approach Slope Indicator has its merits, but, as the "Caution" note says, the pulsating lights can be mistaken for ground vehicles or another aircraft.*

- *Taxiway lights* lead off from the runway centerline to an exit taxiway as a means to expedite landing traffic from the active runway. The lights alternate green and yellow from the centerline to the holding position on the taxiway.

- *Land and hold short lights (LAHSO)* indicate the hold-short point on certain runways that have been approved for land-and-hold-short operations (LAHSO). The system consists of a row of pulsating white lights installed across the runway at the hold-short point. When LAHSO is not in effect, the lights are turned off.

- *Other.* Many more lighting systems and visual glide slope indicators exist than those just summarized above. If you'll check the Directory Legend at the beginning of any A/FD, you'll find a listing and an explanation of those other systems. Also, to determine what lighting facilities are available at a given airport, refer again to the A/FD and the entries immediately above the AIRPORT REMARKS section. You'll find the answer right there.

Ground control of the lighting systems. At airports with an operating control tower, the lighting system is controlled by the tower personnel. Also, at some locations where there is a Flight Service Station but no Tower, or the Tower is closed, the FSS controls the lighting.

In either situation, pilots may request that lights be turned on or off. Runway edge lights, in-pavement lights, and approach lights also have intensity controls that can be varied according to pilot requests. In addition, sequence flashing lights (SFLs) can be turned on or off, and some of these have intensity control.

The *Medium Intensity Approach Lighting System* with *Runway Alignment Indicators (MALSR)* is installed at many airports. This system is also controlled by the ATCT or, if closed, by a transceiver microphone from approaching aircraft.

Pilot control of airport lighting. At many airports where there is no Tower or FSS, or the Tower is closed, the pilot can control the lighting by keying the aircraft's microphone on the airport's published communication frequency. The lighting system at a given airport is listed in the *Airport/Facility Directory* in the runway data section and, if applicable, further information or instructions are included under "Airport Remarks."

The radio control keying system is standardized: key (meaning push or deflect the mike button) the mike seven times within five seconds for highest intensity available; five times within five seconds for medium or lower intensity (Lower REIL or REIL-off); and three times within five seconds for lowest intensity available (Lower REIL or REIL-off).

The suggested technique is initially to key the mike seven times. This assures that all controlled lights are turned to the highest intensity level available. Then, if desired, and where the capability exists, adjustments to a lower intensity can be made by keying the mike five or three times. Once activated, the lights remain on for 15 minutes.

Because of the proximity of some airports using the same frequency (particularly unicom airports), radio controlled lighting receivers may be set at a low sensitivity, requiring the aircraft to be relatively close to activate the system. Consequently, even if the lights are already on, always key the mike as directed when overflying an airport of intended landing, or just prior to entering the final segment of an approach. This ensures that the aircraft is close enough to activate the system and that the full 15 minutes of lighting duration will be available.

Further discussion of pilot-controlled lighting is found in *AIM* and the "Directory Legend" of the *Airport/Facility Directory*. The *A/FD* also provides any pertinent lighting instructions for a given airport.

Airport runway marking aids

From the point of view of airport markings, there are basically three categories of runways. The three are: precision instrument runways, nonprecision instrument runways, and visual approach runways, and each, for ready identification, has its own distinctive markings. Any of three runways can, of course, be used in visual meteorological conditions (VMC), assuming the airport has more than just one category. In instrument conditions (IMC), however, traffic is obviously directed to the runway compatible with aircraft equipment and pilot qualifications. As to the various runway markings, there are always exceptions, but one or more of those summarized here, taken largely from the 1999 issue of FAR/AIM will be found in one form or another at almost every airport, small or large.

Runway designators. Runway numbers and, if required, letters, are based on the magnetic heading of the runway: For example, refer to

Fig. 9-14. The "23" located at the approach end of the runway identifies the heading of a runway as 23, or really 230 degrees. The reading at the opposite end of the same runway would be the reciprocal, or "5" (50). Should there be parallel runways at a given airport, each will be marked "L" (left), "C" (center, if there are three runways), and "R" (right). Keep in mind, though, that runways will be L and R in one direction and R and L in the opposite heading (Fig. 9-15).

Centerlines. Almost everywhere, even on narrow runways at some of the very small airports, the middle of a runway is identified by a painted centerline of uniformly spaced stripes and gaps. The purpose of the line is to guide pilots when taking off or landing, with the object of keeping the aircraft right on the centerline during either operation as well as when on the final approach for landing.

Threshold. A threshold marks the beginning point on the runway that is available and suitable in all respects for landing aircraft.

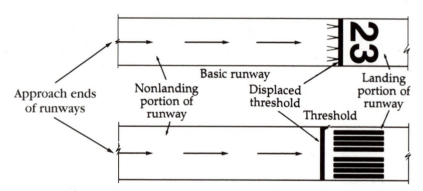

Fig. 9-14. *Runways are numbered according to their magnetic heading, as "23" in this figure.*

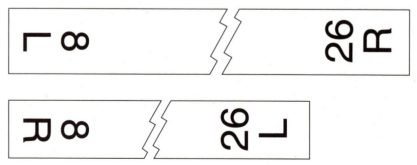

Fig. 9-15 *The identification of parallel runways.*

Displaced threshold. A displaced threshold is one that has been moved a certain distance down a runway from its actual beginning, usually because of physical factors that would make that portion of the runway unsuitable for landing purposes. At the same time, though, it could be entirely satisfactory for taxiing, takeoffs, or landing rollouts from the opposite direction. As indicated in Fig. 9-16, white arrows lead from the start of the runway along the centerline to a horizontally placed wide white bar identifying the beginning point of the approved runway. The white arrows just prior to the bar further identify the end of the displaced area.

Threshold markings. To clearly identify the beginning of the usable runway, two types of markings are used. As illustrated in Fig. 9-17, one is composed of eight solid bars, four either side of the centerline, while the other consists of a number of stripes which indicates the width of the runway, as per Fig. 9-18.

Stopway areas. This is any area extending beyond the regular runway that may appear usable but is not because of its strength, physical condition, or structure (Fig. 9-19).

Closed runway. A closed runway is one that, for whatever reason, is unusable and hazardous. The closing may be temporary or permanent, but the runway is usually so identified by a large painted X at either end (Fig. 9-20).

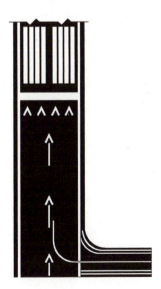

Fig. 9-16 *Note the white arrows and the broad white stripe as identifiers of the start of the approved runway.*

Precision Instrument Runway Markings

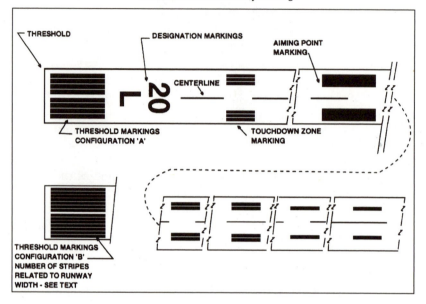

Fig. 9-17   *The two types of stripe markings that establish the beginning of the useable runway.*

Runway side stripe markings. To clearly establish the outer edges of the runway, continuous white stripes are painted down each side of the runway between thresholds.

Touchdown and aiming point markings. Precision instrument runways have both types of these markings. The aiming point, serving as a visual landing, consists of a broad white stripe on either side of the centerline and placed approximately 1000 feet from the landing threshold. The touchdown point markers represent the touchdown zones for landing operations (Fig. 9-21). To assist in the second function, the markers are three, two, or one bars located on either side of the centerline and are spaced at 500-foot increments to provide distance information. If the runway has touchdown points at both ends of the same runway, these markers extend to within 900 feet of the midpoint between the two thresholds.

The usual markings for *visual runways* (those for operations under Visual Flight Rules) (Fig. 9-22) are: centerline marking; runways designation (number, plus "L," "C," or "R," if there are parallel runways); fixed distance markings (on runways 4000 feet or longer used by jet aircraft); and holding position marking (for taxiway/runway intersections).

Number of Runway Threshhold Stripes

Runway Width	Number of Stripes
60 feet (18m)	4
75 feet (23m)	6
100 feet (30m)	8
150 feet (45m)	12
200 feet (60m)	16

Fig. 9-18 *How the number of threshold stripes identifies the width of the runway.*

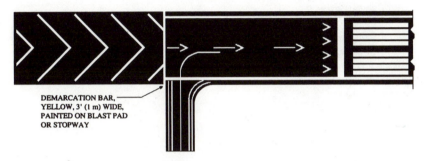

DEMARCATION BAR,
YELLOW, 3' (1 m) WIDE,
PAINTED ON BLAST PAD
OR STOPWAY

Fig. 9-19 *An example of the stopway area and a displaced threshold that follows or immediately precedes the usable portion of the runway.*

Fig. 9-20 *Large painted Xs identify runways that are unsafe and hence closed.*

Nonprecision runway (a runway with a nonvisual navigation aid and intended for landings under instrument weather conditions [Fig. 9-23]). Markings, in addition to those identified, are: centerline marking; runway number (26); fixed distance marking (on runways 4000 feet or more used by jet aircraft); and holding position markings (for taxiway/runway intersections and instrument landing system critical areas).

Precision instrument runway (Fig. 9-24) markings are: centerline; runway designation (20 Left); threshold; fixed distance; touchdown zone; side stripes; and holding position markings (for taxiway/runway intersections and ILS critical areas).

Precision Instrument Runway Markings

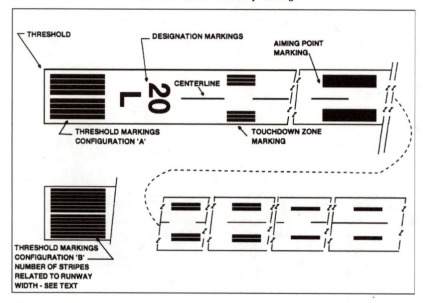

Fig. 9-21. *A repeat of Fig. 9-17 to illustrate additional markings, including those for touchdown zones and runway distance information.*

Fig. 9-22. *These are the simple markings that identify a visual runway.*

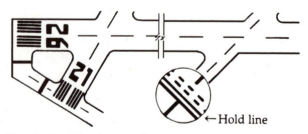

Fig. 9-23. *This figure illustrates nonprecision runway markings (26) and (21), plus the hold line for taxiway/runway intersections.*

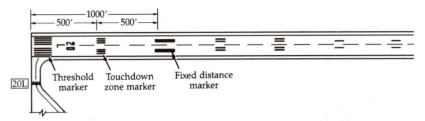

Fig. 9-24. *The markings of a precision instrument runway.*

Taxiways: The taxiway centerline is a continuous yellow line, and the taxiway edge might be marked with two continuous yellow lines, six inches apart. The HOLD line is identified by two continuous and two dashed lines that are perpendicular, or at a 90-degree angle, to the centerline. For further identification, there may also be large signs at the hold line that identify the runway with which the taxiway intersects, as **17** (white numbers on a red background), designating runway 17.

Airport taxiway marking aids

Getting from a runway to the parking ramp, or vice versa, involves moving the aircraft along certain stretches of geography that are designated for taxi operations. At small airports, taxiways or taxi strips (the terms are synonymous)—if, indeed, they exist at all—are usually easy to locate, but such is not always the case at the larger, more complex, airports. Regardless of the situation, however, knowledge of and alertness to the taxiway signage system are just as important as those related to the airport's runways. Even with that said, I'm not going to try to illustrate or discuss all of the 15 or so situations involving taxiway signs or markings. Section 2 of AIM does a very good job of that.

Another reason for a somewhat limited discussion is the types of airport(s) you would normally operate in or intend to visit. If you typically fly out of Class E or G airports but want to go to one of the Class B, C, or D airports, I'd highly recommend a study of the Class B, C, or D runway layout, including the taxiways and the possible signage related thereto. I'll say this, though: If you ever do have a locate-the-taxiway problem at any towered airport, those ground controllers are usually most willing to help you, guide you, give you progressive taxi instructions, or whatever. Just as you want to get to where you're going after landing, the ground controller is equally anxious to help you achieve that objective.

Accordingly, let's look briefly at the more common signs you'd find at the majority of airports—small or large. Best source references for current taxiway information? AIM (Section 2-3), the A/FD (Airport/Facility Directory), the sectional chart, and, if you're a member of AOPA (the Aircraft Owners and Pilots Association), the Association's annual Airport Directory. The Airport Directory has diagrams of many (but not all) of the nation's 5,000 plus public-use airports, including their physical layouts, runway lengths and widths, their directional heading numbers, taxiways, ramp areas, and buildings—plus information relative to lighting, pattern altitudes, weather contacts, restaurants, FBOs, and the like. So, in several alternate sources, you can find what you would need if you were going into a strange airport or one with which you might not be currently familiar.

Despite these other sources, a review of some of the typical taxiway situations you could encounter is in order.

Centerlines. As with the runways, taxiways have their own set of markings, including the centerline. This is a solid yellow line that (quite obviously) establishes the center of the strip. Just as you should try to straddle the runway centerline when taking off or landing, so should it be the same rule in all taxiing operations. While doing so is indicative of your attention to detail, the line (1) primarily provides direction, and (2) indicates that you have adequate wing tip clearance of any off-taxiway obstacle, such as a snowbank, motorized ground equipment, aircraft parked along the edge or shoulder, posted warning or informational signs, and the like.

Continuous taxiway markings. These are continuous yellow lines painted along the taxiway edges when that edge is not the same as the edge of the paved area. In other words, the taxiway is narrower than the pavement itself (Fig. 9-25).

Dashed taxiway markings. Sometimes a taxiway will abut another paved surface, such as a ramp, a tie-down area, an area where aircraft could taxi without any ground control approval, an area for fueling trucks or other pieces of equipment, and so on. When such an abutment exists, 6-inch-wide double yellow lines, 15 feet long, are painted both sides of the taxiway (Fig. 9-25). The gap between those markers is 25 feet.

Holding position markers. Three principal holding positions typically exist at the larger, busier airports. One is on taxiways, another is on

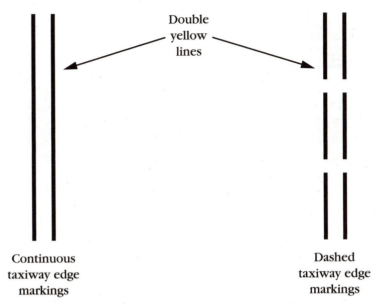

Fig. 9-25. *Samples of the taxiway edge lines.*

runways, and a third is when a taxiway is located in a runway approach area.

The first (on the taxiway) is typically located some thirty yards or so back from the runway to which the taxiway is leading. The marker consists of four yellow stripes—two solid and two dashed or segmented—that are painted across the width of taxiway, with the solid lines first and the dashed lines on the runway side of the hold area (Fig. 9-26). Unless specifically cleared by ground control or the tower at a Class B, C, or D airport, don't let any part of your aircraft extend beyond the solid lines.

After contacting ground control for taxi permission, you could expect to hear from ground something like this:

"Cherokee 1234 Bravo, turn left on Charlie (a taxiway) and taxi to runway two zero." This automatically means that you're cleared to taxi TO the hold line once you are finally ready to depart.

Accordingly, you move to the holding area, or holding "bay" (Fig. 9-26), where you complete the standard engine runup, magneto check, aileron and elevator movements, instruments and gauges, seat belts tight, and so on. When you're satisfied that all is well and, assuming that you're number one in line, taxi TO but do not cross

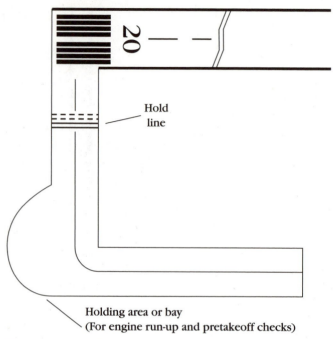

Fig. 9-26. *Another example of a taxiway hold line and a holding bay.*

the taxiway hold line. Come to a full stop and then call the tower—not ground control—for takeoff clearance. The exchange would follow this general pattern:

> **Pilot:** Smithtown tower, Cherokee 1234 Bravo ready to go two zero, west departure.
> **Tower:** Cherokee 1234 Bravo, cleared for takeoff. West departure approved.
> **Pilot:** Roger, west approved. 34 Bravo.

Now cross the hold line, move to the runway as quickly and safely as you can, and get going.

One other thing about this type of hold: Holding areas or bays adjacent to the various runways for those final pretakeoff checks exist at every controlled field—and at many of the uncontrolled as well. So, as you approach the hold point, taxi into the holding area and begin the check. Once you've completed it and are ready to go, move up to the hold line before contacting the tower (Fig 9- 26). The reason? Back in the holding area, you could be another 30 yards or so from the hold line and are thus that much further from the active runway itself. The tower wants you as close to the runway as possible to minimize the time lapses between the controller's takeoff approval and your actual takeoff roll. Another operational reason for this positioning is that on a busy day the controller might be able to clear you for an immediate takeoff between landing aircraft, whereas that wouldn't be possible if you were still sitting back there in the holding area, and, yes, all the time burning up fuel.

A second holding position marker is located on runways that cross or intersect each other at some point. In these instances, the hold position is further identified by a large white number of the runway on a red background that is painted on the surface just behind the hold marker and typically to the left of the center line. Where runway intersections exist and these markers are located, pilots landing on the hold-marker runway may be cleared to land on runway yy but are told to "hold short of runway xx." Usually that means that another aircraft is about to take off or land on the xx crossing runway. Should you be the pilot coming in on runway yy, plan your approach accordingly and either exit yy on a taxi strip before reaching the marker or continue your rollout until you reach that point. Then stop and await further taxi instructions.

A third holding marker is at some airports where a taxiway is located in the approach or departure area of an instrument runway. In such circumstances, an ILS hold marker (Fig. 9-27) might well be located on the taxiway but, for added safety's sake, further back from the runway than the normal hold area symbol. Thus, when circumstances dictate, ground control could hold a taxiing aircraft at the ILS marker to protect a landing aircraft from any interference in what is called the "ILS/MLS critical area" (MLS = Microwave Landing System).

Other markings and signs. What I've summarized here describes the more common airport signs and symbols that should be of meaning to you as a student, or in your early hours as a newly-certificated private pilot, or for the more experienced who feel they need a review of the basics of the marking system. Meanwhile, several other examples of airport signage are again located in AIM, Section 3, for pilots who seek additional information on VOR receiver check locations, roadway signs for motorized equipment, helicopter landing sites, and so on. Indeed, every pilot should review each new annual issue and midyear update of AIM, because changes in procedures, processes, rules, etc., coming as frequently as they do, are clearly identified in the page margins by heavy black bars opposite the revision(s). Keeping current is a major pilot responsibility, and AIM is one of the best tools you have for that.

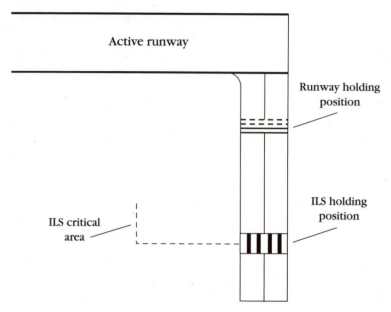

Fig. 9-27. *An illustration of an ILS hold marker on a taxiway leading to an ILS approach runway.*

Quickie quiz questions
Chapter 9

1. Before landing at a no-tower airport or one where the tower is closed, what are the minimum radio calls you should make, and where or when should you make them?

2. Define "CTAF."

3. What is "ATIS" and what does it do?

4. What are the pilot and aircraft equipment requirements to enter a Class C airspace?

5. What is the basic purpose of the Approach/Departure Control facility?

6. For a VFR pilot to enter a Class B airspace, what instruction must the controller specifically communicate to the pilot?

7. How can a pilot control runway lighting, where it has been installed, at the smaller nontower airports?

8. What is the purpose of the VASI light system?

9. What is a "displaced threshold"?

10. Describe the taxiway holding position design.

Answers in Appendix, pages 580-581.

10

VFR flight planning

Careful preflight planning is extremely important—which is an obvious statement. With it, though, you can complete your flights with greater confidence, ease, and safety. Without it, too many pilots have become statistics; and figures show that inadequate preflight planning is a significant cause of fatal accidents.

FAA regulations state, in part, that before beginning a flight, the pilot in command of an aircraft shall become familiar with all available information concerning that flight. For flights not in the immediate vicinity of an airport, this includes current weather reports and forecasts, fuel requirements, alternatives available if the planned flight cannot be completed, and any known traffic delays reported by ATC.

(**Note:** What follows recognizes the inevitability of some duplication, but the intent of this chapter is to discuss a few additional aspects of VFR flight planning that can make the task easier and yet more complete. In so doing, and to the extent feasible, the logical sequence of actions in the planning responsibility are followed.)

The elements of flight planning

The first step, of course, is to assemble the materials required to plan the flight. Depending on its nature, i.e., route, distance, destination (if other than departing point), and the like, you should have:

- The *current* sectional chart(s)
- A VFR terminal area chart, if any portion of the flight will penetrate even just a small segment of a Class B airspace

- A current *Airport/Facility Directory* for intermediate or destination airport information and communication frequencies
- If radio navigation and requesting traffic advisories from a Center are planned, the En Route Low Altitude Chart will be helpful
- The aircraft Flight Manual or Pilot's Operating Handbook— for weight and balance data and performance charts

These are the basics, plus a manual or electronic computer, a Navigation Flight Plotter, a yellow highlight marker, some sort of flight planner, either homemade or an FAA form (Fig. 10-1), the official Flight Plan form itself (Fig. 10-2), and a copy of the alphabetized listing of special equipment on the aircraft (Fig. 10-3). Additionally, the form illustrated in Fig. 10-4 can be helpful for recording weather briefing data.

The preliminary weather check

Before spending time meticulously plotting and planning a flight, particularly if it is to be some distance, a preliminary weather check might be in order. One method for doing this is a visit to a flight service station, if one happens to be on the airport property. In-person briefings, however, are becoming increasingly rare because of the consolidation of FSSs into the 61 Automated Flight Service Stations (AFSSs). Consequently, the other, and more common briefing, is a telephone call to a FSS or a computerized briefing through DUAT (Direct User Access Terminal).

Relative to the last, though, and for purposes here, let's assume one of two situations: (1) You want to plan a flight, get a briefing, and file a flight plan, but you're at home and don't have a computer to access DUAT; or, (2) you're at an airport that has neither a computer nor a Flight Service Station on the property. Hence, in either case, your only alternative is to phone the FSS that is responsible for the area in which you are located. Certainly, if you can access DUAT, that's the way to go—except for one thing: you lose the advantage of discussing a given condition with another human being—someone who might be able to offer some insights that could affect your go/no-go decision or the flight route you intended to take.

Whichever the case, you're on the phone with an FSS briefer. If, at any time, he or she suggests that "VFR is not recommended," (and this would likely come early in the briefing), that should be enough

PREFLIGHT				EN ROUTE					
DEPARTURE PT	ROUTE			ESTIMATED			ACTUAL		
CHECK POINTS	VIA	CRS	DIST	GS	ETE	ETA	GS	ATE	ATA

	FUEL MANAGEMENT						TIME EN ROUTE	
							TOUCH DOWN	
OFF							TAKE-OFF	
ON								
TIME							ATE	

FAA Form 8740-2 (10-84) SUPERSEDES PREVIOUS EDITION

Fig. 10-1. *This is one of several possible forms to use in planning the flight.*

FLIGHT PLAN

1. TYPE OF FLIGHT PLAN		2. AIRCRAFT IDENTIFICATION
	VFR	
IFR	DVFR	

3. AIRCRAFT TYPE/SPECIAL EQUIPMENT 1/	4. TRUE AIRSPEED	5. POINT OF DEPARTURE	6. DEPARTURE TIME		7. INITIAL CRUISING ALTITUDE
			PROPOSED (Z)	ACTUAL (Z)	
	KNOTS				

8. ROUTE OF FLIGHT

9. DESTINATION (Name of airport and city)	10. REMARKS

11. ESTIMATED TIME EN ROUTE		12. FUEL ON BOARD		13. ALTERNATE AIRPORT(S)	14. PILOT'S NAME
HOURS	MINUTES	HOURS	MINUTES		

15. PILOT'S ADDRESS AND TELEPHONE NO. OR AIRCRAFT HOME BASE	16. NO. OF PERSONS ABOARD	17. COLOR OF AIRCRAFT	

CLOSE FLIGHT PLAN UPON ARRIVAL

1/ SPECIAL EQUIPMENT SUFFIX
A—DME, TRANSPONDER, ENCODING
B—DME, TRANSPONDER, NO ENCODING
D—DME WITH NO TRANSPONDER
F—RNAV, TRANSPONDER, ENCODING
T—TRANSPONDER NO ENCODING
U—TRANSPONDER WITH ENCODING
X—NO TRANSPONDER

Fig. 10-2. *The actual flight plan, as communicated to an FSS, should follow the sequence of information illustrated here.*

SPECIAL EQUIPMENT SUFFIX

A - DME, transponder with altitude encoding

B - DME, transponder with no altitude encoding

C - RNAV, transponder with no altitude encoding

D - DME, no transponder

R - RNAV, transponder with altitude encoding

T - Transponder with no altitude encoding

U - Transponder with altitude encoding

W - RNAV, no transponder

X - No transponder

EST	+5=UTC	EDT	+4=UTC
CST	+6=UTC	CDT	+5=UTC
MST	+7=UTC	MDT	+6=UTC
PST	+8=UTC	PDT	+7=UTC

Fig. 10-3. *Be sure to indicate in box number 3 the type(s) of special equipment on the aircraft in the appropriate box.*

right there to forget the flight for now— even though the final go/no-go decision is always yours. Yes, the FSS briefer/specialist can recommend but cannot deny you the right to go. You're the chief decision-maker, and the FSS is not a controlling agency.

To obtain a preliminary telephone weather check from an FSS, even before contacting a briefer, a service called TIBS (Telephone Information Briefing Service), mentioned briefly in Chapter 6, is available. This is a recorded synopsis of conditions just within the FSS's geographic area, including adverse weather, if any, precipitation, thunderstorms, winds aloft, and a summary of current and forecast weather for principal locations in the area. Reaching TIBS is a matter of dialing the universal FSS number (1-800-WX-BRIEF), then listening to a recorded menu of services available, and how to access them.

TIBS replaces what has been known as PATWAS (Pilot Automatic Telephone Weather Answering Service) at the FSSs. PATWAS is still available at nonautomated FSSs, but its weather data are limited to conditions within a 50-mile radius of the station. TIBS, on the other hand, provides more information over a much broader geographic area.

Although limited to the FSS's area, the primary purpose of TIBS is to give the pilot the basic data for preliminary flight planning and to assist in making the go/no-go decision. It is not intended, nor should it be used, as a substitute for a standard briefing by a specialist.

If the flight is a "go". . .

If the TIBS recordings indicate a "go" decision, with the necessary charts and materials on hand, now is the time to plan the flight. Admitting some duplication of Chapter 7, the planning involves at least the use of the sectional, the *Airport/Facility Directory (A/FD)*, depending on the route of the flight and/or airports of intended landing, and, unless the operating features of the aircraft to be flown are well-known, the Aircraft's Flight Manual or the Pilot's Operating Handbook for that particular aircraft.

Using the sectional chart

First, draw the course to be flown on the sectional chart or charts. The course line should begin at the center of the departure airport and end at the center of the destination airport. If the route is direct,

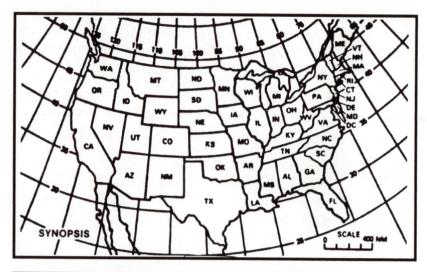

LOCATION	WEATHER DATA:	
	time: _____	time: _____

EN ROUTE WEATHER SUMMARY	time: _____

EN ROUTE WEATHER SUMMARY	time: _____

(A)

Fig. 10-4. *This form simplifies the recording of weather conditions given by the FSS briefer. (Form continues on page 499).*

ROUTE SEGMENT	EN ROUTE FORECASTS

DESTINATION(S)	TERMINAL FORECASTS

LOCATION	WINDS & TEMPERATURES ALOFT FORECASTS	
	alt _____	alt _____

LOCATION	SIGNIFICANT WEATHER/NOTAMS

OTHER DATA:

PILOTS WEATHER "GO OR NO GO" CHECKLIST

SYNOPSIS & AREA WX	DESTINATION WX FORECAST	TEMP DEW POINT SPREAD (FOG)
ADVERSE WX INCLUDING SIGMETS AIRMETS	WINDS & TEMPERATURES ALOFT FORECAST	BETTER WX AREA FORECAST
CURRENT EN ROUTE WX	PIREPS INCLUDING TOP REPORTS	ALTERNATE AIRPORT WX FORECAST
FORECAST EN ROUTE WX	FREEZING LEVELS	NOTAMS

(B)

Fig. 10-4. *Continuation of Fig. 10-4.*

as the crow flies, the course will be a single straight line. If it is not direct, as with a dog leg, it will have two or more straight line segments—for example, a line to a VOR station that is off the direct route but will make navigating easier.

Appropriate checkpoints should be selected along the route and noted in some way. These should be easy-to-locate points, such as large towns, lakes, rivers, or combinations of recognizable points such as towns with an airport, towns with a network of highways, and railroads entering and departing, etc. Normally, choose only towns indicated by splashes of yellow on the chart. Don't pick those represented by a small circle—these may turn out to be only a half-dozen houses. (In isolated areas, however, towns so represented can be meaningful checkpoints.)

The areas on either side of the planned route should be checked for alert, warning, restricted, prohibited, and Military Operations Areas, or Air Defense Identification Zones (ADIZ). Each area, as you'll recall, has its restrictions printed on the sectional, usually on the reverse side on the legend flap.

Next, study the terrain along the route to determine the highest and lowest elevations so that an appropriate altitude, which conforms to FAA regulations, can be selected. Check the route for particularly rugged terrain so it can be avoided. With the help of the *A/FD*, study the airports where landings and takeoffs will be made for tall obstructions such as television towers that can rise to altitudes over 1500 feet above the surrounding terrain. Obstacles like these can be dangerous, and you should be alert to their presence and location.

Also, make a list of the radio navigation aids you will use along the route and the frequencies on which they can be received. In the process, indicate the aids that have voice facilities so that you'll know what stations have weather broadcasts.

Using the airport/facility directory

The *A/FD* has much valuable information in it, so use it as another essential flight planning tool. For instance, make a list of the Flight Service Stations along the intended route and their various frequencies, in addition to the navigation aid frequencies recorded from the sectional.

Then study the information about each airport where you intend to land. To the extent pertinent to the flight, record and become familiar with the *A/FD data* such as: the airport location, field elevation, traffic pattern altitude, runway and lighting facilities, services provided, the existence of unicom, types of fuel available, class of airspace, Control Tower and Ground Control frequencies, traffic information, remarks, NOTAMs, if any, and other pertinent information. Just be sure the *A/FD* is the most current issue. A lot can change between publications.

Weight-and-balance calculation

The weight-and-balance calculation, as discussed in Chapter 5, involves knowing the empty weight of the aircraft, to which is then added the weight of fuel, oil, passengers, and baggage or cargo to be carried. The total weight, then, must not exceed the allowable maximum, and the distribution of the load must not exceed the center of gravity limits. Be sure to use the latest weight-and-balance information in the FAA-approved Airplane Flight Manual or subsequent aircraft maintenance logs and records to obtain empty weight and empty-weight center of gravity information.

Next, determine the takeoff and landing distances from the appropriate charts, based on the calculated load, the elevation and temperature of the airport, then compare these distances with the amount of runway available. Remember: the heavier the load and the higher the elevation, temperature, or humidity, the longer the takeoff roll and landing roll and the lower the rate of climb.

Finally, review the fuel consumption charts to determine the rate of fuel consumption at the estimated flight altitude and power settings. Then calculate the rate of fuel consumption and compare it with the estimated time for the flight, so that refueling points along the route can be included in the plan.

Completing the flight plan form

The computed FAA Flight Plan form illustrated in Fig. 10-5 is basically self-explanatory. Be sure to fill it out, however, *before* calling an FSS or an AFSS.

Blocks 1 and 2 are self-evident.

Block 3. The aircraft type, too, is obvious, but the slash followed by a letter identifies the special equipment on board as listed in Fig.

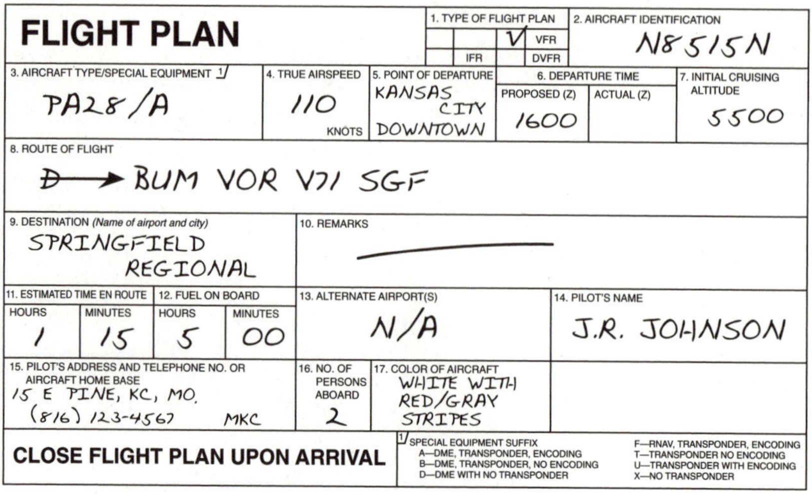

FLIGHT PLAN		1. TYPE OF FLIGHT PLAN		2. AIRCRAFT IDENTIFICATION
		☑ VFR ☐ IFR ☐ DVFR		N8515N

3. AIRCRAFT TYPE/SPECIAL EQUIPMENT 1/	4. TRUE AIRSPEED	5. POINT OF DEPARTURE	6. DEPARTURE TIME		7. INITIAL CRUISING ALTITUDE
PA28/A	110 KNOTS	KANSAS CITY DOWNTOWN	PROPOSED (Z) 1600	ACTUAL (Z)	5500

8. ROUTE OF FLIGHT
D⟶ BUM VOR V71 SGF

9. DESTINATION *(Name of airport and city)*	10. REMARKS
SPRINGFIELD REGIONAL	

11. ESTIMATED TIME EN ROUTE		12. FUEL ON BOARD		13. ALTERNATE AIRPORT(S)	14. PILOT'S NAME
HOURS	MINUTES	HOURS	MINUTES	N/A	J.R. JOHNSON
1	15	5	00		

15. PILOT'S ADDRESS AND TELEPHONE NO. OR AIRCRAFT HOME BASE	16. NO. OF PERSONS ABOARD	17. COLOR OF AIRCRAFT
15 E PINE, KC, MO. (816) 123-4567 MKC	2	WHITE WITH RED/GRAY STRIPES

CLOSE FLIGHT PLAN UPON ARRIVAL

1/ SPECIAL EQUIPMENT SUFFIX
A—DME, TRANSPONDER, ENCODING
B—DME, TRANSPONDER, NO ENCODING
D—DME WITH NO TRANSPONDER

F—RNAV, TRANSPONDER, ENCODING
T—TRANSPONDER NO ENCODING
U—TRANSPONDER WITH ENCODING
X—NO TRANSPONDER

Fig. 10-5. *A completed VFR flight plan.*

10-3. In this sample Flight Plan, Fig. 10-5, 8515 November has a DME and a transponder with altitude encoding.

Block 4. The true airspeed is determined from the Pilot's Operating Handbook (POH) or the Aircraft Flight Manual. That airspeed is close enough for preliminary flight planning purposes.

Block 5. Self-evident, but enter the name of the departure airport. To say "Minneapolis" won't do. From which of the several airports in the Minneapolis area are you departing?

Block 6. The proposed departure time is what you report to the briefer. Be sure, though, to convert local time to "Z" time, or UTC (Coordinated Universal Time).

Block 7. You may have a desired cruising altitude in mind, but the actual altitude and time en route (Block 10) will depend on the briefing of winds aloft, temperatures, cloud conditions, and so on. Following the briefing, some recalculations are often required to compute a more accurate airspeed and estimated time en route (ETE).

Block 8. The "D" with an arrow means "Direct," in this case to BUM, the VOR at Butler, Missouri. "V71" indicates that at Butler the pilot will fly Victor 71 to SGF (Springfield).

Block 9. Again, the entry is self-evident, but see more in "Filing to the First Point of Landing" below.

Block 10. This block is usually of little concern to the VFR flight plan pilot.

Block 11. You reported an ETE of 1:15 during the briefing, based on a 110-knot true airspeed. The briefing could change the ETE, however, and if the time is extended appreciably, advise the FSS accordingly when you contact the FSS to open the flight plan. The reason: If you fail to close your flight plan 30 minutes after the ETE has elapsed, the FSS in whose area the destination airport is located will telephone that airport to see if you have arrived. If not, the first steps of the FSS and FAA search-and-rescue (SAR) procedures will be initiated. This is why keeping the appropriate FSS advised of later-than-planned arrivals and why closing out the flight plan immediately after landing are so important.

Block 12. Record the fuel on board in terms of hours and minutes of flight time based on the usable gallons of fuel.

Block 13. It's not necessary to list an alternate airport on a VFR flight plan unless you so desire.

Blocks 14, 15, 16, and 17 are self-explanatory.

At all of the automated FSSs, the briefer/specialist enters the data on the form in the computer as you report it. In effect, the flight plan is being recorded, stored, and filed even before the actual briefing. Once filed, it's held by the FSS until one hour after the proposed departure and then canceled unless: (1) the actual departure time has been received; (2) a revised proposed departure time is received; (3) at the time of filing, the briefer is informed that the proposed departure time will be met, but the actual time can't be immediately reported because of inadequate communications.

Upon actual departure, the FSS sends only Blocks 2, 3, 9, and 10 to the destination FSS. The balance of the Flight Plan information is transmitted if the pilot does not arrive or does not close the flight plan at the stated destination. When either happens, the first steps of the formal search-and-rescue efforts are initiated.

Filing to the first point of landing

Assume that the pilot in the Fig. 10-5 illustration is merely stopping over in Springfield for an hour or so and then continuing on to a more distant final destination. Should he or she file to that final destination, or just to Springfield? The FAA recommends filing only to the first airport of landing if the ground time is expected to exceed one hour. In the event of an emergency, the search area is then limited to the terrain between that airport and the point of departure instead of along the whole route of flight, which might be several hundred miles. That, in itself, could literally be a lifesaver.

Fast file

Depending on the nature of the flight, and if the TIBS briefing indicates that the weather between departure and destination is clearly VFR, the FSS has a system that allows pilots to FAST FILE. This means that they can enter their flight plan directly onto a recording, eliminating the need to talk to a briefer.

Using FAST FILE expedites service because the specialists can be briefing other pilots while you are simply recording your flight plan. To use this service, after making contact with the FSS, simply follow the recorded instructions that access you to FAST FILE. Once accessed, read off the pertinent Flight Plan data. The flight plan is then retrieved from the recording and entered into the computer.

FSS briefing and flight plan filing

Unfortunately, there are still many general aviation pilots who are inclined to scoff at or ignore aviation weather forecasts and briefings, since the weather information they received has not always proved entirely accurate. The adequacy or accuracy of the forecasts concerned in more than 1000 cases has been examined in considerable detail and it was determined that in 80 to 85 percent of these cases, the forecasts effectively depicted the weather conditions with which the pilots would have been faced if they had received these forecasts.

Based on these odds, it's simply not logical for a pilot to start on a flight without full knowledge of the available weather data, including the forecasts. At the same time, though, as any briefer would tell you, weather briefings can report only what's happening right now, and forecasts are only forecasts—not fixed absolutes. In that light, it's almost as bad to have blind faith in weather information and forecasts as to have no faith at all. Suffice it to say, though, that thorough briefings, properly understood and interpreted, are the best bases for deciding whether a flight should be conducted as planned, postponed, altered, or canceled. By any standard, safety is still the most important consideration of all.

Other statistics indicate that on a national basis more than 25 percent of all fatal accidents and more than 31 percent of all fatalities result from taking off or continuing into adverse weather and the subsequent loss of aircraft control. Without instrument training, it is also a fact that the average pilot will lose control of the aircraft in a matter of seconds when outside references are lost. In other words, statistics say that weather-related accidents continue to account for an unnecessarily high number of VFR-pilot fatalities.

The inescapable conclusion, then, is that VFR pilots *must* stay out of weather, and to do this, the limitations as well as the capabilities of present day meteorology must be understood. In that light, and based on even more studies, consider these odds, facts, or conclusions.

- For up to 12 hours and even beyond, a forecast of good weather (ceiling 3000 feet or more and visibility three miles or greater) is much more likely to be correct than is a forecast of conditions below 1000 feet or below one mile.
- However, if below VFR is forecast for three or four hours in advance, the probability that below VFR conditions will occur is more than 80 percent accurate.
- Forecasts of single reportable values of ceilings or visibility instead of a range of values imply an accuracy that the present forecasting system does not possess beyond the first two or three hours of the forecast period.
- Forecasts of poor flying conditions during the first few hours of the forecast period are most reliable when there is a distinct weather system, such as a front, a trough, precipitation, etc., which can be tracked and forecast.
- The weather associated with fast-moving cold fronts and squall lines is the most difficult to forecast accurately.
- Forecasting the specific time of occurrence of bad weather is less accurate than forecasting whether or not the weather will occur within a span of time.
- Surface visibility is more difficult to forecast than ceiling height, and snow increases the visibility forecasting problem.

Available evidence shows that forecasters CAN predict the following at least 75 percent of the time:

- The passage of fast-moving cold fronts or squall lines within plus or minus 2 hours, as much as 10 hours in advance
- The passage of warm fronts or slow-moving cold fronts within plus or minus five hours, up to 12 hours in advance
- The rapid lowering of ceilings below 1000 feet in prewarm front conditions within plus or minus 200 feet and within plus or minus 4 hours
- The onset of a thunderstorm 1 or 2 hours in advance, if radar is available
- The time rain or snow will begin within plus or minus 5 hours
- Rapid deepening of a low pressure center

Although improvements in forecasting have been made, there are still limitations to predicting the following with an accuracy that completely satisfies present aviation operational requirements:

- The time freezing rain will begin
- The location and occurrence of severe or extreme turbulence
- The location and occurrence of heavy icing
- The location or the occurrence of a tornado
- Ceilings of 100 feet or zero before they exist
- The potential development of a thunderstorm
- The position of a hurricane center to nearer than 100 miles for more than 12 hours in advance.
- The occurrence of ice/fog.

These indications of what can and cannot be predicted vary, depending on the climatology and prevailing conditions of the area. Quite logically, rare events are more difficult to predict than common events. Conditions common to an area, such as nighttime radiation fog or afternoon convective clouds, can be forecast more reliably than conditions that occur only sporadically.

Similarly, weather that depends on the interaction of wind flow with mountain ranges, coastal areas, or large bodies of water, are more reliably forecast than similar conditions that are associated with cyclonic storms moving slowly over flat, uniform terrain.

In looking at these statistics and probabilities, it should be apparent that the pilot who predicates safety over several hours of flying on one forecast or briefing is definitely playing Russian roulette. Don't gamble with the weather. It can be a powerful opponent!

Information to give the briefer

When obtaining a live briefing, the information to give the briefer at the very outset is the following and in this sequence:

a. Pilot qualifications, as student, private, commercial, and if instrument rated

b. Type of flight—VFR or IFR

c. Aircraft N-number

d. Aircraft type and special equipment

e. True airspeed

f. Departure point

g. Proposed departure time

h. Proposed cruising altitude

i. Route of flight

j. Destination or first point of landing

k. Estimated time en route

l. Type of briefing desired: Outlook; Abbreviated; Standard.

Note that except for items a and l, the information follows the Flight Plan form sequence from blocks 1 through 10. The balance of the blocks—12 through 17—is given following the briefing, as-suming the weather permits a "go" decision. Just limit your initial contact with a FSS briefer to these a through l items—nothing more. If you do this, you will make your briefer very happy, be-cause one of their common complaints is the lack of information pilots initially supply and/or the disorganization of the informa-tion. If the Flight Plan form is followed from blocks 1 through 12, such complaints will cease.

Remember, though, that the FSS specialist is entering the data in a computer as you read it (or a specialist is writing down the data at a nonautomated FSS). Consequently, speak slowly enough so that the specialist can digest and record what you are saying.

Types of briefings

As suggested in item l above, three types of briefings are available: *Outlook, Abbreviated,* and *Standard.*

An Outlook should be requested when the proposed flight is more than six hours in advance. This generally is a briefing to help determine whether a proposed flight is practical from a weather point of view. The Outlook, however, should always be followed by a Standard briefing closer to the flight departure time.

An Abbreviated is usually requested perhaps an hour or so *after* receiving a Standard and when the pilot wants an update or certain specific information.

The Standard is the complete briefing relative to the route of flight and proposed altitude. When it is requested, the specialist provides the information in the following sequence.

(**Note**: I'd suggest that you make a photocopy of this sequence, or commit it to memory. By so doing, you'll know the flow of the briefing and will be better prepared to copy and understand what is being communicated to you.)

1. Adverse weather conditions.

2. A synopsis of existing fronts and other weather systems along the line of flight. If conditions are unfavorable, the briefer will probably state at this point that "VFR is not recommended." Otherwise, or if you want more information, the briefing will continue.

3. A summary of current weather along the route of flight, based on surface observations, radar observations, and PIREPs.

4. A summary of forecast en route weather.

5. Detailed forecast destination weather.

6. A summary of forecast winds at the proposed altitude range, and if requested, temperatures at that range.

7. NOTAMs, if requested, that could affect the flight.

8. If requested, additional information, such as active MOAs or Military Training Routes.

Remember that this is not a recording. Any time during the recitation that you have questions, don't hesitate to break in. In reality, the briefing is a conversation between two parties, but it's an organized conversation that follows the pattern outlined.

Types of NOTAMs

NOTAMs vary in importance and are classified accordingly into one of three types: *FDC, NOTAM D*, or *NOTAM L*.

FDC NOTAMs are issued by the National Flight Data Center and are regulatory in nature. Most amend standard instrument procedures, designate restricted airspace, or alter the airway structure. They are transmitted nationwide to all FSSs, and FSSs maintain a file of FDC NOTAMs affecting the airspace within 400 nautical miles of their facility.

NOTAM D (Distant NOTAMs) and *NOTAM L (Local NOTAMs)* communicate changes to the published status of airspace obstructions or components of the national airspace system, such as radio or TV tower light outages, runway closures/commissionings, navigational aids out of service, or other system operational deviations.

NOTAM Ds generally contain information that can affect the decision of many pilots about the proposed flight. They are given *distant* (wide) dissemination and are available to FSSs and other weather subscribers nationwide. Current NOTAM Ds are sent by the weather computer network and are compiled and retransmitted every hour, appended to the weather of the affected station.

Something to keep in mind about FDC and NOTAMs D is that conditions reported that are expected to exist for a period of time are published in the next upcoming biweekly issue of the *Notices to Airmen* publication (NTAP). Once published, those NOTAMs are *not* volunteered during weather briefings. Consequently, if you don't have access to the latest NTAP, be sure to ask if there are any two-week-old or longer NOTAMs that would affect your planned flight.

NOTAM Ls contain "nice to know" information or are of interest to relatively few pilots. They are thus given only local dissemination and are usually available only at FSSs with responsibility for the flight plan area in which the NOTAM L applies.

Replotting the flight, if necessary

Now that you've had the standard briefing, do whatever replotting of the flight might be necessary, such as its route, altitude, airspeed calculation, or estimated time en route. If changes are made, simply advise the specialist you talk to when you radio the FSS to open the flight plan. For the most part, assuming the weather permits the flight, the changes should be minor, such as a different altitude to take advantage of better winds or an ETE revision. There is no need to recontact a briefer by phone or in person to submit changes such as these.

Opening the flight plan

If the radio communication facilities to an FSS at a given airport exist, the flight plan should be opened while still on the ground, preferably at the ramp before taxiing out. The only important thing is to mention at the very outset of the call the frequency that you are calling on and the name of the airport. The specialist responding, who is not a briefer, could be monitoring up to as many as 48 different frequencies and almost as many geographic points. As a result, he or she might not know which frequency to activate and reply on unless it is stated in the initial call. The opening call, then is simply:

> **Pilot:** Columbia *Radio*, Cherokee 1234 Alpha on 122.6, Kansas City Downtown.

Remember that "Radio" is always the address when calling Flight Service Stations. The *only* exception is Flight Watch, where the designation *Flight Watch* is included in the address.

If the departing airport has no RCO (Remote Communications Outlet) to the FSS, open the flight plan as soon as possible when airborne by contacting the FSS on the nearest RCO frequency or over a VOR on which the FSS transmits.

En route position reports

While there is no requirement for the VFR pilot to do so, periodic position reports to the nearest FSS is a sound insurance policy. That statement applies even if the pilot is in contact with a Center and receiving traffic advisories. While a Center can be of immeasurable assistance in the event of an emergency, it exists primarily for IFR operations and is not designed to keep an en route progress check of VFR traffic.

On the other hand, the FSS maintains a recording of all position-reporting radio contacts. Consequently, if an emergency develops and the pilot is unable to squawk the 7700 emergency code or contact another facility, the FSS would have a record of the last report. That one call would at least narrow the search between that point and the pilot's filed destination.

The FSS has an almost immediately-retrievable record of a position report, while a Center might have to replay minutes or hours of tape to find any radio transmission with the VFR aircraft. Keeping these facts in mind, whether on a filed flight plan or not, periodic position reports to the nearest en route FSS could be a life saver if you had to be the subject of a search-and-rescue mission. Remember, though, that this type of call goes to an FSS specialist on one of the published FSS frequencies— NOT to Flight Watch on the common 122.0 frequency.

Inflight visibility and the VFR pilot

The obvious meaning of "Visual" Flight Rules is that the pilot can maintain control of the aircraft by visual reference to the ground, ground obstacles, cloud formations, and other aircraft in the area of operation. The clarity of that visual reference is, of course, dependent on how far the pilot can see ahead, below, and to either side of the aircraft. For one not qualified to control the aircraft solely by reference to the instruments, the dangers of reduced external visibility, when coupled with the speed of even small aircraft, are severe. Consequently, as part of the flight planning and arriving at a go/no-go decision, the following might help in the decision-making process.

Visibility vs. time

In order to stay out of clouds, VFR pilots are often forced down to low altitudes. Even when they can remain clear of the clouds, visibility is frequently marginal. In this situation, visibility, in a very real sense, relates to time as much as to distance. Meaning: How many seconds ahead can you see with one mile visibility? How many seconds do you have to perceive, interpret, act, and obtain aircraft reaction?

Cruising at 109 miles per hour (95 knots), an aircraft travels 160 feet per second. Related to one mile visibility, that means you can see 33 seconds ahead. Matters get worse as speed increases and/or visibility decreases! If you're cruising at 177 mph (154 knots), you can see ahead only 20 seconds with one mile visibility. You might think that this is plenty of time to turn before running into zero-zero conditions or to miss an obstruction, but is it? Consider these factors:

Reaction time. It takes time, very precious time under marginal conditions of visibility, for the eye to see something, for the brain to interpret what the eye sees, for the brain to send a message for the muscles to react, and finally for the airplane to respond to control movements. On the average, all this consumes from 4 to 5 seconds. Now subtract those seconds from the 20 to 30 seconds that you can see ahead, and it's obvious that at certain speeds it would be impossible to miss the zero-zero conditions or an obstruction. At 184 mph (160 knots), with a reaction time of 5 seconds, the aircraft travels 1350 feet before anything even begins to happen in the way of evasive action.

Radius of turn. Suppose you must turn away from a range of hills or a mountain, or a low-lying cloud bank. If flying at 154 knots, the aircraft will have moved in the direction of this obstruction approximately 3700 feet by the time a 90° turn is completed (1298 feet for reaction time, plus 2457 feet for radius of turn). If visibility is less than three-quarters of a mile, it would be impossible to miss the obstruction without the help of a strong headwind. With a tailwind and only one mile visibility, it would be even more hazardous. If you ever get caught in such restricted visibility, low-altitude conditions, about the only thing you can do to maximize any possible maneuvering room is to fly at a reduced speed.

The cockpit cutoff angle and inflight visibility

All too often, adequate visibility at the surface becomes marginal, or even below minimums, at altitude, yet the VFR pilot may continue on simply because surface visibilities are reported at values comfortably above minimums. Some method of determining inflight visibility with reasonable accuracy is, therefore, important. A rule of thumb (Fig. 10-6) that is not equally accurate for all airplanes but is better than guessing is as follows:

The approximate visibility in miles equals the number of thousands of feet above the surface when the surface is just visible over the nose of the airplane. In other words, at the point where the surface first appears over the nose of the airplane, the slant-range visibility is approximately two miles if the flight is at 2000 feet above the surface. This rule of thumb is based on the cockpit cutoff angle. Of course, since all airplanes don't have the same cutoff angle, the

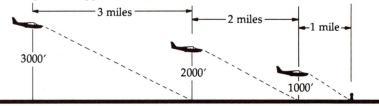

Rule of Thumb when surface is just visible over nose of aircraft the forward visibility will be approximately 1 mile for each 1,000 feet altitude.

Fig. 10-6. *The rule of thumb for determining forward visibility.*

rule of thumb is not equally accurate for all airplanes. But, as is explained in a moment, the cockpit cutoff angle for any airplane can be rather easily determined on the ground. Once established for a given airplane, it remains constant as long as the eye level of the pilot is not changed. The steps in establishing this cutoff angle on the ground are:

1. Adjust the aircraft's ground attitude to correspond as closely as possible to its typical cruise pitch attitude.

2. While seated normally, adjust the pilot's seat to the same position used in flight.

3. Measure the vertical distance from eye level to the ground (six feet in the example).

4. Look straight out over the nose of the airplane (cockpit cutoff angle) and determine the spot where the surface is first visible.

5. Measure the distance from directly under the eye position to the spot established in step 4 (30 feet in the example).

6. At this point the visibility can be determined either by establishing a simple proportion, or by solving for the tangent value, using the information in the following table in Fig. 10-7. In either case, the result represents the least slant-range visibility that could be obtained when flying at 1000 feet above the ground.

Tangent Value Method (Fig. 10-7): The tangent value (tan ϖ) is equal to 6 feet divided by 30 feet or, tan $\theta V = 6/30$, tan $\theta V = .20$.

Referring to the information in the table and locating the value closest to .2, it is apparent that the cutoff angle is somewhere between 11° and 12°. Accurate interpolation reveals that with this cutoff angle the visibility is 5000 feet.

Proportion Method: Six feet is to 30 feet as 1000 feet is to "X" feet.

$$\frac{6 \text{ feet}}{30 \text{ feet}} = \frac{1000 \text{ feet}}{X \text{ feet}} \text{ (or)}$$

$$6X = 30,000 \text{ feet}$$
$$X = 5,000 \text{ feet}$$

Please understand that in either case the visibility would be the very least that could be obtained from the cockpit to the ground straight ahead. It can, of course, be more than this in respect to slant range, but if the ground can be seen at this altitude, it cannot be less. Horizontally or laterally, visibility might be more or significantly less, de-

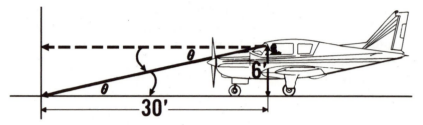

All measurements are from pilot's eye level

Tangent value	Angle (°)	Approximate visibility at 1000 feet agl
0.052	3	19,000 ft. (5280 feet = 1 statute mile)
.070	4	14,280
.087	5	11,500
.105	6	9530
.123	7	8130
.141	8	7090
.158	9	6330
.176	10	5750
.194	11	5150
.213	12	4710
.231	13	4320
.249	14	4010
.268	15	3730
.287	16	3480
.306	17	3270
.325	18	3070
.344	19	2910
.364	20	2750

Note: At 500 feet above the ground, visibility in feet would be approximately half of the 1000-foot value.

Fig. 10-7. *You can determine the cockpit cutoff angle and the tangent value for forward visibility based on pilot's eye level—all on the ground.*

pending on inflight weather conditions. However, the visibility to the ground ahead (a primary VFR reference for aircraft control) would, in the example cited, be at least 5000 feet. If the pilot must descend in order to see the ground over the nose of the airplane, the slant-range visibility is proportionally less.

Some general planning recommendations

In summary, and to contribute further to arriving at a wise go/no-go decision in VFR flight planning, I offer the following recommendations as well as warnings:

- Access the FSS facilities, (TIBS, PATWAS, briefing specialists), to determine if the flight can be conducted safely. Consider personal skills, experience, and aircraft equipment in making the go/no-go decision. If there is any doubt, DON'T GO. Otherwise, once the flight has been started, get current weather updates through HIWAS, TWEBs, and Flight Watch. Give Flight Watch Pilot Reports (PIREPs) if conditions other than forecast are encountered (icing, turbulence, precipitation, clouds, etc.).

- File a flight plan, either through the briefer or via FAST FILE.

- Request an ARTCC to give you en route traffic advisories.

- Give periodic position reports to the nearest FSS on its published frequency or on 122.2, the universal frequency to all FSSs.

- Amend or extend the filed plan with the nearest FSS over the published frequency or 122.2, if it appears that the ETA will be 30 minutes or more later than originally filed.

- If flying over extended areas of swampland, mountains, or water, request "Flight Following" (not previously mentioned) from the nearest FSS. This requires position reports every 10 minutes to the FSS. When a report is not received, or if the FSS cannot contact the pilot, the initial search-and-rescue steps are taken.

- Become thoroughly familiar with inflight emergency procedures, frequencies, and transponder codes, (many of which are discussed in the next chapter).

- If not instrument rated, avoid "VFR on Top" flight. Being caught above an overcast when it comes time to descend for whatever reason places the VFR pilot in a very hazardous position. There is not only the danger of IFR aircraft operating in the clouds or overcast and the potential midair collision, but the strong possibility that the noninstrument-trained pilot will experience total disorientation, with disastrous results.

- Avoid flight through or near thunderstorms. Research has proven beyond any doubt that all thunderstorms are potentially dangerous and should be given a wide berth.

- Avoid flight through areas of known or forecast severe weather, because tornadoes, squall lines, hail, and severe or extreme turbulence might be encountered. At the same time, severe or extreme clear air turbulence (CAT) could be encountered at low and intermediate levels up to 20 miles ahead of squall lines. The "roll cloud" ahead of such a line is a visible sign of violent turbulence, but the absence of a roll cloud doesn't necessarily mean that no turbulence exists.

- Avoid flight through areas of known or forecast icing conditions, unless the aircraft is equipped with deicing/anti-icing devices. Ice accumulation through areas of freezing precipitation and wet snow can be rapid and heavy. In addition to airframe icing, carburetor icing can occur when visible moisture is present and/or when moisture is not visible under the right atmospheric conditions (i.e., low temperature, high humidity).

- Avoid flight at low altitudes over mountainous terrain, particularly near the leeward slopes. If the wind velocity near the level of the ridge is in excess of 40 knots and approximately perpendicular to the ridge, mountain wave conditions are likely over and near the lee slopes. If the velocity at the level of the ridge exceeds 50 knots, a strong mountain wave is probable with strong up and down drafts and severe or extreme turbulence. The worst turbulence will be encountered in and below the rotor zone, which is usually 8 to 10 miles downwind of the ridge. This zone is characterized by the presence of "roll clouds" if sufficient moisture is present. Altocumulus standing lenticular clouds are also visible signs that a mountain wave exists, but their presence is likewise dependent upon moisture. The mountain wave downdrafts may well exceed the climb capability of the aircraft.

- Avoid areas of low ceilings and restricted visibility, unless instrument-proficient and flying an instrument-equipped aircraft. Even then, proceed with caution and have planned alternates.

- Use caution when landing on runways that are covered with water or slush, either of which can cause hydroplaning (aquaplaning). This is a phenomenon that renders braking and steering ineffective because of the lack of sufficient surface friction. Snow- and ice-covered runways are obviously also hazardous.

- Use caution when taking off or landing during gusty wind conditions.
- Avoid taking off or landing too close behind large aircraft. "Wake turbulence" caused by these aircraft can be hazardous.

These are just a few of the recommendations and warnings relative to VFR flight. In addition to the others that have been previously suggested, and those that follow in the next chapters, the hope is that new as well as experienced pilots will heed the various suggestions and thereby enjoy the full measure of pleasure that flight can bring.

Quickie quiz questions
Chapter 10

1. What are the three types of weather briefings and the purpose of each?

2. What information, and in what sequence, should you give an FSS briefer when you want a standard briefing.

3. You're planning a 400-mile trip, with a stop about halfway for fuel and a bite of lunch. Should you file your flight plan to that stop or to your final destination? Explain your answer.

4. If you open a flight plan by radio, what should you keep in mind about the FSS specialist's workstation and information the specialist needs before he or she can promptly respond to your call? How would you phrase the introductory portion of that call?

5. What factors, features, and weather phenomena should you consider if a proposed flight will take you over or near mountainous terrain?

6. If you are cruising at a 95-knot airspeed in one-mile visibility,

   A. How many seconds ahead of you can you see?

   B. How many additional seconds would it take to see an object one mile ahead, interpret what you saw, act, and allow for aircraft reaction?

7. If an FSS briefer says, "VFR is not recommended," how should you interpret the statement? Can you legally still make the flight, despite that recommendation?

8. What is "Fast File?"

9. "NOTAM" is the acronym for what? What are the three types of NOTAMs?

10. What charts, references, or manuals should you have on hand when planning a cross-country flight?

Answers in Appendix, pages 581-583.

11

Emergency procedures

If you fly long enough, the possibility that you will sooner or later encounter a nonroutine situation is fairly good. If that time comes, how you handle the situation may have a critical bearing on the final outcome and the extent to which a relatively minor problem remains just a minor problem.

The unexpected is always a possibility, and no one can unfailingly have the very best solution to every crisis at one's fingertips. Each of us can, however, mentally conjure up the more likely crises we could face as pilots—crises such as an engine failure during the various stages of takeoff, at cruising altitude, in the traffic pattern, or on final approach; fuel shortage on a cross-country; radio failure just before entering a Class B airspace; an unexplained vibration in the airplane; the beginning of wing-ice accumulation; a lowering overcast that keeps forcing you down and down; and so on. The list does have an end, but at times it may seem endless.

Preparation for the expected is a routine part of flight planning; preparation for the unexpected should be just as much a routine, even if you're only going around the pattern.

Whatever the situation, though, the pilot in command of an aircraft is directly responsible for and is the final authority on the operation of the aircraft. That means, basically, that rules and regulations become secondary to getting the airplane safely back on the ground. As FAR 91.3(b) states it: "In an inflight emergency requiring immediate action, the pilot in command may deviate from any rule of this Part to the extent required to meet that emergency." In the process, though, the FAA stresses that the pilot should immediately request help through radio contact with a Tower, an FSS, or a Center.

Of course, there's a bit of catch to the freedoms 91.3 permits, in that a pilot who does deviate from the rules may be requested by the Administrator to submit a report of the deviation. The potential of receiving such a "request" should discourage anyone from violating Part 91 rules under the pretense of an emergency when, in fact, there was no emergency at all.

Aviation emergencies defined

The FAA classifies emergencies as *distress* or *urgency*. A distress condition is one of fire, mechanical failure, or structural failure. An urgency is not necessarily immediately perilous but could be potentially catastrophic, as being lost, a low fuel supply, weather, pilot illness, or any other condition that could affect flight safety. When an *urgency* develops, ask for help *now* before it becomes a distress situation.

While AIM, in Chapter 6, reviews the appropriate emergency procedures in detail, the following summarizes some of the essential elements for the VFR land pilot. Several of the elements have been previously discussed or emphasized, but, to one degree or another, are repeated here because of the importance of the subject to pilot safety and well-being.

Transponder operation in an emergency

When a *distress* or *urgency* situation arises, pilots with a coded aircraft transponder should immediately enter the 7700 emergency code and then attempt to establish radio communications with an ATC facility.

The 7700 code appears on the screens of all radar-equipped facilities within range of their radar coverage and, by sound as well as a flashing blip on the screen, attracts the controllers' attention. Even if not in radio contact with the aircraft, the facility, or facilities, are alerted to the existence of an aircraft in trouble and, if nothing else, can at least track it on radar and notify other agencies of the emergency situation.

Radio communications in an emergency

If you are in contact with a Tower, a Center, or an FSS when either a *distress* or an *urgency* develops, the communications would obviously be directed to that facility. A *distress* message should start with the word "Mayday" and be repeated at least three times. (Mayday comes from the French, "M'aidez," is pronounced "Mayday," and means "help me.") In an *urgency*, the term "Pan-pan," again repeated three times, starts the radio transmission.

- *Distress* messages have absolute priority over all others, and the word "Mayday" commands radio silence on the frequency in use.

- *Urgency* messages have priority over all others except *distress*. "Pan-pan" warns other stations not to interfere with *urgency* transmissions.

If, as the pilot, you have not been receiving services from an ATC facility, and if time permits, you should immediately try to contact the center, tower, or FSS in whose area of responsibility you are flying. By so doing, a more rapid response to your call is likely—which is another reason for listing the various en route frequencies in the preflight planning and having the list immediately available in the cockpit.

Conditions might be such, though, that there is no time to search for the correct frequency, even though a list had been prepared. In that event, two other frequencies can be used: the *emergency-only* frequencies of 121.5 or 243.0. Both have a range that is generally limited to line of sight. 121.5 is guarded by direction finding stations and certain military and civil aircraft, while 243.0 is guarded by military aircraft. In addition, both frequencies are guarded by military towers, most civil towers, FSSs, and radar facilities.

Again, if time permits, the most logical facility to try to reach first is the ARTCC in whose area you are flying, but the ARTCC's emergency frequency capability does not normally extend to its radar coverage limits. If the ARTCC does not respond when called on 121.5 or 243.0, address the call to the nearest Tower or FSS.

Time is crucial in a *distress* condition, but as much of the following as possible, preferably in the order suggested, should be communicated:

1. Mayday, Mayday, Mayday or Pan-pan, Pan-pan, Pan-pan.
2. Name of facility addressed

3. Aircraft identification and type

4. Nature of distress or urgency

5. Weather

6. Pilot's intentions and request

7. Present position and heading, or if lost, last known position, time, and heading since that position

8. Altitude or flight level

9. Hours and minutes of fuel remaining

10. Any other useful information, as visible landmarks, aircraft color, emergency equipment on board, number of people on board

11. Activate the ELT (Emergency Locator Transmitter) if installation permits.

Pilot responsibilities

Once in contact with a ground facility, the pilot's responsibilities are:

- Comply with advice and instructions, if at all possible.
- Cooperate.
- Ask questions or clarify instructions not understood or that you cannot comply with.
- Assist the ground facility in controlling communications on the frequency. Silence interfering stations.
- Do not change frequencies or change to another ground facility unless absolutely necessary.
- If you do change frequency, always advise the ground facility of the new frequency and station before making the change.
- If two-way communication with the new frequency cannot be established, return immediately to the frequency where communication last existed.

Remember the four Cs:

1. Confess the predicament to any ground station.

2. Communicate as much of distress/urgency message as possible.

3. Comply with instructions and advice.

4. Climb, if possible, for better radar detection and radio contact.

The emergency locator transmitter (ELT)

Emergency Locator Transmitters (ELTs) are required by FAR 91 for most general aviation aircraft, although certain exceptions are allowed. The purpose of the ELT is to help locate downed aircraft. These are battery-operated transmitters that, when subjected to crash-generated forces, transmit a distinctive and continuous audio signal on 121.5 and 243.0. The life of a transmitter is 48 hours over a wide range of temperatures.

Depending on its location in the aircraft, some ELTs can be activated by the pilot. In other installations, the ELT is secured elsewhere in the fuselage and can't be accessed in flight. This type of ELT is activated by impact.

Because of their importance in search-and-rescue (SAR) operations, ELT batteries are legal for 50 percent of their manufacturer-established shelf life, after which they must be replaced. Periodic ground checks of an ELT should be made, but only in accordance with the procedures outlined in AIM.

Direction-finding help

Direction Finding (DF) equipment has long been used to locate and guide lost aircraft to airports, areas of good weather, or just to orient a lost pilot as to his or her location. When lost, either a DF fix ("Tell me where I am") or a DF steer ("Direct me to good weather or to an airport") should be requested from the nearest facility (Tower, Center, or FSS).

Even in instrument conditions, DF-equipped facilities can help VFR pilots in a distress or urgency situation. Because most emergencies requiring DF assistance involve pilots with minimum flight experience, the DF specialist gives the pilot headings to fly and when to begin to let down, using small turns and wing-level descents to provide maximum flight stability.

There need not be a literal emergency to request a DF fix or steer. For example, you're flying in clear weather with an ample fuel supply, but you're just plain lost. For whatever reason, trying to obtain a position fix by tuning to VORs, NDBs, or any combination of ground radio aids proves futile. Before matters deteriorate, you think it would be wise to contact the nearest FSS or ATC facility, explain the situation, and ask for either a DF fix or a DF steer.

The facility, let's say an FSS, has various means—some more sophisticated than others—to determine the aircraft's position, and all the pilot really has to do is provide the minimum information the specialist wants: aircraft identification and type, if transponder-equipped, nature of the emergency, general geographic location, and the pilot's intentions. From then on, it is just a matter of following the specialist's instructions. Perhaps keying the mike (depressing the button) without saying anything for 10 seconds, squawking 7700, resetting the directional gyro to the magnetic compass heading, turning the aircraft to certain headings, and so on.

If the facility is equipped with current state-of-the-art DF equipment, a DF fix can be almost immediate. Otherwise, position-determination might require certain maneuvering, tuning to a VOR or an NDB, or obtaining radials off two VORs. Some of these you can do without contacting any ground facility, if you have the navigation equipment and a sectional chart on board (which you should); but, inexperience, heightening anxiety, or other factors, might require the immediate help of an FSS or ATC, for either just a position fix or vectors and guidance to the nearest airport.

The National Search and Rescue (SAR) Plan

While I've referred several times to the National Search and Rescue Plan (SAR), a general understanding of the system can be helpful to the VFR pilot. In essence, the services provided under the Plan include search for missing aircraft, survival aid, rescue, and emergency medical aid for survivors after location of the accident site.

The operational resources are provided by the Coast Guard, DOD (Department of Defense) components, the Civil Air Patrol, the Coast Guard Auxiliary, state, county, and local law enforcement, other public safety agencies, and private volunteer organizations. Through federal interagency agreement, the Plan provides for the effective use of all available facilities in all types of SAR missions. These facilities include aircraft, vessels, pararescue and ground rescue teams, and emergency radio fixing.

The United States Coast Guard is responsible for SAR coordination in the Maritime Region and has Rescue Coordination Centers (RCCs) in Boston, New York, Portsmouth, Virginia, Miami, Cleveland, St. Louis, New Orleans, Long Beach, California, San Francisco, Seattle, Juneau, Alaska, Honolulu, and San Juan. The USAF is responsible for the Inland Region, with its RCC based at Langley Air Force Base, Virginia, Elmendorf AFB, Alaska, and a Joint Rescue Coordination Center in Hawaii. The various RCCs are established to direct SAR activities within their region.

Overdue aircraft

ARTCCs and FSSs alert the SAR system when information is received from any source that an aircraft is in difficulty, overdue, or missing. As *AIM* states, "A filed flight plan is the most timely and effective indicator that an aircraft is overdue," and the flight plan information is invaluable in the SAR efforts. *AIM* further advises that prior to departure on any flight, local or otherwise, someone at the departure point should know your intentions or, if on a cross-country, your destination and route of flight.

To receive search and rescue protection, the advice, once again, is to file a flight plan but only to the first point of intended landing, not the final destination on a multistop itinerary.

SAR action steps

To illustrate the steps of the Search and Rescue Plan, let's assume that the pilot has filed a flight plan but fails to close it on arrival at the destination. Beginning at the very beginning so that the whole scenario is clear, these are the step-by-step actions:

1. The pilot radios Flight Service Station "A" at departure point to activate his filed flight plan.

2. The inflight specialist sends the basic flight plan information to the FSS, say FSS "B," responsible for the area in which the pilot's destination airport is located. All that "A" transmits are Blocks 2, 3, 9, and 10 of the Flight Plan form: the aircraft N-number, type, destination, and ETA.

3. The pilot lands at the airport named as the destination, or at some other airport, and fails to close out the flight plan with any FSS.

4. Thirty minutes after the ETA, the computer in FSS B flashes the flight plan data sent by A, indicating the flight is overdue and the pilot hasn't closed the flight plan.

5. FSS B sends a query to A to determine if the pilot actually departed or had been delayed.

6. FSS A calls the pilot's departure airport to verify his actual departure.

7. Because the pilot did depart, A so notifies B and sends the balance of the flight plan: route of flight, fuel on board, number of passengers, the pilot's name and address, and so on.

8. FSS B calls the Tower or FBO at the pilot's intended destination to see if the flight has landed.

9. If so, and the aircraft is located, the search is ended. If not, or if the aircraft can't be located or the pilot landed at another airport, the search continues.

10. One hour after the ETA, B initiates an INREQ (Request for Information) to all facilities along the route of flight, including Center(s) and Towers, to determine if any facility had heard from the pilot. If so, the search can be focused on the geography between the last reporting point and the pilot's intended destination. A copy of the INREQ is also usually sent to the applicable SAR unit, Coast Guard or USAF, alerting it to the possibility of a downed aircraft.

11. If there has been no recorded or immediately available evidence of any en route contact, all FSSs along the route of flight begin telephoning every airport 50 miles either side of the pilot's route.

12. If these efforts prove futile, an ALNOT (Alert Notice) is sent to every FAA facility along the flight route.

13. Each facility does further checking, such as playing back tapes to try to find any record of a radio contact with the pilot. The SAR unit alerts the Civil Air Patrol. The Air Force also might enter the investigation at this point, contacting family or business associates to determine if anyone has heard from the pilot or if he or she had indicated any possible route deviation before departing. All FSSs in the area broadcast over the VORs each hour that an aircraft has been lost and ask pilots to monitor 121.5 (the emergency frequency) for an activated ELT.

14. The physical search begins.

Depending on the situations listed below, pilots could prevent the first SAR steps from ever being activated if they would just follow these suggestions:

- If you land and terminate your flight for any reason at a location other than your intended destination, call the nearest FSS immediately, explain the situation, inform the briefer of your original destination, and request that your flight plan be closed. Nationwide, all you have to do to reach an FSS is dial 1-800-WX-BRIEF.

- If you land en route and are delayed more than 30 minutes, revise your ETA as necessary, call the nearest FSS and advise the specialist of your original destination and the new ETA. Remember that the first SAR step begins 30 minutes after your estimated time of arrival.

- If your estimated time en route changes by 30 minutes or more while in flight, and the change will affect your Flight Plan ETA, radio the nearest FSS and report your new and revised ETA.

- After arrival at the intended destination, immediately close your flight plan with the FSS designated to you when you filed it. This is the pilot's responsibility. The flight plan will not automatically be closed by any ATC facility.

- The SAR procedures can be time-consuming and costly, should you have an emergency and no one knows where you were going, when you left, or where you are. Failure to file a flight plan, or to close it out, if you did file one, or to keep the FSSs informed of unscheduled landings, revised ETAs, and the like, start the same SAR actions as if it were a bona fide accident. If we would think of all the people who could become involved in an S&R, the ground and air costs associated with a search, the time consumed, perhaps we would be more attentive to the importance of closing out our flight plans and keeping the related agencies informed as to our status.

Observance of a downed aircraft

An SAR mission can be greatly expedited if a pilot happens to observe a downed aircraft and follows the steps outlined in *AIM*:

1. Determine if the crash is marked with a yellow cross. If so, the crash has already been reported and identified.

2. If possible, determine the aircraft type and N-number and if there is evidence of any survivors.

3. Fix the position as accurately as possible with reference to a navigational aid. Also, provide geographic or physical descriptions of the area to assist ground search parties.

4. Transmit the information to the nearest FAA or appropriate radio facility.

5. If circumstances permit, circle the scene to guide other assisting units or until you are relieved by another aircraft.

6. Immediately after landing, make a complete report to the nearest FAA facility or Air Force or Coast Guard Rescue Coordination Center. The report can be made by long distance collect telephone.

Figure 11-1 illustrates the ground-air visual codes for use by survivors and by ground search parties, while Fig. 11-2 sketches the visual emergency signals from ground-to-air and from air-to-ground. Having a copy of these figures aboard the airplane could be a lifesaver for a downed pilot as well as assisting ground SAR parties whom you have observed from the air.

When the radio fails

When partial or complete radio failure occurs or appears probable, the first thing to do is to check the ammeter to see if it is showing a charge. If so, then check the circuit breakers. If a navcom button has popped, let it cool off for a couple of minutes before resetting it. Perhaps that will correct the problem.

If the ammeter shows no charge at all, test it by turning on the landing light. If the needle doesn't move, the alternator has probably failed or its belt has broken. In either case, any electrical power that remains is coming only from the battery. If that's the situation, turn off all nonessential electrical equipment, except the transponder and one radio (assuming any reception is possible), and head for the nearest airport. You won't lose the engine, because the ignition system is independent of the battery-alternator system, but a functioning engine, as essential as that is, is about all you'll have left.

At this point, change the transponder squawk to 7600. This squawk alerts all FAA facilities within radar coverage that an aircraft is out there with partial or total radio failure. While contact with the pilot might not be possible, the aircraft can be tracked and the airport, particularly a tower-controlled airport, to which the aircraft appears to be proceeding can be alerted to the situation.

While direct help from the ground is unlikely, especially with a complete radio failure, the 7600 squawk and adherence to the radio failure

NO.	MESSAGE	CODE SYMBOL
1	Require assistance	V
2	Require medical assistance	X
3	No or Negative	N
4	Yes or Affirmative	Y
5	Proceeding in this direction	↑

IF IN DOUBT, USE INTERNATIONAL SYMBOL **S O S**

INSTRUCTIONS

1. Lay out symbols by using strips of fabric or parachutes, pieces of wood, stones, or any available material.
2. Provide as much color contrast as possible between material used for symbols and background against which symbols are exposed.
3. Symbols should be at least 10 feet high or larger. Care should be taken to lay out symbols exactly as shown.
4. In addition to using symbols, every effort is to be made to attract attention by means of radio, flares, smoke, or other available means.
5. On snow covered ground, signals can be made by dragging, shoveling or tramping. Depressed areas forming symbols will appear black from the air.
6. Pilot should acknowledge message by rocking wings from side to side.

GROUND-AIR VISUAL CODE FOR USE BY GROUND SEARCH PARTIES

NO.	MESSAGE	CODE SYMBOL
1	Operation completed.	L L L
2	We have found all personnel.	L L
3	We have found only some personnel.	╫
4	We are not able to continue. Returning to base.	X X
5	Have divided into two groups. Each proceeding in direction indicated.	⚡
6	Information received that aircraft is in this direction.	━ ━►
7	Nothing found. Will continue search.	N N

"Note: These visual signals have been accepted for international use and appear in Annex 12 to the Convention on International Civil Aviation."

Fig. 11-1. *Having a copy of these emergency signals in the cockpit might help save someone's life, perhaps—just perhaps—even your own.*

procedures outlined earlier in this handbook (overflying the airport, watching for light signals, acknowledging light signals by wing dips, etc.) will contribute to a safe landing. In all cases, however, it is far preferable to head for an uncontrolled field rather than one that has a tower and the activity that warrants such a traffic controlling facility.

NEED MEDICAL ASSISTANCE– URGENT Used only when life is at stake	**ALL OK– DO NOT WAIT** Wave one arm overhead	**CAN PROCEED SHORTLY–WAIT IF PRACTICABLE** One arm horizontal	**NEED MECHANICAL HELP OR PARTS– LONG DELAY** Both arms horizontal
USE DROP MESSAGE Make throwing motion	**OUR RECEIVER IS OPERATING** Cup hands over ears	**DO NOT ATTEMPT TO LAND HERE** Both arms waved across face	**LAND HERE** Both arms forward horizontally, squatting and point in direction of landing—Repeat
NEGATIVE (NO) White cloth waved horizontally	**AFFIRMATIVE (YES)** White cloth waved vertically	**PICK US UP– PLANE ABANDONED** Both arms vertical	**AFFIRMATIVE (YES)** Dip nose of plane several times

NEGATIVE (NO)
Fishtail plane

HOW TO USE THEM

If you are forced down and are able to attract the attention of the pilot of a rescue airplane, the body signals illustrated on this page can be used to transmit messages to him as he circles over your location. Stand in the open when you make the signals. Be sure that the background, as seen from the air, is not confusing. Go through the motions slowly and repeat each signal until you are positive that the pilot understands you.

Fig. 11-2. *A copy of these, also in the cockpit, could materially help you or someone else in the search-and-rescue operation.*

Be prepared

Preparing for an emergency, whatever the nature, should be the highest priority of every pilot, whether VFR, IFR, experienced, or inexperienced. A first key question to ask before any flight is: "What could go wrong?" Then the next key question: "If 'What could go wrong' did go wrong, what would I do?" Or, said in other ways, what actions should I take to handle the problem? What options have I considered to counteract the situation? Do I *know* what to do if I had an engine fire, an electrical fire, a cabin fire? Do I know what to say in a Mayday call? Do I have a list of the key emergency frequencies? Do I know in what sequence I would do things if I had engine problems, a fire, structural failure, or any other serious inflight problem? What would I do if a passenger had all the symptoms of a heart attack? And on and on the questions could go. Before launching forth, we might well ask one more: Do I have the answers?

All of which is only a discipline called *Potential Problem Analysis* (PPA), or the process of anticipating potential problems, developing solutions, and then having plans of action should the problem ever materialize.

The pilot who lives to a ripe old age is always ahead of the airplane and is always as prepared as possible to prevent emergencies from ever occurring at all. Persons and machines, however, being what they are, problems can still arise. This is where potential problem analysis enters the picture and where it can be so critical when *distress* or *urgency* situations are no longer potentials but suddenly become the real thing.

Quickie quiz questions
Chapter 11

1. In a bona fide emergency, you can violate any Federal Aviation Regulation. True or False: _____

2. What is the difference between a distress and an urgency situation?

3. What are the two universal emergency-only radio frequencies?

4. What does this V ground-to-air symbol emergency symbol mean?

5. From the pilot's point of view, the four Cs in an emergency are: _____ ; _____ ; _____ ; _____

6. What are the transponder squawk codes for:

  A. Radio failure? _____

  B. A distress or urgency? _____

7. The radio call, "Mayday," means what and is used when?

8. You have made a forced landing and one of your passengers is severely injured. To communicate the need for help to any aircraft in the vicinity, what visual code could you use and/or what body position could you assume?

9. The Emergency Locator Transmitter (ELT):

  A. Transmits on what frequencies? _____

  B. Is legal for what percentage of its shelf life? _____

  C. Transmits what sort of signal? _____

10. In being mentally prepared for an emergency, what should every pilot ask him/herself before taking off? After mentally answering that question, what follow-up question should he or she then ask?

Answers in Appendix, pages 584-586.

12

Wake turbulence

Every airplane generates a wake while in flight. Years ago, when pilots initially encountered this phenomenon, it was attributed to, or called, "prop wash." It's known now, though, that the disturbance is primarily caused by a pair of counterrotating vortices trailing from the wing tips. These vortices generated by large aircraft can pose serious problems to encountering aircraft, such as the wake creating rolling movement that exceeds the roll control capability of certain aircraft. Further, turbulence generated within the vortices can damage aircraft components and equipment if encountered at close range. Considering the risks, the only answer for pilots is to learn to visualize the location of the vortex wake generated by large aircraft and then stay out of it!

Jet blast turbulence

Wake turbulence is a function of an aircraft in motion, whether it be in a takeoff, landing, or inflight mode. Meanwhile, back on the ground, there is another form of "turbulence," if you will, that also has the potential to be highly destructive. Call it "thrust stream turbulence," or more simply, just "jet blast."

During ground operations, this jet engine blast can cause severe damage if encountered at close range. Exhaust velocity versus distance studies at various thrust levels have shown the need for light aircraft to maintain a healthy ground separation from jets during taxi or breakaway (from a standstill position) operations. For instance, below are examples of the distance requirements to avoid exhaust velocities of greater than 25 mph, created by some of the older jets:

25 MPH Velocity	B-727	DC-8	DC-10
Takeoff thrust	550 feet	700 feet	2,100 feet
Breakaway thrust	200 feet	400 feet	850 feet
Idle thrust	150 feet	350 feet	350 feet

Engine exhaust velocities generated by large jet aircraft during initial takeoff roll and the drifting of the turbulence as a result of the crosswind component indicate how important it is for lighter aircraft awaiting takeoff to hold well back of the taxiway hold line. These exhaust velocities also make it clear that lighter aircraft should align themselves in tandem fashion behind jets rather than being caught at right angles where the blast would strike the full exposed side of the smaller plane. At the same time, in the course of taxiing and applying breakaway power, the pilots of the large aircraft should consider the effects of their jet blasts on other aircraft in their vicinity.

To minimize the potential of damage caused by jets taking off, the FAA has established these standards for the location of taxiway hold lines: Hold lines are 100 feet from the edge of the runway, except at locations where "heavy" jets (those capable of takeoff weights of 300,000 pounds or more) are operating. There, the hold line markings are 150 feet.

Vortex generation

Lift is generated by the creation of a pressure differential over the wing surface. The lowest pressure occurs over the upper wing surface and the highest pressure under the wing. This pressure differential triggers the roll-up of the airflow aft of the wing, resulting in swirling air masses trailing downstream of the wing tips. After the roll-up is completed, the wake consists of two counterrotating cylindrical vortices (Fig. 12-1).

Vortex strength

The strength of the vortex is governed by the weight, speed, and shape of the wing of the generating aircraft. The vortex characteristics of any given aircraft can also be changed by extension of flaps or other wing

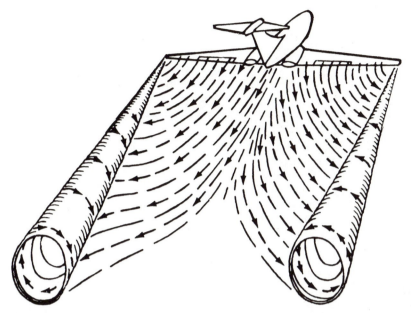

Fig. 12-1. *The pressure differential over the wing culminates in two counterrotating vortices.*

configuring devices, as well as by change in speed. However, since the basic factor is weight, the vortex strength increases proportionately. During one test, peak vortex tangential velocities were recorded at 24 feet per second, or about 133 knots. The greatest vortex strength occurs when the generating aircraft is heavy, clean, and slow.

Induced roll. In rare instances, a wake encounter could cause inflight structural damage of catastrophic proportions. However, the usual hazard is associated with induced rolling moments that can exceed the rolling capability of the encountering aircraft. Aircraft have been intentionally flown directly up trailing vortex cores of large aircraft, and the experiments indicated that an aircraft's capability to counteract the vortex roll depended primarily on the encountering aircraft's wingspan and its countercontrol responsiveness.

Countercontrol is usually effective and induced roll minimal in cases where the wingspan and ailerons of the encountering aircraft extend beyond the rotational flow field of the vortex. It's more difficult for aircraft with a short wingspan (relative to the generating aircraft) to counter the imposed roll induced by vortex flow. Pilots of short span aircraft, even of the high performance type, must be especially alert to vortex encounters (Fig. 12-2).

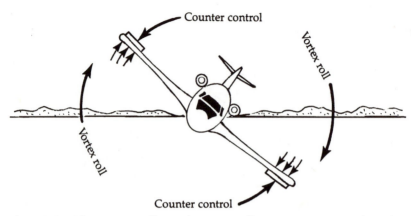

Fig. 12-2. *The vortex roll can be especially serious in aircraft with short wingspans.*

Said simply, the wake of large aircraft requires the respect of all pilots.

Vortex behavior

Trailing vortices have certain behavioral characteristics that can help you visualize the wake location and take avoidance precautions accordingly. Vortices are generated from the moment aircraft leave the ground because they are a by-product of wing lift. When viewed from either ahead or behind the generating aircraft, the vortex circulation is outward, upward, and around the wing tips. Tests with large aircraft have shown that the vortex flow field in a plane cutting through the wake at any point downstream covers an area about two wingspans in width and one wingspan in depth.

In landing or taking off, even when drifting with the wind, the vortices remain so spaced (about a wingspan apart) at altitudes greater than a wingspan from the ground. In view of this pattern, and assuming you're following a departing or arriving jet, note where the jet rotates for takeoff or touches down when landing. Then, to avoid the wake turbulence, plan to take off *before* the spot where the jet rotated and land further down the runway from where it touched down (Fig. 12- 3). If you're then encountering persistent vortex turbulence, a slight change of altitude and lateral position (preferably upwind) should smooth things out for you.

Flight tests have shown that the vortices from large aircraft sink at a rate of about 400 to 500 feet per minute and then tend to level off at

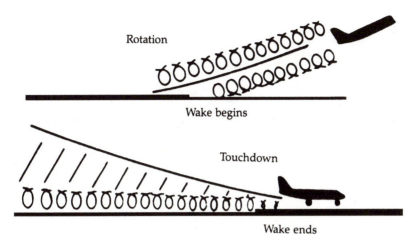

Fig. 12-3. *To avoid wake turbulence, note the rotation and touchdown points of large aircraft then remember the principles. "Take off before, land after" (those respective points).*

about 900 feet below the flight path of the generating aircraft. Their strength, of course, diminishes with time and distance behind the generating aircraft. Also, atmospheric turbulence hastens breakup. Based on that behavior pattern, you should fly at or above the large aircraft's flight path, altering course as necessary to avoid the area behind and below it (Fig. 12-4).

One other factor to keep in mind when large aircraft are near the ground (within about 200 feet), whether taking off or landing: As the vortices sink to the ground, they tend to move laterally over the surface at a speed of about five knots (Fig. 12-5). A crosswind will then decrease the lateral movement of the upwind vortex while increasing the movement of the downwind vortex. Thus a light wind of three to seven knots could result in the upwind vortex remaining stationary in the touchdown zone for a period of time and hasten the drift of the downwind vortex toward another runway. Similarly, a tailwind condition could move the vortices of the preceding aircraft forward into the touchdown zone, as in Fig. 12-6, thus producing a full or quartering tailwind—a condition that requires maximum caution.

Some vortex-avoidance procedures

While a wake encounter could be very serious, it's certainly not always so. An encounter might be only a couple of jolts of varying

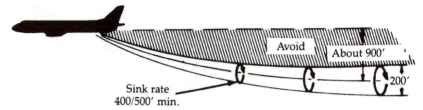

Fig. 12-4. *Be alert to the vortex sink rate and area when in flight.*

severity, depending on how far back, above, or below the generating aircraft you happen to be. The probability of induced roll, of course, increases when the encountering aircraft's heading is basically aligned with the vortex trail or flight path of the generating aircraft. To preclude getting caught in such a situation, the obvious precaution is to avoid the area below and behind the generating aircraft, especially at a low altitude. It's there where even a momentary wake encounter could be hazardous.

In the airport vicinity itself, be particularly alert in calm wind conditions and situations where the vortices could:

- Remain in the touchdown area.
- Drift from aircraft operating on a nearby runway.
- Sink into the takeoff or landing path from a crossing runway.
- Sink into the traffic patterns from other airport operations.
- Sink into the flight path of VFR flight operating at the hemispheric altitude 500 feet below.

In essence, the more you can visualize the location of vortex trails behind large aircraft, the better you will be able to apply proper vortex avoidance procedures. At the same time, it's equally important that pilots of large aircraft plan or adjust their operations, on the ground or in the air, to minimize vortex exposure to other aircraft.

Air traffic wake turbulence separations

Under certain conditions, airport traffic controllers apply procedures for separating aircraft from heavy jet aircraft. They also provide VFR aircraft, with whom they are in communication and that might be adversely affected by wake turbulence from a large aircraft, the position, altitude, and direction of flight of the large aircraft, followed by the phrase "Caution—wake turbulence." Regardless of a warning or

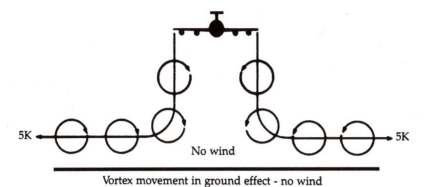

Vortex movement in ground effect - no wind

Fig. 12-5. *The vortex movement in ground effect with no wind.*

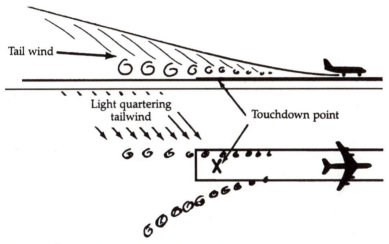

Fig. 12-6. *An illustration of how tail and quartering tail winds affect the vortex movement in a landing.*

not, however, the pilot is expected to adjust operations and flight path of the aircraft as necessary to preclude serious wake encounters.

In addition, air traffic controllers are required to apply specific separation intervals for aircraft operating behind heavy jets because of the possible effects of wake turbulence. To make these separations more meaningful, remember the aircraft classifications:

1. A "heavy" aircraft is capable of takeoff weights of 300,000 pounds or more;

2. A "large" aircraft is of 12,500 pounds certificated takeoff weight up to 300,000 pounds;

3. "Small" aircraft are of 12,500 pounds or less certificated take-off weight.

The following separation is applied to aircraft operating directly behind a heavy jet at the same altitude or directly behind and less than 1000 feet below: heavy jet behind another heavy jet—four miles; small/large aircraft behind a heavy jet—five miles.

Also, controllers provide a six-mile separation for small aircraft landing behind a heavy jet and a four-mile separation for small aircraft landing behind a large aircraft. The separation is based on the time the preceding aircraft passes over the landing threshold.

Aircraft departing behind heavy jets are provided two minutes, or the appropriate 4- or 5-mile radar separation. Three-minute intervals are established for a variety of other takeoff situations that are itemized in *AIM*, Chapter 7-3-9.

Controllers can frequently waive certain separations if the pilot of a departing aircraft so requests and indicates acceptance of responsibility for avoiding the possible wake turbulence hazard. There are occasions or situations, however, when the controller must still hold the aircraft in order to provide separation required for other than wake turbulence purposes.

More avoidance recommendations

In summary, the following vortex avoidance procedures are recommended for these situations: (Note: as used here, "large" also means "heavy" aircraft.)

1. Landing behind a large aircraft—same runway: Stay at or above that aircraft's final approach flight path—note its touchdown point—land beyond it.

2. Landing behind a large aircraft, when a parallel runway is closer than 2500 feet: Consider possible drift to your runway. Stay at or above the large aircraft's final approach flight path and land beyond its touchdown point.

3. Landing behind a large aircraft, crossing runway: Cross above the large aircraft's flight path.

4. Landing behind a departing large aircraft, same runway: Note the aircraft's rotation point and land well before that point.

5. Landing behind a departing large aircraft crossing your runway: Note the large aircraft's rotation point. If it is past the intersection, continue the approach and land prior to the intersection. If the large aircraft rotates prior to the intersection, avoid flight below the aircraft's flight path. Abandon the approach unless a landing is assured well before reaching the intersection.

6. Departing behind a large aircraft: Note the large aircraft's rotation point and rotate prior to it. Continue your climb above and upwind of the large aircraft's climb path until turning clear of its wake. Avoid subsequent headings that will cross below and behind the aircraft. The principle: Avoid any takeoff situation that could lead to a vortex encounter.

7. Intersection takeoffs, same runway: Be alert to adjacent large aircraft operations, particularly upwind of your runway. If an intersection takeoff clearance is received, avoid any subsequent heading that would cross below a large aircraft's path.

8. Departing or landing after a large aircraft executing a low missed approach or a touch-and-go landing: Because vortices settle and move laterally near the ground, the vortex hazard might exist along the runway and in your flight path after a large aircraft has executed a low missed approach or a touch-and-go landing, particularly in light quartering wind conditions. You should assure yourself that an interval of at least two minutes has elapsed before your takeoff or landing.

9. En route VFR (thousand-foot altitude plus 500 feet). Avoid flight below and behind a large aircraft's path. If a large aircraft is observed above you, either crossing, meeting, or overtaking you, deviate laterally from your position, preferably upwind.

Helicopters

A hovering helicopter generates a downwash from its main rotor(s) similar to the prop blast of a conventional aircraft. However, in forward flight, this energy is transformed into a pair of trailing vortices similar to wing-tip vortices of fixed wing aircraft. Pilots of small aircraft should avoid these vortices as well as the downwash.

Pilot responsibility—in the final analysis

Government and industry groups are making concerted efforts to minimize or eliminate the hazards of trailing vortices. Until that happy day, though, it is up to the pilot to exercise the flight disciplines necessary to assure vortex avoidance during VFR operations. To go a step further, it's not too much of an exaggeration to say that vortex avoidance deserves the same level of attention we should be paying to collision avoidance.

In that context, just remember that in operations conducted behind any aircraft, acting on information from ATC, obeying instructions to follow a specific aircraft, being cleared to land or take off, or whatever the case, is an acknowledgment that we will provide our own wake turbulence separation. Once again, the pilot in command is totally responsible for the safe operation of his or her aircraft.

Quickie quiz questions
Chapter 12

1. Wake turbulence and jet blast are really the same thing.

   A. True?_____ False?_____

   B. If false, what is the difference between the two?

2. What causes the formation of vortices?

3. What are the three broad "classifications" of aircraft and the weight factors that lead to the classifications?

4. If you are flying a light plane and are landing or taking off behind a large or heavy jet, where should you plan to touch down or rotate to avoid wake turbulence?

5. The greatest vortex strength occurs when the generating aircraft is which of the following?

A. _____Heavy	**C.** _____Light	**E.** _____Slow
B. _____Fast	**D.** _____Clean	**F.** _____Dirty

   (**Definitions:** "Clean" means gear up, flaps retracted. "Dirty" means just the opposite: gear is down and flaps are extended to traffic pattern and final approach settings.)

6. Which aircraft has more difficulty countering a vortex-generated roll or turbulence—one with a short wing or a long wing?

7. Vortices from large or heavy aircraft tend to sink at what rate of feet per minute and level off at approximately how many feet below the generating aircraft's flight path?

8. How long are controllers authorized to hold a light aircraft from taking off following the departure of a large or heavy jet, and what reason does the controller give?

9. Relative to question number 8:

   A. Can the pilot reject the takeoff delay and request approval for an immediate departure?

   B. Can the controller then rescind the instruction and approve the takeoff?

   C. If the answer to B is "yes," what responsibility does that place on the pilot?

10. What precautions should a light plane pilot exercise when taxiing behind a large or heavy jet, crossing its path after it has passed by, or parking behind the jet on a taxi strip or in the hold bay area?

Answers in Appendix, pages 585-586.

13

Medical facts for pilots

Getting an automobile driver's license is usually a relatively simple process—one that arouses few concerns, including the only so-called "physical" part, the eye exam. It's another matter, though, when it comes to a pilot's certificate and being authorized to operate an airplane from engine start up to shutdown. Now we're talking about not only vastly different kinds of vehicles but of functioning in a vastly different environment. Among the many differences is an environment in which oxygen, or lack thereof, can significantly alter mental alertness; where the effects of drugs, medicinal or otherwise, alcohol, cigarette smoking, the common cold, ear infections, stress are multiplied and can materially affect one's judgment and ability to fly not only well but fly wisely; where fear, joy, exhilaration, confusion, disorientation are but a few of many possible emotional reactions to the immediate surrounding circumstances.

Because of the differences between flying and driving, we have federal control of pilot certification, federal control of pilot operating standards, federal control of medical requirements, federal responsibility for disciplining and disciplinary action for federal regulation violations. None of our 50 states can revise, disregard, or otherwise alter any of what the Federal Aviation Administration has ultimately enacted into "law," nor is there any such thing as a "state" pilot's license.

Perhaps this federal role is self-evident, but I raise it here because we're talking about something that is critical to whether or not you can legally operate as pilot in command of an airplane. No matter what your rating—recreational pilot to airline transport—if you can't pass one of the periodic medical exams, you won't be given your medical certificate; without that, you're grounded until you can pass the exam. Your pilot's rating means nothing in that regard; your medical certificate means everything.

Consequently, considering the importance of the subject to all pilots, and especially to those just starting out, let's begin with...

A few words about the physical exam

Because the environment is so different, and because you can't just pull off the road if you don't feel up to par, a pilot's health is a serious matter with the FAA, both before and after a medical certificate has been issued. And please note this well: You must have a current certificate to be legal to serve as pilot in command of any aircraft other than balloons or gliders. Caught without that certificate could mean trouble.

As to obtaining medical certification, I'd suggest that every student pilot who might have any doubts about his or her vision, hearing, cardiovascular, or other physical condition check with an FAA aviation medical examiner (AME) before investing too much money in any ground or flight training. AMEs are fully qualified physicians, many of whom are pilots in their own right and have had special training in aviation medicine. Only physicians designated as AMEs are authorized to issue medical certificates, and you can usually get names of recommended local examiners from any airport fixed base operator. The third class (private) certificate is valid for 36 months through age 39. Then, after your 40th birthday, the certificate must be renewed every 24 months. I'd further suggest, though, if you eventually hope to enter commercial aviation, that you apply for the highest class of certificate required for the type of position you would like to obtain. The three classes are Class III, Recreational and Private Pilot; Class II, Commercial Pilot; Class I, Airline Transport Pilot. Keep in mind that each exam gets progressively more strict, with Class III the easiest and Class I the most stringent.

Just one thing when you go for the actual physical: The AME will give you a questionnaire-type form to complete, which I urge you to fill out fully and accurately. This applies to all medical questions, plus those related to alcohol or drug usage, including motor vehicle convictions. The FAA will contact the National Driver Register to check your responses against your driving record, and false answers—on a new application or a renewal—will almost inevitably result in denial or suspension of your certificate—plus the possibilities (probability?) of more severe penalties. It might be well to review FARs 61.14, 61.15, and 61.16 in this regard.

The standards for medical certification are contained in Part 67 of the Federal Aviation Regulations. Pilots who have a history of certain medical conditions described in these standards are mandatorily disqualified from flying. These medical conditions include a personality disorder manifested by overt acts, a psychosis, alcoholism, drug dependence, epilepsy, an unexplained disturbance of consciousness, myocardial infarction, angina pectoris, and diabetes requiring insulin or any other hypoglycemic for its control. Other medical conditions might be temporarily disqualifying, such as acute infections, anemia, or peptic ulcers. Pilots who do not meet medical standards can still be qualified under special issuance provisions or the exemption process. This might require that either additional medical information be provided or practical flight tests be conducted.

A Word of Caution: The Federal Aviation Regulations prohibit a pilot who possesses a current medical certificate from performing crewmember duties while the pilot has a known medical condition or increase of a known medical condition that would make him or her unable to meet the standards for the medical certificate.

Fitness for flight

Aircraft accident statistics show that pilots ought to be conducting preflight checklists on themselves as well as their aircraft, because pilot physical impairment contributes to many more accidents than failures of aircraft systems. A personal checklist that can be easily committed to memory includes all of the categories of pilot impairment discussed in this section.

Illness

Even a minor illness suffered in day-to-day living can seriously degrade performance of many piloting tasks vital to safe flight. Illness can produce fever and distracting symptoms that impair judgment, memory, alertness, and the ability to make calculations. Although symptoms from an illness may be under adequate control with a medication, the medication itself may decrease pilot performance.

The safest rule is not to fly while suffering from any illness. If this rule is considered too stringent for a particular illness, you should contact an Aviation Medical Examiner for advice.

Medication

Pilot performance can be seriously degraded by both prescribed and over-the-counter medications, as well as by the medical conditions for which they are taken. Many medications, such as tranquilizers, sedatives, strong pain relievers, and cough-suppressant preparations, have primary effects that could impair judgment, memory, alertness, coordination, vision, and the ability to make calculations. Others, such as antihistamines, certain blood pressure drugs, muscle relaxants, and agents to control diarrhea and motion sickness, have side effects that could adversely affect the same critical functions. Any medication that depresses the nervous system, as a sedative, tranquilizer, or antihistamine, can make a pilot much more susceptible to hypoxia.

The Federal Aviation Regulations prohibit pilots from performing crewmember duties while using any medication that affects the faculties in any way contrary to safety. The safest rule is not to fly as a pilot while taking any medication, unless approved to do so by the FAA.

Alcohol

Extensive research has provided a number of facts about the hazards of alcohol consumption and flying. As little as one ounce of liquor, one bottle of beer, or four ounces of wine can impair flying skills, with the alcohol consumed in these drinks being detectable in the breath and blood for at least three hours. Even after the body completely destroys a moderate amount of alcohol, you can still be severely impaired for many hours by hangover. Alcohol also renders a pilot much more susceptible to disorientation and hypoxia. There is simply no way to speed up the destruction of alcohol in the system or alleviating a hangover.

A consistently high alcohol-related fatal aircraft accident rate serves to emphasize that alcohol and flying can be a deadly combination. The Federal Aviation Regulations prohibits pilots from performing crewmember duties within eight hours after drinking any alcoholic beverage or while under the influence of alcohol. However, due to the slow destruction of alcohol, you may still be under the influence eight hours or more after drinking even a moderate amount. Therefore, the smart rule is to allow at least 12 to 24 hours between "bottle and throttle," depending on the amount of alcoholic beverage consumed.

Fatigue

Fatigue continues to be one of the most treacherous hazards to flight safety because it might not be apparent to a pilot until serious errors are made. Fatigue is best described as either acute (short-term) or chronic (long-term).

A normal occurrence of everyday living, acute fatigue is the tiredness felt after long periods of physical or mental strain, including strenuous muscular effort, immobility, heavy mental workload, strong emotional pressure, monotony, or lack of sleep. Consequently, under any of these influences, coordination and alertness, so vital to safe pilot performance, could well be affected. Acute fatigue is prevented by adequate rest and sleep, as well as regular exercise and proper nutrition.

Chronic fatigue occurs when there is not enough time for full recovery between episodes of acute fatigue. Performance continues to fall off, and judgment becomes impaired so that unwarranted risks might be taken. Recovery from chronic fatigue requires a prolonged period of rest.

Stress

Stress from the pressures of everyday living can impair pilot performance, often in very subtle ways. Difficulties, particularly at work, often occupy thought processes enough to markedly decrease alertness. Distraction can so interfere with judgment that unwarranted risks are taken, such as flying into deteriorating weather conditions to keep a schedule. Stress and fatigue can be an extremely hazardous combination.

Most of us don't leave stress on the ground. Consequently, if you are experiencing more than the usual, or rather normal, emotional problems, you would be wise to consider delaying flying until the problems, whatever they are, have been satisfactorily resolved.

Emotion

Certain emotionally upsetting events—a serious argument, death of a family member, separation or divorce, loss of job, financial difficulties—can cause a person to be an unsafe pilot. The emotions of anger, depression, and anxiety from such events not only decrease alertness but may lead to taking risks that border on self-destruction.

Any pilot who experiences an emotionally upsetting event should stay on the ground until his or her emotions are back to normal and under control.

The effects of altitude

Altitude, and its accompanying decrease in oxygen and pressure, can have several potentially debilitating or dangerous effects on the unwary pilot, the most critical being hypoxia, ear block, and sinus block. While hypoxia is associated with higher altitudes, ear and sinus blocks can occur at any altitude, particularly during descents and especially during rapid descents.

Hypoxia

Hypoxia is a state of oxygen deficiency in the body sufficient to impair functions of the brain and other organs. It is due only to the reduced barometric pressures encountered at altitude, because the concentration of oxygen in the atmosphere remains about 21 percent from the ground out to space.

Although a deterioration in night vision occurs at a cabin pressure altitude as low as 5000 feet, other significant effects of altitude hypoxia usually don't occur in the normal healthy pilot below 12,000 feet. From 12,000 to 15,000 feet of altitude, judgment, memory, alertness, coordination and ability to make calculations are impaired, and headache, drowsiness, dizziness, and either a sense of well-being (euphoria) or belligerence occurs. The effects appear following increasingly shorter periods of exposure to increasing altitude. In fact, pilot performance can seriously deteriorate within 15 minutes at 15,000 feet.

At cabin pressure altitudes above 15,000 feet, the periphery of the visual field grays out to a point where only central vision remains (tunnel vision). A blue coloration (cyanosis) of the fingernails and lips develops. The ability to take corrective and protective action is lost in 20 to 30 minutes at 18,000 feet and 5 to 12 minutes at 20,000 feet, followed soon thereafter by unconsciousness.

The altitude at which significant effects of hypoxia occur can be lowered by a number of factors. Carbon monoxide inhaled in smoking or from exhaust fumes, lowered hemoglobin (anemia), and certain medications can reduce the oxygen-carrying capacity of the blood to the degree that the amount of oxygen provided to body tissues will already be equivalent to the oxygen provided to the tissues when exposed to a cabin pressure altitude of several thousand feet. Small amounts of alcohol and low doses of certain drugs, such as antihistamines, tranquilizers, sedatives, and analgesics can, through their depressant actions, render the brain much more susceptible to hypoxia. Extreme heat and cold, fever, and anxiety increase the body's demand for oxygen and hence its susceptibility to hypoxia.

The effects of hypoxia are usually quite difficult to recognize, especially when they occur gradually. Because its symptoms don't vary in individuals, the ability to recognize hypoxia can be greatly improved by experiencing and witnessing its effects during an altitude chamber "flight." The FAA provides this opportunity through aviation physiology training, which is conducted at the FAA Civil Aeromedical Institute and at many military facilities across the United States.

Hypoxia is prevented by heeding factors that reduce tolerance to altitude, by enriching the inspired air with oxygen from an appropriate oxygen system, and by maintaining a comfortable, safe cabin pressure altitude. For optimum protection, pilots are encouraged to use supplemental oxygen above 10,000 feet during the day and above 5000 feet at night. The Federal Aviation Regulations require that the minimum flight crew be provided with and use supplemental oxygen after 30 minutes of exposure to cabin pressure altitudes between 12,500 and 14,000 feet and immediately on exposure to cabin pressure altitudes above 14,000 feet. Every occupant of the aircraft must be provided with supplement oxygen at cabin pressure altitudes above 15,000 feet.

Ear block

As the aircraft cabin pressure decreases during ascent, the expanding air in the middle ear pushes the Eustachian tube open and, by escaping down it to the nasal passages, equalizes in pressure with the cabin pressure. But during descent, the pilot must periodically open the Eustachian tube to equalize pressure. This can be accomplished by swallowing, yawning, tensing muscles in the throat or, if these do not work, by the combination of closing the mouth, pinching the nose closed and attempting to blow through the nostrils (Valsalva maneuver).

Either an upper respiratory infection—a cold, a sore throat—or a nasal allergic condition can produce enough congestion around the Eustachian tube to make equalization difficult. Consequently, the difference in pressure between the middle ear and aircraft cabin can build up to a level that holds the Eustachian tube closed, making equalization difficult if not impossible. This problem is commonly referred to as an ear block.

An ear block produces severe ear pain and loss of hearing that can last from several hours to several days. Rupture of the ear drum is possible in flight or after landing, and fluid can accumulate in the middle ear and become infected.

An ear block is prevented by not flying with an upper respiratory infection or nasal allergic condition. Adequate protection is usually not provided by decongestant sprays or drops to reduce congestion around the Eustachian tube. Also, oral decongestants have side effects that can significantly impair pilot performance.

If an ear block doesn't clear shortly after landing, consult a physician.

Sinus block

During ascent and descent, air pressure in the sinuses equalizes with the aircraft cabin pressure through small openings that connect the sinuses to the nasal passages. Either an upper respiratory infection, such as a cold or sinusitis, or a nasal allergic condition can produce enough congestion around an opening to slow equalization and, as the difference in pressure between the sinus and cabin mounts, eventually plug the opening. This happens most frequently during descent.

A sinus block can occur in the frontal sinuses, located above each eyebrow, or in the maxillary sinuses, located in each upper cheek. It usually produces excruciating pain over the sinus area, perhaps cause the upper teeth to ache, or bloody mucus might discharge from the nasal passages.

How is a sinus block prevented? By not flying with an upper respiratory infection or nasal allergic condition. Adequate protection is usually not provided by decongestant sprays or drops to reduce congestion around the sinus openings. As with ear blocks, oral decongestants have side effects that can impair pilot performance.

If a sinus block does not clear shortly after landing, consult a physician.

Decompression sickness after scuba diving

A pilot or passenger who intends to fly after scuba diving should allow the body sufficient time to rid itself of excess nitrogen absorbed during diving. If not, decompression sickness due to involved gas can occur during exposure to low altitude and create a serious in-flight emergency.

The recommended waiting time before flight to cabin pressure altitudes of 8000 feet or less is at least two hours after diving that has not required controlled ascent (nondecompression diving) and at least 24 hours after diving that has required controlled ascent (decompression diving). The waiting time before flight to cabin pressure altitudes above 8000 feet should be at least 24 hours after any scuba diving.

Hyperventilation in flight

Hyperventilation, or an abnormal increase in the volume of air breathed in and out of the lungs, can occur subconsciously when a stressful situation is encountered in flight. As hyperventilation "blows off" excessive carbon dioxide from the body, you can experience symptoms of lightheadedness, suffocation, drowsiness, tingling in the extremities, and coolness—and react to them with even greater hyperventilation. Incapacitation can eventually result from uncoordination, disorientation, and painful muscle spasms. Finally, unconsciousness could occur.

The symptoms of hyperventilation subside within a few minutes after the rate and depth of breathing are consciously brought back under control. The buildup of carbon dioxide in the body can be hastened by controlled breathing in and out of a paper bag held over the nose and mouth.

Early symptoms of hyperventilation and hypoxia are similar. Moreover, hyperventilation and hypoxia can occur at the same time. Therefore, if a pilot is using an oxygen system when symptoms are experienced, the oxygen regulator should immediately be set to deliver 100 percent oxygen, and the system should then be checked to assure that it is functioning effectively before giving attention to rate and depth of breathing.

Carbon monoxide poisoning in flight

Carbon monoxide is a colorless, odorless, and tasteless gas contained in exhaust fumes. When breathed in minute quantities over a period of time, it can significantly reduce the ability of the blood to carry oxygen. Consequently, effects of hypoxia occur.

Most heaters in light aircraft work by air flowing over the manifold. Use of these heaters while exhaust fumes are escaping through manifold cracks and seals is responsible every year for several non-fatal and fatal aircraft accidents from carbon monoxide poisoning.

A pilot who detects the odor of exhaust or experiences symptoms of headache, drowsiness, or dizziness while using the heater should suspect carbon monoxide poisoning and immediately shut off the heater and open the air vents. If symptoms are severe, or continue after landing, be sure to seek medical treatment.

Illusions in flight

Something else every pilot must be very aware of and alert to are the various types of illusions he or she could experience in flight. Potentially fatal if not recognized and acted upon, the majority of these illusions occur when the pilot gets into clouds, overcasts, or conditions that blot out all visual reference to the world beyond the cockpit windows.

To counteract the illusions and avoid ending up a statistic, you first need to understand each type of illusion and what causes it; next, even as a student pilot, you should insist on being given some training in flying solely by your instruments, including recovering from instructor-induced unusual positions; and finally, based on that introduction to instrument flight, it is critical to learn to trust your instruments. You may *feel* that you're flying straight and level, but if your instruments tell you you're in a steep turn to the left and losing altitude, believe those instruments—the turn indicator, altimeter, heading indicator, attitude indicator (artificial horizon), vertical speed indicator, airspeed indicator. They don't lie, but even if one or more of those pressure, gyroscopic, or electrical gauges should go belly up on you, you still have a combination of other instruments to tell you what is really happening to your aircraft.

It's often difficult to believe a mechanical gadget that says you're doing one thing when every bodily instinct says you're doing something else. Nevertheless, trust those instruments that are sitting in front of you. Get them under control and you'll have your aircraft under control. Otherwise, your illusions might result in a rather hard arrival on mother earth.

With that, a few words about some of these common illusions in flight.

Illusions leading to spatial disorientation

Various complex motions and forces and certain visual scenes encountered in flight can create illusions of motion and position. Spatial disorientation from these illusions is prevented only by visual reference to reliable, fixed points on the ground or to flight instruments.

The leans. An abrupt correction of a banked attitude, which has been entered too slowly to stimulate the balance organs in the inner ear, can create the illusion of banking in the opposite direction. The disoriented pilot will roll the aircraft back into its original dangerous attitude or, if level flight is maintained, will feel compelled to lean in the perceived vertical plane until this illusion subsides.

Coriolis illusion. An abrupt head movement in a constant-rate turn that has ceased stimulating the balance organs can create the illusion of rotation or movement in an entirely different plane. The disoriented pilot will maneuver the aircraft into a dangerous attitude in an attempt to stop rotation. This most overwhelming of all illusions in flight can be prevented by not making sudden, extreme head movements, particularly while in prolonged constant-rate turns under IFR conditions.

Graveyard spin. A proper recovery from a spin that has ceased stimulating the balance organs can create the illusion of spinning in the opposite direction. The disoriented pilot will tend to return the aircraft to its original spin.

Graveyard spiral. An observed loss of altitude during a coordinated constant-rate turn that has ceased stimulating the balance organs can create the illusion of being in a descent with the wings level. If disoriented, the pilot will pull back on the controls, tightening the spiral and increasing the loss of altitude.

Somatogravic illusion. A rapid acceleration during takeoff can create an illusion of being in a nose-up attitude. The disoriented pilot will push the aircraft into a nose-low, or dive attitude. A rapid deceleration by rapid reduction of the throttles can have the opposite effect, with the disoriented pilot pulling the aircraft into a nose-up, or stall attitude.

Inversion illusion. An abrupt transition from climb to straight and level flight can create the illusion of tumbling backwards. Once disoriented, the pilot will push the aircraft abruptly into a nose-low attitude, possibly intensifying this illusion.

Elevator illusion. An abrupt upward vertical acceleration, usually by an updraft, produces the illusion of being in a climb. So affected, the pilot will push the aircraft into a nose-low attitude. An abrupt downward vertical acceleration, usually by a downdraft, has the opposite effect, with the disoriented pilot pulling the aircraft into a nose-up attitude.

False horizon. Sloping cloud formations, an obscured horizon, a dark scene spread with ground lights and stars, and certain geometric patterns of ground lights can create illusions of not being aligned correctly with the actual horizon. The pilot, because of disorientation, will then place the aircraft in a dangerous attitude.

Autokinesis. In the dark, a static light will appear to move about when stared at for many seconds. The disoriented pilot will lose control of the aircraft in attempting to align it with the light.

Illusions leading to landing errors

Various surface features and atmospheric conditions encountered in landing can lead to illusions of incorrect height above and distance from the runway threshold. Landing errors from these illusions are prevented by anticipating them during approaches, aerial visual inspection of unfamiliar airports before landing, using electronic glide slope or VASI systems when available, and maintaining optimum proficiency in landing procedures.

Runway width illusion. A narrower-than-usual runway can create the illusion of the aircraft being at a greater height. The pilot who does not recognize this illusion will fly a lower approach, with the risk of striking objects along the approach path or landing short. A wider-than-usual runway could have the opposite effect, with the risk of leveling out high and landing hard or overshooting the runway.

Runway and terrain slopes illusion. An upsloping runway, upsloping terrain, or both, tend to create the illusion of greater height. The pilot who fails to recognize this illusion will fly a lower approach. A downsloping runway, downsloping approach terrain, or both, can have the opposite effect.

Featureless terrain illusion. An absence of ground features, as when landing over water, darkened areas, or terrain made featureless by snow, often creates the illusion of greater height. Unless the illusion is recognized, you may fly a lower approach.

Atmospheric illusions. Rain on the windscreen could produce the illusion of greater height, and atmospheric haze the illusion of greater distance. A pilot not aware of such illusions is likely to fly a lower approach. Penetration of fog can develop the illusion of pitching up, causing you to steepen the approach, often quite abruptly.

Ground lighting illusions. Lights along a straight path, such as a road, and even lights on moving trains are often mistaken for runway and approach lights. Bright runway and approach lighting systems, especially where few lights illuminate the surrounding terrain, may create the illusion of lesser distance. If you don't recognize this illusion, you'll tend to fly a high approach.

Vision in flight

Of all the body senses, vision is the most important for safe flight. Major factors that determine how effectively vision can be used are the levels of illumination and the techniques of scanning the sky for other aircraft.

Vision under dim and bright illumination

In darkness, vision becomes more sensitive to light, a process called *dark adaptation.* Although exposure to total darkness for at least 30 minutes is required for complete dark adaptation, you can achieve a moderate degree of dark adaptation within 20 minutes under dim red cockpit lighting. But, because red light severely distorts colors, especially on aeronautical charts and can cause serious difficulty in focusing the eyes on objects inside the aircraft, its use is advisable only when optimum outside night vision capability is necessary.

Even so, white cockpit lighting must be available when needed for chart and instrument reading, especially under IFR conditions. Dark adaptation is impaired by exposure to cabin pressure altitudes above 5000 feet, carbon monoxide inhaled in smoking and from exhaust fumes, deficiency of vitamin A in the diet, and by prolonged exposure to bright sunlight. Because any degree of dark adaptation is lost within a few seconds of viewing a bright light, you should close one eye when using a light to preserve some degree of night vision.

Excessive illumination, especially from light reflected off the canopy, surfaces inside the aircraft, clouds, water, snow, and desert terrain, can produce glare, with uncomfortable squinting, watering of the eyes, and even temporary blindness. Sunglasses for protection from glare should absorb at least 85 percent of visible light (15 percent transmittance) and all colors equally (neutral transmittance), with negligible image distortion from refractive and prismatic errors.

Scanning for other aircraft

Scanning the sky for other aircraft is a key factor in collision avoidance. It should be used continuously by the pilot and copilot (or right seat passenger) to cover all areas of the sky visible from the cockpit.

Effective scanning is accomplished with a series of short, regularly spaced head and eye movements that bring successive areas of the sky into the central visual field. Each movement should not exceed 10 degrees, and each area should be observed for at least one second to enable detection. Although horizontal back-and-forth eye movements seem preferred by most pilots, each pilot should develop a pattern that is the most comfortable and then adhere to it to assure optimum scanning. But a word of advice: Don't get so involved in chart-reading, talking with a passenger, or flying the instruments in clear VFR weather that you forget about the world beyond the plexiglass windows. If you have your head in the cockpit over 15 seconds at a time, you ought to be getting a little nervous! That's too long to be impervious to what might be going on in the skies around you.

Quickie quiz questions
Chapter 13

1. If you have not reached your 40th birthday, your third class medical certificate is valid for_____ months. If you *have* reached your 40th birthday, how many months is it valid?_____

2. What are the types or names of the three classes of medical certificates?

A. Class I =

B. Class II =

C. Class III =

3. What are some of the prescription or over-the-counter medicines/drugs you should avoid before flying as pilot in command, whether solo or with passengers?

List them: _____

4. Define "hypoxia." _____

5. Describe a "graveyard spiral."_____

6. How much time should elapse between "bottle to throttle?"
_____ to _____ hours

7. What is an "AME" and what is unusual about his or her training?

An AME is _____

Training: _____

8. One of the ways to minimize flight illusions in IFR conditions is to: _____

_____

9. If, for no apparent reason, you begin to feel drowsy or develop a headache while flying at a standard VFR altitude:

A. What is the possible/probable cause? _____

B. What action should you promptly take? _____

_____

10. In VFR weather, what is maximum length of time you should have your eyes in the cockpit instead of scanning the skies around you? _____ mins. or secs.(?)

Answers in Appendix, pages 586-587.

14

Practical operating practices

Well-trained pilots should be able to venture forth safely and with justified confidence—not overconfidence—in their airmanship abilities, especially if that confidence is supported by a knowledge of subjects discussed in the preceding chapters. What follows now is a summary of practices VFR pilots should observe for their own well-being and that of others who might be occupying the same airspace.

Alertness. An obvious admonition is constant alertness, *especially* when the weather is good. Most pilots pay close attention to business when they are operating in full IFR weather conditions, but strangely, midair collisions almost invariably have occurred under ideal, or certainly not IMC, weather conditions. Unlimited visibility appears to encourage a sense of security that is not at all justified.

Aircraft checklists. Most owner's operating manuals contain recommended checklists for that particular type of aircraft. As they vary with different types of aircraft and equipment, one universal list to cover all aircraft is not practical. Consequently, each should be tailored to the individual aircraft, based on the owner's manual and modified as necessary when equipment is added or deleted. The important thing is to use the current checklist every time before starting the engine, before takeoff, and before landing. Relying on memory is dangerous, and overlooking even one listed item could prove to be a serious mistake.

VFR in a congested area? Listen! When operating VFR in highly congested areas, whether you intend to land at an airport within the area or are just flying through, I strongly recommend that you maintain extra vigilance and monitor the appropriate radio frequency. Of course, if you're in, or want to enter, a Class B, C, or D airspace, you have no alternative: you must be in contact with either Approach Control or the Tower. But just flying the fringes of those areas, with no intention of entering them, it's advisable to monitor the frequencies to get a general picture of the traffic near or around you.

At uncontrolled airports in Classes E or G airspace, monitor the unicom CTAF frequency (usually 122.7, 122.8, or 123.0) or the Class G CTAF of 122.9. It's in these areas—these uncontrolled airports— where vigilance is especially critical because of traffic volume and the not-always proper use of radios.

Operation Lights On. The FAA has initiated a voluntary pilot safety program called "Operation Lights On." The purpose of the program is to enhance the "see-and-be-seen" concept to avert collisions in the air and on the ground, and, incidentally, to help reduce bird strikes. Pilots are thus encouraged to turn on their anticollision lights any time the engine(s) is running, day or night. Additionally, they are further encouraged to turn on their landing lights when operating within 10 miles of any airport (day and night) in conditions of reduced visibility and in areas where flocks of birds might be expected, as in coastal, lake, and swamp areas and around refuse dumps.

Although having the lights on does contribute to the "see-and-be-seen" concept, don't become complacent about keeping a sharp eye out for other aircraft. Most, but not all, aircraft are equipped with lights, but some pilots may not even have thought of turning theirs on. So, light up and look out!

Judgment in VFR flight. Use reasonable restraint in exercising the prerogative of VFR flight, especially in terminal areas. The weather minimums and distances from clouds are minimums. Giving yourself a greater margin when conditions are just so-so or barely VFR, is just common sense and good judgment.

Simulated instrument flights. In conducting simulated instrument flights, be sure that the weather is good enough to compensate for the relatively restricted visibility of the safety pilot. Remember that you're glued to the instruments and are blocking a good portion of the observer's vision to the left of the aircraft. Visibility and ceiling ought to be better than marginal VFR under those conditions. Especially give yourself a greater margin when you're practicing instruments on or near a busy airway or close to an airport. Also be sure your observer is a qualified pilot who understands his role and what you are doing.

Obstructions to VFR flight. Extreme caution should be exercised when flying less than 2000 feet above ground level (agl) because there are several hundred skeletal structures (radio and television antenna towers) around the country that exceed 1000 feet agl, with some higher than 2000 feet. Also, most skeletal structures are supported by guy wires—wires that are hard enough to see in good weather and can be totally invisible during periods of dusk and reduced visibility. To prevent any possibility of contact with these supports, all skeletal structures should be avoided by at least 2000 feet horizontally.

Before takeoff. Prior to taxiing onto a runway or landing area in preparation for takeoff, especially at uncontrolled airports, be sure to scan the approach areas for possible landing traffic. Make this visual check upwind and downwind. Pilots have been known to land downwind at these uncontrolled fields either because they haven't checked the wind tee, or the wind is very light, or they're just above such mundane things as flying the prescribed traffic pattern. And these last, of course, are equally above using the radio and communicating their intentions.

Climbs and descents. During VFR climbs and descents—particularly climbs, when it is hard to see what's ahead over the nose of the aircraft—make gentle banks, left and right, at a frequency that permits continuous visual scanning.

Straight and level. Keep scanning the skies in as much of a 360° sweep as the aircraft and human limitations will permit. If you keep your head in the cockpit more than 15 seconds without an outside scan, you should be getting just a little nervous.

Traffic pattern. Always enter traffic patterns at the published pattern altitude—especially at Class E and G airports. Entering a pattern while descending is highly dangerous as you might be letting down on top of another aircraft that you couldn't see in the descent.

Traffic at VOR sites. Be particularly watchful in the vicinity of VORs and airway intersections. These are often areas of heavy traffic convergence.

Training operations. Operators of pilot training programs are urged to adopt the following practices:

- Student pilots at all levels should be taught to speak clearing procedures by calling out, "clear" (left), (right), (above), or (below) to instill and sustain the habit of vigilance during maneuvering.

- In a high-wing airplane, momentarily raise the wing in the direction of the intended turn and look.
- In a low-wing, momentarily lower the wing in the direction of the intended turn and look.
- Appropriate clearing procedures should precede all turns, chandelles, lazy eights, stalls, slow flight, climbs, straight and level spins, and other combination maneuvers.

Giving way. If you think another aircraft is too close to you, give way instead of waiting for the other pilot to respect the right-of-way to which you might be entitled. You can worry about manners and the proper protocol at some other time.

Use of federal airways. VFR pilots in level cruising flight above 3000 feet are *always* expected to conform to the VFR cruising altitudes appropriate to direction of flight (WEEO, for: West Even, East Odd). During climbs or descents along an airway, fly to the right side of the airway to avoid opposite traffic operating along the airway's centerline.

Follow IFR procedures even when operating VFR. Whether IFR- or VFR-rated, it is a smart practice to follow some of the IFR operating procedures whenever possible. Accordingly, it's recommended that VFR pilots:

- Obtain a complete preflight and weather briefing, and check the NOTAMs.
- File a flight plan. This is an excellent low-cost insurance policy. The cost is the time it takes to fill it out and communicate it. The insurance includes the knowledge that someone will be looking for you if you become overdue at destination.
- Use current charts. You are not required to have any charts on board, but an out-of-date chart is illegal.
- Use the navigation aids. Practice maintaining a good course—keep the VOR needle centered.
- Maintain a constant altitude (appropriate for the direction of flight). Try to hold your altitude within a plus or minus 25-foot range.
- Estimate and then keep track of your en route position times.
- Make accurate and frequent position reports to the FSSs along your route of flight.
- Make it a practice on cross-country flights to contact a Center for en route traffic advisories.

VFR at night. When flying VFR at night, in addition to the altitude appropriate for the direction of flight, maintain an altitude that is at or above the minimum en route altitude (MEA), as shown on charts, particularly the *En Route Low Altitude Chart.* This is especially critical in mountainous terrain where there is usually very little ground reference. Don't depend on being able to see those built-up rocks or TV towers in time to miss them.

Student pilot's radio identification. The FAA wants to help the student in acquiring sufficient practical experience in the environment in which the pilot will be required to operate. To receive additional assistance while operating in areas of concentrated air traffic, the student need only identify himself or herself as such during the initial call to an FAA radio facility. For instance, "Dayton Tower, this is Fleetwing 6789, Student Pilot, ready to take off." This special identification alerts ATC personnel and enables them to give the student what extra assistance or consideration might be needed. The identification procedure, however, is not mandatory. Don't be embarrassed to let it be known that you're new to flying—if you are. Every pilot was once—or is now.

Operation of aircraft rotating beacon. There have been several incidents in which small aircraft were overturned or damaged by prop or jet blast forces from large taxiing aircraft. In the interest of reducing such incidents and injuries to ground personnel, the FAA has recommended to air carriers and commercial operators that they turn on their rotating beacon any time the engines are in operation.

General aviation pilots utilizing aircraft equipped with rotating beacons are also encouraged to participate in this same program by turning on the beacon any time the engine is running. The purpose, of course, is to alert ground personnel and other aircraft that prop or jet blast forces might be present and that a propellar is spinning. All personnel should be warned, though, not to rely solely on the rotating beacon as an indication that aircraft engines are running. The reason: participation in the program is voluntary.

Ask for assistance. "I'm not lost, I just don't know where I am." "Maybe something familiar will show up if I just go on for a few more minutes." "I think I've got enough fuel to get there." "I'll bet it's smoother above that overcast. Maybe I can sneak through it." "I'd looked kinda stupid if I asked for help and then found I didn't need it."

The first time one of these thoughts pops into your mind, it's time to ask for help. Don't wait until the situation has deteriorated into an emergency before letting ATC know of your predicament. Put your hopeful optimism, your "I've gotta get home-itis," your fear of being embarrassed aside. The fact that pride might goeth before a fall should be enough motivation to ask for help when you first need it. The "fall" isn't worth trying to preserve your ego.

To contact an FSS. Flight Service Stations are allocated frequencies for different functions. As examples, the Airport Advisory Service frequency is 123.6 MHz, 122.0 is Flight Watch, and 122.2 reaches an inflight specialist for routine communications. Other FSS frequencies are listed in the Airport/Facility Directory. If you're in doubt about what frequency to use to contact an FSS, transmit on 122.2 MHz and tell the specialist what frequency you're calling on (he or she can be monitoring as many as 48 frequencies).

Altimeter errors. The importance of frequently obtaining current altimeter settings can't be overemphasized. If you don't reset the altimeter when flying from an area of high pressure or high temperatures into an area of low temperatures or low pressure, you'll be closer to the ground than the altimeter indicates. An inch error on the altimeter equals 1000 feet of altitude. To quote an old saw: "Going from a high to a low, look out below."

A reverse situation: Without resetting the altimeter when going from a low temperature or low-pressure area into a high temperature or high-pressure area, the aircraft will be higher than the altimeter indicates.

The possible result of the first situation is obvious, particularly if operating at low altitudes. In the second, the result might not be as spectacular, but consider an instrument approach: If your altimeter is in error, you could still be on instruments when reaching the minimum altitude (as indicated on the altimeter), whereas you might have been in the clear and able to complete the approach if the altimeter setting were correct. FAR 91 defines current altimeter setting practices.

Avoid flight beneath unmanned balloons. The majority of unmanned free balloons currently being operated have, extending below them, either a suspension device to which the payload or instrument package is attached, or a trailing wire antenna, or both. In many instances, you might not even see these balloon subsystems until you were almost on top of them, and by then it might be too late. Good judgment thus dictates that aircraft should remain well clear of all unmanned free balloons, and flight below them should be avoided at all times.

Because of their danger to aviation, pilots are urged to report any sighted unmanned free balloons to the nearest FAA ground facility with which communication can be established. That information helps the facility identify and flight-follow those balloons that are floating about in the airspace.

Parks, refuges, and forest service areas. Aircraft landings are prohibited on lands and waters administered by the National Park Service, U.S. Fish and Wildlife Service, or U.S. Forest Service without authorization from the respective agency. Emergencies are obvious exceptions. Accordingly, before going out on a flight over (to you) new geography, check the sectional and other charts for these prohibited areas along your route of flight, and then, unless you find exceptions, maintain an absolute minimum of 2000 feet agl when flying over these reserves.

Parachute jump aircraft operations. Pilots of aircraft engaged in parachute jump operations are reminded that all reported altitudes must be with reference to mean sea level, or flight level as appropriate, to enable ATC to provide meaningful traffic information.

Mountain flying. Your first experience of flying over mountainous terrain (particularly if most of your flight time has been in the flatlands of the Midwest) could be a never-to-be-forgotten nightmare if proper planning is not done and if you're not aware of the potential hazards awaiting. Those familiar section lines aren't present in the mountains; those flat, level fields for forced landings are practically nonexistent; abrupt changes in wind direction and velocity occur; severe updrafts and downdrafts are common, particularly near or above abrupt changes of terrain such as cliffs or rugged areas; even the clouds look different and can build up swiftly. With it all, though, mountain flying need not be hazardous if you follow these recommendations:

1. File a flight plan. Plan your route to avoid topography that would prevent a safe forced landing. Also, to the greatest extent possible, plan the route over populated areas and well-known mountain passes. Finally, plan to fly at altitudes that would always give you a chance to glide to a safe landing in the event of engine failure.

2. Don't fly a light aircraft when the winds aloft, at your proposed altitude, exceed 35 miles per hour. Expect the winds to

be of much greater velocity over mountain passes than reported a few miles from them. Approach mountain passes with as much altitude as possible, keeping in mind that downdrafts from 1500 to 2000 feet per minute are not uncommon on the leeward side.

3. Don't fly near or above abrupt changes in terrain. Severe turbulence can be expected, especially in high wind conditions.

4. Some canyons run into a dead-end. Don't fly so far up a canyon that you get trapped. Always be able to make a 180-degree turn.

5. Plan your trip for the early morning hours. As a rule, the air starts to get bad at about 10 A.M. and grows steadily worse until around 4 P.M., then gradually improves until dark. Mountain flying at night in a single engine light aircraft is asking for trouble.

6. When landing at a high-altitude field, the same indicated airspeed should be used as at low-elevation fields. Remember: due to the less dense air at altitude, this same indicated airspeed actually results in a higher true airspeed, a faster landing speed, and more important, a longer landing distance. During gusty wind conditions that often prevail at high-altitude fields, a power approach and power landing is recommended. Additionally, due to the faster groundspeed, your takeoff distance increases considerably over that required at low altitudes.

7. Effects of Density Altitude: Performance figures in the aircraft owner's handbook for length of takeoff run, horsepower, rate of climb, etc., are generally based on standard atmospheric conditions (59°F, pressure, 29.92 inches of mercury) at sea level. However, both experienced and inexperienced pilots might run into trouble when they encounter an altogether different set of conditions. This is particularly true in hot weather and at higher elevations.

8. Take a course in mountain flying before venturing forth the first time. That's the best advice of all.

Aircraft operations at altitudes far above sea level and at higher than standard temperatures are commonplace in mountainous areas. Such operations usually result in drastic reductions in aircraft performance because of the changing air density. Density altitude is a measure of air density. It is not to be confused with pressure altitude, true altitude, or absolute altitude. It is not to be used as a height reference but as a determining criterion in the performance capability of an aircraft. Air density decreases with altitude. As it does, density altitude increases. The further effects of high temperature and high humidity are cumulative, resulting in an increasingly higher density altitude condition. Said simply, high-density altitude reduces all aircraft performances.

To the pilot, this means that the normal horsepower output is reduced, propeller efficiency is reduced, and a higher true airspeed is required to sustain the aircraft throughout its operating parameters. It means an increase in runway length for takeoff and landings and a decreased rate of climb. (Note: A turbocharged aircraft engine provides some advantage in that it produces sea level horsepower up to a specified altitude above sea level.) An average small airplane, for example, requiring 1000 feet for takeoff at sea level under standard atmospheric conditions needs a takeoff run of approximately 2000 feet at an operational altitude of 5000 feet.

Flight beyond United States. When conducting flights, particularly extended flights, outside the United States and its territories, full account must be taken of the amount and quality of air navigation services available in the airspace to be traversed. Every effort should be made to secure information on the location and range of navigational aids, availability of communications and meteorological services, the provision of air traffic services, and the existence of search and rescue services.

Filing a flight plan takes on added significance for extended flights outside United States airspace and is, in fact, usually required by the laws of the countries being visited or overflown. It's also particularly important that pilots leave a complete itinerary and schedule of the flight with someone directly concerned and that they keep that person advised of the flight's progress . . . which is always a good practice, wherever that flight may take you.

With these thoughts, sort of in summary, enjoy your venture into flight and the new horizons that await you. Most important, though, fly safely, fly wisely so that you may reap the benefits and pleasures open to the very few who can justifiably be called "pilot in command."

Appendix

Quickie quiz answers
Chapter 2

The letters in parentheses indicate the correct answer. The numbers at the end of each answer refer to the page(s) where the subject is discussed.

1. Relationship of lift, drag, thrust, and weight in straight-and-level, constant speed flight: (B) Lift equals weight and thrust equals drag. (22)

2. The three axes of rotation: Longitudinal (roll), Lateral (pitch), Vertical (Yaw). (36)

3. What makes an airplane turn or bank? The ailerons and aileron trim tabs. (44)

4. The effects of high density altitude on takeoff or landing performance: Longer takeoff run, decreased rate of climb, less engine horsepower, reduced propeller efficiency, slower speed acceleration. (28-29)

5. Purpose of the rudder: (A) To control yaw. (47)

6. Angle of attack: It is the acute angle between the chord line of the wing and the direction of the relative air. (11)

7. Three factors that affect lateral stability: Dihedral, wing sweepback, keel effect. (42)

8. Load factor defined: (C) Ratio of load supported by the aircraft's wing to actual weight of the aircraft and its contents. (49)

9. Four conditions that affect load factor: Turns, aircraft speed, maneuvers, turbulence. (51 to 57)

10. Factors that affect amount of lift by the wing: Speed of wing through the air, angle of attack, planform of wing, wing area, and air density. (16 and 17)

Quickie quiz answers
Chapter 3

1. Primary and secondary flight control systems: (71)

Primary: Elevators, ailerons, and rudder.

Secondary: Trim tabs, flaps.

2. Reciprocating engine elements: (80)

Cylinder chamber, Piston

Air intake valve Connecting rod

Exhaust valve Crankshaft

3. Meaning of "dual ignition: system: (84)

With two magnetos, one supplies electrical current to one set of spark plugs per combustion chamber, while the second system does the same to the other set.

4. The purpose of flaps: (71)

To change the lifting characteristics of the wing;

To decrease the speed at which the wing stalls.

5. To reduce high indicated engine temperature: One or more of the following: (83):

Increase air speed;

Enrich fuel/air ratio mixture;

Reduce power;

Establish shallow climb;

Open cowl flaps (if the aircraft is so equipped)

6. To minimize possibility of fuel contamination and water: (96)

Drain each sump and gascolator three or four times in preflight check;

Fill tanks at end of flying day;

Don't fuel from cans or drums;

Don't use a chamois as a filter;

7. Performance differences between climb and cruise fixed-pitch propellers: (101)

Climb (low pitch): Higher engine rpms, less drag on the engine, greater horsepower, better takeoff and climb performance.

Cruise (high pitch): Higher drag for engine to overcome, lower horsepower capability. But lower rpms needed because propeller blades, with the greater pitch, take bigger bites of air.

8. Symptoms of carburetor ice with fixed pitch propeller: (90) Loss of rpms.

   Engine roughness.

9. What to do when ammeter shows minus value or needle fluctuates: (78) Turn off all nonessential lights, radios, and navigation equipment to conserve battery power.

10. Operating conditions conducive to carburetor icing: (90) Temperature between 20 degrees F and 70 degrees F with visible moisture or high humidity and low throttle setting, as in the traffic pattern or on final approach.

Quickie quiz answers
Chapter 4

1. Pitot tube system affects what instrument(s)?
   Airspeed indicator. (124 and 132)

2. Five types of altitudes. (129-130)
   Absolute; Indicated; Pressure; True; Density

3. Gyroscopic instruments. (136)
   Turn and bank (needle and ball) or turn coordinator
   Heading indicator (directional gyro)
   Attitude indicator (artificial horizon)

4. The altimeter white and yellow bands: meanings of. (134)
   White: Flap operating range; power-off stall speed (lower range) ;
   Maximum flaps extended speed (upper range)
   Yellow: Caution range. Avoid this arc except in smooth air

5. The three designations or "types" of airspeed: (132-133) Indicated (IAS); Calibrated (CAS); True (TAS)

6. Magnetic compass turning characteristics: (149-150) Turning to the south: the compass lags, or is behind, the turn. Roll out about 30 degrees past the 180-degree heading--150 degrees or 210 degrees.

Turning to the north, the compass leads, or is ahead, of the turn. Roll out about 30 degrees before the 360" heading or at 330 degrees

7. Typical gyroscopic instruments on most light planes: (136) Attitude indicator (artificial horizon), heading indicator, (gyro compass), turn and bank indicator (although this may also be electrically driven).

8. Conditions that affect airspeed indicator readings. (124 and 132)

   A. Changes in airspeeds that increase or decrease the pitot impact pressure versus the undisturbed cockpit static pressure. Those changes are immediately sensed by the instrument's sensitive pressure gauge, and thus the movement of the airspeed needle.

   B. Pitot-static chamber icing thus blocking inflow of air.

   C. Pitot tube protective cover not removed during pre-flight inspection.

9. The meanings of the V velocities: (135)

   Vy = Speed for best rate of climb

   Vx = Speed for best angle if climb

   Vso = The stalling speed or the minimum steady flight speed in the landing configuration

   Vne = Never-exceed speed

   Vfe = Maximum flap extended speed

10. The two basic gyroscopic properties: (138)

   Rigidity in space

   Precession

Quickie quiz answers
Chapter 5

1. Standard weights for W&B calculations: (160)

   Crew and passengers: 170 lbs. each (but always use estimated actual weights in real life):

   Fuel: 6 lbs. per U.S. gallon;

   Oil: 7.5 lbs. per U.S. gallon

   Water: 8.35 lbs per U.S. gallon.

2. Definitions: Arm, Moment, Datum (159-160)

Arm: The longitudinal distance/inches from a reference datum line to the center of gravity of an item.

Moment: The product of the weight of an item multiplied by its arm.

Datum: An imaginary vertical line or plane from which all measurements of arms are taken.

3. Effects of high-density altitude on engine performance and propeller efficiency: (180) Power output and efficiency of both engine and propeller can be seriously diminished.

4. Effects of ground effect on takeoffs and landings: (182)

Can produce a greater rate of climb while the aircraft is still only a few feet off the ground and within the the influence of ground effect.

Can cause floating when landing, perhaps landing dangerously long, if the pilot is not aware of the ground effect phenomenon.

5. The role of wind in takeoffs and landings: (181)

Headwind: Shortens takeoff roll, the angle of climb, the approach to landing, and the post-landing roll.

Tailwind: Lengthens takeoff run, decreases angle of climb. Lengthens approach, increases ground speed, increases possibility of landing long and overshooting the runway.

Quickie quiz answers
Chapter 6

1. The two atmospheric layers and their altitudes: (218)

Troposphere--Sea level to 35,000 feet msl;

Stratosphere--35,000 feet msl and up.

2. The standard atmospheric pressures and temperatures: (219)

Pressure: 29.92 inches of mercury

Temperature: 59 degrees Fahrenheit; 15 degrees Celsius

3. The potential affect of convection currents on an airplane: (229-230)

Mild to moderate turbulence at low altitudes in warm weather;

Overshooting the runway on landing or landing short.

4. Significance of the temperature-dewpoint relationship: (237)

When temperature meets dewpoint, water vapor condenses and becomes dew or frost on the ground or fog, clouds, rain, snow, or hail in the air.

When fuel tanks are not filled at end of the flying day, the temperature cools to the dewpoint, the moisture in the empty space in the tanks condenses into water and sinks to the bottom of the tanks--water being heavier than gasoline.

5. Characteristics of cumulonimbus clouds: (243-246) They contain rising air currents, extreme turbulence, lightning, large hail, heavy rains, icing, wind shear.

6. Primary characteristics of cold fronts and warm fronts. (248)

Cold front:

Cumulus or cumulonimbus clouds

Unlimited ceilings, except during precipitation

Excellent visibility, except during precipitation

Unstable air, pronounced turbulence at lower altitudes

Precipitation: occasional heavy thunderstorms, hail, sleet, snow flurries

Warm front

Stratus, stratocumulus clouds (fog, haze)

Poor visibility (smoke, dust held at lower levels)

Smooth, stable air

Precipitation: drizzle

7. The main elements of a METAR in sequence: (270-273)

   1. Type of report and time
   2. Surface winds
   3. Visibility
   4. Present weather
   5. Sky conditions
   6. Temperature/dewpoint
   7. Altimeter setting
   8. Remarks

8. Weather information in an ASOS report: (278 and 280)

Cloud heights and amount, up to 12,000 feet

Visibility, to at least 10 miles

Precipitation

Barometric pressure and altimeter setting

Ambient temperature and dewpoint

Wind direction, speed, character (as gusty, variable, etc.)

Rainfall accumulation

Selected significant remarks

9. Five critical weather service reports or advisories: (282)

Severe Weather Forecast Alerts (AWW) and Bulletins (WW)

Significant Meteorological Information (SIGMETs [WS])

Airman's Meteorological Information (AIRMETs [WA])

Convective Meteorological Advisories (SIGMETS [WST]

Center Weather Advisories (CWA)

10. The name and radio frequency of the normal ground facility to contact for en route weather advisories: (215-216) The En Route Flight Advisory Service (EFAS), also known as "Flight Watch," in the nearest Flight Service Station on the universal frequency of 122.0.

Practice problem answers
Chapter 7

(Problems pp. 348-349-350)

A1. 23 mph	**B**1 113kts	**C**1. 28°
A2. 18 mph	**B**2. 136kts	**C**2. 4°
A3. 30 mph	**B**3. 83 kts	**C**3. 36°
A4. 46 mph	**B**4. 96 kts	**C**4. -8°
A5. 54 mph	**B**5 105 kts	**C**5 -18°

D1. 54°	**E**1. 4653 feet	**F**1. 137 kts
D2. 19°	**E**2. 6604 feet	**F**2. 122 kts^2
D3. 72°	**E**3. 3537 feet^2	**F**3. 155kts; 178mph
D4. 59°		
D5. 81°		

	WCA	TH	GS
G1. 5:20	**H1.** 21.0 gallons	**I**10° R	020°	150

	WCA	TH	GS
G1. 5:20	**H1.** 21.0 gallons	**I**10° R	020° 150
G2. 4:14 (rounded)	**H2.** 38.5 gallons	**I**0°	267° 164
	H3. 22.2 gallons	**I**6°L	039° 143
	H4. 43.8 gallons		
	H5. 71.8 gallons		

J1. Wind direction is 109° and wind speed is 31 knots.

---

1. Did you remember to convert Fahrenheit to Celsius?
2. Did you convert Fahrenheit to Celsius?

Quickie quiz answers
Chapter 8

1. Staying clear of clouds in what controlled airport airspace: (397) Ans. Class B airspace.

2. Types of Special Use Airspace (400-407)

   Prohibited

   Restricted

   Warning Area

   Military Operations Area (MOA)

   Military Training Routes (MTRs)

   Air Defense Identification Zones

   Alert Area

3. Finding out if a given SUA will be active: Who to contact. (Various references)

   The applicable Flight Service Station before departure and en route;

   The applicable Air Route Traffic Control Center en route.

4. Local versus UTC times. (413)

   3:00PM PST = 11:00PM UTC

   10:30AM EDT = 2:30PM UTC

   8:00PM CST = 2:00AM CST (next day)

5. Conversion to or from the 24-hour clock. (413)

   4:00PM = 1600 hours

7:30PM = 1930 hours

1:48AM = 0148 hours

1:48PM = 1348 hours

1650 hours = 4:50PM

2130 hours = 9:30PM

1200 hours = 12:00 noon

0000 hours = 12:00 midnight

6. When to give your full N-number and when you can eliminate some of the digits. (411)

   A. The full number: On initial contact with a ground
   facility, as "Cessna four three two one Alpha." Also, if the
   controller calls you, using that full ID;

   B. The abbreviated number on subsequent calls to the
   same controller, as "Cessna two one Alpha."

7. Landing at a Class D airport with radio problems (421): try
to communicate your positions and intentions to the tower.
Enter area above traffic pattern. Watch for light signals. If
given green light, enter pattern for standard landing. (421)

8. Basic responsibilities of Air Route Traffic Control Centers:
(423) Control all aircraft on IFR flight plans and assist VFR
aircraft when working conditions permit.

9. What sort of military action usually takes place in Restricted
Areas? (400-401) Artillery fire, aerial gunnery, guided missiles

10. What "TRSA" stands for and its main difference from Class
B, C, or D airspaces. (392-395)

   "TRSA" = "Terminal Radar Service Area"

   Main difference: The pilot can accept or reject radar service
   into the TRSA, and no clearance or approval to enter the
   controlled area is necessary. Clearance to enter the five-
   statute mile radius of the airport itself, however, is required.

Quickie quiz answers
Chapter 9

1. Minimum radio calls when landing at a non-tower or
closed-tower airport. (440-443)

   1) Initial call, 10 to 15 miles out

2) Entering downwind leg

3) Entering base leg

4) Entering final approach

5) Down and clear of the runway

2. Define "CTAF:" (440) "Common Traffic Advisory Frequency"

3. "ATIS"--What it is and does: (448)

Is an acronym for "Automatic Terminal Information Service"

Is a recorded summary, updated at least once every hour, of the local airport weather

Each summary includes:

Airport name

Information code name (phonetic alphabet)

UTC time of preparation

Sky conditions

Visibility

Temperature and dewpoint

Wind direction and velocity

Altimeter setting

Information code repeated

4. Pilot and aircraft equipment required to enter a Class C airspace. (457)

Pilot: no minimum requirements

Equipment: Operating two-way radio; operating Mode C transponder

5. The purpose of the Approach/Departure Control facility. (453) To ensure the orderly flow of traffic into and out of the terminal area but not the control of traffic within the 5-mile radius of the principal Class B (or C) airport.

6. What the VFR pilot must hear from Approach Control before entering a Class B airspace: (464 and 468) The pilot may not enter the Class B airspace until he hears the controller specifically state that "Cessna 1324 is *cleared* into the Chicago Class B airspace. *Cleared* is the important word. Without that approval,, the VFR pilot must remain clear of the 30-mile or so radius of the airspace.

7. How you can control runway lighting at the smaller non-tower airports: (479) Key the microphone on the CTAF

frequency 7 times for 5 seconds for high intensity lighting, 5 times for 5 seconds for medium intensity, 3 time for 5 seconds for low intensity. Also check the Airport/Facility Directory under AIRPORT REMARKS for any other lighting information.

8. The purpose of the VASI light system: (472) To provide visual descent guidance during the approach to a runway.

9. What is a "displaced threshold?" (481) The initial portion of a runway that has been moved a certain distance from one end or the other because of its physical condition (broken concrete, pot holes, rough, loose pavement, etc.) that make that portion unsafe for landing. Depending on its condition, however, the displaced area could be used for taxiing, takeoffs, or other light-load operations.

10. Describe the taxiway holding position design. (487) Two yellow stripes--one solid, one dashed or segmented--painted across the taxiway 30 yards or so back from the runway to which the taxiway leads.

Quickie quiz answers
Chapter 10

1. What are the three types of weather briefings, and for what purpose should you use each? (507-508)

   Outlook: When the flight is six hours or more in advance and you want a preliminary and general picture of the possible/probable conditions at your proposed departure time.

   Standard: You will be ready to go shortly, if weather conditions permit, and you want a complete FSS specialist briefing..

   Abbreviated: You had a standard briefing an hour or so ago and just want an update.

2. What information should you give an FSS specialist at the beginning of a weather briefing? (507)

   A. Refer to the Flight Plan form and give the information in boxes 1 through 12.

   B. Following the briefing, the briefer will ask for the data in boxes 13 through 17.

3. In planning a 400-mile cross-country flight, you decide to make a fuel stop at about the halfway point. Should you file your flight plan to that stopover airport or to your final destination airport? (503-504) It depends: If you know that you will be on the ground less than one hour, then file to your final destination. If there is any possibility, however, that the ground time could exceed one hour, file only to the refueling point and then file another flight plan for the balance of the trip with the FSS in whose area the stopover airport is located

4. Things to remember about the FSS specialist when opening a flight plan by radio and wording the introductory portion of the call. (510)

The specialist may have up to 48 frequencies to handle, and some locations can have the same frequency. Unless you identify who you are, the name of the airport you're calling from, and the frequency over you are transmitting, the specialist may not know on which of the frequencies he should try to respond.

The initial call should be this; "Lakewood Radio, Cherokee 6789 Alpha on 123.45 at Jonestown Municipal." Then wait for the FSS to respond.

5. Factors to consider if the flight will take you over or near mountainous terrain. (516)

Avoid low altitudes, especially near leeward slopes because of mountain wave conditions, strong updrafts, downdrafts, and potentially extreme turbulence.

6. Cruising at 95 kts per hour in one-mile visibility. (511)

A. How many seconds ahead can you see? 33 seconds.

B. How many additional seconds to perceive an obstacle one mile ahead, interpret what you saw, act, and allow aircraft reaction? 4 to 5 seconds.

7. "VFR not recommended:" Interpretation, and can you legally go, despite that recommendation? (494 and 497)

Interpretation: The FSS specialist knows weather. If he or she says "VNR," the careful pilot will terminate the briefing at that point, thank the briefer, and call back another time or another day.

Can you legally go, no matter what the briefer says? Yes. The briefer is not a controller. He or she has no authority over any pilot, so you can accept or reject offered advice or recommendations. Is it wise to do so? Well, that's another subject.

8. What is Fast File? (504) It's a system whereby the pilot can access FAST FILE in the FSS and enter a flight plan into a recording, thus eliminating the need to talk to a briefer. The recording is then entered into the computer for normal flight plan handling.

9. NOTAMs: What there are and the types. (508-509)

The acronym stands for "Notices to Airmen."

The three types are:

FDCs, issued by the National Flight Data Center and are regulatory in nature

NOTAMs D, or Distant NOTAMs relate to airspace or airport condition changes that could affect many pilots and their decisions about operating into a given area or airport

NOTAMs L, or Local NOTAMs, are of the "nice to know" nature that affect relatively few pilots and that are usually disseminated only to the FSS responsible for the airport or area in which the NOTAM applies.

10. References, etc. to have on hand for planning a cross-country flight. (493)

Current sectional chart(s) for the entire flight

VFR Terminal Area Chart(s), if any portion of the flight will penetrate even just a small segment of a Class B airspace

A current Airport/Facility Directory

An En Route Low Altitude Chart for radio navigation and Center flight-following

Aircraft Flight Manual or Pilot's Operating Handbook--for weight and balance data and performance charts

Quickie quiz answers
Chapter 11

1. In a bona fide emergency, you can violate any Federal Aviation Regulation. True or false? (519-520) Answer: True. But

be sure it's a real emergency. You may have to explain what happened and the FAR violation to the FAA.

2. The difference between a *distress* and an *urgency*. (520):

Distress is a fire, engine failure, a structural failure, and the like.

Urgency is a situation that could become catastrophic, as being lost, low on fuel, a rough engine, a severe engine or airframe vibration, rapidly accumulating ice, etc...

3. What are the two universal emergency-only radio frequencies? (521) Answer: 121.5 and 243.0

4. The meaning of this V ground-to-air symbol: (529)

Ans. "Require assistance"

5. The four Cs to remember in an emergency: (522)

Confess

Communicate

Comply

Climb

6. The transponder squawk for:

A. Radio failure is: 7600 (528)

B. An emergency is: 7700 (520)

7. The radio call "Mayday" means what and is used when? (521) "HELP ME" and used in a *DISTRESS* situation

8. You have a forced landing. one passenger severely hurt. What symbols to use to communicate the situation to an aircraft perhaps circling overhead?

X drawn or marked by some means on the ground; (529)

Stretch out face up on the ground (530)

9. The Emergency Locator Transmitter (ELT): (523)

A. Transmits on 121.5 and 243.0 frequencies

B. Is legal for 50 percent of its shelf life

C. Transmits a distinctive and continuous signal

10. Two questions every pilot should ask him/herself before taking off: (530-531)

"What could go wrong?"

"If what could go wrong did go wrong, what would I do?"

Quickie quiz answers
Chapter 12

1. Wake turbulence and jet blast: the same?

(A) *False* (533)

(B) *The difference:* Wake turbulence is the product of the wing in motion, while jet blast, or thrust stream, is generated by the engine(s)

2. What causes the formation of vortices? (534)

The pressure differential over the wing, which produces lift, beginning at the instant the aircraft leaves the ground and creates two counter-rotating vortices.

3. The three broad "classifications" of aircraft and their weights. (540)

Heavy = 300,000 pounds or more

Large = 12,500 pounds to 300,000 pounds

Light = 12,500 pounds or less

4. Landing or taking off behind a large or heavy jet and where to touch down or rotate to avoid wake turbulence (536)

A. Landing: Land beyond the point at which the jet touched down

B. Takeoff: Rotate before the point at which the jet broke ground

5. The greatest vortex strength occurs when the generating aircraft is: (535)

Heavy--Slow--Clean

6. Which aircraft has more difficulty countering a vortex roll or turbulence? (535)

One with a short wing as opposed to a long wing.

7. Vortices sink rates and eventual leveling-off altitude below the generating aircraft. (536-537)

A. Sink rate is about 400 to 500 feet per minute;

B. Leveling-off altitude is approximately 900 feet below the aircraft's flight path.

8. Controllers' authority to hold departing aircraft for wake turbulence avoidance: How long and for what reason. (540)

A. Controllers can hold aircraft up to 3 minutes

B. Reason: Wake turbulence avoidance after a jet has just landed or taken off. The communication is little more than this:

"Cessna 78 Delta, hold three minutes, wake turbulence."

9. Relative to question #8: (540)

A. The pilot can reject the takeoff hold and request immediate departure.

B. Yes. The controller can rescind the wake-avoidance hold order and approve the takeoff

C. The pilot now assumes sole responsibility for wake avoidance

10. Light plane precautions when taxiing behind a heavy jet, crossing its path, or in the hold bay area awaiting takeoff clearance. (533-534)

Follow a taxiing large or heavy jet by at least 200 feet or more. If the jet has to stop, its breakaway thrust to overcome inertia could be dangerous and damaging to light aircraft only a few yards back in trail.

Stay at a minimum of 200 feet behind a parked jet on a taxiway or in a holding bay.

Avoid exposing the side or profile of the light plane to the jet and to nothing more severe than idle thrust.

Quickie quiz answers
Chapter 13

1. Class III medical certificate validity period: Through age 39, 36 months; from age 40 on, 24 months. (546)

2. Classes and types of medical certificates: (546)

Class I: Air Transport Pilot

Class II: Commercial pilot

Class III: Private and/or recreational pilot

3. Medications/drugs to avoid if flying as pilot-in-command: (548) Antihistamines, certain blood pressure drugs, muscle relaxants, diarrhea, motion sickness controlling agents.

4. Define "hypoxia." (550)

A state of oxygen deficiency sufficient to impair functions of the brain and other organs.

5. Describe a "graveyard spiral:" (555)

The illusion during a constant speed turn of being in a descent with the wings level. The pilot pulls back on the controls, which tightens the spiral and increases the loss of altitude.

6. The minimum time lapse between "bottle to throttle." (548)

12 to 24 hours

7. An "AME" and his or her training: (546)

An AME is an "Aviation Medical Examiner," appointed by the FAA, who is a qualified physician in his own right and has also received specialized training in aviation medicine.

8. A way to prevent most illusions in actual or simulated IFR conditions: (555)

Avoid sudden, abrupt head movements, particularly in prolonged constant-speed turns

9. The possible cause and action to take if you feel drowsy or develop a headache in flight. (554)

Cause: Possible carbon monoxide poisoning

Action: Turn off the heater, if it's on. Open fresh air vents or window wing vent. If your physical condition does not improve, land as soon as possible and get medical attention.

10. In VFR weather, maximum length of time to have your head in the cockpit: (558)

No more than 15 seconds without scanning the skies ahead, above, below, and to either side of you

Acronyms and abbreviations

AD	Airworthiness Directive
ADF	Automatic Direction Finder
ADIZ	Air Defense Identification Zone
A/FD	Airport/Facility Directory
AFSS	Automated Flight Service Station
A/G	Air/Ground Communications
agl	Above ground level
AIM	Aeronautical Information Manual
AIRMET	Airmen's Meteorological Information
ALNOT	Alert Notice
ALS	Approach Light System
AME	Aviation Medical Examiner
AMOS	Automatic Meteorological Observing System
APU	Auxiliary Power Unit
ARTCC	Air Route Traffic Control Center
ARSA	Airport Radar Service Area (now obsolete)
ARSR	Air Route Surveillance Radar
ARTCC	Air Route Traffic Control Center
ARTS	Automated Radar Terminal System
ASDE	Airport Surface Detection System
ASOS	Automated Surface Observation System
ASR	Airport Surveillance Radar
ATA	Airport Traffic Area
ATC	Air Traffic Control
ATCRBS	Air Traffic Control Radar Beacon System
ATCT	Air Traffic Control Tower
ATIS	Automatic Terminal Information Service
AWC	Aviation Weather Center
AWW	Severe Weather Report
AWOS	Automated Weather Observing System
BRITE	Bright Radar Indicator Tower Equipment
CAS	Calibrated Air Speed
CD	Clearance Delivery
CDI	Course Deviation Indicator
Center	Air Route Traffic Control Center
CFCF	Central Flow Control Function
CG	Center of gravity

CH	Compass Heading
CT	Control Tower
CWA	Center Weather Advisory
CWSU	Central Weather Service Unit
CZ	Control Zone
DEV	Deviation
DF	Direction Finding
DME	Distance Measuring Equipment
DOD	Department of Defense
DUAT	Direct User Access Terminal
EFAS	En Route Flight Advisory Service (Flight Watch)
EGT	Exhaust Gas Temperature
ELAC	En Route Low Altitude Chart
ELT	Emergency Locator Transmitter
ETA	Estimated Time of Arrival
ETE	Estimated Time En Route
FA	Area Forecast
FAA	Federal Aviation Administration
FAR	Federal Aviation Regulations
FBO	Fixed Base Operator
FCC	Federal Communications Commission
FD	Winds Aloft Forecast
FDC	Flight Data Center
FSS	Flight Service Station
FT	Terminal Forecast
GC	Ground Control
GOES	Geostationary Operational Environmental Satellite
GPS	Global Positioning System
GRI	Group Repetition Interval
GS	Ground speed
HF	High frequency
HG	Inches of mercury
HIRL	High Intensity Runway Lights
HIWAS	Hazardous Inflight Weather Advisory Service
IAS	Indicated airspeed
ICAO	International Civil Aviation Organization
IFR	Instrument Flight Rules
ILS	Instrument Landing System
IMC	Instrument Meteorological Conditions
INREQ	Request for Information (or Information Request)
IR	Military Instrument Flight Route
IVRS	Interim Voice Response System
kHz	Kilohertz
KTs	Knots
LAAS	Local Area Augmentation System
LORAN	Long Range Navigation

LIRL	Low Intensity Runway Lights
LIFR	Low Instrument Flight Rules (weather conditions)
LLWS	Low Level Wind Shear
MAC	Mean Aerodynamic Chord
MALSR	Medium Intensity Approach Light System with Runway Alignment
METAR	Meteorological Reports-Aviation Routine
MEF	Maximum Elevation Figures
MH	Magnetic heading
MHz	Megahertz
MIRL	Medium Intensity Runway Lights
MOA	Military Operations Area
msl	Mean sea level
MTR	Military Training Route
MULTICOM	Nongovernment air/air radio communication frequency
NASP	National Airspace Plan
NAVAID	Navigation aid
NAWAU	National Aviation Weather Advisory Unit
NDB	Nondirectional Beacon
NESDIS	National Environmental Satellite Data and Information Service
NFCT	Non-Federal Control Tower
NHC	National Hurricane Center
NM	Nautical miles
NMC	National Meteorological Center
NOAA	National Oceanic and Atmospheric Administration
NOSUM	NOTAM Summary
NOTAM	Notice to Airmen
NSSFC	National Severe Storm Forecast Center
NWS	National Weather Service
OAT	Outside air temperature
OBS	Omnibearing Selector (Also "Observation")
OMNI	"All"
OVC	Overcast
PAPI	Precision Approach Path Indicator
PAR	Precision Approach Radar
PATWAS	Pilot's Automatic Telephone Weather Answering Service
PIREP	Pilot Report
PPS	Precise Positioning Service
RADAT	Rawinsonde Freezing Level
RAICG	Rawinsonde Icing Level
RAIM	Receiver Autonymous Integrity Monitoring
RAWIN	Upper Air Wind Observation (by Radio Methods)
RCLS	Runway Centerline Light System
RCC	Rescue Coordination Center
RCO	Remote Communications Outlet

RDT&E	Research, Development, Testing, and Evaluation
REIL	Runway End Identification Lights
RF	Radio Failure or Radio Frequency
RMI	Radio Magnetic Indicator
RRWDS	Remote Radar Weather Display System
RVR	Runway Visual Range
SA	Surface Observations
SAR	Search and Rescue
SCTD	Scattered
SFLS	Sequenced Flashing Light System
SIGMET	Significant Meteorological Information
SM	Statute miles
SPECI	"Special" Forecast
SPS	Standard Positioning Service
Squawk	Activate specific number code in the transponder
SUA	Special Use Airspace
SVFR	Special Visual Flight Rules
TAC	Terminal Area Chart
TACAN	Tactical Air Navigation
TAF	Terminal Area Forecast
TAS	True Airspeed
TC	True Course
TCA	Terminal Control Area (now obsolete)
TD	Time Difference
TDZL	Touchdown Zone Lights
TIB	Transcribed Information Briefing Service
TML	Television Microwave Link
TRACON	Terminal Radar Approach Control
TRSA	Terminal Radar Service Area
TWEB	Transcribed Weather Broadcast
UA	Pilot Report
UUA	Urgent Pilot Report
UHF	Ultra high frequency
UNICOM	Nongovernment air/ground radio communication facility
UTC	Coordinated Universal Time
VAR	Variation
VASI	Visual Approach Slope Indicator
VFR	Visual Flight Rules
VHF	Very High Frequency
VOR	Very High Frequency Omnidirectional Range
VOR/DME	VOR with Distance Measuring Equipment
VORTAC	VOR with TACAN
VOT	VOR Test
VR	Visual Range
VV	Visibility Value
WA	AIRMET

WAAS	Wide Area Augmentation System
WFO	Weather Forecast Office
WH	Hurricane Warning
WMSC	Weather Message Service Center
WS	SIGMET
WSO	Weather Service Office
WSR	Weather Service Radar
WST	Convective SIGMET
WX	Weather
ZULU	Sometimes used to mean UTC: "1530 Zulu."

Index

595

About the Author

Paul E. (Pete) Illman is the author of *The Pilot's Air Traffic Control Handbook*, 3rd Edition, and *The Pilot's Radio Communications Handbook*, 5th Edition. An active private pilot for over 50 years, he holds a certificate with single-engine commercial and multi-engine ratings. Employed by TWA for more than 30 years in various management capacities, he is a member of the Aircraft Owners and Pilots Association, the United States Pilots Association, and the Kansas Pilots Association.